T0303873

Inverting the Paradox of Excellence

How Companies Use Variations for
Business Excellence and How Enterprise
Variations Are Enabled by SAP

Inverting the Paradox of Excellence

How Companies Use Variations for Business Excellence and How Enterprise Variations Are Enabled by SAP

Vivek Kale

CRC Press
Taylor & Francis Group
Boca Raton   London   New York

CRC Press is an imprint of the
Taylor & Francis Group, an **informa** business

A PRODUCTIVITY PRESS BOOK

CRC Press
Taylor & Francis Group
6000 Broken Sound Parkway NW, Suite 300
Boca Raton, FL 33487-2742

Printed on acid-free paper
Version Date: 20140514

International Standard Book Number-13: 978-1-4665-9216-2 (Hardback)

Library of Congress Cataloging-in-Publication Data

Kale, Vivek.
   Inverting the paradox of excellence / Vivek Kale.
      pages cm
   Includes bibliographical references and index.
   ISBN 978-1-4665-9216-2 (hardback)
   1. Organizational effectiveness. 2. Organizational change. 3. Success in business. 4. Management. I. Title.

HD58.9.K353 2014
658.4'013--dc23
                                                            2014016289

**Visit the Taylor & Francis Web site at
http://www.taylorandfrancis.com**

**and the CRC Press Web site at
http://www.crcpress.com**

Contents

SECTION II   Evolution of Excellence

SECTION III *Dimensions of Excellence*

SECTION V   Industry Excellence through Variations

SECTION VI   Business Excellence and SAP

Preface

In Search of Excellence started a trend of comprehensive efforts worldwide to identify the prescriptive characteristics for *excellent companies.* However, time and again, corrective measures adopted by companies, based on such prescriptions, have belied expectations. An analysis of Fortune 1000 corporations shows that between 1973 and 1983, 35% of the top 20 companies are new. The number of new companies rises to 45% when the comparison is between 1983 and 1993. It increases even further, to 60%, when the comparison is between 1993 and 2003. It seems that the very strategies that contribute to the competitiveness, success, and excellence of an enterprise, in time, lead to its decline resulting from organizational inertia, complacence, and inflexibility because of overemphasis and adherence on these very *proven* routines. Companies end up focusing exclusively on a singular or a small set of guiding principles to the exclusion of all others, way beyond the limits of their validity and time.

The best-run and most widely admired companies are unable to sustain their market-beating levels of performance for an extended period of time. Large successful firms have greater resources and the forward momentum of established products and customers to carry them through times of distress, disruptions, and disasters. However, many of what were once the biggest, best financed, and most professionally managed companies have slid from the pinnacles of excellence. The book presents one of the most proven and effective models of success in the world: evolution by natural selection. The world of business can be understood in terms of individual companies, the market environment, and variations: the generation of variations and the selection and retention of advantageous variations. Thus, companies are systems that struggle for survival in the environment of the *market.*

This book proposes inverting the paradox of excellence by advocating that a company must continuously monitor the market environment and competitors to ascertain excellence and reconfigure and reframe continuously. To maintain excellence, the company must be in a constant state of flux! Thus, competitiveness and resulting excellence is not a state of *being* but of *becoming* excellent—it is a continuous process. This is the most important takeaway of this book—it proposes companies actively seeking out changes or variations on a continuous basis as essential for ensuring excellence by testing out a continuum of opportunities and advantages, with failures being learning experiences that enable them to tackle unexpected pitfalls or disasters in the future. The success or failure of variation(s) is tested out by surviving in the actual environment, and the duration of the test (including the commitment of capital, resources, etc.) is benchmarked against the evolutionary life cycle of concerned industry measured by the rate at which that industry introduces new products, processes, skill sets, and organizational structures.

Biological evolution provides a useful model for the evolution of companies because it implies, on the one hand, that a variety of unique events are important and, the other hand, that these unique, microlevel events and diversity still add up to an aggregate identifiable pattern of business change—that of survival and growth of companies. The book also discusses the coevolution of companies and the market environment to highlight the mutual interdependence for the growth and development of companies.

WHAT MAKES THIS BOOK DIFFERENT?

This book presents various dimensions of business variations that are available for any company to explore in its continual quest for opportunities and advantages to sustain excellence. As long as it collectively and effectively covers the various aspects of an operational company, the exact set of the chosen dimensions of variations is immaterial. This book chooses and extends a set inspired by *McKinsey's 7S model* as a tribute to its pioneering effort in focusing interest on the challenges of sustaining excellence in enterprise performance, namely, shared values, strategy, structure, stuff, style, staff, skills, systems, and sequence. The variations could be in any combinations of these dimensions, that is, the variations could be of products, services, business or production process, organization structures, organizational rules and procedures, and so on. These variations are affected simultaneously in multiple dimensions to different degrees of strength, so that at any moment of time the company is always in a state of flux under the resultant variations.

The following are the characteristics of the approach being proposed here that should be noted:

a. *Paradox of excellence* is a *hard* problem

The problem of business excellence is a hard problem like the perennially unsolved problems in neurosciences (*memory*), psychology (*mind, consciousness*), sociology (*citizen*), etc., that are intractable not only because of the inherent complexity, multiplicity, and interdependency of factors but also because of the fundamental problems arising out of *self-reference, definitional circularity, etc.*

b. Consistency

This book proposes an approach to business excellence based on changing how we look at change, that is, variation; this approach itself must be self-consistent. As a counter to attributes of excellence proposed in *In Search of Excellence* or *Built to Last*, we cannot give another set of definitive prescriptions that would in turn become obsolete in a couple of years. Thus, the approach suggested here has to be and is inherently iterative, recursive, and self-consistent.

By the same standard, paradoxically, it also cannot negate all the past progress made in identifying and addressing the challenges of the *paradox of excellence* made in these and numerous other works listed in the reference section at the end of the book. Does that make it vulnerable to attack on account of being "viable for all but testable for none" (not unlike the criticism faced by Darwin's "theory of evolution by natural selection" in the biosciences)? The answer to this is in the negative—though it is too involved an issue to be tackled here and is out of scope for the objectives of this book.

c. Conjectures on *patterns of excellence*

This book is not aiming for a precision engineering accuracy to tackle the problem of business excellence since the nature of the problem itself is much more subtle and not amenable to quantitative formulation. However one should not doubt the efficacy of such an approach, because in nature the evolutionary process has given rise to such sophisticated systems like the *eyes*, which are critical for navigation and survival of a majority of animal life. The approach adopted in this book is more in the nature of highlighting the patterns of development and evolution for business excellence. The fallacy of the opposite approach can be seen in the repeated failures of the definitive and prescriptive treatments proposed in the earlier works on business excellence cited earlier and in the references at the end of the book. Darwin's theory of evolution by natural selection has been invoked by other authors in the past, but this is the first book to focus on the *variations* component of this theory. The idea of variations, going against the mainstream of received wisdom of the last 30 years, is radical enough. Hence, instead of newer case studies, the book presents the usual and long familiar case studies through the prism of the *variations* to experience the difference of the *case history* approach presented here.

d. Enterprise change management using enterprise systems like SAP

Enterprises routinely miss altogether or underestimate the power and potential for enterprise change management enabled by enterprise systems like SAP ERP. Initiating change and confronting change are the two most important issues facing today's enterprises. The ability to change business processes contributes directly to the *innovation* bottom line.

The traditional concept of change management is usually understood as a one-time event or at least a nonfrequent event. But if an enterprise is looking for the capability to handle not only change management but also management of changes on a continual basis, then establishing an enterprise system like SAP is a must!

This brings us to the next significant aspect of this book—customary treatments of business excellence seldom highlight the change-enabling aspects of IT. Conventional works in this area have the now familiar refrain on the notion of business and IT alignment to assure optimal creation of business value, but they seldom discuss the very key enabler role of IT: "IT makes enterprise-wide change (i.e., variation) possible, more easily and effortlessly!" This is the second-most important takeaway of this book.

As will be discussed in Chapter 1, there is an essential tension between stability (or inertia) and instability (or variation) within the companies. To succeed both today and tomorrow, companies must play these two different games simultaneously. Similarly, as discussed in Chapter 4, there is again an essential tension between mechanistic and organismic perspectives on enterprises, both of which are also essential for enterprise excellence. Such essential tensions can be resolved by deploying suitable IT systems, in particular enterprise systems like SAP.

This is one of the first books to stress continually on the power and potential of enterprise systems like SAP to be a huge enabler of enterprise-wide iterative change. It is phenomenally important to realize that business processes that *reside* or are internalized within an organization's employees are difficult to change simply because human beings naturally find it more difficult to change. However, processes that reside within any computerized systems are easy to change because they are not thwarted by problems of inertia, fatigue, or lack of motivation. SAP enables the essential and continual changing of processes that are so critical to the successes of the enterprise. The last chapter discusses the change-enablement aspects (i.e., *Built-for-Variation* aspects) of a SAP implementation.

The book's argument is valid for any of the enterprise systems available on the market like SAP, Oracle, J.D. Edwards, Baan, PeopleSoft, and others. However, the book focuses on SAP as an example because

- SAP is closest to what a canonical enterprise system should be: it enables the enterprise to operate as an "integrated, enterprise-wide, process-oriented, information-driven, and real-time enterprise"
- In the past few years, all other systems have fallen way behind SAP in the market; currently, SAP is the predominant ERP system in the market with more than 70% of the installed base (both large enterprises and small and medium businesses) across the world

The book introduces SAP's vision of an enterprise-wide, integrated, and near-real-time performance platform for realizing these variations by enabling continuous reframing and reconfigurations. The existing IT infrastructures not only fail to support fast, flexible, and cost-effective adaptation to new business strategies and processes, but they actually impede such adaptation. SAP provides a solution to help meet the three central requirements of an optimal business platform, namely, a software platform that fulfills the demand for flexibility and innovation at manageable costs. SAP business applications, and SAP NetWeaver, which is based on a service-oriented architecture approach, result in much greater degree of agility—flexibility and innovation—at dramatically reduced total cost of ownership (TCO).

The last part of the book describes how SAP enables customary variations required of enterprises. However, it must be highlighted that SAP enables even disruptive changes in the enterprise's business processes and logic via the service-oriented architecture (SOA) nature of SAP NetWeaver, but the requisite rationale and supporting details are too technical to be tackled here and are out of scope for the objectives of this book, which is essentially focused on business management.

Finally, a remark for those who focus more on what is not in the book. This book proposes a new idea *necessity to vary*, explains why it is important and how to realize, via SAP, continual variations that are essential for the continual growth and success of enterprises. However, this book does not address the issue of what to do in your particular enterprise—it does not present (say) a 7-step method to be adopted for the continual journey of excellence. That will be addressed by the next book project that is underway.

HOW IS THIS BOOK ORGANIZED?

This book is divided into three major portions. In the first portion, Sections I through III present the paradox of excellence followed by the evolutionary model of excellence, finally rounding up with elaborating on the various dimensions of excellence. In the second portion, Sections IV and V present real-life cases of maintaining business and industry-level excellence through variations. Finally, in the third portion, Section VI presents how enterprises can achieve excellence by implementing enterprise systems like SAP.

SECTION I: PARADOX OF EXCELLENCE

The chapters in the first section of this book give the context and significance of the paradox of excellence experienced by enterprises. Chapter 1 introduces the key idea of variations for resolving the paradox of excellence. Chapters 2 and 3 acquaint the readers with the patterns and antipatterns of business excellence proposed by the major pioneers in this area.

SECTION II: EVOLUTION OF EXCELLENCE

Chapter 4 introduces Darwin's "theory of evolution by natural selection." In the context of change of theories in sciences, it also acquaints the readers with Popper's thesis of falsification, Kuhn's concept of paradigms, and Peter Drucker's theory of business. The later part of the chapter looks at the mutually contradictory perspectives on the enterprises which can be reconciled by implementing enterprise systems like SAP within the enterprises.

SECTION III: DIMENSIONS OF EXCELLENCE

This section presents the characteristics of the dimensions of excellence. Chapter 5 details the characteristics of Built-for-Variation enterprises, the nature of core and context of enterprises, and the extended 9S model of enterprise excellence. Chapter 6 introduces, with illustrations, the three sources of variations, namely, invention (or pioneering), imitation, and innovation variations. Chapter 7 illustrates the significance of each of the dimension of variation with specific examples from various businesses across the world.

SECTION IV: BUSINESS EXCELLENCE THROUGH VARIATIONS

In this section, we look at enterprises through their entire life spans to highlight the variations they had to undergo to maintain and sustain excellence. Chapter 8 on General Electric looks at one of the longest-lasting excellent company that operates in the most traditional manufacturing sectors of the economy. Chapter 9 presents the travails of IBM, a typical high-technology company that had to renew itself multiple times to remain at the forefront of the new-era excellent companies. Chapter 10 recounts UPS as an example of a traditional transportation and delivery company that has reframed itself as the premier logistics and supply chain company for the burgeoning world of e-businesses.

SECTION V: INDUSTRY EXCELLENCE THROUGH VARIATIONS

Chapter 11 presents variations witnessed by a particular industry, namely, the automobile industry, in its transition toward business excellence as a whole.

SECTION VI: BUSINESS EXCELLENCE AND SAP

This section starts with Chapter 12 explaining the business variations through which SAP became the world's premier vendor of enterprise resource planning software. Chapter 13 then introduces SAP's vision of an enterprise-wide, integrated, and real-time performance platform called SAP Business Suite, which is empowered to realize enterprise variations for reframing and reconfiguring enterprises. Chapter 14 demonstrates the changeability of SAP-driven enterprises and describes how business variations in all dimensions of variations—shared values, strategy, structure, stuff, style, staff, skills, systems, and sequence—can be achieved by using SAP.

WHO SHOULD READ THIS BOOK?

This book should be of interest to business executives, business and technology managers, and program managers, as also to corporate consultants who are interested in issues related to business strategy, company performance, corporate innovation and renewal, and challenges of ensuring corporate resilience and change.

The broad areas of interest are given as follows:

a. Business excellence, visionary, value creation, sustained growth, high performance, accelerating growth, supremacy, lasting/enduring performance, business models, dominant design
b. Driving and managing change, competitiveness
c. Offerings, that is, products/services/experiences, marketing and sales, communication strategies
d. Radical innovation, differentiation, discontinuity, disruption, breakthroughs, resilience, renewal, competitive advantage
e. Business evolution, business Darwinism, adaptive enterprise, complexity, complex adaptive systems, symbiosis, business ecosystems, coevolution and co-creation, competion and cooperation, biology of business, corporate life cycles
f. Paradoxes, myths or riddles of excellence, greatness and success of companies
g. Value creation, addition and assurance by implementing enterprise-wide systems like SAP ERP

Vivek Kale

Author

Vivek Kale has more than two decades of professional IT experience, during which he has handled and consulted on various aspects of enterprise-wide information modeling, enterprise architectures, business process redesign, and, e-business architectures. He is also a seasoned practitioner in transforming the business of IT, facilitating business agility and enabling the process-oriented enterprise. He has been group CIO of Essar Group, the steel/oil and gas major of India, as well as, Raymond Ltd., the textile and apparel major of India. He is the author of *Implementing SAP R/3: The Guide for Business and Technology Managers*, Sams, Indianapolis, IN (2000) and *A Guide to Implementing the Oracle Siebel CRM 8.x*, McGraw-Hill, New Delhi, India (2009).

Acknowledgments

I acknowledge all those who have helped me with their clarifications, criticisms, and valuable information during the writing of this book and those who were patient enough to read the entire or parts of the manuscript and made many valuable suggestions. They include Dr. B. Srinivas and Heman Cholke of Citibank. I was also fortunate to get advice and feedback on several chapters of this book from Prof. Phil Rosenzweig, IMD Business School, and Prof. Gregory G. Dess, University of Texas at Dallas.

I thank my friend Nilesh Acharya, who, since I returned from the United States in the early 2000s, has been providing unstinted support in procuring books and references required for my numerous book projects. B. Srinivas, Nilesh Acharya, and Prashant Jagtap have been the pillars of support for my continual progress on various book projects.

I thank my editor Kristine Mednansky for initiating this book's journey and then shepherding it through the publication process.

My deepest values and patterns of thought have evolved in the close partnership and understanding I have shared for over 24 years with my wife, Girija. She has believed in me and supported me for all these years. Her encouragement helped me accomplish so much, and I could not have done any of it without her. I would not be the person I am without her, and I would not think the way I do but for her. Our beloved daughters, Tanaya and Atmaja, were also very supportive while I chased my dreams. I thank God for the opportunities I have been given and for my wonderful family and friends who have made all these efforts meaningful.

Vivek Kale

Section I

Paradox of Excellence

One of the prime reasons for failures of companies is that they end up focusing exclusively on a singular or a small set of guiding principles to the exclusion of all others, way beyond the limits of their validity and time. It seems that the very strategies that contribute to the competitiveness, success, and excellence of an enterprise, in time, lead to their decline resulting from organizational inertia, complacence, and inflexibility because of overemphasis and adherence on these very *proven* routines. The first chapter introduces the concept of *paradox of excellence* using the example of the decline of Motorola; the inversion of this paradox is illustrated through the example of production systems and operations at Toyota. In the following two chapters, the book acquaints the readers with the patterns and antipatterns of business excellence proposed by the major pioneers in this area.

1 Introduction

The best-run and most widely admired companies are unable to sustain their market-beating levels of performance for an extended period of time. No enterprise can build a competitive advantage that is sustainable indefinitely—every advantage erodes. The very processes that enable them to survive over the long term thwart them from renewal and reinvention and, finally, fossilize them. It is unlikely that a singular set of approaches or principles would resolve permanently all issues faced by companies and also remain a valid panacea for all future times. This book takes inspiration from the most proven model of success in the world: evolution by natural selection. It proposes companies actively seeking out changes or *variations* on a continuous basis as essential for ensuring excellence by testing out a continuum of opportunities and advantages, with failures being learning experiences that enable them to avoid unexpected pitfalls or disasters later.

The *success case* decision on variation(s) is decided by introducing them to the actual environment to test out their acceptance or rejection, and the duration of the test (including the commitment of capital, resources, etc.) is benchmarked against the evolutionary life cycle of the concerned industry measured by the rate(s) at which the industry introduces new products, processes, and organizational structures.

1.1 PARADOX OF EXCELLENCE

It appears that the very strategies that contribute to the competitiveness, excellence, and success of an enterprise, in time, lead to their decline resulting from organizational inertia, complacence, and inflexibility because of overemphasis and adherence on these very *proven* routines. In a trend identified with the publication of *In Search of Excellence*, comprehensive efforts have been undertaken worldwide to identify the prescriptive characteristics for *excellent companies*. However, time and again, corrective measures adopted by companies, based on such prescriptions, have belied expectations. This is because the companies end up focusing exclusively on a singular or a small set of guiding principles to the exclusion of all others, way beyond the limits of their validity and time. No enterprise can build a competitive advantage that is sustainable indefinitely—every advantage erodes. In fact, fine-tuned systems for today's success may actually *increase* the chances of failure tomorrow! Short-term effectiveness can sow the seeds of failure by hindering long-term adaptability. Most declining companies did not lack the technology to succeed; rather, these resulted from companies failing to embrace variations and change effectively.

Large successful firms have greater resources and the forward momentum of established products and customers to carry them through times of distress and mismanagement. However, many of what were once the biggest, best financed, and most professionally managed companies have slid from the top ranks. Others have dropped from the lists altogether. Still others, who were earlier small or nonexistent, have risen to displace them. Many of the new entrants are formed around semiconductors, software, supercomputers, and biotechnology—technologies that few had imagined were commercially viable a generation ago. And the few who survived like IBM and Apple have so altered their products and technologies that they are scarcely recognizable as the same companies. For instance, Texas Instruments (TI) had taken the momentous decision to exit out of the traditional chip business to concentrate more on design and development of digital signal processing (DSP) chips.

> We are proposing that there is nothing fundamentally wrong *per se* with any of the traditional strategies and techniques. However, it is unlikely that a single approach or principle will resolve permanently all issues faced by companies and also remain a valid panacea for all times in the future. Adherence to one or a small set of guiding principles way beyond its relevance or time is singularly responsible for the decline or even destruction of enterprises.

Failure to *vary* is a prime source of business failure. There is an essential tension between variation (or instability) and stability (or inertia) within the companies. Initiating change and confronting change are the two most important issues facing the companies today. To succeed both today and tomorrow, companies must play two different games simultaneously. First, they must continually get better at competing in the short term, which requires increasing alignment among strategy, structure, processes, culture, and people. Second, they must also simultaneously introduce strategic changes to ensure long-term competitiveness, which requires increasing variation, innovation, and disruption. However, this balancing game alone will not ensure long-term success: short-term effectiveness can sow the seeds of failure by hindering long-term adaptability. As companies grow, they develop structures, processes, and systems that are interlinked, making further changes difficult, costly, and time-consuming to implement. Structural inertia rooted in size, complexity, and such interdependence sets in. In fact, fine-tuned systems for today's success may actually increase the chances of tomorrow's failure. While consistency, reliability, and efficiency are crucial, so, too, are characteristics such as flexibility and responsiveness (i.e., variation).

In a sense, this is the more fundamental version of the universally recognized *productivity paradox*, which results from a tension arising from trying to achieve two mutually contradictory goals. On one hand, companies strive for economies of scale; on the other hand, they are confronted increasingly with the dilemma of the economies of scope. For companies, an unhappy by-product of success in one dimension has been a rapid deterioration in the other, which have led to their decline, if not demise, much sooner than anticipated. Rather than work toward competitive responses (possibly entailing even radical changes), with unfailing regularity, companies have chosen to defend from their traditional bastions. They keep building upon, reinforcing, and modifying what has made them successful. Time and again, they have demonstrated remarkable creativity in defending their entrenched products, technologies, and processes, which have often reached unimaginable heights of productivity and performances. The evolutionary metaphor and model, based on biological evolution, goes a long way to unravel the mystery of the solution to the problem of growth and development of businesses. The evolutionary model readily explains, in analogy with the decline, decay, and death of species in the biological world, the trauma associated with the change management within companies and its consequences like downsizing. Similarly, according to this model, excessive proliferation of companies, along with their products, is thwarted either because of the competition or because of the limited capacity of the market environment.

Traditionally, the pursuit of sustainable advantage has long been the focus of strategy. But advantages can last only until competitors have duplicated or outmaneuvered them. No enterprise can build a competitive advantage that is sustainable; every advantage erodes. The configuration of markets and competition are constantly threatened by uncertainty, dynamism, and heterogeneity because of short product life cycles, short product design cycles, new technologies, frequent entries by new entrants, repositioning by incumbents, and so on. Protecting advantages becomes increasingly difficult; therefore, disruption of the competitor's or even one's own advantages is the approach for long-run survival. The traditional goal of strategies has been to find a grand and long-term strategy that sustains itself for years, if not for decades. However, such strategies take too long to create the assets needed to pull off this grand strategy. Such long-term strategy is often outmaneuvered or rendered irrelevant because of the dramatic changes in the circumstances and the environment. Instead of long-range plans and competitive advantages, companies aim for a series of small and short-term advantages, which, when combined together effectively, create a long-term sustainable advantage for the companies. It is much easier and less risky to create a home run rather than a series of base hits.

 An organization may have multiple business models to address multiple businesses or divisions or market segments. It is not necessary for a company to have an overarching unified single business model across the whole company.

Thus, the only true solution for longevity of companies is to *vary*. As indicated earlier, the world of business can be understood in terms of individual companies, the market environment, and variations: the generation of changes, retention, and selection. Competitiveness is not a state that can be reached once and for all and held on to; competitiveness is a process. Thus, the approach suggested here involves a fundamental transition of viewing business from a state of *being* to a process of *becoming* competitive.

This approach can help structure the understanding of the opportunities and the challenges that confront companies. Variations are the engine of business development and growth. Variation is the process whereby business agents act to transform new knowledge, inventions, and/or scientific techniques, that is, know-how into business value, often through products, production processes, and/or changes to the organization. The variations may be technological, organizational, and/or market environment in orientation. Thus, the variations could be in products, services, business or production process, organization structures, procedures, processes and rules, and so on.

In the evolutionary model to be discussed in the next section, business variations can be understood to lead to sustenance and growth of companies. It provides a way of conceptualizing variation, not as a final result but as a complex process involving many stages through which the companies respond to environmental conditions and in turn effect or even create newer states of environmental conditions.

1.1.1 Darwin's Theory of Evolution

Darwin's theory of evolution has been deployed as a model for application in diverse fields ranging from *hard* sciences (like physical sciences) to *soft* sciences (like ecology, economics, social and political sciences, and even in philosophy for the allied problems of growth of knowledge, theory selection, etc.). We explore the interesting possibility of applying this model to the growth and development of enterprises. Thus, businesses or companies are primarily organic systems that struggle for survival in the environment of the *market*. This is not to suggest that companies are organisms with characteristics of sex, reproduction, etc., but primarily to throw more light on our understanding of the problem of change and sustained competitiveness, performance, growth, and development of companies. It may also be fascinating to see the many common business terms interpreted in a new light. We are proposing that the only true solution for longevity and success of companies is to *vary*!

Using the evolutionary model, the world of business can be understood in terms of individual companies, the market environment, and variations: the generation of variations, selection, and retention. These variations, unlike the more familiar innovations, are not necessarily confined to products alone but can extend to visions, goals, objectives, plans, services, business or production processes, organizational structures, communications, systems, rules and procedures, partnerships, and so on. We are suggesting here that it is the result of such continuous and experimental variations, at varied levels of the enterprise or time scales wrought by an enterprise in itself and its surrounding environment, that may result in its continued competitiveness and, therefore, long-term performance, survival, and success. The success or failure of variation(s) is tested out by surviving in the actual environment, and the duration of the test (including the commitment of capital, resources) is benchmarked against the evolutionary life cycle of the concerned industry measured by the rate(s) at which the industry introduces new products, processes, and organizational structures.

1.1.2 EVOLUTION OF COMPANIES

In our model, in response to the changes in the market environment, not unlike mutations in the biological evolution, it is the variations or differentiations that are wrought by the companies that increase their effectiveness to perform and survive in the changed environment or, in other words, their competitiveness. These changes or variations undergone by the companies for increased competitiveness could be in terms of their strategies, structures, functions, resources consumed, and outputs produced. These variations, and the resulting differentiations, are different for different companies. The variations (or breakthroughs) could manifest in terms of new products, product improvisations, relaunching of products (or services), new strategies, diversifications, mergers, acquisitions, and so on. The variations or differentiations themselves could be enforced by the market environment or originate internally. The variations can be perceived at four levels, namely, the individual, the firm, the industry, and the economy. The focus in this book will be on the firm level; in real economy, firms don't really die; firms don't have to destruct but they no longer have to remain the same, either. In the process of being in flux to survive and succeed, the firms may so alter their products, processes, organizational structures, and technologies that they may be scarcely recognizable as the same companies.

All segmentation and positioning strategies employed by the companies as also the consequent promotional strategies like advertising are similar to the differentiation strategies brought to play in the biological environment. The market scanning, competitor intelligence, business forecasting, and, at the extreme, scenario planning exercises undertaken by companies are similar to the constant scanning or sensing done by organic systems both for food and for sensing any approaching danger.

The response of the market for such introductions or changes may be negative or affirmative. Since there are many companies in the market environment addressing similar situations, this is the corporate analog of the process of natural selection—the market response may either encourage or discourage the continuation of these variations. For a company as a whole, the total effect of such variations is the sum total of all such variations for the various products and services provided by the company (or group of divisions or companies). An organization may have multiple business models to address multiple businesses or divisions or market segments. It is not necessary for a company to have an overarching unified single business model across the whole company. In case of the positive market response as a whole, companies may reinforce these variations even further and may perform better and emerge stronger and more successful; alternatively, if they face rejections of these variations as a whole, the company performance may be affected adversely and may have to identify and work on other variations. The *success case* decision on variation(s) is based on introducing them to the actual environment to test out its acceptance or rejection (the duration of the test is benchmarked against the evolutionary life cycle of the concerned industry measured by the rate(s) at which that industry introduces new products, processes, and organizational structures).

The interaction between the companies and the market is dynamic and constantly undergoes changes in an endless cycle: the market environment influences and selects the best-fit companies, and in turn, the variations introduced by the competing companies affect this very market environment. This may happen because of the following:

1. Changes brought about in the configuration of the market by all the companies constantly competing against each other
2. Changes that occur fundamentally in the market environment
3. Changes brought about by customers

Changes of the second category may occur because of several reasons like the following:

- Natural cataclysms or sudden changes in political situations (like military coups, landslide victories for opposition parties after a prolonged periods as in Britain, or dramatic changes in demographics because of the large influx of refugee populations into or from neighboring countries)
- The sudden promulgation or withdrawal of regulatory frameworks (like license policies and export policies) by the governments
- Discovery of radically new resources of energy like atomic energy or sudden depletion of traditionally derived energy sources like petroleum

 According to this model, not only suppliers but even customers compete among themselves for providing their custom—in other words, competition among customers!

However, there are some major differences between the biological and business evolution being proposed here:

1. Unlike biological evolution, business evolution can be faster by many orders of magnitude. Entrepreneurs, who are the agents of the business evolution, and, therefore, companies can try out a large range of alternatives, which can be subjected much more rapidly to selection.
2. Unlike biological evolution where mutations in genes are essentially random in nature, companies can direct variations along certain directions or paths or directly control the generation of novelties or variations corresponding to their perceptions of the market environment. Thus, companies internalize some selection mechanisms in order to generate variations that they hope will be successful in the market.
3. The alternative that is ultimately selected is better than other alternatives only in relation to the localized market environment and not necessarily to any ideal, universally best alternative. This implies that success and progress is not general and permanent but can only be discussed in relation to specific and local conditions—it is context specific and ephemeral.

The business variations are the outcome of a myriad of knowledge-seeking activities whereby the agent's perceptions and actions are translated into practice. The resulting pattern of business change is characteristically *evolutionary* because it involves the development and diffusion of business variations, as well as novelty and selection among alternatives. Biological evolution provides a useful model for the evolution of businesses because it implies, on one hand, that a variety of unique events are important. On the other hand, it also implies that these unique, microlevel events and diversity still add up to an aggregate identifiable pattern of business change—that of survival and growth of business firms or companies. Correspondingly, in evolution of businesses through variations, the unit of variation is the know-how, the unit of selection is the product or service or experience delivered to the customer, and, finally, the unit of evolution is the development and growth of the enterprise. Corporate evolution like biological evolution is not goal-directed.

This completes the basic characteristics of the evolutionary model of businesses. Within this general framework, it is fascinating to map the standard business issues into the evolutionary model and seek solutions within this evolutionary model and then retranslate them into the normal business framework for comparison with conventional wisdom. Many a time, even if this does not result in a solution radically different than the traditional one, it at least unfolds a completely new perspective on the concerned issues—which in itself is extremely fulfilling and satisfying.

1.1.3 APPLICATIONS

For sustainable success, companies must also understand how and when to initiate variations and/
or change. Variations are a central determinant of longer-run success and failure for commercial
enterprises. Most of the declining companies did not lack the technology to succeed; rather, these
resulted from companies failing to embrace variation and change effectively. As we have stated
earlier, initiating change and confronting change are the two most important issues facing the companies today, and the ability to manage for today and for tomorrow simultaneously is critical for
long-term survival and success.

We are suggesting here that it is the result of such continuous and deliberate variations, at varied
levels of the enterprise or time scales wrought by an enterprise in itself and its surrounding environment, that may result in its continued competitiveness and, therefore, long-term performance,
survival, and success. The book proposes inverting the paradox of excellence: to maintain excellence, the company must be in a constant state of flux! It proposes companies actively seeking out
changes or *variations* on a continuous basis as essential for ensuring excellence by testing out a
continuum of opportunities and advantages with failures being learning experiences that enable
them to tackle unexpected pitfalls or disasters later. The success or failure of variation(s) is tested
out by surviving in the actual environment, and the duration of the test is benchmarked against the
evolutionary life cycle of the concerned industry (measured by the rate at which it introduces new
products, processes, and organizational structures). A company must continuously monitor the market environment and competitors to ascertain excellence and reconfigure and reframe continuously.
Thus, competitiveness and resulting excellence is not a state of *being* but of *becoming* excellent; it
is a continuous process.

> While it may be true that remaining inflexible cannot lead to sustained success, it may
> seem implausible that the opposite leads to success, either. Business leaders and man-
> agers may find it implausible that success means merely being in a constant state of
> flux. Foster and Kaplan, Raynor, and others have identified a conundrum, namely, that
> a degree of commitment is needed to be successful but that same degree of commitment
> makes long-term success unlikely; yet to know that flux is needed may actually make short-
> term success impossible. The resolution for all such and other dilemmas is critically depen-
> dent on the efficacy of generation of variations, that is, costs, durations, and assessment of
> usefulness of the generated variations (see Chapter 5, Subsection 5.3, "Aspects of Variations").
> This can be thought of at four levels: the individual, the firm, the industry, and the economy
> (see Chapter 5, Subsection 5.2, "Core and Context" for discussion regarding the latter three
> levels). For example, creative destruction is beneficial for the economy and even the industry,
> yet not for the firm; on the other hand, firms live and die for the benefit of the industry and the
> economy. We discuss real-life case histories at the firm level in Section IV (Chapters 8 through
> 10) and at the industry level in Section V (Chapter 11).

In the motorcar industry, at the turn of the century, bicycles and horse-driven carriages were
threatened by the horse-less carriage, soon to be called the automobiles. There were several competing alternative energy sources and different steering mechanisms and arrangement of passenger
compartments. In a very short period, however, a dominant design emerged epitomized by Model
T Ford. This design consisted of an internal combustion engine, steering wheel on the left, brake
pedal on the right, and clutch on the left. Once this standard emerged, the focus of competition
shifted primarily to the optional feature, cost, or power of the engine. This lasted until General
Motors introduced the radically new concept in car—the fully enclosed steel automobile. A majority of the companies continue to make gasoline engines, whereas some are experimenting with
electric engines. They are quite different technologies but competing paths for similar functions.

IBM successfully entered the personal computer (PC) market through a separately dedicated unit set up far from the firm's headquarters, an independent Team Taurus put Ford Motor Company back on the map, and General Motors entered the small-car market through the Saturn Motor Company. In each instance, the task of creating the competencies needed to successfully bridge into chosen markets hinged on creating organizational units with clear mandate and a great deal of independence from the staffs, committees, and other encumbrances of the parent company. Predictably, spinning off separate and independent organizational units does not always lead to success. Xerox's attempt to revitalize itself through Xerox Palo Alto Research Center (PARC) facility is a notable example. PARC was the ultimate fount of creative genius, creating technology for the modern PC, the fax machine, the Ethernet, the now ubiquitous Windows user interface, and the laser printer. However, most have found way to the marketplace and undoubtedly astounding market success not through Xerox but via other newer companies.

The importance of business vision can be understood in its ability to sometimes overcome the limitations imposed by the core competence of the corporations. For companies facing major opportunities or threat, current competencies may cloud the companies' field of vision and hence limit its ability to perceive the potential. With a strong vision, often driven by entrepreneurial individuals with authority to implement it, the enterprise may develop new competencies and thereby move into new technologies. This implies, first, that while radical change is taken to be disruptive and incremental change less so, the perception of change as being *radical* or *incremental* is dependent on a vision of where the business is going. If a vision correctly anticipates a market change in the future path of a business or technology, then radical may seem or become incremental. Second, this also implies that only newer or existing companies with related competencies or those with strong incentives/disincentives are likely to move quickly into a new technology.

In the past, other authors have talked about variation–selection–retention as it comes to companies. The problem arises in that small-scale variations—the sort of portfolio of options—may not be sufficient for success in some industries, where big bets are called for. The nature of some strategic decisions is in fact to make large-scale bets under uncertainty, and those not prepared to make such bets can never hope to win. This results in what is termed as the *strategy paradox*—making big bets does not guarantee success, but the unwillingness to do so almost guarantees failure.

Per the framework presented in this book, all variations or change starts small: radical change is taken to be disruptive and incremental change less so; the perception of change as being *radical* or *incremental* is dependent on a vision of where the business is going. If a vision correctly anticipates a market change in the future path of a business or technology, then radical may become incremental.

If a company is required to take large-scale bets, it indicates that it has already missed the signals from the market at earlier stages. Admittedly, it is difficult to read or identify a market-defining variation at its inception; but if enterprises are in the business of routinely generating or scouting for variations (as this book suggests), they are unlikely to miss it altogether. Ultimately, notwithstanding all alertness, the company may miss some of the variations—that would account for the difference between close competitors even in narrowly defined segments of the market (see Chapter 5, Subsection 5.3, "Aspects of Variations").

1.2 ENTERPRISES AND PARADOXES OF EXCELLENCE

The word paradox derives from the Greek *paradoxos*—with *para* denoting against or over and *doxos* meaning contrary to received wisdom or common sense. It is used today to refer to instances where meanings appear to be contradictory and yet where there is also a sense that there is a hidden truth entwined within the opposites. In conventional everyday use, the terms *dilemma, contradiction*, and *paradox* are often deployed more or less interchangeably. However, more analytically, it is possible to draw some important distinctions. A dilemma is more of an either–or situation where one alternative has to be selected. However, the essence of the idea of paradox is the precise opposite of this. The whole point of paradox is that no either–or choice needs to be made or should be made. Indeed, the key to the idea is that two apparent contradictory notions are held and worked with simultaneously. The value to be derived from paradoxical thinking stems from this duality. Dilemmas derive from perceived polarities—but these may disguise the opportunity to exploit simultaneity. Leaders and managers can learn how to exploit the tensions between seemingly conflicting priorities and use the energy to transcend the fixation on dualities. This entails working with rather than against the dilemmas and paradoxes that in turn means overcoming learned reactions and responses. It means finding advantage in the seemingly *opposing* options and seeking to harness their logics into a new, higher-level form. If paradox is integral to enterprise, and if paradox means that apparently sensible and rational means can produce unanticipated and contrary outcomes (so that, e.g., actions taken to control or limit undesired behaviors actually generate an increase in these behaviors), then it is important to analyze how leaders can better handle paradoxes so that not only their negative possibilities are pruned but also their beneficial qualities are enhanced.

One of the most well-recognized and indeed classic dilemmas is the tension between managing for today versus planning for tomorrow. In other words, the pressure on organizational leaders to deliver efficiencies and results from the current business model and the current product and service offerings is set against the need to prepare to supplant these *answers* by looking for new ones to meet changing times and circumstances. This type of paradox and dilemma revolves around the exploitation of a given combination of resources in order to yield optimal efficiency versus the need to prepare for the future by innovation and making other forms of change. This dilemma has been expressed in various ways—most notably in the succinct contrast between *exploitation* and *exploration*. The dilemma becomes all the more acute when the issue of radical rather than *mere* incremental innovation is contemplated.

A paradoxical solution would look to ambidextrous or dual organizational forms—organizational architectures that build in both tight and loose coupling simultaneously. That is, they manage both process-efficient exploitation units and more loosely managed exploration units. The management of these different units enterprises needs to be *consistently inconsistent* as they strive to be both focused on the long term and the short term, to be both centralized and decentralized, tightly focused on process and efficiency by driving out variation through conformance to written process rules, yet loose enough to promote variation in the discovery units. Variation-decreasing units (process-focused production and service units), it is argued, need to be decoupled at least to some degree from variation-seeking units.

However, there may be exceptions. An alternative way to achieve dual objectives such as high exploitation and high exploration may be to pursue a *punctuated equilibrium* strategy. This would mean devoting some periods of time to a concentrated emphasis on one and then switching for a while to a concentrated emphasis on the other. These options again indicate a further managerial dilemma. If the organizational unit is considered as a relatively unified whole system, then the punctuated equilibrium approach may be sensible; if, however, the enterprise is framed as a number of loosely coupled units, then it is possible to pursue process efficiency (exploitation) and radical innovation (exploration) simultaneously.

As an example of paradox, take the emphasis on process management techniques and process improvement using techniques such as TQM, BPR, and Six Sigma. These process and quality improvement approaches can reduce costs and provide reliable services to customers. Independent auditing through ISO 9000 ensures consistent follow-through of documented processes. However, while this approach can certainly deliver improvements to existing products and customers, the same values and techniques can unfortunately impede variation and innovation. It has been noted that winners of the Baldrige Award and similar other awards that signal strong adherence to process improvement values and behaviors often tend to suffer subsequent poor financial performance out-turns. The reason is that the clarity of focus that is a merit also carries within it a fatal flaw. It is both a strength and a weakness. A firm's competitiveness over time requires both a capability to conduct current processes in an efficient manner and the development of new capabilities and thus, by defini-tion, a departure from the current suite of routines and capabilities. An example of the exploitation of paradox in management is the idea of Just-in-Time manufacturing. JIT competes with the con-ventional Western idea of trade-offs; instead, quality, low cost, service, and efficiency are deemed to be mutually reinforcing rather than opposing values requiring trade-off. For example, JIT prompts new, creative ways to interact with suppliers.

Organizations can expect to face continually—at least at regular intervals—alternative pulls between a relatively common set of choices. These relate, for example, to familiar dilemmas such as whether to compete on price or on quality, whether to centralize or decentralize, whether to out-source or bring services in-house, whether to focus on the drive for efficiency (current exploitation of resources), or whether to explore and search for new opportunities and to innovate. Rather than oscillating between these polarities, we suggest that an alternative path is to go beneath the surface dilemma and to actively search out and even embrace the inherent nature of the presenting dilemma or paradox and, by reaching a deeper level of understanding, to exploit its potential. Managing through paradox should ideally be neither a compromise nor a split between competing tensions. Rather, it seeks to be aware of both and to utilize the strength of both. As a result, managers may counteract their tendency to overrationalize and oversynthesize by simultaneously holding and even exploring opposing views. The challenge for managers of enterprises lies in learning how to manage the tensions or dualities between traditional and new forms of organizing, a process demanding the arbitration of continuity and change.

> Regarding Enterprise Performance
>
> Some kinds of performance are absolute—notably things like cycle time, prod-uct quality, and measures of efficiency—but others are better understood as relative, including market share, sales, profits, and share price. They are relative precisely because the performance of one company is affected by the actions of others. This is critical to understanding business excellence: why some companies achieve it, why some achieve it but do not maintain it, and so forth. It is also crucial whenever we recommend actions that may lead to performance excellence. Enterprise responses (and performance), being resul-tant of multiple dimensions of variations, would be uniquely defined by its context of uncer-tainty, complexity, and variety acting on the company's historical trajectories of business architecture, configurations, and dynamics. There is an inherent limit to the applicability of an absolutist framework, formulaic approach, or precision engineering accuracy because it is contrary to the situation in real life. Corporate evolution like biological evolution is not goal directed per se and can be as effective as natural evolution.

To be effective, enterprises need to exhibit contradictory attributes simultaneously. For exam-ple, they need to be both controlling and autonomous, to have both internal and external focus, to manage for today, and to prepare for tomorrow. It is possible, theoretically at least, to distinguish between alternative choices (i.e., either/or choices) on the one hand and dilemmas on the other. The either/or choices may sometimes be resolved by close attention to the context. However, dilemmas may not be amenable to such a fit; managing with dilemmas thus means going beyond the idea of *fit*. Dilemma theory seeks to avoid pendulum swings and to be more in tune with ongoing dynamics. The idea is to seek to avoid maximizing along any dimension. Enterprises they say need both agree-ment and disagreement. Managers, by implication, need to design enterprises that have attributes in tension such as aspects of rules driven and values driven, planned and emergent, control and autonomy, products and experiences, administrational and transformational, challenging and nurturing, focus and breadth of skills, mandatory and discretionary systems, and, finally, mass production to mass customization (see Chapter 7, *Dimension of Variations*). To be capable of successfully handling *both* rather than *either/or* requires some form of ambidexterity. Ambidextrous enterprises allow apparently inconsistent tendencies to coexist.

There is a series of dilemmas and paradoxes that relate to types of business and organizational decision making. The first relates to dilemmas and paradoxes in the domain of business strategy, the second to dilemmas and paradoxes in the domain of decisions about organizational structuring, the third to dilemmas and paradoxes inherent in performance management and control, the fourth concerns dilemmas about innovation, the fifth is concerned with the realm of underlying frames of management knowledge, and the sixth and final one concerns change management.

Critical to making sense of the myriad developments is the ability to relate parts to the whole and vice versa: a movement, back and forth, between the whole conceived through the parts that actualize and comprise it, and the parts conceived through the whole that consists of and is made up of them. Running alongside that is the theme of dilemmas and how to manage them. In order to manage a dilemma, the answer is not necessarily *balance*: choices still have to be made that lean more toward one end of a dimension rather than another. However, it does mean attending to the merits of both ends of the spectrum.

1.3 PARADOX OF EXCELLENCE AT MOTOROLA

Motorola's stunning results in the 1980s and the early to mid-1990s put at the heart of the high-potential electronic business. The company's claim to fame at that time was its excellence in TQM; consequently, Motorola conducted courses in TQM for other companies. It was widely recognized for its decentralized management approach, training, business reengineering, and self-directed teams. Motorola also made ground-breaking contributions to the electronics industry; the company built some of the first car radios and first battery-powered consumer radios. Motorola leveraged these technologies to provide walkie-talkies during World War II and played a sterling role in putting man on the moon. It is credited with basically inventing the cell phone industry; in 1996, Motorola's highly successful StarTAC cell phone captured more than half of the global cell phone market. An institutionalized focus on innovation propelled the company from battery eliminators and car radios to televisions, microprocessors, cellular communications, satellites circling the earth, and pursuit of the daunting *six sigma* quality standard (only 3.4 defects per million). Galvin encouraged dissent, discussion, and disagreement and gave individuals the latitude to show what they could do largely on their own. He set challenges and gave people immense responsibility so as to stimulate the organization and its people to grow and learn, often by failures and mistakes. In fact, Galvin's son and successor used the word *renewal* to capture the idea of continual transformations, often (although not exclusively) attained through commitments to audacious projects.

1.3.1 EXCESSES OF SUCCESSES

No major corporation has been more committed to decentralized empowerment than has Motorola. Motorola had built a culture based on rampant—if not rabid—entrepreneurial activity. Famed for its *warring tribes*, Motorola's culture promoted internal competition even within its many tribes and clans. That competition was nowhere more apparent than in product development. Would-be product champions engaged in intense competition for budgets, engineering manpower, and other resources to feed product development efforts. The problem was that hundreds if not thousands of individuals pulled Motorola's product development activity in a multitude of competing and often conflicting directions. Compounding the chaos, Motorola had no common product development or quality assurance processes and—most important—had disjointed or nonexistent group and corporate product portfolios and roadmaps. In contrast to IBM's famed *shootout* exercise between competing technologies, products, or solutions, Motorola had no structured process for managing internal competition. Without a formal process, wannabes and losers lingered around while winners failed to reach critical mass. Many redundant initiatives consumed vital resources while critical programs languished, and obvious if unexciting opportunities were ignored altogether. Everyone was too busy doing his or her own thing to notice that this company was in trouble. Motorola was dissolving into chaos.

By 1997, legacy practices were clearly getting entrenched within Motorola with detrimental effect on its focus on market realities and competitiveness. This was clearly exemplified by its wrong focus on perfecting and launching its smart card offerings when in reality they never became mainstream business in the United States. It also misread the market completely when it positioned StarTAC as the first *wearable* phone. Similarly, persisting with legacy practices and slow-moving culture also caused Motorola to miss the movement of cellular phone technology from analog to digital. It even justified its limiting to the analog technology because of paucity of resources to drive the digital effort. It allowed itself to be completely blindsided on the digital telephony. Despite the declining position of Apple's Macintosh against the ever-increasing onslaught of Windows on PCs, Motorola chose to ignore enabling the Windows NT operating system (OS) to run on its PowerPC chip (which was majorly used in Apple's Macintosh computer). It missed realizing a huge market by opting to miss out the opportunity on the IBM PCs. Motorola's culture, which lacked customer and market focus, was also causing it to rupture its relationships with its top mainstay customers. Motorola arrogantly made the availability of its popular StarTAC phone to the wireless networks contingent on them using Motorola call phones for a majority of their requirements.

Motorola built its mobile division on technology innovation. When it launched, there was no one else even close to developing a competitive offering, and indeed it took years for the competition to catch up. The very first *clamshell* mobile phone, the Motorola StarTAC, was considered by some to be one of the greatest gadgets in the last 50 years. Despite this phenomenal market leadership, the shine was starting to come off by 1998. Motorola had always had central to its commercial platform the capabilities of the handset from a functional perspective—the core technology and functionality. This comes from the strong engineering pedigree of its mobile phone division. This functional-led approach enabled Motorola to excel with the smallest and most capable platform in the 1990s. But by the mid-1990s, Nokia was hammering at Motorola's door, particularly with the launch in 1996 of the 8110 and then shortly thereafter with the 9000 Communicator. Motorola had only a few variations in its range at the time, so Nokia's approach to try to attract different segments and demographics worked well, but Nokia also focused on innovating around the software interface. Nokia's phones were easier to use, which appealed to a wider audience and attracted a whole new set of customers. A shift in user preferences occurred in the mid-1990s to emphasis form overfunction, devastating Motorola, which did not deviate much from purely function-led hardware. Motorola found a brief resurgence in brand popularity with the RAZR, pushing the phone as a fashion accessory, but that too was short lived. The shift in user preferences has again morphed with an emphasis on device usability and connectivity, largely as a result of the iPhone's popularity and more capable devices with MP3 and wireless capability. The success of the BlackBerry in the corporate arena; new handsets from LG, Samsung, and Sony Ericsson; and the iPhone's launch left the RAZR wanting.

1.3.2 REWIRING FOR WIRELESS

By 1998, Motorola's market share had fallen from the traditional level of 50%–30% and further downward to 13% by 1999. While Motorola was still fixated on the analog phones market, the market rapid movement toward digital phones was profitably exploited by Nokia and Ericsson, who made major strides in capturing this market. Its slow-moving retarded moves were in stark contrast to the speed and conviction required for being an effective player in the market. Sensing that many centrifugal forces were pulling the company apart, scion Chris Galvin took the drastic step of pulling together all its cell phone, wireless, satellite, and cable modem business units into a new communications enterprise (CE) group. CE was charged to create a common look and feel for all Motorola's wireless products, a common brand identity, a single strategy for the entire CE, coherent product planning and development roadmaps, common technology platforms, and integrated network equipment offerings. Motorola aimed to reestablish itself as the leader in wireless communications, and it had a lot of ground to make up. Motorola's new enterprise strategy for its wireless businesses created a set of critical common priorities. These new priorities described a fundamental shift in Motorola's management world. Its new approach emphasized enterprise strategies, platforms, processes, and management practices like alignment. These new rules place the customer and the enterprise ahead of the business unit and individual interests. Motorola redefined the contract between the company and its executives, and it reset the limits of autonomy and empowerment within the context of a common enterprise strategy. It wanted to establish to the internal and external stakeholders that the enterprise comes first. One important new initiative established a program management office within CE, staffed with more than 400 project management professionals, to ensure disciplined execution of key initiatives. Motorola's transformation included expansionary thrusts in several new directions as well. Long a product-centric company, its unidimensional focus on product innovation had led it to neglect the market and customers in favor of a singular focus on products and technologies. To reverse this imbalance, the company formed a new group called the services and solutions organization (SSO) within CE specifically to focus on repairing and building relationships with key customers.

But Motorola was not only intent on renewing its existing wireless business. It also established a new business unit to capture market leadership for Motorola in the emerging wireless web world. The personal networks group was created from whole cloth under Janiece Webb, former head of Motorola's network services group. Webb and her team set out to create a master plan for market leadership in the wireless web arena. The plan identified all the key elements of the wireless web market, including wireless servers, content distribution networks, location systems, synchronization technologies, unified messaging, electronic agents, and end-user applications. Webb and her team then set out to build or buy all the major elements to support an aggressive market leadership strategy. The firm spared no resources in supporting this aggressive program. By 2001, Motorola began to show critical mass in this space, realizing significant progress toward its goal of becoming a market leader in one of the most promising growth markets of the twenty-first century. Motorola's attempted transition from rampant decentralization to an architected enterprise approach was traumatic; this resulted in all kinds of infighting as teams yearned to execute their businesses the way they had in the old days. Turnover among its talented executive ranks soared in the face of new disciplines; tension between traditional entrepreneurial forces and the new enterprise focus remained uncomfortably high.

Motorola had slid from being number one in the wireless infrastructure equipment industry to a distant number four, with Ericsson taking the number one position. Its revenues from cable companies had been cut in half as the company lagged behind the competition in delivering new products. It had sunk $2.6 billion in 10 years on Iridium satellite network, which required brick-sized phones and an impractical cost for international calls (several dollars per minute); Iridium went bankrupt. Motorola also had immense problems in executing. In 2002, with the advent of color-screen cell phones, Motorola was beaten by its competitors Nokia and Samsung to emerge victorious as the top two cell phone players. Motorola was late in the TV setup box business, because of which it lost out to rival Scientific Atlanta. It had previously been the leader in chips for personal digital assistants (PDAs), but Intel overtook it in that business. Finally, in 2004, realizing that it had gone from leading the industry to being viewed as an antiquated player, the Motorola board hired Ed Zander, the former president of Sun Microsystems, as the new CEO.

1.4   INVERTING THE PARADOX OF EXCELLENCE AT TOYOTA

Toyota has defied the paradox of excellence by resorting to deliberate variations even in the proven successful routines in all aspects of its strategy (strategy, structure, shared values, and stuff), organization (style, staff, skills, and system), and generating value (sequence). There are a number of *radical contradictions* at the heart of the Toyota system. Enterprises are under increasing pressure to meet multiple, often inconsistent, demands. Increasing technological change, global competition, and workforce diversity reveal and intensify the paradox; and these kinds of disruptions expose tensions within enterprises. Also, Toyota's phenomenal record in productivity gains at the same time as its impressive achievements in innovation has cast doubts on earlier conventional thinking—that there is a necessary trade-off between productivity and innovation. Toyota's unorthodox manufacturing system has enabled it to make the world's best automobiles at the lowest cost and to develop new products quickly. The company creates contradictions and paradoxes in all aspects of organizational life. In many areas, it deliberately fosters contradictory viewpoints and challenges its managers and employees to find answers that transcend differences rather than settle for compromises—they are simultaneous variations along the different dimensions mentioned earlier, namely, strategy, structure, shared values, stuff, style, staff, skills, systems, and sequence.

Examples of its paradoxical nature include the following: it takes big leaps yet is patient and moves slowly; it grows steadily and yet maintains a state of never satisfied and indeed even a degree of paranoia; it has outstandingly efficient operations and yet seems to use employees' time wastefully (e.g., including large number of people in meetings at which they often do not directly participate); it is frugal and yet spends heavily in select areas; and it maintains a strict hierarchy and yet prompts employees to challenge. Consider some other examples of the contradictions: it thinks and acts both globally and locally—it has a global knowledge center and yet goes to extraordinary lengths to learn from and adapt to local cultures and settings. It combines hard and soft modes of management. It strives for short-term efficiency and associated incremental wins while also striving for long-term step-change gains. It cultivates frugality, yet it is willing to spend large sums on selected projects. It cultivates stability and yet is also a mindset of paranoia. It is characterized by bureaucracy and hierarchy yet fosters a spirit of dissent. It maintains both simple and complex modes of communication. It sets very hard-to-achieve goals, yet it emphasizes the need for a strong sense of reality. It expects small-scale experimentation and occasional audacious leaps. The company is constantly in a state of flux.

In order to foster these *contradictions*, Toyota combines both forces of disruption with complementary forces of integration. Its forces of disruption include the setting of highly stretching and near-impossible goals. Second, there is a huge emphasis on experimentation—most notably, Toyota encourages all employees to search for improvements by highlighting mistakes and failures. Third, despite its huge emphasis on efficiency and a standardized system, it also promotes and encourages local customization. These forces of disruption are complemented by forces of integration: the values of the founders are held in high esteem; these values are inculcated; the company is loathe to make any layoffs even in times of economic downturn and even when this policy costs money; Toyota also invests in communication across the board. Thus, the forces of expansion are balanced by the forces of integration in a manner that allows a restless forward momentum.

Above all, this system has been widely emulated not only by the world's leading automobile companies and manufacturing forms but also by enterprises in service industries such as hospitals.

1.5   SUMMARY

The best-run and most widely admired companies are unable to sustain their market-beating levels of performance for an extended period of time. It seems that the very strategies that contribute to the competitiveness, success, and excellence of an enterprise, in time, lead to their decline resulting from organizational inertia, complacence, and inflexibility because of overemphasis and adherence on these very *proven* routines. The chapter introduced one of the most proven and effective model of success in the world: evolution by natural selection. Thus, companies are systems that struggle for survival in the environment of the *market*. The book proposes inverting the paradox of excellence by advocating that it must continuously monitor the market environment and competitors to ascertain excellence and reconfigure and reframe continuously. To maintain excellence, a company must be in a constant state of flux! of *paradox of excellence* is illustrated using the example of Motorola; the inversion of this paradox is illustrated through the example of production systems and operations at Toyota.

2 Patterns of Excellence

2.1 IN SEARCH OF EXCELLENCE*

Tom Peters catapulted to international fame when he coauthored, along with Robert Waterman, *In Search of Excellence: Lessons from America's Best-Run Companies* (Peters and Waterman, 1982), which is the best-selling management book of all time. It is difficult to overestimate the impact this book has had. At the time when Western economies were on the rocks and Japanese companies appeared to be sweeping all before them, *In Search of Excellence* seemed to offer a way, perhaps the only way, for Western companies to regain their competitiveness.

2.1.1 BIAS FOR ACTION

One of the main identifiable attributes of excellent companies is their bias for action. Even though they may be analytical in approach, they also favor methods that encourage rapid and appropriate response. One of the methods devised for achieving quick action is what Peters and Waterman term *chunking*. Chunking is an approach whereby a problem that arises in the organization is first made manageable (i.e., broken into *chunks*) and then tackled by a small group of staff brought together specifically for that purpose. The main reason for the use of such groups, variously called project teams, task forces, or quality circles, is to facilitate organizational fluidity and to encourage action. Key characteristics of these groups are as follows:

- They usually comprise no more than 10 members.
- They are voluntarily constituted.
- The life of the group is usually between 3 and 6 months.
- The reporting level and seniority of the membership is appropriate to the importance of the problem to be dealt with.
- The documentation of the group's proceedings is scant and very informal.
- These groups take on a limited set of objectives, which are usually determined, monitored, evaluated, and reviewed by themselves.

Chunking is merely one example of the bias for action that exists in excellent companies and reflects their willingness to innovate and experiment. These companies' philosophy for action is simple: "Do it, fix it, try it." Therefore, excellent companies are characterized by small, ad hoc teams applied to solving designated problems that have first been reduced to manageable proportions. Achieving smallness is the key, even though the subject or task may be large. Smallness induces manageability and a sense of understanding and allows a feeling of ownership.

2.1.2 CLOSE TO THE CUSTOMER

Excellent companies really do get close to the customer, while others merely talk about it. The customer dictates product, quantity, quality, and service. The best organizations are alleged to go to extreme lengths to achieve quality, service, and reliability. There is no part of the business that

---

* Thomas J. Peters and Robert H. Waterman, *In Search of Excellence: Lessons from Americas Best-Run Companies* (Oxford, U.K.,: Oxford University Press, 1980).

is closed to customers. In fact, many of the excellent companies claim to get their best ideas for new products from listening intently and regularly to their customers. The excellent companies are more "driven by their direct orientation to the customers rather than by technology or by a desire to be the low-cost producer. They seem to focus more on the revenue-generation side of their services."

2.1.3 AUTONOMY AND ENTREPRENEURSHIP

Perhaps the most important element of excellent companies is their ability to be big and yet to act small at the same time. Product champions are allowed to come forward, grow, and flourish. Such a champion is not a blue-sky dreamer or an intellectual giant. The champion might even be an ideal thief. But above all, the champion is the pragmatist, the one who latches onto someone else's idea and doggedly brings something concrete and tangible out of it. In fostering such attitudes, the excellent companies have what they label *championing systems*, consisting of the following:

- The product champion—a zealot or fanatic who believes in a product
- A successful executing champion—one who has been through the process of championing a product before
- The godfather—typically an aging leader who provides the role model for champions

The essence of this system is to foster, promote, and sustain the budding entrepreneur. It is claimed that the three elements of the championing system are essential to its operation and credibility.

Another key part of this system is that, in some companies, product champions tend to be allocated to their own *suboptional divisions.* These are similar to small, independent businesses and comprise independent new venture teams, run by champions with the full and total support of senior management. The suboptional division is independent in that it is responsible for its own accounting, personnel activities, quality assurance, and support for its product in the field. To encourage entrepreneurship further, teams, groups, and divisions are highly encouraged by the companies' reward structures to compete among themselves for new projects.

Autonomy and entrepreneurship are also encouraged by the type of no-holds-barred communications procedures adopted by excellent companies. These exhibit the following characteristics.

Communication is informal—even though there are lots of meetings going on at any one time, most meetings are informal and comprise staff from different disciplines gathering to talk about and solve problems.

- The communication system is given both physical and material support—blackboards, flip charts, and small tables that foster informal small group discussions are everywhere. The aim is to encourage people to talk about the organization: what needs changing, what is going on, and how to improve things around the place. There are also people, variously described as dreamers, heretics, gadflies, mavericks, or geniuses, whose sole purpose is to spur the system to innovate. Their job is to institutionalize innovation by initiating and encouraging experimentation. They can also call on staff in other divisions of the organization to assist them in this process, as well as having financial resources at their disposal.
- Communication is intensive—given the freedom, the encouragement, and the support (financial, moral, and physical) in the organizations, it is no wonder that the level of communication between and among workers is not only informal and spontaneous but also intense. This is borne out by the common occurrence of meetings without agendas and minutes. Also, when presentations are made in these meetings, questioning of the proposal is unabashed and discussion is free and open. Those present are expected to be fully involved in such meetings and there are no *sacred cows* that cannot be questioned.

This intense communication system also acts as a remarkably tight control system, in that people are always checking on each other to see how each is faring. This arises out of a genuine desire to keep abreast of developments in the organization rather than any untoward motive. One result of this is that teams are more prudent in their financial expenditure on projects. Another is that the sea of inquisitors act as *idea generators*, thereby ensuring that teams are not dependent entirely on their own devices to innovate and solve problems. This usually also ensures that all options are considered before a final decision is made. The concomitant result of this fostering of creativity is that senior management is more tolerant of failure, knowing full well that champions have to make many tries and consequently suffer some failures, in the process of creating successful innovations.

2.1.4 PRODUCTIVITY THROUGH PEOPLE

A cherished principle of the excellent companies is that they treat their workers with respect and dignity; they refer to them as partners. This is because people, rather than systems or machines, are seen as the primary source of quality and productivity gains. There is a closeness and family feeling in such companies; indeed many of the *partners* see the organization as an extended family. The slogans of such companies tend to reflect this view of people: "respect the individual," "make people winners," "let them stand out," and "treat people as adults."

2.1.5 HANDS-ON, VALUE-DRIVEN

Excellent companies are value-driven; they are clear about what they stand for and take the process of value shaping seriously. There is an implicit belief that everyone in the organization, from the top to the bottom, should be driven by the values of the organization, hence the great effort, time, and money spent to inspire people by and inculcate them with these values.

Implanting these values is a primary responsibility of the individual members of the management team. They set the tone by leading from the front. Coherence and homogeneity must, however, first be created among senior management by regular meetings (both formal and informal). The outcome of this is that management speak with one voice. They are passionate in preaching the organization's values. They unleash excitement, not in their offices, but mainly on the shop floor where the workers are. Inculcating these values, however, is a laborious process and persistence is vital in achieving the desired goal.

2.1.6 STICK TO THE KNITTING

Acquisition or internal diversification for its own sake is not one of the characteristics of excellent companies. They must stick to the knitting—do what they know best. But when they do acquire, they do it in an experimental fashion, by first "dipping a toe in the water." If the water does not feel good, they get out fast. Acquisitions are always in fields related to their core activities and they never acquire any business that they do not know how to run. As a general rule, they "move out mainly through internally generated diversification, one manageable step at a time."

2.1.7 SIMPLE FORM, LEAN STAFF

A guiding principle in excellent companies is to keep things simple and small. Structurally, the most common form is the *product division*. This form, which is rarely changed, provides the essential touchstone that everybody understands and from which the complexities of day-to-day life can be approached. Since the use of teams, groups, and task forces for specific projects is a common stock-in-trade of these companies, most changes in structure are made at the edges, such as by allocating one or two people to an ad hoc team. By adopting this approach, the basic structure is left in place, while all other things revolve and change around it. This gives these organizations great flexibility but still enables them to keep their structures simple, divisionalized, and autonomous.

Such simple structures only require a small, lean staff at the corporate and middle management levels. Therefore, in excellent companies, flat structures, with few layers, and slimmed-down bureaucracies—which together allow flexibility and rapid communication—are the order of the day.

2.1.8 Simultaneous Loose–Tight Properties

This is the *firm and free* principle. On the one hand, it allows the excellent companies to control everything tightly while, on the other hand, allowing and indeed encouraging individual innovation, autonomy, and entrepreneurship. These properties are jointly achieved through the organization's culture—its shared values and beliefs. By sharing the same values, self-control and self-respect result in each person becoming their own, and everyone else's, supervisor. The individual members of the organization know they have the freedom, and are encouraged, to experiment and innovate. They also know that their actions will be scrutinized and judged, however, with the utmost attention paid to the impact they have on product quality, targets, and, above all, the customer. The focus is on building and expanding the frontiers of the business. The ultimate goal is to be the best company, and in the final analysis, this is the benchmark against which the discipline and flexibility of the individual will be measured. Therefore, Peters and Waterman maintain that the main attributes of excellent companies are flat, antihierarchical structures, innovation and entrepreneurship, small corporate and middle management staffs, reward systems based on contribution rather than position or length of service, brain power rather than muscle power, and strong, flexible cultures.

Peters and Waterman's vision of the organization of the future, based on their study of leading American companies, has proved extremely influential, not only in the business world but in academia as well. This is not to say (as will be shown later) that they are without their critics; however, there is little doubt that they laid the groundwork, especially in highlighting the important role played by culture, for other leading thinkers whose work draws on and gels with theirs.

2.2 BUILT TO LAST*

This is a book about visionary companies. All individual leaders, no matter how charismatic or visionary, eventually die; and all visionary products and services eventually become obsolete. Indeed, entire markets can become obsolete and disappear. Yet visionary companies prosper over long periods of time, through multiple product life cycles and multiple generations of active leaders.

They took a set of truly exceptional companies that have stood the test of time—the average founding date being 1897—and studied them from their very beginnings, through all phases of their development to the present day; and they studied them in comparison to another set of good companies that had the same shot in life but didn't attain quite the same stature.

Generated long-term superlative financial returns:

- Premier institution in its industry
- Widely admired by knowledgeable businesspeople
- Made an indelible imprint on the world in which we live
- Had multiple generations of chief executives
- Been through multiple product (or service) life cycles
- Founded before 1950

---

* Jim Collins and Jerry I. Porras, *Built to Last: Successful Habits of Visionary Companies* (New York: Harper Business, 2002).

In a 6-year research project, they set out to identify and systematically research the historical development of a set of visionary companies, to examine how they differed from a carefully selected control set of comparison companies, and to thereby discover the underlying factors that account for their extraordinary long-term position.

They selected the comparison companies using the following criteria:

- Same founding year
- Similar founding products and markets
- Not a dog company

This book presents the findings of our research project and their practical implications.

The objectives of this study were the following:

1. To identify the underlying characteristics and dynamics common to highly visionary companies (and that distinguish them from other companies) and to translate these findings into a useful conceptual framework
2. To effectively communicate these findings and concepts so that they influence the practice of management and prove beneficial to people who want to help create, build, and maintain visionary companies

One aspect of this book that most separates it from all previous management books, we would point to the fact that we looked at companies throughout their entire life spans and in direct comparison to other companies (Table 2.1).

They decided to examine the companies throughout their entire histories as they evolved from small- to midsized on to large-sized enterprises; only an evolutionary perspective could lead to understanding the fundamental dynamics behind visionary companies. They undertook the comparison analysis from a historical perspective. Their aim was to use the long range of corporate

---

TABLE 2.1

Companies in Research Study

Visionary Company	Comparison Company
3M	Norton
American Express	Wells Fargo
Boeing	McDonnell Douglas
Citicorp	Chase Manhattan
Ford	GM
General Electric	Westinghouse
Hewlett-Packard	Texas Instruments
IBM	Burroughs
Johnson & Johnson	Bristol-Myers Squibb
Marriott	Howard Johnson
Merck	Pfizer
Motorola	Zenith
Nordstrom	Melville
Philip Morris	RJR Nabisco
Procter & Gamble	Colgate
Sony	Kenwood
Wal-Mart	Ames
Walt Disney	Columbia

---

history to gain understanding and develop concepts and tools that will be useful in preparing organizations to be visionary in the twenty-first century and beyond. They looked for underlying, timeless, fundamental principles and patterns that might apply across eras—they aimed to identify those concepts that would explain the historical trajectory of the visionary companies and would provide practical guidance to managers building their companies for the twenty-first century.

The kernel of their findings comes from comparison analyses; this analytic process was further combined with the creative processes. One outstanding result that emerged was that almost anyone can be a key protagonist in building an extraordinary business institution. The lessons of these companies can be learned and applied by the vast majority of managers at all levels. The study belied the myth that the trajectory of a company depends on whether it is led by people ordained with rare and mysterious qualities that cannot be learned by others.

A few other myths that were shattered were as follows:

Myth 1: It takes a great idea to start a great company.
Myth 2: Visionary companies require great and charismatic visionary leaders.
Myth 3: The most successful companies exist first and foremost to maximize profits.
Myth 4: Visionary companies share a common subset of *correct* core values.
Myth 5: The only constant is change.
Myth 6: Blue-chip companies play it safe.
Myth 7: Visionary companies are great places to work, for everyone.
Myth 8: Highly successful companies make their best moves by brilliant and complex strategic planning.
Myth 9: Companies should hire outside CEOs to stimulate fundamental change.

2.2.1 CLOCK BUILDING, NOT TIME TELLING

Having a great idea or being a charismatic visionary leader is *time telling*; building a company that can prosper far beyond the presence of any single leader and through multiple product life cycles is *clock building*. The findings demonstrate how the builders of visionary companies tend to be clock builders, not time tellers. They concentrate primarily on building an enterprise—building a ticking clock, not a standardized clock but one specific for the company—rather than on hitting a market just right with a visionary product idea and riding the growth curve of an attractive product life cycle.

Visionary leaders, instead of concentrating on acquiring the individual personality traits of visionary leadership, take an architectural approach and concentrate on building the organizational traits of visionary companies. The primary output of their efforts is not the tangible implementation of a great idea, the expression of a charismatic personality, the gratification of their ego, or the accumulation of personal wealth. Their greatest creation is the company itself and what it stands for—if you see the ultimate creation as the company, not the execution of a specific idea or capitalizing on a timely market opportunity, then you can persist beyond any specific idea and move toward becoming an enduring enterprise.

As noted earlier, one of the most significant findings of the study was that creating and building a visionary company absolutely does not require either a great idea or a great and charismatic leader. Hewlett-Packard (HP), Sony, and Wal-Mart belie the widely held mythology of corporate origins that paints a picture of a far-seeing entrepreneur founding his or her company to capitalize on a visionary product idea or visionary market insight. This mythology holds that those who launch highly successful companies usually begin with a brilliant idea (technology, product, market potential) and then ride the growth curve of an attractive product life cycle. Yet this mythology does not show up as a general pattern in the founding of the visionary companies. Instead of seeing the company as a vehicle for the products, being a visionary company entailed seeing the products as a vehicle for the company: exactly the stance that was in line with the difference between time telling and *company-specific* clock building.

The continual stream of great products and services from highly visionary companies stems from them being outstanding organizations, not the other way around. All products, services, and great ideas, no matter how visionary, eventually become obsolete; but if a visionary company has the organizational ability to continually change and evolve beyond existing product life cycles, it may not ever become obsolete.

2.2.2 No "Tyranny of the OR"

 A key aspect of highly visionary companies is the "Tyranny of the OR"—the rational view that cannot easily accept paradox, which cannot live with two seemingly contradictory forces or ideas at the same time. The "Tyranny of the OR" pushes people to believe that things must be either A or B, but not both at the same time.

We're not talking about mere balance here; a visionary company doesn't seek balance between short term and long term, for example. It seeks to do very well both in the short term and in the long term. A visionary company doesn't simply balance between preserving a tightly held core ideology and stimulating vigorous change and movement; it does both to an extreme. A visionary company doesn't simply balance between clear vision and sense of direction and opportunistic groping and experimentation; it strives to plan and also explore emerging opportunities (Table 2.2).

TABLE 2.2
Magic of *AND*

On the One Hand		On the Other Hand
Purpose beyond profit	AND	Pragmatic pursuit of profit
A relatively fixed core ideology	AND	Vigorous change movement
Conversations around the core	AND	Bold, committing, risky moves
Clear vision and sense of direction	AND	Opportunistic groping and experimentation
Big Hairy Audacious Goals	AND	Incremental evolutionary progress
Selection of managers steeped in core	AND	Selection of managers that initiate change
Ideological control	AND	Operational autonomy
Extremely tight culture (almost cult-like)	AND	Ability to change, move, and adapt
Investment for the long term	AND	Demands for short-term performance
Philosophical, visionary, futuristic	AND	Superb daily execution *nuts and bolt*
Organization aligned with a core ideology	AND	Organization adapted to its environment

2.2.3 More than Profits

For many of the visionary companies, profitability is a necessary condition for existence and a means to more important ends, but it is not the end in itself. In contrast to the doctrine taught in business schools, the study did not find *maximizing shareholder wealth* or *profit maximization* as the dominant driving force or primary objective throughout the history of most of the visionary companies. They have tended to pursue a cluster of objectives, of which making money is only one—and not necessarily the primary one. Indeed, for many of the visionary companies, business has historically been more than an economic activity, more than just a way to make money. Most of the visionary companies had a core ideology that transcended purely economic considerations; and they have had the core ideology to a greater degree than the comparison companies in the study.

Visionary companies have generally been more ideologically driven and less purely profit driven than the comparison companies.

In 1935, George Merck II articulated ideals that would guide and inspire it throughout thereafter, "[We] are workers in industry who are genuinely inspired by the ideals of advancement of medical science, and of service to humanity." Driven by these ideals as a backdrop, we're not surprised that Merck elected to develop and give away Mectizan, a drug to cure *river blindness*, a disease that infected over a million people in the Third World with parasitic worms that swarmed through body tissue and eventually into the eyes, causing painful blindness. A million customers is a good-sized market, except that these were customers who could not afford the product. Knowing that the project would not produce a large return on investment (ROI), the company nonetheless went forward with the hope that once available, some government agencies or other third parties would purchase and distribute the product. However, since none of this materialized, Merck elected to give the drug away free to all who needed it. At its own expense, Merck also involved itself directly in distribution efforts to ensure that the drug did indeed reach the millions of people at risk from the disease. Merck has been more ideologically driven than its comparison company Pfizer even though it was also in the same industry and also made drugs that save lives, cure diseases, and relieve suffering.

Core ideology does not come from mimicking the values of other companies—even highly visionary companies; it does not come from following the dictates of outsiders; it does not come from reading management books; and it does not come from a sterile intellectual exercise of *calibrating* what values would be most pragmatic, most popular, or most profitable. When articulating and codifying core ideology, the key step is to capture what is authentically believed, not what other companies set as their values or what the outside world thinks the ideology should be.

Core ideology is a conjunction of core values and a purpose. Core values are the organization's essential and enduring tenets, not to be compromised for financial gain or short-term expediency. The purpose is the set of fundamental reasons for a company's existence beyond just making money; a visionary company continually pursues but never fully achieves or completes its purpose. Both the core values and purpose need not be wholly unique: it's entirely possible that two companies can both share a rock-solid belief in a value like integrity, just as it's entirely possible that two companies could have a very similar purpose. The primary role of purpose is to guide and inspire, not necessarily to differentiate. For example, many companies could share HP's purpose of making a contribution to society via electronic equipment for the advancement of science and the welfare of humanity. The question is, would they hold it as deeply and live it as consistently as HP? The key is authenticity and not uniqueness.

The existence of a core ideology is a primary element in the historical development of visionary companies. The visionary companies don't merely declare an ideology; they also take steps to make the ideology pervasive throughout the organization and transcend any individual leader.

2.2.4 PRESERVE THE CORE/STIMULATE PROGRESS

A company can have the world's most deeply cherished and meaningful core ideology, but if it just sits still or refuses to change, the world will pass it by. It is absolutely essential to not confuse core ideology with culture, strategy, tactics, operations, policies, or other noncore practices. Over time, cultural norms must change; strategy must change; product lines must change; goals must change; competencies must change; administrative policies must change; organization structure must change; reward systems must change. Ultimately, the only thing a company should not change over time is its core ideology—that is, if it wants to be a visionary company.

Core ideology in a visionary company works hand in hand with a relentless drive for progress that impels change and forward movement in all that is not part of the core ideology. The drive for progress arises from a deep human urge—to explore, to create, to discover, to achieve, to change, and to improve. It is the drive for progress that pushed 3M to continually experiment and solve problems that other companies had not yet even recognized as problems, resulting in such pervasive innovations as waterproof sandpaper, Scotch tape, and Post-it notes.

The interplay between core and progress is one of the most important findings from the study:

- The core ideology enables progress by providing a base of continuity around which a visionary company can evolve, experiment, and change. By being clear about what is core (and therefore relatively fixed), a company can more easily seek variation and movement in all that is not core.
- The drive for progress enables the core ideology, for without continual change and forward movement, the company—the carrier of the core—will fall behind in an ever-changing world and cease to be strong or perhaps even to exist.

The essence of clock building is the creation of tangible mechanisms aligned to preserve the core and stimulate progress like the following:

  I.   Big Hairy Audacious Goals (BHAGs): Commitment to challenging, audacious goals and projects toward which a visionary company channels its efforts (stimulates progress).
 II.   Cult-like cultures: Great places to work only for those who buy in to the core ideology; those who don't fit with the ideology are ejected like a virus (preserves the core).
III.   Try a lot of stuff and keep what works: High levels of action and experimentation—often unplanned and undirected—which produce new and unexpected paths of progress and enable visionary companies to mimic the biological evolution of species (stimulates progress).
 IV.   Home-grown management: Promotion from within, bringing to senior levels only those who have spent significant time steeped in the core ideology of the company (preserves the core).
  V.   Good enough never is: A continual process of relentless self-improvement with the aim of doing better and better, forever into the future (stimulates progress).

2.2.5 BIG HAIRY AUDACIOUS GOALS

All companies have goals. But there is a difference between merely having a goal and becoming committed to a huge, daunting challenge—like a big mountain to climb. Boeing Corporation is an excellent example of how highly visionary companies often use bold missions as a particularly powerful mechanism to stimulate progress. A BHAG is not the only powerful mechanism for stimulating progress, nor do all the visionary companies use it extensively. Nonetheless, we found more evidence of this powerful mechanism in the visionary companies and less evidence of it in the comparison companies.

Boeing has a long and consistent history of committing itself to big, audacious challenges. As far back as the early 1930s, it set the goal of becoming a major force in the military aircraft market and gambled its future on the P-26 military plane and then bet the company on the B-17 Flying Fortress. In 1952, Boeing was building aircraft primarily for the military (B-17 Flying Fortress, B-29 Superfortress, B-52 jet bomber), and four-fifths of their business came from only one customer—the Air Force. Boeing virtually had no presence in the commercial market, and commercial airlines in both the United States and Europe have expressed little interest in the idea of a commercial jet from Boeing. It was under such circumstances that Boeing management decided to defy the odds, commit to the audacious goal of developing a prototype for the jet aircraft 707, and establish itself as a major player in the commercial aircraft industry. In the early 1960s, Boeing turned the demands of a potential customer (Eastern Airlines) into a clear, precise—and nearly impossible—challenge for its engineers: build a jet that could land on runway 4-22 at LaGuardia Airport (only 4860 feet long—much too short for any existing passenger jet) and be able to fly nonstop from New York to Miami and be wide enough for six-abreast seating and have a capacity of 131 passengers and meet Boeing's high standards of indestructibility. They achieved all these mutually opposing goals in the 727. Against the original estimate of a market demand of 300, Boeing sold over eighteen hundred 727s.

In contrast, initially Douglas Aircraft made the explicit decision to stick with piston propellers and take a cautious wait-and-see approach to commercial jet aircraft and believes that propeller-driven planes will continue to dominate the commercial market. Belatedly, Douglas introduced the DC-8 only in 1958. They were again slow to respond to 727 and did not introduce the DC-9 until 2 years after 727, putting it even further behind Boeing in the commercial jet aircraft market. Even by their own standards, Boeing overstretched itself—financially, psychologically, and publicly—when it decided to go forward with the 747 jumbo jet. Being slow again to commit to a jumbo jet project, McDonnell Douglas was left behind again with its introduction of DC-10.

We should emphasize here that a BHAG only helps an organization as long as it has not yet been achieved. Once this has been achieved, the company must set a new BHAG, again and again, else it may get afflicted with "we've arrived" syndrome characterized by complacent lethargy.

BHAGs and the consequent progress alone do not make a visionary company. A company should be careful to preserve its core while pursuing BHAGs. For example, the 747 was an incredibly risky venture, but along the way, Boeing maintained its core value of product safety and applied the most conservative safety standards, testing, and analysis ever to a commercial aircraft.

2.2.6 CULT-LIKE CULTURES

Visionary companies tend to be more demanding of their people than other companies, both in terms of performance and congruence with the ideology. Because the visionary companies have such clarity about who they are, what they're all about, and what they're trying to achieve, they tend to not have much room for people unwilling or unsuited to their demanding standards. It's binary: you're either in or out, and there seems to be no middle ground. It's almost cult-like.

Commonly, a *cult* is a body of persons characterized by great or excessive devotion to some person, idea, or thing (which certainly describes many of the visionary companies). The study observed four common characteristics of cults that the visionary companies display to a greater degree than the comparison companies:

- Fervently-held ideology
- Indoctrination
- Tightness of fit
- Elitism

Unlike many religious sects or social movements that often revolve around a charismatic cult leader (a *cult of personality*), visionary companies tend to be cult-like around their ideologies, for example, how Nordstrom created a zealous and fanatical reverence for its core values, shaping a powerful mythology about the customer service heroics of its employees, rather than demanding slavish reverence for an individual leader. Cultism around an individual personality is time telling; creating an environment that reinforces dedication to an enduring core ideology is clock building.

The heavy-duty indoctrination processes at Nordstrom began with the interview and continue with Nordie customer service heroic stories, reminders on the walls, chanting affirmations, and cheering. Nordstrom gets its employees to write heroic stories about other employees and engages peers and immediate supervisors in the indoctrination process. (A common practice of cults is to actively engage recruits in the socializing of others into the cult.) The company seeks to hire young people, mold them into the Nordstrom way from early in their careers, and promote only those who closely reflect the core ideology. Nordstrom imposes a severe tightness of fit—employees that fit the Nordstrom way receive lots of positive reinforcement (pay, awards, recognition)—and those who don't fit get negative reinforcement (being *left behind*, penalties, black marks). Nordstrom also draws clear boundaries between who is *inside* and who is *outside* the organization and how it portrays being *inside* as being part of something special and elite—again, a common practice of cults. Indeed, the very term *Nordie* has a cultish feel to it. We found no evidence that Melville, the corresponding comparison company, cultivated and maintained through its history anywhere near such clear and consistent use of practices like these.

Nordstrom presents an excellent example of what we came to call *cultism*—a series of practices that create an almost cult-like environment around the core ideology in highly visionary companies. These practices tend to vigorously screen out those who do not fit with the ideology (either before hiring or early in their careers). They also instill an intense sense of loyalty and influence the behavior of those remaining inside the company to be congruent with the core ideology, consistent over time, and carried out zealously.

A cult-like culture can actually enhance a company's ability to pursue BHAGs, precisely because it creates that sense of being part of an elite organization that can accomplish just about anything. IBM's cultish sense of itself contributed greatly to its ability to gamble on the IBM 360. Also, visionary companies impose tight ideological control and simultaneously provide wide operating autonomy that encourages individual initiative. In fact, as we will discuss in the next chapter, we found that the visionary companies were significantly more decentralized and granted greater operational autonomy than the comparison companies as a general pattern, even though they have been much more cult-like.

2.2.7 TRY A LOT OF STUFF AND KEEP WHAT WORKS

Visionary companies often make some of their best moves not by detailed strategic planning but rather by experimentation, trial and error, opportunism, and—quite literally—accident. What looks in hindsight like a brilliant strategy is often the result of opportunistic experimentation and *purposeful accidents*.

In 1890, Johnson & Johnson—then primarily a supplier of antiseptic gauze and medical plasters—received a letter from a physician who complained about patient skin irritation from certain medicated plasters. Fred Kilmer, the company's director of research, quickly responded by sending a packet of soothing Italian talc to apply on the skin. He then convinced the company to include a small can of talc as part of the standard package with certain products. To the company's surprise, customers soon began asking to buy more of the talc directly. J&J responded by creating a separate product called *Johnson's Toilet and Baby Powder*, which became a famous household staple around much of the world. According to J&J's own official history, "the Johnsons got into the baby powder business quite by accident." Even more significant, the company thereby took a tiny incremental step that eventually mushroomed into a significant strategic shift into consumer products—an *accident* that eventually grew to become 44% of J&J's revenues—and as important to its growth as medical supplies and pharmaceutical products.

Later, J&J stumbled upon another famous product by accident. In 1920, company employee Earle Dickson created a ready-to-use bandage—made of surgical tape with small pieces of gauze and a special covering so that it would not stick to the skin—for his wife who had a knack for cutting herself with kitchen knives. When he mentioned his invention to the marketing people, they decided to experiment with the product on the market. Eventually, after a slow start and a never-ending process of tinkering, Band-Aid products became the biggest selling category in the company's history and further solidified J&J's *accidental* strategic move into consumer products.

Apart from BHAG, this is a second kind of progress stimulated by the visionary companies to a greater degree than the comparison companies: evolutionary progress. The word *evolutionary* describes this type of progress because it closely resembles how organic species evolve and adapt to their natural environments. Evolutionary progress differs from BHAG progress in three key ways:

1. Whereas BHAG progress is planned and deterministic, evolutionary progress is unplanned and opportunistic.
2. Whereas BHAG progress involves clear and unambiguous goals, evolutionary progress involves ambiguity or tentativeness.
3. Whereas BHAG progress involves bold discontinuous leaps, evolutionary progress usually begins with small incremental steps or mutations, often in the form of quickly seizing unexpected emerging opportunities that eventually result into major strategic shifts.

After the Darwinian revolution, biologists came to understand that species were not directly created in a specific preplanned and deterministic form but they evolve. The central concept of evolutionary theory—and Charles Darwin's great insight—was that species evolve by a process of undirected variation (*random genetic mutation*) and natural selection. Through genetic variation, a species attains *good chances* that some of its members will be well suited to the demands of the environment. As the environment shifts, the genetic variations that best fit the environment tend to get *selected* (i.e., the well-suited variations tend to survive and the poorly suited tend to perish—that's what Darwin meant by *survival of the fittest*). The selected (surviving) variations then have greater representation in the gene pool and the species will evolve in that direction (see Chapter 4, Subsection 4.2, "Darwin's Theory of Evolution through Natural Selection").

However, the process of variation and selection in human organizations differs from a purely Darwinian process in the natural world. Darwinian selection with species is natural selection—an entirely unconscious directed process whereby the variations that best fit with the environment survive and the weakest variations perish. Furthermore, evolution in the natural world has no goal or ideology other than sheer survival of the species. Human organizations, on the other hand, can make predefined, conscious, and predetermined selections. Thus, visionary companies stimulate evolutionary progress toward desired ends within the context of a core ideology, hence termed as *purposeful evolution*.

By the early twentieth century, American Express found its traditional freight business under siege. Government regulators eroded the company's monopolistic rate structure, and in 1913, the U.S. Post Office began a competing parcel-post system; consequently, profits plummeted 50%. Then in 1918, the U.S. government nationalized all freight express businesses, creating a cataclysmic industry change; as the government snatched away their core business, most freight companies had to close shop. But for American Express, though unplanned, its experiments in financial and travel services proved to be favorable variations that were better suited to the changed environment than its traditional freight business. These variations were then selected as the path to evolve beyond its traditional line of business and on which to base its future businesses in money orders and *travelers' check*.

2.2.8 HOME-GROWN MANAGEMENT

Visionary companies develop, promote, and carefully select managerial talent grown from inside the company to a greater degree than the comparison companies. They do this as a key step in preserving their core. It is not the quality of leadership that most separates the visionary companies from the comparison companies. It is the continuity of quality leadership that matters. Both the visionary companies and the comparison companies have had excellent top management at certain points in their histories, but the visionary companies have had better management development and succession planning. They thereby ensured greater continuity in leadership talent grown from within than the comparison companies.

The study concluded that it is extraordinarily difficult to become and remain a highly visionary company by hiring top management from outside the organization. On the other hand, there was absolutely no inconsistency between promoting from within and stimulating significant change.

The management-succession process that placed venerable General Electric (GE) in Welch's hands exemplifies the best and most vital aspects of the old GE culture. The result ranks among the finest examples of succession planning in corporate history. Prior CEO Reginald Jones took the first step in that process by creating a document entitled A *Road Map for CEO Succession* in 1974—7 years before Welch became CEO. After working closely with GE's Executive Manpower Staff, he spent 2 years paring an initial list of 96 possibilities—all of them GE insiders—down to 12, and then 6 prime candidates, including Welch. To test and observe the candidates, Jones appointed each of the six to be *sector executives*, reporting directly to the Corporate Executive Office. Over the next 3 years, he gradually narrowed the field, putting the candidates through a variety of rigorous challenges, interviews, essay contests, and evaluations. Welch eventually won the grueling endurance contest from a group of candidates so highly qualified that almost all of them ended up heading major corporations.

2.2.9 GOOD ENOUGH NEVER IS

In a highly visionary company, there is no ultimate finish line. There is no point where they feel they can coast the rest of the way, living off the fruits of their labor. Visionary companies attain their extraordinary position not so much because of superior insight or special *secrets* of success but largely because of the simple fact that they are so terribly demanding of themselves. Becoming and remaining a visionary company requires oodles of plain old-fashioned discipline, hard work, and a visceral revulsion to any tendency toward smug self-satisfaction. At the visionary companies, the concept of *continuous improvement* has been commonplace for decades. Rather than as a program or management fad, in a visionary company, it is an institutionalized habit ingrained into the fabric of the organization and reinforced by tangible mechanisms that create discontent with the status quo. Furthermore, visionary companies apply the concept of self-improvement in a much broader sense than just process improvement. It means long-term investments for the future; it means investment in the development of employees; it means adoption of new ideas and technologies.

Visionary companies thrive on discontent. They understand that contentment leads to complacency, which inevitably leads to decline. So visionary companies install powerful mechanisms to create discomfort and discontent—to counter complacency—and thereby stimulate change and improvement before the external world demands it.

Richard Deupree at Procter & Gamble (P&G) pondered these exact questions, worried that P&G's rise to prominence in the early twentieth century might cause the company to become complacent. In 1931, he created a brand management structure that would allow P&G brands to compete directly with other P&G brands, almost as if they were from different companies. If the marketplace doesn't provide enough competition, why not create a system of internal competition that makes it virtually impossible for any brand to rest on its laurels? Implemented in the early 1930s, the competing brand management structure became a powerful mechanism at P&G for stimulating change and improvement from within. The structure proved so effective that it was eventually copied in one form or another by virtually every American consumer products company, including Colgate—but not until nearly three decades later.

Visionary companies simply do not accept the proposition that they must choose between short-term performance and long-term success. They build first and foremost for the long term while simultaneously holding themselves to highly demanding short-term standards. HP versus TI illustrates one of the key differences we saw between the visionary and comparison companies. In the 1970s, TI's quest for sheer size and growth in the short term (squeezing quality and thus cost) eroded its foundation and heritage as a creator of excellent and innovative products and severely damaged its long-term prospects. Visionary companies habitually invest, build, and manage for the long term to a greater degree than the comparison companies in our study. *Long term* at a visionary company does not mean 5 or 10 years; it means multiple decades—50 years is more like it. Yet, at the same time, they do not let themselves off the hook in the short term.

Visionary companies invested for the future to a greater degree than the comparison companies. Visionary companies consistently invested more heavily in new property, plant, and equipment as a percentage of annual sales than the comparison companies; they invested more heavily in R&D as a percentage of sales. They also plowed a greater percentage of each year's earnings back into the company, paying out less in cash dividends to shareholders. The visionary companies also invested much more aggressively in human capital via extensive recruiting, employee training, and professional development programs. The visionary companies tended to have much more elaborate and extensive recruiting and interviewing processes than the comparison companies, requiring a significant professional and managerial time investment. Finally, the visionary companies invest earlier and more aggressively than the comparison companies in such aspects as technical know-how, new technologies, new management methods, and innovative industry practices.

2.3 SUMMARY

This chapter introduced the patterns of excellence proposed by pioneers in this area. First, it presents the patterns of excellence first proposed by Tom Peters and Robert Waterman in their 1980 book *In Search of Excellence: Lessons from Americas Best-Run Companies*. This refers to the McKinsey 7S model that inspired this book's extended 9S framework consisting of strategy, structure, shared values, stuff, style, staff, skills, systems, and sequence. We present the 9S framework in detail in Chapter 5, *Variations and Enterprise Excellence*. In the latter part of this chapter, we presented another set of patterns proposed by Jim Collins and Jerry Porras in their 2002 book *Built to Last: Successful Habits of Visionary Companies*. Both of these books, in respective times, led to a deluge of books on this and related topics.

3 Antipatterns of Excellence

3.1 SEVEN STRATEGIC TRAPS*

The authors believe that there is much to be gained from examining the strategic failures of others. After shifting through the ashes of numerous failures, they have observed that root causes are often similar with minor changes in each individual case. They have identified seven of the most common causes of strategic failure, which are described in the following.

Strategic Trap #1: Business blind spots that are related to failing to recognize and understand the implications of events and changing conditions in the competitive environment. Even though this is equivalent to an ostrich avoiding danger by burying its head in the sand, it is not very uncommon to find examples of companies whose strategies have foundered because they failed to register or understand the changing circumstances in their environment. Enterprises often ignore environmental signals that are inconsistent with their assumptions about the *formula* for success. Notwithstanding the changing market conditions, there is a natural tendency to persist with strategies that have successes in the past. Britannica was clearly aware of the availability and the potential of CD-ROM technology; their subsidiary Compton's Encyclopedia was one of the first to enter the market with a true multimedia product. While Britannia's strengths were in the depth of editorial content, Compton's strengths were in fewer words and more pictorial format. But Britannica failed to understand the impact the CD-ROM technology would have on their flagship product. Not only did they miss on an opportunity, but management unnecessarily drove themselves in the corner by opting out of this emerging market segment, which could have significantly expanded the market for their entire product line.

Strategic Trap #2: Flawed assumptions that are related to basing strategies on a flawed set of assumptions or premises or failing to react when changing circumstances render the initial assumptions and premises invalid. This focuses on the assumptions and premises on which strategies are devised and evaluated. Given the initial assumptions and premises, the strategies and products seemed to be sound and well thought out; however, in each case, these enterprises fell into the trap of basing a strategy on a flawed set of assumptions that in hindsight proved to be invalid. Strategies frequently go awry when management's internal frame of reference is out of sync with the realities of the business situation. Misled by the fundamental assumptions and biases of their individual and collective assumption sets, the managers of each of these companies embarked upon and then persisted in a failing strategy long after it was recognized as fallacious. In other cases, strategies fall short of achieving sustainable competitive advantage not because their initial assumptions and premises were wrong, but because these were overtaken by events that could not have been foreseen at the time. Testing the validity of a set of assumptions is not always easy; managers often become so locked into a particular view of the world that they lose sight of *why* they believe *what* they believe.

GM and the rest of the domestic automobile industry have learned a great deal from the 1983 joint venture with Toyota known as New United Motor Manufacturing, Inc. (NUMMI) that in the beginning produced a line of nearly identical vehicles—the Toyota Corolla and GM's Geo

---

* Joseph Picken and Gregory Dess, *Mission Critical: The 7 Strategic Traps That Derail Even the Smartest Companies* (Irwin: Chicago, IL, Irwin, 1997).

Prism—sold in the United States through two separate distribution channels. It was assumed that NUMMI would provide a number of advantages for GM and Toyota, such as the following:

1. By building the cars on a common assembly line, GM would achieve manufacturing cost and quality parity with GM.
2. GM would learn how to build automobiles the *Japanese way* and would be able to lever this knowledge into improved competitive position for its other product lines.
3. Toyota would reduce the threat of punitive import duties on one of its most popular models.

NUMMI appears to have been a success for both companies in that the initial objects have been achieved. As GM has focused on quality and adopted the same lean production techniques, the Japanese edge in product cost and quality has been nullified. But in the meanwhile, the market has varied and the competitive advantage has now shifted to design, marketing, and supply chain management. The GM and other U.S. automakers are lagging behind again in the new arena, and Toyota has regained the high ground in the redefined market.

In the early 1980s, the Beech Aircraft was taken over by Raytheon Co. who was keen to reduce its dependence on the highly cyclical defense business. However, Beech's traditional core *light aircraft* business had collapsed under the burden of huge payouts to victims of private aviation mishaps. Beech continued to operate with the manufacture of King Air, the leading corporate turboprop aircraft. Raytheon conceived of a bold plan—an advanced turboprop design based on latest materials technology that would provide performance competitive with low-end business jets at a fraction of the cost. Originally conceived as a competitor to the small corporate jets from Cessna and Learjet, a 10-seater aircraft capable of 400-knot speed, the all-composite aircraft would be more fuel efficient than a jet, require only a pilot, be ready for shipment in 2 years, and sell only for about $3 million (versus $4.5–$6 million for a comparable business jet). This was quite similar to Ford's initial conception of Model T vehicle (see Chapter 6, Subsection 6.1, "Enigma of Xerox"). Raytheon's strategy for Beech was to move up in performance with an advanced-design turboprop based on the latest defense-industry technologies that could compete effectively and win market share from its competitors at the low end of the business jet market.

But Raytheon's strategy was based on a number of key assumptions, which turned out to be invalid:

1. Raytheon would complete the design of the all-composite aircraft called *Starship*.
2. Raytheon will achieve Federal Aviation Administration (FAA) certification for the all-composite aircraft in 2 years.
3. There would be a significant market for the all-composite aircraft.

Moreover, they had assumed that they would not be struck by Murphy's law. The key to the design lies in the anticipated weight savings: carbon fiber composites are 350% stronger than aluminum but 15%–20% lighter. By building the plane from these stronger but lighter materials, the aircraft could carry more payload further and faster than the conventional turboprop but significantly better economy than a jet. However, the FAA had never certified an all-composite aircraft and began to insist on compliance with certain existing standards for metal aircraft. This resulted in an incredibly strong composite fiber aircraft that weighed about as much as a metal one. With increase in weight, bigger engines were required, which meant more fuel, which in turn meant additional weight, requiring the redesign of the structure, and so on. As the weight increased upward, the Starship outgrew the *light aircraft* category and moved into the *commuter aircraft* weight class requiring two pilots.

The Starship finally made to the market, delayed by more than 4 years. But it did not come close to meet the original performance expectations. Most importantly, the anticipated market never materialized and the production line was shut down by 1994.

Strategic Trap #3: Creating competitive (dis)advantage that is related to pursuing a 1D strategy that fails to create or sustain a long-term competitive advantage. Many enterprises base their strategies on organizational strengths that do not create competitive advantages or rely so heavily on a single source of competitive advantage that they fail to recognize the need for a different approach when environmental conditions change. Many a times, the enterprise's dominant strength contributed to a significant strategic failure. The root of the problem is the vision that carried a strategy of cost cutting to a dysfunctional extreme or led to a valueless attempt at differentiation or pushed ahead with an innovation that the market neither wanted nor appreciated. In 1980, Michael Porter introduced the notion that there were three potentially successful generic strategies—cost leadership, differentiation, and focus—that enable firms to outperform their rivals. Southwest Airlines' 15 min turnaround time between flights is an example of how one key element can enhance all three forms of competitive advantage. This quick turnaround results in a cost saving of $25 million per airplane in capital expenditures alone through more efficient utilization of their aircraft. Ensuring such tight turnarounds requires superb coordination among several activities, including ticketing, catering, baggage handling, fuelling, maintenance, and flight plans and local clearances. Moreover, greater utilization enables the airline to offer more flights; this is a source of differentiation because it provides their customers with a more frequent arrival and departure times at each destination serviced.

Apple has historically competed on the basis of differentiation and quick response through product introductions like Apple II, the first successful PC in 1977; Lisa, the first PC with a GUI in 1983; Macintosh PC with its numerous technological innovations in 1984; LaserWriter printer for desktop publishing 1985; and PowerBook notebook in 1991. In 1993, Apple launched Newton PDA as an organizer with built-in e-mail, fax capability, and a host of other features. After the initial surging sales of more than 50,000 Newtons, the sales quickly dropped to negligible quantity per month. Given the weak returns on a $100 million investment for this product, Apple eliminated one-fifth of its workforce including CEO John Scully. In the rush to lever the first mover's advantage, Apple made several mistakes:

1 There was too much of hype rather than reality, and Apple leadership bought into its own hype.
2. Newton was released before it was ready because of internally generated publicity and excessively heightened expectations that ruled out any delays in the launch.
3. Suboptimal ability to decipher handwriting.
4. Inability to connect to office network or a PC.

Subsequent releases addressed these issues with improved handwriting recognition and a complete communications package, but Newton as an exciting product was already dead.

Strategic Trap #4: Subtracting value by adding businesses that is related to diversifying for all the wrong reasons, into areas of activity that fail to add value for investors. Mergers and acquisitions must be justified by the generation of value for shareholders. The related value of synergy is defined as the incremental value created by business units working together as part of a corporation as compared to the value generated by the units operating independently, that is, as separate companies. Synergy may be generated by

1. Capitalizing on core competencies (R&D expertise, marketing skills, etc.)
2. Sharing infrastructures (production facilities, marketing channels, procurement processes, and the like)
3. Increasing market reach and power (creating a stronger bargaining position vis-a-vis suppliers and customers)

Value chain analysis is an essential tool for analyzing and understanding the potential sources of synergy in a diversification strategy. Managers must look at their existing business as part of a broader value chain system that encompasses the firm, its suppliers, its customers, and the potential acquisition or joint venture candidate and identify the sources of synergy. What important relationships exist or can be created among the primary and support activities of the value chain of entities that comprise the firms' *extended* value chain? How can such relationships enhance competitive advantage through cost leadership, differentiation, focus, or quick response? GE pursues technology across its entire organization. GE's business units share technology, design expertise, compensation practices, and customer and country knowledge across its various businesses. Thus, gas turbine unit shares manufacturing with aircraft engines; motor and transportation systems work together on new locomotive propulsion systems; lightning and medical systems collaborate to improve x-ray tube processes; and GE Capital provides innovative financial products that help all GE businesses across the world.

Rather than continuing to focus on Novell's highly successful networking system business, Novell CEO Ray Noorda decided to challenge Microsoft's dominance in operating systems and applications. Accordingly, Novell acquired WordPerfect Corporation, a leader in word-processing applications, at the cost of $1.4 billion in 1994. Novell's goal was to integrate WordPerfect's then popular word-processing software, Borland's Quatro Pro spreadsheet, and other applications with Novell's networking software. However, the smooth integration of the acquisition foundered because of the severe clashes between the Novell and WordPerfect cultures. Novell's sales force was oriented toward corporate market, while the WordPerfect's sales force was focused on the retail channel; thus, the anticipated synergies in marketing and distribution were not realized. Moreover, as most of the WordPerfect's top management team left shortly after the acquisition, Novell's comparatively limited resources were spread thin. Novell's performance suffered and the stock price fell sharply.

Strategic Trap #5: Tripping over the barriers, which is related to failing to structure and implement mechanisms to ensure the coordination and integration of core processes and key functions across enterprise boundaries. Boundaries are an essential element in the description and definition of enterprises. Enterprise boundaries are defined in a variety of ways: by product, by function, by geography, and ultimately by ownership, control, and enterprise's existence as a legal entity. For the most part, enterprise boundaries serve useful and essential functions but, when the boundaries become barriers to effective coordination and integration, often emerge as major impediments to the successful implementation of strategy. High degree of organizational specialization and the optimization of processes and procedures to maximize local efficiencies may create strong organizational barriers that limit flexibility, impede communications, and create intolerable delays in accomplishing even routine tasks. Major strategic programs, such as the development and introduction of a complex system or a new product, are particularly dependent upon effective cross-functional integration of activities. Such complex tasks require the close coordination and integration of R&D, engineering, manufacturing, marketing, and sales activities and are virtually impossible to achieve under the traditional structure, which became a millstone around the enterprise's neck, sapping its productivity and constraining its ability to compete.

Therefore, a key management challenge is to design more flexible enterprises. Three new architectures promise greater flexibility than the traditional model: modular, virtual, and barrier-free organizations. The choice of an organizational architecture creates different opportunities and constraints on subsequent managerial choices, including strategic objectives, its core competencies and limitations, and its need to retain, or willingness to relinquish, strategic control over the key activities in its value chain.

Also, management must select and implement an appropriate mix of tools and techniques to achieve the desired mix and balance of coordination, integration, and strategic control. Some are focused on achieving more effective coordination, others address the barriers to more effective integration, and some provide new approaches to strategic control. GE's description of the boundaryless organization suggests that a number of different approaches can be successful within an enterprise:

1. Experimenting with new ideas
2. Adopting *best practices* from other organizations

3. Involving customers and suppliers in design and production decisions
4. Using multifunctional teams
5. Developing cooperative labor-management practices
6. Sharing expertise throughout the organization

Others advocate leveraging core competencies, using information technology (IT) to facilitate cross-functional integration, outsourcing nonstrategic functions, and developing strategic partnerships and alliances. No one tool or technique, by itself, is likely to be the total solution; rather a combination of several techniques must be used, as building blocks, to attain an effective organization. The actual mix would be specific to each particular enterprise and its strategic environment.

Strategic Trap #6: Arbitrary goals that are related to setting arbitrary and inflexible goals and implementing a system of controls that fails to achieve a balance among culture, rewards, and boundaries. This fundamental strategic error results from the blind pursuit of an arbitrary and inflexible set of objectives and an unbalanced system of strategic controls that drives the enterprise with culture and rewards but fails to define the boundaries of acceptable behavior.

The traditional approach to strategic control is rigid and sequential and involves a single feedback loop. Strategies are formulated and goals are set, plans are implemented, and performance is measured against predetermined goal. Although simple and easy to implement, the traditional approach is flexible, and the long time lag between goal setting and performance measurement limits the usefulness of the approach in dynamic and rapidly changing environments. Consider the case of the subsidiary of a manufacturer of heavy mining, oilfield, and construction equipment; multimillion-dollar pieces of equipment were designed and built in the United States and shipped in pieces to one of the 14 sales companies around the world. The sales companies were responsible for assembly and delivery of the equipment to the customer and subsequent ongoing support and warranty service. Each unit's performance was measured against predetermined profit objectives; all costs incurred in the field for warranty support were charged back to the factory through the intercompany accounts and immediately credited against the sales company's operating expenses, because of which each plant scrutinized the charge-backs in detail. Thus, one way to solve a short-term profit optimization problem at the factory was to slow down the processing of warranty claims by leaving them unresolved in the intercompany accounts; in turn, a sales company could *better* its profit by overcharging the factory for warranty work—an overcharge that would not be detected for months because of the procedural time lag involved. In retaliation, the factory frequently *disallowed* warranty claims for minor discrepancies and charged them back to the relevant sales company (which would correct the problem and rebill it to the factory). When uncovered, this warranty-claim *ping-pong* had been going on for years and involved unreconciled *warranty claims in process* amount that exceeded the sales company's cumulative earnings of a few years.

In the contemporary approach to strategic control, both the premises of strategy formulation and the results of strategy implementation are monitored more or less continuously. *Informational control* monitors both premises and the current strategic context to ensure that the organization's strategy continues to be focused on *doing the right things*, while *behavioral control* focuses on ensuring that the organization is *doing things right*. Effective strategic control requires the use and balancing of three separate elements or *levers* of behavioral control: culture, rewards, and boundaries. Culture is a system of shared values (what is important) and beliefs (how things work) that shape a company's member employees, organizational structures, and control systems to produce behavioral norms (the way we do things around here). If culture, rewards, and boundaries are not consistent, they will work at cross purposes; if one or more of these elements are neglected or overemphasized, the resulting distortions may render the entire system dysfunctional. Each of these elements plays a different role in the development and implementation of an effective system of strategic controls, and alignment and balance among these elements become essential.

Traditional enterprises have relied heavily on boundaries and constraints—rules, policies, procedures, and the sanctions of enforcement—to exercise operational and strategic control.

The downside is that organizations that rely too heavily on rules and regulations are inflexible and often suffer from a lack of motivation on the part of the employees. An overreliance on rules may lead to difficulties with customers, indifferent performance, and constant conflicts among departments and functions. As firms downsize and eliminate layers of management and as the marketplace requires greater flexibility and responsiveness, increased coordination and integration of activities across enterprise boundaries are essential. Reliance on boundaries and constraints as the primary means of strategic control may no longer be feasible, and the use of rewards and culture to align individual and enterprise goals becomes increasingly important. Monitoring is expensive and a pure overhead cost, which many enterprises cannot afford; culture and awards are often less costly, although they involve investment of a different kind. They expect different kinds of behavior from top executives; the development and reinforcement of culture involves managers in personnel selection, training and indoctrination, and the ongoing reinforcement of organizational values through their writings, speeches, and leadership by example. Well-designed rewards and incentives can go a large way to align individual and organizational objectives and to ensure that the entire enterprise is focused on *doing the right things*.

Effective rewards and incentive programs have a number of common characteristics:

1. Objectives are clear, well understood, and broadly accepted.
2. Rewards are clearly linked to performance and desired behaviors.
3. Performance measures are clear and highly visible.
4. Performance feedback is prompt, clear, and unambiguous.
5. The compensation system is perceived as fair and equitable.
6. The structure is flexible to be able to adapt to changing circumstances.

Strategic Trap #7: A failure of leadership that is related to ignoring basic principles and failing to provide the leadership essential to the successful implementation of strategic change. The role of leadership is crucial in the effective implementation of strategy. We have focused on leadership primarily in the context of organizational transformation: leadership is about the process of transforming organizations and institutions from what they are to what the leader would have them become.

Transformational change involves much more than only cultural change. Xerox Corporation's competitive position was seriously eroded in the early 1980s by aggressive Japanese manufacturers. Upon visiting their Japanese counterparts, Xerox discovered that its Japanese competitors were able to manufacture, ship, and sell copiers in about the same cost that it took Xerox to only manufacture them. Consequently, under the leadership of David Kearns, Xerox embarked on an enterprise-wide transformation program called *Leadership through Quality*: Xerox's function-driven matrix structure was revamped into three strategic business units (SBUs); estimation and reward systems were changed to monitor how it effectively supported the program; an extensive training program was rolled out covering all of the 100,000 Xerox employees; new standard and measurements were introduced to make the language of TQM part of the everyday business process; the language and symbols of TQM were widely disseminated through training, videotape messages, and company publications and became an essential part of the culture; finally in 1986, David Kearns rearranged the order of corporate goals on company literature to quality, return on assets, and market share.

The characteristics of transformational leaders are as follows:

1. Move quickly and decisively and create a sense of urgency: Change is greatly facilitated when people throughout the enterprise share an awareness of a crisis and a need for immediate action. Sometimes, a leader may have to deliberately create a sense of crisis, to energize an enterprise, and get it moving in the right direction.
2. Develop and communicate both a vision and a plan: A leader needs to develop a vision and a plan and then communicate them broadly and effectively across the enterprise.

     The vision must be focused on the future and what the enterprise needs to do to succeed, and it must provide a framework within which goals and objectives can be developed.
3. Set stretch goals and empower others to act: A leader must challenge the enterprise by setting stretch goals and then to empower it to achieve them. Effective stretch goals require an organization to change what it does and how it does it.
4. Consolidate the gains by institutionalizing change.

3.2 SELF-DESTRUCTIVE HABITS OF GOOD COMPANIES*

Success is huge business vulnerability. It can destroy an enterprise's ability to understand the need for change and can also destroy the motivation to change when their external environment changes; underlying this inability or unwillingness to change are the self-destructive habits that companies acquire on their way to success and greatness. Sometimes these habits become worse overtime and become, in effect, addictions. But self-destructive habits can also be broken and overcome, and companies can be put back on the road to improved health. Great leadership is crucial for helping a company avoid or break self-destructive habits. Good leaders provide vision for the company, but great leaders, in addition to being visionaries, must be grounded in the reality of current and potential vulnerabilities posed by hostile and constantly changing external environment. Great leaders are constantly looking out for self-destructive habits that will get in the way of the existing vision.

3.2.1 SELF-DESTRUCTIVE HABIT #1: DENIAL—THE COCOON OF MYTH, RITUAL, AND ORTHODOXY

Denial is a disbelief in the existence of reality of a thing or refusal to recognize or acknowledge that reality. This destructive habit prevents companies from being reminded that they have arrived at their success through good fortune as much as through their own brilliance and that they may still prove to be fallible after all.

     Things that lead to denial are as follows:

1. Emerging technologies
2. Changing consumer tastes
3. New global environment

The warning signs of denial are as follows:

- "I am different" syndrome
- "Not invented here" syndrome
- "Looking for answers in all wrong places" syndrome

3.2.2 SELF-DESTRUCTIVE HABIT #2: ARROGANCE—PRIDE BEFORE THE FALL

Arrogance is an overblown self-image that doesn't square up with the facts; it leads to the downfall of great heroes. The same flaw causes mighty companies to stumble as well.

     Things that lead to arrogance are as follows:

1. Exceptional achievement in the past warped perception of reality.
2. David conquers Goliath.
3. Pioneer a product or service or experience that is not duplicable.

---

* Jagdish Sheth, *The Self Destructive Habits of Good Companies... and How to Break Them* (New York:, Wharton Sh. Pub, 2007).

The warning signs of arrogance are as follows:

1. Stop listening.
2. Flaunt it.
3. Browbeat it.
4. High-handedness.
5. Curry approval.

3.2.3   SELF-DESTRUCTIVE HABIT #3: COMPLACENCY—SUCCESS BREEDS FAILURE

Complacency rests on three main factors: success in the past, belief in predictable future, and belief in *much more of the same* will resolve all problems. Complacency is the sense of security and comfort that derives from the belief that the success in the past will continue indefinitely. It gives rise to the assumption that the future will be like the present and past and that nothing will change substantially. A jolt will come, but you would not be shaken. Complacency settles easily into large institutions, where size and scale provide a natural bulwark against the demanding and competitive world outside.

Things that lead to complacency are as follows:

1. Past success comes via a regulated monopoly.
2. Past success was based on a distribution monopoly.
3. *Chosen* for success by the government.
4. Government owns or controls the business.

The warning signs of complacency are as follows:

- No hurry to make decisions.
- Processes are overly bureaucratic.
- Bottom-up, decentralized, consensus-based culture.
- Vertically integrated structure.
- Enormous cross-subsidies by functions, by products, by markets, and by customers.

3.2.4   SELF-DESTRUCTIVE HABIT #4: COMPETENCY DEPENDENCE—THE CURSE OF INCUMBENCY

When you are competency dependent, your strength becomes your weakness. Most enterprises depend on a core competency for success, but this competency dependence becomes a liability when it limits your vision and blinds you from other opportunities. It's hard to change when you are no. 1. Your competency is deeply rooted in your culture; it is what you are and what you stand for—it becomes your identity. That is hard to change when the market for your iconic product is in decline.

Things that lead to competency dependence are as follows:

1. R&D dependence
2. Design dependence
3. Sales dependence
4. Service dependence

The warning signs of competency dependence are as follows:

- Efforts to transform the company prove futile.
- The thrill is gone.
- Stakeholders jump ship.

3.2.5 Self-Destructive Habit #5: Competitive Myopia—A Short-Sighted View of Competition

You suffer from this destructive habit when you make the mistake of defining your competitors too narrowly; you acknowledge only those competitors whose challenge is direct and immediate. You lack the peripheral vision that would discern less obvious challengers; their threat is not on radar screen today but is nonetheless real and dangerous.

Things that lead to competitive myopia are as follows:

1. The natural evolution of the industry
2. The clustering phenomenon
3. When no. 1 is also the pioneer
4. The opposite scenario: when no. 2 chases no. 1

The warning signs of competitive myopia are as follows:

- Small niche players coexist with you.
- Supplier's loyalty is won by nontraditional competitor(s).
- Customer's strategy shifts from buy to make.
- Underestimated new entrants, especially from emerging economies.
- Helplessness against a substitute technology.

3.2.6 Self-Destructive Habit #6: Volume Obsession—Rising Costs and Falling Margins

This self-destructive habit is usually a by-product of growth. This comes about when your costs are too high for the revenue you are generating. In a free-market situation, this occurs when prices crash because of intense competition or excess industry capacity, but your costs remain the same.

Things that lead to volume obsession are as follows:

1. The high-margin pioneer
2. The fast-growth phenomenon
3. The paradox of scale
4. The ball and chain of unintended obligations

The warning signs of volume obsession are as follows:

- Guideline-free, ad hoc spending: You have other more interesting and challenging things to think about than controlling your costs.
- Functional-level cost centers: You have always calculated profit and loss at the corporate level, even though it may no longer be efficient or even sensible.
- A culture of cross-subsidies: You allow the success of one business unit to conceal the failure of another one.
- Truth in numbers: Your auditors, your stock price, or industry analyst is telling you that the numbers are not in your favor.

3.2.7 Self-Destructive Habit #7: The Territorial Impulse—Culture Conflicts and Turf Wars

As companies grow and become successful, they tend to organize themselves into *functional silos*; successful growth requires rules, policies, and procedures, and it requires organization and structure. For the sake of efficiency, growth necessitates organization into silos, which threaten to become factions, fiefdoms, or territories. In the absence of a strong leader who can instill his or her vision in the minds of chieftains, the company is likely to find itself expending its time and resources resolving conflicts between warring tribes.

Things that lead to the territorial impulse are as follows:

1. The corporate ivory tower.
2. Growth requires the institution of formal policies and procedures.
3. The founder's culture is submitted within a larger corporate culture.
4. A company's culture is dominated by one functional specially.

The warning signs of the territorial impulse are as follows:

- Dissension: Instead of one strong general, your company has a lot of headstrong lieutenants.
- Indecision: Decision making is an agonizing or even impossible process.
- Confusion: The left hand doesn't know what the right hand is doing.
- Malaise: Nobody's happy, especially the rank and file.

3.3 SEDUCED BY SUCCESS*

Success creates a huge business vulnerability. It can destroy an enterprise's ability to understand the need for change and can also destroy the motivation to creatively attack the status quo. Enterprises and people become trapped by legacy practices and thinking. They fail to notice that the world is changing around them; this fallout is one of the most crippling phenomena that enterprises face. Instead of building on all things they have done well in the past, managers become complacent, comfortable, and mediocre. All are susceptible to success-induced traps.

3.3.1 SUCCESS-INDUCED TRAP #1: NEGLECT—STICKING WITH YESTERDAY'S BUSINESS MODEL

Business model includes questions like what is the industry that the enterprise will be competing? Would they manufacture in-house or outsource? How will they sell the products or services? What is the structure of support staff? What is the approach to distribution and inventory? Enterprise should be consistently reviewing all aspects of their business model, looking for areas that are weak and need to be overhauled. For example, Michael Dell scrutinized the PC industry to see if he could create a unique business model in what looked like a commodity business. He observed that all the PC manufacturers were using the retail channel as a way to get their products into the consumer's hands. Dell envisaged that there was potential for a business model that sold unsurpassed products using a direct-to-the-customer approach and a just-in-time manufacturing approach, avoiding the costs and complexity of both a sales force and inventories.

3.3.2 SUCCESS-INDUCED TRAP #2: PRIDE—ALLOWING YOUR PRODUCTS
TO BECOME OUTDATED

Success compels you to believe that once you have studied consumer behavior, analyzed and identified the optimal sales approach, upgraded to the latest technology to generate improved products, and everything else that is required to stay ahead, things are going to be fine thereafter. But you have to assume that your product and service are going to become inferior to the competition very soon; and you have to be on the guard to repeat the process again and again. Until the early 1970s, typewriters were used to prepare documents and IBM Selectric model was the

---

* Robert Harbold, *Seduced by Success* (New York, McGraw-Hill, 1997).

industry standard. In 1976, Wang Laboratories introduced its word processor incorporating all characteristics of a modern word processor. It basically invented the word-processing segment of this industry.

Then, during early to mid-1980s, the PC emerged and PC-based word processors like WordPerfect and Microsoft Word became the rage. Wang made no attempt to modify its software for the PC and died out. Wang fell into the trap of not updating its products, even though it basically had invented this segment of the industry.

3.3.3 Success-Induced Trap #3: Boredom—Clinging to Your Once-Successful Branding after It Has Become Stale and Dull

Maintaining a vibrant brand requires constant hard work because the brand must be kept fresh and vital. Once a brand achieves some success, the tendency is to sit back and relax, allowing your brand to become dull and ordinary. In 1928, Chrysler introduced the Plymouth automobile as the competitor to Ford and Chevrolet. It earned a solid brand reputation in the low price range of being a reliable, sturdy, and durable car but having a bit more flair than Chevrolet and Ford. In the 1960s, the Plymouth brand began to lose its uniqueness; Chrysler also decided to reposition the Dodge, reducing its price so that it was quite close to that of Plymouth. By 1982, Dodge was outselling Plymouth, and finally, Chrysler announced discontinuation of the Plymouth brand in 1999.

3.3.4 Success-Induced Trap #4: Complexity—Ignoring Your Business Processes as They Become Cumbersome and Complicated

Many a times when enterprises experience weak financial results, they end up laying off thousands of people and streamlining the structure and organization. Under the pretext of refining the management, business units seeking more autonomy often develop their own processes and staff resources; they add more and more people, resulting in increasing nonstandardization and fragmentation of processes. Such bloated processes, instead of increasing efficacy of the processes, only add extra costs to the basic processes of the enterprise.

3.3.5 Success-Induced Trap #5: Bloat—Rationalizing Your Loss of Speed and Agility

Enterprise's bloated processes thwart its ability to respond to changes rapidly, which consequently results in loss of agility. Even in precisely definable areas like IT, the autonomic tendency for proactiveness results within short time in a proliferation of heterogeneous solutions across the enterprise that are incompatible with each other. Such disparate collection of systems prevent the enterprise to function as a unified entity, reducing drastically its ability to respond decisively to competitive challenges of the market.

3.3.6 Success-Induced Trap #6: Mediocrity—Condoning Poor Performance and Letting Your Star Employees Languish

Successful enterprises are especially vulnerable to this trap, since enterprises that achieve success often have high morale and pride. Lacking any sense of urgency, successful enterprises find it difficult to deal with poor performances; on the other hand, the really strong performers tend to get ignored; they also do not feel challenged enough. This discourages them to feel involved and engaged in the effort for defining and realizing the future.

3.3.7 SUCCESS-INDUCED TRAP #7: LETHARGY—GETTING LULLED INTO A CULTURE OF COMFORT, CASUALNESS, AND CONFIDENCE

Success, and the resulting tendency to become complacent, often leads enterprises and individuals to believe that they are talented, have figured out all the answers, and no longer need to reanalyze the situations and problems afresh to devise innovative solutions expeditiously.

3.3.8 SUCCESS-INDUCED TRAP #8: TIMIDITY—NOT CONFRONTING TURF WARS, INFIGHTING, AND OBSTRUCTIONISTS

Success often leads to the hiring of too many people and fragmentation of the enterprise, which results in turf wars and infighting of warring groups to have their way; there is a clear lack of direction for the enterprise and slow decision making on critical issues.

3.3.9 SUCCESS-INDUCED TRAP #9: CONFUSION—UNWITTINGLY PROVIDING SCHIZOPHRENIC COMMUNICATIONS

Communications from the head of the enterprise, be it a small group or a corporate company, are critical. Member employees want to know where they are headed and want to be reassured that things are going fine. When an enterprise is successful or stable, considering the environmental uncertainty, there are inherent tendencies for the managers to keep all the options open; consequently, they are reluctant to state clearly where the enterprise is going in the future. Such behaviors lead to speculation by the troops based on often conflicting statements emanating from folks in leadership positions in the organization.

3.4 SUMMARY

This chapter introduced the antipatterns of excellence proposed by some of the pioneers in this area. First, it presented the antipatterns of excellence proposed by J. Picken and G. Dess in their 1997 book *Mission Critical: The 7 Strategic Traps That Derail Even the Smartest Companies.* This is followed by next set of antipatterns proposed by Jagdish Sheth in his 2007 book *The Self Destructive Habits of Good Companies... and How to Break Them.* In the latter part of this chapter, we discussed another set of antipatterns proposed by Robert Herbold in his 2002 book *Seduced by Success.*

Section II

Evolution of Excellence

Biological evolution provides a useful model for the evolution of companies because it implies, on one hand, that a variety of unique events are important. On the other hand, it also implies that these unique, microlevel events and diversity still add up to an aggregate identifiable pattern of business change—that of survival and growth of companies. After recounting briefly the voyage, it introduces Darwin's "theory of evolution by natural selection." In the context of change of theories in sciences, it also acquaints the readers with Popper's strategy of disconfirmation, Kuhn's concept of paradigm shifts, and Peter Drucker's theory of business. The later part of the chapter looks at the broad characteristics of enterprises and contrasts the mechanistic and organismic perspectives on the enterprises. A case is made for the simultaneous cocombination of both these perspectives, which is achievable by implementing enterprise systems like SAP within the enterprise.

As mentioned in the Preface, I am not aiming for an absolutist framework or precision engineering accuracy or formulaic approach because it is contrary to the situation in the real world—it is futile to aim for absoluteness or precision or clarity or formulaic approach when it does not exist in the real world or real life. I must hasten to add—this is not as much of a disaster as it may seem considering that the same reality is mirrored even in the most proven and *effective* model of success: evolution by natural selection. Corporate evolution like biological evolution is not goal directed per se (*in an absolute sense*) and can still be as effective as evolution in nature.

For a company, every event is unique, but all such unique, microlevel events and diversity still add up to an aggregate identifiable pattern of business change—that of survival and growth of companies.

4 Variations and Theories of Excellence

4.1 VOYAGE OF CHARLES DARWIN*

It was Erasmus Darwin's grandson Charles (1809–1882) who worked out a detailed and correct theory of evolution and supported it by a massive weight of evidence. As a boy, Charles Darwin was passionately fond of hunting and collecting beetles, but he was a mediocre student. Darwin's father, a wealthy physician, sent him to Edinburgh University to study medicine; but finally, he gave up the idea of making him a doctor and sent him instead to Cambridge to study for the clergy.

Thus, it happened that on December 27, 1831, Charles Darwin sailed from Devonport on HMS Beagle, a small brig of the British navy. The Beagle's commander, Captain FitzRoy, was 27 years old (4 years older than Darwin), but he was already an excellent and experienced sailor. He had orders to survey the South American coast and to carry a chain of chronological measurements around the world. It was to be 5 years before the Beagle returned to England.

Soon Darwin found a collaborator and close friend in none other than Sir Charles Lyell, the great geologist whose book had so inspired him. The years between 1836 and 1839 were busy ones for Darwin. He found lodgings in London, and he worked there with Lyell on his geological collection. During these years, he edited a five-volume book on the zoological discoveries of the voyage; and in 1839, his journal of researches into the geology and natural history of various countries visited by the HMS Beagle was published. Originally, Darwin's journal formed part of a multivolume work edited by Captain FitzRoy, but the publisher, John Murray, recognized the unusual interest of Darwin's contribution, bought up the copyright, and republished the journal. It immediately became a bestseller, making Darwin famous. Under the shortened title, The Voyage of the Beagle, Darwin's journal has been reprinted more than a hundred times.

In 1839, Darwin married his cousin, Emma Wedgwood; Emma and Charles Darwin were to have ten children together (of whom three were knighted for their contributions to science). Darwin was beginning to show signs of the ill health that was to remain with him for the rest of his life, and to escape from the social life of the capital, he moved to the small country town of Down, about 16 miles south of London. Darwin's illness was probably due to a chronic infection picked up in South America. For the remainder of his life, his strength was very limited, and his daily routine at Down followed an unvarying pattern that allowed him to work as much as possible within the limits imposed by his illness. The early mornings were devoted to writing (even Sunday mornings), while correspondence and experimental work were done in the afternoons and scientific reading in the evenings.

4.1.1 ORIGIN OF SPECIES

In 1837, Darwin had begun a notebook on transmutation of species. During the voyage of the Beagle, he had been deeply impressed by the great fossil animals that he had discovered, so like existing South American species except for their gigantic size. Also, as the Beagle had sailed southward, he had noticed the way in which animals were replaced by closely allied species. On the Galapagos Islands, he had been struck by the South American character of the unique species found there and

---

* Peter J. Bowler, *Evolution: The History of an Idea* (Berkeley, CA, University of California Press, 1989).

by the way in which they differed slightly on each island. It seemed to Darwin that these facts, as well as many other observations that he had made on the voyage, could only be explained by assuming that species gradually became modified. The subject haunted him, but he was unable to find the exact mechanism by which species changed. Therefore, he resolved to follow the Baconian method, which his friend Sir Charles Lyell had used so successfully in geology. He hoped that by the wholesale collection of all facts related in any way to the variation of animals and plants under domestication and in nature, he might be able to throw some light on the subject. He soon saw that in agriculture, the key to success in breeding new varieties was selection; but how could selection be applied to organisms living in a state of nature?

In October 1838, 15 months after beginning his systematic inquiry, Darwin happened to read Malthus' book on population. After his many years as a naturalist, carefully observing animals and plants, Darwin was very familiar with the struggle for existence that goes on everywhere in nature; and it struck him immediately that under the harsh conditions of this struggle, favorable variations would tend to survive while unfavorable ones would perish. The result would be the formation of new species! Darwin had at last got a theory on which to work, but he was so anxious to avoid prejudice that he did not write it down. He continued to collect facts, and it was not until 1842 that he allowed himself to write a 35-page sketch of his theory. In 1844, he enlarged this sketch to 230 pages and showed it to his friend Sir Joseph Hooker, the director of Kew Botanical Gardens. However, Darwin did not publish his 1844 sketch. Probably, he foresaw the storm of bitter hostility, which his heretical theory was to arouse.

In England at that time, Lamarckian ideas from France were regarded as both scientifically unrespectable and politically subversive. The hierarchal English establishment was being attacked by the Chartist movement, and troops had been called out to suppress large-scale riots and to ward off revolution. Heretical ideas that might undermine society were regarded as extremely dangerous. Darwin himself was a respected member of the establishment, and he was married to a conservative and devout wife, whose feelings he wished to spare. So he kept his work on species private, confiding his ideas only to Hooker and Lyell.

Instead of publishing his views on evolution, Darwin began an enormous technical study of barnacles, which took him 8 years to finish. Hooker had told him that no one had the right to write on the question of the origin of species without first having gone through the detailed work of studying a particular species. Also, barnacles were extremely interesting to Darwin: they are in fact more closely related to shrimps and crabs than to molluscs. Finally, in 1854, Darwin cleared away the last of his barnacles and began to work in earnest on the transmutation of species through natural selection, arranging the mountainous piles of notes on the subject that he had accumulated over the years. By 1858, he had completed the first part of a monumental work on evolution. If he had continued writing on the same scale, he would ultimately have produced a gigantic, unreadable multivolume opus.

Fortunately, this was prevented: a young naturalist named Alfred Russell Wallace, while ill with a fever in Malaya, also read Malthus on population; and in a fit of inspiration, he arrived at a theory of evolution through natural selection that was identical with Darwin's! Wallace wrote out his ideas in a short paper with the title: On the Tendency of Varieties to Depart Indefinitely from the Original Type. He sent this paper to Darwin with the request that if Darwin thought the paper good, he should forward it to Lyell.

Lyell had for years been urging Darwin to publish his own work on natural selection, telling him that if he delayed, someone else would reach the same conclusions. Now Lyell's warning had come true with a vengeance, and Darwin's first impulse was to suppress all of his own work in favor of Wallace. Darwin's two good friends, Lyell and Hooker, firmly prevented this however; and through their intervention, a fair compromise was reached: Wallace's paper, together with an extract from Darwin's 1844 sketch on natural selection, was read jointly to the Linnean Society. At the urging of Lyell and Hooker, Darwin now began an abstract of his enormous unfinished book. This abstract, entitled *On the Origin of Species by Means of Natural Selection*, or *The Preservation of Favoured*

Races in the Struggle for Life, was published in 1859. It ranks with Newton's Principia as one of the two greatest scientific books ever written.

4.1.2 WHAT IS *EVOLUTION THROUGH NATURAL SELECTION?*

Darwin reminds us of the way in which mankind has produced useful races of domestic animals and plants by selecting from each generation those individuals that show any slight favorable variation and by using these as parents for the next generation. Darwin believed that a closely similar process occurs in nature, wild animals and plants exhibit slight variations, and in nature, there is always a struggle for existence. This struggle follows from the fact that every living creature produces offspring at a rate that would soon entirely fill up the world if no check ever fell on the growth of population. We often have difficulty in seeing the exact nature of these checks, since living organisms are related to each other and to their environment in extremely complex ways, but the checks must always be present. Accidental variations that increase an organism's chance of survival are more likely to be propagated to subsequent generations than are harmful variations. By this mechanism, which Darwin called *natural selection*, changes in plants and animals occur in nature just as they do under the artificial selection exercised by breeders.

If we imagine a volcanic island, pushed up from the ocean floor and completely uninhabited, we can ask what will happen as plants and animals begin to arrive. Suppose, for example, that a single species of bird arrives on the island. The population will first increase until the environment cannot support larger numbers, and it will then remain constant at this level. Over a long period of time, however, variations may accidentally occur in the bird population, which allow the variant individuals to make use of new types of food; and thus, through variation, the population may be further increased.

In this way, a single species *radiates* into a number of subspecies that fill every available ecological niche. The new species produced in this way will be similar to the original ancestor species, although they may be greatly modified in features that are related to their new diet and habits. Thus, for example, whales, otters, and seals retain the general structure of land-going mammals, although they are greatly modified in features that are related to their aquatic way of life. This is the reason, according to Darwin, why vestigial organs are so useful in the classification of plant and animal species.

The classification of species is seen by Darwin as a genealogical classification. All living organisms are seen, in his theory, as branches of a single family tree. This is a truly remarkable assertion, since the common ancestors of all living things must have been extremely simple and primitive; and it follows that the marvelous structures of the higher animals and plants, whose complexity and elegance utterly surpasses the products of human intelligence, were all produced, over thousands of millions of years, by random variation and natural selection!

Each structure and attribute of a living creature can therefore be seen as having a long history; and knowledge of the evolutionary history of the organs and attributes of living creatures can contribute much to our understanding of them. For instance, studies of the evolutionary history of the brain and of instincts can contribute greatly to our understanding of psychology, as Darwin pointed out.

An interesting chain of ecological relationships involves clover, bumblebees, mice, cats and cat-loving people: Red clover is much more common near to towns than elsewhere. Why should this be so? Darwin's explanation is that this type of clover can only be pollinated by bumblebees. The underground nests of bumblebees are often destroyed by mice; but near to towns, mice are kept in check by cats. Hence, Darwin notes, the presence of cats in a district might determine, through the intervention first of mice and then of bees, the frequency of certain flowers in that district.

Among the many striking observations presented by Darwin to support his theory are facts related to morphology and embryology. For example, Darwin includes a quotation from the naturalist, von Baer, who stated that he had in his possession two embryos preserved in alcohol, which he had forgotten to label. Von Baer was completely unable to tell by looking at them whether they were embryos of lizards, birds, or mammals, since all these species are so similar at an early stage of development.

4.1.3 Publication of *On the Origin of Species*

Darwin's *On the Origin of Species*, published in 1859, was both an immediate success and an immediate scandal. Darwin had sent an advance copy of his book to The Times to be reviewed; and because of the illness of the usual reviewer, T.H. Huxley (1825–1895) was asked to comment on the book. Huxley, who was one of the most brilliant zoologists of the period, immediately recognized the validity and importance of Darwin's work and exclaimed: "How exceedingly stupid not to have thought of that!" He wrote a long and favorable review for The Times, and partly as a result of this review, the first edition of *On the Origin of Species* (1200 copies) was sold out on the day of publication. A second edition, published 6 weeks later, also sold out quickly; and new editions, reprintings, and translations have been published ever since in a steady stream.

> Darwin had avoided emphasizing the emotionally charged subject of man's ancestry, but he did not think that it would be honest to conceal his belief that the human race belongs to the same great family that includes all other living organisms on earth. As a compromise, he predicted in a single sentence that through studies of evolution "light would be thrown on the origin of man and his history." This single sentence and the obvious implications of Darwin's book were enough to create a storm of furious opposition. One newspaper commented that "society must fall to pieces if Darwinism be true."

The storm of scandalized opposition was still growing in June 1860, when three anti-Darwinian papers were scheduled for reading at an open meeting of the British Association for the Advancement of Science at Oxford.

The meeting hall was packed with 700 people as Samuel Wilberforce, Bishop of Oxford, took the floor to *smash Darwin*. Darwin himself was too ill (or too diffident) to be present, but T.H. Huxley had been persuaded to attend the meeting to defend Darwin's ideas. After savagely attacking Darwin for half an hour, the bishop turned to Huxley and asked sneeringly, "Is it through your grandfather or your grandmother that you claim to be descended from an ape?" Huxley, who was 35 at the time and at the height of his powers, rose to answer the bishop. He first gave scientific answers, point by point, to the objections that had been made to the theory of evolution. Finally, regarding the bishop's question about his ancestry, Huxley said: "If I had to choose between a poor ape for an ancestor and a man, highly endowed by nature and of great influence, who used those gifts to introduce ridicule into a scientific discussion and to discredit humble seekers after truth, I would affirm my preference for the ape." His retort caused inextinguishable laughter among the people.

The debate at Oxford marked the turning point in the battle over evolution. After that, Huxley and Hooker defended Darwin's theories with increasing success in England, while in Germany, most of the prominent biologists, led by Professor Ernst Haeckel, were soon on Darwin's side. In America, the theory of evolution was quickly accepted by almost all of the younger scientists, despite the opposition of the aging *creationist* Louis Agassiz. However, opposition from religious fundamentalists continued in most parts of America, and in Tennessee, a school teacher named John T. Scopes was brought to trial for teaching the theory of evolution. He was prosecuted by the orator and three-time presidential candidate William Jennings Bryan and defended by the brilliant Chicago lawyer Clarence Darrow. In this famous *Monkey Trial*, Scopes was let off with a small fine, but the anti-evolution laws remained in force. It was only in 1968 that the State Legislature of Tennessee repealed its laws against the teaching of evolution.

4.2 DARWIN'S THEORY OF EVOLUTION THROUGH NATURAL SELECTION

Darwin combined reflection from his field research with two ideas—evolution and competition—from two other disciplines to formulate his theory of evolution by natural selection. Darwin first thought of natural selection in 1838 while reading Thomas Malthus's *Essay on Population*, a dire prophecy of the effects of competition between individuals for food. Malthus in turn had been influenced by Adam Smith's theories of economic competition in *The Wealth of Nations* published in 1776. Darwin published *On the Origin of Species by Means of Natural Selection* in 1859. The idea of evolution had been widely mooted in the early nineteenth century. Fossils showed that species had evolved from earlier, more primitive species. K.E. von Baer (1792–1876) encapsulated a major insight when he stated that "less general characters are developed from the most general, until the most specialized appear"; evolutionists talked about "heterogeneity emerging from homogeneity." Darwin's big advance was to explain the mechanism of evolution through natural selection in an elegant and extremely economical manner.

This was based on the following assumptions:

1. All creatures systematically overproduce offspring.
2. All creatures vary; they are all unique.
3. All creatures inherit a summation of all variations from the earlier generation.

Those creatures survive that fit in best with the *context of life*, that is, physical environment. As many more individuals of each species are born than can possibly survive and as there is a frequently recurring struggle for existence, it follows that any being, if it varies however slightly in any manner profitable to itself, will have a better chance of surviving and, thus, be naturally selected. Plants and animals that have been naturally selected will have had the most successful parents and in turn will have more offspring than other organisms. Natural selection critically depends on the very occurrence of variations—natural selection is this preservation of favorable variations and the rejection of injurious variations. Plants and animals that have been naturally selected will have had the most successful parents and in turn will have more offspring than other organisms. So driven by the natural selection of the survivors, and by the relative reproductive success in that generation of survivors, in each generation, there is *improvement*.

Modern biologists stress that there is no implicit evolutionary process leading naturally to improvement; evolution does not imply any immanent purpose or historical progress. Organisms adapt themselves to the conditions of life, but the fact that *better adapted* organisms thrive at the expense of the *less adapted* implies no value judgment: better means more likely to survive and multiply, not superior.

 Darwin's big idea in 1838 was natural selection—that there was competition for life between individuals and that traits were conserved through their relative adaptability to life's conditions. The controversy was only regarding the universal idea of evolution, especially humanity's decent from animal species.

Darwin's theory of evolution by natural selection has the following characteristics:

- The odds against survival are high, leading to a struggle for life.
- The context of life, that is, physical environment determines whether species and individuals survive or not.
- Evolution involves coevolution of the context of life and other species.
- The process of natural selection is characterized by high degree of luck, randomness, and arbitrary development.

As conceived by Darwin, the process is very simple: variation, then selection, then further variation ad infinitum. This is how species evolve. If a species is diverse, it can survive and prosper; if a species is homogeneous, it is vulnerable. Diversity works; it always leads to even greater diversity and to sustainable growth.

Variations and improvements occur continually within species, but occasionally, a mutation occurs, when an individual has a new characteristic. This mutation may improve or worsen the odds of survival—if the former, the individual mutant will prosper, and leave plenty of offspring, who will inherit and pass on the advantage; if the latter, the mutation will die out. When the environment changes, new characteristics may be required—and the whole process is iterated again:

1. Variation is a key to development.
   New species are formed from an existing species. This is a universal principle: in knowledge, through speciation, one branch gives rise to one or more new branches; in the economy, one industry gives rise to more specialized branches thereof or when one firm spawns spin-offs, each of which develops its own particular variations.
2. Variation never stops.
   Each differentiation becomes a new generality, which can then result in new differentiation; overall, this results in increasing complexity and diversity.

Darwin held that the environment was the determining factor, which was in contrast to the French naturalist Jean Lamarck (1744–1829), who claimed that species adapted to the demands of the environment. For Darwin, species naturally evolve, and the environment decides whether or not they survive; for Lamarck, species evolve to survive—though subtle, this is a critical distinction.

Darwin implies that species, and to even greater degree individuals, cannot hope to control their own destiny. This is a key insight for business—if a business is failing, there are only two possible remedies: to change the environment or to change the character of the business or the individual. Markets usually evolve by changing the winners (whether the *winners* are firms, technologies, or nations), not by changing the way that the incumbent winner or incipient loser behaves.

In the evolution by natural selection, the environment is more powerful than the species, and the species is more important than the individual. In economic development, the market is more important than any particular industry, and the *species* of producers or consumers is more important than any individual firm or consumer.

4.2.1 Evolution through Selection in Business

We can now parallel this process in thinking about the business world. The development of economies, industries, individual corporations, and individual careers follows the same evolutionary path described by Darwin and earlier evolutionists. The principle of natural selection can be observed in business. The only way to win is to be exposed to competition, to pursue variation relentlessly and continuously, to accept the environment's verdict, and to be quick. New products and services will emerge from somewhere, from the organization itself or from competitors. Therefore, leave no niche unfilled to be exploited by competitors; cannibalize your own products and markets before you are cannibalized by others. Products and services can be accelerated; encourage failure as a necessary part of the process of experimentation. Individuals, technologies, products, team, brands, firms, and markets that experiment the most and produce most variants will improve faster, and faster improvements lead to faster market growth. What adapts faster to the *context of life* gains market share and earns superior margin.

At the level of the enterprise, focus on a group of customers that has some internal homogeneity and some differentiation from the rest of the current market. Work out how to serve that customer group better, so that extra value is created for them at the same cost or preferably at a lower cost.

At the level of products, depending on how well adapted is the product to its market, relative to competing products, products will either prosper or die. Products live in families across generations. All products will eventually die, but the most successful products will live long enough to generate at least one *offspring*, a next-generation product or a same-generation variant. The more successful products will generate more of both. However, for every successful product, there will be many that never get off the drawing board, never survived the test market, died shortly after launch, or never produced any offspring.

Back in 1930, Procter & Gamble, one of the world's most successful consumer goods firms, took the revolutionary and apparently wasteful step of allowing direct competition between its own brands. This effectively provided the challenge that did not exist in the actual marketplace; discomfort stimulated improvement and cut complacency. P&G also has an extremely rigorous and structured product development process, including mandatory test marketing to see whether product marketing expectations are met and whether product sales are sustainable. Even successful products are subject to routine, ongoing consumer research, to aid in further product refinement and innovation. P&G has a far higher ratio of potential products to actual products than most of its competitors and a far greater propensity to produce new generations of successful products.

Competitive selection drives evolution faster and evolution proceeds by new and better genera-tion of older products: not just new variants but also new and better versions of older product. Cost reduction is both a cause and a result of growth. Only by reducing costs or improving features or providing other forms of extra value can markets expand faster than other markets. Above-average growth is the reward for above-average improvement in delivering value. Firms that grow faster than the market can increase their accumulated production faster than the laggards and can therefore cut cost or increase value faster. By gaining market share, they actually also underpin the basis for defending and building further market share: they improve their relative costs position or relative value position. In a profitable market, it is therefore an excellent strategy to build market share even at the expense of short-term profits.

In evolutionary terms, markets, firms, brands, teams, products, technologies, and individuals who gain experience at above-average rates are actually speeding up the evolutionary process. They are packing in more generations in a shorter time. Each generated variation offers scope for improvement. Yet improvement actually occurs if there is an adaptive variation, that is, if each suc-ceeding generation or version (markets, firms, brands, teams, products) produces something that consumers like better, by doing something different that enables the market or firm to deliver better value—and to deliver improvement at a faster and faster rate.

Time is a proxy for the passing of generations; competitive advantage flows from minimizing the time it takes a firm to complete its activities and provide goods and services to the market and the time taken to introduce a new product. The higher the time taken, the greater the cost, and the lower the degree of customer satisfaction. Compressing time therefore lowers costs and raises market share.

Tolerating, even encouraging failures, is an intrinsic part of the process; market progresses via selection. This necessarily requires the deselection or death of most of what is tested. This clearly happens at the product or subproduct level. But, if there is a free market in companies, deselection will also happen to corporations—they will go bust or be taken over. In nature, a failed organism becomes food for more successful creatures. The same thing happens in business: when a company fails, or is taken over, its resources are freed up for more productive use.

In natural selection, failure is endemic. In business, the lesson that failure is endemic is invalu-able. Failure implies a lack of fit between the organism and the environment. Natural selection implies that failure is the most normal course of events, and that slight modifications will not be enough for a turnaround. If a poor fit has to be turned into a good fit, either the environment must change or the *lack of fit* circumstances must change or both must change.

Hoping that the exiting environment will change is the prevalent strategy of failing businesses. This strategy nearly always fails because of reasons that Darwin gives—the businesses have little or no control over the environment. Thus, expecting the transformation of the environment is futile.

Therefore, the only feasible solution is to relocate to a different environment and to change the circumstances of *lack of fit*. In other words, if a company is losing out in one market, it had better find another market more aligned to its capabilities or change its character radically to serve the existing market in a radically different way. Since the existing capabilities have been built and fine-tuned across an extended period of time, it is unlikely that there just happens to be another market out there for which the failing businesses' capabilities are an exact fit.

Thus, the only solution possible is variations in both the core and context of the enterprise. The latter implies a changed market segment entailing at least one of the following: different customers, different businesses, different products or services, different competitors, and different locations. The former implies changed business model(s) entailing at least one of the following: different strategy, different structure, different shared values, different stuff, different style, different staff, different skills, different systems, and different sequence.

4.3 THEORIES OF EXCELLENCE

4.3.1 POPPER'S THEORY OF FALSIFICATION*

Karl Popper (1902–1995) was born in Vienna, Austria. He enrolled in the University of Vienna in 1918, where he studied physics, mathematics, and philosophy. In 1928, he received his PhD for a dissertation titled *On the Problem of Method in the Psychology of Thinking*. He never returned to the subject of psychology again during his professional career, because he became convinced that methodology of science is exclusively a matter of logic and objective knowledge instead of psychology. Popper was personally acquainted with Rudolf Carnap and other members of the Vienna Circle, and although he had been invited to address the group at a meeting in which he set forth his philosophy of science, he was never a member of the circle.

Popper's philosophy is a milestone in the history of philosophy, because it represents a fundamental problem shift. While Carnap and other positivists continued their efforts to establish theoretical science including Einstein's theory, on firm ontological foundations, Popper rejected the naturalistic theory of meaning that supposedly supplies such a foundation and accepted the revision of scientific explanation as a matter of course. Positivist foundational problems, such as the problem of the meaningfulness of theoretical terms, became pseudo problems as a result of Popper's problem shift, while the problem addressed by Popper, the rational growth of science without foundations, has become central to the philosophy of science. Popper's philosophy comprehensively addresses the four basic topics of the philosophy of science: criticism, explanation, aim of science, and discovery.

4.3.1.1 Thesis of Falsification

In 1919, Popper concluded that the critical attitude, which does not look for verifications but rather looks for crucial tests that can refute the tested theory, is the correct attitude for science, even though the crucial tests can never establish the theory. This is Popper's falsificationist philosophy of scientific criticism, the central thesis of his philosophy of science. His falsificationist thesis is not only a philosophy of scientific criticism but also a philosophy of scientific explanation and of the growth of scientific knowledge. As a philosophy of scientific criticism, it says that the empirical test outcome can never establish or *verify* a scientific theory, but can only refute or *falsify* the theory. And even before theory's claims are considered for testing, it is possible to determine whether or not it is a scientific explanation: it is not a scientific explanation if it is not empirically testable. Another way that Popper describes this condition is that what makes a theory scientific is its power

---

* Karl Popper, *The Logic of Scientific Discovery* (London, U.K., Routledge, 1992).

to exclude the occurrence of some possible events, and he calls the singular statements that describe these excluded events *potential falsifiers*.

This way of speaking introduces his idea of various degrees of explanatory power: the more that a theory forbids or excludes and therefore the larger the class of potential falsifiers, then the more the theory tells us about the world. Popper calls the variability of degree of explanatory power the *amount of information content* of a theory or explanation. The idea of the amount of information content may be illustrated by reflection on the logical conjunction of two statements α and β. It is intuitively evident that the conjunction $\alpha\beta$ has no lesser amount of information content than do the component statements taken separately, and it usually has more information content than its components. This is because there are more potential falsifiers for the conjunction than for the component statements taken separately; the conjunction is false if either component is false. In some contexts, Popper calls information content *empirical content*, and he calls the falsifiability of the theory its *testability*. All of these terms refer to a logical relation between a theory or a hypothesis and its class of potential falsifiers.

4.3.1.2 Progress in Science

The concepts of relatively greater or lesser degrees of information content and falsifiability provide the basis for Popper's ideas on scientific progress, the growth of scientific knowledge, and the aim of science. He advances a *metascientific* criterion of progress that enables the scientist and methodologist to know in advance of any empirical test, whether or not a new theory would be an improvement over existing theories, where the new theory is able to pass crucial tests, in which its performance is compared to older existing alternatives. He calls this criterion the *potential satisfactoriness* of the theory, and it is measured by the degree or amount of information content. Simply stated, his thesis is that the theory that tells us more is preferable to one that tells us less, and the theory that tells us more is also one that is most falsifiable. From this, it follows that the aim of science is high empirical information content as well as successful performance in tests.

It is the criterion of high information content that makes the growth of science rational. The aim of science is not high probability, and the rationality of science does not consist of constructing deductive axiomatic systems, since there is little merit in formalizing a theory beyond the requirements for testing it. Nor does the growth of science consist of the accumulation of observations. Rather it consists of the repeated overthrow of scientific theories and their replacement by more satisfactory theories. The continued growth and progress of science is essential to the rational and empirical character of scientific knowledge. The growth is continuous, because criticism of theories, which are proposed solutions, in turn generates new problems. Scientific problems occur when expectations are disappointed. Science starts from problems, not from observations, although unexpected observations give rise to new problems.

Popper views science as progressing from old problems to new problems, to new problems having increased depth as it progresses from old theories to new theories having increased information content. He also views progress in science as approaching more and more closely to the truth, where truth is understood as a correspondence with the facts and as a regulative idea. Just as there are degrees of information content, so too there are degrees of approach to the truth that he calls *verisimilitude*.

As a basis for empirical science, Popper proposes the idea of the *basic statement*, which he defines as a singular statement that together with the universal statements of theory can serve as a premise in an empirical falsification of a theory. Basic statements are objective in the sense that they can be intersubjectively tested by repetition of the conditions that occasioned them. And they can be falsified, since they operate as premises from which other statements can be deduced, which in turn can be tested. As a result, there can be no ultimate statements in science, as the positivists believed; all statements in empirical science can be refuted by falsifying some of the conclusions that may be deduced from them. But it is not necessary that a basic statement should be tested in order for it to be accepted; it is only necessary that the basic statement be testable. The function of basic statements is to test theories.

Every test of a theory must stop at some basic statement, which the scientists have agreed to accept at least for the present time. To the extent that the basic statements are accepted on the basis of agreement, they are conventional. But the agreement is not arbitrary or capricious; the decision is made by reference to a theory and the problem that the theory is proposed to address. Theory dominates experimental work from its initial planning to its completion in the laboratory. Popper summarizes his views on the empirical basis of science by means of a memorable metaphor: There is nothing absolute about science; it does not rest upon solid bedrock, as it were. The bold structure of its theories rises as it were above a swamp like a building erected on piles, which in turn are driven down to whatever depth is found to be satisfactory to carry the structure for the time being.

Popper's reconceptualization of the empirical basis of science is also a reconceptualization of the concept of theory in science. Unlike the positivists, Popper does not define the concept of scientific theory in terms of theoretical terms. Instead, he views theories as universal statements and rejects any distinction between empirical laws and theories, since there is no longer any distinction between theory language and observation language based on a distinction between theoretical terms and observation terms. All the universal statements in science are conjectures that are testable and falsifiable, and these conjectures are invented by the human mind; none of them are produced by inductive generalization. To give a causal explanation of an event means to deduce a statement that describes the event using as premises the deduction of one or more universal laws as theories together with singular basic statements that describe the initial conditions. Popper's ideas for such terms as *theory*, *law*, and *cause* are fundamentally different from the positivists' ideas for these terms, because Popper's ideas are separated from the subject matter or ontologies described by the sciences.

Popper maintained that falsification is never finally and permanently conclusive, because the singular basic statements that are potential falsifiers may be revised, thus occasioning the revision of a falsifying test outcome. The empirical test may be said to be conclusive only to the extent that interested scientists agree to accept certain basic statements. Popper states that in some cases, it has taken scientists a long time before a falsification is accepted and that it is usually not accepted until a falsified theory is replaced by the proposal of a new and more adequate theory.

4.3.2 Kuhn's Theory of Paradigms*

Thomas Kuhn gained his master's degree in physics in 1946 and his doctorate in 1949, also in physics (concerning an application of quantum mechanics to solid state physics) from Harvard. In 1962, Kuhn published his *The Structure of Scientific Revolutions*. The central idea of this extraordinarily influential book is that the development of science is driven, in normal periods of science, by adherence to what Kuhn called a *paradigm*. The function of a paradigm is to supply puzzles for scientists to solve and to provide the tools for their solution. A crisis in science arises when confidence is lost in the ability of the paradigm to solve particularly worrying puzzles called *anomalies*. Crisis is followed by a scientific revolution if the existing paradigm is superseded by a rival.

Kuhn claimed that science guided by one paradigm would be *incommensurable* with science developed under a different paradigm, which meant that there is no common measure of the different scientific theories. This thesis of incommensurability rules out certain kinds of comparison of the two theories and consequently rejects some traditional views of scientific development, such as the view that latter science builds on the knowledge contained within earlier theories or the view that latter theories are closer approximations to the truth than earlier theories. Most of Kuhn's subsequent work in philosophy was spent in articulating and developing the ideas in The Structure of Scientific Revolutions, although some of these underwent transformation in the process.

Kuhn's claim that scientists do not employ rules in reaching their decisions appeared tantamount to the claim that science is irrational. This was highlighted by his rejection of the distinction between discovery and justification (denying that we can distinguish between the psychological

---

* Thomas Kuhn, *The Structure of Scientific Revolutions* (Chicago, IL, University of Chicago Press, 3rd ed., 1996).

process of thinking up an idea and the logical process of justifying its claim to truth) and his emphasis on incommensurability—the claim that certain kinds of comparison between theories is impossible. The negative response among philosophers was exacerbated by an important naturalistic tendency in *The Structure of Scientific Revolutions* that was then unfamiliar. A particularly significant instance of this was Kuhn's insistence on the importance of the history of science for philosophy of science.

In *The Structure of Scientific Revolutions*, Kuhn paints a picture of the development of science quite unlike any that had gone before. According to the traditional account of scientific change, science develops by the addition of new truths to the stock of old truths or the increasing approximation of theories to the truth and, in the odd case, the correction of past errors. Such progress might accelerate in the hands of a particularly great scientist, but progress itself is guaranteed by the scientific method. However, it was becoming clear that scientific change was not always as straightforward as the standard, traditional view would have it. Since the standard view dovetailed with the dominant, positivist-influenced philosophy of science, a nonstandard view would have important consequences for the philosophy of science. Kuhn was the first and most important author to articulate a developed alternative account.

4.3.2.1   Normal and Revolutionary Science

According to Kuhn, the development of a science is not uniform but has alternating *normal* and *revolutionary* (or *extraordinary*) phases. The revolutionary phases are not merely periods of accelerated progress, but differ qualitatively from normal science. Normal science does resemble the standard cumulative picture of scientific progress, on the surface at least. Kuhn describes normal science as *puzzle-solving*. While this term suggests that normal science is not dramatic, its main purpose is to convey the idea that like someone doing crossword puzzles or chess puzzles or jigsaws, the puzzle solver expects to have a reasonable chance of solving the puzzle; that his doing so will depend mainly on his own ability; and that the puzzle itself and its methods of solution will have a high degree of familiarity. A puzzle solver is not entering completely uncharted territory. Because its puzzles and their solutions are familiar and relatively straightforward, normal science can expect to accumulate a growing stock of puzzle solutions. Revolutionary science, however, is not cumulative in that, according to Kuhn, scientific revolutions involve a revision to existing scientific belief or practice.

In the standard picture, revolutionary science will at all times be regarded as something positive, to be sought after, and to be promoted and welcomed. Revolutions are to be sought on Popper's view also, but not because they add to the positive knowledge of the truth of theories but because they add to the negative knowledge that the relevant theories are false. Kuhn rejected both the traditional and Popperian views in this regard. He claims that normal science can succeed in making progress only if there is a strong commitment by the relevant scientific community to their shared theoretical beliefs, values, instruments and techniques, and even metaphysics. This constellation of shared commitments Kuhn terms as a *paradigm* or a *disciplinary matrix*. Because commitment to the disciplinary matrix is a prerequisite for successful normal science, an inculcation of that commitment is a key element in scientific training and in the formation of the mind-set of a successful scientist.

This conservative resistance to the attempted refutation of key theories means that revolutions are not sought for except under extreme circumstances. Popper's philosophy requires that a single reproducible, anomalous phenomenon be enough to result in the rejection of a theory. Kuhn's view is that during normal science, scientists neither test nor seek to confirm the guiding theories of their disciplinary matrix. Nor do they regard anomalous results as falsifying those theories. It is only speculative puzzle solutions that can be falsified in a Popperian fashion during normal science. Rather, anomalies are ignored or explained away if at all possible. It is only the accumulation of particularly troublesome anomalies that poses a serious problem for the existing disciplinary matrix. A particularly troublesome anomaly is one that undermines the practice of normal science. For example, an anomaly might reveal inadequacies in some commonly used piece of equipment, perhaps by casting doubt on the underlying theory. If much of normal science relies upon this piece of equipment, normal science will find it difficult to continue with confidence until this anomaly is addressed. A widespread failure in such confidence Kuhn calls a *crisis*.

The most interesting response to crisis will be the search for a revised disciplinary matrix, a revision that will allow for the elimination of at least the most pressing anomalies and optimally the solution of many outstanding and unsolved puzzles. Such a revision will be a scientific revolution. According to Popper, the revolutionary overthrow of a theory is one that is logically required by an anomaly. According to Kuhn, however, there are no rules for deciding the significance of a puzzle and for weighing puzzles and their solutions against one another. The decision to opt for a revision of a disciplinary matrix is not one that is rationally compelled, nor is the particular choice of revision rationally compelled. For this reason, the revolutionary phase is particularly open to competition among differing ideas and rational disagreement about their relative merits—based primarily on the puzzle-solving power of the competing ideas.

4.3.2.2 Progress in Science

Kuhn makes it clear that science does progress. The phenomenon of Kuhn-loss does, in Kuhn's view, rule out the traditional cumulative picture of progress. The revolutionary search for a replacement paradigm is driven by the failure of the existing paradigm to solve certain important anomalies. Any replacement paradigm had better solve the majority of those puzzles, or it will not be worth adopting in place of the existing paradigm. Hence, we can say that revolutions do bring with them an overall increase in puzzle-solving power, the number and significance of the puzzles and anomalies solved by the revised paradigm exceeding the number and significance of the puzzle solutions that are no longer available as a result of Kuhn-loss. Kuhn is quick to deny that there is any inference from such increases to improved nearness to the truth.

Kuhn favors an evolutionary view of scientific progress. The evolutionary development of an organism might be seen as its response to a challenge set by its environment. But that does not imply that there is some ideal form of the organism that it is evolving toward. Analogously, science improves by allowing its theories to evolve in response to puzzles and progress is measured by its success in solving those puzzles; it is not measured by its progress toward to an ideal true theory.

4.3.3 DRUCKER'S THEORY OF BUSINESS*

Peter Drucker proposed the concept of *theory of business*, which is the assumptions on which the organization has been built. "These are the assumptions that shape any organization's behavior, dictate its decisions about what to do and what not to do, and define what the organization considers meaningful results."

The theory of the business has three parts:

1. There are assumptions about the environment of the organization.
2. There are assumptions about the specific mission of the organization.
3. There are assumptions about the core competencies needed to accomplish the organization's mission.

Drucker identifies four specifications to a valid theory of the business. First, the assumptions about environment, mission, and core competencies must fit reality. Second, the assumptions in all three areas have to fit one another. Third, the theory of the business must be known and understood throughout the organization. Fourth, the theory of the business has to be tested constantly. Some theories of the business are so powerful that they last for a long time, but they do not last forever. There is a need for building into the organization systematic monitoring and testing of its theory of the business. The author also introduces preventive measures (abandonment and

---

* Peter Drucker, Theory of Business, *Harvard Business Review.*

walk-around management), early diagnosis (unexpected success and unexpected failure), and a cure (hard work and being conscientious).

4.4 THEORIES OF ENTERPRISE

Future enterprises will have to operate in an even more dynamic and global environment than the current ones. They would need to be more agile, more adaptive, and more transparent. A core reason for strategic failures is the lack of coherence and consistency among the various components of an enterprise, which precludes it from operating as a unified and integrated whole; unity and integration between various enterprise components—the business and organizational, informational, and technological arrangement or *design*—have to do with the design of the enterprise as a whole. The requirements posed by the modern enterprise context—to operate in a unified and integrated manner over increased operational extendedness—necessitate a focus on design (and architecture). The higher the degree of fit among the various components of the enterprise, the more effectively the enterprise is likely to operate; enterprise unity and integration does not come or happen by default, it has to be designed.

Design must be interpreted broadly and regarded as any intentional action to create desired enterprise arrangements or enable desired enterprise developments. Service and customer orientation, quality, productivity, flexibility, process excellence, lean production, compliance, motivated and involved employees, or lower operational costs do not come of their own accord or by an edict from the above. The enterprise must be designed such that these areas of attention are successfully operationalized. However, the term *design* in the context of enterprises has uncomfortable connotations. The term is associated with mechanistic approaches to enterprises: arranging them as if they are machines. This approach essentially equates management with control, with the associated conviction that by using certain *controls* management is able to steer the enterprise top-down within the desired range of control. The enterprise is thereby assumed to be an objective entity (and external to management) that, like a machine, merely needs to be controlled.

A radically different view acknowledges the nonplanned and emerging character of many enterprise developments. Such developments rest for a large part on the capacity for self-organization. Nonmechanistic or organismic enterprise characteristics are essential for enterprise strategic and operational success, as well as for the ability to innovate and change. Innovation, flexibility, the ability to change, and the capacity for self-organization are not provided by any incidental set of enterprise characteristics but rest on specific enterprise conditions. The creation of these conditions cannot be left to chance, that is, spontaneous or incidental developments—these conditions must be created intentionally: they must be designed. Hence, enterprise design (and architecture) must also enable future, yet unknown, enterprise change and adaptation.

Thus, the notion of enterprise design should be interpreted broadly and seen as devising courses of action aimed at changing existing enterprise situations (and contexts) into preferred ones. Design concerns both, on one hand, understanding the intentions that are to be operationalized and, on the other hand, arranging to realize them. All these paradoxically opposing objectives of enterprise design can be enabled through enterprise-wide systems like SAP enterprise resource planning (ERP) (see Chapter 13, *Understanding SAP ERP*, and Chapter 14, *Business Excellence through Variations Using SAP*).

4.4.1 BIRTH OF ENTERPRISES

Various parallels can be noticed between the development of the industrial revolution and the development of enterprises as we know them today. The industrial revolution turned out to be a period of enormous technological, socioeconomical, and cultural transformation. Often, the period from 1760 through 1830 is termed as the era of the first industrial revolution, whereby (initially the British and European) civilization changed from an agrarian into an industrial society with manual labor being increasingly replaced by machines.

The industrial revolution must be characterized as an evolutionary and emergent development. Since various developments contributed to the industrial revolution, there is no single development or innovation that can be considered as the prime driving force behind the industrial revolution. However, the advancement of machines and tooling that enabled the development of machines for producing goods appears most significant. The innovation of the steam-driven machine by Thomas Newcomen (1663–1729) was followed later by the rotating steam engine of James Watt (1736–1819), which made the powering of many production machines in factories possible. This also made possible the large-scale factory-oriented production of goods. Consequently, many enterprises emerged in areas such as textiles, gas, mining, oil refinery, transport (train and ship), and communication (telegraph). Construction of roads and canals made concentrated factory production of goods possible at locations distant from those where products were eventually used or where the basic raw or production materials were available.

Associated with the appearance of such industrial enterprises and the rising need for capital, was the emergence of financial markets. At the end of the eighteenth and beginning of the nineteenth century appeared the first instances of enterprises gaining access to capital through issuance of shares. As a necessary function within the financial markets, the development of financial enterprises like stock exchanges followed subsequently; the New York stock exchange was established in 1792. Employment offered by factories and mines led to migration of people from rural areas to rapidly developing cities. Urbanization also led to the creation of new social classes and changing social and cultural circumstances. Generally, the first industrial revolution was associated with large-scale increase in productivity, welfare, and health. Many parallel, supporting, and reinforcing technological, demographic, sociological, geographical, and economic developments contributed to the transformation of especially the European society. This transformation was in large measure due to competent technicians that were able to translate their insights into practical applications, like the production machines and tooling mentioned previously.

The industrial revolution can be viewed as the transformation that also led to the origination of most of the organizational forms that are currently prevalent. Core aspects of enterprises—and their theory development—find their origin here. For a long time, factory-oriented production was directed toward delivering standard products and services. This type of production was associated with mass demand, whereby customers appeared to be satisfied with supplier-defined products or services. Markets were relatively static, so mass demand could be answered through mass production and its associated ways of organizing. These ways of organizing were *mechanistic* in nature: the enterprise was envisaged as a machine; attention was focused primarily on economically optimal ways of production rather than the satisfaction of the end user of the products or services. Eventually, an increase in wealth led to increased demand for more product variety; consequently, the market became less static—since larger product variety entailed more dynamic demand. Eventually, technological progress especially in IT enabled customization of products suitable to the requirements of individual customers. Gradually, this led to a shift from the mass production of standardized products toward individualized production of customized products and from a static toward a dynamic market.

> The period from 1830 onwards is considered as the onset of the second industrial revolution that was initiated primarily by the freight and transport capabilities offered by the railways.
>   The beginning of the mid-1970s is considered as the onset of the third industrial revolution triggered mainly due to the revolutionary developments in IT.

An enterprise is an intentionally created entity of human endeavor with a certain purpose. Enterprises are organized complexities: they are highly complex, as well as highly organized entities. The core problem with organized complexity is the necessity of taking into account numerous aspects and interdependencies that jointly form an organic whole. The system approach is the only meaningful way to address the core problem of organized complexity.

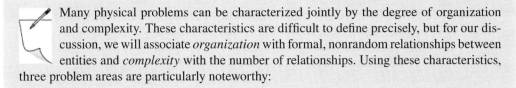 Many physical problems can be characterized jointly by the degree of organization and complexity. These characteristics are difficult to define precisely, but for our discussion, we will associate *organization* with formal, nonrandom relationships between entities and *complexity* with the number of relationships. Using these characteristics, three problem areas are particularly noteworthy:

1. Organized simplicity: The first area concerns problems characterized by relatively limited complexity but a high level of organization termed as *organized simplicity*. The limited complexity signifies that there are few interdependencies—relationships between certain aspects that manifest being organized—while the high level of organization indicates that these relationships are formal and predictable. Examples are problems associated with the operation of machines and mechanisms. The limited complexity (few interdependencies) allows these problems to be addressed through analytical (mathematical) methods.

2. Organized complexity: Next, there is a large area of problems of *organized complexity* that are characterized by a high level of complexity, hence, many interdependencies, as well as a high level of organization, indicating that the interdependencies have a formal relationship to a significant extent. The problems in this area are therefore too complex for analytical methods and too organized for statistical methods. Consequently, a core problem confronting modern science is developing a theory and associated methodology for addressing problems of organized complexity. Many biological and societal problems are problems of organized complexity.

3. Unorganized complexity: The other extreme problem area is that of problems characterized by a high level of complexity but a low level of organization. The high level of complexity indicates that there are numerous interdependencies, but the low level of organization implies that the interdependencies are nonformal and random in nature. This is the area of *unorganized complexity*, whereby the random nature of the numerous interdependencies allows these problems to be addressed through statistical means. So, despite the random, unpredictable character of individual interdependencies, the totality of the unorganized complexity can be understood and predicted. For example, gas molecules in a closed space, certain aspects of (car or telephone) traffic, or life insurance pose problems that can be addressed this way.

4.4.2 ENTERPRISE PERSPECTIVES

This section discusses two fundamentally different perspectives on enterprises: the mechanistic and organismic perspective. These different perspectives define the way enterprises are organized and thus define the characteristics of governance, strategy development, design, and operation of enterprises. In view of the limits of mechanistic thinking in dealing with dynamics, complexity, and the associated uncertainty, the importance of the organismic perspective is emphasized.

4.4.2.1 Mechanistic Perspective

Building on the ancient Greek intellectual heritage, an enormously influential contribution to the considerable impact of rational and deterministic reasoning came from the work of the French mathematician and philosopher René Descartes. Through a pure reductionistic process of methodical doubt, assumed truths about the world as it was experienced were declared as possibly being untrustworthy; only the act of thinking itself was considered to be *clear and distinct* and, therefore, certain. Hence, rational thinking as a method of obtaining knowledge gained its primacy. Fundamental truths about the world could thus be discovered through processes of rational thought.

The views expressed by Descartes clearly manifest themselves in the four modes of thinking. Reductionism holds that complex *wholes* can only be understood through knowledge of—simpler—constituent aspects or elements. Conversely, knowledge of parts implies understanding the whole. Closely related is the notion of logical-deductive thinking, which might be viewed as moving rationally from *the general to the specific*. This leads to rationalism, expressing the belief that reason is the prime source of knowledge and the route to an objectively knowable world. Finally, the notion of determinism boils down ultimately to the belief in identifiable causes that necessitate the current state of affairs, which in turn, through a set of causal relationships, determines the future state of affairs.

Two basic dichotomies emerged from Cartesianism, namely, the separation between mind and body and the separation between the thinking subject and the world. As a consequence of the second dichotomy, the thinking subject and the external world were not seen as dynamically interrelated; rather, the external world was considered a separate object governed by deterministic laws and already and forever *filled* with absolute truths awaiting to be discovered by the rational mind.

Thus, it is not the meaning of things that is the object of scientific study, but their orderly relations—as expressed by certain deterministic and mathematical laws. The separation created by the Cartesian split between the inquiring subject and the world, combined with the need to regain certainty, gave rise to a value pattern to proactively investigate and control the world. Hence, the mechanistic view became associated with a value pattern to control everything.

 All too often, unforeseen developments, opportunities and threats, complex and hardly discernable mutual dependencies and relationships between actors, and internal and external forces, as well as various forms of nonlinear feedback, make predictability and control an illusion. The mechanistic way of organization is based exactly on such an illusion.

The mechanistic perspective is exemplified by the following characteristics:

- Enterprise complexity can only be understood and managed through breakdown into, and knowledge about, fundamental parts. The more detail and the more knowledge is available on the parts, the higher is the ability to control the overall enterprise complexity.
- This devolves into minute and fixed division of labor, detailed task and job descriptions, and the managerial control hierarchy, including the associated measurements. The fixed task patterns define the fixed and machinelike rigidity of the enterprise's operational structure.
- The objective and deterministic enterprise reality is inherently measurable; enterprise reality can (thus) be captured objectively and unambiguously through measurement.
- Measurements define reality; reality exists independently of management that merely controls the enterprise as an object. Through measurement, developments can be controlled and guided into the desired direction.
- Through planning, strategy can be defined and executed, whereby the enterprise future is determined and secured.
- The effects of initiatives (causes) are inherently predictable because there are identifiable deterministic cause/effect relationships. The enterprise future is thus under intentional human control: courses of action can be planned and controlled, while risks can be identified and managed.

- Events have identifiable causes that necessarily determine the current state of affairs, which state in turn determines the future state of affairs. Clear cause and effect relationships can be established.
- Enterprises can thus be controlled through a management structure of top-down cause and effect relationships that secures the contribution of individual workers.
- Control proceeds top-down, whereby higher levels control lower levels. Unit and personal targets as well as performance-related pay are seen as incentives (causes) that drive performance (effect).
- Complex tasks or goals can be broken down into elementary units of activity that can be planned and controlled, thereby securing the accomplishment of the complex tasks or goals. Hence, a sequence of actions (linear cause/effect relationships) can be determined that will produce a predefined result.
- Employees are instruments: elements of the enterprise machine. The more they behave according to predefined task descriptions, the better the enterprise performance.

The mechanistic view treats the enterprise as a machine, leading to a high degree of enterprise rigidity and inertia. The mechanistic approach is deterministic with an unquestioned belief in the predictability of enterprise developments and a denial of the ever-present internal and external dynamics and complexity with its irreducible uncertainty.

4.4.2.2 Organismic Perspective

The organismic perspective is exemplified by the following characteristics:

- Enterprise complexity shows overall, aggregated behavior that cannot be inferred from knowledge about the constituent parts.
- Enterprise reality is socially constructed. Communication plays an essential role. Employees interpret reality through concepts and language established and agreed through social interaction. People are products of the enterprise context in which they operate, while also being participants in shaping that context.
- Cause and effect relationships vanish in enterprise complexity, dynamics, and the associated uncertainty. Measurements are therefore often symbolic in nature, with no identifiable link to enterprise performance, and often lead to unproductive goal replacement.
- With the vanishing of enterprise predictability, detailed task and job descriptions—based on the assumed predictability of task execution—are unproductive.
- The lack of detailed task and job descriptions underplays the rigid and machinelike characteristics of the enterprise and imbues it with the inherent ability to adapt and change.
- Enterprises are cognitive systems that learn and develop knowledge. Enterprise learning is crucial for the capacity to adapt and change.
- Enterprise change is not the result of planning but of learning. The learning process is emergent: results become manifest in evolutionary, unplanned, and unpredictable ways.
- Self-control and self-organization are essential for enterprise performance and the ability to innovate, change, and renew.
- Unlike the instrumental, machinelike view, the capacity for self-organizing is essential for enterprise adaptation and change.
- Employee involvement is essential for
    - Enhancing productivity, quality, and service
    - Resolving the fundamental tension between enterprise stability, on the one hand, and the ability to change and adapt, on the other
    - Addressing the nonmechanistic character of enterprises
    - Dealing with complexity, dynamics, and the associated uncertainty

- Addressing strategic transition barriers
- Constituting the foundation for enterprise learning and emergent enterprise developments
- Employee involvement and local freedom are essential for constituting the self-organizing capacity.

The two perspectives are compared in Tables 4.1 and 4.2.

TABLE 4.1
Mechanistic and Organismic Perceptions of the Enterprise

Factor	Mechanistic	Organismic
Reality	Objective reality	Perceptive reality
Thinking	Either-or	All-and, inclusive
Analysis	Reductionism	Holism
Method of analysis	Logic	Paradox
Causality	Linear causality	Nonlinear causality, multiple interdependencies
Observation	Observer and context	Observer and context
Focus	Separate discreet entities and tasks	Mutually dependent relationships
Forecasting	Deterministic	Uncertain, indeterminate
Strategy development	Planning	Learning
Behavior	Directed top-down	Emerges bottom-up

TABLE 4.2
Mechanistic and Organismic Perspectives of the Enterprise

Factor	Mechanistic	Organismic
Market	Mass, static, regulated	Individual, dynamic, open
Enterprise context	Stable, orderly	Dynamic, uncertain
Customers	Anonymous, mass marketing, product focus	Identified, one-to-one marketing, relationship focus
Competitors	Same domain	Different domains
Business relationships	Transaction based	Relationship based, support
Business boundaries	Clear and fixed	Diffuse and dynamic
Enterprise boundaries	Fixed, local	Dynamic, extended
Products and services	Distinct	Complementary
Management	Formal control	Support, values
Enterprise perspective	Reductionist	Holistic
Assets	Financial, physical	Intellectual
Organization	Mechanistic	Organismic
Enterprise development	Planned	Emergent
Employees	Costs	Asset
	Labor	Knowledge
	Managed	Empowered
Employee relationships	Transaction focus	Commitment focus
Work	Place and time dependent directed	Anywhere, anytime informated

4.4.3   COCOMBINATION OF MECHANISTIC AND ORGANISMIC PERSPECTIVES

Mechanistic enterprises show the rigid, machinelike characteristics previously discussed, whereas the organismic enterprises have opposite characteristics, and show flexibility and responsiveness, based on fundamentally different perspectives on control. These fundamentally different perspectives are necessary for providing counter to the deleterious effects of traditional control. The organismic perspective is not only because of the (human-centered) organismic concept itself but also in view of the avoidance of either-or thinking and the procedural (adaptive, learning, emerging) notion of enterprise variation.

The mechanistic perspective on enterprises treats the enterprise as an isolated entity and obscures seeing the enterprise and its environment as a whole of interrelated areas. This stance entails a focus on functional units rather than having a process orientation, hence, division of labor rather than integration of labor. Departments are evaluated and analyzed in isolation with locally oriented financial criteria that inherently do not support major process and value-added improvements. Such a lack of integral, unified, and holistic perspective results in local *gain* at the expense of much larger whole. Determinism also underlies many of the views on strategic and operational planning; the enterprise future is assumed to be predictable and controllable through planned activities: causal chains to secure a desired outcome. Further, determinism seems to drive a short-term orientation, since the shorter the time horizon, the more easily deterministic relationships can be assumed. So, enterprise performance is measured in lagging indicators through a limited set of short-term financial parameters that are supposed to predict future performance. Such short-term measures are innately in conflict with inherently long-term investment commitments and continual improvements related to quality, the reduction of throughput time, the design of new processes, and the development of human resources.

A singular focus on mechanistic perceptions is likely to be counterproductive due to the resulting one dimensional approaches to multidimensional problems. Unwillingness to use an inclusive enterprise perspective will further the either-or mode of thinking that perpetuates seeing enterprises as full of irreconcilable opposites or trade-offs. For example, freedom and order are recognized in the inclusive view as two essential aspects of all enterprises; the either-or approach treats them as an irreconcilable dilemma. However, freedom and order are not necessarily opposites: given complexity and uncertainty, more freedom in self-organizing could address uncertainty to create overall emergent order.

In view of a number of essential enterprise success areas, an exclusive mechanistic approach is dysfunctional since it undervalues human capacities, the very essence of the organismic approach to enterprises. Undervaluing human capacities entails that people should behave like machine parts carrying out predefined tasks. Work that requires only mechanical input stifles creativity and initiative. This absence of mentally involved employees created in itself a justification for the existence and continuation of the mechanistic approach. The inherent undervaluation of human capacities and contributions within the mechanistic mind-set essentially detaches employees from enterprise activities in an emotional sense, since these activities are not perceived as part of their responsibilities. Carrying out tasks *set before them* amounts to no more than mechanical behavior and is distant from participation and the expression of personal involvement with, and integration into, enterprise activities. Hence, at the employee level, the mechanistic approach to enterprises induces the attitude of not taking responsibility for what is happening. Employee involvement is thus extremely limited.

The lack of employee involvement is detrimental to enterprise success and excellence. The drive for further productivity and quality improvements, as well as a customer- and service-oriented operation, rests on employee involvement to a critical degree. Similarly, this holds for the need for enterprise learning and innovation and the moral and ethical aspects related to the responsibility of enterprises beyond shareholder profit maximization. Finally, the focus on employee involvement is also driven by the shift from manual-intensive to knowledge-intensive work. Different enterprises having virtually identical technology, and producing similar products, nonetheless show dramatically different results in various areas such as productivity, quality, customer and service orientation, and innovation. Customarily, the response to completion has been to add technology, cut costs, or seek favorable government regulation and intervention. However, the only sustainable resource for competitive advantage, which is also the best, cheapest, and easiest to employ, is people. The phenomenon can only be understood by focusing on human resources development and human behavior in enterprises.

Enterprises face considerable complexity and dynamics caused by technological, social, economic, political, commercial, environmental, or competitive developments. Globalization and deregulation, and the emergence of new business models (e-business, network economy, networked enterprises) likewise play an important role. Increasing complexity and dynamics necessitate a shift from the mechanistic toward the organismic way of organizing and, hence, a shift from top-down control to bottom-up empowerment. As environmental uncertainty increases, organizations tend to become more organic, which means decentralizing authority and responsibility to lower levels, encouraging employees to take care of problems by working directly with one another, encouraging teamwork, and taking an informal approach to assigning tasks and responsibility.

This discussion on organismic perspective should not be interpreted as a plea to disregard principles of rationalism, reductionism, or determinism altogether, nor to devalue logical-deductive thinking as the reliable foundation for our customary thinking and actions. To a large measure, our own thinking is based on these principles; the mechanistic perspective of reality works very well to a large extent. Complex technical systems, on which society depends for its functioning on a daily basis, show clearly the utility of this type of thinking, because in case of a system breakdown, the search for rectification or a solution to the problem is based on an assumption that the rational (and deterministic) cause and effect relationships are in play. The traditional notion of progress is also driven by mechanistic thinking to a considerable degree—the mechanistic approach has created considerable growth in productivity, employment, and wealth. Various activities in an enterprise benefit from rational planning and the application of analytic tools, including adequate measurements.

> The problem arises only with the exclusive and isolated use of mechanistic thinking that even precludes awareness about its dominant use, thereby contributing to the continuation of problems that cannot be solved within this domain of thinking. Mechanistic thinking has practically become the exclusive way of thinking in modern enterprises. Mechanistic approaches are often virtually unquestioned, and irregularities are not considered as evidence for the importance of different views, but rather seen as an anomaly that can be attributed to improper insight into the deterministic relationships or are attributed to poorly established initial conditions. Erroneous results thus are understood to create a practical problem, not one of principle. Mechanistic thinking by its very nature precludes viewing the enterprise as an integrated whole, with a multitude of interrelated, mutually influencing aspects, wherein employees play a crucial role.

The mechanistic approach is also a prerequisite for sustaining a human-centered focus within the enterprise; it enables the opportunity to address systematically the various aspects of human development and utilizing the full potential of human capabilities and capacities available within the enterprise. For example, adequate processes and technology allow decentralization and self-management while simultaneously ensuring unified efforts toward common goals of the enterprise. A mechanistic approach can significantly raise the level of competence of employees, as is the case in the area of information distribution and the generation of knowledge to support local decision making and autonomy. Customers would not be satisfied with suboptimal products or customer services on account of the dynamics, complexity, and the associated uncertainty faced by the enterprise in the market environment. Customers would expect best value for their money regardless of the challenges faced by the enterprise internally or externally. Thus, both the mechanistic and organismic perspectives (entailing employee involvement) are equally critical.

Enterprises can be conceptualized as potentially being able to apply seemingly mutually exclusive concepts; enabling holistic, integrative, and inductive thinking; simultaneously using apparently contradictory concepts; and obviating the need to perceive enterprises as full of irreconcilable trade-offs. The all-and principle enables a perspective of enterprise as being both control and people oriented, seeing people aspects both as ends and means, being control oriented while maintaining an adequate level of flexibility, focusing on quality as well as on efficiency, or showing both a humanistic and a mechanistic focus.

Technology, especially IT, resolves the paradox between the requirements for adequate control and the requirements to enable involved and committed employees. Technology can be extremely supportive in the form of information and decision support systems, which improve quality of knowledge and enhance employee involvement by allowing local decision making and the use of cognitive capacities of employees. In particular, ERP systems like SAP enable coexistence of both mechanistic and organismic perspectives of operations, management, and governance of enterprises (see Section VI, *Business Excellence and SAP*).

4.4.4 ENTERPRISE CORE AND CONTEXT

Rather than the structural analysis of internal assets and market structures, it is the unique sources of practice, know-how, and culture, at the firm and industry level, that is seen as the source of competitive advantage. Hamel and Prahalad characterized an enterprise competence as the integrated whole of enterprise skills, knowledge, and technology. They believed that an enterprise must not be seen as portfolio of individual business units, but rather more as a portfolio of competencies. It is the competencies that uniquely determine enterprises' opportunities and corresponding capabilities required to exploit them. Thus, strategic issues are not only concerned with what has to be done to maximize revenue or market share for a given product–market combination, but are also concerned with competencies that must be acquired for the envisaged future revenue and opportunities. Failures of enterprise strategies are attributed to enterprises entering new business domains that require core competencies that the enterprise does not have.

Within this framework, they introduced the concept of core competencies that underpin the dominant position of the enterprise for the delivery of their specific products and services; new opportunities entail the development of new core competencies. Hence, strategy development is not only about defining possible initiatives pertinent to the products and services but also about defining the requisite competencies.

Central to the notion of competence is the integration of various enterprise resources. In the earlier view, we define an enterprise competence as an integrated whole of enterprise skills, knowledge, and technology. Understandably, competencies must be organized—they are thus an organizational capacity or ability to produce something. And mentioned earlier, unity and integration does not occur spontaneously but has to be guided by the enterprise design enabled through top-of-the-line enterprise-wide system like SAP (see Chapter 13, *Understanding SAP ERP*).

The notion of enterprise competencies is closely related to the resource-based view on enterprises, which holds that the different resources enable them for different strategies. Accordingly, within this framework, different resources can be associated with different core competencies.

The broad spectrum of available resources can be classified into

1. Physical resources, such as buildings, machines, technology, and other means
2. Human resources with their skills, knowledge, and experience
3. Cognitive resources such as shared values or enterprise culture

Enterprise evolution is a pattern of co-creation between the enterprise and its environment: enterprises are able to influence the nature of their environment, whereas conversely, their environment shapes the nature of enterprises. The enterprise and its environment are seen as two independent entities: the enterprise delivers products and services to the environment and reacts to stimuli from that environment (which are considered to exist independent of the enterprise). However, an enterprise organizes the environment as part of itself: it chooses the environmental domain of interaction, whereby the nature and number of relationships with its environment coevolve. Both the environment and its enterprise must be seen as a unity of mutual relationship.

4.5 SUMMARY

In the introductory chapter, the world of business was interpreted in terms of individual companies, the market environment, and variations: the generation of variations and selection and retention of advantageous variations. Thus, companies were seen as systems that struggle for survival in the environment of the *market*. This chapter gave the requisite background on Darwin's theory of evolution. After recounting briefly the Beagle's voyage, it introduces Darwin's *Theory of Evolution through Natural Selection*. In the context of change of theories in sciences, it also acquainted the readers with Popper's thesis of falsification, Kuhn's concept of paradigm, and Peter Drucker's theory of business. We presented these theories of change (of models or of theories) so as to get a proper context for the Built-for-Variation enterprises discussed in the next chapter. Since SAP implemented in an enterprise is a working model and operating kernel of that enterprise, any variation envisaged in the enterprise can be realized by affecting the same on the SAP implemented within the enterprise. In the later part of the chapter, we looked at the broad characteristics of enterprises and contrasted the mechanistic and organismic perspectives on the enterprises. While the mechanistic perspective of enterprises is based on the traditional Cartesian understanding of reality, the contrasting organismic perspective, though not as easy to comprehend with its simultaneous cocombination can be realized easily by implementing an ERP system like SAP within the enterprise. These aspects are handled in detail in Section VI, *Business Excellence and SAP*.

Section III

Dimensions of Excellence

This section introduces the various dimensions of excellence to assess its progress toward achieving and maintaining excellence. It introduces the concept of Built-for-Variation enterprises that enable companies to seek a string of temporary competitive advantages through an approach to strategy, organization design, products or services, etc., that assumes variation is normal. Instead of having to create change efforts, disrupt the status quo, or adapt to change, enterprises should be built for variations. To collectively and effectively cover the various aspects of an operational company, the book chooses a set inspired by *McKinsey's 7S model* as a tribute to its pioneering effort in focusing interest on the challenges of sustaining excellence in enterprise performance, namely, the 9S framework constituting shared values, strategy, structure, stuff, style, staff, skills, systems, and sequence. The variations could be in any combinations of these dimensions, that is, the variations could be of products, services, business or production process, organization structures, organizational rules and procedures, and so on. These variations are affected simultaneously in multiple dimensions to different degrees of strength so that at any moment of time, the company is always in a state of flux under the resultant variations. It then introduces the three sources of variations, namely, pioneering, imitation, and innovation variations. In the last chapter of this section, the significance of each of these dimensions is illustrated with specific examples from various businesses across the world.

The 7S framework (and the extended 9S framework proposed here) is not very germane to the main thesis of the book. As mentioned in the Preface, as long as it collectively and effectively covers the various aspects of an operational company, the exact set of the chosen dimensions of variations is immaterial. *This is analogous to the use of coordinate system (or frame of reference) in sciences: technically any coordinate system would do, be it Cartesian, spherical, etc. But in practice one uses the coordinate system in which the system under consideration can be described most easily. Thus, we use Cartesian coordinates for rooms and buildings but use spherical coordinates for a system with spherical symmetry.*

However, "dimensions of variations" are different from a list of "attributes of excellence" proposed in *In Search of Excellence* (*ISoE*) (and dozens of similar works in the following decades). The focus on the latter is bound to encounter serious problems sooner than later. The fallacy of the latter approach can be seen in the repeated failures of the definitive and prescriptive treatments proposed in the earlier works on business excellence. Every few years you may need a new laundry list of "attributes of excellence" because of changes in the context or environment. My approach would not be afflicted with this malice.

The objective of the approach suggested here was to be inherently iterative, recursive, and self-consistent. I couldn't have suggested another list of "attributes of excellence" (like many other authors since 1980) that would have to be updated every few years by me or someone else. I only understood that was a wrong way to go.

5 Variations and Enterprise Excellence

5.1 BUILT-FOR-VARIATION ENTERPRISES

Most large-scale change efforts in established enterprises fail to meet expectations because nearly all models of organization design, effectiveness, and change assume that stability is not only desirable but also attainable. The theory and practice in organization design explicitly encourage organizations to seek alignment, stability, and equilibrium. The predominant logic of organizational effectiveness has been that an organization's fit with its environment, its execution, and its predictability are the keys to its success. Organizations are encouraged to institutionalize best practices, freeze them into place, focus on execution, stick to their knitting, increase predictability, and get processes under control. These ideas establish stability as the key to performance. Stability of distinctive competitive advantage is a strong driver for organization design because of its expected link to excellence and effectiveness (see Subsection 5.2.3.1, "Vantage Time"). Leveraging a vantage requires commitments that focus attention, resources, and investments to the chosen alternatives. In other words, vantage results when enterprises finely hone their operations to perform in a particular way. This leads to large investments in operating technologies, structures, and ways of doing things. If such commitments are successful, they lead to a period of high performance and a considerable amount of positive reinforcement. Financial markets reward stable vantages and predictable streams of earnings: a commitment to alignment reflects a commitment to stability.

Even the traditional approaches to change management reinforce the assumption of stability. The overwhelming change logic for decades has been a model of unfreezing, changing, and refreezing. *Unfreezing* presumes some form of equilibrium exists that needs to be disrupted. Once enterprises implement variations that move them to a new and desired future state, they are supposed to *refreeze*, which involves institutionalizing the variation and returning back to semblance of stability. The idea of unfreezing and refreezing is widely accepted because it supports traditional views of how enterprises can be effective—that is, by being stable and predictable and by executing effectively. The fallacy in this approach is that it assumes that variation is a one-time occurrence, when in actuality it is a continuous occurrence.

Consequently, enterprises are built to support stable strategies, organizational structures, and enduring value creations, not to vary. For example, the often-used strengths, weaknesses, opportunities, and threats (SWOT) analysis encourages the firm to leverage opportunities while avoiding weaknesses and threats. This alignment among positive and negative forces is implicitly assumed to remain constant, and there is no built-in assumption of variation. When environments are stable or at least predictable, enterprises are characterized by rules, norms, and systems that limit experimentation, control variation, and rewarded consistent performance. They have many checks and balances in place to ensure that the organization operates in the prescribed manner. Thus, to get the high performance they want, enterprises put in place practices they see as a good fit, without considering whether they can be varied and whether they will support variation in future, that is, by aligning themselves to achieve high performance today, enterprises often make it difficult to vary, so that they can have high performance tomorrow. When the environment is changing slowly or predictably, these models are adequate. However, as the rate of change increases with increasing globalization, technological breakthroughs, associative alliances, and regulatory changes, enterprises have to look for greater agility, flexibility, and innovation from their companies.

Instead of pursuing strategies, structures, and cultures that are designed to create long-term competitive advantages, companies must seek a string of temporary competitive advantages through an approach to organization design that assumes variation is normal. When vantage increasingly rests on the company's people and its ability to organize its human capital, the situation is dramatically different than when enterprises compete on the basis of tangible assets. With the advent of the Internet and the accompanying extended *virtual* market spaces, enterprises are now competing based on intangible assets like identity, intellectual property, ability to attract and stick to customers, and their ability to organize, reorganize frequently, or organize differently in different areas depending on the need. Thus, the need for variations in management and organization is much more frequent, and excellence is much more a function of possessing the ability for variation. Enterprises need to be built around practices that encourage variation, not thwart it. Instead of having to create change efforts, disrupt the status quo, or adapt to change, enterprises should be built for variations.

To meet the conflicting objectives of performing well against current set of environmental demands and changing themselves to face future business environments, enterprises must engender two types of variations: the natural process of evolution, or what we will call strategic adjustments, and strategic reorientations. Strategic adjustments involve the day-to-day tactical variations required to bring in new customers, make incremental improvements in products and services, and comply with regulatory requirements. This type of variation helps fine-tune current strategies and structures to achieve short-term results; it is steady, incremental, and natural. This basic capability to evolve is essential if an enterprise is to survive to thrive. Strategic reorientation involves altering an existing strategy and, in some cases, adopting a new strategy. When the environment evolves or changes sufficiently, an organization must significantly adjust some elements of its strategy and the way it executes that strategy. More often than not, enterprises have to face a transformational variation that involves not just a new strategy but a transformation of the business model that leads to new products, services, and customers and requires markedly new competencies and capabilities. However, operationally all these variations can be seen as manifestations of the basic variations only differing in degrees and multiple dimensions.

For example, a challenge faced in understanding GE across the generations stems from the complexities of *simultaneity*. Simultaneity pertains to a number of paradoxical trade-offs that have to be kept in tension. It would have been much easier if each of the domains of contention could have been isolated and treated one at a time. Unfortunately, as our quest for the new mindset frequently confirms, isolating one effect, investigating an interlocking systems by dissecting it into discrete parts, is illusory. Thus, in most real-life cases, we see the combined effects of several imbalances. This makes our story harder to sell, but the additional complexity pays off in greater accuracy and a more trustworthy understanding of the factors that lead to sustained performance. This will be evident at GE as we note the trade-offs being managed within and between successive administrations.

Maintaining a variable enterprise is not a matter of searching for the strategy but continuously strategizing, not a matter of specifying an organization design but committing to a process of organizing, and not generating value but continuously improving the efficiency and effectiveness of the value generation process. It is a search for a series of temporary configurations that create short-term vantages. In turbulent environments, enterprises that string together a series of temporary but adequate vantages will outperform enterprises that stick with one vantage for an extended period of time. The key issue for the Built-for-Variation enterprise is orchestration, or coordinating the multiple changing subsystems to produce high levels of current enterprise performance.

A Built-for-Variation enterprise is constantly in flux comprising of three aggregate dimensions, namely, strategizing, organizing, and generating value; strategizing is related to the dimensions of strategy, structure, shared values, and stuff (products, services, or experiences); organizing is related to the dimensions of style, staff, skills, and systems; and, finally, generating value is related to the dimension of sequence of production or delivery. Strategizing, organizing, and creating value are each viewed as dynamic processes changing in response to or in anticipation of an environmental variation. An enterprise's external environment includes general business conditions and industry structures. Built-for-Variation enterprises look at both the current environment and the potential environments that might emerge in the future. An enterprise has little choice but to anticipate its future environments and position it to succeed in those environments. Enterprises must deal with uncertainty by making reasoned guesses about the future—and, where possible, hedging their bets by being able to vary in sync with environmental variations. Since anticipating the exact nature of the environment is difficult, organizing a Built-for-Variation enterprise to respond quickly to unexpected environments is an important part of the organizing process.

 We would like to highlight that the various case histories are meant to highlight the variations during the life span of these companies rather than to illustrate either effective or ineffective handling of administrative situations.

5.1.1 Strategizing: Shared Values, Strategy, Structure, and Stuff

Strategizing describes how an organization achieves and maintains competitive parity—that is, how close an organization's outputs are to the demands of its environment. As the environment shifts and changes, the enterprise's responses must shift and change to drive effectiveness. Thus, instead of pursuing a single sustainable advantage, a Built-for-Variation enterprise seeks a series of momentary advantages that can create and maintain competitive parity; this involves the relationship among the environment, strategic intent, and enterprise performance. To achieve and maintain competitive parity, a Built-for-Variation enterprise first must develop a sense of the future by closely interfacing with the external environment to identify key trends. Rather than scheduling static annual reviews of the environment, enterprise members on an ongoing basis need to observe and report on trends and to identify competitive opportunities. They need to think constantly about potential alternative futures and create a variety of short- and long-term scenarios. To achieve and maintain competitive parity, a Built-for-Variation enterprise must define strategy in a new way. Success within a range of possible futures requires Built-for-Variation enterprise to seek a robust strategy that will succeed under a variety of conditions and yet be flexible enough to adjust to those conditions. A robust strategy is created by tinkering with the tension between identity and strategic intent.

Strategizing represents a continuous search for a string of temporary competitive advantages that will drive its effectiveness.

Strategic review: a diagnosis of the determinants of current performance and an assessment of the strategy's fitness for the future. The frequency of the strategic reviews should be a function of pace of technological, global, regulatory, and competitor moves or on the occurrence of an unexpected development. Processes and techniques that involve enterprise members aid in the diagnosis of the causes of poor performance or the reasons future performance may be at risk. Small gaps between desired and actual performance are usually indicative of execution problems; it usually calls for an assessment of the organizing or generating value processes (or both) and may require only tactical variation. Large gaps between desired and actual performance suggest that some aspect of the strategy is not responding to current environmental demands; careful analysis of the existing strategy can determine if the problem is with the strategic intent or (most seriously) the identity.

Strategic choice: working with the information generated by the strategic review, the organization decides whether or not it needs to alter its identity, the elements of strategic intent, or both. One possible decision is to affirm the current identity and strategic intent and pursue strategic adjustment; or the enterprise might decide to pursue strategic reorientation or even transformation. A reorientation reformulates one or more elements of strategic intent with an affirmed identity; a transformation involves changing both identity and intent.

Strategic variation: the orchestration process leads as the enterprise reconfigures its strategic intent (in the case of reorientation), varies its identity, or both (in the case of transformation). This resetting of the identity or intent must be initiated by the orchestration process. When an organization engages in a reorientation, it redefines one or more of the elements of strategic intent: breadth, aggressiveness, differentiation, logic, and orchestration. But changing multiple strategic intent elements is much more complex and often requires change in the enterprise's organization and capabilities. Finally, the orchestration process needs to coordinate the organization and implementation of the changes and see that they become manifest in the competencies, capabilities, and organization of the enterprise. Identities are deeply rooted in the basic assumptions of an enterprise and are very difficult to vary. When and how these changes are implemented requires carefully orchestrated timing. When should the firm lead the variation in the industry, and when should it move with the variation in the industry? The orchestration process must also address the speed of the variation process and the amount of effort needed to make it happen.

In the pursuit of a series of short-term advantages, Built-for-Variation enterprises need to avoid exhorting members toward perfection, excellence, and other sensationalist metaphors. A strategic transformation that changes identity is needed when the strategic review shows that the enterprise's identity is not viable. This happens when the review has identified an environmental shift or organizational event of such magnitude and importance that the very core of the organization is viewed as obsolete. The identity conversations include debates about the core values and assumptions driving the enterprise's growth, discussions of important biases and tendencies in decision making, and reflections on the organization's strengths and weaknesses. The issues involved in thinking through a new identity and strategy are so complex and difficult that it is a good choice only when no other options exist. Successful change of a firm's identity is a rare event, but it does occur. More often than not, it coincides with dramatic shifts in technology, a fundamental change in the environment, or a merger or acquisition.

5.1.1.1 Shared Values

Identity is what enables the enterprise to maintain its unique characteristics and sense of purpose despite being responsive (with appropriate variations) to the environmental demands for variation in its strategic intent. Identity—a combination of sense of purpose, core values, culture, image, and perspective—is a central concept in the Built-for-Variation approach because it is what holds constant in the midst of constant state of flux. A simple way to think about identity is to ask how an enterprise prioritizes and addresses the often conflicting demands of the environment and its key stakeholders; for instance, investors' preferences for higher dividends can conflict with customers' demands for new products, employees' demands for higher wages, and the community's demands for corporate social responsibility. How a company reconciles these conflicting expectations is the key part of its identity. It is an important foundation of future performance and the ability to vary; it is an important source of effectiveness and is potentially a primary reason why a Built-for-Variation enterprise can reorient itself easily.

Like an individual's personality, an enterprise's identity is a defining characteristic that does not vary, except perhaps through slow evolution or as the result of a disruptive variation. Establishing what can change and that change is normal is an important part of establishing credibility and realistic employee expectations when variation occurs. It is a major mistake for an organization to announce change efforts that consistently call for transformational variation, radical departures, or fundamental shifts in its strategy. An enterprise that boasts of making discontinuous variations in its strategy can create too much uncertainty for enterprise members and threaten an important source of performance. When enterprises know their identity, they are less likely to propose adjustments to their strategic intent that will not be supported by its culture or that are not in line with its brand image. For example, an organization that prides itself on legendary customer service is in a good position to identify strategic adjustments that enhance its service and to say no to a strategic adjustment that would cut costs but decrease good service. When organization members know that announced or intended changes honor the firm's identity, they find it easier to support and commit to new structures and new processes or to building new capabilities. This is particularly true when an organization's identity includes responding to change in the external world. Thus, the best Built-for-Variation enterprises have strong identities that incorporate commitment to both stability and change.

5.1.1.1.1   Shared Values at NUMMI

In 1963, GM opened an automobile assembly plant in Fremont, California. By 1978, the Fremont plant employed over 7200 workers. GM Fremont ranked at the bottom of the GM's plants in productivity and was producing one of the worst-quality automobiles in the entire GM system. The plant was characterized by high incidence of sick leave, slowdowns, wildcat strikes, and even sabotage. Daily absenteeism was almost 20%, and drug abuse and alcoholism plagued the workforce. There was a climate of fear and mistrust between management and the union. First-line managers were known to carry weapons for personal protection. Owing to such prevailing conditions, Fremont plant was closed down in 1982.

In 1983, Toyota and GM signed a letter of intent to reopen the plant, now named NUMMI with an investment of $100 million each coupled with another $200 million in debt. Toyota was to operate and manage the facility. Toyota's objective in entering the joint venture was to gain a foothold in the U.S. market, learn about working with U.S. suppliers, and see if their manufacturing and management approaches could work with U.S. employees. GM needed a small car (the Nova) to add to its product line and also hoped to learn about Toyota's famed manufacturing system. Toyota assumed the responsibility for all plant operations, including product design and engineering as well as marketing, sales, and service for Toyota-branded vehicles (initially the Corolla); GM assumed responsibility for the marketing, sales, and service of GM-branded vehicles (initially the Chevy Nova). GM was to assign on a rotation basis a limited number of managers to learn the Toyota manufacturing system. NUMMI's management was initially headed by Tatsuro Toyoda, son of Toyota's founder. The then Union of Auto Workers (UAW) president and head for GM also committed the union to work with the new venture. GM pushed to keep the UAW to avoid trouble with the union for operations at its other facilities (though Toyota had preferred to operate a nonunion plant). Toyota agreed to recognize the union and to offer recall rights, at union-scale wages, to the workforce laid off when GM had closed the plant. In turn, the UAW agreed to accept the Toyota production system (TPS), to greatly increase the flexibility of work rules, and to rationalize the job classifications to a simple structure. Correspondingly, Toyota agreed to reappoint the same 25-member union bargaining committee that existed at the erstwhile plant, to assume the same role at NUMMI. Since there was a significant risk associated with this, reestablishing the same committee was the beginning of the establishment of a new culture at NUMMI based on trust and respect. Eighty-five percent of the initial workforce of 2200 came from the pool of GM employees laid off in 1982. The only category of employees that was not offered employment at NUMMI was former first-line supervisors. At the outset, Toyota sent 400 trainers from Japan to teach the TPS. NUMMI spent more than $3 million to send 600 of its employees to Japan for training, including 3 weeks of classroom and on-the-job training side by side with Toyota workers.

In the very first year, NUMMI built 65,000 Novas—a car that was rated by Consumer Reports as one of the highest-quality small cars in the world. Absenteeism was less than 3%, and only a handful of grievances were filed (as against an average of 5000–7000 grievances under the erstwhile GM system). By 2000, the plant employed 4000 unionized workers and produced an average of 85 vehicles per worker, far above the average of 50 vehicles per worker at both Saturn and Buick city, the most efficient GM facilities. NUMMI produces the same number of automobiles as the erstwhile GM plant but with a much higher quality and half the workforce (for an overall investment of $1.2 billion). In 1998, NUMMI plant won the National Association of Manufacturer's award for excellence. The award cited that this plant managed a changeover to a new model in the remarkable period of only 5 days and took only 30 days to attain full production. The quality of the vehicles was nearly 50% better than the old version (which itself was already highest rated), while the cost-reduction targets through the launch were exceeded by 86%. Additionally, over 86% of the workforce made over 3.2 suggestions per person, of which 81% were adopted.

> Since 1983, GM has spent more than $80 billion on automation to improve the quality of its automobiles and enhance productivity. Yet in spite of the large technology investments, in 1998 the most efficient GM plants were still lagging NUMMI in productivity to the extent of 40%. Moreover, GM and its unions continue their bitter and costly labor disputes; poor union–management relations resulted in a 50-day strike at two spare parts plants in Flint, Michigan. Part shortages resulting from the strike idled more than 200,000 UAW members and resulted in a shutdown of most of GM's automobile assembly plants, with an estimated loss to GM of $2.5 billion—enough for GM to build two brand-new assembly plants.

The primary goal of the Toyota manufacturing system is to reduce costs and maximize profits through the systematic identification of waste. This goal was broadened from reducing the cost per vehicle to include continually improving quality and safety. The vision for NUMMI was to produce the highest-quality, lowest-cost vehicle in the world. *Kaizen* places an unrelenting emphasis on the identification and elimination of waste in all of its various forms: inventory, buffer stocks, equipment, material flow, man power, and work design. These forms of waste stem from poorly designed plans and processes, poor standardization, a lack of communication, poor cost accounting practices, and so on. Importantly, waste is seen as having adverse effects on people, leading to physical and emotional fatigue, lack of attention or concentration, a tendency to be careless or sloppy, and a tendency to blame others. The shared belief is that everything can be improved and that all improvements, no matter how small, are significant. This approach further recognizes that people are the foundation of this system and that their ideas are the true source of improvements. The NUMMI production system is characterized by a constant tension and quest for improvement. Balancing this tension necessitates consistency in adhering to the principles of the system and requires maintaining a level of cooperation and trust between management and employees. Building this trust requires a genuinely open, data-driven decision-making management style, but not necessarily one that is democratic or permissive—this kind of trust is indispensible in the NUMMI system. Managing this process also requires continual change; to do this effectively over long periods of time requires that managers continuously renew their resolve and find new ways to reenergize employees to push for improvement and to avoid the complacency that success invariably brings.

How can one management achieve extraordinary results when the previous management failed miserably with the same people? It was not because of any special workforce: the NUMMI plant employed ex-GM workers. It was not because of technology: the NUMMI plant relied on old technology. It was not a nonunion workplace. the NUMMI has the same union as at the erstwhile GM plant (in fact, it also had even the same union leaders).

5.1.1.1.2 Shared Values Differential

The NUMMI approach begins with a different set of basic values and assumptions. The underlying belief is that all the people in the plant have a common interest and a rationale of mutually beneficial relationship. Under the NUMMI system, the basic assumption is that all people are responsible and want to contribute. In the highly competitive global automobile market, success for everyone requires that NUMMI produce the highest-quality car at the lowest possible cost. This will ensure profits for the company and secure jobs for all the employees. To realize this, management believes that the line employees are the key to accomplishing this goal. The assumption has led to design of a system calculated to unleash the power of the workforce ranging from how people are selected, to how jobs are designed and improved, to how the people are trained, and to how employees are supervised and rewarded. The system is critically based on the belief in a common fate and one that rests on mutual trust and respect for the contribution of all members of the organization. The practices that foster mutual trust and respect, equity, involvement, and teamwork include the following: job security (a no-layoff policy), concern for safety in the plant, individual responsibility for quality, active involvement in the decision-making process, no time clocks, common eating and parking areas, and no differentiation in attire.

Under the erstwhile GM system, the basic assumption seemed to be that people do not want to work hard and will take advantage of any opportunity to shirk. These implicit assumptions lead managers to design a system that produces the behavior they were designed to prevent. These assumptions about people produced narrow job designs that required little training or thought from workers; the thinking and job designing was reserved for industrial engineers and managers. Because the employees needed little skill, no real effort was made to select those with positive attitudes. Instead, the dominating assumption was that all people were lazy and needed close supervision; hence, supervisors and strong punishment systems played large roles. The tendency of managers was to rely on the use of external controls. Management began to see that employees really could not be trusted, and employees began to learn that the rhetoric about trust and common goals were more words than real belief. The reaction from employees and the union was to increasingly test the system and sincerity of the management. Efforts by managers to correct any abuses tended to tighten the controls even further. With strong management control, people felt the need for strong union representation as a countervailing force. Very soon, employees and management seemed to have little interest in common. Management's role became to coerce unwilling workers to produce more for less, while workers and their union wanted less work for more money and benefits. This led to a rapidly growing chasm between the employees and the management at the erstwhile GM plant that very soon became unbridgeable and led to the final breakdown.

The success of NUMMI (and Toyota's manufacturing system) is difficult to replicate unless the underlying values and philosophies are deeply held and there is a genuine commitment to live those values. The core values that are constantly reinforced include customer satisfaction (quality and cost), dignity, trust, teamwork, consistency, frugality, continual improvement, simplicity, and harmony. After studying NUMMI, a competitor may conclude that mystery of NUMMI's success can be explained by the careful alignment and consistency of its management policies and practices and the NUMMI production system. Further, this competitor may replicate all the NUMMI production system as also the NUMMI policies and practices at another plant location, but without embracing the underlying values, this would be a futile effort. The success of NUMMI comes from an integrated set of manufacturing and human resource processes that align the interests of employees, managers, and company and involve the workforce in a way that simultaneously empowers them while managing the inherent interdependences in a complex manufacturing system.

5.1.1.2 Strategy

Strategic intent is a constellation of organizational choices about breadth, aggressiveness, differentiation, orchestration, and logic. It provides the flexibility and describes the enterprise's breadth of products and services, the vigorousness with which it pursues its vantages, and the product and services that distinguish its offerings from those of competitors. Thus, for any temporary set of product or service features, an organization can have a broad or narrow product line and can be relatively aggressive or passive in its approach; these elements can be varied quickly. A robust strategic intent should be relatively stable but much more variable than identity. The elements of intent may need to be reconfigured relatively quickly in a Built-for-Variation enterprise. On the one hand, a Built-for-Variation enterprise needs to make strategic choices that will work out under any of the most likely scenarios it foresees; on the other hand, the individual elements of intent may need to change and therefore must be relatively easy to change.

Strategic intent also includes a road map for how offerings will be orchestrated over time in response to environmental variations and in concert with an enterprise's capabilities and organization. The key components of strategy relate the environmental scenarios to the generating value process (competencies and capabilities). Environmental scenarios provide the context for formulating strategy. Identity bridges scenarios and the five elements of strategic intent—breadth, aggressive, orchestration, differentiation, and logic—which are the relationships within critical configuration that must be specified. Finally, strategic intent guides the process of generating a value that is codependent on the characteristic competencies and capabilities of the enterprise; that is, capabilities dictate strategic intent that in turn determines the required capabilities and competencies. If requisite capabilities and competencies do not exist, they will have to be acquired or created anew:

1. Breadth: The breadth of a company's strategy describes the choices it makes with respect to the range of products or services offered, the different markets served, the different technologies supported, the different segments of the value chain occupied, and so on. The broader the company's strategy, the more complex and diversified it is.
2. Aggressiveness: A company's aggressiveness defines how it develops new products, grows its business, and battles its competitors. It refers to an organization's commitments to courses of action and is reflected in an organization's goals, objectives, and policies.
3. Differentiation: The differentiation elements of a strategy are concerned with the features of a company's product or service and how they match up against competitors' products or services. A product (we'll use the term product generically to refer to either products or services) can vary in quality, warranty promises, reliability, or price.
4. Orchestration: It refers to how variations in breadth, aggressiveness, and differentiation are managed together to bring the enterprise into competitive parity with environmental demands over time. Orchestration represents a planning process for how different strategic and organization initiatives are executed sequentially or concurrently or staggered. The orchestration process needs to coordinate changes not only in the elements of strategic intent but also in the processes for organizing and generating value.
5. Strategic logic: Strategic logic refers to the underlying business model used to generate revenue, manage costs, and produce profits. An enterprise, for example, that chooses an aggressive and broad strategy may be attempting to capture market share and lower unit costs. This volume strategy may seek to establish a low-cost position within the industry and a small margin over many units. Linking the strategic intent to such economic concepts as the experience curve, economies of scale, economies of scope, or global product mandates lends credibility to its specification.

5.1.1.2.1 Strategic Transition at Kodak

George Fisher, who joined as chairman and CEO of Eastman Kodak in 1993, established the digital imaging strategy for Kodak that set the direction of the company up until 2004. Fisher leveraged on Kodak's traditional competencies and capabilities to formulate a vision beyond the traditional photographic business to embrace a much larger business of imaging. He opinioned that Kodak was not in the photographic film business or in the electronics business, but was really in the *picture* business. He followed this up with divestments of its pharmaceutical and chemical businesses to enable Kodak to focus all of its resources on its core imaging business. Kodak adopted a hybrid approach where Kodak introduced those aspects of digital imaging that could offer truly enhanced functionality for users. Thus, in the consumer market, Kodak recognized that image capture would continue to be dominated by traditional film for some time—digital cameras did not offer the same sharpness of resolution as conventional photography. However, digital imaging offered the potential for image manipulation and transmission that were quite beyond traditional photography.

This hybrid approach involved Kodak in providing facilities in retail outlets for digitizing and editing images from conventional photographs, then storing, transmitting, and printing these digital images. In 1994, Kodak launched its Picture Maker, which allowed digital prints to be made either from conventional photo prints or from a variety of digital inputs. Picture Maker allowed customers to edit their images (zoom, crop, eliminate red-eye, and add text) and print them in a variety of formats. A particular advantage of these retailer-based digital photography systems was that they allowed Kodak to exploit a key resource—its extensive distribution presence. By the end of 2000, some 30,000 retail locations worldwide offered Picture Maker facilities. In addition, Kodak introduced a wide range of purely digital photographic products that extended from image capture to image printing. For the consumer market, Kodak viewed its huge retail presence as a means of bringing digital imaging to the mass market.

It was in the commercial and professional markets where Kodak launched its major innovations in digital imaging. The sophisticated needs of the government in satellite imaging, planning military campaigns, weather forecasting, and surveillance activities favored digital technologies for transforming, transmitting, and storing images; medical imaging (especially CT, MRI, and ultrasound) required digital technologies for 3D imaging, diagnosis, and image storage; publishers and printers needed digital imaging to complement the new generation of computerized publishing and printing systems for newspapers and magazines. For commercial applications ranging from journalism, to highway safety, to real estate, digital imaging provided the linkage to the Internet and sophisticated IT management systems. For example, in the medical field, Kodak's Ektascan Imagelink system, which included the capability of converting medical images to digital images that could then be transmitted via phone lines to local hospitals, was launched in 1995. Kodak established world leadership in medical laser imaging through its Ektascan laser printer, introduced in 1996. This leadership was extended with the acquisition of Imation's DryView laser imaging business in 1998. By the end of the 1990s, Kodak had built a powerful position in digital health imaging based upon both laser imaging and digital radiography. In 2000, Kodak launched its application service provider business to the medical, community allowing images to be captured and managed via Kodak's digital systems to Intel Online Services' data center.

5.1.1.2.2 Transition from DRAMs to Microprocessors at Intel

Intel is a leading manufacturer of microprocessors, but it started out as a semiconductor company. Intel was founded in 1968 by Robert Noyce and Gordon Moore, both of whom had been senior executives at Fairchild Semiconductors. The company's initial strategy was to develop semiconductor memory chips for mainframe and minicomputers. In 1971, Intel introduced the 1103, a 1 kbit dynamic random access memory (DRAM) chip that very quickly became a best-selling product, accounting for more than 90% of the company's sales revenue; following this, within a year, it invented the microprocessor. Intel's strategy was to be the first to market with the newest innovative devices; this strategy necessitated maintaining strong capabilities in product design. Intel also had to be on the leading edge of process technology because semiconductor manufacturing processes were enormously complex and directly influenced the distinctive characteristics of the products. With each new generation of product technology, the company was forced to invest heavily in upgrading to equipment capable of producing ever-more-complex devices. But with the introduction of newer and unfamiliar processes, production yields would suffer and fall dramatically. Only as the plant gained experience with the new process, identified and resolved trouble spots, and exploited opportunities for process optimization and improvement would the yields begin to rise appreciably. Thus, Intel's strategy not only necessitated maintaining strong capabilities in product design but also necessitated capabilities in execution and rapid scaled-up production.

Until around 1979, Intel's strategy seemed to be working well when Intel introduced four generations of DRAMs (1K, 2K, 4K, and 16K) and related process technologies, which were ahead of the competition and commanded significant price premiums. However, the product-led leadership strategy was under threat and became increasingly vulnerable. For example, in 1979, Intel introduced a

16K DRAM to which Fujitsu responded by introducing a 64K DRAM that quickly captured a significant share of the DRAM market; Fujitsu's higher market share translated into higher cumulative production volumes, which in turn gave the company a manufacturing cost advantage. This scenario was repeated again in 1982 when Intel introduced an improved version of the 64K DRAM that was responded by Fujitsu and Hitachi by introducing 256K DRAMs. Japanese company's investments in new plant and equipment were almost double of that for the U.S. companies. Japanese competitors in DRAMs were much faster at developing process technologies and ramping-up production capacities (and improving yields) than their American counterparts. Consequently, Japanese production yields were as high as 70%–80% against 50%–60% at best of the American companies. In 1984, Intel scientists designed a 1 Mbit DRAM; but they knew that this would be successful only if Intel reached the market and achieved commercially viable manufacturing yields before Japanese competitors could introduce their own 1M DRAMs. Finally, Intel decided to halt further development of its 1M DRAM and exited from the DRAMs market. This resulted in microprocessors becoming the core of Intel's business and Intel became to be known as a microprocessor company.

5.1.1.3 Structure

5.1.1.3.1 Structural Building Blocks

An enterprise's structure is a critical determinant of enterprise effectiveness and in most cases needs to be altered when it's strategic intent changes. Traditionally, an enterprise structure is primarily a way to distribute the work and authority. In actuality, an enterprise needs a structuring process that enables it to develop the competencies and capabilities it needs to execute its strategic intent. It is important to create a structure that is flexible enough to allow for strategy-driven variations; a number of structural *building blocks* make strategy-driven variations easier, namely, jobs, teams, virtual teams, and business units. Traditional job descriptions cover what the job holder is supposed to do, the kind of skills needed, and, in some cases, how performance can be measured. However, job descriptions are not only costly to maintain but also thwart any variation. Built-for-Variation enterprises do away with job descriptions altogether, resulting in a structure that is characterized by dynamic work assignments and relationships. As people's skills change and the needs of the organization vary, the task mix that individuals are responsible for is adjusted. The kind of projects individuals work on and the kind of tasks they perform change depending on what is happening with a particular customer or a particular product. We often see this kind of structure in consulting firms and in other professional service organizations where individuals are continually moved from project to project with a different project lead for each assignment. Instead of reporting to a single manager of marketing, production, or other function, individuals report to multiple managers—for example, one who represents a function and another who is managing a customer relationship or a product development process.

Clearly, this approach to organizing puts a heavy demand on individuals; however, it is far better than the alternative of having job descriptions that are limiting, out of date, and difficult to vary. Working in a team helps individuals develop skills they will need when the enterprise varies. Temporary teams can greatly enhance the agility of an enterprise by enabling them to focus quickly on new products, customers, capabilities, and competencies. To be effective, project teams need to have clear accountability and produce results that are visibly tied to customer satisfaction and business performance. Permanent teams can facilitate tactical variation like responding to unusual customer requests, equipment breakdowns, new processes, and service failures. Virtual teams constituted of members at different locations connected through electronic means can be very effective in providing seamless 24×7 support; members can also work at home. With virtual structures, reporting relationships and team formations can be changed without many of the usual problems and, hence, are less resistant to variations.

Business units are a way to get the parts of a large organization focused on the external environment and tied into performance results that they can control. They usually have considerable autonomy and employees take ownership for results and willingly adapt to variation. Matrix organizations can develop competencies and capabilities that more traditional structures simply cannot. A matrix structure gives the organization both a focus on current performance and the ability to vary; thus, it can be a structure that supports tactical as well as major strategic variation. The combination of many close-to-the-customer business units and a matrix structure is often the best way to design a large Built-for-Variation enterprise. Business process outsourcing (BPO) model is popular in finance, accounting, HR management, and information systems management. BPO arrangements can produce real cost savings because of the economies of scale an outsourcing firm can achieve. There is also a core competency advantage that argues that an outsourcing firm, because of its scale and focus, will always have more of a core competency in an area like HR management than any single company is likely to have. The outsourcing firm creates and runs the systems that provide information services, HR, or whatever traditional internal staff services the organization decides can be done better by an outsourcer. The outsourcer is then also responsible for handling any variations: by shifting responsibility from an internal staff group to an outsourcer, the firm makes its own variation effort much easier and painless. The enterprise that is either upsizing or downsizing doesn't have to worry about whether its systems need to be revised or whether new knowledge and skills are required to operate them with its new business model. It relies on its outsourcing firm to provide this kind of expertise and indeed to revise processes so that they fit the new business model.

5.1.1.3.2 *Built-for-Variation Structures*

New businesses: Built-for-Variation enterprises must constantly attend to the processes of the day while also developing scenarios based on the variations that will define their future. Most enterprises are much better at exploiting their existing capabilities rather than at looking forward and determining which new capabilities to develop for the future; they often falter in developing and marketing new products and services. Usually, start-up firms often win out because existing businesses often have practices and policies that are built to serve an existing set of environmental demands (and are designed for stability), whereas start-ups don't have a burdensome legacy of practices and policies. New businesses in old enterprises are often weighed down by expenses and controls imposed by the existing corporate structure; existing enterprises particularly stumble in implementing transformational variations that require a new identity. Moreover, when start-ups are a part of a large existing enterprise, they often lack the decision-making authority for the quick *make or break* decisions that are characteristic of new businesses.

New business units: Often, the only viable approach to starting new businesses within an existing organization is to create a special business unit that is *independent* of the existing corporation, much like emerging business opportunities (EBOs) at IBM (see Chapter 7, Subsection 7.3.2, "Organizing for Innovation at IBM"). The people in the new business were transferred from the existing business. In addition, their compensation followed the practices of the existing organization rather than being like that of the typical start-up venture in which individuals could lose everything or become very wealthy. But perhaps the biggest limitation of the venture was that most individuals came to it laden with a *big corporation* mind-set. Overall, new business units are a way to produce major variation in a Built-for-Variation enterprise. They are particularly appropriate when the future scenarios and strategic intent favor getting into a new business area and the company realizes that its existing business units do not possess the appropriate competencies and capabilities. It is probably the best approach for existing organizations to use when they want to make a major entry into a new business area, but there is no guarantee of success. The risk of failure is quite high.

Joint ventures: These are an approach to creating new businesses that is often favored by built-to-change companies. GM, for example, has successfully used them as a way to bring operational and production variations to market at NUMMI (see Chapter 7, Subsection 7.7.3, "Fruits of Empowerment at NUMMI"). Joint ventures typically benefit from having relatively high levels of autonomy, and when this is combined with the right transfer of competencies and capabilities, they can be very successful.

Acquisitions and mergers: These are two of the most obvious and frequently used ways to produce major strategic variation in a company. They have a number of obvious and very attractive advantages. They can, for example, provide an entrée into a new market, allow an enterprise to increase its scale, and provide new core competencies. They seem to offer quick and easy reorientation and in some cases transformational variation. They can indeed vary the very identity of a firm, but, more often than not, they fail—the failure rate being between 60% and 80%.

Mergers are difficult to manage because there is often extreme competition for jobs between the members of the two merged organizations as also conflict on adopting practice and policies of the respective companies for the combined entity. Acquisitions represent a better way for Built-for-Variation enterprise to grow and develop. Built-for-Variation enterprises typically employ one of two acquisition strategies. The first is a hands-off approach that rarely creates synergies that enhance the value of the acquiring company. The second approach is to look for the synergies that can occur when a Built-for-Variation enterprise buys a smaller business to bring in a key technology, skill, or group of customers. When this type of acquisition is handled correctly, it can indeed create a new core competency or at least supplement the core competency of the existing Built-for-Variation enterprise. They usually make clear to everyone that an acquired company is going to become part of the acquiring company and is going to operate like the acquiring company. It rarely changes the operating procedures of the acquiring company, though it may change elements of its business model. In this type of acquisition, integration can be quick, thorough, and strategic (see Chapter 7, Subsection 7.1.1.2, "Perfecting the Acquisition Strategy").

Alliances, like acquisitions, can be a quick and effective way for Built-for-Variation enterprise to add to its capabilities and competencies. There are many different kinds of alliances, but most of them have in common an agreement between two or more enterprises that is seen as mutually beneficial; they may market each other's products or share technologies and core competencies, potentially gaining such advantages as market share and visibility. Alliances are often difficult to create and are certainly not an automatic success. Before Built-for-Variation enterprises enter into alliances, they need to conduct a great deal of due diligence on their prospective partners and protect themselves against their alliance partner eventually becoming a competitor as a result of what it learns from the alliance. The ability to form effective alliances may best be thought of as a capability that an organization needs to develop. For example, it is easier to grow into a new market by forming an alliance than it is by following a build-from-nothing strategy. Equally, it is much easier to exit a market if it means severing an alliance than if it means closing down your own operations in that market. Companies use alliances where the competency or capability it needs is not central to the organization's future; alliance can often be activated and terminated with less cost.

5.1.1.3.3 Unfettered Exuberance at HP

Perhaps one of the very best symbols of corporate entrepreneurship would be HP. HP built its success on a philosophy that emphasized autonomous business units created out of the entrepreneurial efforts of highly decentralized development teams. The prime career path at HP began with product development. HP's junior executives aspired to lead a development effort that would result in the creation of a new business unit, and the company has successfully focused and harnessed the entrepreneurial energies of its talented executive corps to do just that. The HP Way created one of the world's greatest companies, but in the early 1990s, this approach created serious difficulties in its computer business.

HP's 50+ divisions operated as highly decentralized, autonomous units that largely defined their own directions: 36 separate divisions had decided to enter the computer market, and each had designed and developed distinct product offerings. HP's highly entrepreneurial culture spawned a dysfunctional *family* of computing systems that used more than 30 distinct central processing units (CPUs) and more than 30 OSs. It interacted with customers via a variety of divisional sales and service organizations. Corporate customers were surprised and disappointed to find that buying two computer systems bearing the HP logo reduced enterprise connectivity and information sharing. In short, HP's excessively diverse technology base and product offerings placed it at a distinct disadvantage in the enterprise computing market as customers vocally demanded integrated computing solutions.

HP's response was to design a new-generation reduced instruction set computing (RISC) family intended to replace all existing computing platforms with a series of products incorporating a single architecture and OS. Its attempts to implement this new platform, however, were thwarted by the need to coordinate 36 historically autonomous product divisions active in the computing market, each with different market positions, technology platforms, and customer applications. Further examination revealed that HP owned and operated more than 100 circuit board assembly plants to feed its computing product lines, while the entire company's needs could have been met with only 6 plants. Each division had built its own capacity in manufacturing and many other areas without considering how to optimize the activities of HP as an enterprise.

HP experienced great difficulty attempting to migrate from its diverse technology, product, and organizational base to an integrated next-generation system. After several years of delays in implementing the RISC architecture, HP broke with its own made-here tradition and acquired Apollo Computer in an attempt to jump-start the changeover. Even that strong and uncharacteristic move could not overcome the underlying problem. HP was simply unable to sustain a leadership position in the enterprise computer systems business because of its culture of autonomy.

Computer Peripherals Organization (CPO), which had been merely a fledgling business in 1990, introduced a series of printing products based on Canon's printer engine that vaulted HP into a leadership position in several segments of that market. HP's new-product introduction skills were then brought to bear, spawning a large number of successful new printer offerings, and HP quickly established itself as market champion in the desktop printer business. Over time, CPO gradually pulled together the various printer technologies, facilities, and products within HP to create an integrated family of platforms and offerings. That itself was no small feat in HP. Spinning discrete product technologies is the natural focus of highly entrepreneurial, autonomous enterprises like HP. The firm's entrepreneurial style facilitated its success in printers but kept it from becoming an effective systems vendor.

5.1.1.4 Stuff

5.1.1.4.1 From Products to Services to Experiences

By the middle of the last century, products, goods, and property came to increasingly mean an individual's exclusive right to posses, use, and, most importantly, dispose of things as he or she wished. By the 1980s, the production of goods had been eclipsed by the performance of services. These are economic activities that are not products or construction, but are transitory, consumed at the time they are produced (and, thus, cannot be inventoried), and primarily provide intangible value. In a service economy, it is time that is being commodified, not prices, places, or things— this also leads to a transition from profit and loss to market cap as the base metric of success; what the customer is really purchasing is the access for use rather than ownership of a material good. Since the 1990s, goods have become more information intensive and interactive, are continually upgraded, and are essentially evolving into services. Products are rapidly being equated as the cost of doing business rather than as sales items; they are becoming more in the nature of *containers* or *platforms* for all sorts of upgrades and value-added services (see Subsection 5.2.5.3.1, "Paying with Card"). Giving away products is increasingly being used as a marketing strategy to capture the attention of potential customers. But with the advent of electronic commerce, feedback, and workflow mechanisms, services are being further transformed into multifaceted relationships between the service providers and customers, and technology is becoming more of a medium of relationships. In the servicized economy, defined by shortened PLCs and an ever-expanding flow of competitive goods and services, it is the customer attention rather than the resources that is becoming scarce.

The true significance of a customer's attention can be understood the moment one realizes that time is often used as a proxy for attention. Like time, attention is limited and cannot be inventoried or reused. In the current economy, attention is the real currency of business and, to be successful, enterprises must be adept in getting significant and sustained mindshare or attention of their prospects or customers. As with any other scarce and valuable resource, markets for attention exist both within and outside the enterprise. For extracting optimum value, the real-time and intelligent enterprises must impart optimal attention to the wealth of operational and management information available within the enterprise. This fact alone should automatically put a bar on overzealous reengineering and downsizing efforts (although reengineering and other cost-cutting tactics are necessary, it is essential to ascertain if undertaking such tactics will contribute to the delivery of superior or at least *on par* value to the customers) (see Chapter 14, Subsection 14.2, "Background of BPR"). This is the fundamental vision underlying the emergence of outsourcing strategies (see Chapter 13, Subsection 13.4.4, "Virtual Enterprise.")

One major result of this trend toward the importance of experience has been the blurring of lines between the content (the message) and container (the medium) in the market (Figure 5.1). *Convergence* describes the phenomenon in which two or more existing technologies, markets, producers, boundaries, or value chains combine to create a new force that is more powerful and more efficient than the sum of its constituting technologies. The value chain migration alludes to the development of real-term systems that integrate supply chain systems and customer-facing systems, resulting in a single and unified integrated process.

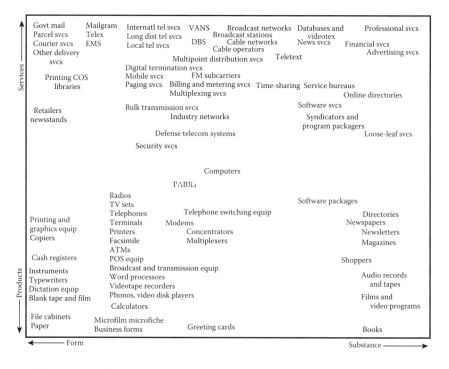

FIGURE 5.1   Spectrum of offerings (products/services) versus medium (container or form)/message (content or substance).

This convergence occurs primarily because of three factors:

1. The digitization of information to enable the preparation, processing, storage, and transmission of information regardless of its form (data, graphics, sound, and video or any combination of these).
2. The rapidly declining cost of computing that has enabled it to become ubiquitous and available with sufficient power (see *Moore's law* in Subsection 5.2.4.2.1, "Intel's Microprocessor Platform").
3. The availability of broadband communications is critical to convergence because multimedia is both storage intensive and time sensitive.

5.1.1.5 Coffee as an Experience at Starbucks

In 1975, Starbucks was a single store in Seattle's Pike Place Market selling premium roasted coffee. Today, it is a global roaster and retailer of coffee with more than 12,000 retail stores, some 3,000 of which are to be found in 40 countries outside the United States. Starbucks Corporation set out on its current course in the 1980s when the company's director of marketing, Howard Schultz, came back from a trip to Italy enchanted with the Italian coffeehouse experience. Schultz, who later became CEO, persuaded the company's owners to experiment with the coffeehouse format—and the Starbucks experience was born. Schultz's basic insight was that people lacked a *third place* between home and work where they could have their own personal time-out, meet with friends, relax, and have a sense of gathering. The business model that evolved out of this was to sell the company's own premium roasted coffee, along with freshly brewed espresso-style coffee beverages, a variety of pastries, coffee accessories, teas, and other products, in a coffeehouse setting.

5.1.1.5.1 Home Office Away from Home Experience

The company devoted, and continues to devote, considerable attention to the design of its stores to create a relaxed, informal, and comfortable atmosphere. Underlying this approach was a belief that Starbucks was selling far more than coffee—it was selling an experience. The premium price that Starbucks charged for its coffee reflected this fact. From the outset, Schultz also focused on providing superior customer service in stores. Reasoning that motivated employees provide the best customer service, Starbucks executives developed employee hiring and training programs that were the best in the restaurant industry. Today, all Starbucks employees are required to attend training classes that teach them not only how to make a good cup of coffee but also the service-oriented values of the company. Beyond this, Starbucks provides progressive compensation policies that gave even part-time employees stock option grants and medical benefits—a very innovative approach in an industry where most employees are part time, earn minimum wage, and have no benefits. Unlike many restaurant chains, which expanded very rapidly through franchising arrangements once they established a basic formula that appears to work, Schultz believed that Starbucks needed to own its stores. Although it has experimented with franchising arrangements in some countries and in some situations in the United States such as at airports, the company still prefers to own its own stores whenever possible. This formula met with spectacular success in the United States, where Starbucks went from obscurity to one of the best-known brands in the country in a decade. As it grew, Starbucks found that it was generating an enormous volume of repeat business. Today, the average customer comes into a Starbucks store around 20 times a month. The customers themselves are a fairly well-heeled group—their average income is about $80,000.

As the company grew, it started to develop a very sophisticated location strategy. Detailed demographic analysis was used to identify the best locations for Starbucks stores. The company expanded rapidly to capture as many premium locations as possible before its imitators could. Astounding many observers, Starbucks would even sometimes locate stores on opposite corners of the same busy street—so that it could capture traffic going in different directions down the street. By 1995, with almost 700 stores across the United States, Starbucks began exploring foreign opportunities. The first stop was

Japan, where Starbucks proved that the basic value proposition could be applied to a different cultural setting (there are now 600 stores in Japan). Next, Starbucks embarked on a rapid development strategy in Asia and Europe. By 2001, the magazine Brandchannel named Starbucks 1 of the 10 most influential global brands, a position it has held ever since. But this is only the beginning. In October 2006, with 12,000 stores in operation, the company announced that its long-term goal was to have 40,000 stores worldwide. Looking forward, it expects 50% of all new store openings to be outside the United States.

5.1.2 ORGANIZING: STYLE, STAFF, SKILLS, AND SYSTEMS

Organizing is concerned with how the enterprise's features (e.g., structure, processes, people, rewards) are orchestrated over time to support each other and the company's strategic intent, identity, and capabilities. To support a dynamic alignment among these features, each one needs to be changeable, flexible, and agile because they will be varying all the time. The organizing process must support the idea that the implementation and reimplementation of a strategy is a continuous process. What Built-for-Variation enterprises need is organization design and management practices that support variation and an enterprise's strategic intent. Though the strategic intent is different from one enterprise to another, it is possible to identify characteristic features that are common to most Built-for-Variation enterprises.

5.1.2.1 Style

Built-for-Variation enterprises must be in close touch with the market and other environmental demands in order to continually define and redefine a series of short-term competitive advantages. To achieve that high level of external awareness, all employees—not just senior managers—must observe and report on market trends and identify competitive opportunities. They need to think constantly about potential alternative futures, creating a variety of short- and long-term scenarios. Thus, instead of scheduling static annual reviews of the environment, Built-for-Variation enterprises must adopt a strategy development process that continuously monitors the environment. The key design principle here is to connect as many employees as possible with the external environment. Structures that accomplish this sharpen the external focus of its members; bring in critical information about trends, opportunities, and issues; and prevent people from becoming ossified in their roles. Thus, as many employees as possible should have contact with regulators, suppliers, the local community, watchdog groups, and, most importantly, customers. Built-for-Variation firms are anxious about being caught off guard, so they place everyone close to customers and the environment. That way, when the time comes to alter the direction of the enterprise, everyone moves together based on a common understanding and felt need for the variation. Network structures consist of individual organizations (or units within a company) that have been pulled together to exploit specific opportunities. An integrating organization coordinates the activities of the different entities, much as a hospital assembles and coordinates the work of doctors, anesthetist, nursing personnel, and other groups necessary to conduct and operation.

Built-for-Variation enterprises often choose front–back structures because customers want to deal with only one representative even when the company sells a complex array of products and services. IT firms (e.g., IBM, HP) and financial services institutions (e.g., Merrill Lynch, Citibank) sell a wide variety of products and services. Many of their best customers want to deal with a single representative who manages the overall interface between the two organizations. The same situation exists with many individual customers: they want a single person when interfacing with other complex service delivery organizations. Customers don't want to have to work their way through the various product offerings and the individuals representing the products to buy a mix of services and products.

5.1.2.1.1 Just Do It Style at Nike

Nike, headquartered in Beaverton, Oregon, was founded over 30 years ago by Bill Bowerman, a former University of Oregon track coach, and Phil Knight, an entrepreneur in search of a profitable business opportunity. Bowerman's goal was to dream up a new kind of sneaker tread that would enhance a runner's traction and speed, and he came up with the idea for Nike's waffle tread after studying the waffle iron in his home. Bowerman and Knight made their shoe and began selling it out of the trunks of their car at track meets. From this small beginning, Nike has grown into a company that sold over $12 billion worth of shoes in the $35 billion athletic footwear and apparel industries in 2004. Nike's amazing growth came from its business model, which has always been based on two original functional strategies: to create state-of-the-art athletic shoes and then to publicize the qualities of its shoes through dramatic guerrilla-style marketing.

Nike's marketing is designed to persuade customers that its shoes are not only superior but also a high fashion statement and a necessary part of a lifestyle based on sporting or athletic interests. A turning point came in 1987 when Nike increased its marketing budget from $8 to $48 million to persuade customers its shoes were the best. A large part of this advertising budget soon went to pay celebrities like Michael Jordan millions of dollars to wear and champion its products. The company has consistently pursued this strategy: in 2003, it signed basketball star LeBron James to a $90 million endorsement contract, and many other sports stars, such as Tiger Woods and Serena Williams, are already part of its charmed circle. Nike's strategy to emphasize the uniqueness of its product has obviously paid off; its market share soared and its revenues hit $9.6 billion in 1998. However, 1998 was also a turning point because in that year, sales began to fall. Nike's $200 Air Jordans no longer sold like they used to, and inventory built up in stores and warehouses. Suddenly, it seemed much harder to design new shoes that customers perceived to be significantly better. Nike's stunning growth in sales was actually reducing its profitability; somehow, it had lost control of its business model.

Phil Knight, who had resigned his management position, was forced to resume the helm and lead the company out of its troubles. He recruited a team of talented top managers from leading consumer products companies to help him improve Nike's business model. As a result, Nike has changed its business model in some fundamental ways. In the past, Nike shunned sports like golf, soccer, rollerblading, and so on, and it focused most of its efforts on making shoes for the track and basketball markets to build its market share in these areas. However, when its sales started to fall, it realized that using marketing to increase sales in a particular market segment can grow sales and profits only so far; it needed to start selling more types of shoes to more segments of the athletic shoe market. So Nike took its design and marketing competencies and began to craft new lines of shoes for new market segments. For example, it launched a line of soccer shoes and perfected their design over time, and by 2004, it had won the biggest share of the soccer market from its archrival Adidas. Also in 2004, it launched its Total 90 III shoes, which are aimed at the millions of casual soccer players throughout the world who want a shoe they can just *play* in. Once more, Nike's dramatic marketing campaigns aim to make their shoes part of the soccer lifestyle, to persuade customers that traditional sneakers do not work because soccer shoes are sleeker and fit the foot more snugly.

To take advantage of its competencies in design and marketing, Nike then decided to enter new market segments by purchasing other footwear companies offering shoes that extended or complemented its product lines. For example, it bought Converse, the maker of retro-style sneakers; Hurley International, which makes skateboards and Bauer in-line and hockey skates; and Official Starter, a licensor of athletic shoes and apparel whose brands include the low-priced Shaq brand. Allowing Converse to take advantage of Nike's in-house competencies has resulted in dramatic increases in the sales of its sneakers, and Converse has made an important contribution to Nike's profitability. Nike had also entered another market segment when it bought Cole Haan, the dress shoemaker, in the 1980s. Now it is searching for other possible acquisitions. It decided to enter the athletic apparel market to use its skills there, and by 2004, sales were over $1 billion. In making all these changes to its business model, Nike was finding ways to invest its capital in new products where it could increase its market share and profitability. Its new focus on developing new and improved products for new market segments is working.

The front–back structure is not well known, but it can be the right approach for a Built-for-Variation enterprise. As the name suggests, the organization has a *front*: a customer-facing piece that deals with all customer-related activities, including sales, most of marketing, and the delivery of products and services. The rest of the organization, the *back*, produces the products and services that the front sells and delivers to the customer. In essence, the front of the enterprise becomes a customer to the back. In some respects, the front is not the best customer for the back, because no internal customer is, but it can be a reasonable proxy for an external customer. When the front is properly designed, it can reflect the needs and desires of the ultimate end user of the enterprise's products and services. The front–back organization is relatively easy for variation, because it has a kind of modular structure. This is particularly true when variation affects the customer-facing part of the organization, which has a good sense of how the market is changing and therefore is motivated to adapt. For many types of tactical variation, such as eliminating selling to particular segments of the market or discontinuing products, or if the organization no longer wants to sell to a particular kind of consumer or to a particular geographical area, it has to merely eliminate or reassign those employees who are the *front* for that particular type of customer. A similar situation exists with respect to the back of the enterprise. If the enterprise wants to reduce its services and products, it has to merely eliminate the particular piece or pieces of the back that produces them, or, if the enterprise wants to add a new product and enter a new market, it can simply add a production module or a sales unit. The rest of the enterprise does not need to vary.

The strengths of the front–back enterprise usually do outweigh its complexity and the disadvantages that stem from it. Those organizations that have tried this model find managing the interface between the front and the back to be a major challenge. All too often, the back does not want to listen to the front, and the front is frustrated by its relationship with the back. In many respects, it is not surprising that enterprises using this structure are in complex businesses, with customers who buy multiple, often complex products and services. Customers usually prefer to have a supplier manage complexity and will pay accordingly.

5.1.2.2   Staff

When hiring people, Built-for-Variation enterprises seek individuals who are quick learners and like variation; they specifically look for people with initiative and the right attitude, including the desire for professional growth. Built-for-Variation enterprises need to have an employment contract that states that change is to be expected and that support for change is a condition of long-term employment. Of course, people should be made aware of the Built-for-Variation employment deal before they are hired, so that they can make an informed decision about whether they want to work in such an environment. Once they join, training should be a normal, ongoing process, focused on the skills and knowledge necessary to support change and other organizational capabilities and aimed at the competencies that will help the company add value both now and in the future.

Pay and other rewards that are based on seniority stifle variation; they do little but reward people for surviving. In contrast, Built-for-Variation enterprises utilize a variety of reward practices, including person-based pay, bonuses, and stock that encourage both current performance and variation. Companies should shift the basis of pay from the job (and seniority) to the individual (and what he or she can do). In work environments that call for changing task assignments, paying the person—as opposed to paying the job—is a much more effective approach, particularly when it comes to retaining the right people. After all, people have a market value; jobs do not. People can change companies for higher pay; jobs cannot.

Bonus systems can be particularly effective motivators during periods of variation; they establish a clear line of sight between results and rewards. For example, individual plans that offer relatively large bonuses can provide powerful incentives for employees and alter their individual behaviors when a new element of strategic intent calls for it. Group and business unit bonuses can be very helpful in focusing team performance and creating a shared need for variation. One-time bonuses can be awarded for the completion of a strategic variation effort; for example, members of a new product development team can be given bonuses when the product ships or reaches a sales goal.

Similarly, broad-based stock ownership can be an incentive for change because everyone is rewarded for performance improvement. It is superior to a stock program that includes only senior managers, because under those conditions, employees cannot be faulted for thinking why they should listen to calls for variation that only benefit those at the top.

5.1.2.2.1 Nurturing Staff at HP

HP has gone to great lengths to continually immerse employees in the tenets of what became known as the *HP Way*. HP took all of their managers off-site in the 1950s to the *Sonoma Conferences*, where they penned HP's ideology and ambitions into a document expressing basic ideals subject to current interpretation and to amendment. Soon thereafter, HP began a strict promote-from-within policy, implemented extensive interviewing processes that emphasize *adaptability and fit* to the HP Way, and created a program to indoctrinate first-line supervisors. HP took many steps to reinforce the importance of technological contribution and to promote an entrepreneurial environment. Beginning in the 1950s, HP sought to hire only top 10% graduating seniors from respected engineering schools, rather than hiring more experienced but less talented engineers from industry.

HP has a long history of showing respect for employees in a multitude of tangible ways. In the 1940s, it introduced a *production bonus* (essentially a profit sharing plan) that paid the same percentages to the janitor as to the CEO and created a catastrophic medical insurance plan for all employees—actions virtually unheard of at that time, especially in a small company. When the company went public in the 1950s, all employees at all levels with 6 months of tenure received an automatic stock grant and became eligible for a stock option program. Soon thereafter, HP instituted an employee stock purchase program, with a 25% subsidy from the company. To reduce the chance of layoffs, HP passed up large government contract opportunities—profitable as they might be—if they would lead to *hire-and-fire* tactics. It required divisions to hire HP insiders first before looking to the outside, providing further secure employment across the entire company (not to mention keeping the culture tight). When facing corporate-wide downturns, HP generally asked all employees to take every other Friday off and reduce their pay by 10%, rather than imposing a 10% layoff. HP was one of the first American companies to introduce flexitime opportunities for employees at all levels and to conduct extensive employee surveys to gauge and track employee concerns. It was also one of the first American companies to introduce an open-door policy in which employees could bring grievances all the way to the top without retribution. To promote communication and informality and to deemphasize hierarchy, HP created a wide open-door plan; no manager at any level would be allowed to have a private office with a door—a very unusual practice in the 1950s.

5.1.2.3 Skills

Instead of rewarding people for expanding their jobs or for moving up the hierarchy, the enterprise recognizes them for increasing their skills and for developing themselves. This reinforces a culture that values growth and personal development; the result is a highly talented workforce that is receptive to variation. Those characteristics are particularly valuable when an enterprise needs to improve its competencies and capabilities, because the company can adjust its reward system to encourage individuals to develop the necessary skills. Person-based pay can have a reinforcing effect on organizational culture and on employees' motivation to vary. The implementation of a person-based pay system must start with a clear model of the competencies required to meet current customer and environmental demands, as well as a notion of the kinds of skills and knowledge that employees will need in the future. This information can guide professional development activities that are tied to the reward system. One indirect effect of person-based pay is a decreased emphasis on hierarchy, because individuals don't need to be promoted to receive a significant raise. Instead, they can develop a new expertise. Among the positive results of that change are fewer individuals jostling for promotions merely because they want higher salaries.

5.1.2.3.1 Multiskilling at Toyota

Taiichi Ohno interpreted productivity improvement as a crucial goal for Toyota very early on. However, because of his concern with ensuring smooth material flow without excess work in process (WIP), productivity improvements could not be achieved by having workers produce large lots on individual machines. It rapidly became clear that a JIT system is much better served by multifunctional workers who can move where needed to maintain the flow. Furthermore, having workers with multiple skills adds flexibility to an inherently inflexible system, greatly increasing a JIT system's ability to cope with product mix changes and other exceptional circumstances. To cultivate a multiskilled workforce, Toyota made use of a worker rotation system. The rotations were of two types. First, workers were rotated through the various jobs in the shop. Then, once a sufficient number of workers were cross-trained, rotations on a daily basis were begun.

Daily rotations served the following functions:

1. To keep multiple skills sharp
2. To reduce boredom and fatigue on the part of the workers
3. To foster an appreciation for the overall picture on the part of everyone
4. To increase the potential for new idea generation, since more people would be thinking about how to do each job

These cross-training efforts did indeed help the Japanese catch up with the Americans in terms of labor productivity. But they also fostered a great deal of flexibility, which Americans, with their rigid job classifications and history of confrontational labor relations, found difficult to match. With cross-training and autonomation, it becomes possible for a single worker to operate several machines at once. The worker loads a part into a machine, starts it up, and moves on to another machine while the processing takes place. But remember, in a JIT system with very little WIP, it is important to keep parts flowing. Hence, it is not practical to have a worker staffing a number of machines that perform the same operation in a large, isolated process center. There simply will not be enough WIP to feed such an operation. A better layout is to have machines that perform successive operations located close to one another, so that the products can flow easily from one to another. A linear arrangement of machines, traditionally common to American facilities, accommodates the product flow well, but is not well suited to having workers tend multiple machines because they must walk too far from machine to machine. To facilitate material flow and reduce walking time, the Japanese have tended toward U-shaped lines or cells.

The use of cellular layouts in JIT systems precipitated a trend that gathered steam in the United States during the 1980s. One now sees V-shaped manufacturing cells in a variety of production environments, to the point where cellular manufacturing has become much more prevalent than the JIT systems that spawned it.

5.1.2.4 Systems

Instead of relying on annual budgets to control costs, Built-for-Variation companies deploy profit centers and activity-based costing; each business unit is governed by P&L. To ensure good decision making, information needs to be transparent and up to date, indicating the current condition of the enterprise's capabilities and providing a clear view of how the company is performing relative to its competitors and its strategy. Performance-based information systems are a particularly effective way to motivate and empower employees in a Built-for-Variation enterprise because such systems facilitate moving decision making to wherever decisions can best be made and implemented. Each employee can log on to an information system and gain access to corporate, market, and competitor information, data on current projects, and quarterly objectives for any individual in the organization. This widely available information allows everyone throughout the organization to make customer-related decisions with the most up-to-the-minute data available, and it helps people align their individual behaviors with corporate objectives. The system thus facilitates the goal setting, performance review, and reward processes.

5.1.2.4.1 Becoming Future-Enabled at Charles Schwab

In December 1998, Charles Schwab's market capitalization first surpassed that of Merrill Lynch, $25.5–$25.4 billion. Merrill had $11.4 billion in equity versus Schwab's $1.9 billion; $1.5 trillion in customer assets versus Schwab's $600 billion; and 66,000 employees versus Schwab's 17,400. But Schwab was worth more to investors. To the uninformed, it might have appeared to be an overnight e-commerce success, but Schwab's success was the result of decades of often frustrating efforts to achieve a breakthrough in the brokerage business.

Charles (Chuck) Schwab started his business in 1971 with a mission of providing individual investors with low-cost, high-quality service minus selling pressure. Seeing a new market materializing for cost-sensitive customers, Schwab cut its fees and—along with several other upstarts—got the discount brokerage industry on its way.

Schwab went beyond cutting rates; he concentrated on quick and efficient execution of customer orders. Bucking the standard 35%–40% commission the big houses paid brokers on trading fees, he paid his brokers a fixed salary plus a bonus based on company performance. A decade after its founding, Schwab was king of the bargain-basement brokers, with 29 offices, 160,000 clients, and $40 million in revenues. Schwab was at the head of the class of some 50 discount brokers who together garnered 10% of all retail brokerage transactions and 5% of commissions.

A person who wished to trade 300 shares of a $35 stock in 1983 would have paid Merrill Lynch $191.69 and Schwab only $88.50. A number of discount competitors were in the same ballpark, but Schwab differentiated itself by pioneering 24 h service, offering no-load mutual fund supermarkets and establishing automated, self-service trading operations. Big bets on IT were an essential aspect of Schwab's strategy from the beginning. In the 1970s, for example, the company spent a year's worth of revenue on an IBM mainframe to automate trading and reporting. Such investments in back-office technology paid off as Schwab service reps confirmed orders in 90 s and handled most trades in a paperless fashion. By 1989, Schwab could accept automated trades via push-button telephones and PCs.

Schwab's aggressive and innovative approach to technology led to numerous failures over the years. In retrospect, Chuck Schwab calls them *noble failures*, flawed attempts to achieve a vision that endured until a sustainable breakthrough was achieved. Noble failures have been something of a tradition at Schwab since the company's founding. Many of them have been attempts to use the latest technology to provide Schwab customers with the most timely financial and market information. Among them were the following:

- Pocketerm—a handheld device that was supposed to act like a portable stock quotation machine. The gadget never worked properly and was dropped.
- Schwabline—an electromechanical desktop device for printing out a customer's portfolio value, which used to break down frequently.
- Financial independence—this software product enabled users to manage all personal financial information but required one to be computer savvy and did not permit account management.
- The equalizer—Schwab's attempt to let customers issue orders from their desktop computers via modem. Once again, users needed computer knowledge and the product was buggy, but it later appeared in a Windows version as StreetSmart.

This undying interest in using technology to help customers manage their investments and do business more conveniently led directly to Chuck Schwab's early interest in the Internet. The first output of the company's Internet push was e.Schwab, an independent division focused on the web. In 1995, it also began offering trading through America Online (AOL), thus gaining access to the 7 million people who were then using AOL. Sensing a breakthrough, the firm expanded its online capacity eightfold to enable 80,000 simultaneous log-ons. Growth followed quickly. Online accounts leaped to 2.2 million in 1996, exactly 40% of total accounts. Furthermore, by offering sophisticated online services and tools to independent investment managers, the company opened up an important indirect channel.

Assets in wholesale accounts from investment managers reached $146 billion by 2000. Schwab, king of discounters, thus morphed itself as a full-service click-and-mortar brokerage house.

As the twentieth century came to a close, a flood of investor dollars inundated the nation's stockbrokers. Customer assets at the top four brokerage firms/mutual funds companies—Merrill Lynch, Vanguard, Fidelity Investments, and Schwab—equaled more than half of all the deposits in U.S. banks. More than 1.8 million new online trading accounts (with about one-fifth of the bank deposits) were opened in the last quarter of 1999; and Schwab had the lion's share of that market.

At the turn of the millennium, Schwab, a brokerage firm that had pioneered discount brokerage a quarter century earlier, was the number one online stockbroker with a 22% market share and $350 billion in assets from online investors. Achieving substantiated leadership in the next-generation business model is the surest way to win Wall Street recognition and valuation as an emerging market leader. With its bricks-and-clicks combination of frontline human and online customer service, Schwab was the big winner in the booming brokerage decade of the 1990s.

Schwab continues to expand its range of services and offerings. The acquisition of U.S. Trust in 2000 positions Schwab to compete ever more effectively with both its established and insurgent competitors. The retail brokerage industry has become the preserve of investment banks, as one after another brokerage house has been gobbled up by the likes of Salomon (Smith Barney), Morgan Stanley (Dean Witter), and UBS (Paine Webber). Schwab is positioning itself to be a full-line financial services house able to compete across the board with established players.

5.1.3 GENERATING VALUE: SEQUENCE

For generating value for the customer, the best approach to operations planning (or flow of product) is highly dependent on the nature of that business. Indeed, finding the right approach to planning its operations is part of the way a business should differentiate itself from its competitors and achieve competitive advantage. While manufacturing issues historically have dominated the development of planning concepts, contemporary thinking often places manufacturing in the context of serving customers. It is certainly time to close the gap between manufacturing planning and nonproduction supply chain planning; manufacturing is very much a part of the supply chain. It is often the most expensive, complex, time-consuming part of the supply chain—its dynamics may even dictate the structure of the entire supply chain—but ultimately it is performed because of its supply-chain function. In the product flow realm, planning can be defined as the process of deciding how we will use all the kinds of resources that ultimately provide product to end customers: manufacturing resources, labor, supplier commitments, multiple levels of inventories, transportation, warehousing facilities, and so on.

Supply-chain management is the process of managing multiple steps along the path from raw materials to final consumers in an integrative way that helps achieve an enterprise's objectives. Since first identified by Keith Oliver of Booz Allen Hamilton in 1982, the concept of the supply chain has become widely accepted. It is the mechanism by which goods are moved and transformed from raw materials to delivery of value to the final customer. Figure 5.2 is a classic picture of the supply chain, showing the flow of product from left to right, the flow of payment from right to left, and the integrating movement of information and control in both directions to make it all work. *Directing product flow* is, of course, part of the information and control realm.

While the details will vary based on specific business circumstances, in general, the objectives of product flow planning are to help the enterprise and its primary supply chain(s)

1. Provide the customer service required by their business strategy
2. Maintain an appropriate speed of product flow that encourages sales by having product to market in a timely fashion and also minimizes product obsolescence and shelf-life expiration costs

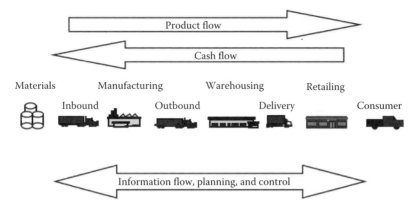

FIGURE 5.2 A classic view of the supply chain.

3. Have a minimum cost of procurement, manufacturing, and physical distribution
4. Employ the minimum quantities of assets, both fixed assets like plants and distribution centers and working assets like inventory

5.1.3.1 Approaches to Planning

If the resources that we need to create and deliver product would always, spontaneously, be available for immediate use, we would have little planning to do. If manufacturing capability was always ready for our use, if the right number of production operators spontaneously walked in the door every day, if materials magically appeared when we needed them, if finished-goods inventory was somehow always ready when a customer needed product right now, we would not have to plan. But the reality is such that for all those activities to happen smoothly requires planning, working through all the logical relationships in material flow, and utilizing resources based on actual or expected requirements for product. When planning is not being performed well, there are some typical symptoms:

- Too much or too little inventory; short-lived product growing old
- Mediocre results in customer service surveys
- Many customer service calls per sale
- Lengthy cycle times for customers or for our own inventory replenishment
- Knowing we are not a low-cost provider—high manufacturing or logistics costs
- Poor utilization of labor
- Frequent last-minute changes to schedules
- Facility capacity utilization too low or too high
- Inconsistent material availability
- Complaints from suppliers
- Harried operations management—constant reacting or firefighting

It takes knowledge of planning tools, understanding of the enterprise and its context, imagination, and persistence to design and evolve good planning approaches. The *best* planning approach for an enterprise will probably continue to vary, both because it will evolve as we try to perfect it and because it will need to be adapted (and occasionally rethought from top to bottom) as the business varies. If an enterprise conducts operations with physical goods, it will, one way or another, make decisions (i.e., plans) about how to direct the flow of that product, based on some expectations for the future. Good planning is planning that

- Uses all the available information and uses it in a timely way (some of it near real time) from a comprehensive view of the data available to the enterprise fully integrated from customer through manufacturing (or other product source) to supplier
- Quickly works out all the logical relationships correctly, including correctly making trade-offs across the supply chain among costs, asset requirements, and service
- Creates plans that reflect those logical relationships and trade-offs, plus takes account of uncertainty and risks

Many authors date the beginning of mathematical methods for managing operations to Ford W. Harris's economic order quantity (EOQ) model of about 1913. Harris was one of the first to explicitly recognize the trade-off between the fixed cost associated with configuring machinery to make a specific part and the cost of holding inventory of that part and then to turn that trade-off into a mathematical model: a lot size formula. Subsequently, it was discovered that this model has very limited applicability in manufacturing. As computers became powerful, reliable, and cost effective enough during the 1960s to be applied directly to operations, manufacturing planners realized that relying on probabilistic models (inventory theory) to maintain reorder point systems for WIP inventory and for purchased material was no longer necessary. Manufacturing resource planning (MRP) was a much more powerful technique for planning *dependent* material requirements, that is, direct materials that depend on a production schedule (that is controllable), rather than relying on the statistical techniques that were still generally the best way to manage supply to meet *independent* demand (over which there was no control).

It was now possible to support maintaining an accurate bill of material (BOM) for each product manufactured, including all the layers of components back to raw materials, and accurate inventory records for finished goods, WIP, and materials. We could regularly *explode* that BOM by multiplying it by the entries in a production schedule to compute time-phased, consolidated material requirements across all the products scheduled and net those requirements against current inventories to identify the need for additional subassembly and parts fabrication and for additional material purchases. This logic could be applied recursively down through as many levels of the BOM as appropriate, each time applying a *lead time* offset representing the time allowed to produce or acquire material in that next lower level. However, users of simple MRP quickly discovered that they needed to have additionally the right processes (*master production schedule*) and systems (*rough-cut capacity planning*) in place around the core MRP calculations to make the technique generally workable. MRP with these additional modules was named as MRP II.

The product flow scheduling processes, of course, depend on the higher-level decisions about how the business will be run; business strategy drives supply–demand policy, which then determines what is required from flow planning. One cannot effectively design a supply-chain facility, be it a manufacturing plant or a distribution center, without simultaneously considering how the operations (product flow and scheduling) of that facility will be planned. Scheduling is essentially the short-term execution plan of a plan; a schedule is an assignment problem that describes into details (in terms of minutes or seconds) which activities must be performed and how the factory's resources should be utilized to satisfy the plan. Detailed scheduling is essentially the problem of allocating machines to competing jobs over time, subject to the constraints. Each work center can process one job at a time and each machine can handle at most one task at a time. A scheduling problem, typically, assumes a fixed number of jobs and each job has its own parameters (i.e., tasks, the necessary sequential constraints, the time estimates for each operation, and the required resources). All scheduling approaches require some estimate of how long it takes to perform the work. Scheduling affects, and is affected by, the shop floor organization.

MRP II represents the most precisely defined *universal* structure for product flow planning that has ever been created. It was advocated by most experts and was the basis for the *MRP Crusade* promoted by the American Production and Inventory Control Society in the 1970s and 1980s. Much packaged software was created by many providers to implement this standard specification.

These MRP II software packages grew to include the software to track inventory and manage customer orders as well, that is, to perform some of the core day-to-day transactions by which the business was executed—not just planning anymore. By the early 1980s, the software was being extended to add distribution resource planning (DRP) capabilities to plan for products that must be stocked in many locations. However, progressively it became clear that MRP was not the definitive planning approach for many environments.

Many of its problems are due to logic that does not adequately address manufacturing capacity or material constraints. The master production schedule as initially generated is based on the assumption that there is infinite production capacity available, and multiple passes between the master production schedule, rough-cut capacity planning, material requirements, capacity requirements planning, and sometimes finite scheduling logic (for individual departments or machines) are usually necessary to generate a truly feasible master production schedule. But in real operations, there is typically little time for these multiple passes, and plants would often try to execute master schedules that were not feasible. The inability of MRP scheduling to truly understand capacity relative to demand (the dynamic supply–demand balance) makes it very difficult to produce valid schedules, and, of course, it is impossible to stay on invalid schedules! The use of substantial material lead times to try to deal with capacity constraints led to a guarantee that total lead times for finished goods would be long (even when the plant was not in fact very busy). Process variability could produce even longer production times. Thus MRP-controlled plants tended to have manufacturing orders sit in the plant for a very long period. This tendency, of course, both drove manufacturing costs up and created unhappy customers.

5.1.3.2 Toyota Production System

The TPS used kanbans (cards) to implement a type of pull operation on the plant floor. TPS has two important parts, namely, JIT to manage inventories in production and heijunka to *level* or *smooth* product mix and quantity in production plan. JIT is a stock replenishment policy that aims to reduce final product stocks and WIP; it coordinates requirements and replenishments in order to minimize stock-buffer needs, and it has reversed the old make-to-stock production approach, leading most companies to adopt *pull* instead of *push* policies to manage material and finished product flows (in case of unleveled demand, stock levels in JIT may spiral out of control). Contrary to MRP that schedules the production run much in advance compared to its time of requirement, JIT replenishes a stock only after it is consumed. JIT is part of a much broader philosophy of lean production, which is designed to eliminate waste at every step of product flow: transportation, inventory, motion, waiting, overprocessing, overproducing, and defects. JIT is devised to ensure the right products, in the right quantities, just in time where they are needed. Main pillars of JIT are

1. One-piece flow
2. Demand-pull production
3. Takt time
4. Mixed-model production

The traditional JIT technique to manage production flow is named kanban. A kanban system is a multistage production scheduling and inventory control system. Kanban is a card that contains information on a product in a given stage of the production process and details on its path of completion; kanban cards are used to control production flow and inventories.

5.1.3.3 Toyota

Toyota set out over 40 years ago to bridge the apparent trade-off between meeting the demands for variety and achieving satisfactory company profitability. They focused attention on mastering a disciplined pattern of work that is known as TPS. TPS has enabled Toyota to produce greater varieties of higher-quality cars at lower cost than any other auto makers in the world. Toyota's approach to organizing work solves the perennial problem of how to produce variety and high quality at low cost for large markets. TPS does this by shifting from the batch-oriented mass-production way of organizing work in accordance with the general principles of scale and speed toward the natural way of organizing work, where each minute particular reflects the patterns that shape the whole. Toyota achieves low cost by integrating flexibility and problem solving into the flow of direct work itself; Toyota organizes work so that variety-producing and quality-producing activities become integral part of the direct work that is done to fill each order. Moreover, the system achieves low costs by managing the quantities of resources used—material and labor hours—by producing only vehicles that customers have ordered and paid for and consuming only the resources needed to make each vehicle.

The JIT ideals suggest an aspect of the Japanese production techniques that is truly revolutionary: the extent to which the Japanese have regarded the production environment as a control. Rather than simply reacting to such things as machine setup times, vendor deliveries, quality problems, and production schedules, they have worked proactively to shape the environment. By doing this, they have consciously made their manufacturing systems easier to manage. This is in sync with the constructal law that applies to all flow systems: for a finite-size (flow) system to persist in time (to live), its configuration must evolve such that it provides easier access to the imposed currents that flow through it (Bejan and Zane 2012). The constructal theory of global optimization under local constraints explains in a simple manner the shapes that arise in nature. The theory allows one to design and analyze systems under constraints in a quest for optimality. This law was proposed by Adrian Bejan in 1976. He coined the term constructal from the Latin verb construere (to construct).

From a theoretical point of view, constructal is to construct—in order to designate the naturally optimized forms. Examples include rivers, trees and branches, lungs, and the engineered forms that come from an evolutionary process that maximizes flow access in time. The constructal theory posits that in nature the generation of design (configuration, pattern, geometry, etc.) is a phenomenon of physics that unites all animate and inanimate systems. The two worlds of inanimate and animate matter are connected by a theory that flow systems—from animal locomotion to the formation of river deltas—evolve in time to balance and minimize imperfections; flows evolve to reduce friction or other forms of resistance, so that they flow more easily with time. Constructal theory also explains the reason and a scientific basis for the prevalence of S-curve (also known as the sigmoid function) in nature and man-made systems like biological populations, chemical reactions, contaminants, language, information, and economic activity; the ubiquitous S-curve can be viewed as a natural design of flow systems. A new technology, for example, begins with slow acceptance, followed by explosive growth, only to level off before hitting the wall. When plotted on a graph, this pattern of growth takes the shape of an *S*. For the example of a new technology, per constructal theory, after a slow initial acceptance, the rise can be imagined moving fast through established, though narrow, channels into the market place. This is the steep upslope of the *S*.

5.2 CORE AND CONTEXT

The dynamics of a company can be better understood in terms of the interplay between the core and the context. The core corresponds to the core offerings (products, services, etc.), business processes, and direct stakeholders, which are the kernel of the commercial viability of the enterprise. The context corresponds to all the support offerings, processes, and allied stakeholders that enable the efficient and profitable functioning of the core. This includes offerings, processes, and stakeholders of its partners and external entities that are part of the extended ecosystem of the enterprise. Variations along the dimensions of variations alternate between the core and context of an enterprise resulting in the myriad configurations that are then assessed for their usefulness.

The strength of a force of variation is reflected in the rate of variation it creates in the environment; forces of variation are associated with recurring patterns that reflect different rates of variation.

5.2.1 Trends and Trajectories

Trends represent forces of variation to the extent that they change the business environment. For example, ever wider diffusion of microprocessor technology has implications for innovation in many industries. Or, on a shorter time scale within one industry, a declining cost curve has pricing implications for all competitors.

5.2.1.1 Turning Points, Stimuli, and Limits

A turning point (or transpoint) shows up as a shift in the direction of a trend, which corresponds to a strong force of variation. It is worth recalling the number of discontinuities that IBM stimulated with successive generations of mainframe computers, reflecting the transitions from the vacuum tube to the transistor, further on to integrated circuits.

The stimuli of an upturn take many different forms:

- Innovation of all forms, especially new technology or products
- Emergence of a dominant design or standard product offering that enables shifting to much larger output levels
- Specialization or customization that opens up new and niche market segments
- Deregulation unleashes the stimulus of free competition
- New management ushering a more dynamic organization

The limits that presage a downturn take many different forms:

- Natural laws of the sciences defining a physical limit on a trend
- Carrying capacity or resource exhaustion
- Saturation or fragmentation of markets
- Underinvestment that cuts off growth
- Negative feedback effects that undermine growth

When stimuli and limits are oriented in the same direction, they may combine to create a transpoint or discontinuity. The most common example is the transition from one technology development curve to another. The higher potential return on alternative technologies increases the chance of a jump to a new generation of technology; major technology shifts often have their origin in the year of weak returns. The limits become increasingly apparent, for example, before competitive behavior shifts away from value competition: the return to product enhancement and customization declines; the offerings of competitors in the marketplace begin to look alike; customers are less and less willing to pay for purely perceived value. At the same time, the stimuli for a shift toward more cost-based competition begin to make themselves felt; the convergence of the products favors the development of a dominant design that can be used to standardize the production delivery and service process. A broad potential market emerges sharing an implicit consensus about the basic features of a standard offering.

The development of the generic drugs business in the pharmaceutical industry of the 1980s illustrates this interplay between limits and stimuli:

- For some time, fewer new products were being launched, despite higher R&D spending.
- While the NPD process slowed to an average of 10 years, the cost of introducing new products has ballooned to $100 million.

- Average volume growth decreased from 15% in the 1970s to about 5% in the 1980s.
- There was growing worldwide political pressure for lower drug prices, which helped open door for generics.
- Imminent expiration of many major patents.
- The Waxman bill greatly facilitated the FDA approval process.
- Increasing older population created a groundswell for cheaper medicine.

5.2.1.2 Cycles and Recurring Turning Points

Cycles comprise major turning points that involve reversals in the direction of trends, which make the forces of variation even greater. There is a basic pattern in cyclical phenomenon that can be used to anticipate cyclical turning points. Cyclical variations involve repeated turning points between opposing poles of behavior; the limits inherent in too much of one behavior create the opening for stimuli supporting the opposite type of behavior. Cycles incorporating the tension between opposing behaviors crop up everywhere, on the sociopolitical, economic, industry, enterprise, and organizational levels; underlying each of these areas is the tension between variety creation, on one hand, and efficient and standardized use of scarce resources, on the other. Sensitivity to the characteristics of typical cycles, like the sensitivity to stimuli and limits, is a key to identifying the forces of change as early as possible.

5.2.1.2.1 Basic Pattern in Cyclical Phenomenon

The key to isolating strong forces of variation is clearly in the ability to anticipate cyclical turning points. Anticipating a transpoint requires seeing the limits and stimuli that provoke it—here the recognition of cyclical patterns is central, because cycles suggest the kinds of limits and stimuli to watch out for. The behavior preceding transpoints has identifiable patterns: the behavior reflects the creation of greater variety on one hand (innovation, value competition, technology development, economic expansion, sociopolitical individualism) and an improved ability to manage scarce resources (efficiency, price competition, technology diffusion, economic consolidation, sociopolitical cooperation) on the other.

The transpoints of the market-related cycles (economic, technology, and competitive) and hierarchy-related cycles (sociopolitical and organizational) are similar: all involve either convergence or divergence. The typical behavior of industry variation agents prior to competitive divergence (which often leads to a new product breakthrough) and competitive convergence (which often results in a price war) is outlined in the following.

Leading indicators of divergence:

- Customers: an increasingly saturated market for the standardized commodity product reflects itself in declining growth rates.
- Competitors: declining returns because of cost reduction and rationalization force competitors to look elsewhere.
- Potential competitors: restless customers attract new entrants.
- Supply chain: new sources of supply and new resources, especially new technology, are frequently the source of new product development.
- Channels: variation in the distribution channels is mostly a lagging rather than leading indicator of competitive product divergence.

Leading indicators of convergence:

- Customers: the segmentation between customer groups looks increasingly blurred or artificial and starts to crumble.
- Competitors: convergence is visible in increasingly similar products, service, and image.

- Potential competitors: very few, if any; new entrants on the horizon.
- Supply chain: suppliers and resources cannot easily be used as a source of competitive advantage.

5.2.2 INDUSTRY LEVEL

The convergence of computers, data communication and telecommunications, and media industries has resulted in the emergence of one of the biggest market spaces with possibly the largest growth opportunities in recent times. Convergence describes the phenomenon in which two or more existing technologies, markets, producers, boundaries, or value chains combine to create a new force that is more powerful and more efficient than the sum of its constituting technologies. The value chain migration alludes to the development of real-term systems that integrate supply chain systems and customer-facing systems, resulting in a single and unified integrated process.

This convergence occurs primarily because of three factors:

1. The digitization of information to enable the preparation, processing, storage, and transmission of information regardless of its form (data, graphics, sound, and video or any combination of these).
2. The rapidly declining cost of computing that has enabled computing to become ubiquitous and available with sufficient power.
3. The availability of broadband communications is critical to convergence because multimedia is both storage intensive and time sensitive.

The merging of previously disparate technologies, products, and information to give rise to compelling new products and services also underscores the concept of the merging of the container and content that we referred to earlier.

5.2.2.1 Business Cycle

The pattern of (radical) innovation stimulating financial investments and economic growth is a basic pattern in the history of modern economies. Technological innovation and subsequent economic cycles have happened since the beginning of the industrial revolution in England. The first economist to empirically document this pattern was the Russian economist Nikolai Kondratiev (1892–1938), who in the 1920s studied the economic development of the English economy of the late 1800s and early 1900s. He plotted a correlation between times of basic innovation to times of economic expansion. Overall, the capitalistic economies were expanding rather than contracting because of periodic innovations of new technologies. This economic idea is now called a long economic cycle, or a Kondratiev wave (K wave). The idea is that long periods of economic expansion in modern economies are stimulated by the invention of a new basic technology—such as the airplane or radio or computers or biotechnology. New businesses begin to economically exploit the new technology, and new markets emerge to purchase the new-technology (or high-technology) products and services. This expansion of businesses and markets drives the economy over a long time during the rising part of a K wave.

The K wave is a 60-year cycle with internal phases that are sometimes characterized as seasons: spring phase, a new factor of production, good economic times, and rising inflation; summer phase, hubristic *peak* war followed by societal doubts and double digit inflation; autumn phase, the financial fix of inflation leads to a credit boom, which creates a false plateau of prosperity that ends in a speculative bubble; and winter phase, excess capacity worked off by massive debt repudiation, commodity deflation, and economic depression. A *trough* war breaks the psychology of doom. The English economy expanded from 1792 to 1825 but then contracted from 1825 to 1847. Kondratiev argued that temporary excess production capacity in iron production, steam engine production, and textile production increased economic competition and drove prices down for an economic recession. After the second economic expansion in England from 1847 to 1873, there followed another economic contraction from 1873 to 1893 due to excessive investments in the new industries of railroads, steamships, and telegraph industries. The third economic expansion from 1893 to 1913 was interrupted by World War I in Europe. Then the economic expansion was renewed in North America and Japan, only to end in a worldwide depression in 1929—due, in part, to a collapse in the stock market in the United States and excessive inflation in Germany. The global depression did not end in several countries until military production in their economies restarted their industries—for weapons production.

> In addition to technology being a major factor in K cycles, credit and banking also play a crucial role. This is due to the fact that new technology spurs growth, initiative, and risk taking. This mind-set encourages investment and lending; thus, when the multiplier effect kicks in, economies expand rapidly. In modern times, we find that periods of "K" expansion and contraction bring with them phases of bigger booms and busts. The picture is doubly exacerbated by increasingly integrated world funding mechanisms which mean these booms and busts are global rather than local and increasingly more political than economic. It is the innovative interaction between science and technology and economy that provides the basis for long-term economic expansion. In the normal business cycle, after periods of economic expansion, often excess production capability develops. This lowers prices as any new technology-based industry matures and many competitors enter the new market; this will always cut profit margins, even in a relatively new industry. High-tech industry will never be a high-profit-margin industry for long, because competition will intensify after the technology begins maturing.

If we accept the fact that most winters in K cycles last 20 years, following the 2007 systemic collapse of world banking and credit, things are likely to get much worse before they get better. Per this pattern, we are about halfway through the Kondratieff winter that commenced in the year 2000; thus, in all probability, we will be moving from a *recession* to a *depression* phase of the cycle about the year 2013 and would last until approximately 2017–2020. The good news is that after this creative destruction period is over, the world economy will be ready for a new epoch-making spring boom that will propel it to new levels of political, social, and economic development (Figure 5.3).

The nine stages in this K long wave are as follows:

1. Science discovers phenomena that can provide for a new manipulation by technological invention of nature.
2. New basic technology provides business opportunities for new industries.
3. A new high-tech industry provides rapid market expansion and economic growth.
4. As the new industry continues to improve the technology, products are improved and prices decline and the market grows toward large volume.
5. Competitors enter the growing large market, investing in more production capacity.
6. As the technology begins to mature, production capacity begins to exceed market demand, triggering price cuts.
7. Excess capacity and lower prices cut margins and increase business failures and raise unemployment.
8. Turmoil in financial markets may turn recession into depression.
9. New science and new basic technologies may provide the basis for a new economic expansion.

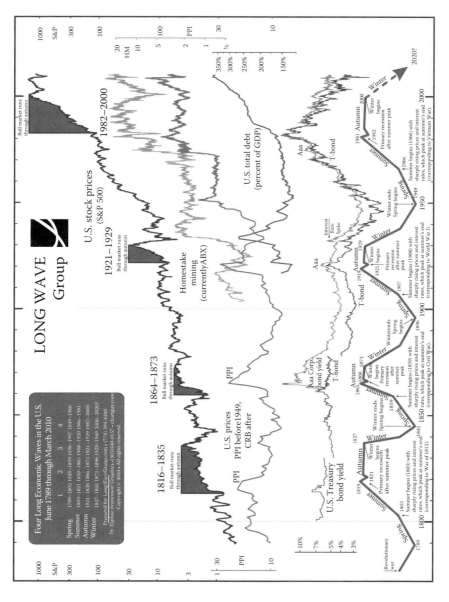

FIGURE 5.3   K wave © Longwave Group (www.longwavegroup.com).

There is no historical inevitability in Kondratiev's long-wave pattern. It can begin only after scientists discover new natural phenomenon and after technologists invent new basic or component technologies based on the same; then component technological innovation can provide business opportunities for economic expansion. But there is no guarantee that new science and new technologies will always be invented.

5.2.2.2 Network Effects

There are many markets for goods and services that satisfy the characteristics of what we call network products. These markets include the telephone, e-mail, Internet, computer hardware, computer software, music players, music titles, video players, video movies, banking services, airline services, and legal services. The main characteristics of these markets that distinguish them from the market for grain, dairy products, apples, and treasury bonds are as follows:

- Complementarity, compatibility, and standards
- Network externalities
- Switching costs and lock-in
- Significant economies of scale in production

5.2.2.2.1 Complementarity, Compatibility, and Standards

Computers are not useful without having monitors attached or without having software installed. CD players are not useful without CD titles, just as cameras are not useful without films. Stereo receivers are useless without speakers or headphones, and airline companies will not be able to sell tickets without joining a particular reservation system. All these examples demonstrate that, unlike bread that can be consumed without wine or other types of food, the markets we analyze in this book supply goods that must be consumed together with other products (software and hardware). In the literature of economics, such goods and services are called complements. Complementarity means that consumers in these markets are shopping for systems (e.g., computers and software, cameras and film, music players and cassettes) rather than individual products. The fact that consumers are buying systems composed of hardware and software or complementary components allows firms to devise all sorts of strategies regarding competition with other firms. A natural question is to ask, for example, whether firms benefit from designing machines that can work with machines produced by rival firms.

On the technical side, the next question to ask would be how complements are produced. In order to produce complementary products, they must be compatible. The CD album must have the same specification as CD players, or otherwise it can't be played. A parallel port at the back of each computer must generate the same output voltage as the voltage required for inputting data into a printer attached to this port. Trains must fit on the tracks, and software must be workable with a given OS. This means that complementary products must operate on the same standard. This creates the problem of coordination as how firms agree on the standards. The very fact that coordination is needed has the potential of creating some antitrust problems. As in some cases, firms may need to coordinate their decisions, and while doing that, they may find themselves engaging in price fixing.

Complementarity turns to be a crucial factor in the markets for information goods. For example, people who subscribe to the Private Pilot Magazine are likely to be interested in fashion clothing catalogs, just like people who read the New York Times are likely to be interested in real-estate and interior decoration magazines. Advertising agencies have understood these complementarities for quite some time and make use of these complementarities to attract more customers. For example, the publishers of real-estate magazines could benefit from purchasing the list of names and addresses of the subscribers to the New York Times and send them sample copies to attract their attention. These information complementarities become more and more important with the increase in the use of the Internet for advertising and shopping purposes. For example, those who browse in commercial Internet sites offering toys for sale, such as www.etoys.com, are likely to be interested in browsing through Internet sites offering children clothing. Thus, the toy sites are likely to sell the list of their site visitors to children clothing stores.

5.2.2.2.1.1 Bell Systems   In the mid-1890s, with several key Bell patents expiring and the country emerging from a depression, the result was a proliferation of many non-Bell independent companies. By 1903, independents and rural corporations had a majority, and Bell companies controlled less than half of the phones in America. In the normal course of development, many of these independent companies should have survived and thrived in the twentieth century. In contrast, it led to the emergence of a dominant long-distance or national telephone company, the Bell System. The key to Bell System's success was long-distance telephone service, even though long-distance service was not apparently a decisive competitive advantage at that time—in 1900, a mere 3% calls were long distance. Accordingly, many telephone companies did not even offer long-distance service because it was also plagued by many technical problems.

But in due course, there was increasing demand for long-distance services; local phone companies were finding it more profitable to combine adjacent towns and extend their reach to more and more longer distances. The Bell System with the most extensive long-distance network allowed access to its affiliates and only those nonaffiliated companies that met Bell's technical and operating standards and that were not direct local competitors. This strategy stimulated traffic throughout the Bell network, enhanced the value of the Bell service by increasing the number of parties that could be reached, and made Bell stronger at the expense of the independent corporations. Bell System denied local rivals access to its long-distance network, arguing that interconnection with independents with inferior standards (driven by the economics of completion) could compromise the integrity of its entire network. This turned the tide against the independents; since Bell already controlled key cities, the independents could not establish a viable national alternative to the Bell System. This allowed the Bell System to grow into the dominant local and long-distance carrier, to be renamed as AT&T. AT&T pushed for a natural monopoly model for the telephone system, including acquiring many of its local competitors, which were accepted to support universal service. But, this has its downside on account of *excesses of successes* (see note "Bankruptcy of AT&T" in the following).

5.2.2.2.2 Network Externalities

What use will anyone have from having a telephone for which there is no one to talk to? Would people use e-mail knowing that nobody else does? Would people purchase fax machines knowing that nobody else has such a machine? These examples demonstrate that the utility derived from the consumption of these goods is affected by the number of other people using similar or compatible products. Note that this type of externalities is not found in the market for tomatoes, or the market for salt, as the consumption of these goods does not require compatibility with other consumers. Such externalities are sometimes referred to as adoption or network externalities.

The presence of these standard-adoption effects can profoundly affect market behavior of firms. The precise nature of the market outcome (e.g., consumers' adoption of a new standard) depends on how consumers form expectations on the size of the network of users. The reliance on joint-consumer expectations generates multiple equilibria where in one equilibrium all consumers adopt the new technology, whereas in the other no one adopts it. Both equilibria are *rational* from the consumers' viewpoint as they reflect the best response to the decisions made by all other consumers in the market. A good example for this behavior is the fax machine, which has been used in the 1950s by flight service stations to transmit weather maps every hour on the hour (transmission of single page took about 1 h that time). However, fax machines remained a niche product until the mid-1980s. During a 5-year period, the demand and supply of fax machines exploded. Before 1982, almost no one had a fax machine, but after 1987, the majority of businesses had one. The Internet exhibited the same pattern of adoption. The first e-mail message was sent in 1969, but adoption did not take off until the mid-1980s. The Internet did not take off until 1990; however, from 1990, Internet traffic more than doubles every year. All these examples raise a fundamental question,

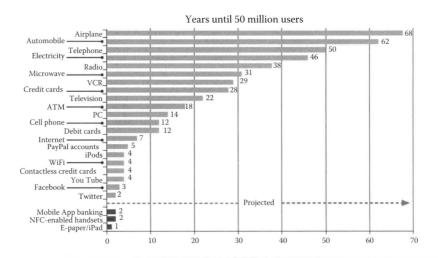

FIGURE 5.4 Surging contexts of innovations.

which is when to expect a new technology to catch on. A related question to ask is in the presence of adoption externalities, what should be the minimal number of users (the critical mass) needed for inducing all potential consumers to adopt the technology (Figure 5.4).

5.2.2.2.2.1 Switching Costs and Lock-In Learning to master a particular OS such as Windows, UNIX, DOS, or a Macintosh takes time (depending on the level of the user). It is an established fact that users are very much annoyed by having to switch between OSs. To some consumers, switching OSs is as hard as learning a new language. On the production side, producers heavily depend on the standards used in the production of other components of the system. For example, airline companies rely on spare parts and service provided by aircraft manufacturers. Switching costs are significant in service industries as well. Several estimates provided in this book show that the cost associated with switching between banks (i.e., closing an account in one bank and opening an account and switching the activities to a different bank) could reach 6% of the average account balance. In all of these cases, we say that users are locked-in. Of course, lock-in is not an absolute term. The degree of lock-in is found by calculating the cost of switching to a different service or adopting a new technology, since these costs determine the degree in which users are locked in a given technology. We call these costs switching costs.

There are several types of switching costs that affect the degree of lock-in:

- Contracts: Users are sometimes locked into contracts for service, supplying parts, and buying spare parts. Switching costs amount to the damages and compensation that must be paid by the party who breaks the contract.
- Training and learning: Consumers are trained to use products operating on a specific standard. Switching costs would include learning and training people, as well as lost productivity resulting from adopting a new system.
- Data conversion: Each piece of software generates files that are saved using a particular digital format. Once a new software is introduced, a conversion software may be needed in order to be able to use it. Notice that the resulting switching cost increases over time as the collection of data may grow over time.
- Search cost: One reason why people do not switch very often is that they would like to avoid the cost of searching and shopping for new products.
- Loyalty cost: Switching technology may result in losing some benefits such as preferred customers' programs, for example, frequent-flyer mileage.

Switching costs affect price competition in two opposing ways. First, if consumers are already locked-in using a specific product, firms may raise prices knowing that consumers will not switch unless the price difference exceeds the switching cost to a competing brand. Second, if consumers are not locked in, brand-producing firms will compete intensively by offering discounts and free complimentary products and services in order to attract consumers who later on will be locked in the technology. In the presence of switching costs, once the critical mass is achieved and the sales of the product take off, we say that the seller has accumulated an installed base of consumers, which is the number of consumers who are locked in the seller's technology. For example, AT&T's installed base is the number of customers subscribing to its long-distance service, where switching costs include the time and trouble associated with switching to, say, MCI's long-distance service.

> *Bankruptcy of AT&T.* As noted earlier, AT&T had been established in the early twentieth century and granted a monopoly for phone service in the United States. AT&T established a research lab, Bell Laboratories (much earlier, but inventive like Xerox's PARC). Bell Labs made major inventions, including transistor in the 1940s. In the 1960s, it invented the basic concepts of cellular phone systems. But then, AT&T did not commercialize and start a cellular phone business. AT&T top management was looking backward—at how to maximize profits from pricing local and long-distance phone services. Managers got into legal arguments about AT&T's phone monopoly with the U.S. Department of Justice. Consequently, AT&T agreed to divide its fixed-line phone business between one long-distance phone company (AT&T) and several regional local phone services. The regional phone services thrived but long-distance AT&T shrank. Eventually, AT&T went bankrupt. But two of the local phone services looked ahead and established cellular phone services as Verizon and Cingular. Then Cingular bought out the old AT&T and changed its name to AT&T. Reincarnated, the new AT&T is a cellular phone service.
>
> It is one of the great ironies of big business that management has often looked backward to yesterday's technologies and focused only on maximizing short-term profits from these old technologies. Even while their researchers might be envisioning and creating a new technical future, sometimes top executives have failed to look forward toward a strategic future of innovation (see Chapter 6, Subsection 6.1, "Enigma of Xerox").

5.2.2.2.2.2 Significant Economies of Scale in Production Software, or more generally any information, has the highly noticeable production characteristic in which the production of the first copy involves a huge sunk cost (cost that cannot be recovered), whereas the second copy (third, fourth, and so on) costs almost nothing to reproduce. The cost of gathering the information for the Britannica encyclopedia involves more than 100 years of research as well as the lifetime work of a good number of authors. However, the cost of reproducing it on a set of CDs is less than $5. The cost of developing advanced software involves thousands of hours of programming time; however, the software can now be distributed without cost over the Internet. In economic terms, a very high fixed sunk cost, together with almost negligible marginal cost, implies that the average cost function declines sharply with the number of copies sold out to consumers. This by itself means that a competitive equilibrium does not exist and that markets of this type will often be characterized by dominant leaders that capture most of the market.

5.2.3 ENTERPRISE LEVEL

5.2.3.1 Vantage Time

Markets have become unpredictable; the rapid pace of technologies, deregulation, and globalization is changing the business landscape. In the new economy, the speed and means by which advantage grows and declines are becoming increasingly diverse. As an enterprise, you seek and gain advantage; value flows for a time. But then that advantage is lost and must be renewed again. Even managers in the most powerful companies find that success is not enduring; obsolescence is inevitable and nothing lasts forever. Vantage time is the transforming insight that business time moves at different speeds; business time splits markets apart, as well as the companies that compete in them. It predicts the means by which advantage evolves through the mechanism of generating value that are distinctive for each company. The growth engine of every enterprise has its distinguishing competitive mechanics and its own dynamic signature that tells how value is generated, how products age, and how advantage is potentially renewed. A vantage time zone is a segment of a market where the styles of management needed to renew advantage are similar. Within a vantage time zone, managers learn customer needs, see threats, build control systems, and leverage capabilities with similar competitive logic. Vantage time zones are the dynamic analogs to the traditional idea of strategic groups regions of market where competitors behave similarly toward each other. In similar vantage time, the growth engines of companies have similar dynamic mechanics at work to sustain growth. Most value-generating relationships that companies have with their suppliers, customers, and competitors are grounded finally in the corresponding vantage time.

The automobile industry provides a clear example of the changing nature of competitive advantage. Japanese manufacturers have consistently gained market share in the U.S. market, despite the fact that they face a significant location disadvantage and well-established competitors. Initially, the Japanese manufacturers gained market share by charging lower prices, but that did not prove to be a sustainable competitive advantage, so they began to focus on quality. Until recently, they had a clear-cut quality lead over their American competitors. Beginning in the early 2000s, U.S. auto manufacturers began to equal Japanese quality; as a result, quality has ceased to be a significant competitive advantage. Consumers now take quality for granted. As a result, the competition has shifted to intangibles, such as design, customer experience, service, and image. There is also growing evidence that customers want a car company to exhibit a sense of social responsibility by producing energy-efficient, low-pollution cars. Perhaps the best way to summarize this is that customers want to make a purchase that not only provides reliable, high-quality transportation but also makes a statement. The Japanese manufacturers once again have adjusted their strategies. They now lead in service, design, and social responsibility. Once again, the U.S. manufacturers appear to be behind.

5.2.3.1.1 *Microsoft IE versus Netscape Navigator*

Consider case of the competition between Netscape's Navigator and Microsoft's Internet Explorer (IE). Netscape's Navigator is based on HTML, a freely available standard in the industry. Netscape has no proprietary technology or other supporting strength that could shield its products from fast imitation. Its vantage time is small; and the pace of innovation must be fast and relentless. Netscape has a lot at stake with each new product introduction. In contrast, for Microsoft, IE is only one of many interconnected applications built upon the MS-DOS and MS Windows OSs. For example, Windows 95 growth engine, because it has created dynamic lock-in with customers, runs in a slower vantage time.

Vantage time characterizes the emergence of multispeed competition. The heart of vantage time is the understanding that competitive forces drive the value of products (or services or experiences) down to zero at different rates of speed. The classification of markets by vantage time refers to how quickly and by what means this happens. Rather than relying on one or a few drivers of competition, vantage time subsumes a wide range of competitive options in terms of how aging advantage can be renewed. The key idea in vantage time is to manage products (or services), companies, and markets by the speed and means by which economic value arises, decays, and is renewed. Vantage time is a concept universally applicable to all markets, companies, and products. Vantage time provides a unifying business language for comparing renewal opportunities of a constellation of markets, companies, and products. Up to three vantage time zones can be formed depending on the diversity and stability of isolating mechanisms or barriers at work—slow, standard, and fast cycle. The isolating mechanisms or barriers are features of the market, company, and products (or services) that delay its obsolescence.

> The central measure of vantage time itself is the product (or service) half-life, which is the amount of time that passes before the per-unit profit margin for a product drops to one-half of its highest value.
>   Vantage time can be treated as a measure of the longevity of the competitive advantage of companies and as such can be used for classifying them into distinct zones of sustainability.

5.2.3.1.2 Slow-Cycle Vantage Time

Companies operating in this first renewal class, like Microsoft with its Windows OS, pursue renewal opportunities that are shielded from traditional competitive pressures. This is characteristic of companies like Microsoft, Disney, and Merck, which thwart competition through a segregating mechanism or barrier. These barriers are based on one-of-a-kind advantages such as geography, copyrights, patents, or ownership of patent resource. Slow-cycle companies achieve enduring dominance of the market in their vantage time zone because of a competitive effect called a phase transition, whereby a market transits all the way toward dominance by one competitor. Slow-cycle vantage time zone companies are characterized by stable long-running pricing strategies.

5.2.3.1.3 Standard-Cycle Vantage Time

Companies operating in this second renewal class are found midway on the spectrum of vantage time. They are typically mass-market companies, market share oriented, and process focused. What distinguishes their success is their ability to replicate the same usage experience for customers every time. This is characteristic of companies like Wal-Mart, Toyota, and Starbucks, whose isolating mechanisms or barriers are less powerful than those in slower-cycle time. Vantage time is smaller for these companies because their capabilities are less specialized; competitors have greater ability and incentive to duplicate them, improve upon them, or render them obsolete. Still standard-cycle companies achieve extended dominance of the market in their vantage time zone by harmonizing a range of technical and organizational elements with economies of scale. Standard-cycle vantage time zone companies are characterized by competitive cost-plus pricing strategies.

5.2.3.1.4 Fast-Cycle Vantage Time

Companies operating in this third renewal class, like Samsung, rely on new ideas, novelty, and innovation products that are quickly duplicated. This is characteristic of companies like Samsung, Motorola, and Sony, whose isolating mechanisms or barriers are almost nonexistent and the advantage is based on nonproprietary ideas realized with easily available standardized components and interfaces. Vantage time is smallest for these companies because their capabilities are devoid of embedded specialties and do not necessitate specialized services and support that are challenging to deploy. Fast-cycle companies may achieve short-lived dominance of the market in their vantage zone because of rapid changes in customer preferences, pricing, styling (as against distinctive features), and perceived comparative advantages. Fast-cycle vantage time zone companies are characterized by rapidly changing market-responsive pricing strategies.

Vantage time helps to forecast life-cycle manufacturing goals, to know the extent to which the manufacturing process will come under pressure to meet productivity and time-to-market objectives, to determine product-specific success factors like quality and standardization, to match control systems with cultural norms, to guide policies on innovation and renewal, to compare different styles of management as to whether they work for or against each other, and to establish meaningful human resource policies.

5.2.3.2   Bandwagon Effect

Bandwagon effect is a phenomenon resulting from the combination of *platform effect* with the *network effects*. The history of Microsoft illustrates how bandwagon effects can lead to market concentration and market power. A successful proprietor of a bandwagon technology generally has the ability to abuse market power. The U.S. Department of Justice, in its antitrust case, alleged that Microsoft did, indeed, abuse its market power. Bandwagon effects, notwithstanding their pressure toward uniformity and their potential for abuse of market power, can be viewed in a positive light. They enable consumers to benefit if they can somehow contrive to do the same thing. Suppliers in bandwagon markets are band conductors who try to get consumers to play in concert to achieve that goal.

The largest and most successful bandwagon, apart from telephone service, has been the Internet. It has, indeed, achieved unstoppable momentum. The Internet makes available to most computer users a huge range of information on just about any subject. It has become indispensable to universities and other research institutions. In some recent years, Internet stocks have been among the hottest on Wall Street. Perhaps most important, the Internet serves as a vast resource to facilitate free speech and free expression across the globe.

Bandwagons have dynamics that differ from those of conventional products and services. They are quite difficult to get started and often end up in a ditch before they can get under way. Once enough consumers have gotten on a bandwagon, however, it may be unstoppable. Not surprisingly, firms in high-technology industries clearly understand the importance of bandwagon effects. When a new service is first introduced, competitors often wage a fierce battle. Each tries to have its own technology become the industry standard (or platform). The contenders all know that the lion's share of the profits will go to the bandwagon technology. The whole nature of competitive rivalry depends on whether the products or services of suppliers are interfaced. Bandwagon markets without interfacing have a tendency to gravitate toward a dominant supplier; bandwagon markets with standardized interfaces have no such tendency.

Technical standards play an important role in bandwagon markets. An agreed-upon technical standard interlinks the products of all suppliers. Technical standards can be set through industry agreement or through government intervention. For example, several major producers of CDs and CD players successfully agreed to a single technical standard. Such agreements avoid the economic waste associated with producers' developing a losing standard and consumers' being stuck with products that embody it. A supplier with a truly superior technology may, however, prefer to go for broke and battle it out in the market. Sony did precisely that, to its own regret, by introducing the Beta videocassette recorder (VCR) without getting industry consensus on a technical standard. Such battles take quite a different form when governments become involved in setting technical standards. Each market participant then competes to persuade public policymakers that its technology is superior. The alternative is for multiple suppliers to promote their own proprietary standards. Each then tries to become the dominant supplier in the non-interlinked bandwagon market.

In 1972 when Sony introduced their ½ in. tape machine called Betamax (smaller than earlier ¾ in. device called U-Matic), company executives tried to persuade other firms to adopt the technology as the new industry standard—but they refused to alter the Betamax design to accommodate other firms in Japan or in the United States. For example, GE wanted a much longer recording time for American consumers than the original recorded time of only 1 h. Sony's competitor JVC came out with its own product VHS in 1976, which offered 2 h recording time. Even though VHS was perceived to be technically inferior to the Betamax machine, eventually, it was the VHS format that prevailed and became the market standard for home VCR.

VHS triumphed over Betamax because of the bandwagon effects arising out of multiple factors. There was a lack of real differentiation between the two offerings in terms of the basic technology or features. Though Betamax and VHS were both based on Sony's U-Matic device, they used different cassette sizes and incompatible signal-recording formats; since they were sufficiently expensive, it was unlikely that the consumers would own more than one format. But JVC (and its giant parent Matsushita Electronics) had better success in its efforts for making VHS as the industry standard and maneuvering the network effect to impart extra momentum for this effort of standardization. First, JVC executives and development team visited competitors and potential partners, seeking support and suggestions for improvement and incorporating them to the extent possible. JVC and Matsushita also broadly licensed the new technology on inexpensive terms to some 40 firms (contrary to about a dozen in the case of Sony Betamax); they also provided essential components (like the helical scanner, which was very difficult to mass produce) until the licensees were able to manufacture it themselves (contrary to Sony continuing to do bulk of the manufacturing itself).

Second, JVC and Matsushita aggressively cultivated a complementary market in prerecorded tapes and retail distribution. Matsushita even leveraged its engineering resources to build machines that replicated tapes at very high speeds for the prerecorded market. The network effects increased in strength as the much larger number of firms licensing VHS brought more production capacity *in play* for this standard, which in turn encouraged more tape producers and distributors to make many more prerecorded VHS tapes. Retailers increasingly used their limited shelf space to stock VHS machines and prerecorded tapes. Users responded and bought more VHS machines, which encouraged more firms to license the VHS standard and then more tape producers, distributors, and consumers to opt for VHS. Beginning with a 0% market share in 1975, VHS went to a 100% market share by late 1980s.

5.2.3.2.1 Paying with Card

Humankind has seen only four major innovations in the most routine aspect of economic life—how we transact with one another—(1) the switch from barter to coin around 700 BC; (2) the introduction of checks by the Venetians in the twelfth century; (3) the shift to paper money in the seventh century; (4) the payment card. In the early 1950s, Frank McNamara of American Express gave cards to a few hundred people in Manhattan and talked to some local restaurants into paying his company 7% of the meal tab billed to the Diners Club card. From this small beginning platform, the industry has expanded slowly over time. Indeed, payment cards have become a global common currency, especially for the Internet transactions—though more than 70% of the payments by U.S. households are still made with cash or checks. This industry is what economist term as a *bandwagon effect* (i.e., platform effect + network effect) because a payment card needs both consumers and merchants: the consumers gradually attract merchants, who in turn gradually attract consumers.

The card systems are the hubs in a vast interconnected network of businesses and consumers. After a consumer presents his or her card to a merchant, the clerk swipes the card through an electronic terminal near the cash register. Within seconds, the terminal connects to a computer miles away and verifies the willingness of the entity that issued your card to pay for your purchase, that is, MasterCard or Visa. MasterCard and Visa, which are associations of financial institutions, are two brands that account for more than 70% of all U.S. payment card transactions. Over the course of an average year, these computers process more than tens of billions of transactions between the millions of merchants who take payment cards and the hundreds of millions of consumers who use payment cards. If the consumer had used the MasterCard credit card, the following strings of actions follow: (1) the system has to transfer money to the merchant from the entity or member that signed up the merchant; (2) it has to transfer money from the member that issued the card to the member that signed up the merchant; (3) and, finally, the member that issued the card must obtain all the information necessary to bill the cardholder. And all along the way, the system must work to collect and distribute various fees among the parties that have participated in each transaction.

In practice, how a payment card actually works varies depending upon the specific type of the card. For example, consider the case of MasterCard issued by one of its largest members—Citibank. Suppose a consumer goes to an Apple Store to purchase a new iPhone and swipes the MasterCard issued by Citibank (*issuer*) through the card reader. The card reader takes data off the magnetic stripe on the back of the card. It combines these data with information about the merchant and the dollar value of the purchase to create an electronic message. It then dials the telephone number of a computer maintained by Apple Store's *acquirer* (the bank that handles its MasterCard transactions). Once connected, a message is sent to the acquirer's computer. This computer reads the message and figures out that the consumer has used a MasterCard. It dials up MasterCard's computer system. After reading the message, MasterCard's computer knows to check with Citibank's computer to see whether consumer has enough money on his or her credit line to cover the purchase. If so, Citibank's computer will send a message back to Apple Store's acquirer, which in turn sends a message back to the terminal at the store; the terminal prints out the receipt that the consumer signs as *authorization*. This authorization process takes just a few seconds. Since, the entire transaction is captured electronically, the main purpose of the receipt is to help resolve disputes when cards are stolen and signatures are forged.

Apple Store then automatically submits a request for payment to its acquirer, which in turn sends it on to MasterCard's computer. The MasterCard computer passes on the request to Citibank's computer, which posts the transaction to the consumer's account. MasterCard's computer consolidates all such transactions and settles accounts among banks. For our example purchase, Citibank pays the acquirer, which then pays Apple Store. This process is completed within 2 or 3 days from the time the consumer makes his or her purchase. The Apple Store receives about 98% of the amount charged for the iPhone. The remaining 2% difference is called the *merchant discount*, which is the fee paid to the acquirer for providing its services. The acquirer in turn pays about 1.7% of the purchase amount to the issuer, in this case Citibank. That 1.7% *interchange fee* is set by MasterCard. This is how the card businesses make money.

The previous process is the same whether the consumer used a MasterCard credit or debit card until almost the end. With a credit card, the issuer compiles information on consumer charges over the course of the billing cycle (usually 30 days) and sends the consumer a statement. The issuer expects full or partial payment typically within 25 days of the end of the billing cycle; if consumer decides to make a partial payment, that is, finance the purchases via the credit card, he or she will have to pay the finance charges. With a debit card, the issuer simply deducts the charge from your checking account—generally within a day or 2 of the purchase. The consumer's monthly checking account statement, in addition to other account activity, will contain his or her debit card purchases.

Thus, in the normal scenario, the net effect is that the consumer gets the convenience of paying with the card; obviating the need to always carry adequate cash on person (with its attendant risks) and the merchant gets a customer *enabled to pay* at the cost of parting with the *merchant discount*. This is a typical bandwagon effect—no different than Adobe giving away its *reader* software free and charging companies only for the *editor* software or Microsoft charging little for its developer tools and making its money from computer purchasers.

5.2.4 Product Level

5.2.4.1 Product Life Cycle

If you put a pair of rabbits in a meadow, you can watch their population go through an exponential growth pattern at first. As with every multiplication process, one unit brings forth another. But the population growth slows down later as it approaches a ceiling—the capacity of a species' ecological niche. Over time, the rabbit traces an S-shaped niche. Over time, the rabbit population traces an S-shaped trajectory. The rate of growth traces a bell-shaped curve that peaks when half the niche is filled. The bell-shaped curve for its rate of growth and the S-shaped curve for the total population constitute a pictorial representation of the natural growth process; that is, how a species population grows into a limited space by obeying the laws of survival.

A product's sales follow the same pattern as the product fills its market niche, because competition in the marketplace is intrinsically the same as in the jungle. The cumulative number of units sold is shown in Figure 5.5; it also shows the PLC and the number of units sold each quarter. Table 5.1 lists characteristic product cycle times by industry.

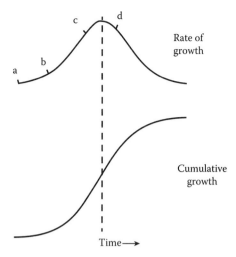

FIGURE 5.5 S-curve and the PLC.

TABLE 5.1
Characteristic Product Cycle Times by Industry

Description	Life Cycle (Years)	Development Cycle (Years)
Financial services	0.2	0.2
Silicon foundries	0.5	0.5
Retailing, entertainment	1.0	1.0
Fashion and textiles	1.5	1.5
Software	2.0	2.0
Electronics	2.5	2.5
Computers	3.0	3.0
Medical and dental	3.5	3.5
Automobiles	4.0	4.0
Metal products	4.5	4.5
Photographic	5.0	5.0
Chemicals, paper	6.0	6.0
Publishing	7.0	2.0
Aircraft	7.0	7.0
Biotechnology	8.0	3.0
Pharmaceuticals	10.0	10.0
Mining	11.0	6.0
Lodging, hotels	11.0	3.0
Foods	11.0	2.0
Tobacco	11.0	1.0
Forestry, oil, and gas reservoirs	12.0	12.0
Military weapons	12.0	2.0
Communication systems	20.0	20.0
Transportation systems	20.5	20.5

The PLC is used to map the life span of a product. There are generally four stages in the life of a product. These four stages are the introduction stage, the growth stage, the maturity stage, and the decline stage. There is no set time period for the PLC and the length of each stage may vary. One product's entire life cycle could be over in a few months; another product could last for years. Also, the introduction stage may last much longer than the growth stage and vice versa.

Figure 5.5 also illustrates the four stages of the PLC:

1. Introduction: The introduction stage is probably the most important stage in the PLC. In fact, most products that fail do so in the *introduction* stage. This is the stage in which the product is initially promoted; public awareness is very important to the success of a product. If people don't know about the product, they won't go out and buy it. There are two different strategies you can use to introduce your product to consumers. You can use either a penetration strategy or a skimming strategy. If a penetration strategy is used, then prices are set very high initially and then gradually lowered over time. This is a good strategy to use if there are few competitors for your product: profits are high with this strategy but there is also a great deal of risk. If people don't want to pay high prices, you may lose out. The second pricing strategy is the skimming strategy. In this case, you set your prices very low at the beginning and then gradually increase them. This is a good strategy to use if there are a lot of competitors who control a large portion of the market. Profits are not a concern under this strategy: the most important thing is to get your product known and worry about making money at a later time.

2. Growth: The growth stage is where your product starts to grow. In this stage, a very large amount of money is spent on advertising. You want to concentrate on telling the consumer how much better your product is than your competitors' products. There are several ways to advertise your product—TV and radio commercials and magazine and newspaper ads— or you could get lucky and customers who have bought your product will give good word of mouth to their family and friends. If you are successful with your advertising strategy, then you will see an increase in sales. Once your sales begin to increase, your share of the market will stabilize. Once you get to this point, you will probably not be able to take anymore of the market from your competitors.

3. Maturity: The third stage in the PLC is the maturity stage. If your product completes the introduction and growth stages, then it will spend a great deal of time in the maturity stage. During this stage, sales grow at a very fast rate and then gradually begin to stabilize. The key to surviving this stage is differentiating your product from the similar products offered by your competitors. Due to the fact that sales are beginning to stabilize, you must make your product stand out among the rest.

4. Decline: This is the stage in which sales of your product begin to fall. Either everyone that wants to has bought your product or new more innovative products have been created that replace yours. Many companies decide to withdraw their products from the market due to the downturn: the only way to increase sales during this period is to cut your costs and reduce your spending.

Very few products follow the same life cycle. Many products may not even make it through all four stages; some products may even bypass stages. For example, one product may go straight from the introduction stage to the maturity stage. This is the problem with the PLC—there is no set way for a product to grow. Therefore, every product requires a great deal of research and close supervision throughout its life; without proper research and supervision, your product will probably never get out of the first stage.

5.2.4.1.1 Polaroid at the Terminus of Its Product Cycle
Polaroid was a pioneer in the development of instant photography. It developed the first instant camera in 1948 and the first instant color camera in 1963 and introduced sonar automatic focusing in 1978.

In addition to its competencies in silver halide chemistry, it had technological competencies in optics and electronics and mass manufacturing, marketing, and distribution expertise. The company was technology-driven from its foundation in 1937, and the founder Edwin Land had 500 personal patents. When Kodak entered the instant photography market in 1976, Polaroid sued the company for patent infringement and was awarded $924.5 million in damages. Polaroid consistently and successfully pursued a strategy of introducing new cameras but made almost all its profits from the sale of the film (the so-called razor/blade marketing strategy also used by Gillette), and between 1948 and 1978, the average annual sales growth was 23% and profit growth 17% per year.

Polaroid established an electronic imaging group as early as 1981, as it recognized the potential of the technology. However, digital technology was perceived as a potential technological shift rather than as a market or business disruption. By 1986, the group had an annual research budget of $10 million, and by 1989, 42% of the R&D budget was devoted to digital imaging technologies. By 1990, 28% of the firm's patents related to digital technologies. Polaroid was therefore well positioned at that time to develop a digital camera business. However, it failed to translate prototypes into a commercial digital camera until 1996, by which time there were 40 other companies in the market, including many strong Japanese camera and electronics firms. Part of the problem was adapting the product development and marketing channels to the new product needs. However, other more fundamental problems related to long-held cognitions: a continued commitment to the razor/blade business model and pursuit of image quality.

A species population may begin growing into an ecological niche that is already filled to the capacity. In this case, the new population can grow only to the extent that another one decreases. Thus, a process of substitution occurs, and under conditions of natural competition, the transition from occupancy by the old to occupancy by the new should follow the S-shaped pattern. For 40 years after their invention in 1880, telephone switches were operated by human operators. Then in 1920, mechanical switches were introduced that reduced the labor content to 50%; in 1940, electromechanical switches reduced the labor content to 25%; in the 1960s, with analog switches, the labor content dropped further until the 1980s when the integrated circuit switching the labor content was 5%. Meanwhile, the development cost rose from $10 million for electromechanical switches in the 1940s to $1 billion for digital switches in the 1980s.

Figure 5.6 shows the market share transfer from an old technology to the new one; the regularity of the transition is remarkable, considering that the overall market increased many times during this period and that a world war took place in the background. The advantage of market share is its deeply rooted competitive origin; one competitor's gains bear directly on another competitor's losses. The description thus becomes free of external influences: economy, politics, earthquakes, and seasonal effects such as vacations and holidays. However, sometimes the natural character emerges only when seen as a composite of competitors substitute for another set of composition. An example of a nonobvious natural replacement is the loss of market value by IBM and DEC in favor of Microsoft and Intel.

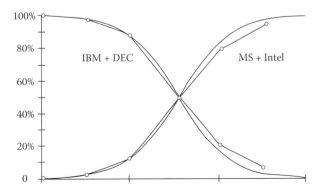

FIGURE 5.6   Market share transfer from IBM + DEC to Microsoft + Intel.

5.2.4.2 Platform Effect

What differentiates innovative companies from others is the constancy of generating a stream of strong products—they understand that long-term success does not hinge on any single product. They know that they must generate a continuous stream of value-rich products that target growth markets. Such products form a product family with individual products sharing common technology and addressing related market applications. It is such product families that account for the long-term success of an enterprise. Product families do not emerge one product at a time; they are planned so that a number of derivative products can be efficiently created from the foundation of common core technology or product platform.

A product platform is a set of subsystem and interfaces that form a common structure from which a stream of derivative products can be efficiently developed and produced. A platform approach to product development dramatically reduces manufacturing costs and provides significant economies in the procurement of components and materials, because so many of these are shared among individual products. The building blocks of product platforms can be integrated with new components to address new market opportunities rapidly.

Platforms and families are powerful ways for companies to recoup their high initial investments in R&D by deploying the technology across a number of market fields. For example, P&G invested heavily in their cyclodextrin development for original application in detergents but then was able to use this technology or variants on it in a family of products including odor control (*Febreze*), soaps and fine fragrances (*Olay*), off-flavor food control, disinfectants, bleaches, and fabric softening (*Tide, Bounce*, etc.). They were also able to license out the technology for use in noncompeting areas like industrial-scale carpet care and in the pharmaceutical industry.

> In 1798, gun making was considered a complex craft, with each gun being produced by a single craftsman. Eli Whitney devised a method whereby the parts for rifles became standard rather than being individually produced by a gunsmith. As a result, the army could use standard produced rifles, at a great cost savings and with greater efficiency. It was then possible to assemble a musket from the parts he produced rather than to build each one individually. He obtained a contract to produce rifles during the War of 1812, although his success was only modest. In such a manner, he became the father of *mass production*, although his legacy centers almost entirely on the invention of the cotton gin.

Product platforms must be managed. If a platform is not rejuvenated, its derivative products will become dated and will fail customers in terms of function and value. If a company's platforms are renewed periodically to incorporate new functions, components, and materials, the product family will remain robust through successive generations. But, product platforms do not become robust by accident—they are the result of a unique methodology and of strategies for designing, developing, and revitalizing them over time.

5.2.4.2.1 Intel's Microprocessor Platform

On April 19, 1965, Gordon Moore, the cofounder of Intel Corporation, published an article in *Electronics Magazine* entitled *Cramming more components onto Integrated Circuits* in which he identified and conjectured a trend that computing power would double every 2 years (this was termed as *Moore's law* in 1970 by the CalTech professor and VLSI pioneer, Calvin Mead). This law has been able to predict reliably both the reduction in costs and the improvements in computing capability of microchips, and those predictions have held true (Figure 5.7).

In 1965, the amount of transistors that fitted on an integrated circuit could be counted in tens. In 1971, Intel introduced the 4004 microprocessor with 2300 transistors. In 1978, when Intel introduced the 8086 microprocessor, the IBM PC was effectively born (the first IBM PC used the 8088 chip)—this chip had 29,000 transistors. In 2006, Intel's Itanium 2 processor carried 1.7 billion

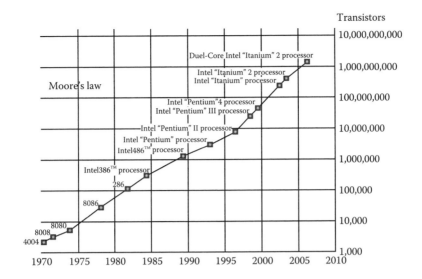

FIGURE 5.7   Increase of the number of transistors on an Intel chip.

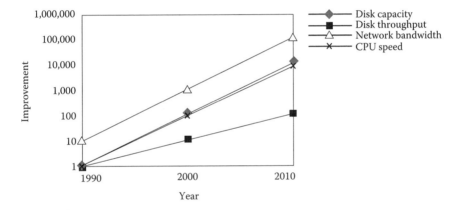

FIGURE 5.8   Hardware trends in the 1990s and the current decade.

transistors. In the next 2 years, we'll have chips with over 10 billion transistors. What does this mean? Transistors are now so small that millions of them could fit on the head of a pin. While all this was happening, the cost of these transistors was also exponentially falling, as per Moore's prediction (Figure 5.8).

In real terms, this means that a mainframe computer of the 1970s that cost over $1 million had less computing power than your iPhone has today. The next generation of smartphone we will be using in the next 2–3 years will have 1 GHz processor chips. That is roughly one million times faster than the Apollo Guidance Computer. Theoretically, Moore's law will run out of steam somewhere in the not too distant future. There are a number of possible reasons for this. Firstly, the ability of a microprocessor silicon-etched *track* or circuit to carry an electrical charge has a theoretical limit. At some point when these circuits get physically too small and can no longer carry a charge or the electrical charge *bleeds*, then we'll have a design limitation problem. Secondly, as successive generations of chip technology are developed, manufacturing costs increase. In fact recently, Gordon Moore said that each new generation of chips requires a doubling in cost of the manufacturing facility as tolerances become tighter. At some point, it will theoretically become too costly to develop the

manufacturing plants that produce these chips. The usable limit for semiconductor process technology will be reached when chip process geometries shrink to be smaller than 20 nanometers (nm)
to 18 nm nodes. At those nodes, the industry will start getting to the point where semiconductor
manufacturing tools are too expensive to depreciate with volume production; that is, their costs will
be so high that the value of their lifetime productivity can never justify it. Lastly, the power requirements of chips are also increasing. More power being equivalent to more heat equivalent to bigger
batteries implies that at some point, it becomes increasingly difficult to power these chips while
putting them on smaller platforms.

Greater power in product development can be achieved if these building blocks are leveraged
across product platforms of multiple product lines. For example, Intel's advances in microprocessors are leveraged into new versions of its servers and supercomputers. Many firms fail to leverage
their capabilities across product lines—diversified businesses of most large enterprises typically do
not share core technologies across its product lines.

A robust product platform is based on a number of building blocks that can be grouped into four
areas:

1. Customer insights: Insights into the minds and needs of the customers and the processes
of customer and competitive research that uncover and validate those insights. Marketers
have many techniques for determining customer needs, perceptions, and preferences. The
resulting knowledge gained cannot be a preserve of one function within the enterprise, but
should be available enterprise-wide—no function within the enterprise can be allowed to
own the customer.
2. Product technologies: Product technologies in materials, components, subsystem interfaces, and development tools. Product technologies can encompass chemistries, material
properties, programming languages and algorithms, hardware or logic design, and so
forth. One level up from these basic or component technologies is the actual implementations of proprietary knowledge and skills in the form of chemical formulations, material
assemblies, software modules, or chips. Rapid platform design, development, and renewal
must incorporate latest advances in the areas of component technologies. Just as derivative
products should be rapidly developed through incremental improvements to existing platforms; new platforms should be created by integrating latest advances in the component
technologies, either from within or external suppliers or partners.
3. Manufacturing processes and technologies: Processes and technologies that make it possible for the product to meet competitive requirements for cost, volume, and quality. In
many industries like glass and refining, the firms with the best manufacturing technologies have an edge; for such industries, the manufacturing process is itself the platform.
For both assembled and nonassembled products, the tendency is to consider traditional
variations in volume or capacity for improvements; but innovation or flexibility improvements in manufacturing process can result in much better dividends. Flexible manufacturing has enormous implications for the design of plant and equipment, patterns of
resource allocation, and the range of product variety that a company can bring to the
market.
4. Organizational capabilities: Capabilities that include infrastructures for distribution and
customer support, as well as information systems for customer centricity, customer responsiveness, and operational control (including market feedback). Firms must have strong
channels through which to distribute their products or services. For many firms, packaging also is a distinct focus of achieving competitive advantage and lies at the confluence
between product design and distribution. Likewise, customer support must be available
both to help customers to realize the full value of the firm's products and as a listening
post for gathering customer insights. Remote diagnostics built into industrial and medical
equipment can greatly facilitate and improve customer support.

5.2.4.2.2   Microsoft's Platforms Strategy

Microsoft is a classic example of successful employment and deployment of platform strategy for extending market ownership. This approach consists of extending advantage while maintaining customer lock-in. Although MS-DOS was only one of three OSs initially offered by IBM, Microsoft priced MS-DOS lower than its competitors. MS-DOS quickly became the de facto OS on the IBM PC. Microsoft transformed this into a platform by treating it as part of a platform of functions tied to the original MS-DOS. While maintaining the MS-DOS OS, Microsoft developed a proprietary GUI that emulated the look and feel of the popular Macintosh computer. Microsoft used Windows to lure customers to stay with MS-DOS and MS-DOS-based applications while they were upgraded progressively. As customers were persuaded to adopt newer products, the MS-DOS installed base was nurtured and protected; the strategy was always to provide a strong bridge between earlier and later product releases. The next step of Microsoft was built on applications. Competitors for applications like WordPerfect dominated word processing, Lotus 1-2-3 dominated spreadsheets, and Harvard Graphics dominated presentation software. But through the linkage of the Windows, Microsoft made its word processing (MS Word), spreadsheet (MS Excel), and presentation software (MS PowerPoint) attractively compatible with each other and with Windows. Customers were encouraged to purchase the entire suite of Microsoft applications (MS Office) by highlighting the ease with which customers could interchange documents between any of these applications—which was not possible with the competitor's applications. Microsoft introduced Windows NT OS for office PC market.

In the fall of 1995, Microsoft introduced Windows 95, which was a 32-bit OS. It was a vastly improved OS while maintaining backward compatibility with the early-generation MS-DOS OS and applications; it was also cross-platform compatible with Windows NT bridged again via Windows. With Windows 95 and Windows NT compatibility, Microsoft became the first company to offer high-performance, cross-platform connectivity between the home and office markets to consolidate the customers from these two markets by promoting third-party applications that worked on both Windows 95 and Windows NT. In order to get their product qualified for Windows 95, third-party developers were required to write applications that would work on both Windows 95 and Windows NT.

With the advent of the Internet, HTML along with Sun Microsystem's Java had the potential of becoming an alternate OS for PCs that could also communicate with each other. In response, Microsoft enabled Internet access through Microsoft's browser IE that was similar to Netscape's Navigator. However, with the introduction of Windows 98, IE was embedded into Microsoft OS, MS Office, and third-party applications, thus rendering Netscape's browser irrelevant.

5.3   ASPECTS OF VARIATIONS

This section addresses the analytical side of variation proficiency of the enterprise. It highlights the fundamental principles that underlie an enterprise's ability to vary, and by indicating how to apply these principles in real situations, it illustrates what it is that makes a business and any of its constituting systems easy to vary.

> Inertia and Agility: As indicated in the Preface, this book does not discuss the process related to the realization of variations. However, in the context of variations, we would like to briefly highlight two aspects of an enterprise, namely, inertia and agility. Inertia is the resistance encountered by the enterprise affecting variations in any combination of the dimension of variations; accordingly an enterprise may have to encounter nine types of inertia (independently or in combination):
>
> • Shared values (rules-driven to values-driven) inertia e.g. Motorola's focus on quality
> • Strategy (planned to emergent) inertia e.g., Sun Microsystems focus on workstations with proprietary O/S

- Structure (control to autonomy) inertia e.g., GM's multi-divisional organization
- Stuff (products to services to experiences) inertia e.g., Kodak films and camera business or IBM mainframes business
- Style (administrational to transformational culture) inertia e.g., HP's 'HP Way'
- Staff (challenging to nurturing people) inertia e.g., GM's unionized staff
- Skills (focus or breadth of skills) inertia e.g. UPS's foray into Air Carrier Services
- Systems (mandatory to discretionary) inertia e.g., Barnes & Nobel's foray into Internet-based selling
- Sequence (mass production to mass customization) inertia e.g., Ford mass production

Agility is the ability to respond to (and ideally benefit from) unexpected change. Agility is unplanned and unscheduled adaption to unforeseen and unexpected external circumstances. However, we must differentiate between agility and flexibility. Flexibility is scheduled or planned adaptation to unforeseen yet expected external circumstances.

One of the foremost abilities of an agile enterprise is its ability to quickly react to change and adapt to new opportunities. This ability to change works along two dimensions:

(i) The number or "types of change" an organization is able to undergo
(ii) The "degree of change" an organization is able to undergo.

The former is termed as *range*, and the latter is termed as *response ability*. The more response able an enterprise is, the more radical a change it can gracefully address. Range refers to how large a domain is covered by the agile response system; in other words, how far from the expected set of events one can go and still have the system respond well. However, given a specific range, how well the system responds is a measure of response ability.

We can also define agility at the virtual enterprise level, where the virtual enterprise is an aggregation of individual enterprises working together as one entity. Agility then, has an internal context (within each enterprise and within the virtual enterprise as a whole) and an external context (from the virtual enterprise towards the external environment or business opportunities). The overall agility of the virtual enterprise (or supply chain) depends on both internal and external agility–an internal agility is a prerequisite for external agility. Unless we are able to rearrange or reconfigure or reframe the virtual enterprise competencies on demand, one cannot win on the changing battlegrounds that markets are often today.

Built-for-Variation (or variation-able or variable) enterprises are akin to agile enterprises, but we would continue to use the new nomenclature for this book because it enables sharper focus on the variation ability of an enterprise at the most fundamental level rather than the ability to respond predominantly with reference to the existing competencies.

Variation proficiency enables both efficiency programs (e.g., lean production) and transformation programs; if the enterprise is proficient at variation, it can adapt to take advantage of an unpredictable opportunity and can also counter the unpredictable threat. Variation ability or variability can embrace semantics across the whole spectrum: it can capture cycle-time reduction, with everything happening faster; it can build on lean production, with high resource productivity; it can encompass mass customization, with customer-responsive product variation; it can embrace virtual enterprise, with streamlined supplier networks and opportunistic partnerships; it can echo reengineering, with a process and transformation focus; and it can demand a learning organization, with systemic training and education. Being variable (or built for variations) means being proficient at variation. Variability allows an enterprise to do anything it wants to do whenever it wants to—or has to—do it. Thus, a variable enterprise can employ business process reengineering as a core competency when transformation is called for; it can hasten its conversion to lean production when greater efficiencies are useful; and it can continue to succeed when constant innovation becomes the dominant competitive strategy. Variability can be wielded overtly as a business strategy as well as inherently as a sustainable-existence competency.

Variability is a core fundamental requirement of all enterprises. It was not an area of interest when environmental variation was relatively slow and predictable. Now there is virtually no choice; enterprises must develop a conscious competency. Practically all enterprises now need some method to assess their variability and determine whether it is sufficient or needs improvement. This section introduces techniques for characterizing, measuring, and comparing variability in all aspects of business and among different businesses.

Variability derives from both the physical ability to act (variation ability) and the intellectual ability to find appropriate things to act on (knowledge management). Variability can be expressed as the ability to manage and apply knowledge effectively, so that an enterprise has the potential to thrive in a continuously varying and unpredictable business environment. Variation ability, the ability to act, derives from two sources: an enterprise architecture that enables variation and an organizational culture that facilitates variation. The enterprise architecture that enables variation is based on reusable elements that are reconfigurable in a scalable framework.

The concepts of knowledge management and variation ability are not new. Organizations throughout time have practiced both successfully or they have ceased to exist. What is new is that the quickening pace of knowledge development and knowledge obsolescence has created the need for more formal and conscious understandings of these practices, raising them to the level of a recognized competency. What used to be done unconsciously and in its own good time is no longer adequate in competitive enterprise. Volvo's Kalmar plant decided to abandon the chain drive that moved all cars synchronously through the factory from workstation to workstation. They foresaw advantages in an asynchronous movement and placed each car-in-process on its own automated guided vehicle (AVG), capable of independent movement and not in harness to the car in front (see Chapter 7, Subsection 7.6.3, "Enriching Work Life at Volvo"). This promised more flexibility for adding mass-customized features to individual cars without dragging all cars through stations where no work was performed. More importantly, if a workstation was shut down for any reason, cars could be pool buffered or rerouted to other stations first and then return while the rest of the factory continued to operate. However, when the plant went live, the expected high throughput turned out to be considerably less than the traditional chain drive had provided. Under the old system, a failed workstation shut down the entire production line and the silence was deafening—gaining immediate and total attention. With the highly fluid AVG flow, cars simply bypassed out-of-service stations and the comforting noise of industry continued. A classic architecture for increasing variation ability resulted in a major failure because it failed to recognize the knowledge management issues—this situation occurred because of a disproportionate focus on response ability without a balancing knowledge base of how and why to use it.

 In contrast, the situation at Xerox's PARC was exactly the reverse. PARC brought together a group of extremely innovative thinkers and learners, organized around active collaborative learning concepts. Despite some elements of progressive knowledge management techniques, few research results were transferred and applied within the Xerox family.

5.3.1 VARIABLE CONSTRUCTION TOYS

Construction toys offer a useful metaphor because the enterprise systems we are concerned with must be configured and reconfigured constantly, precisely the objective of most construction toys. An enterprise system architecture and structure consisting of reusable components reconfigurable in a scalable framework can be an effective base model for creating variable (or built for variation) systems. For achieving this, the nature of the framework appears to be a critical factor. We illustrate this point and introduce the framework/component concept, by looking at three types of construction toys and observing how they are used in practice: Erector Set Kit, LEGO Kit, and Model Builder's Kit.

You can build virtually anything over and over again with either of these toys; but fundamental differences in their architectures give each system unique dynamic characteristics. All consist of a basic set of core construction components and also have an architectural and structural framework that enables connecting the components into an unbounded variety of configurations. Nevertheless, the Model Builder is not as reusable in practice as Erector Set; and the Erector Set is not as reusable or reconfigurable or scalable in practice as LEGO, but LEGO is more reusable, reconfigurable, and scalable than either of them. LEGO is the dominant construction toy of choice among our preteen builders—who appear to value experimentation and innovation.

The Model Builder's kit can be used to construct one object like an airplane of one intended size. A highly integrated system, this construction kit offers maximum esthetic appeal for one-time construction use; but the parts are not reusable, the construction cannot be reconfigured, and one intended size precludes any scalability. But it will remain what it is for all time—there is zero variability here.

Erector Set kits can be purchased for constructing specific models, such as a small airplane that can be assembled in many different configurations. With the Erector Set kit, the first built model is likely to remain as originally configured in any particular play session. Erector Set, for all its modular structure, is just not as reconfigurable in practice as LEGO. The Erector Set connectivity framework employs a special-purpose intermediate subsystem used solely to attach one part to another—a nut-and-bolt pair and a 90° elbow. The components in the system all have holes through which the bolts may pass to connect one component with another. When a nut is lost, a bolt is useless, and vice versa; when all the nuts and bolts remaining in a set have been used, any remaining construction components are useless, and vice versa. All the parts in a LEGO set can always be used and reused, but the Erector Set, for all its modularity, is not as reusable in practice as LEGO.

LEGO offers similar kits, and both toys include a few necessary special parts, like wheels and cowlings, to augment the core construction components. Watch a child work with either and you'll see the LEGO construction undergoes constant metamorphosis; the child may start with one of the pictured configurations but then reconfigures the pieces into all manner of other imagined styles. LEGO components are plug compatible with each other, containing the connectivity framework as an integral feature of the component. A standard grid of bumps and cavities on component surfaces allows them to snap together into a larger configuration—without limit.

The Model Builder's kit has a tight framework: a precise construction sequence, no part interchangeability, and high integration. The Erector Set has a loose framework that doesn't encourage interaction among parts and insufficiently discriminates among compatible parts. In contrast, each component in the LEGO system carries all it needs to interact with other components (the interaction framework rejects most unintended parts) and can grow without end.

 Enterprises primarily aim progressively for efficiency, flexibility and innovation in that order. The Model Builder's Kit, Erector Set Kit and LEGO kit are illustrations of enterprises targeting for efficiency, flexibility and innovation (i.e. agility) respectively (see note on "Inertia and Agility" in Subsection 5.3, "Aspects of Variations").

5.3.2   ARCHITECTING FOR VARIATION

The future of organizational structures is based on small, interacting, self-organizing, autonomous units, sharing a common framework that facilitates reconfiguration and adaptation. And it doesn't matter if we are talking about top-level corporate structure or looking inside at functional subdivisions; the concept of loosely coupled interacting components reconfigurable within a framework is the central design attribute that brings adaptability. You can employ this reconfigurable framework/

component concept just as fruitfully in the design of adaptable production processes, upgradeable products, responsive supply chains, flexible distribution logistics, high-performance teams, evolving information systems, adaptable procedures, reconfigurable facilities, and any other aspect of business that must thrive in a constantly changing environment.

Though variability is a broad enterprise issue, looking at the restricted area of product realization will provide a tangible illustration and some fundamental insight. Decreasing innovation cycles in all market sectors are increasing the product introduction frequency. Bringing new or improved products to market involves variations in the production process. Whether these variations are fairly small or quite sweeping, there is usually a transition period of adjustment and settling in. Simply stated, after we design, build, and install a variation, we must deal with a transition period before we have what we want or decide to settle for what we get. Making this variation incurs cost and takes time. Some of this cost and time involves pure design, development, acquisition, and installation; and some is transition turmoil from integration and shakeout. In the ideal Built-for-Variation or variable enterprises, this transition period takes no time, incurs no cost, is not prematurely terminated, and is not an inhibiting factor on the latitude of variation that one is willing to consider.

In the past, such product variations occurred infrequently and the transition costs were easy to ignore. But product introduction frequency in all markets continues to rise, and already in many markets, ignorance of transition cost and time is intolerable. The toll of the transition period is reflected in true product cost, product quality, and market responsiveness. An obvious way to reduce the toll of transition is to reduce the quantity and complexity of things in transition. If we want to do this while accommodating more new products than ever before, we have to learn how to build new products with old proven process—reusable process and reconfigurable for a new purpose. It may not be as technically appealing as a completely new design, but it will be up and running a lot sooner and a lot cheaper, produce less scrap and rework, reuse prior service training and require less new training, and generally function more predictably.

> The old ideas of integration are dangerous, though still attractive. Just as lean tells us to remove all wastes from the system while ignoring the loss of adaptability if we are highly successful, integration tells us to couple ourselves intimately with everything else while ignoring that single-point failures can have a broad and catastrophic reach. In a static environment, the integrated system will dance with efficient grace; but if one part breaks, the whole mass becomes a whole mess. And forget about modifying or improving an integrated system; the unanticipated side effects will return you to the equivalent of a broken system.

It means an important new focus on the structure of the production elements that must be reconfigurable. And it is physical reconfigurability we need, not programmed reconfigurability. We need the ability to make unanticipated new things from reusable pieces, not simply select some predefined subset of flexible capability or embedded options. Reconfigurable structures, whether they organize subunits in a piece of equipment, equipment relationships in a cell, cell relationships in a production area, or production areas in a plant, require some form of facilitated component reusability. For maximum benefit, these structures must be scalable as well as reusable and reconfigurable. Scalability eliminates size restrictions imposed by the structure, allowing any number of reusable components to be included or omitted as desired.

5.3.3 Principles of Built-for-Variation (or Variation-Able or Variable) Systems

1. Reusable
   a. Self-contained units (components): Components of variable systems are distinct, separable, self-sufficient units cooperating toward a shared common purpose.
   b. Plug compatibility: Components of variable systems share defined interaction and interface standards; and they are easily inserted or removed.

     c. Facilitated reuse: Components of variable systems are reusable/replicable; and responsibilities for ready reuse/replication and for management, maintenance, and upgrade of component inventory are specifically designated.

2. Reconfigurable

     a. Flat interaction: Components within a variable system communicate directly on a peer-to-peer relationship; and parallel rather than sequential relationships are favored.

     b. Deferred commitment: Component relationships in a variable system are transient when possible; decisions and fixed bindings are postponed until immediately necessary; and relationships are scheduled and bound in real time.

     c. Distributed control and information: Components in variable systems are directed by objective rather than method; decisions are made at point of maximum knowledge; information is associated locally, accessible globally, and freely disseminated.

     d. Self-organization: Component relationships in variable systems are self-determined; and component interaction is self-adjusting or negotiated.

3. Scalable

     a. Evolving standards (framework): Frameworks of variable systems standardize inter-component communication and interaction; define component compatbility; and are monitored/updated to accommodate old, current, and new components.

     b. Redundancy and diversity: Duplicate components are employed in variable systems to provide capacity right-sizing options and fail-soft tolerance; and diversity among similar components employing different methods is exploited.

     c. Elastic capacity: Component populations in variable systems may be increased and decreased widely within the existing framework.

5.3.4 VARIATION-ENABLING ENTERPRISE ARCHITECTURE AND CULTURE

Reusable components, reconfigurable within a scalable framework design strategy, can engineer variability into a wide variety of systems. When we define a system as any group of units that work together to achieve a common purpose, we include such business systems as a collection of machines in a manufacturing process, a procedure in an assembly process, an integrated chain of suppliers, a contract full of clauses, a gaggle of partners, a team of people, an organization of departments, and so forth.

Variation-able or variable production requires neither variable nor flexible machines: the variability is a function of how the components of production are permitted to interact. The need for a variable system to be readily reconfigurable can be accomplished simply by having a large variety of compatible but infrequently used production units. This is a common approach in the toy industry. Not knowing from year to year what toys will be the hot items until a few months before they must make volume deliveries, toy manufacturers are either highly vertically integrated (with poor resource utilization) or broadly leveraged on outsourced manufacturing potential. Variability is a relative issue, and the toy industry has few alternatives to either outsourcing or just-in-case vertical integration. The just-in-case alternative does not have to be as onerous as it sounds if these practitioners become proficient at in-sourcing work from other companies.

The dynamics of variable enterprise systems come in two forms: directed and self-organizing. Directed dynamics are generally used where the components of the system are inanimate such as the workstations in an automated assembly process. Self-organizing dynamics are possible when the principal resource components are goal seeking and empowered such as the people in a company. Both the static and the dynamic parts are important: static system architectures that make variation possible and a dynamic organizational culture that makes variation probable. Real competitive potential, however, is not realized until a company is strong in both the possible (greater range) and the probable (more likely to act) dimensions. There is little correlation between variability and the employment of technologies intended to make factories more flexible. There is no relationship between size of a factory and variability, and no relationship between workforce experience and variability. Instead, the variability of these plants was primarily determined by the people and their personal interests and concerns for variable operation.

The corporate culture provides alignment among the employees and between the individual and the organization. Culture is a framework. It can promote or inhibit the reusableness and reconfigurableness of human resources. Simply having a culture is not enough to promote variability. People expect the nature of their jobs to change frequently; if no change occurs, they would be disappointed. But neither is embracing variation alone enough. The culture provides a common set of standards for interaction, relationships, participation, and values. These standards facilitate the mobility of people within the organizations because they provide a common language, common objectives, and open communications that permit someone to enter into new relationships effectively.

5.3.5 FRAMEWORK FOR VARIATION PROFICIENCY

How do we measure enterprise's variation ability or variability? This section establishes a metric framework for proficiency at variation; an enterprise's variation proficiency may exist in one or more of dimensions of variations. And these dimensions of variations can form a structural framework for understanding current capabilities and setting strategic priorities for improvement: how the Built-for-Variation enterprise knows when it is improving its variability or losing ground; how it knows if it is less variable than its competition; and how it sets improvement targets. Thus, a practical measure of variation proficiency is needed before we can talk meaningfully about getting more of it or even getting some of it. Again, it must be highlighted that measuring competency is generally not unidimensional, nor likely to result in an absolute and unequivocal comparative metric. Variation proficiency has both reactive and proactive modes. Reactive variation is opportunistic and responds to a situation that threatens viability. Proactive variation is innovative and responds to a possibility for leadership. An organization sufficiently proficient at reactive variation to respond when prodded should be able to use that competency proactively and let others do the reacting.

Would it be proficient if a short-notice variation was completed in the time required, but at a cost that eventually bankrupted the company, or if the changed environment thereafter required the special wizardry and constant attention of a specific employee to keep it operational? Is it proficient if the variation is virtually free and painless but out of sync with market opportunity timing? Is it proficient if it can readily accommodate a broad latitude of variation that is no longer needed or too narrow for the latest challenges thrown at it by the business environment? Are we variation proficient if we can accommodate any variation that comes our way as long as it is within a narrow 10% of where we already are?

Therefore, variation proficiency can be understood to be codetermined by four parameters:

1. Time: a measure of elapsed time to complete a variation (fairly objective)
2. Cost: a measure of monetary cost incurred in a variation (somewhat objective)
3. Quality: a measure of prediction quality in meeting variation time, cost, and specification targets robustly (somewhat subjective)
4. Range: a measure of the latitude of possible variation, typically defined and determined by mission or charter (fairly subjective)

Completing a variation in a timely manner is the only effective way to respond at all in an environment full of continuous and unrelenting variation. Product development, the time to design and engineer a new car, had been reduced to about 2 years at most automakers by the mid- to late 1990s, with PLCs averaging about 4 years. The cost of a slow variation is not just associated with the money involved in the variation process itself. In the case of new product launches, a slow launch may impact eventual market share heavily. But the time of variation alone does not provide a sufficient metric: you can vary virtually anything if cost is no object.

If the cost of variation is too much relative to your competitor's costs, and variations happen with any frequency, there will be a steady erosion of working capital or shareholder dividends or both. Variation at any cost is not viable; else, we need not restructure anything ever: the enterprise can simply discard the old and buy a new capability assuming that we can bring something new to the operational level quick enough. In the case of new car launches, the profit contribution from lost sales spanning the time that the older model is no longer produced until the newer model is satisfying market demand is a real cost of variation, as is the cost of lost market share because of a poor-quality premature entry. Quick, economical variation, however, is still not a sufficient profile for proficiency.

If after a variation, the result is a house of cards that requires constant attention or repair to remain functional, the variation process quality was inadequate. If we cut corners during the variation process to do it quickly and economically, we are likely to end up with a fragile result that lacks robustness. Getting cars to market fast can dampen subsequent sales considerably if quality problems result; consequently, shortening the launch time would result in greater total cost. Encompassing robustness, quality requires predictability. Measuring the quality of a variation process is similar to measuring the quality of a product or a service. Generally, we want to know how closely the end result conforms to specifications competitive in the market and consistent with customer expectations. You can measure the quality of a product in the amount of scrap, rework, and returns. You can generally measure the quality of a service in customer complaints—a more subjective measure since the customer may have unrealistic or unreasonable expectations. The quality of the variation process is more subjective than either time or cost as it is subject to local circumstances; through quality of the variation process, we, measure perhaps the most critical parameter for making sound business decisions—predictability.

The object of the quality parameter of variation proficiency is to gauge mastery of the variation process. Taking the absolute measures of time and cost of variation is different from measuring the predictability of time and cost of variation. Meeting the performance specification is just as important as meeting the time and cost targets. Performance can always be traded for time and cost, and often is when projects are defined as finished because they exhaust a budget or run out of time before meeting performance goals. Respecifying the finished result as a success is a common occurrence—and a conspicuous indicator of a shortfall in the quality parameter. Less conspicuous is when a specification is met as a result of riskless specsmanship; predicting the ability to meet a noncompetitive goal is not proficiency; it does not make them proficient at variation—just safe and predictable, for example, when a company sees itself negotiating delivery dates while using on-time delivery as a corporate performance metric. Such solutions may produce an on-spec result but lose the market in the end. Though this may sound like the intelligent thing to do, so as not to promise something that cannot be met, it is another form of defining away a variation-proficiency problem.

 Earlier, we saw how the cost of a variation interacted with the time of a variation. Now, we see a similar interactive relationship with quality. Proficient variation is one that is accomplished on time, on budget, and on spec.

Range is a measure of how much latitude a potential variation can accommodate; when this range is small and finite, we typically have a flexible rather than a variation-able or variable capability. Though range is most readily associated with capacity range, capability range is more meaningful; the range of variation is not limited to capacity and capability variations; it applies to the latitude of any type of variation. One way to get a good quality (predictability) score is to simply pass over anything that looks too difficult. Scope measurements counter this effect as they attempt to reflect both opportunities lost and innovations achieved. Lost opportunities are those occasions when a variation could have provided some useful advantage but was declined. An opportunity must fit within the enterprise's mission or charter to qualify as an opportunity. Innovations are an indicator of good range. Lost opportunities are an indicator of poor range. Both are indications of poor range; they do not balance out.

Establishing an actual (or estimated or forecasted) range measurement requires an understanding of mission beyond strategy. In an absolute sense, it is bounded by none on the lower end and infinite on the upper end and measured then as a dimensionless or unitless ratio ranging from 0% to 100%. Useful range is generally bounded well short of infinity and focused on specific units of latitude, like the range in car unit production that could be provided to a market at profit. The focus on variation renders various issues in terms of a system's operating dynamics, forcing us to develop an understanding relative to the real operating environment, as opposed to the hypothetical ideal environment where everything works as planned. An automotive assembly process can be designed to meet forecast; or it can be designed to adjust gracefully when forecasts don't materialize, accommodate transparent next-model launch tests and transitions, and even weather a no-warning major supplier failure.

More than one Japanese automaker sets a strategic target of any car in any plant, to meet uncertain demand. This entailed conscious plant design to permit a high-demand model, whatever it might be, to be inserted in additional plants along with whatever else they were producing. One U.S. automaker looked at the cost of such an open-ended strategy and decided the problem was bounded at a more reasonable level. Historical data showed that a car producible in three plants should be able to meet virtually any unexpected high demand and that a plant able to produce three different cars should be able to stay profitable in the face of virtually any unexpected low demand. These probabilistic assumptions leave very little exposure, greatly increase the range of potential variation, and are affordable. Designing plants for three cars and cars for three plants may well add a cost that would otherwise not occur, but this cost can be offset by the profits from meeting otherwise lost demand and by the elimination of losses in plants operating below breakeven.

 Range is closely associated with the concept of variability and often is associated with the expectation that variability is costly. There was also a time when it was known that quality would be costly as well, until people realized that cost added to boost quality was more than recovered from reduced cost in other areas like scrap, warranty repairs, and sales (replacing lost customers).

Range is the principal difference between flexibility and variability. Flexibility is a characteristic fixed at specification time; it is a range of planned variation to anticipated contingencies. Variation ability or variability, on the other hand, is capable of dealing effectively with unanticipated variation. At the heart of range is the architectural issue: rather than design something that anticipates a defined range of requirements, or 10 or 12 contingencies, design it so it can be deconstructed and reconstructed as needed. Design it with a reusable, reconfigurable and scalable strategy. Range is only a statement about the magnitude of variation that can be accommodated: it is useless if it can't be done in time to matter, at a cost that is reasonable, and with a surety of completeness. Thus, for any element to be truly proficient at variation, it must have some effective capability across all four dimensions of time, cost, quality, and scope.

5.3.6 FRAMEWORK FOR ASSESSING VARIATIONS

Range is not hard to measure once you select the important issues. You specify precisely what to measure (production capacity, rapid staffing ability) and how to measure it (units of product per month, hiring ramp-up). What may be difficult, however, is understanding where the important competitive issues lie and where to set the boundaries—this is what strategy and mission are really all about. Right at the outset, the most vocalized variation issues were concerned with meeting production demand when it soared and introducing new products when the market hit a downturn; these are identified as two distinctly different response situations or domains of variation. Variation proficiency is now recognized in a variety of variation domains:

- On the proactive side:
  - Creation (make something new)
  - Improvement (make it better)
  - Migration (move on to something completely different)
  - Modification (change its capabilities)
- On the reactive side:
  - Correction (fix it)
  - Dispersion (deal with its variance)
  - Expansion (get more of it)
  - Reconfiguration (reorganize it)

This framework offers more than just a vocabulary. At the enterprise level, it is a way of categorizing the strategic issues faced by the company, seeing how they group, and sensing where difficulties clump together in certain domains but not others. This helps prioritize improvement strategies. Below the enterprise level, in any of the various business systems, the framework provides a structure for focused measurement and analysis. It also provides a context framework for defining problems and opportunities in terms of their dynamic operational environment from a consistent and comprehensive perspective. The framework establishes requirements for solutions and evaluation criteria for sorting among competing solutions and strategies.

5.4   GENERATION OF VARIATIONS

An enterprise's ability to innovate or vary relies on a process of experimentation whereby new products and services are created and existing ones are improved. A major development project involves literally thousands of experiments, all with the same objective: to learn, through rounds of organized testing, whether the product concept or proposed technical solution holds promise for addressing a problem or need. The information derived from each round is the incorporated into the next set of experiments and so on until the final product ultimately emerges. Experimentation is the means through which various technologies like simulation and computer modeling and combinatorial technologies enable rapid and inexpensive generation and testing of new product (or service or experience) possibilities.

All experimentation generates knowledge; the knowledge, however, comes as much from failure as it does from success. Thus, experimentation encompasses both success and failure; this emphasizes the fact that in experiments, learning what does not work is as important as what does work. But a relentless enterprise focus on success makes true experimentation all too rare. Because experiments that reveal what does not work are frequently deemed failures, tests may be delayed, rarely carried out, or simply positioned toward verification of a predefined and predetermined results. Consequently, if there is a problem in the experiment, the feedback on what does not work comes effectively so late that not only can costs of corrective measures spiral out of control but with the emphasis on *getting it right first time* may render opportunities for variation to be lost forever. However, when managers understand that effective experiments are supposed to reveal what does not work early, that is, *getting it wrong first time*, the knowledge gained can then benefit the next round of experimentation and lead to more varied ideas and concepts—early *failures* can fuel more powerful successes faster. Because few resources have been committed in these early stages, decision making is still flexible, and other approaches can be experimented with quickly. In the absence of learning from failure, because of experimental capacity constraints and/or the number of possible iterations, experimentation itself becomes a bottleneck to variation. In fact, new information-based technologies have driven down the marginal costs of experimentation, just as they have decreased the marginal costs in some production and distribution systems. An experimental system that integrates new information-based technologies does more than lower costs; it also increases the opportunities for variation (innovation, imitation, etc.). Thus, some technologies can make existing experimental activities more efficient, while others introduce entirely new ways of discovering novel concepts and/or solutions.

Traditionally, the high cost of experimentation has limited generation of variations (innovations, imitations, etc.). Statistical methods of designing experiments have helped companies get more out of each experiment—making them more efficient. Alternatively, new technologies like computer simulation and modeling are lifting the cost constraint by changing the economics of experimentation. These technologies drastically reduce the cost and time to free up testing capacity as well as make possible what-if experiments that in the past have been either prohibitively expensive or nearly impossible to carry out. They amplify the impact of learning, thus creating the potential for higher R&D performance and breakthrough products. Thus, not only are experimentation and variation intimately linked, but it is only through the process of experimentation that new technologies can generate higher R&D performance, variation, and new ways of creating value for customers. But mastering and integrating new technologies also pose grave challenges. In particular, processes and people limit the impact of new technologies, organizational interfaces can get in the way of experimentation cycles, and technologies often change faster than human and organizational behavior. Unlocking the potential of new technologies requires changes in the processes, organization, and management of variation.

Learning from experiments is maximized when they can link cause and effect while minimizing the impact of noise and other factors that obscure the phenomenon they are interested in; the rate of learning is influenced by a number of factors, some effecting the process and others affecting how the process is managed. Experiments can be of different types: observation entails waiting for variations to be induced and then carefully studying the presented phenomenon; exploration assumes more proactive role but still lacks the manipulative character of an experiment; and, finally, experimentation entails directed effort to manipulate or change variables of interest. In an ideal experiment, experimenters separate an independent (the cause) and dependent (the effect) variable and then manipulate the independent variable to observe variations in the dependent variable. The manipulation, followed by careful observations and analysis, then gives rise to learning about relationships between cause and effect, which, ideally, can be applied to or tested in other settings. In the real world, things are much more complex: environments are constantly changing, linkages between variables are complex and poorly understood, and often the variables are themselves uncertain or unknown. Therefore, the environment has to be treated as a collective of all such variables and we must iterate multiple times between the experiments.

An experiment consists of four stages, namely, design, build, run, and analyze. During the design stage, a firm defines what it expects to learn from the experiment; during the build stage, prototypes and testing apparatus that are needed to conduct the experiment are constructed; during the run stage, the experiment is conducted in either controlled conditions or a real setting; finally, during the analyze stage, the experimenter analyzes the result to compare it against the expected outcome and adjusts the understanding of what is under investigation. Most learning happens during the analyze stage and forms the basis of the experiments in the next cycle: effective learning depends on many factors that require strategic and managerial commitment and organizational flexibility.

The factors that are common across all experimentations are the following:

- Type: the degree to which the experiment manipulates the variable(s) ranging from observation, exploration, to full experimentation
- Capacity: the number of same fidelity experiments that can be carried out at a time
- Execution strategy: the degree to which experiments are run in parallel or series
- Fidelity: the degree to which a model and its testing conditions represent a final product, process, or service under actual use conditions

- Cost: total cost of experimentation including expenses for prototype
- Iteration time: time for planning another experiment
- Noise: the degree to which the variable of interest is obscured by experimental noise

Today's processes, organization, and management of variation often impede experimentation. When new technologies amplify the impact of learning, managing experimentation becomes very important:

1. Anticipate and exploit early information through *front-loaded* variation process: New technologies are most powerful when they are deployed to test what works and what does not work as early as possible—the *frontloading* effect. These experiments can reveal what does not work before substantial resources are committed and design decisions are locked in. With more experimentation capability during early development, teams are also more likely to experiment with many ideas and concepts that will ultimately result in much more enhanced products and services.
2. Experiment frequently but do not overload your organization: Experimenting more frequently reveals what does and does not work with minimal delay and problems can be addressed right away, thus minimizing the cost of redesign. In contrast, the quest for efficiency combined with an incomplete understanding or measurement of the benefits of early problem solving has been driving out experimentation.
3. Integrate new and traditional technologies to unlock performance: New technologies like computer simulation may not achieve more than 70% or 80% of their traditional counterpart's technical performance—but they can achieve that much more quickly. Thus, by combining new and traditional technologies, enterprise can avoid performance gap while simultaneously benefiting from cheaper and faster experimentation.
4. Organize for rapid experimentation: Rapid feedback shapes new ideas by reinforcing, modifying, or complementing existing knowledge. Thus, teams must be organized for rapid feedback across functional groups in order to speed up learning from experimentation.
5. Fall early and often but avoid *mistakes*: Early failures are not only desirable but also needed to eliminate unfavorable options quickly and build on the learning they generate. However, failures should not be confused with mistakes. Failures can be desirable outcome of an experiment, whereas mistakes should be avoided as they produce little new or useful information and are therefore without value.
6. Manage projects as experiments: Projects are powerful mechanisms for managing change, knowledge creation, and the introduction of new technologies and processes; projects themselves can be conceived as experiments. Thus, learning from experiments, like projects, can be maximized in terms of following factors: type of experiment, fidelity, cost, iteration time, capacity, sequential and parallel strategies, and signal-to-noise ratio.

Development strategies are optimized around the cost and time of making design iterations and variations. Environments in which iterations are difficult and costly inhibit experimentation and foster strategies that emphasize planning and risk minimization. In contrast, the ability to iterate and make variations quickly and at low cost invites experimentation and tolerates risk and rapid variation. These two different development approaches give rise to two different variation cultures. In one culture, the risk of variation is eschewed and frozen specifications drive incremental experiments that are predominantly confined to computer simulation; this linear specification-driven development is a rational response to the constraints that technology poses: variations are costly and should be avoided. In the other culture, changes are considered natural and experimentation is invited as a way of resolving customer need uncertainty and technical uncertainty. This evolutionary experimentation-driven development starts with a specification that is good enough and uses computer simulation combined with frequent prototype iterations to address problems as quickly as they occur. The outstanding characteristic of this approach is more frequent prototyping.

Highlight of the observed pattern in product requirements: fewer than 5% products have a complete design specification before beginning product design.

Two important areas where advances in technology have dramatically decreased the marginal cost of experimentation are computer modeling and simulation and combinatorial and high-throughput testing technologies. Simulation is the representation of selected characteristics of the behavior of one physical or abstract system by another system. In a digital computer system, simulation is done by a software that uses mathematical models through equations and/or approximations that represent the behavior of the system. The rapid emergence of semiconductor industry accelerated the trend toward low-cost *digital* experiments and the advancement of tools and methodologies. Computer simulation involves representing experimental objects and experimental environments in digital form (through numerical models) and then simulating their interaction by means of a virtual experiment; for example, one might model an automobile and a crash barrier inside the computer, simulate a virtual crash, and then calculate the effects of the crash on the structure of the car via finite element analysis. The steady decrease in computational cost per Moore's law and the associated knowledge in modeling complex phenomenon allowed for rapid increases in simulation capacity. These simulation models will not only allow researchers to run experiments faster and cheaper but will also make possible experiments that cannot be done today because of practical or ethical issues. Similarly, combinatorial technologies have dramatically reduced the cost and time of generating physical artifacts of an idea or concept, thus enabling many combinations to be generated in a very short period of time. Thus, rapid prototyping is usually an inexpensive and fast way to build models that preserve the advantages of working in the physical world and thus overcome any limitations that simulation may have.

5.4.1 Rational Drug Design

In the discovery of new drugs, cost and time of generating some drug candidate and its related testing have dropped dramatically; combinatorial chemistry (combichem) and high-throughput screening methods enable drug developers to quickly generate numerous variations simultaneously and screen them at a small cost fraction of traditional tests. The three-phase drug development and approval process begins with preclinical phase devoted to the discovery of one or few *lead* chemical compounds that appear to hold sufficient promise as drugs to merit investment in clinical testing. The second phase, clinical development, is dedicated to determining and documenting the safety and efficacy of the proposed drugs. The final phase involves regulatory New Drug Approval (NDA) review processes of the clinical trial outcome. The entire process represents a long and costly commitment.

The goal of drug discovery or drug design is to discover or create a molecule that will bind to a specific receptor. Drugs achieve their effect by binding with very specific molecule or enzymes that are present in the human body or disease-causing agents such as bacteria, fungi, and viruses. The discovery process involves either trying out many candidate molecules until one finds one that binds properly with the target disease receptor (without any prior knowledge of its structure) or one can first determine the structure of the target disease receptor (with biophysical methods) and then attempt to evaluate and select a molecule that will bind to it. Until the 1970s, lacking the ability to determine the structure of the target disease receptor, most pharmaceutical firms adopted the first approach—have continued with it since then—by setting up a systematic trial-and-error system called as *mass screening*, wherein masses of chemical compounds are applied one at a time to the screen receptor with a goal of identifying compounds that cause the screen to exhibit binding to the receptor (or killing of the disease-causing bacterium).

The sources of input materials are either proprietary archival library of known chemical compounds that have been collected by the firms over the years or extract of plants, microorganisms, and animals, each of which contain tens of thousands of unknown chemical compounds. In the former case, the known compounds are tested against the target disease screen one by one for the desired effect; in the latter case, the entire extract is tested against the screen. If the desired effect is observed, the compound responsible for that effect must then be isolated via a complex series of fractionations and retesting. Many a times, the identified compound may display unacceptable side effects. The drug discovery process then creates and tests a number of variations (or analogs) of the identified molecule—by adding, exchanging, or removing a chemical group—in order to find one or more that appear to have all the attributes needed for a successful drug. This lead compound is then advanced into the clinical development phase where its effects are tested on humans.

> To discriminate sharply between very similar target disease receptors, the pharmaceutical companies have to develop as much as 6,000 analogs for each successful drug that makes to the market—as compared with more than 150,000 compounds in the archival libraries. Of these, only 1000 compounds make it to more extensive trials in vitro (outside living organisms in settings such as test tubes), of which 20 are then tested even more extensively in vivo (in the body of living organism such as a mouse), of which less than 10 make it to clinical trials with humans.

5.4.2 COMBINATORIAL CHEMISTRY FOR GENERATION OF VARIATIONS

Until the late 1980s, leading pharmaceutical firms could test and analyze about 20 chemical compounds per week against a drug target. As the synthesis of compound prototypes was very costly and time consuming, this rate was perhaps adequate; but it was not adequate enough to screen through all the compounds in the archival library to tap into knowledge and information that has been accumulated over decades from other projects in the form of diverse chemicals: this represented a serious bottleneck to drug discovery. However, in the last 10 years, using combichem, firms have been enabled to quickly generate numerous variations simultaneously around a few lead compounds, which in turn led to the need for screening all those generated compounds quickly. So laboratories developed test-tube-based screening methodologies that could be automated. This technology called *high-throughput screening* not only enabled screening of all members of the archival library simultaneously, but it also enabled firms to test these very libraries for promising new leads at the same time. Combichem will complement rather than completely replace the traditional chemistry. The purity and diversity of compounds generated via combichem have been lower when compared to traditional synthetic chemistry. All major pharmaceutical companies are using combichem and traditional synthesis in concert with other technologies, and the companies that are best able to manage the new and mature technologies together so that they fully complement each other have the greatest opportunity to achieve the higher gains in productivity and variations.

5.4.3 CO-CREATION

Product or service definition, development, and delivery are often difficult because the *need* information (what the customer wants) resides with the customer and the *solution* information lies with the provider; the translation of these needs into suitable solutions is fraught with innumerable hazards. Traditionally, the onus has been on the provider to collect the customer need information through various means, including market and field research. The process can be time consuming, costly, and often erroneous or misleading because customer needs are often complex, subtle, and fast changing, thus rendering the gathered information to be invalid, incorrect, incomplete, or ambiguous. Since customers often firm up their needs while using new products or services, tapping into the innovativeness and imagination of customers can generate tremendous value. Technologies, by deploying user-friendly toolkits, enable management via the value co-creation systems and processes to lever possibly the largest and most effective source of experimentation capacity: the customer. Co-creation of products or services could not only result in faster development of offerings better suited to their needs, but unfettered by any preconceived notions, it could generate variations that providers cannot even imagine today. Such co-created and customized offerings can result in more satisfied customers since the customers are able to customize the offerings to their specific requirements and preferences. However, toolkits may not satisfy every type of customer because co-creation systems or even mass customization systems cannot handle every type of design or configuration. Toolkits create products that are typically not as sophisticated as those developed by experienced engineers at a manufacturer using conventional methods. Above all, if homogeneous markets require standard products, the traditional approach of deep market research probably gives the most robust results.

5.5 McKINSEY 7S MODEL

This section discusses the McKinsey 7S model that was created by the consulting company McKinsey & Company in the early 1980s. Since then, it has been widely used by practitioners and academics alike in analyzing hundreds of companies. We explain each of the seven components of the model and the links between them. It also includes practical guidance and advice for the students to analyze companies using this model.

The McKinsey 7S model was named after a consulting company, McKinsey & Company, which has conducted applied research in business and industry. All of the authors worked as consultants at McKinsey & Company; in the 1980s, they used the model to analyze over 70 large enterprises. The McKinsey 7S Framework was created as a recognizable and easily remembered model in business. The seven variables, which the authors term *levers*, all begin with the letter "S."

These seven variables include structure, strategy, systems, skills, style, staff, and shared values. Structure is defined as the skeleton of the company or the organizational chart. The authors describe strategy as the plan or course of action in allocating resources to achieve identified goals over time. The systems are the routine processes and procedures followed within the company. Staff are described in terms of personnel categories within the company (e.g., engineers), whereas the skills variable refers to the capabilities of the staff within the company as a whole. The way in which key managers behave in achieving organizational goals is considered to be the style variable; this variable is thought to encompass the cultural style of the company. The shared values variable, originally termed superordinate goals, refers to the significant meanings or guiding concepts that organizational members share. The shape of the model was also designed to illustrate the interdependency of the variables. This is illustrated by the model also being termed as the *managerial molecule*. While the authors thought that other variables existed within complex companies, the variables represented in the model were considered to be of crucial importance to managers and practitioners (Peters and Waterman).

Table 5.2 shows that the McKinsey 7S model involves seven interdependent factors, which are categorized as either *hard* or *soft* elements:

1. *Hard* elements are easier to define or identify and management can directly influence them: these are strategy statements, organization charts and reporting lines, and formal processes and IT systems.
2. *Soft* elements, on the other hand, can be more difficult to describe and are less tangible and more influenced by culture. However, these soft elements are as important as the hard elements if the organization is going to be successful.

TABLE 5.2
McKinsey 7S Model *Hard* and *Soft* Elements

Hard Value Elements	Soft Value Elements
Strategy	Shared values
Structure	Skills
Systems	Style
	Staff

The analysis of several companies using the model revealed that American companies tend to focus on those variables that they feel they can change (e.g., structure, strategy, and systems) while neglecting the other variables. These other variables (e.g., skills, style, staff, and shared values) are considered to be *soft* variables. Japanese and a few excellent American companies are reportedly successful at linking their structure, strategy, and systems with the soft variables. The authors have concluded that a company cannot merely change one or two variables to change the whole company. For long-term benefit, they feel that the variables should be changed to become more congruent as a system.

Figure 5.9 depicts the interdependency of the elements and indicates how a change in one affects all the others.

Let's look at each of the elements specifically:

- Strategy: the plan devised to maintain and build competitive advantage over the competition.
- Structure: the way the enterprise is structured and who reports to whom.
- Systems: the daily activities and procedures that staff members engage in to get the job done.
- Shared values: called *superordinate goals* when the model was first developed, these are the core values of the company that are evidenced in the corporate culture and the general work ethic.

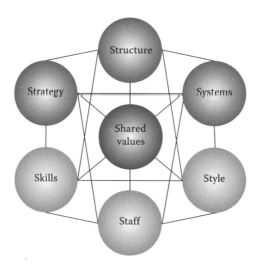

FIGURE 5.9 The McKinsey 7S model.

- Style: the style of leadership adopted.
- Staff: the employees and their general capabilities.
- Skills: the actual skills and competencies of the employees working for the company.

 The external environment is not mentioned in the McKinsey 7S Framework, although the authors do acknowledge that other variables exist and that they depict only the most crucial variables in the model. While alluded to in their discussion of the model, the notion of performance or effectiveness is not made explicit in the model.

5.5.1   Using the McKinsey 7S Model to Analyze a Company

A detailed case study or comprehensive material on the company under study is required to analyze it using the 7S model. This is because the model covers almost all aspects of the business and all major parts of the company. It is therefore highly important to gather as much information about the company as possible from all available sources such as organizational reports, news, and press releases although primary research, for example, using interviews along with literature review is more suited. The researcher also needs to consider a variety of facts about the 7S model. Some of these are detailed in the paragraphs to follow.

The seven components described earlier are normally categorized as soft and hard components. The hard components are the strategy, structure, and systems that are normally feasible and easy to identify in a company as they are normally well documented and seen in the form of tangible objects or reports such as strategy statements, corporate plans, organizational charts, and other documents. The remaining four Ss, however, are more difficult to comprehend. The capabilities, values, and elements of corporate culture, for example, are continuously developing and are altered by the people at work in the company. It is therefore only possible to understand these aspects by studying the company very closely, normally through observations and/or through conducting interviews. Some linkages, however, can be made between the hard and soft components. For example, it is seen that a rigid, hierarchical organizational structure normally leads to a bureaucratic organizational culture where the power is centralized at the higher management level.

It is also noted that the softer components of the model are difficult to change and are the most challenging elements of any change-management strategy. Changing the culture and overcoming the staff resistance to changes, especially the one that alters the power structure in the company and the inherent values of the company, is generally difficult to manage. However, if these factors are altered, they can have a great impact on the structure, strategies, and systems of the company. Over the last few years, there has been a trend to have a more open, flexible, and dynamic culture in the company where the employees are valued and innovation encouraged. This is, however, not easy to achieve where the traditional culture is been dominant for decades and therefore many companies are in a state of flux in managing this change. What compounds their problems is their focus on only the hard components and neglecting the softer issues identified in the model, which is without doubt a recipe for failure.

Similarly, when analyzing an company using the 7S model, it is too easy to fall into the trap of only concentrating on the hard factors as they are readily available from companies' reports. It is important to address the real dynamics of the company's soft aspects as these underlying values in reality drive the companies by affecting the decision making at all levels. For being more effective, it is essential to analyze in depth the cultural dimension of the structure, processes, and decision made in a company. Moreover, it is sufficient to analyze these components not only individually but also collectively: how they interact and affect each other. This will enable in understanding how one component is affected by changes in the other. Especially, the *cause and effect* analyses of soft and hard components would provide insight that could result in an in-depth understanding of what caused the change.

5.6 EXTENDED 9S MODEL

5.6.1 SHARED VALUES

These are appropriate culture and beliefs that support the needs and environment of the business. These are ideas of what are right and desirable. For example,

- Quality and customer satisfaction (John Lewis)
- Entrepreneurialism (Virgin)
- Customer service (IBM)
- Innovative culture (HP/3M)
- Willingness to change

5.6.2 STRATEGY

This is the clear and communicated direction and goals for the enterprise supported by a coherent set of actions aimed at gaining a sustainable advantage over competition. The orientation of each other factor must be evaluated and changes introduced to ensure compatibility with the strategy.

5.6.3 STRUCTURE

This is the management and overall organizational structure to match the future needs. For example,

- Responsibilities and accountabilities defined
- Clear, relevant, and simple
- Provides for career development and motivation of staff
- Flexible and responsive to change
- Organizational hierarchy

5.6.4 STUFF

- Product
- Service
- Experience

5.6.5 STYLE

This also reflects aspects of culture. It is linked to the management paradigm—*the way we do things here*. For example,

- Autocratic versus democratic
- Concentration on consensus building to ensure commitment to change
- Enthusiasm
- Focus on external achievement and continuous progress
- Integrity
- *Open* culture

5.6.6 STAFF

These are appropriate resources to meet the demands of the existing business and future strategy. For example,

- Ability to recruit, develop, and retain staff of sufficient quality
- Staff retention
- High fliers versus team players
- Quality of resources
- Old versus young
- Levels of competence
- Creative versus analytical

5.6.7 SKILLS

These are the capabilities possessed by the enterprise as a whole as distinct from those of individuals. Some companies perform extraordinary feats with ordinary people. For example,

- Strategic thinking ability
- Responsiveness to change
- Ability to analyze based on fact not opinion
- Ability to turn ideas into action
- Product development capability
- Entrepreneurial focus
- Marketing competence
- Production control

5.6.8 SYSTEMS

These are the techniques, working procedures, computer systems, communication systems, etc. They may be formal or informal *customary practices*. These are processes through which things get done on a day-to-day basis. For example,

- Management information systems
- Customer information systems
- Authority levels
- Manpower planning

5.6.9 SEQUENCE

- EOQ
- Safety stock/cycle stock/reorder point
- Production planning
- Material requirements planning
- Master production scheduling (MPS)
- Master planning
- Final assembly scheduling
- Lot sizing
- Shop floor scheduling
- Finite capacity scheduling (FCS)
- Rough cut capacity planning

- Capacity requirements planning
- Supply management
- Demand planning
- Demand-based management
- Distribution requirements planning
- Inventory deployment
- Adaptive supply chain networks
- APS
- Order profitability
- Order sourcing
- Hierarchical planning
- Strategic planning
- Tactical planning
- Sales and operations planning
- Workforce planning
- Supply planning
- Collaborative planning (and CPFR)
- Operational planning/scheduling
- Shop floor control
- Warehouse management
- Pick wave optimization
- Available to promise/capable to promise
- TPS
- JIT
- Kanban
- Zero inventories
- Drum–buffer–rope scheduling (theory of constraints)
- Pull versus push inventory management
- Transportation management
- Load building
- Carrier assignment
- Routing
- Vendor-managed inventory/continuous replenishment

5.7 SUMMARY

This chapter introduces the concept of Built-for-Variation enterprises that enable companies to seek a string of temporary competitive advantages through an approach to strategy, organization design, products or services, etc. that assumes variation is normal. We then discussed the core and the context at the variations at all levels, namely, product, enterprise, and industry level. Per the model proposed in the book, companies actively seek out changes or variations on a continuous basis by testing out a continuum of opportunities and advantages with failures being learning experiences that enable them to tackle unexpected pitfalls or disasters later. We discussed the process of generating useful variations including the procedure to weed out variations that are not acceptable. In the latter part of the chapter, we refer to the McKinsey 7S model that inspired this book's extended 9S framework—consisting of shared values, strategy, structure, staff, stuff, style, systems, skills, and sequence—that was discussed next.

6 Sources of Variations

This chapter looks at sources of variations that an enterprise can employ for achieving business excellence, namely, inventions, imitations, and innovations. The chapter has three parallel running tracks of subsections that describe examples from domains (and functions) ranging from automobiles to electronics to computers onto the phenomenon of the Internet and the World Wide Web (WWW). These illustrate the kind of variations that are instrumental in bringing about the evolution of markets and enterprises.

The three sections are as follows:

1. Invention or pioneering variations: Lenoir internal combustion engine, AT&T Bell Labs germanium transistor, Ford production system, Sony pocket transistor radio, 3M Thermofax, Psion PDAs, Xerox Alto and MITS Altair, and CERN WWW
2. Imitation variations: Otto four-stroke-cycle internal combustion engine, TI silicon transistor, TPS, Sony Walkman, Xerox 914 and Canon copiers, Apple Newton and Palm PDAs, IBM PC, and Yahoo!
3. Innovation variations: Wankel rotary engine, TI ICs, theory of constraints (TOC), Apple iPod, Xerox laser printers, Blackberry PDAs, Apple II and Toshiba laptop, and eBay

6.1 ENIGMA OF XEROX

But before getting onto these tracks, we look at the enigma of Xerox to highlight the challenges faced while organizing for invention, imitations, or innovations within enterprises. The enigma of Xerox Palo Alto Research Center (PARC) is characterized by birthing of a host of breakthrough technologies and products coupled with dismal failure in commercializing most of them. By the late 1960s, Xerox's success with copiers had transformed the firm into a giant, highly profitable corporation, with a virtual monopoly over the copier market. As a result, Xerox strove to ensure that its copiers remained the very best in the market: research at the laboratory at Webster, New York, and other facilities focused on fine-tuning the current portfolio of copiers to make them faster, more reliable, and less costly. However, success with copiers had brought a large measure of complacency, bureaucracy, and short-term thinking. Such an approach was more conducive to business as usual than to a creative search for new technologies for the office of the future. The atmosphere at Webster was not inspiring; nearly all of the research was geared to improving current products; there was little attempt to bring in new research ideas or methods or technologies. In large enterprises, an important hindrance to enterprise variations is managerial preoccupation with current customers and competitors. As a result, managers get preoccupied with the present technology and customers at the cost of emerging markets, causing them to overlook promising innovations that enable a firm to leapfrog competitors by harnessing new technologies for emerging mass markets. Thus, preoccupation with the present may lead to loss of a promising future.

Xerox's CEO Joe Wilson was concerned regarding the potential of digital technologies replacing optical imaging. Having seen how xerography rendered coated paper and carbon copying obsolete, Wilson feared that some new technology would arise to make xerography obsolete too. Xerox's president at that time, Peter McColough, was concerned that Xerox's reliance on perfecting the old technology of optics for its existing line of copiers would not enable it to withstand competition for more than a decade.

Bureaucracy can be a formidable barrier to enterprise variations. Large successful firms tend to have a large staff to manage their current business; this requires establishing rules, routines, and procedures for evaluating variations and making decisions, resulting in bureaucracy that slows the review processes and tends to kill innovations. Autonomy can be a great antidote to bureaucracy and results from the creation of small units with an independent mission, goal, and budget. Guided by the right vision, they can quickly identify and respond to emerging markets without interference from central bureaucracies. Similarly, another hindrance to variation is a firm's emphasis on institutionalized talent over individual talent, which is a huge dampener on the process of birthing breakthrough products. A firm's talent is the strongest force it can marshal in pursuit of variation. A firm can sustain the momentum of variation by regularly hiring fresh talent from the market. It then needs to provide an autonomous and supportive atmosphere to enable unfettered collaboration, cooperation, and coordination to stimulate the fusion and cross-fertilization of ideas. Such a context is essential to the development of novel ideas for successful variation. An equally important challenge for all enterprises is retaining creative talent.

At that time, digital and computer technologies held great promise. McColough established the PARC to realize Wilson's vision of the *office of the future*; it was a research laboratory dedicated to fundamental and advanced research in the basic science of digital technologies and the development of leading-edge products for computer age. He envisioned the new lab as a prestigious center of path-breaking research, such as AT&T's Bell Labs and IBM's Watson Research Center at Yorktown Heights.

> PARC was successful in hiring a core of visionary directors, scientists, and engineers for the center. One of the early hires was Robert Taylor, who was the director of the computer research division of the U.S. Defence Department's Advanced Research Projects Agency (ARPA) during the time it launched ARPAnet. He was a firm believer in the vision of future potential of networking and interactive computing; he had a vision of the computer being, more than a number-crunching machine, a much more effective communication and interaction device. This was the vision that inspired the ARPAnet and that was brought to PARC by Taylor. As a director of ARPA, he was familiar with the best researchers in the field; in a short time, he brought many outstanding researches to PARC and continued to motivate and direct them during the next decade.

In PARC, Xerox created the ideal atmosphere for radical variations, namely, a stimulating environment, minimal structure, generous funds, and outstanding talent recruited and directed by visionary leaders. The research center was approved and officially opened on July 1, 1970, in Palo Alto, California. For the next 10 years, Xerox management supported it generously but let it operate independently from any other part of the corporation; by the end of the decade, PARC's budget reached about $30 million with a staff of about 400.

PARC surpassed all these expectations beyond any measure:

1. Laser printer: Gary Starkweather developed the forerunner of desktop laser printer and laser copiers in 1971. This was 4 years before IBM introduced its own laser printer. And today, HP is the market leader in this category.
2. Smalltalk: Alan Kay developed Smalltalk, an object-oriented language that was a precursor to Java.
3. Alto: Ed McCreight, Chuck Thacker, Butler Lampson, Bob Sproull, and David Boggs jointly developed Alto PC in 1973, which was 2 years before MITS commercialized the Altair.

4. Tiled windows: Bit-mapped graphics that allowed overlapping windows, pop-up menus, and graphics on a desktop monitor was developed in 1974; this was 8 years before Apple incorporated these features in Lisa and 11 years before Microsoft included them in its first version of the Windows OS. OS for PCs became a huge category in its own right.

5. Ethernet: Bob Metcalfe developed a system for networking PCs in 1971 and was used to support a network of computers and printers by 1975; with time, networking itself became a huge category in itself.

6. Gypsy: Developed a graphical word-processing program with true fonts (with *what-you-see-is-what-you-get* display) in 1975; with time, word processing itself became a huge category in itself.

7. NoteTaker: A suitcase-size portable computer was developed in 1978; this was 3 years before the introduction of Osborne.

8. Gyricon: Nick Sheridon developed an e-paper in the 1970s.

Gyricon consisted of polyethylene spheres embedded in a transparent silicon sheet. Depending on whether a negative or positive charge is applied, the spheres would translate into a pixel that emits either a black or white appearance, thus looking a lot like normal paper. The Amazon Kindle and Barnes & Noble Nook are both examples of implementations of e-ink technology; they implement a type of technology known as electrophoretic display. This is essentially an information display that forms images by rearranging charged pigment particles using an applied electric field. The Kindle and Nook devices use a hi-res active matrix display constructed from electrophoretic imaging film manufactured by E Ink Corporation.

6.2 INVENTION OR PIONEERING VARIATIONS

The firm that pioneers a market is believed to have enormous advantages in terms of success, enduring market share, and long-term market leadership. The order of entry is assumed to be the principal driver of enduring market leadership, which is termed as the pioneering advantage or first entrant advantage or first-mover advantage. Enduring leadership is of paramount importance to managers for several reasons. First, enduring brands are very attractive to consumers; such brands can charge premium prices while incurring relatively low marketing costs and capture a higher market share. In contrast, new brands or those with smaller share must resort to costly marketing in order to get visibility and foothold into the market. Second, because of economies of scale, a market leader can operate at a more efficient volume and earn higher profits than a rival that commands a narrow market niche. Third, market leaders that dominate a category can easily extend their franchise into a new related category and dominate that too at comparatively much lower cost. Consequently, companies are advised to rush to enter, beat the competition, and be first to market; managers assume being first to market is critical to short- and long-term success. The first mover and only the first mover, the company that acts decisively while the others dither, has a true opportunity to gain a head start over its competitors and gains market share at the cost of their competitors:

1. Ease of recall: The leading product or service (or brand or company) in any category is always the first company that comes first into the prospect's mind. It is also the name that is repeated most often and is most deeply embedded in their memory. The simplest reason offered in favor of pioneers is the ease of recalling the first company name in a category.

2. Brand loyalty: This also becomes the basis of comparison for new, later entrants. If the new entrants are different, they may not win favors with the customers; if they are similar,

they may be dismissed as me-too followers of the pioneers. Thus, the pioneer has the great advantage of shaping preferences in favor of its unique formulation. As a result, it would develop an enduring preference or loyalty for its specific formulation. Brand loyalty is a preference for a brand that develops from a consumer's prior purchase of the brand.

3. Consumer inertia: Brand loyalty generates consumer inertia that refers to the reluctance of consumers to switch brands except for compelling reasons. Such inertia can reinforce the endurance of pioneering brands.

4. Economies of experience: This refers to reduction in costs or improvement in quality that accrues to a firm as it gains experience producing and marketing a product. Costs decline with experience primarily because workers learn to produce more efficiently or with more efficient technology or with cheaper materials or with less waste. This can give pioneers a cost advantage over later entrants so that pioneers can either sell the product at a lower price, or gain a higher margin themselves, or reinvest these profits to keep ahead of later entrants into the market. In either case, pioneers have a competitive advantage over later entrants. For example, the experience Toyota has accumulated with auto production has resulted in Toyota's dominance in the automobile market; this experience enables it to produce at a lower cost, introduce new designs earlier, and earn higher margins and profits on a series of newly introduced products (or services).

5. Resource mobilization: Because pioneers are the first to the market, they are in the best position to quickly corner significant resources and deny them accordingly for the subsequent rivals. By entering first, pioneers can corner the best resources, such as rich supplies of raw materials, best suppliers, large consumer segments, and best distributors.

6. Patent barriers: A patent is a legal ownership over a design that prevents a rival from using that design for a set period of time (which in the United States is 20 years from the first U.S. filing for most common patents). The goal of patents is to reward companies that carry out the costly and inherently risky research for a new product (while preventing competitors from replicating these designs and products), giving them a monopoly in that product's market for a reasonable time to recover and profit from their investments. For example, Xerox held so many patents in the copier market that it seemed impossible for others to compete.

6.2.1 Lenoir Internal Combustion Engine

Etienne Lenoir was the first to build an internal combustion engine and to commercially produce the engine. Prior to Lenoir's work, inventors had concentrated on perfecting steam engines, which created pressure and heat outside of the cylinder. The heat then entered the cylinder and moved the piston. Several of these inventors had drawn diagrams of an engine within which the combustion would occur, but no internal combustion engine had actually been built. Lenoir envisioned an engine that would create its power by using a combustible gas mixture. In 1858, Lenoir invented a two-stroke internal combustion engine that used an electric spark ignition and was fueled by illuminating gas (also known as coal gas). The engine was very similar to a double-acting steam engine; however, Lenoir had made important modifications to the engine, namely, having the combustion occur inside the engine.

In 1859, while he was working as a consulting engineer for Gauthier etCie, he succeeded in building the first internal combustion engine. Lenoir's internal combustion engine had stemmed valves through which a mixture of coal gas and air entered the engine. The mixture was drawn into the engine by the movement of a piston operated by a flywheel. Once the piston was partially drawn down in the cylinder, an electric spark ignited the gas and air mixture. The combustion then forced the piston the rest of the way down the cylinder. The flywheel then returned the piston to its original firing position. The valves that let the air into the cylinder also provided for the escape of the gas created by the explosion. The single-cylinder two-stroke engine fired on every revolution of the crankshaft. The engine was noisy and produced a considerable amount of pollutants. It was primarily useful for running pumps and small machines. Lenoir obtained a patent for his internal combustion engine in January 1960.

The engine that Lenoir built was relatively weak and fairly large in size. It required 18 L of the gas mixture to produce a horsepower rating of two. Although his engine had a number of drawbacks, it was very reliable and was particularly suited to run pumps and other small machinery. With a capital of two million francs, he established a Paris-based company named Société des Moteurs Lenoir. He succeeded in selling more than 500 engines in France, Germany, and the United States during a 5-year period. A considerable additional number of the engines were built and sold in Germany as a licensed product.

His engine so impressed the German inventor Nikolaus August Otto that Otto did further research and eventually built a four-stroke internal combustion engine that ran on liquid fuel. Otto's engine became the standard engine for all liquid-fueled automobiles.

6.2.2 BELL LABS GERMANIUM TRANSISTOR

As extraordinary as the electron vacuum tube was, still it had technical limitations. The tubes were relatively big and used a lot of electricity to heat the anode (to boil off the electrons). By the middle of the twentieth century, there was a need for an electronic control—a device better than an electronic vacuum tube. The research laboratory that took on the task of replacing the electronic vacuum tube was AT&T Bell Laboratories (*Bell Labs*) in the United States. This was the challenge that Mervin Kelly undertook when he was appointed as director of research of the Bell Labs in 1936 and established a research group to search for a way to replace the electron vacuum tube. Kelly had gone to work for the Western Electric engineering department, after he had received a PhD in physics from the University of Chicago in 1918. As Kelly was trained as a physicist, he had been following the exciting developments in physics of that decade of the new quantum mechanics. Kelly saw a technological opportunity in quantum mechanics, as it was providing theory to explain the behavior of electrons in materials. Kelly envisioned that the new theory applied to certain semiconducting materials, germanium and silicon, might provide a way to invent something to replace the electron vacuum tube. Both these interesting materials had been called semiconducting materials, because their electronic conductivity was between the high conductivity of metals and the nonconductivity of dialectic materials. Kelly created a new research program in Bell Labs in solid-state physics—to explore the further use of the materials of germanium and silicon, understanding these with the new theory of quantum mechanics.

After the war, Kelly also appointed James Fisk as assistant director of physical research at Bell and told him to make a major and broad research effort in all aspects of solid-state physics and the underlying quantum mechanical theory. Fisk set up three research groups: physical electronics, electron dynamics, and solid-state physics. William Shockley and Stanley Morgan led the solid-state physics group. They hired John Bardeen and Walter Brattain, also new solid-state physicists, into the group. Shockley's group learned how to alter the conductivity of germanium by adding other atoms (doping) to the germanium crystal during its growth. Next, Shockley proposed an artifact (transistor) to control the current in doped germanium crystals—by applying an external electric field perpendicular to the direction of the current in the crystal. This was to work similarly to how a voltage applied to the grid of an electron vacuum tube controls the flow of electrons in the tube. The reason Shockley thought this was practical for germanium was that he had used the new quantum mechanics theory to calculate the expected effect of the controlling field on the electron flow. His calculations showed that it would be large enough to provide amplification. Amplification meant that the electron flow through germanium would closely follow the increases and decreases of the controlling field, thereby mimicking its form but with much larger amplitude.

They tried different configurations of the artifact. One of the configurations placed two closely spaced gold strips on the surface of a doped germanium crystal and an electrical connection on its base. Relative to that base, one gold strip had a positive voltage (called the emitter) and the other a negative voltage (called the collector). They applied a signal between emitter and base. There was sufficiently large amplification in the voltage between the collector and the base. It could do everything the old electron tube could do; they called this a transistor.

6.2.3 FORD PRODUCTION SYSTEM

A key event in the history of the U.S. auto industry was Henry Ford's introduction of his famous Model T. In 1902, the Olds Motor Works constructed and sold 2500 small two cylinder gasoline cars priced at $650. But Ford had in mind a large, untapped market—a car for people living on farms; around 1900, half of Americans still lived on the farm. The rural application required an inexpensive, reliable, and durable car, which also had a high clearance for dirt roads and easy maintainability by mechanically minded farmers. Ford wanted to build a practical, high-quality automobile priced at $450; his commercial strategy was price and his technical strategy was durability. The key to his technical innovation would be in the weight and strength of the chassis of the automobile structure. Material costs in the early automobile were a very large part of its cost. If Ford could reduce the weight of the Model T by at least one-half of competing designs, that technology would produce an enormous competitive advantage for his grand strategy of a *car for the people*. Ford's innovation for decreasing the weight of the automobile would be to use high-strength steel for the chassis, made of the element vanadium as an alloy. Henry Ford learned of this new steel when attending an automobile race. Making the chassis of this steel meant that he could reduce the weight of the chassis by nearly a third and get the same strength. It was a technological breakthrough that allowed Ford to imagine an innovative new product design.

Ford used the new vanadium steel to fabricate the chassis of the automobile, which reduced the overall weight of the Model T to about half that of then existing automobiles. In addition, Ford innovated the design by mounting the motor to this chassis with a three-point suspension. The prior practice had been to bolt the engine directly to the frame, and often, even the cylinder blocks of those engines were twisted in half by the enormous strain that occurred when the automobile bounced over a hole or rut. Ford also designed the Model T to be a *best of breed*. He used many other best ideas in other contemporary automobiles. For example, he replaced the then traditional dry-cell batteries for starting the car with a magnet-powered ignition (one cranked the Model T to start it). The Model T became a *dominant design* or *design standard* for automobile technology. Ford's Model T was the right product at the right time for the right market at the right price. Performance, timing, market, and price—these are the four factors for commercial success of Model T. Ford captured the auto market from 1908 to 1923, selling the majority of automobiles in the United States in those years.

Henry Ford's plants were organized according to the principle of flow, in particular single-product flow, that extended from the assembly line to all other processes and is singularly responsible to reduce the production lead time. Each part was attached to the moving chassis in order, from axles at the beginning to bodies at the end of the line. Since some parts took longer to attach than others, there must be differently spaced intervals between the deliveries of different parts along the line to maintain the evenness of the flow. This necessitated fine-tuning and rearrangement until the flow of parts and the speed and intervals along the assembly line meshed into a perfectly synchronized operation throughout all stages of production; it is the complete synchronization that accounts for the difference between an ordinary and a mass production assembly line. The organizing principle for achieving acceptable flow was timing. The challenge was to regulate the material flow so that just the right amount of each part would arrive at just the right time—making one part too few slowed the flow; making one part too many produced waste in the form of inventory. All materials entering the Ford plant went into operation and stayed there; they never came to rest until they had become part of a unit like an engine, an axle, or a body!

6.2.3.1 Principles of Flow

The vision of a flow line concentrated the attention of engineers on barriers to throughput. A barrier, or bottleneck, occurred wherever a machining operation could not process material at the same pace as the previous operation. The bottleneck machine was the activity that constrained not only the throughput at that machine but of the production system as a whole. Increasing the pace of work on any other machining activity could not increase output, only inventory. Henry Ford's assembly lines can be seen in this light: it was not the speed of the line that was revolutionary in concept; it was the idea of synchronizing production activities that effectively made the bottleneck to disappear so that bottlenecks did not constrain the whole production system. Unfortunately, all too often, the basis of mass production was mistakenly defined in terms of economies of size when it was really synchronized production that drove the rate of throughput up and the per unit costs down. Flow requires synchronization that, in turn, requires system integration. A conveyor line is a physical linkage system that integrates all of the requisite machining and other operations required to convert material into finished product. Before a conveyor can be connected, operations must be revamped one by one to equalize the cycle time for each constituent operation (a cycle time is the time it takes to complete a single operation, usually on a single piece part). Ford's engineers equalized cycle times for one-product flow so that the right parts would arrive at the right place at the right time; but they did not equalize cycle times for one-piece flow. The principle of flow yields a simple rule to concentrate the attention of engineers: equalize cycle times. Optimally, every operation on every part would match the standardized cycle time, the regulator of the pace of production flow. Failure to synchronize appears as inventory buildup in front of the slower operation. Any activity that takes more time does not meet the condition and requires engineering attention. The way to increase the flow of material is not to speed the pace of the conveyor belt but to identify the bottleneck, or slowest cycle time, and develop an action plan to eliminate it (see *TOC*). Ford's assembly line, from the perspective of flow, was primarily a signaling device or a visual information system for continuous advance in throughput performance; with the near-zero inventory system, the work assignments of engineers were signaled by material buildup on the line. It established a standard cycle time: the engineering task was to revamp each operation into conformity with the standard cycle time. Every time a bottleneck was removed, productivity and throughput advanced.

Ford did not achieve complete synchronization that would require one-piece flow or transfer lot sizes of one throughout the production system. In certain fabrication stages, Ford's shops produced in large lot sizes; lot sizes of more than one entail inventory if single car absorbs less than the lot size. In these cases, the process was fragmented into separated operations with the resulting interruption in flow and throughput inefficiencies. The reasons that Ford did not produce each of the 6000 distinct parts in the same cycle time are not hard to understand: engineers can direct the practice of equalizing cycle times, but it is best accomplished by a management system in which workers take on a quasitechnology management role that was completely alien to Ford. This would have necessitated a revolution in Ford's management philosophy.

 A failure to understand Ford's assembly line as a visual scheduling device, backed by standardized cycle times, is what led American volume producers to build huge, centralized planning and scheduling departments. Their efforts have effectively demonstrated that no amount of IT can avoid bottlenecks in such systems.

6.2.3.2 Implementation and Execution

Scheduling, too, was decentralized in Ford's system. At an output rate of 8000 cars per day, production of the Model A, with 6000 distinct parts, involved 48 million parts in motion. But instead of chaos, Ford's plants were orderly. Schedules were met and order was achieved by the application of the synchronization rule: equalize cycle times. Once the system was in synchrony, increasing the speed of the line, the operational efficiency of individual machines, or the intensity of work could not produce more cars. Production rates could be increased in two ways: reduce the cycle time of the slowest operation (successive elimination of bottlenecks) and driving down the standardized cycle time.

Contrary to the simplicity of the principle of flow, its implementation demands a revolution in the organization of production and the management of technology. Ford simplified the organizational challenge, including coordination, by constraining the production system to one product. Equalizing cycle time for more than one product was inconceivable without organizational innovations that go well beyond Ford's system. In fact, the conveyor line itself precludes multiproduct low. Synchronization and the equal cycle time concept necessitate two technology management activities both for Ford and for today. First, adjustments are required in operational activities to meet the synchronization constraint. Achieving the narrow time and timing specifications required by the principle of flow involved Ford engineers in continuously *revamping*, searching for new technologies, adjusting, regearing, retooling, fitting new jigs and fixtures, and redesigning machines and plant layout. This was a never-ending process for Ford, as it is for practitioners of the management philosophy of continuous improvement today. Second, the reduction of the standard cycle time can be accomplished through pursuit of new technologies.

Ford attacked the standard cycle time by addressing generic technologies that impacted on all machines, for example, electric power. Implementation of the principle of flow depended upon and was intertwined with technological innovations in electric power; the dynamo was not seen as a means to reduce the cost of power but as a means to redesign production to apply the principle of flow. The result was an order of magnitude leap in productivity. Flow applied to car production is impossible without the electric motor: the [unit drive] electric motor meant that plant layout and machine location could be freed from the dictates of a central power system and the associated shafts and belts. Power, for the first time, could be distributed to individual machines, and machinery could be arranged on the factory floor according to the logic of product engineering and the material conversion process. Ford's innovation in electricity supply enabled his engineers to organize the plant according to the logic of material flow; competitors departmentalized factories according to machining activity. For Ford, the independently powered machines went to the material; for his competitors, material went to the machine and the machine was located by the power system. Flow meant redesigning machines to incorporate unit drive motors. The fusion of the electric motor with machines offered enormous potential to expand productivity but only with a prior commitment to a radical reorganization of the factory. Ford systematically pursued innovations in processes, procedures, machines, and factory layout to exploit the productivity potential of the principle of flow. The electric motor was a tool in the process; but technological change in electric power awaited organizational change. Unit drive, in turn, created unforeseen opportunities in advancing productivity when integrated with production redesign.

Technology management for Ford meant integrating technology and production in pursuit of the principle of single-product flow. While imitators of Ford could take advantage of innovations developed by technological leaders, the synchronization requirement will always demand a technology management capability. Even though Ford simplified the coordination problem by constraining the production system to one basic product and even though Ford's engineers equalized cycle times for some of the fabrication activities, the implementation of the simple concept of synchronization demanded a revolution in the organization of production and the management of technology. But Ford failed to conceptualize the principle of flow and institutionalize it as a pioneering American effort. Ford, unlike American industrial imitators, had no interest in measuring labor productivity, conducting time and motion studies, or devising piece-rate systems; in the Ford's system, the rate of production only depended on throughput efficiency and associated cycle times.

Ford's *principle of flow* was the basis for world-renowned systems like TPS and TOC. But, instead of enshrining Ford's pioneering principle of flow, the industrial engineering manuals adopted and highlighted the more mundane *scientific management* paradigm. Even less surprising was the complementary practice in economic research of focusing on capital and labor to the exclusion of production and organizational issues. Both obscured the sources of productivity gains in America's most celebrated production system for roughly a half century after Ford's engineers first applied the principle of flow.

6.2.4 SONY POCKET TRANSISTOR RADIO

In the early 1950s, radios depended on vacuum tubes; even if one could come up with a consumer product with transistors, who could afford to buy such a machine with such expensive devices? People believed that transistors cannot be commercially viable. However, Sony went on to make the pocketable radio and fulfilled its dream of creating a product that became pervasive worldwide. Akio Morita read about the invention of the transistor at Bell Labs. In 1953, Morita went to America to purchase a license to the transistor from Western Electric for $25,000, which was a big sum for their new company in those days. Ibuka had appreciated the inherently great performance advantage that transistors potentially had over vacuum tubes—compared to a vacuum tube, a transistor could operate at a fraction of the size and with a fraction of operating current. Ibuka and Morita knew that any business that made portable consumer electronic products would have eventually change from vacuum tube circuits to transistorized circuits. This was the beginning of Sony's strategic plan to become a world leader in consumer electronics—transistorized circuitry and miniaturization.

Ibuka and Morita's strategic plan focused upon a core technology competency—transistorized electronics. But the transistor invention had to be improved to use it in a radio: they had to improve the frequency response of the transistor to a wider range. The problem with the original transistor invented at Bell Labs was its poor frequency response. The original transistors were constructed out of two kinds of semiconductors, arranged like a sandwich, in which the middle slab controls the current flow between the outer two slabs. Since current in semiconductors can be carried either by electrons or by holes (holes are effectively unfilled electronic orbits around atoms), one can design the sandwich in either of these two ways: either hole–electron–hole carrier combinations (positive–negative–positive [pnp]) or electron–hole–electron combinations (negative–positive–negative [npn]). The original Bell Labs transistor had a pnp sandwich of germanium–indium–germanium. Electrons (the negative carriers) inherently move faster through a semiconductor than holes (the positive carriers). The physical reason for this is that holes wait for an electron to put into its empty orbit from a neighboring atom before that empty orbit appears to have moved from one atom to another. This is inherently a slower process than a relatively freely moving electron passing by one atom after another. So the first thing the Sony researchers had to do to make the new technology of the transistor useful was to speed up the signal processing capability of the transistor by using electrons rather than holes as carriers. The Sony researchers accordingly reversed the order of the transistor sandwich: from a pnp structure to an npn structure (indium–germanium–indium). The development of the transistor by altering its phenomenal basis from hole conduction to electron conduction is an example of an innovative technological strategy. This became possible because of the combined background of scientific and engineering mind-set at the leadership level of the company.

 Leo Esaki, one of the transistor researchers on the Sony team, discovered a new fundamental phenomenon of physics called quantum tunneling (in which electrons can sometimes tunnel through physical barriers that would normally bar them, if they obeyed classical physical laws rather than quantum physical laws). Esaki won the Nobel Prize in Physics in 1973.

The next problem the researchers faced was the choice of materials for the bases (or *substrate*) of the transistor and its impurities. Without adding a small quantity of different atoms (or *doping*), neither germanium nor indium can conduct electricity; but adding *doping* atoms as impurities makes these materials semiconducting. They decided to discard the indium, used in Bell Labs' original version of the transistor, because indium had too low a melting point for use in a commercial transistor. They tried working with the combination of gallium as a substrate with antimony as its doping atom. Next, they tried replacing the doping element of antimony in the gallium substrate with phosphorus. Eventually, they found just the right level of phosphorus doping in the gallium substrate that made it semiconducting. Thus, they had an npn transistor of gallium–germanium–gallium structure, with just the right amount of phosphorus atoms doping the substrate gallium material, which made it semiconducting. Sony researchers had developed a high-frequency germanium transistor, which was commercially adequate for their pocket transistor radio model TR-63 launched in 1957.

The U.S. consumer electronics industry, which in the 1950s was the greatest electronics industry in the whole world, had almost completely disappeared by 1980. And the reason for this debacle was a failure of their technology strategy. The U.S. consumer electronics firms failed to transform their products from tubes to transistors in a timely, committed manner. That little transistor—an American invention (and its follow-on key invention, the IC semiconductor chip)—was the technical key to the rise to world dominance of the Japanese consumer electronics industry and the corresponding demise of the American consumer electronics industry. This pattern of acquisition of a foreign-originated technology and subsequent improvement of this technology for commercialization was the recurring pattern in both early and later industrial development of Japan that led to its emergence as a world economic power.

6.2.5 3M Thermofax

3M's Thermofax was a photocopying technology introduced in 1950. It was a form of thermographic printing and was considered a significant advance because no chemicals were required, other than those contained in the copy paper itself. Thermofaxing involved specially manufactured paper sensitive to infrared energy. The original was laid on top of the sensitized sheet and inserted into a machine that applied heat to the original. In all those places where the original had carbon, or print, the carbon itself heated up and passed this heat onto the sensitized sheet. White areas did not heat up. The copy reproduced the image by darkening under the impulse of heat. The method was widely used because it was very handy, simple, and did not include solvents or inks. Costs of the process were low, around 1 cent per copy or less, and the equipment was not expensive either. But nobody much liked the product. Thermofax paper had a tendency to curl, to grow dark, and to become brittle with time.

6.2.6 Psion PDAs

Psion was a pioneer in the handheld PDA market. Founded in 1980 by David Potter, it was in the business of software publishing for Sinclair microcomputers. David built a core team of technically competent and highly skilled engineers that were focused on developing and selling both applications and gaming software for Sinclair micros. Profits from software publishing were invested into an ambitious new project to build the first portable handheld computer. The new device—the Psion Organizer I—was introduced into the market in 1984. Psion became the world's first volume manufacturer of a handheld computer and the global pioneer of an important new sector. By the end of 1987, handheld computers and associated peripherals and software accounted for 90% of Psion's revenues, which had reached £11 million Sterling, with a profit of £1.9 million and 80 employees.

In early 1990s, major competitors such as HP, Amstrad, and Casio entered the market with competing products in different geographic markets like Asia where Psion did not have a major presence. Sharp Zaurus became dominant in Japanese market, and HP's LX series entered with a price point that was thrice that of the entry level of Psion Series 3. However, none of these had any major impact on Psion's overall market leadership, and in 1996, Psion was still on top with a 30% market share with an estimated sales volume of 1.6 million units.

Following a major drop in its stock price, Psion announced the formation of Symbian, a joint venture of Psion, Ericsson, Nokia, and Motorola with the purpose of establishing the industry-standard OS for the next generation of integrated mobile communication and computing devices. But, in early 2001, the stock market collapsed, signaling the end of the technology boom. After Motorola pulled out of the partnership, Psion exited the handheld market. The early adopter had been forced out of the market that it had pioneered in 1984.

Despite it having been an initially successful early adapter, Psion's leadership in the handheld PDA market did not sustain. First, although Psion managed to dominate the then nascent market for handheld PDAs in Europe, it failed to make real major inroads into the much larger U.S. market. Psion's management should have invested more aggressively to get better traction and mindshare in the American market and users. Second, although the design of Psion's PDA had superior functionality, the PalmPilot design had greater and wider consumer appeal because of its simplicity and functionality.

6.2.7   XEROX ALTO AND MITS ALTAIR

The Alto was a highly innovative, relatively powerful PC, although it was never sold commercially in the market. It was the fruit of PARC's engineering abilities and Taylor's vision that the future lay in *personal distributed computing.* By that term, he meant that each person had his or her own computer, which was linked to similar computers of others. As such, the computer will be a communicating device rather than only a computing device. Taylor believed that an essential characteristic for this purpose was the presentation of information. He pressed for video display, which allowed for instantaneous and easy communications between the computer and the user. In contrast, at that time, time-sharing of minicomputers or mainframes was gaining in importance from the earlier mode of batch processing. In time-sharing and batch processing, users had to rely on a single large, remote, and expensive computer.

By using materials already available and drawing on the experience of PARC's earlier minicomputer, PARC's engineers built the Alto in about 4 months. It was an immediate hit in the lab. It was small enough to fit on a desk, yet allowed for independence and networking. It rivaled the minicomputer in its power and functions, though it lagged in speed; it was inexpensive enough for each person to have his or her own machine. The estimated cost of Alto was less than the per-user cost of building PARC's minicomputer. The Alto had an Ethernet port that allowed it to be networked with other Altos and to the laser printer. Perhaps its most attractive feature was its monitor, which could display text and pictures. That display allowed navigation with a mouse, also developed in the lab, based on earlier work done at Doug Engelbart's lab.

The Alto was operational in April 1973, which was 2 years before MITS commercialized the relatively basic Altair, 3 years before Apple I computer was introduced, 8 years before IBM's first PC came into the market, and 11 years before the Macintosh. The Alto became an even more useful machine by 1975, with the incorporation of PARC's bit-mapped graphics, overlapping windows, and the Gypsy word processor. The next year, small-scale production was started at Xerox's SDS unit in Southern California producing 60 Altos, though no large-scale production ever took place. John Ellenby was entrusted with the responsibility of supervising the manufacturing of Alto on a limited scale. Ellenby redesigned the machine for reducing cost and enabling easier maintenance. Called Alto II, Xerox produced about 1500 of these machines, which were distributed to users in Xerox and at select research centers and universities. Alto II was hailed by the users as a great computer.

Thus, it happened that Xerox invented the PC that the world would not see for another decade. Xerox invented the Ethernet-connected PC, along with the graphic interface and mouse and object-oriented OS. Xerox's research was 10 years ahead of Apple's Mac and 20 years ahead of Microsoft's Windows software. But then, Xerox never produced PCs and lost its future as a commercially dominant company.

6.2.7.1 Altair 8800

Altair was the first commercially available PC in the market. After the first microprocessors had come onto the market, Ed Roberts, an engineer at MITS, a small calculator company in Texas, decided to build a kit computer, which he intended to sell to hobbyists. He chose Intel's 8080 as the CPU for his computer, since this chip was the most advanced and powerful at the time. As Roberts wanted to sell his computer for less than $500 and the official price for the 8080 was already at $360, he contacted Intel and could finally receive the chip for only $75 apiece.

By the end of 1974, Roberts finished his computer, which was named Altair. When the Altair was introduced on the cover of the January 1975 issue of Popular Electronics as the first PC, which would go for $397 only, the market response was incredible. The low price was the actual sensation, because it was largely known that the price for the Intel 8080 CPU powering the Altair was already at $360. So many hobbyists, engineers, and programmers who had keenly waited for their own PC, which they could experiment on at home, welcomed the new product and ordered *their* Altair on the spot.

Altair was one of those *switches and lights computers*. It was programmed by arranging a set of switches in a special order, and the results appear as different combinations of lights. Roberts had never expected such a great response and his small firm was flooded by those immediate orders (more than 4000). He boosted up the production, but still could not meet the huge demand. The Altair was a success at first, and Roberts sold many of them.

However, he had increased production at the expense of quality and further refinement of his computer, so the Altair brought along a lot of trouble and was finally supplanted by other computers that were superior. Nevertheless, the Altair, as the first successful microcomputer, contributed a lot to the PC revolution, since it encouraged other people to build PCs (e.g., IMSAI, Apple).

6.2.8 WORLD WIDE WEB

By the early 1990s, the Internet had realized the dream of linking many of the world's computers. But the retrieval of information was slow and difficult because of the variety of incompatible systems. This was a problem that Tim Berners-Lee had begun to think of at CERN in the 1980s.

CERN had a number of visiting scientists from all over the world spending a few years at the center and then returned home. These scientists brought to the center their own computers and programs. Over the years, the center grew to encompass thousands of affiliated scientists all over the world, working on various computers, yet needing a common way to collaborate. He wondered whether the information stored on all the computers in the world could somehow be linked together. Hypertext, initially proposed by Ted Nelson in 1965, was a text format that included links between documents. Horizontal linkages between documents based on keywords could open up a web of limitless information. Berners-Lee realized that the combination of the Internet with hypertext could provide a solution to the problem of disparate and unconnected information around the world.

Berners-Lee discovered a British company Owl Ltd., which had developed a program called Guide that could do just that. But it was not Internet based nor was Owl interested in transporting it to the Internet. After much thought, Berners-Lee designed the WWW, an integrated system for posting and retrieving the information in documents that resided on any computer anywhere in the world. The WWW constituted of three key components: uniform addresses to locate where documents were located (*uniform resource locator* [URL]), links in the documents that let one get from one document to another (HTML), and a standard protocol for exchanging the information in document across sites (*hypertext transfer protocol* [HTTP]). Berners-Lee envisioned two pieces of compatible software that made the system viable. The server resided on the site's *server* computer and made the information available to various client browsers or users. The browser resided on the other *client* computers and retrieved the information. Keywords in any document stored on the server that had the address of any other related document on the server would be marked or highlighted to become noticeable. By clicking on these marked or highlighted keywords or hyperlinks, a client could get the address URLs and access the other documents. But the hyperlinks on the keywords need not be limited to the documents on the same server but could also address documents on other servers. By hopping from document to document across servers, a user had limitless access to information without relying on any one central server or computer. These links between sources were continuous and unlimited and not hierarchical as in Gopher. This was the essence of the powerful logic of the WWW.

It is important to emphasize that there is no central computer *commanding and controlling* the WWW. The WWW is not a *thing* that existed in a certain locatable *place*; there was nothing else beyond the URLs, HTTP, and HTML. WWW was nothing more than a web of interconnections!

By merely reconfiguring conventions and software available at that time, Berners-Lee had defined a new medium in which information could be meaningfully accessed and shared all across the world. All of these three constituting elements had existed independently before; but it was Berners-Lee who put them together in a meaningful way to enable accessing and sharing of that information limitlessly. It was based on the principle that once one made a *hyperlink* or reference available to a document (which could be text, graphic, sound, screen, or video), it should be accessible seamlessly by any computer across the world. Evidently, the key component to do so effectively was the address URL. In the WWW, each server or computer that stored information had a unique address (URL). The address had three parts separated by slashes, "/", for example, http://www.amazon.com/books. The first part indicated which protocol to use, such as Gopher, WAIS, ftp, and http. The second part (e.g., www.amazon.com) indicated the name of the server. The periods delineated the type and location of the servers. The third part (e.g., books) indicated the specific page within the server. By using the uniform address and the standard protocol, HTTP, the WWW allowed for accessing documents irrespective of the type of the system, protocol, or language in which the information was stored.

In August 1991, with the objective of people to experience the value of the web, Berners-Lee released on the Internet the WWW browser for the NeXT computer and the basic server software for any machine. He also wrote and released a rudimentary line-mode version of the browser that would work on any machine. He had programmed the WWW browser to run on a NeXT computer because that was his working computer at CERN; both his server and the browser ran only on the NeXT computers. He wrote the code for URLs, HTML, and HTTP. He intentionally designed the system to be compatible with the two popular protocols of the time, Gopher and WAIS, so as to enable users to access information available on those servers as well. He also wrote the software for the browser to create and edit pages. He wrote the code for the server at CERN, which he called info.cern.ch. This server became the first site on the newly designed web and WWW was the first browser to navigate the web.

Berners-Lee took to personally promoting the system, talking about it at conferences and seminars. Like his experience in the past decade of propagation and discussions on this system, he did not get much of a response. This was the traditional *push* system and, not surprisingly, there was no response. Finally, he began posting notices about the system on several Internet chat groups. Being a *pull* system, this finally turned the tide, though it was characteristically slow in the beginning. Interest began to pick up gradually. People who liked the web downloaded the server, posted their own information, and added links of their own. Thus, the web began to develop its own community and momentum. By August 1991, his site got 100 hits per day; the hits began to increase exponentially, doubling every few months. Within a year, the number of hits had increased 100 times.

One constraint on the growth of the WWW was the absence of a graphical browser that could run on the more widely used computer systems, such as UNIX, Apple, and Windows. His first browser WWW was graphical but it ran only on the NeXT PC, which was not widely used. Realizing this, Berners-Lee went around encouraging others to develop such a program, especially in the university environments. The Mosaic graphical browser that was developed by the students at the University of Illinois and released in early 1992 clearly demonstrated the superiority of the web. From then on, the system took off. It spread so rapidly and completely that the web became ubiquitous, and the WWW became synonymous with the Internet.

The WWW was one of the greatest of the inventions of all times. At the same time, the vision did not necessarily involve a radical transformation in available tools and methods. All the key constituent elements for the design of the web were already in existence. What Berners-Lee brought to the table was a unique vision for standardizing and integrating all these elements to enable quick, easy, and limitless sharing of information. What is even more remarkable is that Berners-Lee neither patented his invention nor charged for any of its aspect. He was interested neither in profits nor proprietary ownership. He freely distributed the specification of the web as well as the server and the client software to use it. It was his specific goal that the web be free to all individuals. This zero-cost pricing was really the cause for the eventual explosive growth of the Internet.

6.2.8.1 Battle of Browsers

6.2.8.1.1 NCSA Mosaic

The browser war of the 1990s clearly demonstrates the futility of first-mover advantage for companies dealing with inferior or immature product. For high-technology markets like Internet or electronic commerce, strategic speed outweighs the importance of the order of entry. A company entering the market with a distinctive product needed by the customers could see its market share rise rapidly. But this also works in reverse in that a pioneer that does not keep up with the pace of innovation could also see its market share eroding equally rapidly.

In early 1990s, developing browsers became the favorite research project of computer science students at many universities. Several browsers became available, including the Lynx 2.0 developed at the University of Kansas, Cello developed at Cornell University, and Viola developed at the University of Berkeley. In 1992, Marc Andreessen and Eric Bina were working with the software developing group at the National Centre for Supercomputing Applications (NCSA) at the University of Illinois at Urbana–Champaign. Realizing that user-friendly web programs would have worldwide demand, they took upon themselves to improve the available browsers. To start with, they rewrote the code of Berners-Lee's line-mode browser to make it run faster and enhance it to a screen-mode browser called Mosaic to enable full-page formatting (including fonts and color) and incorporating multimedia elements like graphics, sound, and video. Mosaic was easy to download, install, learn, and use. It allowed users to easily navigate among websites—merely by clicking over a highlighted hypertext link, the user could switch over to a new webpage. They worked in tandem; Andreessen served more as an architect, evaluating available programs and features, acting as single point of contact and participating in discussions on these features, and recommending new features for incorporation and keeping everyone on the same page. Bina served as the programmer writing the code, testing and rectifying technical problems. Andreessen kept in touch with users, incorporated features people wanted, and debugged the programs in response to reported problems. He was passionate about Mosaic becoming the browser of choice of the Internet users and it was this zeal that everyone responded positively. Subsequently, more members joined the team and Mosaic was ported to function on Windows and Macintosh desktops, which were more popular with users worldwide. When Mosaic took off in 1993, the university was swamped with requests for the software, licensing, and support. Realizing that it was neither capable of serving the tremendous demand for the product nor positioned to exploit its commercial potential, NCSA contracted with Spyglass to handle all licensing of the software. Late in 1994, Spyglass had licensed 10 million copies of Mosaic. Prompted by this success, Spyglass went public with an initial public offering (IPO) that was valued at $25 million in June 1994.

6.2.8.1.2 *Netscape Navigator*

Upon graduation in December 1993, Marc Andreessen was asked to stay on as an NCSA employee, but he was asked to keep away from the Mosaic project. Overall, Andreessen and his core team did not feel acknowledged and adequately rewarded for their contribution. He not only felt that the university tried to take credit due to his team, but they were also denied any share in the royalties or bonuses for their work. In frustration, Andreessen left and shifted to Silicon Valley. Jim Clark was the founder and CEO of Silicon Graphics Inc. (SGI), which was the producer of high-end 3D graphics workstations. The company owned a niche, selling its workstations at high prices like $50,000 a piece, but lost its position as rivals like Sun Microsystems and HP introduced increasingly better workstations at much more competitive prices. Feeling constrained and unable to agree with the strategy of the company to reverse its declining fortunes, he had quit SGI in frustration. He was on the lookout for starting another company that would be more attuned to the rapid changes that new technologies brought to the new market and met Andreessen at an opportune time. On April 4, 1994, Jim set up Netscape with himself and Marc Andreessen as cofounders. While NCSA overlooked its talent, Jim Clark perceived its true value; he strongly believed that in this market, the key to success was the talent that could do the job. In a few rapid moves, Jim Clark signed up the key talent responsible for creating the major browsers at that time, Mosaic and Lynx. In addition to Eric Bina, they also recruited Lou Montulli, one of the key programmers who developed the Lynx 2.0. Clark won the talent that was intimately familiar with Mosaic and most capable of improving on it to an extent that it radically changed the browser market and the shape of the Internet.

Right from the start, Clark gave very clear instructions to the programmers he hired from the Mosaic project that they should start the project completely fresh—they could not use any code from the Mosaic program even though it was publicly available. Notwithstanding all these measures and precautions, NCSA insisted that its former employees used proprietary knowledge to develop Netscape's new browser and were expecting Netscape to pay a royalty on every copy of the program that was downloaded, sold, or licensed. This was further complicated by the fact that the company was initially called Mosaic Communications and their browser was called Netscape Mosaic. Netscape development team had erred in believing that they had the right to the name merely because they had developed the code of Mosaic at NCSA. But they had developed the code as employees of NCSA and, thus, the use of Mosaic name by Clark and his team seemed a clear infringement of NCSA's copyright. In late December 1994, the University of Illinois and NCSA agreed to settle their long-standing copyright dispute with Netscape for a one-time royalty fee of about $3 million. Within a fortnight of this settlement, the university gave Microsoft a license to Mosaic on favorable terms. About a year later, Spyglass sold the lifetime rights to the PC version of the Mosaic for $8 million to Microsoft; effectively, this gave Microsoft a head start that they had denied to Netscape, a start-up that was created by its own former students.

Netscape Navigator's beta release in October 1994 was very successful because it was 10 times faster than Mosaic. As servers began offering richer material on the web, with graphics, sound, and video, download speed became a key criterion for consumer's choice of the browser. Netscape's superior speed would pretty much kill Mosaic, and Spyglass and NCSA could see their steady stream of royalties soon drying up. Netscape introduced its first version of the browser in December 1994. By June 1995, total downloads and sales had reached 40 million copies. Prompted by this strong performance, Netscape Communications went public with an IPO in August 1995 that was valued at $2.2 billion.

6.2.8.1.3   Microsoft Internet Explorer

Microsoft initially ignored the Internet like any other large incumbent facing a radically new technology. But the rapid increase in the number of web users and the media attention surrounding Netscape's success underscored the growing importance of the WWW. The Internet represented a new revolution in personal computing. The browser was a sort of OS by itself, while sufficiently powerful servers with rich content and numerous applications threatened to render traditional application obsolete. This was a direct threat to Microsoft's dominance in the market of PC OSs and software applications. In the prior 15 years, the explosion of PC sales and Microsoft's superior products in OSs and applications had transformed the company into a colossus. Microsoft's intent to address the challenge of the Internet was signaled in mid-1995 by a memo titled *The Internet Tidal Wave* in which Gates was proclaimed highest level of importance to the Internet market. In March 1996, Microsoft signed a contract with AOL, offering the latter the option of an icon on the Windows desktop in exchange for AOL making IE its preferred choice of browser. The deal offered IE a good chance of becoming the browser of choice for AOL subscribers, which were 10 million in number; in return, AOL won immediate presence on the desktop of 90% of all new PCs sold (and all old ones that upgraded to Windows 95) to offer consumers the option of signing up for the AOL service with every new installation of Windows. At that time, Windows desktop represented some of the most expensive real estate on consumer's PCs. In effect, Gates had sacrificed the MSN for the future and fortunes of Microsoft's IE. He set up a full-fledged task force of 80 programmers headed by Benjamin Slivka who were tasked with developing a strong and innovative version of IE. For the benefit of speed, Microsoft had foregone the option of developing its own solutions from scratch and opted to embrace and extend the prevailing Internet standards and protocols. Microsoft embraced HTML that was developed by Berners-Lee and further developed by Netscape. It also contracted with Sun Microsystems to license its Java software.

Overall, Microsoft invested about $500 million in the development of the first few versions of the IE. Not surprisingly, IE 3.0 was rated equal or even better than Netscape Navigator 3. To build its market share in the browser market, Microsoft decided to leverage its strong position in the PC OSs and software applications market by distributing both IE and the accompanying server software free. As a next step, it bundled IE with Windows 95; whether or not consumers were explicitly going to choose IE over Netscape, making IE available (free of cost) through the OS greatly increased the probability of them choosing it as their default browser. Microsoft also began integrating IE with Windows, so that the linkages between the two programs would become seamless. This was a master stroke because it skewed the economics of the browser market totally in favor of Microsoft: in comparison to Netscape's installed base of 10 million users in March 1996, Microsoft had a worldwide-installed base of 150 million users along with sales of 50 million new copies of Windows every year. By bundling IE with Windows, Gates had staked out a market that was 15 times bigger than Netscape's market. By December 1996, IE's market share had risen from 4% to 24%, while Netscape's market share declined from a peak of about 87% to 70%. Thereafter, IE's share grew rapidly until it dominated the browser market.

6.3   IMITATION VARIATIONS

Imitation is usually associated with products or services; but imitation is not restricted to these alone; it is also possible to imitate procedures, processes, and strategies of competitors. Traditionally, Japanese competitors have excelled at copying American products and selling them on world market at lower prices. In recent years, American firms have been especially interested in copying the procedures that have made Japanese firms so competitive on world markets. For a variety of reasons, it is more difficult to reverse engineer intangible processes than it is to copy physical products. Not only are process inventions or innovations intangible and rooted in organization and culture, they are also easier to keep secret. The Japanese have had more success in copying Western pioneering product or innovations than American companies have had in copying Japanese processes and operational innovations. Processes, procedures, and strategies are often culturally bound, and consequently, imitations of them often must be tailored to fit a particular social context.

Established companies find it difficult to pioneer or innovate new products; they rely on pioneers or smaller agile competitors to venture into risk-prone variations of products. Some companies are caught off guard by the introduction of new and innovative products; they fail to recognize the potential of a new product introduced by a small, entrepreneurial firm until demand for that product explodes. Typically, the incumbent is forced to catch up and catch up quickly. It imitates because it has no other choice.

There are numerous advantages of imitating variations:

1. Avoiding low-potential products or services: Imitation enables avoidance of products with low customer acceptance and, hence, market potential. This reduces their risks and lowers their cost considerably; they may have to spend heavily for differentiating their products or services to overcome the pioneer's advantages or lead time.

2. Leapfrogging to latest technology: Imitators have an opportunity to leapfrog the pioneers or innovators. The first-generation technology presents both a risk and an opportunity for pioneers; typically, a pioneer picks the cutting-edge technology at the time of entry. But that choice may become defunct quickly; the pioneers may find it difficult to switch technologies once they have invested so much in the first generation.

3. Lower research and development (R&D) expenditures: Imitation is less expensive than pioneering or innovation; pioneers or innovators spend heavily on R&D in order to identify and bring to market new or innovative products. This expense is justified by the assumption that pioneers or innovators gain a long lead on imitators; in practice, competitors know of a new product development projects within 6 months of their inception (which is quite early in the product development cycle of about 3 years). Companies learn about each other's new product development projects by monitoring each other's patent applications, papers and presentations at professional and academic conferences, and technical and marketing jobs spreading knowledge through job switching to other companies.

4. Lower costs of educating consumers: Pioneers or innovators spend heavily to inform and persuade customers as to the merits of a new or innovative product; this is specially so for products (or services) with which customers are unfamiliar. Imitators have the benefit of accessing an identified need and educated and appreciative customers.

5. Compliance with enduring standards: Pioneers are able to impose its standard on the market, forcing followers into the subservient position of imitating its pioneering design; but pioneers do not set long-enduring standards. Eventually, a standard emerges that defines the entire product category and many providers rally around that standard. Imitators have the opportunity of being compliant with the industry standards right from the beginning, thus, avoiding a separate effort that is invariably incurred by the pioneers. For example, in PCs, there were competing and propriety OSs until IBM largely standardized the design and architecture of the PC around the MS-DOS standard in 1981.

6.3.1 Otto Four-Stroke-Cycle Internal Combustion Engine

Nikolaus August Otto invented the four-stroke-cycle internal combustion engine in 1876. It was marketed by the Gasmotoren-Fabrik Deutz firm as *Otto's new motor*, although it soon became known as the *Silent Otto* engine because it was less noisy than the Otto–Langen atmospheric engine. Unlike the Lenoir internal combustion engine, the compression occurred within the working cylinder; he thought that his major contribution was that he used a stratified layer of gas/air mixture that cushioned the shock to the piston. Otto's engine was a horizontal, stationary machine, designed primarily for shops, printing presses, power stations, and other similar facilities. The Silent Otto established the internal gas combustion engine as the most important new power source for industry and consumers, rivaled only by the massive expansion of the use of electrical power.

Otto's new engine established the basic principles that defined all future four-stroke-cycle internal combustion engines, regardless of size or horsepower. During the first stroke, the piston moves downward toward the crankshaft. Because of the resulting drop in pressure, a fuel and air mixture enters through the intake valve. When the cylinder obtains its maximum volume, the valve closes and the piston returns toward the top of the cylinder, compressing the gas/air mixture. This compressed mixture is then ignited by a spark, and the resulting force creates the third stroke, which forces the piston downward in the direction of the crankshaft and delivers the direct workforce. When the piston reaches the bottom, the exhaust valve opens, allowing the gas to exit the cylinder. After the piston returns to the top of the cylinder, the four-stroke process is repeated.

The first Otto engine delivered only three horsepower, but by the time of Otto's death in 1891, his engines were producing as much as 100 horsepower. Because the first engine weighed 1450 lb per horsepower and was dependent on urban gas supply, it was limited to urban stationary use. Otto's engine, however, evolved both in terms of power and size. By increasing the compression ratio, the engine became more powerful and the size and weight of the engine were reduced significantly, allowing it to become mobile. Between 1877 and 1889, the Deutz firm produced 8308 four-stroke engines. In the United States, the introduction of the Otto engine in Philadelphia in 1876 stimulated massive interest in this new source of power; 15 years later, 18,500 Otto cycle engines were operating in the United States. In 1885, Otto's old colleagues Wilhelm Maybach and Gottlieb Daimler produced a petrol gas engine weighing only 88 lb and producing one-half horsepower. This was only the beginning of a series of developments in the emerging automobile industry. After Otto lost his German patent in 1886, his four-stroke engine became available to all entrepreneurs, helping to launch the automobile revolution in the 1890s.

6.3.2 Texas Instruments Silicon Transistors

The germanium transistor suffered from a serious technical performance problem: sensitivity to temperature. What good would transistorized electronics be if their circuit performance changed dramatically from the heat of day to the cool of night, from the hot of summer to the cold of winter? So the historical setting of this case study is about 10 years after the original invention of the germanium transistor. Many electronic engineers appreciated the new technology but needed a more reliable, less temperature-sensitive version of the transistor. Most researchers felt that the obvious route was to try to make a transistor not from germanium but from its sister element silicon.

One of the groups looking for a silicon version of the transistor was based in a then small U.S. company, TI. In 1952, Patrick Haggerty was president of TI, and the company was a maker of seismographic detection instruments, sold to oil companies for use in oil exploration. Their instruments used electron vacuum tubes but needed to be portable and rugged and use little power. It was obvious to Haggerty that transistors would be a desirable replacement for tubes in TI's products. Haggerty had assigned a research project to one of his employees, Mark Shepard, to develop a germanium transistor that could be sold for U.S. $2.50 at that time. Shepard developed it; TI produced a pocket radio with it in 1954. But TI did not follow through with this product, and Sony very soon introduced its own independently developed germanium transistor and pocket radio and proceeded to commercially exploit this new product.

Still, Haggerty knew the germanium transistor needed to be replaced. He hired a physicist from Bell Labs, Gordon Teal, who had been researching silicon. Haggerty told Teal and another researcher, Willis Adcock (a physical chemist), to develop a silicon transistor. Many other research groups were seeking the silicon transistor; and it was not an easy artifact to make: it was brittle and difficult to purify as a material for making transistors. But Teal and Adcock achieved this in 1954.

6.3.3 Toyota Production System

Actually, TPS was inspired by the Ford production system. In 1950, when Toyota Motor Company was in trouble, Eiji Toyoda went to Detroit to learn from the legendary Ford Motor Company how to improve his family's business. He spent 3 months in Detroit, studying Ford's manufacturing techniques in detail and looking for ways to transport them to Toyota. His conclusion was that while Henry Ford's concept of mass production was probably right for 1913, it was not responsive to the demands of the 1950s. The result was the design of a fundamentally different system, the TPS, which enabled the Japanese automobile industry to overtake Detroit. Toyota is now recognized as a benchmark of superior performance among the world's best-run, most successful manufacturing companies.

The new production system known variously as JIT, the TPS, and lean production was not the consequence of large investments in capital. The new system was based on the development, application, and diffusion of new principles of production and organizational capabilities that enabled Japanese manufacturing enterprises to compete on more comprehensive performance standards combining cost, quality, time, and flexibility. The new performance standards put industrial enterprises and regions throughout the world on notice, much as Henry Ford had done a half century before: failure to adapt to, or counter, the new production system would lead to industrial decline. The central organizing concept of Toyota can be described as multiproduct flow. The major difference with Ford, and it is a major one, is that Toyota was not constrained to one product. Toyota applied the principle of flow to a range of products: different models go down the same line without preventing the goals of minimal throughput time and of low inventory targets. Toyota still achieved an inventory turn (ratio of sales divided by WIP) approaching 300 (compared to Ford's inventory turns of about 200 and GM's inventory turns of about 8). Toyota took Ford's challenge of synchronization two steps beyond Ford: the first step was to introduce multiproduct flow, and the second was equalization of the cycle times for every part.

The work organization ideally suited to the challenge of multiproduct flow is cellular manufacturing. The idea harks back to the concept of group technology in which work *cells* are organized by the logic of the product. Multiproduct flow requires equalizing cycle times and the flexibility to have different, but equal, cycle times. This enables the product mix to be varied in response to demand shifts. While cycle times vary according to the product, they are the same for each specific product. Flexibility comes from first, being able to adjust the number of workers in a cell; second, quick setup and changeover designed machines; and third, multiskilled workers. Each worker must operate not one machine but three or four machines and also do setups (and maintenance activities) on the machines.

What was revolutionary at Toyota was not JIT production but the idea of single-minute exchange of die (SMED). To produce multiple products on the same line, it is necessary to make the machines capable of being programmable (mechanically or electronically) for different products. The challenge at Toyota was to go beyond multiple products on the same line to the idea of multiple products on the same line in batch sizes of one. This meant the worker had to be able to set up the machine and, in certain circumstances, set up several machines. By establishing cellular production, Toyota was able to achieve the same high-performance standards in terms of equal cycle time as Henry Ford, but with multiple products. Machines, as along Ford's assembly line, are laid out and reconfigured according to the dictates of the routing sheet or flow chart but in U-shaped cells and without a conveyor line.

This new management paradigm makes possible the organizational capability of continuous, incremental innovation in the form of an accumulation of thousands of tiny improvements and an unrivaled persistence to production detail built into the organization of production. The plan–do–check–act (PDCA) management paradigm of W. Edwards Deming was an organizational corollary to the principle of multiproduct flow. While Deming's focus was not on innovation but on continuous improvement of product and process, his approach to integrating thinking and doing on the shop floor introduced a new dimension to the management of technology. For Deming, the discovery of knowledge is not the preserve of science just as thinking is not the preserve of management; the business challenge became to build the discovery process into every level and activity of the organization. For example, the workers involved can discover knowledge about the causes of product defects if the organization is properly designed. The purpose of statistical process control was not only to distinguish systemic from special causes of defects but also to focus attention on improvement of the organization as the means to advance quality and productivity. The idea was to design quality into the system, not inspect it into the product. This required innovation capability on the shop floor.

Multiproduct flow is the mirror image of a new organizational principle that appears in a range of variants and goes under the popular names of continuous improvement, TQM, kaizen, small group activity, and self-directed work teams (SDWTs). Deming considered each of these management practices to be aspects of the *theory of system*, which, for him, meant replacing the hierarchical, up/down, vertical information flows and functional departmentalization with cross-functional relations and horizontal, interactive information flows of process integration. The new principles of production (multiproduct flow) and corollary organizational capability (kaizen) are interdependent and self-reinforcing; neither can be successfully applied without the other. Successful implementation, however, depended upon a prior or simultaneous development of specific organizational capabilities and investments in the skills required to apply and convert the new production principle into production capabilities and pursue the new technological opportunities.

6.3.4 SONY WALKMAN

In 1946, with his father's investment from their family's brewery business and a university colleague named Masaru Ibuka as his partner, Akio Morita formed Tokyo Telecommunications Engineering Corporation (Tokyo Tsushin Kogyo K.K. [TTK]). Akio was a graduate in applied physics from Tokyo University and Ibuka was an engineer from Waseda University. Ibuka was inventive and had always been fascinated with technology. Morita viewed science as source of ideas for new technologies. Ibuka was committed to a high-tech consumer electronic product—he had no plan, just a commitment. He was looking for a new high-tech product with which to compete with the bigger but slower-moving established Japanese electronics firms. He saw a new American high-tech product, a Wilcox-Gay tape recorder, which the U.S. occupation forces had brought from the United States. He looked it over and could see immediately that it had technical advantages over wire recorders prevalent in Japan at that time. Ibuka understood what kind of electronics, physics, and chemistry would be required to copy and develop the new technology. Ibuka decided that tape recorder was to be their product.

There are many technical problems in innovating a new product, but Ibuka and Morita were confidant they could duplicate it successfully. They realized the critical part of the system that they did not know how to make was the recording tape. Earlier, they had worked on wire recorders as a possible high-tech product and understood how to make the mechanical and electrical components of a recorder. The tape was a subsystem of the new high-tech product, providing the recording medium. The tape would be composed of materials that were physical and chemical based. The rest of the system was based in electronic circuitry and mechanical processes. Ibuka and Morita wanted to produce the tape as well as the machine, in order to obtain a follow-on sales business. This commercial strategy to produce tape as well as tape recorders occurred to them immediately after they had made a decision to produce tape recorders.

Ibuka and Morita's first technical problem was the base material for the tape, but there was a severe supply problem in postwar Japan. The American firm 3M was then the source of the base tape material, but they were also the major tape producer. Moreover, Ibuka and Morita thought 3M might not wish to supply tape to a small Japanese competitor at that time. They tried cellophane, which turned out to be totally inadequate as they had anticipated. They cut it into long quarter-inch-wide strips and coated it with various ferromagnetic materials. The cellophane stretched hopelessly after only one or two passes as a tape on the machine. They even hired chemists to improve cellophane but without success.

They also experimented with paper tapes coated with magnetic material, but the resulting fidelity was very poor. They really needed plastic tape. Finally, they got a supply of plastic tape. With a supply of plastic tape and the ferric oxide coating, they had a recording-tape technology. This was the critical technology for their new product.

Ibuka and Morita's first tape machine, which used their new plastic-based magnetic tape, had turned out to be very bulky and heavy (about 75 lb) and expensive (170,000 yen). Japanese consumers simply wouldn't buy it. They had to look for another market. At the time, there was also an acute labor shortage of stenographers, because during the war, so many students had been pushed from school into war materials production. Ibuka and Morita demonstrated their new tape recorder to the Japan Supreme Court and immediately sold 20 machines. It was the breakthrough sale for their new high-tech product. They redesigned their tape recorder into a medium-sized machine (a little larger than an attache case). They also simplified it for a single speed and sold it at a much lower price. They then sold their modified product to schools for English language instruction to Japanese students.

To obtain a high-quality recorded signal, they had purchased a license to an invention patented by Dr. Knszo Nagai, which was a high-frequency AC bias system for recording: this demagnetized the tape before it reached the recording head, reducing background and prior recording noise. At that time, the patent was owned by Anritsu Electric, and they bought half rights in the patent from them in 1949. Eventually, when Americans imported U.S.-made tape recorders into Japan using the AC bias system technology, the U.S. firms had to pay royalties to Sony. This encouraged Sony to be aggressive about intellectual property in future. By 1950, the new company had products, tape recorders, magnetic recording tapes, and intellectual property. They continued to put heavy development into it (many years later, in 1965, IBM chose Sony magnetic tape as their suppliers for IBM computer magnetic data storage).

With the advent of transistors, the focus shifted from the tape recorder business to the radio transistor business. In the meanwhile, competitors such as Panasonic and Olympus were selling a new breed of mini and micro tape cassette recorders. At the other end of the spectrum, large boom boxes had also become very popular. In general, these devices were bellwethers for the personalization of music, which was already in full swing with the abundance of diversity and new genres. But nobody was pulling far enough ahead of the pack. Radios and cassette players were being repackaged in every way to make them more portable. However, they were still not personal. Without a truly personal experience, the market did not know what to ask for. Yet providers feared venturing too far into the unknown and losing the market they understood.

This situation changed after the success of pocket transistor radio model TR-63 introduced in 1957. In the next couple of years, Sony brought out no less than eight additional generations of the pocket transistor radio, each one the result of the numerous lessons learned earlier. By then, it had sold more than a million pocket transistor radios. The breakthrough pace of Sony's innovations was unprecedented, and it quickly became the hallmark of its agile brand. In this changed context, the idea of a personal space became easier to imagine: a cocoon in which you could go out in public and isolate yourself from your friends and family or to go out in traffic and to shopping malls without hearing the cars or people within inches of you. Its tape recorder division stumbled on a refinement to its Pressman personal recorder: someone got the bright idea to add a simple stereo player and miniature headphones. This was the basic idea of Sony's best-known product introduced in 1979—the Walkman.

6.3.5 XEROX 914 AND CANON COPIERS

Xerox 914, so called because it could make copies on plain paper that was 9 in. × 14 in., was shipped in March 1960 at a list price of $29,500. The product took 14 years of research, during which Haloid spent $75 million on the research effort, which was almost twice its earnings during this extended period. To ensure that firms would accept the product, Haloid decided to lease the product for $95 a month that included service and 2000 free copies for the month; additional copies cost 4 cents each. The product had to compete with copiers from 30 other companies including Kodak and 3M. However, it was simpler, faster, and easier to use than its competitors: It did not use liquid but dry toners, and it could produce copies on ordinary paper (unlike for the competitor's copiers that required special paper supplied by these companies for their proprietary machines). Xerox 914 was a huge success and within 2 years of its introduction, the company had installed 10,000 copiers. The company changed its name to Xerox Corporation.

The story of the Xerox 914 reveals how a small firm can grow to dominate a market through focus and persistence. It begins with Charles Carlson, a patent attorney, who had a vision of a *dry copier* for making copies with powder and static electricity. He started experimenting in a makeshift laboratory and, after 3 years with the help of a German physicist, developed a dry copying machine that could make crude image on regular paper. Hoping to interest some firm in commercializing his invention, he demonstrated his machine to major technology firms of the day including IBM, Kodak, and RCA (who already had products closely related to this technology, namely, office, copier, and communication equipment, respectively). They clearly had the resources, funding, and identified need for Carlson's technology, but they declined interest in exploring it any further. Eventually, he found a sponsor in a nonprofit institute called Battelle Memorial Institute, which took him on employment and also bought 60% interest in his invention. In 1945, based on his prior search, Joseph Wilson, owner of a small photographic manufacturing company called Haloid Corporation, approached Battelle for purchasing the rights to this technology.

In the commercial model, Carlson's zinc plate is a drum whose surface can be charged. The document is laid print side down on glass. Powerful light is directed at the document and reflected down on the drum as it turns. A precise reflection is ensured by using mirrors. Where light reaches the drum, thus where the document is white, the charges on the drum's surface are neutralized. The printed or other dark areas of the document remain charged on the drum. The drum, as it turns, passes a source of toner that corresponds to the yellow lycopodium spores (in Carlson's original invention). The toner is oppositely charged and adheres selectively to the drum. As the drum continues to turn, it touches the sheet that will hold the copy. The sheet itself is also given a charge but greater than that of the drum so that the toner transfers to the paper, also by electrostatic attraction. A strong source of heat is then applied to the paper to cause the toner to melt and fuse into the fibers of the sheet.

Wilson had a vision for this technology called xerography (Greek for dry copying) and set himself the task of developing it into a viable product. In 1949, he introduced the Model A, which consisted of three separate machines; the operator had to manually carry a heavy plate from one machine to another and the whole process took 2–3 min for a single copy. The product was not very successful. The need was for all of these parts to work together seamlessly and without any glitches, every time. There were numerous potential problems relating to the copy paper not moving aligned to the guide, copy paper jamming in the machine, toner residue building up on the photoreceptor, copy paper sticking to the photoreceptor, the machine itself overheating periodically, and so forth. Above all, the marketing people regularly gave a pessimistic prognosis that they were dealing with a market of no more than a few thousand machines. Through all these years of frustrations and slow progress, Wilson held steadfast to his vision and championed the project wholeheartedly. He had the research department systematically file for all patents emerging from the research. He persuaded the board to sell stock to pay for the cost of manufacturing the machine. He and some executives made personal sacrifices by putting up their savings and mortgages on their homes to support the project; some of them even took part of their pay in company stock.

As stated in the beginning, the Xerox 914 was eventually launched in 1961 and was a huge success. By 1966, sales crossed a half billion dollars and Xerox held 61% of the copier market.

That year, Xerox also won its 500th patent. The research effort paid off in a constant stream of new products that helped Xerox to dominate the copier market for many years.

6.3.5.1 Digital Copying

Toner for copiers is made of tiny, spherical carbon and polymer particles in size between 5 and 7 µm. A micron is one millionth of a meter and thus is extremely tiny. Printer resolution is defined in dots per inch (dpi). A good quality printer will have a 600 dpi resolution meaning that a square inch will hold 600 dots—any one of which may be black or white (or some other color and white). A standard 8.5 × 11 in. sheet of paper at 600 dpi will accommodate 56,100 dots. In preparing documents on a computer, the machine can readily divide the page into many thousands of sequential dot lines, known as rasters, and send these lines to a printer dot by dot and line by line. Similarly, a high-resolution scanner can look at a document raster by raster and capture what it sees as 56,100 separate bits of data, storing them in computer memory as 0s or as 1s depending on whether the tiny areas are white or dark. These modern capabilities in combination have produced both laser printers and digital copiers.

Since the development of digital copying, ordinary copiers are called analog, which reflect light from the entire page to be copied, or digital, which send light in dot-sized increments. The advantage of digital copying is that in making many copies, less energy is used; less light is used. The scanned image can also be faxed, permitting functions to be combined. The digital copier can thus be used as a fax machine, a scanner, and as a printer. Such devices are often referred to as multifunction printers (MFPs). In the first decade of the twenty-first century, digital printers were rapidly displacing analog machines. Furthermore, the two categories, copiers and printers, were converging into a common imaging technology.

6.3.5.2 Canon Copiers

In the 1960s, Xerox put a lock on the copier market by following the well-defined and successful strategy: having segmented the market by volume, Xerox decided to go after the corporate reproduction market by concentrating on copiers designed for high-speed, high-volume needs. This inevitably defined Xerox's customers as big corporations, which in turn determined its distribution method: the direct sales force. At the same time, Xerox decided to lease rather than sell its machines, a strategic choice that had worked well in the company's earlier battles with 3M. Throughout the 1960s and early 1970s, Xerox maintained a return on equity (ROE) of around 20%. Xerox's strategy proved so successful that several new competitors, among them IBM and Kodak, tried to enter this market by adopting similar strategies; but without adequate differentiation, they were not able to make any dent on Xerox's position which also had the benefit of first-mover advantage.

Canon, on the other hand, segmented the market by end user and decided to target small- and medium-sized businesses (SMBs) while also producing PC copiers for the individual. At the same time, Canon decided to sell its machines through a dealer network rather than lease them, and while Xerox emphasized the speed of its machines, Canon selected to concentrate on quality and price as its differentiating features.

Canon achieved a successful entry in established markets by attacking the entrenched competitor Xerox through unorthodox strategies.

6.3.6 APPLE NEWTON AND PALM PDAS

PDAs are handheld computers originally designed to manage the personal information of the user. Since their introduction in the 1990s, many features have been added, including calculators, video games, and Internet web browsers. The devices can also be used to check e-mails, create and manage spreadsheets, and store phone numbers, appointments, tasks, and notes. They can also hold maps and city guides and display photos. The most recent models, as of 2007, have wireless capabilities, which allow them to act as global positioning satellite (GPS) devices, mobile phones (smartphones), or portable media players. PDAs are about the size of a deck of cards. They have black and white or color liquid crystal display (LCD) screens. Users access the PDA's various functions by using a stylus (pen) and writing on the screen; all PDAs employ some form of handwriting-recognition software. Users can also tap on the keyboard or scroll through the menu to access functions. PDAs come with expansion slots, which allow the device to be programmed with extra functions, such as GPS. The device comes with a port so that its battery can be recharged; the first PDAs, however, ran on standard alkaline batteries. PDAs can be synchronized with a user's home computer; that is, information can be passed between computer and device.

Apple Computer released the Apple MessagePad in August 1993. It ran on Apple's Newton OS and featured 640 kB of random access memory (RAM); it ran on four AAA alkaline batteries. The MessagePad was often called the Newton because of the OS on which it ran. The key features of the Newton were its ability to send faxes and e-mails, its built-in personal organizer applications, its calendar, and its ability to recognize and interpret words written on its screen. It is most remembered for its handwriting-recognition software Calligrapher, which was licensed from the Russian company Paragraph International. Calligrapher could parse a written sentence and make predictions about what the user was writing based on a programmed database of words. It could sort names and dates in a sentence so that they could be filed into a user's address book.

Palmcomputing and a consortium of partners brought PDAs to the U.S. market by acquiring the failed Casio Zoomer product, which had Geoworks OS similar to Psion's and Palmcomputing's innovative handwriting-recognition software. Both products flopped in the market—not only did they have poor handwriting recognition, they were also expensive, heavy, and overburdened with PC functions (like spreadsheet software and printing) that made them slow.

In 1995, Palmcomputing was eventually bought by U.S. Robotics, which launched PalmPilot in 1996 with a much improved handwriting-recognition technology and touch screen. PalmPilot was an instant and massive success. It had much less functionality than either of Newton or the Psion Series 3 palmtops but it was simple, easy to use, and excellent at synchronizing with PCs. The Newton was like a scaled-down PC, loaded with all kinds of software applications. It was also too thick and awkward to be easily carried around in a shirt pocket as originally intended; the database storage structure made it difficult to synchronize with the file-based system of a user's home computer. By contrast, the PalmPilot was conceived as accessory to the PC, to be used primarily as an organizer with connectivity to the PC. It was less sophisticated than either the Newton or Psion, but was exactly what the mass market wanted and needed!

By the end of that year, it had 60% of the U.S. market, and by 1998, it was shipping 100,000 units per month, compared with 20,000 units per month for Psion's Series 5. Palm, using Microsoft's OS, had expanded its distribution to Europe, and by 1999, Palm was also the market leader in Europe and other parts of the world.

6.3.7 IBM PERSONAL COMPUTER

IBM had become a behemoth with its highly profitable sales and service of large mainframes. Each mainframe cost over a million dollars and required extensive maintenance and service. In contrast, PCs sold in the price range of $600–$3000 a piece. IBM manager's did not see the mass market for PCs and thus did not envision how that business could be profitable as the mainframe business. Similarly, with its professional sales force, an impeccable brand name, and a massive R&D budget, IBM developed an impenetrable position in the mainframe market. As a result, the firm became complacent, bureaucratic, and lethargic and focused myopically on its mainframe market. In contrast, the PC market was characterized by fast-moving companies, rapid innovations, and an intensely competitive climate. Moreover, the market was strongly driven by Moore's law: performance of components, especially microprocessors and memory chips, doubled every 18 months. Thus, a company had to be ready with a new product every 18 months or less. Companies that could keep up the pace of innovation had a competitive advantage, while those that were slow to innovate died out. IBM had the technical expertise, personnel, and facilities to develop a PC from scratch. But the company clearly lacked the entrepreneurial drive to make a sustained success of such an endeavor. IBM of the 1970s was too bureaucratic and slow to succeed in the world of computers.

A PC is a small computer and is capable of rapidly obtaining, manipulating, storing, and calling up information for the user in a changed format if required. For these purposes, it has

1. A CPU
2. A memory
3. Input and output ports

It acquires information and commands through input ports by means of stored data on disk, by keyboard, by mouse movements, and, if the device is so enabled, from any source capable of feeding it digitized information. It communicates through output ports to video terminals, printers, permanent storage disks, sound systems, and other devices capable of receiving digital signals.

Mauchly–Eckert–Von Neumann's concept of the stored program computer used the basic technical idea that a binary number system could be directly mapped to the two physical states of a flip-flop electronic circuit. In this circuit, the logical concept of the binary unit "1" could be interpreted as the on (or conducting state) and the binary unit "0" could be interpreted as the off (or not conducting state) of the electric circuit. In this way, the functional concept of numbers (written on the binary base) could be directly mapped into the physical states (physical morphology) of a set of electronic flip-flop circuits. The number of these circuits together would express how large a number could be represented. This is what is meant by word length in the digital computer. Binary numbers must not only encode data but also the instructions that perform the computational operations on the data. One of the points of progress in computer technology has been how long a word length could be built into a computer.

The design of the early computer used a hierarchy of logical operations. The lowest level of logic was the mapping of a set of bistable flip-flop circuits to a binary number system. A next step up had circuits mapped to a Boolean logic (AND, OR, NOT circuits). A next step up had these Boolean logic circuits connected together for arithmetic operations (such as add and subtract, multiply and divide). Computational instructions were then encoded as sequences of Boolean logic operations and/or arithmetic operations. Finally, at the highest logic level, Von Neumann's stored program concept was expressed as a clocked cycle of fetching and performing computational instructions on data. This is now known as a Von Neumann computer architecture—sequential instruction operated as a calculation cycle, timed to an internal clock.

The modern computer has four hierarchical levels of schematic logics mapped to physical morphologies (forms and processes) of transistor circuits:

1. Binary numbers mapped to bistable electronic circuits
2. Boolean logic operations mapped to electronic circuits of bistable circuits
3. Mathematical basic operations mapped (through Boolean constructions) to electronic circuits
4. Program instructions mapped sequentially into temporary electronic circuits (of Boolean and/or arithmetic instructions)

The core of the computer is an arrangement made of transistors. All information in the computer is held by capacitors, tiny devices able to hold energy or to release it, to be on or off. Computers are digital devices. Everything is created from 0s and of 1s. Every capacitor needs something to switch it on or off. Transistors are such switches. By a convention used universally, the American Standard Code for Information Interchange (ASCII) defines the alphabet, numbers, and many special symbols as fixed binary values. For example, the capital letter A has the value of 10000001. These eight bits of information are treated as one unit, called a byte. To hold this number, eight capacitors and transistors are employed. Indeed, to hold the text of this paragraph, including the spaces that separate the words, 7952 transistors and capacitors will be kept busy until this paragraph is saved and the file is closed.

The heart of the computer is its CPU. Its control circuitry monitors ports and responds to commands, obtained directly from the keyboard, the mouse, or a stored program it has been asked to execute. In carrying out commands, the CPU sends messages to output devices, obtains information from and stores data to memory, interprets programs in memory by reading commands from them sequentially, and manipulates data using its arithmetic/logic unit (ALU) if required by the commands it decodes. The ALU operates on data placed in the CPU's special memory locations, known as registers. The CPU's controls permit it to recognize special interrupts. When an interrupt arrives, the CPU suspends the execution of the currently running program and picks up execution of another, keeping track of everything in specially set-aside areas of memory. The CPU's communication with the rest of the machine takes place via special data highways known as buses.

Three hierarchically arranged instruction sets tell the CPU what to do. A built-in and hardwired program, known as the kernel, becomes operational as soon as the machine is turned on. This program handles the basic functions, including booting of the OS from the hard drive. The OS contains the second layer of instructions. It resides in memory. Once up and running, it displays its own visual interface and responds to user commands. The third level is represented by user-activated software programs. One or more programs may be running at any time. These might be, for instance, a word processor, a spreadsheet, and an Internet connection. In modern PCs, functions such as visual display, printing, and disk operations are distinct units with specialized processors of their own so that the CPU's capacity is not diverted to routine tasks. Very advanced functionalities are available to the user wishing to have high-end graphical, audio, or communication capabilities. These devices are integrated into the computer as cards, which are placed into slots left open for just such add-ons on the computer's motherboard.

The year 1977 saw the introduction of three new PCs: Commodore's PET, Radio Shack's TRS-80, and Apple's Apple II, which quickly became popular. The success of these machines awakened IBM to the potential of the PC market. William Lowe, a manager of a small IBM unit in Boca Raton, made a proposal to IBM's corporate management committee for an IBM PC using readily available parts and software. His proposal was approved subject to the completion of the project in 1 year. That 1-year deadline proved to be a key factor in the product's initial success—and also the key reason for its ultimate demise.

IBM entrusted the design and manufacture of the new PC to the unit at Boca Raton, which was far away from the scrutiny and influence of IBM's headquarters in Armonk, New York. Under the leadership of Lowe, the Boca Raton project was entrepreneurial, free from bureaucracy, and goal driven. Lowe chose to buy almost all parts of the PC from components readily available in the market. Lowe used Microsoft's DOS OS and Intel's 16-bit 8088 processor. Lowe also designed the machine with an *open architecture* and many expansion slots. That way outside vendors could easily sell peripherals for the IBM PC without depending on IBM. He even encouraged manufacturers to supply such peripherals. The basic input output system (BIOS) that functions as the interface between the hardware and software was the only component that was proprietary to IBM and was designed and manufactured by IBM internally.

Lowe entered into fairly generous licensing agreements for the software. For example, he licensed the software from Microsoft, then a small company, on very generous terms.

IBM allowed Microsoft to hold the copyright for the software and to license the same software to IBM's competitors in the PC market. Similarly, it used Intel's microprocessor without seeking any exclusive rights to the chip. So Intel was free to sell the same chip to other firms. Thus, Intel and Microsoft got a foothold in the PC market, while IBM had only the BIOS protecting its uniqueness.

IBM PC was launched in August 1981 and was an instant hit. Because of its brand name, and supported by a massive advertising campaign, retail distribution, and a competitive price, sales exceeded all expectations. In a year, the company's sales totaled over 200,000 units. PC sales revenues soon equaled those of the mainframe and minicomputers combined.

The IBM PC's open architecture ensured healthy competition in components and accessories for the PC. But it also encouraged competitors to clone the PC and introduce models of their own. Within a few years, Compaq followed by Dell, HP, and a host of other companies entered the PC market by reverse engineering IBM's BIOS. IBM followed up with two successful product extensions based on the Intel's 286 processor, namely, the PC XT and the PC AT. However, when Intel introduced the 386 chip, IBM failed to bring out a new model right away. Competitors like Compaq seized the opportunity to take the lead by introducing an IBM-compatible model based on the 386 processor. Thereafter, the market moved too fast and the margins were too low for IBM to reclaim the lost ground.

In a last effort to gain a proprietary hold over its market, IBM tried to enter the market for the OSs, where it was in competition with Microsoft. IBM was confident of reclaiming the lost ground with the design of a graphical OS, OS/2. IBM contracted Microsoft for the development of OS/2 but retained the sole rights to license the program, unlike its policy for DOS. Unfortunately, here too, it was unwilling to let go the seeming primacy of the mainframe market. First, it insisted that OS/2 be compatible with its mainframes enabling seamless connectivity with the mainframes. But ensuring compatibility with mainframes made OS/2 a huge, clumsy, and a slow program. Microsoft did develop OS/2, but not before it had developed its own graphical OS, Windows. Microsoft Windows was free of any burden requiring compatibility with the mainframes and, therefore, was faster and more reliable than OS/2.

When Windows and OS/2 were finally launched, the former was way ahead in terms of performance and quickly took over the market. Thus, IBM finally lost both its hardware and software positions in the PC market.

6.3.8 YAHOO!

Yahoo is the world's best-known interactive web portal or entryway onto the WWW. The portal has its origins in the website directory created as a hobby by its two founders, David Filo and Jerry Yang. Filo and Yang, who were two PhD candidates in electrical engineering at Stanford University, wanted a quick and easy way to remember and revisit the websites they had identified as the best and most useful from the hundreds of thousands of sites that were quickly appearing on the WWW in the early 1990s. They soon realized that as the list of their favorite websites grew longer and longer, the list began to lose its usefulness since they had to look through a longer and longer list of URLs, or website addresses, to find the specific site they wanted. So to reduce their search time, Filo and Yang decided to break up their list of websites into smaller and more manageable categories according to their specific content or subject matter, such as sports, business, or culture. In April 1994, they published their website directory, *Jerry's Guide to the WWW*, for their friends to use. Soon, hundreds, then thousands, of people were clicking on their site because it saved them time and effort to identify the most useful sites. As they continued to develop their directory, Filo and Yang found that each of the directory's subject categories also became large and unwieldy to search, so they further divided the categories into subcategories. Now, their directory organized websites into a hierarchy, rather than a searchable index of pages, so they renamed their directory *Yahoo*. As their directory grew, they realized they could not possibly identify all the best sites that were appearing in the WWW, so they recruited human volunteers to help them improve, expand, and refine their directory and make it a more useful, labor-saving search device.

By 1994, hundreds of thousands of users were visiting the site every day, and it had quickly become the primary search portal of choice for people using the Internet to find the websites that provided the most useful, interesting, and entertaining content. By 1996, Yahoo listed over 200,000 individual websites in over 20,000 different categories, and hundreds of companies had signed up to advertise their products on its portal to its millions of users. This, however, was just the beginning of their efforts. It became clear that they could make money from their directory if they allowed companies to advertise their products on the site. Filo and Yang's business model was based on generating revenues by renting advertising space on the pages of their fast-growing web directory.

They took Yahoo's business model and replicate it around the world. By the end of 1996, there were 18 Yahoo portals operating outside the United States, and Yahoo could be accessed by users in 12 languages. In each country, Yahoo's portal and web directory were customized to the tastes and needs of local users.

Yahoo's success with its global operations convinced Google to craft a new vision of Yahoo, not as an Internet website directory but as a global communication, media, and retail company whose portal could be used to enable anyone to connect with anything or anybody on the Internet. In 1998, Yahoo acquired the Internet shopping portal through web providing services that enabled businesses to quickly create, publish, and manage secure online stores to market and sell goods and services. Over the next decade, Yahoo continuously developed technology and made acquisitions that allowed users to access an increasing number of services such as e-mail, instant messaging, news, stock alerts, personals, and job placement services using digital devices from conventional PCs to wireless laptops to eventually to handheld smartphones. Yahoo also began to work with content providers and merchants to help them build and improve their online content, which in turn increased the value of Yahoo's portal to users who could access the content and merchants through Yahoo. Yahoo also increased its value to advertisers by enabling them to better target their advertising message to specific demographic groups, for example, sports fans, teens, or investors. It began to increase the degree to which users could customize Yahoo's pages and services to better meet their specific needs. Its goal was to lock in users and increase their switching costs of turning to a new portal.

Most of these services were provided free to Yahoo users because the advertising revenues earned from the ads on the millions of webpages on its portal were the main source of its highly profitable business model. In addition, it earned some revenues from the fees it earned from joining sellers and buyers on its shopping and specialized retail sites. However, Yahoo also searched for opportunities to increase revenues by providing specialized, customized services to users for a monthly fee; for example, it established a personal dating service, a streaming stock quotes service, job hunting service, and various premium e-mail and web storage options that provided users with more kinds of value-added solutions. All these helped to increase revenues and earnings.

6.3.8.1 Search Services

One of the most important factors that generates return user visits and stimulates advertising revenues is the quality of a portal's search engine service. Semel recognized that for Yahoo to achieve significant revenue and earnings growth, it also had to maximize the value of its search services to Internet users to generate the high volume of web traffic that leads to significant revenues from online advertising and facilitating e-commerce transactions. As mentioned earlier, Yahoo's original search directory was developed by its own human editors or *surfers*, who identified the best websites and organized them into categories by their content. However, as the WWW grew enormously, its human surfers could not keep up, and from the early1990s, Yahoo partnered with independent *crawler-based* search engine companies to provide answers to user queries when there were no matches within its own human-powered listing directory. The independent search providers were paid by Yahoo according to the volume of queries their engines handled, and since Yahoo was the most popular search site on the web, being Yahoo's provider could earn the search engine company significant revenues. By 2003, Google's growing popularity as the search portal of choice and its fast-developing customized advertising strategy showed Yahoo's managers they had made a major error. Recognizing the increasing threat posed by Google's customized search and advertising strategy, Semel began to look for acquisitions to strengthen and improve Yahoo's search engine. Its past relationship with search engine leader Inktomi made that company an obvious acquisition target. After buying Inktomi in 2002, Yahoo bought Overture Services in 2003, a company that specialized in identifying and ranking the popularity of websites and in helping advertisers find the best sites to advertise on; it also obtained Overture's search engine subsidiaries AltaVista and AlltheWeb.

It is no longer clear what the company is today and what kind of portal it aspires to be since it functions as an entry portal, a web search engine company, a retail portal, a media content and communications company, and a social networking platform service; it also provides companies with a range of online commercial services and customized advertising programs. On top of all these, the push to generate advertising revenues across its entire website is paramount. Others argue that it is Yahoo's unique strength that it operates in all these areas and that as long as it can catch up with Google and other specialized dot-coms, it will perform well in the future.

The real breakthrough in Google's strategy was that it was not advertising on a particular portal that was the main source of revenue; it was the ability to create the advertising that was most closely linked to any specific webpage—the advertising that comes up when a user clicks on the search results from a particular query. Google's advertising model is to help every potential website or advertiser host-customized ads that drive online transactions so that everyone would benefit—website, advertiser, and, of course, Google, which collects a small fee for each click. Google has also improved its advertising system and seems able to maintain its first-mover advantage in customized advertising on other websites as well as improved search engine technology—hence the jump to $500 a share it reached in November 2006. Yahoo is also struggling to catch up with Google's AdSense service, which sells search-based and banner advertisements to other people's websites and blogs. Google is entering new advertising areas, offering package deals for its customers that take in radio and newspaper advertising as well as online ads. Its goal seems to be to become the leading advertiser in every communications media.

6.4 INNOVATION VARIATIONS

Innovation can be defined in several ways, for example, the introduction of something new, a new idea, method, or device; the creation of new products or services; the introduction of a new idea into the marketplace in the form of a new product or service or an improvement in organization or process; a successful exploitation of new ideas, creating value out of new ideas, new products, new services, or new ways of doing things; and the creative force of humankind that allows the progress of the world to advance. The definitions earlier show that there are different views on innovation. It is argued here that an innovation must be differentiated from an (ordinary) improvement. For instance, physical products and services can be improved on the basis of customer feedback, resulting in new versions or releases. Innovations, however, create something new in a more profound sense—for example, new products based on new technologies or on a new combination of existing technologies. Otherwise, there would be no need for another term having exactly the same meaning as the word improvement.

Innovation is the process whereby ideas for new (or improved) products, processes, or services are developed and commercialized in the marketplace. The process of innovation affects the whole business—not just specified products, services, or technologies. Innovation is not just about technology development. Innovation had to be in the way we did our financing, the way we did our marketing and marketing relationships, the way we created strategic partnerships, and the way we dealt with government. The innovative nature of doing business for us had to be pervasive in the company and had to look at more than just technology development. The crucial element of innovation's success may well be related to the way the organization works and serves its customers (e.g., providing turnkey deliveries instead of just selling machinery) or to the revenue logic behind the offering (e.g., revenue sharing instead of fixed license fees).

Companies do not aim to develop new technologies and products for the sake of their novelty value only. The main driver is, naturally, the expected economic yield. A new product or service cannot be regarded successful unless it (1) sells well and (2) produces profits. Technical performance per se does not suffice. Therefore, another basic criterion for innovation is its ability to create new value to the customer as well as to its producer. In this way, the concept of innovation gets linked with the concept of benefit. In other words, the product can be new, but if it doesn't turn out to be beneficial and commercially successful, it cannot be called innovation. When innovation is looked at from the viewpoint of benefits, the picture gets more diverse and complicated.

Innovation involves an act of creating a new product or process. The act includes invention as well as the work required to bring a new idea or concept into the final form. Both inventing and innovating require creativity, which is an individual process. But individuals do not produce innovations; individuals play different roles when building a solution to a problem, but rarely does an individual have the whole answer. Introducing a new product to the market calls for different sorts of competences, resources, and activities. For example, before a new idea or concept may be taken further, it must be considered from various perspectives, such as R&D, production, distribution, marketing and sales, customer service, and, of course, revenue generation.

Innovation is described in many different ways—by scope, level, nature, or depth. An example of describing innovation by its scope could mean dividing innovations into the following categories (the examples in parentheses have been taken from the telecom industry):

- Technology (e.g., radio networks)
- Product (e.g., a mobile phone)
- Service (e.g., location-based services)
- Marketing/culture (e.g., the mobile phone represents personality)
- Organization and process (e.g., automated service procedures)
- Business model/strategy (e.g., long-term package sales)

Very often, if not always, a true innovation incorporates elements from more than one of the aforementioned categories.

The nature of innovation can be described using three different dimensions:

1. Incremental (or continuous or sustaining) versus radical (or discontinuous or disruptive) innovation: This dimension has to do with the scale or magnitude of changes resulting from the innovation. The terms *incremental* and *continuous* encompass the idea of a foreseeable, step-by-step development process, in which particular functional or structural features of the product or service concerned are gradually enhanced or replaced by different features. Therefore, it is actually difficult to say when the question is about *innovation* and when it is about *product enhancement*. If the innovation is sustaining, it usually allows an organization to maintain its current approach to the target market. For example, if the innovation is related to the fuel efficiency of cars, the resulting new car will probably be marketed and used in pretty much the same way as before. Fuel efficiency has been an important development target in the automotive industry for decades, and most new cars have always been marketed as being better in this respect—regardless of the underlying technology.

   A radical innovation would significantly change the supply and demand conditions in the market or product category concerned. For example, introduction of a cheap and safe electric car that could replace existing fuel-based car would certainly do that. Radical innovations typically involve large leaps in understanding, new ways of seeing the problem at hand, and taking bigger risks than many people involved feel comfortable about. In addition, they are often disruptive in the sense that they render earlier success products and/or business models obsolete.

2. Local (or modular) versus systemic (or architectural) innovation: This dimension is closely related to the scope of changes that result from or are necessary for the adoption and diffusion of the innovation. In the case of a local or modular innovation, the functional principles or performance of a product or its component may change, but the way it connects to other surrounding systems remains unchanged. For example, let's assume that someone develops new technology that doubles the power of mobile phone batteries. If the new batteries, based on that technology, can be designed in such a way that they do not necessitate changes in the design or manufacturing of the phones, the innovation can be called modular. Manufacturers and customers may easily change old batteries to the new ones without being forced to vary their behavior in any major way (both can, however, benefit from the development, which provides them with new options for the marketing and use of mobile phones).

   In the case of a systemic or architectural innovation, the introduction of the new technology, product, service, business model, etc., calls for changes in the structural or functional features of other related products or systems and/or in the behavior of other actors, for example, suppliers, distributors, or customers. This may create substantial organizational and marketing challenges for the organization behind the innovation.

3. Closed versus open innovation: This dimension aims to characterize innovations in terms of the nature of interactions between the initiator of the original idea, his or her affiliation or reference group within which the idea is incubated, and the *external world*, including all relevant interest groups and individuals that are expected to contribute to or benefit from the end result of the development work. Closed innovation refers to innovation based on internal and centralized R&D and deep vertical integration of the value chain from research to commercialization. The term *closed* is also used to refer to secrecy and various formal arrangements for the protection of original ideas and all possibly useful intermediate products of the development work. This may be the case if the original idea has been evaluated to bear significant economic potential and if, at the same time, the endeavor is prone to an expensive failure (e.g., due to industrial espionage). For example, the development of new drugs certainly belongs to this category.

   Open innovation, on the other hand, stands for innovation practices designed to take full advantage of the changing knowledge landscape (e.g., abundance of knowledge) and business environment (e.g., availability of venture capital and various services) through a systematic utilization of external knowledge and search for additional commercialization channels for technologies that have been developed but cannot be commercialized in-house. In informal parlance, the term *open* is also associated with the free exchange of ideas and information both within and between organizations, the underlying assumption being that without distributing ideas, crossing borders, and seeking international cooperation, there simply is no way of achieving breakthrough innovations. The advocates of open innovation stress the value of reciprocity: in exchange for ideas and information that one conveys to the community, he or she will be rewarded by additional ideas and information that may prove useful later.

6.4.1 Wankel Rotary Engine

In 1924, Felix Wankel first conceived the notion of an engine whose pistons would be replaced by rotors, and he embarked intermittently on the work that would become his lifelong passion and would result in his invention of the Wankel rotary engine. Wankel was employed in 1951 by the NSU Motorenwerke AG to continue his work on developing a rotary engine, which NSU hoped to use in manufacturing its motorcycles. Wankel completed the first design for a rotary piston engine in 1954 and, on February 1957, completed the first prototype of his rotary engine that turned in slightly over 20 horsepower.

Wankel's rotary engine is housed in a uniquely shaped combustion chamber of an automotive engine, its triangular rotor replacing the pistons that are characteristic of most internal combustion engines. The stages through which the rotor passes are, respectively, intake, compression, expansion, and exhaust. During the intake stage, air is taken in and mixed with fuel that is drawn into the motor through the tiny intake opening. In the next stage, the rotor compresses the mixture of fuel and air as the rotor passes the intake opening. During the next stage, a spark plug ignites the mixture, which causes the burning gases to expand. This, in turn, causes the rotor to move around the output shaft. Finally, the burnt gases are expelled through the exhaust port as soon as the rotor tip uncovers it. When this four-stage cycle has been completed, it automatically repeats itself, resulting in a smooth infusion of power into the engine.

The most important parts of the rotary engine are the triangular rotor and the uniquely shaped chamber in which it rotates. The tips of the rotor are in continuous contact with the chamber's walls and, because of the rotor's triangular structure, separate the chamber into three specific areas. In the four-stroke-cycle gasoline engine, each piston has to move back and forth two times and stop four times to go through its cycle. The rotary engine, on the other hand, operates continuously, completing three cycles of combustion with each complete rotation of its rotor. The single-rotor engine produces one power stroke for each turn of its output shaft, whereas the more conventional piston engine produces one power stroke every time the piston moves down its cylinder. Thus, the dual-rotor engine is able to generate a number of power strokes equal to that of a four-cylinder piston engine. Because all the motion in a Wankel engine is rotary, its operation is remarkably efficient. Whereas in the piston engine, the reciprocating vertical motion has to be converted to rotary motion, in the Wankel engine, there is no need for such a conversion. Every revolution of the rotor results in three impelling power forces.

In 1957, shortly after Wankel unveiled the prototype of his rotary engine, automobile manufacturers throughout the world and particularly in Japan and the United States became extremely interested in this new approach to powering vehicular engines, especially those used to power automobiles, trucks, and motorcycles. Rotary engine automobiles, like piston engine automobiles, require a battery, a starter motor, and a distributor to engage the engine. They also require cooling and lubrication systems to make their engines work efficiently. To this extent, they are similar to automobiles with more conventional engines. One of the major selling points of the Wankel rotary engine is that it has less than half the moving parts of conventional piston engines, meaning that there are fewer parts that can malfunction.

In 1967, the Japanese automobile maker Mazda introduced the Cosmo Sport, one of the world's first dual-rotor rotary engine cars. The company manufactured many rotary engine sports cars that were much in demand because of their dependable power and the infrequency with which they required repairs. In 1971, despite of the international energy crisis that discouraged enthusiasm for new technologies, Mazda continued to experiment with the rotary engine and to refine it in many ways. By the end of the 1970s, the Japanese manufacturer concentrated on producing sports cars with rotary engines for European and American markets.

6.4.2 Texas Instruments Integrated Circuits

The invention of the transistor made possible much more complex circuits thanks to the smaller size and power requirements of the transistor compared to the older electronic tube. In the late 1950s, electrical engineers were using the new silicon transistor for many advanced electronic circuits. The transistors were so useful that a new problem arose in electronics. The new complex circuits engineers could now dream up required so many transistors that it was physically impossible to wire them together with the technology of soldering transistors into printed circuit boards. So a new natural limit was on the horizon for transistorized electronics—the number that could be physically wired together. In 1958, this limit was on the mind of two researchers: Jack Kilby at TI and Robert Noyce at Fairchild.

In 1958, Willis Adcock of TI hired Kilby; he was assigned to a *micromodule* research project that was already under way at TI to approach the problem of integrating transistors rather than handwiring them together. Since TI led in silicon technology, he had this idea: If transistors were made of silicon, could not the other components of a circuit, such as resistors and capacitors, also be fabricated on silicon—which would automatically resolve the problem of integration? Why not make the whole circuit on a silicon chip? It was an inventive idea, for at the time, the technology for fabricating resistors used carbon as the phenomenal material and plastics and metal foil for capacitors.

He entered rough sketches of how to make each component by properly arranging the silicon material. Kilby carved out a resistor on one silicon chip and then carved a capacitor on another and wired the two chips together. They worked, showing resistance and capacitance in the circuit. Adcock gave his approval to build a whole circuit on a chip and Kilby chose to build an oscillator circuit—one that could generate a sinusoidal signal. The circuit on the chip was hooked to an oscilloscope that would display the form of the signal from the circuit. Before the circuit was turned on, the oscilloscope displayed a flat line indicating no signal output; upon switching on the new IC on the silicon chip—a wiggling line appeared on the screen, the sine-wave form of an oscillator circuit. This was the birth of the IC chip, on September 12, 1958.

About the same time, Robert Noyce at Fairchild Semiconductors also hit upon the same idea of making multiple devices on a single piece of silicon, in order to be able to make interconnections between devices as part of the manufacturing process. He achieved and demonstrated this soon thereafter. Both TI and Fairchild Semiconductors filed for the patent on the IC chip. Finally, in 1966, TI and Fairchild agreed to grant licenses to each other and share in inventing the device.

6.4.3 THEORY OF CONSTRAINTS

Over the course of the 1980s, Eli Goldratt introduced a powerful set of concepts called the TOC. The theory represents a philosophy of operations management, a management system, and a set of tools/principles to improve operations. Initially, TOC promotion focused around the fact that most manufacturing operations have a few bottleneck steps that limit the throughput of the plant under typical product mixes. The goal of planning, then, should be to schedule these bottleneck steps efficiently so as to achieve maximum throughput, to schedule steps before and after the bottlenecks in order to best support the bottlenecks, and to *elevate* the constraint by adding capacity there and thus shifting the binding constraints elsewhere in the system. The drum–buffer–rope scheduling methodology was invented to support plant operations to *exploit* constraints to the maximum possible (get maximum throughput through them) and *subordinate* other manufacturing steps to the constrained ones. As TOC evolved, greater emphasis was placed on the fact that the principles apply not just to manufacturing but to supply-chain operations as a whole and even to non-supply-chain activities like project management. These principles led to a universal five-step methodology for business improvement:

1. Identify the system's constraints.
2. Decide how to exploit the system's constraints.
3. Subordinate everything else to the earlier decision.
4. Elevate the system's constraints.
5. If in the previous steps a constraint has been broken, go back to step 1.

TOC has helped us to recognize that while well-managed supply chains operate with less inventory than poorly managed ones, systems that have significant process variability (which is to say almost all operations systems) must plan to operate with some inventory. Corollary concepts that TOC has given us are that not all processes should be fully utilized (we have to leave slack in some steps so that we can focus on a few bottlenecks), that manufacturing lead times cannot be modeled statically and are truly dynamic, that economic order quantities are seldom useful in a manufacturing environment, and that transfer batch sizes (between workstations) can be much smaller than reasonable fabrication batch sizes—thus improving flow and reducing WIP inventory. TOC's emphasis on always increasing throughput has remained more controversial, as has the fact that it disputes decision making based on traditional cost accounting. TOC has also helped raise the level of discourse substantially in product flow planning because it focuses on elements that MRP neglects. Whereas MRP tries to downplay the importance of capacity constraints, TOC points out correctly that planning product flow is, in fact, all about managing around constraints. Constraints are a fundamental part of operations because real businesses have to achieve good asset utilization in order to compete economically, and, hence, simply buying plenty of capacity so that constraints do not impact operations is seldom a feasible strategy.

6.4.4 APPLE IPOD

An MP3 player, often called a digital music player or portable audio player, is a handheld device that plays and stores audio and video files. The device is called an MP3 player because the digital format used most commonly on the device is called an MP3. This format quickly became the standard in audio file downloading and distribution in the late 1990s and into the twenty-first century. In the late 1990s, when consumers were starting to burn their favorite CDs, Macs did not have CD burners or software to manage users' digital music collections. If people were going to maintain the bulk of their music collection on a computer, they needed a portable MP3 player to take music with them—a Sony Walkman for the digital age. This led to the concept of iPod. While there were such devices on the market already, they could hold only a few dozen songs each. To run the iPod, Apple licensed software from Portal Player. Apple also learned that Toshiba was building a tiny 1.8 in. hard drive that could hold over 1000 songs; Apple quickly cut a deal with Toshiba, giving it exclusive rights to the drive for 18 months. Meanwhile, Apple focused on designing the user interface, the exterior styling, and the synchronization software to make it work with the Mac. The attention to detail and design elegance, with requisite financial support, was to turn the iPod into a fashion accessory. When iPod was unveiled in October 2001, the price of $399 was significantly above that of competing devices, and since the iPod worked only with Apple computers, it seemed destined to be a niche product. Jobs made the call to develop a Windows-compatible version of the iPod, which was introduced in mid-2002.

Apple's new player held a small monitor, a scroll wheel to guide the user through various functions displayed on the monitor, and a 5 GB hard drive. It could hold approximately 1000 songs. With later iPod models, the wheel would become stationary and touch sensitive; the user moves through the iPod folders by clicking various places on the wheel. Some models are flash based and hard disk based. Apple continually released new generations and models of iPods from 2003 to 2005. Color screens were added in the middle of 2005 and video was added in October 2005. The fifth generation iPod was released on September 6, 2005. Its 60 GB hard drive could hold more than 10,000 songs. The iPod mini and iPod nano, both released in 2005, sold well because of their compact size and the array of colors in which they were available.

Apple created iTunes, an online store where users can purchase and download individual songs or entire albums. It took Apple approximately 18 months to convince the music labels to sign on to the store. Unlike Napster, these downloads are legal. Users pay for the music they download— typically $0.99 per song. The site, which was introduced on April 29, 2003, allows users to hear a 30 s sample of a song before deciding to purchase it. Users might also rate songs or even create lists of favorite songs called playlists. Other users can view these lists and purchase the songs on them as they wish. iTunes uses jukebox technology, which enables users to create and manage a digital library. Users can burn CDs on their home computer using songs from this library. Users can also upload music from other sources (e.g., a current CD collection) to this library. This upload process is called ripping.

Success at this scale attracts competitors, but with the first-mover advantage, iTunes continued to outsell its rivals by a wide margin. In mid-2006, iTunes was accounting for about 80% of all legal music downloads. iTunes was also the fourth largest music retailer in the United States; the other three all had physical stores. The iPod also had plenty of competition. Many of the competing devices were priced aggressively and had as much storage capacity as the iPod. However, iPod still accounted for 77% of annual sales in the U.S. market because in contrast to the rivals' systems, iTunes and iPod have always worked together seamlessly.

6.4.5   Xerox Laser Printer

Laser printing (and, indirectly, ink-jet printers) came from the invention of xerography—technology based on static electricity. A metallic surface, a platen, is uniformly charged across its entire surface. A document laid over this pattern, but separated from it by glass, is powerfully illuminated. The areas of the platen that light can reach lose their charge, but the areas shaded by the dark print on the document retain their charge. The process is functionally identical to putting a negative over photographic film and exposing it to light, but in photography, the negative would let light through. In xerography, the print prevents light from passing through. The platen is moved over a bed of tiny particles of carbonaceous toner. Where the platen is still charged, particles of toner are drawn by the electrostatic force still on the platen to its surface and cling there. Where no charge is present, no toner sticks. The sheet of paper that will become the copy is brought in contact with the platen. A powerful charge is applied to the paper so that it becomes electrically more attractive than the platen and draws the toner to stick to it. While the toner still clings to the paper, the sheet is subjected to high heat, causing the toner to melt and to fuse to the paper's fibers. In practice, the platen is arranged as a drum. The image is transferred to the drum as it turns, picks up toner as it rotates, and transfers toner to the paper as both are moving together.

Laser printing was invented by Gary Starkweather in 1969; he was an optician working for Xerox. It occurred to him that he could use lasers, capable of producing very tiny beams of light, to inscribe a page on a xerographic drum. He could send light for every dot he wanted to be white and simply withhold the light from dots he wanted to be black. Spots that refused the light would attract the toner. All other areas would be neutral. A computer that had already divided a document in its memory into a matrix of dots could send the signals to the laser sequentially. Digital copying developed from laser printing. A digital copier first scans a document into a copier's memory and then laser prints that digital image to paper by means of drum and toner.

Ink-jet printing technology, invented simultaneously but independently by HP in the United States and by Canon in Japan, built on the software staging of data by the computer as rasterized images, but exploited the fact that tiny droplets of heated ink form bubbles that, in bursting, can be directed precisely to intended, tiny areas of the paper to be imaged. The economist, in a summary of this technology, dubbed it *spitting image* by way of conveying the sensory impression this process would make if people were tiny enough to witness it as observers in the vicinity of the printing head. Electrical signals reading the raster (the dots that form the image) cause individual ink dispensers to boil up briefly to eject the proper amount and color of ink to be deposited as the printing head moves.

6.4.6   Blackberry PDAs

Apple's Newton had no radio transceiver and thus no mobile communication abilities. It could simply synch to a desktop computer using a cradle and wires. Rob Fraser, who had worked on radio design with Motorola and operated his own wireless systems integration company, had already published an article predicting the *wireless* PDA in the July 1991 issue of Communications Magazine. In it, he laid out all the market potential and engineering challenges that had to be met before perfecting what he called the personal communicator, a handheld touch screen Mobitex device with e-mail, computer bulletin board connectivity, and a way to manage your calendar, contact list, and other personal data. Everyone else was trying to add a radio to a PDA, whereas Mike's mind-set was how to add a PDA to a radio. One isn't going to beat everybody in every category, so he decided that focus would be one of the keys to Research In Motion (RIM)'s competitive success, "a focus on the wireless end of the business, playing on the convergence of mobility and digital data." Lazaridis believed that his potential customers craved solutions in the way of small, user-friendly handhelds with a secure and reliable system of transmission—a technology that would keep everyone in the loop, no matter where they were or what access they had to standard computer servers.

In January 1992, Ericsson launched the Viking Express, the world's first commercial wireless e-mail solution. Enveloped in a sleek black leather case, it featured the Ericsson Mobidem, velcroed together with an HP-95 palmtop and bundled with RIM's MobiLib-Plus application programming interface (API) to work with Anterior's gateway to major e-mail systems. Anterior Technology was led by Geoff Goodfellow, the California techie who came up with the whole idea of wireless e-mail in 1982; Goodfellow had this vision of an e-mail system that had a client and a server and he built both. By the time Viking Express shipped, there was a major falling out between RIM and RadioMail. Goodfellow and his group refused to work with the RIM mobile client application and demanded Ericsson use its RadioMail-developed client. Ericsson caved in; Ericsson felt that the sensible thing was to go with RadioMail, since RIM didn't yet have a workable client and server.

But Mike Lazaridis was ready with all the essential requisites—with compression, encryption, synchronization, a thumbwheel, context ribbons, thumbpad, dual destination e-mail, always on, push BlackBerry Enterprise Server (BES), and enough bright minds and capital to get the job done. He merely had to put all of these together to make them work within one device.

RIM relied on Intel Corporation support to build the first Interactive pager prototype. It was designed with a 16-bit OS along with built-in contact manager, scheduler, and form-based messaging applications. It sported a QWERTY keyboard and a small, text-only display screen that showed four lines of text. Network service was provided by RAM Mobile Data and Ardis Co. The network service had all the features of a traditional one-way paging system, but also added two-way features such as peer-to-peer delivery and read receipts. It could also send faxes and leave voice messages on a telephone. The 900 could communicate with the Internet, peer users, and the phone network via a gateway, which also served as the store and forward mailbox for the wireless user. The Interactive pager could send and receive messages and had its own Internet address. It could store 100 kB of data and had some preprogrammed responses, such as *I'll be late*. RIM released its RIM 900 original equipment manufacturer (OEM) radio modem and the RIM 900 Interactive pager in 1996. They marked the last step before the first BlackBerry. RAM Mobile Data was sold and renamed BellSouth Wireless Data in 1995 and later became Cingular Interactive when BellSouth and SBC formed Cingular Wireless (now renamed AT&T). Operator of the Mobitex network in the United States, Cingular Wireless brought the Interactive pager service to market in 1997. Corporate User magazine named it the top wireless product of the year.

Lazaridis was already working flat-out on the successor to RIM 900. He was determined to produce a cheaper, friendlier, and even smaller device termed as RIM 950. Mike Lazaridis hit on a way of messaging using the one big physical factor we share with monkeys and apes—opposable thumbs. The resulting e-mail device, optimized for thumb computing, he still calls RIM's *secret sauce*. The RIM team filed for a patent for the device in June 1998. The network operations center (NOC) was the brains of the whole process. When the client company's desktop redirector (later called the BES) pushed out data or a message, it went to a virtual device on the NOC. The NOC then pushed the message to the real handheld on behalf of the BES.

Another great innovation by Lazaridis and Gary Mousseau was resolving the dual mailbox problem. In those days, mobile users had to have a special, separate wireless mailbox—apart from their corporate e-mail—for e-mail, fax, and text-to-voice services. People didn't know whether to reach users by sending e-mail to their desktop computers or wireless devices. Mike hit upon an integrated, single-mailbox, end-to-end wireless data solution. It mirrored a user's e-mail account, making RIM's handheld as an extension of their PC desktop inbox, with the same e-mail address doing double duty. They also perfected a continuously connected *push model* of e-mail delivery that automatically found the user and notified discretely about its arrival. The *Single Mailbox* patent was filed on May 29, 1998.

RIM also patented a way to compress and reenvelope the message so it was completely secure and opaque as it moved through the NOC to the destination device. They figured out a way to generate a two-to-one compression ratio on small bursts of data and then encrypt the data, which saved lots of bandwidth. Unlike Moore's law, which states that the number of transistors on a semiconductor chip will double every year, neither battery power nor available radio spectrum can be expanded quite so easily. So RIM had to pioneer the rational use of battery power. This meant finding clever uses of bandwidth that wouldn't drain the batteries so quickly.

The 950 became a huge commercial hit when it was rebranded as the BlackBerry, and the successful launch and publicity boosted RIM's sales that year by 80%, to U.S. $85 million. RIM launched its BlackBerry wireless e-mail service across North America in January 1999 through partners Rogers Cantel and BellSouth. The package included the RIM 386-based wireless handheld device with typical PDA organizer software (calendar, address book, task list), along with a docking cradle and synchronizing software to connect with a PC. E-mail was encrypted using Triple DES and remained encrypted at all points between the desktop PC and the handheld device. The BlackBerry was the first wireless device that synchronized with company mail systems so that users did not need a different e-mail address when traveling. This was a very big selling point. Initially set up for Microsoft Exchange, RIM later added Lotus Domino and Novell GroupWise synchronization. The 950 cost more than $500 (including activation fee) or could be rented for $25 per month plus a one-time $69 activation fee. Cost for the service was an additional $50 per month, of which half was rebated monthly for the first 12 months. Soon, RIM had a server farm that filled an air-conditioned cement block warehouse.

In 2000, RIM revenue leapt another 160%, to U.S. $221 million. By February 2000, and even before entering Europe, RIM was boasting 164,000 BlackBerry subscribers in 7,800 companies. Competition between RIM and Apple, Nokia, Samsung, HTC, and their carriers is getting hotter by the day. Yet in spite of Apple's entry on the scene, and the explosion of iClones and me-too devices, RIM is stronger than ever. The early years of the twenty-first century were good for RIM, as its devices went from strength to strength, growing in power and sophistication and morphing into true mobile PCs (MPCs) also known as smartphones. Revenues and profits also skyrocketed. From revenue of $85 million in 2000, RIM was generating $595 million in 2004 and a colossal $6 billion in 2008.

The addictive, immersive properties of smartphone use are now challenging the whole world of work, and we're a long way from being able to cope with the new power it gives us. In offices around the world, workers are drowning in e-mail excess, and BlackBerry use is very much part of the problem. It's now clear that constant BlackBerry checking can actually nullify gains made in productivity. BlackBerry bondage can also make family life suffer, as employees bring their work home and never really leave the office behind. Any gains people make in organizing family messaging and scheduling can get cruelly offset by upsets in work–life balance.

6.4.6.1 Smartphones

Just as the PDA technology was finding favor among consumers, manufacturers were working on the next generation of the technology. IBM released the first smartphone, the IBM Simon, in a joint operation with BellSouth in 1994. A smartphone is a handheld device designed to offer complete phone functions while also operating as a PDA. Smartphones function as phones first and data managers second. The wireless phone had been on the market for a decade in 1994 (the first commercial model was available from Motorola in 1984). By combining a PDA and a wireless phone, manufacturers took communication possibilities to the next level. In short, instead of simply transmitting voice, phones could now transmit data. By 2007, most wireless phones were so multifunctional that the line between smartphones and cellular phones was blurred considerably.

6.4.7 Apple II

On April Fools' Day, 1976, two young electronics enthusiasts, Steve Jobs and Steve Wozniak, started a company to sell a primitive PC that Wozniak had designed. Steve Jobs was just 20; Wozniak, or Woz as he was commonly called, was 5 years older. They had known each other for several years, having been introduced by a mutual friend who realized that they shared an interest in consumer electronics. Woz had designed the computer just for the fun of it. That's what people did in 1976. The idea that somebody would actually want to purchase his machine had not occurred to Woz, but it did to Jobs. Jobs persuaded a reluctant Woz to form a company and sell the machine. The location of the company was Steve Jobs' garage. Jobs suggested they call the company Apple and their first machine the Apple I.

They sold around 200 of them at $666 each. The price point was picked as something of a prank. The Apple I had several limitations—no case, keyboard, or power supply being obvious ones. It also required several hours of laborious assembly by hand. By late 1976, Woz was working on a replacement to the Apple I, the Apple II.4 In October 1976, with the Apple II under development, Jobs and Woz were introduced to Mike Markkula. Only 34, Markkula was already a retired millionaire, having made a small fortune at Fairchild and Intel. Markkula had no plans to get back into business anytime soon, but a visit to Jobs' garage changed all that. He committed to investing $92,000 for one-third of the company and promised that his ultimate investment would be $250,000. Stunned, Jobs and Woz agreed to let him join as a partner. It was a fateful decision. The combination of Woz's technical skills, Jobs' entrepreneurial zeal and vision, and Markkula's business savvy and connections was a powerful one. Markkula told Jobs and Woz that neither of them had the experience to run a company and persuaded them to hire a president, Michael Scott, who had worked for Markkula at Fairchild.

The Apple II was introduced in 1977 at a price of $1200. The first version was an integrated computer with a Motorola microprocessor and included a keyboard, power supply, monitor, and the BASIC programming software. It was Jobs who pushed Woz to design an integrated machine—he wanted something that was easy to use and not just a toy for geeks. Jobs also insisted that the Apple II look good. It had an attractive case and no visible screws or bolts. This differentiated it from most PCs at the time, which looked as if they had been assembled by hobbyists at home (as many had).

In 1978, Apple started to sell a version of the Apple II that incorporated something new—a disk drive. The disk drive turned out to be a critical innovation, for it enabled third-party developers to write software programs for the Apple II that could be loaded via floppy disks. Soon, programs started to appear, among them EasyWriter, a basic word-processing program, and VisiCalc, a spreadsheet, was an instant hit and pulled in a new customer set, business types who could use VisiCalc for financial planning and accounting. Since VisiCalc was available only for the Apple II, it helped to drive demand for the machine. By the end of 1980, Apple had sold over 100,000 Apple IIs, making the company the leader in the embryonic PC industry. The company had successfully executed an IPO, was generating over $200 million in annual sales, and was profitable.

6.4.8 eBᴀʏ

The auction business was changed forever in 1995 when Pierre Omidyar developed innovative software that allowed buyers around the world to bid online against each other to determine the fair price for a seller's product. Until the 1990s, the auction business was largely fragmented; thousands of small city-based auction houses offered a wide range of merchandise to local buyers. And a few famous global ones, such as Sotheby's and Christie's, offered carefully chosen selections of high-priced antiques and collectibles to limited numbers of dealers and wealthy collectors. However, the auction market was not very efficient, for there was often a shortage of sellers and buyers, and so it was difficult to determine the fair price of a product. Dealers were often able to influence auction prices and so obtain bargains at the expense of sellers. Typically, dealers were able to buy at low prices and then charge buyers high prices in the bricks-and-mortar (B&M) antique stores that are found in every town and city around the world, so they reaped high profits.

The magic of eBay's software is that the company simply provides the electronic conduit between buyers and sellers; it never takes physical possession of the products that are listed, and their shipping is the responsibility of sellers and payment the responsibility of buyers. Thus, eBay does not need to develop all the high-cost functional activities like inventory, shipping, and purchasing to deliver products to customers, unlike Amazon.com. eBay generates the revenues that allow it to operate and profit from its electronic auction platform by charging a number of fees to sellers (buyers pay no specific fees). In the original eBay model, sellers paid a fee to list a product on eBay's site and paid a fee if the product was sold by the end of the auction. As its platform's popularity increased and the number of buyers grew, eBay has increased the fees it charges sellers.

From the beginning, eBay's business model and strategies were based on developing and refining Omidyar's auction software to create an easy-to-use online market platform that would allow buyers and sellers to meet and transact easily and inexpensively. eBay's software was created to make it easy for sellers to list and describe their products and easy for buyers to search for, compare, and bid on the products they wanted to purchase. To make transactions between anonymous Internet buyers and sellers possible, however, Omidyar's software had to reduce the risks facing buyers and sellers. It achieved this by a method for building and establishing trust between buyers and sellers—building a reputation over time. This is more difficult because new *unknown* buyers come into the market continuously. After every transaction, buyers and sellers can leave online feedback about their view of the other's behavior and the value of the transaction they have completed. When sellers and buyers consistently act in an honest way in more and more transactions over time, they are able to build a stronger and stronger positive feedback score that provides them with a good reputation for honesty.

This core auction business model worked well for the first years of eBay's existence. Using this basic software platform, every day tens of millions of products such as antiques and collectibles, cars, computers, furniture, clothing, books, DVDs, and a myriad of other items are listed by sellers all around the world on eBay and bought by the highest bidders. The incredible variety of items sold on eBay suggests why eBay's business model has been so successful—the same set of auction platform programs, constantly improved and refined over time from Omidyar's original programs, can be used to sell almost every kind of product, from low-priced books and magazines costing only cents to cars and antiques costing tens or hundreds of thousands of dollars.

6.5 SUMMARY

This chapter presented different sources of variations, namely, pioneering, imitation, and innovation variations. The examples discussed range from pioneering variations like Lenoir internal combustion engine to AT&T transistors to Ford production system to CERN WWW. These illustrate how breakthrough products are pioneered, imitated, and radically innovated for a quantum jump in performance or a novel application inconceivable when the pioneering effort was first conceived. The examples of these variations also highlight the vast chasm that sometimes separates a host of trial ideas and products from an ultimately useful and successful product. In retrospect, sometimes one may not comprehend the challenges and barriers that stalled the development to the next stage—which, with hindsight, looks so obvious today.

7 Dimension of Variations

This chapter discussed variations for Built-for-Variation enterprises in one or several of these dimensions: strategy, structure, shared values, stuff, style, staff, skills, systems, and sequence. It discussed examples of businesses with strategy variations ranging from planned to emergent, structure variations ranging from control to autonomy, shared values variations ranging from rules driven to values driven, stuff variations ranging from products through services to experiences, style variations ranging from administrational to transformational, staff variations ranging from challenging to nurturing people, skills variations ranging from focus to breadth of skills, systems variations ranging from mandatory to discretionary, and sequence variations ranging from mass production to mass customization.

 We would like to highlight that the various life histories are meant to highlight the variations during the life span of these companies rather than to illustrate either effective or ineffective handling of administrative situations. It should also be highlighted that more than case studies, they are case histories or segments of case histories.

7.1 SHARED VALUES VARIATIONS RANGING FROM RULES DRIVEN TO VALUES DRIVEN

Enterprise culture can either support or frustrate enterprise goals. There is a determining relationship between cultural aspects and enterprise performance. Two views on culture can be mentioned. The first is based on a descriptive approach to culture, showing more attention for manifestations of culture and addressing culture on the level of form. Culture is thus seen as something the organization is. Within the second view, the normative aspect of culture is emphasized. Culture is then viewed as something the organization has. From this perspective, culture refers to basic values and beliefs that serve as guidance for behavior. Fundamentally, culture can act as an aggregated form of behavioral regulation and can replace some of the traditional rules-driven levers of control.

As indicated previously, much of the enterprise context and reality is unpredictable, ambiguous, and chaotic. Within enterprises, there are principles that allow them to develop an orderly pattern over time; such principles cohere over time into value patterns of culture. For example, how one should act in a specific service encounter is uncertain and unpredictable. However, the value patterns about quality guides the required behavior into an orderly and predictable fashion. In this sense, culture communicates implicitly what is considered important and acts as a source for uncertainty reduction. But for this to be effective requires trust in employees, as well as trust in the guiding power of values, knowing that they are strong enough influences to guide employee behavior into the desired direction.

Practically, the requirement for internal coherence and consistency is often violated with unfortunate consequences. For example, individual structures and systems are developed independently, leading to mismatches with the intentions of other structures or systems, or even with the intentions of the enterprise as a whole. All too often, mismatches will become manifest in the future or in another part of the enterprise. For example, specific performance-related rewards might lead to a strong narrow task or departmental focus, whereby the quality of the end-to-end process is degraded. The acquisition of unworkable orders because payment is contingent upon sales volume is another well-known example. Similarly, cross-functional process improvements might fail due to departmentally oriented accounting and management information structures, while reward structures focused on individuals might frustrate teamwork. Likewise, achieving quality improvements seems difficult if only productivity is measured. Finally, the needed long-term horizon for quality initiatives might be untenable due to the short-term financial reporting structures.

The requirement for coherence and consistency holds similarly for enterprise culture, management practices, and structures and systems mutually. Inconsistencies within the behavioral context might easily lead to low commitment or even cynicism about enterprise intentions. Multiple examples can be given; for example, it is not to be expected that quality improvements will be successful if the existing culture suppresses an open discussion about failures or when management frustrates improvement suggestions because of their perceived prerogative of decision making. Similarly, an information system for sharing knowledge seems of little value in a culture that encourages an individualistic and competitive working environment. In contrast, ensuring coherence and consistency of the behavioral context is indicative of a unified and integrated enterprise design.

> In the following is the case history of Cisco. It illustrates Cisco's dominant stance of shared values variation through acquisition driven by numbers (and rules of success) like sales and profits, with a continually fine-tune ability to integrate the acquired company with itself. As may be discerned through a careful perusal, these variations were accompanied simultaneously by variations in other dimensions of variations like strategy (emergent acquisitions), structure (biased toward operational autonomy), stuff (progressively enhanced products), style (administrational culture), and staff (nurturing people).

7.1.1 Acquiring Competitiveness at Cisco

Cisco is a 12-billion-dollar high-technology company: the fastest-growing company of its size in history, faster even than Microsoft, with a market capitalization of $200 billion. Cisco competes in markets where hardware is obsolete in 18 months. How has Cisco managed this startling growth in an industry where technology is constantly changing? Cisco has frequently used acquisitions to obtain new technology (and markets and market share). It has completed more than 40 mergers since 1993 and spent more than $18 billion acquiring 9 companies in 1998 and 14 companies in 1999. Normally, most mergers are failures, not only failing to achieve their intended objectives but, in many cases, actually destroying value as companies struggle to combine cultures, systems, and products. A good example was the postmerger failure of Cisco's direct competitors, namely, the number one intelligent-hub company SynOptics with the number two router company, Wellfleet, to create Bay Networks, a 1-billion-dollar business almost as large as Cisco.

7.1.1.1 Triggering an Avalanche

Mergers are difficult, maybe more so in the case of Cisco because Cisco's acquisitions are not just to acquire customers, branches, or plants—its mergers are specifically designed to acquire technology and know-how embodied in people, frequently including the founders of the acquired companies. The answer to the mystery of Cisco's ability to grow successfully by acquisition has to do with several complementary values that permeate the company: the importance of cultural fit and shared vision, speed, frugality, and the need and willingness to change continually.

In the early 1990s, fast Ethernet connections were still the LAN technology, but for WAN networking, asynchronous transfer mode (ATM) switches were becoming preferred by customers. ATM was a hardware-based switching technology that transmitted data faster than routers and could be used to connect a finite number of LANs together, with resulting high-speed communication between LANs. ATM was a hardware-based switching technology that transmitted data faster than routers and could be used to connect a finite number of LANS together, with resulting high-speed communication between LANs. Moreover, ATM allows a digital emulation of traditional switch-based phone networks and could bridge between data communications and telephone communications. Thus, Ethernet technology was hooking up computers into LANs, ATM technology was hooking together LANs into WANs, and routers were hooking all into Internet. The IT challenge was in tying LAN nets into WAN nets.

By 1993, an additional growth spurt began in the router market as the Internet continued to expand nationally and globally. New switches were developed for networks using hardware that did what software in routers was doing but faster. They were also capable of being used to put together larger Ethernet LANs, as switches that could function as better LAN hubs than routers. Cisco's drawback was that it supplied only routers when the market was expecting end-to-end full service provider. Cisco was eager to find companies that could help them offer increased bandwidth. This would improve a network's ability to move traffic smoothly, without delays. Although routers could expand bandwidth, they were slow, expensive, and were hard to manage in larger numbers. Nor did intelligent hubs (devices that make it easier to detect network crashes or faults) increase bandwidth.

The answer came from hardware vendors that began selling LAN switches that switched traffic from point to point and offered huge increases in bandwidth. Boeing had been considering a 10-million-dollar router order from Cisco but wished to use new switches from a new firm called Crescendo Communications. John Chambers learned from Boeing that unless Cisco cooperated with Crescendo, Cisco would not get the Boeing order. Boeing had (and still has) the largest private network in the world. As an early leader in networking, the aircraft maker had a large influence on the networking world as a whole. Its Boeing Computer Services did computer consulting for various customers including the government, managing such projects as Space Station Project Network. Consequently, Cisco decided to buy Crescendo for $97 million in 1990—for a company that had been forecasted to sell only $10 million of equipment the following year. But, in 2000, Cisco's switching business had become a 10-billion-dollar business, almost half of its annual revenues. The LAN switch became the core of their enterprise business. This was the first of Cisco's subsequent strategic policy of acquiring competitors to extend and improve technologies to provide advanced and complete customer solutions. Crescendo taught Cisco how to do acquisitions. Cisco's acquisition strategy got a further boost as more data, graphic, and video were put on the Internet, requiring companies to purchase more routers and switches to direct the overwhelming traffic.

7.1.1.2 Perfecting the Acquisition Strategy

The strategic challenge that Cisco leadership saw was the need to continue to ride the wave of Internet expansion as a dominant and fast-moving player. They studied lessons from GE, IBM, and HP. From GE, they would use Jack Welch's strategy for each business to be dominant as number one or two or not to compete. From IBM, they would use the business strategy to provide complete application solutions to customers but would avoid IBM's rigidity to avoid adaptation to new product lines. From Hewlett-Packard's strategies, they saw the need to periodically reinvent the organization with new products as new technologies emerged. Cisco leadership then devised a strategy: provide a complete solution for businesses, make acquisitions a structured process, define the industry-wide networking software protocols, and form the right strategic alliances.

Cisco refrains from espousing any technology biases. Cisco's philosophy is to listen carefully to customer requests, monitor all technological advancements, and offer customers an informed choice of options. To fulfill this, Cisco attempts to develop products using widely accepted standards. Cisco recognizes that if the company does not have the internal resources to develop a new product within 6 months, it must buy its way into the market or miss the window of opportunity. To do this, they needed to continue to add routinely new technologies and network products and decided to do this through business acquisitions. The stock market grew through the 1990s, and Cisco's stock soared with very high price/earnings (P/E) ratios. John Chambers was able to use Cisco's highly valued stock to acquire other best-in-class networking product companies. In pursuance of an end-to-end strategy for Cisco's hyper growth, Cisco pursued a stream of acquisitions as a way of keeping up with the lightning-fast market transitions that were a trademark of the high-tech industry. This was Cisco's breakaway strategy.

How can Cisco simultaneously adapt to fast-cycle, rapid change, grow to offer the scale and scope demanded by the customers, and effectively integrate new acquisitions without losing control or critical intellectual capital? Chambers implemented systematic procedures for such acquisitions, with tasks to select, acquire, and integrate new businesses. First, a Cisco business-development team scouted for new companies with a technology that would be needed by Cisco to maintain its technology progress and fill out its product lines (so it could be a one-stop network supplier). Throughout the acquisition process, the Cisco team constantly screens the target against the following five principles:

1. Presence of a shared vision
2. The likelihood of a short-term win for both the acquired company and Cisco
3. A long-term win for all stakeholders
4. The right chemistry or cultural compatibility
5. Reasonable geographic proximity

Second, the team looked to see if there could be a shared strategic vision. Third, the team looked for a compatibility of company cultures. Since the acquisition would become part of Cisco, personnel would have to adapt to Cisco policies and conventions. Cisco espouses five core values: a dedication to customer success, innovation and learning, partnership, empowerment and teamwork, and doing more with less. Chambers did not want too large a cultural shock to prevent newly acquired employees from quickly becoming happy with their new home. A third criterion was financial, in which the product line of the acquired company would produce sufficient profits through rapid growth to soon justify the acquisition price. Fourth, the Cisco team would have to persuade a new company to allow it to be bought. Many departments of Cisco would be involved in negotiations so that all aspects of the acquisition would be apparent to both potential partners, such as issues about HR, business development, engineering, and financial and legal points.

Fifth, valuation of the Cisco stock in the acquisition was the critical issue—the buying price. For example, when Cisco acquired Grand Junction in 1995, the company had been planning to go public at a Goldman Sachs estimate of a 200-million-dollar IPO. Cisco offered five million shares of Cisco, then worth $346 million, and Grand Junction accepted. In 1996, Cisco acquired Nashoba Networks to produce and sell token-ring switches. Cisco also used pricing strategy against competitors not acquired. For example, in 1996, Cisco cut by half the price of its networking switches, then undercutting a rival's switches by 50%. Sixth, integrating the new company was the final step. The long-term value of the new acquisition to Cisco was the capability of its employees to manage, design, and produce new cutting-edge products in its product line. Accordingly, retention of the acquisition's management, technical, and sales people was important to the real value of the purchase. Cisco moved quickly to orient and integrate its new employees to its policies, and Cisco stock options were a big attraction. Cisco retained the top executives by letting them continue to run the company within the Cisco fold and play a major role within Cisco.

In most acquisitions, the formal deal is closed quickly because of the amount of honest communication and mutual sizing that has already happened; but time to market is more important than getting things completely right because, if delayed, in a world of short product lifecycles, the market might not even exist anymore. The goal is to ship the acquired company's products under the Cisco label by the time the deal is closed, usually within 3–6 months. With a final agreement in place, the focus shifts immediately to integrate the new company into Cisco as quickly as possible. Integration teams (e.g., products, logistics, MIS, and infra) act immediately to ensure that the new employees are up on the intranet, have office space, and get immediate training in the Cisco way. In a typical acquisition, the engineering, marketing, and sales units will be integrated into the sponsoring unit, while HR, services, manufacturing, and distribution are merged into the Cisco infrastructure. The former takes place at two levels, structural and cultural. The structural part includes the organizational rearrangements needed to ensure operations of the business functions like payroll, information systems, employee services, and other services.

Cultural integration includes the use of integration teams who explain and model Cisco values, the holding of orientation sessions, and the assignment of *buddies*. The buddy system involves pairing each new employee with a Cisco veteran of equal stature and similar job responsibility; the buddy offers personalized attention better suited to conveying the Cisco values and culture. This dispels *insider versus outsider* attitude. Special orientation session involve employees from previously acquired companies who offer their insights, as well as change management sessions to assist the people within the acquired company to support the transition. In the early stages of the transition, all integration processes are monitored and controlled by project management. There is also a careful effort to assess and track 30-, 60-, 90-, and 120-day milestones so that there is no loss of productivity. At the conclusion of this process, there is a *lesson-learned* review designed to improve the acquisition process for the next cycle. Cisco works hard to ensure a fit before an acquisition takes place, then rapidly assimilates the new company and works to ensure that the new employees are satisfied and want to stay with Cisco, not off and create another start-up.

Cisco acquisitions are typically entrepreneurial, fast-growing Silicon Valley companies that thrive in dynamic markets; the fact that Cisco is a player in all the hot network technology areas makes it attractive to the employees of acquired firms. The turnover rate for acquired personnel is same as that of the Cisco population as a whole; over 70% of the senior managers from acquired firms are still with Cisco. These are people who often have multiple start-ups under their belt and have substantial personal wealth; they stay because they now have the corporate resources and backing to pursue their dream projects with a matching role based on merit. Although 70%–80% of Cisco's products are developed in-house, these are often created by engineers who started with smaller firms acquired by Cisco. Cisco understands that obtaining technology is fundamentally about acquiring people—the intellectual capital that is source of this technology. Considering the number of employees who have left and started up their own firms, a summation of the revenue of such spin-offs gives an estimate of the lost intellectual capital from a firm that fails to retain its people. Moreover, considering that Cisco effectively pays between $500,000 and $2 million per employee of the acquired company, the economic rationale for retaining these assets is clear. People, not technology, are the key to winning this game.

Cisco's continued success has to do with two of their core values: the strong belief in having no technology religion and listening carefully to the customer. That is the reason why Cisco has been able to ride several different technology waves, and how they have been able to adapt in spite of disruptive technological change. They have been able to do this and avoid being trapped by an existing technology, by their willingness to provide their customers with what they want (even if at that instant it may be an older or suboptimal technological option) in the time they want (even if Cisco does not have in-house capability to deliver that option or an option that they had rejected earlier) through rapid acquisitions and assimilations. Unlike many other companies, Cisco really understands the difficulties of mergers and the importance of retaining talent after the merger has occurred. Because the purpose of any acquisition is to retain people and their intellectual capital, the processes are designed to empower and retain people, especially the executive management of the acquired company. Retaining the leaders of the acquired company is critical because without retaining the executive management, it is difficult to retain the rank and file.

In the following is a segment of the case history of DuPont. It illustrates DuPont's dominant stance of shared values variation through operations driven by numbers (or rules of success) like sales and profits, along with a phenomenal focus on values like environment-friendly materials, nondepleteable resources, and greenhouse gas reductions. As may be discerned through a careful perusal, these variations were accompanied simultaneously by variations in other dimensions like strategy (planned), structure (biased toward control), and stuff (low-energy and nondepletable resources).

7.1.2 TRANSFORMED PRIORITIES AT DUPONT

DuPont, a 27-billion-dollar company with 60,000 employees, began life in 1802, manufacturing gunpowder and explosives. Since then, it has reinvented itself many times—first by moving into dyes, resins, and paints in the early twentieth century and later becoming an energy company with its acquisition of Conoco in 1983. Still the second largest chemical manufacturer in the United States, it redefined itself once more in the early 1990s as "the world's most dynamic science company, creating sustainable solutions essential to a better, safer, and healthier life for people everywhere."

DuPont is now pursuing business opportunities in agriculture, nutrition, and bio-based materials while shifting away from its traditional lower-growth businesses that rely heavily on fossil fuels. The shift is evident in its sale of the Dacron, Lycra, and Nylon divisions and the creation of The Solae Company (soy foods) and Pioneer Hi-bred International, Inc. (bio-tech seeds) businesses.

DuPont began to mobilize its sustainability efforts in earnest in 1988 after Greenpeace activists scaled the wall of one of its plants and hung a giant banner *DuPont Number* 1 *Polluter* facing a highway used by thousands of commuters.

It was an event that led the company to clean up its act. The fear of being singled out as one of the world's top corporate villains continued to motivate the company's top management during much of the 1990s. In 1990, DuPont was a major producer of nitrous oxides (N_2O) and fluorocarbons such as HFC-23, a by-product of HCFC-22 manufacture. These gases have a global warming potential of 310 times and 11,700 times that of carbon dioxide (CO_2), respectively. By 1991, DuPont's own atmospheric scientists were beginning to sound the alarm bell about the company's emissions and what they might mean down the road for climate change and impending regulation.

A science-based corporate culture forced top management to take seriously the link between greenhouse gas emissions and climate change, much as science had made the case to the international community for phasing out chlorofluorocarbons (CFCs) in the previous two decades. DuPont was the first company to announce a phaseout of CFCs and the first to develop and commercialize CFC alternatives—particularly for refrigeration and air conditioning, which represented about 60% of CFC use worldwide. Its profitable leadership in phasing in CFC alternatives helped demonstrate to management the business benefits of a first-move advantage based on good science.

Energy conservation and emission reductions led to $3 billion in avoided costs between 1991 and 2005. To illustrate the energy conservation efforts, in some cases, DuPont replaced fossil fuels such as natural gas with methane from landfills in its industrial boilers while, in other cases, it redesigned industrial processes to squeeze efficiencies from its chemicals manufacturing. Overall, the company managed to reduce global energy use by 7% below 1990 levels, exceeding early on its goal of holding energy use flat through 2010.

Emissions reductions eventually made money for the company. The sale of emission reduction credits on the London Climate Exchange, based on efforts by UK facilities, is a case in point. Overall, greenhouse gas emissions were reduced by 72% from 1990 levels, also exceeding early targets set at 65% by 2010.

DuPont has a long history in agriculture through its sales of agricultural chemicals. Moving into soy-based nutrition and bio-based seeds, facilitated by its Solae and Pioneer ventures, was a natural extension of that business.

In addition to the $3 billion in avoided costs through energy conservation and greenhouse gas emission reductions, DuPont's shift to high-value low-energy products is helping to position the company for an increasingly carbon-constrained marketplace. Biofuels, solar panels, fuel cells, and green building products are all soaring as markets anticipate tighter carbon regulations and rising fuel prices. New revenue streams from sustainability ventures include the sale of greenhouse gas reduction credits, the sale of soy foods and hybrid seeds to meet new health and nutritional needs, and the growth of business in emerging markets including the base of the pyramid.

Corporate image and reputation went from *worst of* to *best of* in less than a decade. DuPont is still grappling with serious issues, chief among them being a chemical called perfluorooctanoic acid (PFOA) used in Teflon, which is scheduled to be phased out by 2015. DuPont is still targeted by regulators and activists for a range of environmental and health-related impacts of its businesses. However, the image transformation of the company over the last 10 years is nothing short of remarkable. In 2005, it was ranked first on *Business Week*'s list of *the top green companies*. In 2006, it was awarded *best in class* for its approach to climate change by an investor coalition called the Carbon Disclosure Project. Ironically, it was also the recipient of the Presidential Green Chemistry Award (for its Bio-PDO™ materials) from the U.S. EPA, the very same body that had labeled DuPont the top U.S. polluter in the mid-1990s.

DuPont's sustainability strategy is an excellent example of an environmentally smart business model for a world marked by growing ecological disasters. The company's 2015 sustainability goals include doubling investment in R&D programs that offer direct environmental benefits to its customers. They include doubling revenues from nondepletable resources to at least $8 billion. The goals also include growing annual revenues by at least $2 billion from "products that create energy efficiency and/or significant greenhouse gas emission reductions for our customers." These goals have energized the organization and engaged senior executives and line managers in a quest for profitable growth.

> In the following is a segment of case history of Tata that is majorly driven by values, over and above being driven by numbers (or rules of success) like sales and profits. As may be discerned through a careful perusal, these variations were accompanied simultaneously by variations in other dimensions like strategy (planned), structure (business autonomy), stuff (market-led in-demand products), style (biased toward administrational culture), staff (nurturing people), and skills (breadth of skills).

7.1.3 Driven by Values at Tata

The Tata group is 140 years old and is a strong force in the domestic market in India, where it has 98 operating companies and 289,000 staff—more than any other private sector company in India. The group's stand-alone revenue is around $29 billion, with 2.8-billion-dollar profits. Founded by entrepreneur Jamsetji Tata in the mid-nineteenth century, the companies were the first in India, and among the first in the world, to introduce concepts such as company pensions, sick pay, paid annual holidays, and other benefits. When Tata Iron & Steel Company was founded, Tata also built a model town to house his workers and insisted that there be a full range of benefits, including places for exercise and places of worship. He was particularly adamant that there be plenty of trees and green space. The town, Jamshedpur, went on to become a template for other *model towns* in India. The group is controlled by three trusts and is headed by a family member—Ratan Tata, a Cornell-trained architect, from 1981 until 2012.

Although Tata is a conglomerate, it is a lot lighter in structure than a Western equivalent—there is no central strategy or consolidated financial statements. The group is bound together by small staffs at the holding companies Tata Sons and Tata Industries. These two—chaired by Ratan Tata—provide the strategic vision, control the Tata brand, and lend a hand with big deals. Bombay House exerts influence through a Group Corporate Office—nine senior executives sit on the boards of Tata companies and act as *stewards*, mentoring managers and promoting corporate social responsibility. Partly as a result of its trust-based governance, the group has built a long history of enlightened projects to alleviate poverty and hunger by investing in education, health, and agricultural development projects. Tata has ambitions to reinvent solar energy to bring affordable power to villages that are off the power grid.

Tata's international expansion began in earnest in 2000, when Tata Tea, the group's beverage division, bought Britain's Tetley Tea—the company that invented the tea bag—for £271 million.

Since then, almost all parts of the group have made substantial overseas acquisitions: TCS has bought IT businesses from Chile to the United Kingdom, Tata Tea has made purchases in the United States and South Africa, and Tata Motors purchased Daewoo's truck unit in Korea. The group's Indian Hotels, operating under the brand name Taj, has bought hotels in Sydney, New York, and other countries—in 2005 acquiring the Ritz-Carlton in Boston. Tata has purchased stakes in Indonesia's biggest coal mines and steel mills in Singapore, Thailand, and Vietnam. Tata's acquisition of Tyco International's undersea telecom cables for $130 million makes it the world's biggest carrier of international phone calls. Its purchase of British company Icat International makes Tata a major supplier of outsourced industrial design for U.S. car and aerospace companies. After Jaguar and Land Rover consolidation, the Tata group earns more revenue from its UK-based companies than from its India-based units.

7.1.3.1 Whetting the Appetite

Tata is India's most prolific purchaser of international companies. The group's biggest international takeovers between 2004 and 2007 were presented in the following:

Date Announced	Target	Value ($ Billions)
January 2007	Corus	11.30
March 2007	Bumi Resources[a]	1.10
February 2005	NatSteel Asia	0.47
February 2000	Tetley Tea	0.41
July 2005	Teleglobe International	0.24
June 2006	Eight O'Clock Coffee	0.22
November 2006	Ritz-Carlton, Boston	0.17
April 2006	Millennium Steel	0.17
November 2004	Tyco Global Network	0.13
December 2005	Brunner Mond	0.12

[a] Tata acquired a 30% stake in Bumi Resources.

Tata Steel has bought mills in Singapore, Thailand, and Vietnam and is expanding output in India. After full consolidation, Corus has added £9.7 billion in additional revenue. This deal makes Tata the world's fifth largest steelmaker, greatly expands Tata's range of finished products, secures access to U.S. and European auto makers, and boosts its steelmaking capacity fivefold, with steel mills added in Pennsylvania and Ohio. These last acquisitions tilt the balance between Tata's domestic and international sales to the global market.

The group's overseas strategy has been generally to combine low-cost production in emerging economies like India, with sales in the high-margin markets of the West. Tata Steel, for example, has access to cheap supplies of government-allocated iron ore, which it can ship to operations in southeast Asia, and in time to Corus' markets in Europe.

Nonetheless, Tata has found a way to acquire companies across the globe yet to still tread gently. Mergers are more akin to strategic partnership than to aggressive venture capitalism. In all its deals Tata has signaled its respect for workers, and up to 2008, it had not laid off any workers or closed any facilities in its overseas acquisitions (although it has had layoffs at home). For example, in its acquisition of Daewoo's commercial trucks business in Korea in 2004, Tata had to win an auction: Tata executives were enrolled in Korean language classes; company brochures were translated into Korean; and Tata began making presentations to employees, the local mayor, public officials, and even Korea's prime minister. With the auction won, Tata formed a joint board of directors to develop a strategy to expand Daewoo's product line and boost exports. Tata executives from India working with Daewoo were required to shave their moustaches because Koreans prefer a *clean* look. To date, Tata's governance and history has encouraged a *hands-off* approach to its acquisitions.

7.1.3.2   Land Rover and Jaguar

The purchase of Land Rover and Jaguar is an example of how Tata manages its acquisitions. The deal with Ford promises to transform Tata Motors from an emerging markets specialist into a global producer with the full range of vehicles from trucks to small and luxury passenger vehicles. In 2008, Tata Motors concluded the $2 billion purchase of Land Rover and Jaguar from Ford. This is the highest profile takeover of an established European car maker by an emerging Asian manufacturer so far. Ford had acquired Jaguar for $2.5 billion in 1989 and Land Rover for $2.75 billion in 2000. While Land Rover has performed well in recent years, Jaguar had seen huge sales declines in Ford's core U.S. market and has been unprofitable for years. Ford was selling the brands as part of its strategy to refocus on its core Ford and Lincoln brands and to raise cash to help fund Ford's turnaround (the company has lost more than $15 billion in the last 2 years). Contrary to damaging, spoiler rumors that Tata aimed to sell the brands as soon as a deal with Ford was reached, Tata's plan was to retain the brands' British character and leave their management largely intact. Tata has the potential to add value in the supply chain by cooperating on engineering and development, which can be done at lower cost in India. There is also the opportunity to build the brands' business in Asian auto markets in which Tata is highly experienced.

In preparation for the takeover, in March 2008, Tata executives spent 2 days in talks with UK union leaders to assure them that there were no plans to drastically change the business structure of the two businesses when they were bought. The stress was on Tata's long-term investment culture and desire to keep the structure of acquired companies mostly intact. As part of the deal, the UK factories are to remain open until 2011, and Ford becomes the main supplier to the new owner, providing engines, stamping, and other components. However, the terms of the sales preclude passing Ford technology to third parties, which constrains Tata's freedom to do deals with partners like Fiat.

In particular, there was to be no attempt to *Indianize* the companies; Tata does not consider itself capable of micromanaging acquired businesses from India. Tata pledged to preserve the historic identities of the Jaguar and Land Rover brands for competing against luxury manufacturers like BMW, Mercedes, Porsche, and Audi.

7.2   STRATEGY VARIATIONS RANGING FROM PLANNED TO EMERGENT

As discussed in Chapter 4, enterprises are intentionally created, goal-oriented entities. On an overarching level, the intentionality and goal orientation can be expressed by the enterprise mission; this can be seen as a relatively timeless general expression of the enterprise purpose, its reason for existence: the *why* and *whereto* of the enterprise. Within this general expression about the enterprise purpose, more specific, partly time-dependent, goals are relevant.

These goals might relate to, or be determined by, for example,

1. Customers and the sales and interaction channels to be used
2. The type of products and services, their quality, and the effectiveness and efficiency of their internal production
3. The resources required
4. The environmental conditions of the enterprise, such as the market, competitors, as well as general economic developments

Certain conditions and convictions (norms and values) play a role and determine under which principles the enterprise will carry out its mission and realize its goals. Two fundamentally different approaches in this respect have been outlined in Chapter 4. Clearly, an enterprise that also aims to offer meaningful work and aims to contribute to society will most likely formulate associated goals and will bring its internal arrangements (i.e., design and architecture) into correspondence with these objectives. Choices the enterprise makes have to do with its goals and the conditions (among which the internal arrangements) under which these goals are to be achieved. We will define strategy as the totality of choices (or intentions) that provide an overall orientation for the future development of the enterprise. That is not to say that these choices are necessarily totally free. Emerging developments and the interdependence of an enterprise and its context are likely to enhance or limit such strategic choices.

Thus, corporate strategy is the pattern of decisions in a company that determines and reveals its objectives, purposes, or goals, produces the principal policies and plans for achieving those goals, and defines the range of business a company is to pursue. Planning strategy implies seeing management engaged in structured activities leading to a set of strategic initiatives that can be decided upon, and operationalized through, budgets, targets, and the planning of projects. But strategy development is not a planned process, and planning is more about realizing choices already made. Planning refers to decomposition, while strategy development is more about arriving at certain choices and rests on synthesis and integration, aspects that are difficult to conceive as the result of analytic planning process. Formal plans are merely a confirmation of strategic decisions already reached through other informal, bottom-up, intuitive, or political processes that are outside the top-down planning process.

Furthermore, a formal planned strategy is considered to be naïve in the face of uncertainty, indeterminacy, and ambiguity; uncertainty and ambiguity necessitate adopting to emerging, previously unknown contexts or environments. Rather, strategy emerges in a dynamic interplay with contextual or environmental conditions, thus implying an incremental development, whereby strategy is constantly readjusted. Consequently, enterprise variations as a result of adaptation occur not because of the planning process but because of the learning process.

> In the following is the case history of Wal-Mart whose corporate and business strategy was predominantly planned like location of stores, UPC codes, inventory management, procurement strategies, replenishment, and customer analytics. As may be discerned through a careful perusal, these variations were accompanied simultaneously by variations in other dimensions like structure (systemic control but operational autonomy), style (biased toward transformational culture), staff (challenging through empowering ownership but biased toward nurturing), and systems (mandatory).

7.2.1 WAL-MART

Wal-Mart's transformation from a small chain of discount stores in Arkansas, Missouri, and Oklahoma in 1970 to the world's largest retailer was one of the most remarkable corporate success stories of the twentieth century. Emerging after the World War II, discount retailers were large format stores that offered a broad range of products that included apparel, appliances, toiletries, household goods, and sometimes groceries as well. This was possible because of direct supply from manufacturers and low-cost operations in austere settings; manufacturers found that in this buyer's market, discounters represented a more effective means of getting products to consumers because their willingness to accept lower margins enabled them to move large quantities of goods more rapidly than conventional retailers, who required higher markups. Discount stores were located within large towns—it was generally believed that a minimum population of 100,000 was necessary for a discount store to be viable. Sam Walton believed that discount stores could be viable in smaller communities: if the prices were right, the stores would attract customers from a wide area. Because automobiles, cheap gasoline, and the expansion of systems of paved roads running through the countryside meant that almost all people could, at least on occasion, go to larger towns and cities and enjoy what was rapidly becoming the national pastime of shopping, catalog shopping lost its luster. Sam Walton saw the opportunities, and it is this small-town beginning that is most often mentioned in accounts of the creation of Wal-Mart. Walton opened his first Wal-Mart in 1962 and within 8 years had 30 discount stores in small and medium-sized towns in Arkansas, Oklahoma, and Missouri.

In 1970, lacking distributors in these towns, Walton started building his own distribution centers that could buy in volumes at attractive prices and store the merchandise for onward distribution; in the same year, he took the company public in order to finance the heavy investment involved. While most discount retailers relied heavily upon their suppliers to undertake distribution to individual stores, over 80% of Wal-Mart's purchases were shipped to Wal-Mart's own distribution centers from where they were distributed in Wal-Mart trucks. It was also an early adopter of *cross-docking* system where goods arriving on inbound trucks were unloaded and reloaded on outbound trucks without first sitting in warehouse inventory.

A typical distribution center spanned a million square feet and was operated 24 h a day; it was highly automated and designed to serve the needs of about 150 stores within a radius of 200 miles. When orders were pulled from stock, an automated pick-list system guided associates to the correct locations. With this structure of large distribution hubs serving a group of 15–20 discount stores, Wal-Mart began its rapid expansion across the country. Wal-Mart's geographical expansion was incremental. It moved into a new area, first, by building a few stores that were served by extending Wal-Mart's distribution lines from a nearby cluster; eventually, when a critical mass of stores had been established in the new area, Wal-Mart would build a distribution center to serve the newly evolved cluster. At the end of 1980, using this hub-and-spoke strategy, Wal-Mart had 330 stores in 11 states; by the end of 1985, there were 859 stores in 22 southern and mid-western states; and, at the beginning of 1994, there were 1953 stores operating in every state except Vermont, Alaska, and Hawaii.

7.2.1.1 UPC Codes

It was not, of course, sufficient merely to build distribution centers with conveyer belts. Walton and his associates also realized that a coding system was essential, and here, too, they moved quickly to seize the advantage. Before the late 1960s and the introduction of computers into the retailing process, inventory management was highly labor intensive, and the process of reorder slow. An early improvement in department stores involved use of a Bureau of Standards-backed system of optical character recognition (OCR). The bar code system that has become a familiar part of American shopping today was already being used in grocery stores and involved use of a uniform product code (UPC), which allowed simple scanning. In general retailing, the OCR system had been the initial choice of most because the UPC did not have the capacity to handle the large number of different goods carried by most department stores.

Walton and his associates nevertheless made the decision to go ahead and began using UPC, even in the early 1980s, in part because so many of the goods they carried were also sold by grocery stores and so were already part of the UPC system and in part because they thought that capacity would grow. A Voluntary Inter-Industry Commerce Standards (VICS) initiative led by a number of retailers began to pressure suppliers to tag products before they were delivered and to adopt the UPC. As all of this happened, those companies that had not moved quickly to adopt the UPC were forced to catch up and faced higher costs as a result. Whether through foresight or with a degree of luck as well, all portions of the Wal-Mart system were coming together to give them a decided advantage over competitors. Consider that another reason why Wal-Mart moved so quickly to adopt the UPC was that 80% of the goods that Wal-Mart stocked went through their own distribution system where tickets were already put on; it was easy to attach bar codes to these.

7.2.1.2 Efficiency of Transportation Containers

Prior to the time when containers were used internationally, ocean freight costs amounted to 12% of the value of U.S. exports and 10% of the value of imports. To that had to be added the costs of domestic shipping, and as had long been recognized by some students of international trade, such costs were often more significant than the more often discussed tariffs. Particularly important were the port costs; the total of shipping and handling meant that selling internationally often did not make economic sense. The adoption of containers, with all of the related changes involved for ships, trucks, and ports, reduced the cost dramatically and changed the volume and nature of international trade.

The cost of moving goods across oceans had not been the major financial barrier for some time. Rather, what was costly was loading and unloading goods at ports and, as Walton recognized, from trucks to warehouses and back to trucks. Containers, and the ships and trucks designed to haul them, as well as the computer systems that developed to track them and direct the machines responsible for loading and offloading, drastically reduced those costs. These changes also affected the time required to move goods.

Transport efficiencies, though, hardly begin to capture the economic impact of containerization. The container not only lowered freight bills, it saved time. Quicker handling and less time in storage translated to faster transit from manufacturer to customer, reducing the cost of financing inventories sitting unproductively on railway sidings or in pierside warehouses awaiting a ship. Container shipping abolished the advantage that a New York City location once held for manufacturing because of its proximity to ocean shipping but also, and in general, reduced the importance of distance.

Wal-Mart took advantage of this fact of the modern world first by their hub-and-spoke distributional system and also by their management of the shipment of goods. Although the story of Walton's rise to wealth is often told as a story of overcoming what are assumed to be intuitively obvious disadvantages of starting in a remote corner of Arkansas, the context in which he was working meant that locational advantage went to the aggressive and early managers of supply chains. Wal-Mart owned their own fleet of trucks, which were tightly managed. They built their distribution centers to move goods quickly and cheaply from truck to truck. And they required their suppliers to pack in units designed for distribution to the stores to which they were going so that containers could be quickly and easily broken into shipment units within the distribution centers.

Wal-Mart's ability to demand lower costs, tagged products, and, more recently, radio-frequency identification (RFID) tagged products, and to place orders for specified size of shipments to minimize resorting costs in Wal-Mart distribution centers were all a result, in some large measure, of their monopolistic power arising ultimately from the power of their purchase volumes. The size of Wal-Mart's purchases and its negotiating ability meant that Wal-Mart was both desired and feared by manufacturers. Being accepted as a Wal-Mart vendor offered access to a huge share of the U.S. retail market. At the same time, Wal-Mart buyers were well aware of Wal-Mart's ability to take full advantage of economies of scale available to their suppliers and to squeeze their margins to razor-thin level. The requirements that Wal-Mart imposed on its suppliers extended well beyond low prices. Increasingly, Wal-Mart involved itself in its suppliers' employment policies, including workplace safety, working hours, and absence of child labor.

7.2.1.3   Variations on Discount Stores

Sam's Clubs, Wal-Mart's entry into warehouse clubs in the mid-1980s, demonstrated its ability to transfer its retailing capabilities to a very different retail format (though they imitated a distribution concept established by Price Club). The warehouse clubs were not traditional retailers since they were not open to the public; they were clubs where access was through membership. These wholesale outlets offered a narrower range of products—typically around 4,000 stock-keeping units (SKUs) as compared with the 50,000 SKUs for most Wal-Mart discount stores—at prices significantly below those of discount stores. These smaller numbers of items were available in multipacks and catering-size packs. The clubs were literally warehouses with products available on pallets and minimal customer service. The rationale was to maximize economies in purchasing, minimize operating costs, and pass the savings on to members through very low prices. The development Sam's Club demonstrated Wal-Mart's capacity for continuous improvement and innovation.

Supercenters were Wal-Mart stores with larger floor space—typically 120,000–180,000 ft^2, about double the size of the average Wal-Mart discount store. Supercenters were modeled on the European concept of the *hypermarket* that had been pioneered by the French retailer Carrefour. A supercenter combined a discount store with a grocery supermarket; in addition, a supercenter incorporated a number of specialty units such as an eyeglass store, hair salon, dry cleaners, and photo lab. The Supercenters were open for 24 h a day, 7 days a week. The supercenter stores and Sam's Clubs were supplied through a separate distribution network from the Wal-Mart discount stores. In 1990, Wal-Mart acquired McLane, a Texas-based wholesale distributor, that became the basis for Wal-Mart's distribution to Supercenters and Sam's Clubs throughout the United States.

Wal-Mart's international operations comprised a number of separate national subsidiaries, each attempting to interpret the basic Wal-Mart business principles and underlying approach to retailing within a distinctive economic structure and national culture. Wal-Mart's differentiated approach to different countries reflected the different retailing environments of these countries and the different entry opportunities that had presented themselves. In 1992, Wal-Mart established a joint venture with Mexico's largest retailer, Cifra SA, and began opening Wal-Mart discount stores and Sam's Clubs in several Mexican cities. Within 7 years, the 2 companies had opened 416 stores in Mexico, and Wal-Mart had established a dominant position in the venture through acquiring 51% of Cifra. In 1994, Wal-Mart entered the Canadian market by acquiring 120 Woolco stores from Woolworth and converting them to its own discount stores format. In Germany, Wal-Mart acquired the 21-store Wertkauf chain and followed this with the purchase of 21 Interspar stores. In 1999, it purchased United Kingdom's third largest supermarket chain, Asda Stores, with its 232 retail outlets. Wal-Mart's performance in overseas markets was mixed. Its strongest performance was in adjacent countries—Mexico and Canada—and also in Britain, where its Asda supermarket chain enthusiastically adopted Wal-Mart's systems and its culture.

7.2.1.4 Decentralized Operations

Wal-Mart's management structure and management style had been molded by Sam Walton's principles and values. As Wal-Mart grew in size and geographical scope, Walton was determined that corporate executives should keep closely in touch with customers and store operations. The result was a structure in which communication between individual stores and the Bentonville headquarters was both close and personal. Wal-Mart's regional vice presidents were each responsible for supervising between 10 and 15 district managers (who, in turn, were in charge of 8–12 stores). The key to Wal-Mart's fast-response management system was the close linkage between the stores and headquarters.

Individual store managers were given considerable decision-making authority in relation to product range, product positioning within stores, and pricing. This differed from most other discount chains where decisions over pricing and merchandising were made either at head office or at regional offices. Decentralized decision-making power was also apparent within stores, where the managers of individual departments (e.g., toys, health and beauty, consumer electronics) were expected to develop and implement their own ideas for increasing sales and reducing costs. Wal-Mart placed a strong emphasis on management development. Most senior managers were recruited internally, and there was a strong emphasis placed upon developing managers through moving them between line and staff positions and between functions.

7.2.1.5 Centralized Information Systems

Balancing this decentralized management and operations was the sophisticated highly centralized enterprise-wide information systems. Wal-Mart was a pioneer in applying information and communications technology to support decision making and promote efficiency and customer responsiveness within each of its business functions and between functions. In 1974, Wal-Mart was among the first retailers to use computers for inventory control. In 1977, Wal-Mart initiated electronic data interchange (EDI) with its vendors. In the following year, Wal-Mart introduced bar code scanning for point-of-sale and inventory control. To link stores and cash register sales with supply-chain management and inventory control, Wal-Mart invested $24 million in its own satellite in 1984 (by the end of the 1990s, Wal-Mart computer system was receiving 8.4 million updates every minute on the items that customers take home—and the relationship between the items in each basket; its merchants use this database to understand what customers want).

By 1990, Wal-Mart's satellite system was the largest two-way, fully integrated private satellite network in the world, providing two-way interactive voice and video capability, data transmission for inventory control, credit card authorization, and enhanced EDI. By the mid-1990s, Wal-Mart had extended EDI to cover about 70% of its vendors. Wal-Mart pioneered RFID—a system of locating and tracking cases of merchandise by means of electronic tags. Through Wal-Mart's *Retail Link* system of supply-chain management, data interchange included point-of-sale data, levels of inventory, Wal-Mart's sales forecasts, vendors' production and delivery schedules, and electronic funds transfer.

Through collaboration with Cisco Systems, Retail Link was moved to the Internet during the mid-1990s, allowing suppliers to log onto the Wal-Mart database for real-time store-by-store information on sales and inventory for their products. This allowed suppliers to work with Wal-Mart company's buyers to manage inventory in the stores—forecasting, planning, producing, and shipping products as needed. Wal-Mart's buyer benefits from the supplier's product knowledge, while the supplier benefits from Wal-Mart's experience in the market.

> Combine these information systems with their logistics—Wal-Mart's hub-and-spoke system in which distribution centers are placed within a day's truck run of the stores—and all the pieces fall into place for enabling the ability to respond to the needs of Wal-Mart's customers, before they are even in the store. Wal-Mart's ability to turn information into improved merchandising and service to the customer results in a crucial competitive advantage in retailing: speed. The result was faster replenishment, a product mix tuned to the needs of local customers and lower inventory costs for Wal-Mart. By the end of the 1990s, Wal-Mart was pioneering the use of data mining for retail merchandising. Mining the enormous database of purchasing information accumulated across a decade enabled Wal-Mart to place the right item in the right store at the right price. For instance, computer-enabled seasonal merchandising offers many opportunities for product placement based on customer buying patterns.

Wal-Mart's marketing strategy rested primarily upon disseminating its policy of low prices and customer commitment. Central to its marketing was the communication of its slogan *Everyday Low Prices*—the concept that Wal-Mart's price cutting strategy was not restricted to particular products or to particular time periods, but was a basic principle of Wal-Mart's business. As a result of its customer-focused, value-for-money approach, Wal-Mart was able to rely upon word-of-mouth communication of its merits and was able to spend comparatively little on advertising and promotion.

7.2.1.6 Human Resources Development through Ownership

Wal-Mart's HR policies were based closely upon Sam Walton's ideas about relations between the company and its employees and between employees and customers. All employees—from executive-level personnel to checkout clerks—were known as *associates*. Wal-Mart's relations with its associates were founded upon respect, high expectations, close communication, and effective incentives. Associates enjoyed a high degree of autonomy and received continuous communication about their company's performance and about store operations. Every aspect of company operations and strategy was seen as depending upon the close collaboration of managers and shop-floor employees.

Although Wal-Mart's employees received relatively low pay (in common with most of the retail trade), Wal-Mart offered strong profit incentives for employees and encouraged them to share in its wealth creation through its stock ownership scheme. Numerous employees have retired as millionaires as a result of their participation in the plan. Wal-Mart resisted the unionization of its employees in the belief that union membership created a barrier between the management and the employees in furthering the success of the company and its members. Despite strenuous efforts by unions to recruit Wal-Mart employees, union penetration remained low.

Wal-Mart's approach to employee involvement made heavy use of orchestrated demonstration of enthusiasm and commitment. The central feature of Wal-Mart meetings from corporate to store level was the *Wal-Mart cheer*—devised by Sam Walton after a visit to Korea. The call and response ritual (*Give me a W! Give me an A!...*) included the *Wal-Mart squiggly*, which involved employees shaking their backsides in unison. Wal-Mart's success rested upon its ability to offer its customers *Always low prices. Always.* Wal-Mart's success at keeping its costs below those of its competitors rested upon its culture of frugality and the continual striving of its employees to find new ways to reduce costs and better serve customers.

At their stores, Wal-Mart went to great lengths to engage with its customers at a personal level. In order to encourage customer loyalty, Wal-Mart maintained a *Satisfaction Guaranteed* program; this program assured customers that Wal-Mart would accept returned merchandise on a no-questions-asked basis. Stores employed *greeters*—often retired individuals—who would welcome customers and hand out shopping baskets. Within the store, all employees were expected to look customers in the eye, smile at them, and offer a verbal greeting. Wal-Mart cheer's mixture of homespun and corporate themes provided an apt metaphor for what was termed as the *the Wal-Mart paradox*. Its founder, Sam Walton, had combined folksy charm and homespun business wisdom with cutting-edge IT and supply-chain management to create the world's most efficient retail organization.

In the following is the case history of Google that is majorly driven by an emergent strategy to organize information, over and above being driven by planned strategy of growth based on the unique currency of digital economy, namely, impressions. As may be discerned through a careful perusal, these variations were accompanied simultaneously by variations in other dimensions like shared values (to democratize information, i.e., bridge the digital divide), structure (biased toward autonomy), stuff (semantically enhanced or more meaningful products, services, and experiences), style (transformational culture), staff (ideationally challenging but operationally nurturing people), skills (breadth of skills), systems (discretionary), and sequence (targeted for the masses, but biased toward mass customization).

7.2.2 SEARCH ECONOMICS AT GOOGLE

Google started as a research project called BackRub undertaken by Larry Page while he was a computer science PhD student at Stanford in 1996. The goal of the BackRub project was to document the link structure of the web and rank the value of a web page based on which (and how many) pages were linking to it, and if those pages were themselves linked to which (and how many) other pages. At this point, another PhD student, Sergey Brin, became involved in the project. Brin was able to develop an algorithm that ranked web pages according not only to the number of links into that site but also to the number of links into each of the linking sites. They had stumbled onto the key ingredient for a better search engine—rank search results according to their relevance using a back-link methodology. This methodology had the virtue of discounting links from pages that themselves had few, if any, links into them. Brin and Page noticed that the search results generated by this algorithm were superior to those returned by AltaVista and Excite, both of which often returned irrelevant results, including a fair share of spam. Moreover, they realized that the bigger the web got, the better the results would be. In August

1996, Brin and Page released their search engine on the Stanford website. They christened their new search engine Google after googol, the term for the number 1 followed by 100 zeros.

A search engine connects the keywords that users enter (queries) to a database it has created of web pages (an index). It then produces a list of links to pages (and summaries of content) that it believes are most relevant to a query. Search engines consist of four main components: a web crawler, an index, a runtime index, and a query processor (the interface that connects users to the index). The web crawler is a piece of software that goes from link to link on the web, collecting the pages it finds and sending them back to the index. Once in the index, web pages are analyzed by sophisticated algorithms that look for statistical patterns.

Google's page rank algorithm, for example, looks at the links on a page, the text around those links, and the popularity of the pages that link to that page to determine how relevant a page is to a particular query (in fact, Google's algorithm looks at more than 100 factors to determine a page's relevance to a query term). Once analyzed, pages are tagged. The tag contains information about the pages, for example, whether it is porn, or spam, written in a certain language, or updated infrequently. Tagged pages are then dumped into a runtime index, which is a database that is ready to serve users.

The runtime index forms a bridge between the back end of an engine, the web crawler and index, and the front end, the query processor, and user interface. The query processor takes a keyword inputted by a user, transports it to the runtime index, where an algorithm matches the keyword to pages, ranking them by relevance, and then transports the results back to the user, where they are displayed on the user interface. The computing and data storage infrastructure required to support a search engine is significant. It must scale with the continued growth of the web and with demands on the search engine.

7.2.2.1 Developing the Business Model

As a means to generate money to support its operations, Google started to experiment with ads, but they were not yet pay-per-click ads. Google began selling text-based ads to clients that were interested in certain keywords; the ads would then appear on the page returning search results, not in the list of relevant sites but on the top of the page; the ads were sold on an estimated *cost per thousand impressions* basis. It was about this time that they were intrigued by the GoTo.com's business model consisting of the auctioning of search key words coupled with the pay-per-click. However, the purity of GoTo.com's search results was biased by the desire to make money from advertisers, with those who paid the most being ranked highest. For those who paid the most, GoTo.com would give guarantees that websites would be included more frequently in web crawls.

Brin and Page liked the GoTo.com's innovations, but they were ideologically attached to the idea of serving up the best possible search results to users, without being corrupted by any commercial considerations. Thus, Google settled on an approach combining the innovations of GoTo.com with Google's superior relevance-based search engine; they decided to place text-based ads on the right-hand side of a page, clearly separated from search results by a separating line. But unlike GoTo.com, Brin and Page decided that in addition to the price an advertiser had paid for a keyword, ads should also be ranked according to relevance (relevance was measured by how frequently users clicked on ads). More popular ads rose to the top of the list, less popular ones fell. In other words, Google allowed their users to rank ads.

Google's business challenge was to build advertising revenue but not to compromise objectivity. To do this, Google built two separate columns for its search results page. The first column presented its objective ranking of relevant web sites for the search. The second column presented a list of relevant advertisers to the research results. In that second advertisers' column, Google would charge an advertiser, but only if the user actually clicked through to its web page, called click-through. The two marketing ideas were that (1) Google would maintain brand integrity for its search users, while (2) producing a higher probability of sales for an advertiser through click-through pricing.

Google maintained objectivity in the presentation of the ranking of relevance to sites, and Google also charged advertisers not on view but only on click-throughs. The Google search users were not

Google's customers. Google provided a free and objective service to them. That free service was paid for by advertising. Google's customers were the companies who paid Google to list as relevant to the search on the advertising column. Therefore, Google had to provide two kinds of value:

1. Search value to its users, as Google's market base
2. Sales value to its advertisers, as Google's customers

This in essence is the Google's business model.

In February 2002, Google introduced a new version of AdWords that included for the first time the full set of pay-per-click advertising, keyword auctions, and advertising links ranked by relevance. Sales immediately started to accelerate. Google had hit on the business model that would propel the company into the big league. In 2003, Google introduced a second product, AdSense. AdSense allows third-party publishers large and small to access Google's massive network of advertisers on a self-service basis. Publishers can sign up for AdSense in a matter of minutes. AdSense then scans the publisher's site for content and places contextually relevant ads next to that content. As with AdWords, this is a pay-per-click service, but with AdSense, Google splits the revenues with the publishers. In addition to large publishers, such as online news sites, AdSense has been particularly appealing to many small publishers, such as webloggers. Small publishers find that by adding a few lines of code to their sites, they can suddenly monetize their content.

7.2.2.2 Avenues for Growth

In 2001, subsequent to discussions within the core group of early employees, the company declared a vision and list of values that have continued to shape the evolution of the company. The central vision of Google is to *organize the world's information and make it universally acceptable and useful*. The team also articulated a set of 10 core philosophies (values), which are now listed on its website.

Prompted by this vision, Google introduced a wave of new products, including mapping services (Google Maps and Google Earth), a free e-mail service (Gmail), Google Desktop (which enables users to search files on their own computers), and free online word-processing and spreadsheet programs that had much of the look, feel, and functionality of Microsoft's Word and Excel offerings. Apparently, Google was trying to position itself as a platform company that supported an ecosystem that would rival that fostered by Microsoft, long the software industry's dominate player.

Since 2001, Google has endeavored to keep enhancing the efficacy of its search engine, improving the search algorithms and investing heavily in computing resources. The company has branched out from being a text-based search engine. One strategic thrust has been to extend search to as many digital devices as possible. Google started out on personal computers but can now be accessed through PDAs and cell phones. A second strategy has been to widen the scope of search to include different sorts of information. Google has pushed beyond text into indexing and now offers searches of images, news reports, books, maps, scholarly papers, blogs, a shopping network (Froogle), and, in 2006, videos. Google Desktop, which searches files on a user's PC, also fits in with this schema.

Google views video, like print and images, as another form of information that it wants to make available to the world. It is also another medium for which it can sell ads. Google's commitment to video has been obvious for some time. On Google Video, you can search from a collection of millions of indexed videos that include movie clips, documentaries, TV shows, and music videos. When you type in a search term in the Google Video search box, Google puts the same powerful search engine to work to return the highly relevant results we've come to expect from our searches with Google for printed material. In October 2006, Google announced purchase of YouTube for $1.64 billion in stock. YouTube is a website to which anybody can upload video clips in order to share them.

In April 2007, Google reported that it would pay $3.1 billion for the advertising company DoubleClick; Google had been competing with Microsoft for DoubleClick. Over the course of more than a decade, DoubleClick developed a successful online display ad program and software to help its clients increase their revenue from ads. The acquisition was strategically important to Google for several reasons. The acquisition of DoubleClick will help Google to advance toward its goal of diversification into display ads.

Google wants to reach the wireless market more effectively and more thoroughly. Mobile phones are used by three billion people worldwide and that number will continue to grow. Currently, the sales of portable technology are exceeding the sales of personal computers. Market analysts project that the revenue potential from targeted ads to match search queries from smart phones could exceed the revenue generated by advertising on computer-based search. Google is better positioned than its competitors to provide this kind of effective advertising tied to search. One of its significant early moves toward wireless was Google's 1995 acquisition of a young company named Android, Inc. (breakaway from Motorola) that was developing software for mobile phones. Andy Rubin, an Android cofounder, is currently Google's director of mobile platforms.

In November 2007, the Open Handset Alliance, a multinational group of 34 technology and wireless companies, issued a press release to announce its collaboration to develop Android, *the first complete, open, and free mobile platform*. The alliance includes Google, T-Mobile, Qualcomm, and Motorola, among others. The goal of the alliance is to give consumers a better mobile phone experience than what is currently available. To reach this goal, the alliance created a collaborative development environment based on open-source software. Within this environment, it hopes to accelerate the process of bringing innovative products to the consumer and at a much lower cost and to create an alternative to the proprietary platforms of Microsoft and Symbian.

> In the following is the case history of P&G that is majorly driven by brand strategies for innovative and quality household products. As may be discerned through a careful perusal, these variations were accompanied simultaneously by variations in other dimensions like shared values (to be producer of innovative and quality household products), structure (biased toward autonomy), stuff (innovative products), style (transformational culture), staff (challenging people), skills (breadth of skills), systems (discretionary), and sequence (biased toward mass production).

7.2.3 HOUSEHOLD INNOVATIONS AT P&G

William Procter and James Gamble came from different countries but shared the same goal: to seek a new life in America. Procter was an Englishman and Gamble was an Irishman who came to seek a new life in America. Procter was a candle maker by trade while Gamble was a soap maker; both candles and soap had common ingredients, namely lye, animal fat, and wood ashes. Procter ran the store while Gamble handled the manufacturing process in the back room. Candles were the primary product of the new start-up and provided the young company a steady business. Each morning, Gamble visited homes, hotels, and steamboats to retrieve scraps of meat and wood ash; he traded bars of soap for the scraps. In the pre-Edison era, candles were a staple product in America and P&G was only one of many companies in this field. However, the company had distinct logistical advantages in that Cincinnati was well linked to eastern cities by the railroads. It was also located near the Ohio River, which helped expand the business by providing a waterway to ship products down the river. Its second good fortune had to do with its famous trademark. P&G's simple marking was more attractive than most and became well known. After the symbol had established itself, William Procter enhanced it further by adding 13 stars to represent the 13 colonies. A company's logo isn't going to make or break the business; but it can have a powerful impact on customers' impression and memory of the company.

7.2.3.1 Ivory

With the country on the brink of the Civil War, cousins James Norris Gamble and William Alexander Procter were dispatched to New Orleans by their fathers to purchase large quantities of rosin, which is derived from pine sap and only available in the South. This strategic purchase solidified P&G

manufacturing output during the war as their competitors fell short. In addition, the company inno-vated at the end of the war by experimenting with silicate of soda as a viable substitute. It later became a key ingredient in modern soap products. P&G was continuing to research and innovate with new products. Aiming for cost reduction without sacrificing quality, the company developed a new soap that achieved this objective. It was originally called white soap but was soon rebranded as Ivory. It became an instant success and had a very unusual quality: It was the first soap that floated in water.

One day during production, a machine operator forgot to turn off the mixing machine before he left for his lunch break. Upon his return, he noticed that the soap was still churning, which caused more air to be mixed into the product than normal. The product was packaged and shipped as usual, but it received an incredible response from consumers who were tired of fishing around in the bottom of the tub for sunken soap. Everybody wanted the soap that floats. P&G quickly turned the mistake into one of the best marketing strategies of all time. Ivory soap would single-handedly be responsible for growing the company to the prime position in the industry.

The incredible success of Ivory persuaded the company to build a new plant on the outskirts of Cincinnati called Ivorydale and to hire a chemist to lead a more extensive effort of research, innova-tion, and development. The company developed additional soaps geared toward industrial uses and continued to grow at a rapid pace. Cooperation fortified with an insatiable appetite for innovation and complemented by incentives for employees is a formula that has produced results with incred-ible success for many decades.

The Ivory brand also lent itself well to advertising, which was a frowned-upon practice at this time, usually reserved for companies with less than honorable reputations. But Ivory, with its pure image and built-in story, would overcome this cultural hurdle. The first advertising budget for this remarkable product was $11,000 in 1892 and the slogan was *99-percent pure*. This new practice of consumer marketing also convinced the company to begin an extensive quality control and testing program to ensure that they could back their claims with evidence. This became the cornerstone of the famed P&G research and product development program.

This fast-growing business encountered labor problems, which resulted in many strikes over the next several years and had a negative impact on production at a time when the business was growing rapidly. This motivated the company to reexamine the whole approach to employee rela-tions and resulted in a pioneering employee incentive and benefit program. P&G experimented with several employee compensation and loyalty programs during the upcoming year and has been a consistent leader in the development of cutting-edge, innovative employee programs throughout its history.

7.2.3.2   Portfolio of Products

The company developed a cadre of new products, including a revolutionary new cooking oil called Crisco in 1911. After applying the P&G marketing model of promotion and advertising, the product became a huge success. William Procter and James Gamble never forgot the lesson they had learned many years before and made sure the company was well prepared for an ingredient shortage when World War I loomed on the horizon. They stockpiled raw ingredients so that the company would not have production problems during the war. P&G introduced many new products and categories during the next two decades, including Ivory Flakes, Chipso Flakes for industrial laundries, Camay, Oxydol, and synthetic soaps.

7.2.3.3   Origin of Brand Management

During the Great Depression, P&G contributed several key innovations that would set the standard for business operations in the future. It began with the establishment of a distinct method for brand management. The concept was of *one man, one brand* that concentrated attention on a more indi-vidualized approach to running the various products within the company. This became the standard for almost all future consumer product companies in America. Radio advertising became an effec-tive vehicle for the company.

P&G, creator of the first floating bar of soap, pioneered a new soap concept that would become a cultural icon of America. This concept was called the soap opera. By 1939, there were 29 different soap operas on the radio.

World War II brought additional business to P&G as the company's expertise was used to fill military contracts for 60 mm mortar shells. The company was a large producer of glycerin, used in explosives and medicines, which were vital in the war effort.

After World War II, new consumer attitudes demanded more products and P&G was ready for the challenge. The postwar period proved to be a spectacular growth period for the company, and one product in particular was a phenomenal success. P&G had experimented with synthetic soaps and introduced Tide in 1946. Tide, code-named *product-X*, was developed in 1945 through in-house experimentation with the cleansing properties of synthetic compounds. The test results were so compelling that P&G abandoned its exhaustive product- and market-testing procedures in order to steal a march on its competitors, Colgate and Unilever. Resources were quickly ploughed into developing new manufacturing facilities and processes and into refining and communicating the Tide value proposition.

The demand for this revolutionary soap outstripped production immediately as this product—along with a 21-million-dollar advertising campaign—was seen as a modern-day miracle. The product quickly became the most popular soap in America and has stayed that way for decades. Although the success of Tide was incredible, P&G continued to introduce new products, including Cheer, Downy, Bold, Era, and Solo. In time, the financial resources generated through massive sales transformed P&G from a U.S. soap company into a global provider of household products.

7.2.3.4 Profusion of Product Innovations

Over the years, P&G has acquired an array of companies so that it can stay in the forefront of consumer product innovation. It truly has created a culture that encourages, allows, and nurtures innovation. P&G took a lucky situation with a floating bar of soap and turned it into gold. The power of luck is sometimes the result of people making mistakes. Patient innovators benefit from creating cultures where mistakes can happen. Few innovators are successful immediately, and many discover new ways of thinking simply by keeping an open mind to the opportunities that they might just stumble upon.

With its flurry of successful products and market dominance, P&G's organic growth in the 1950s was unprecedented. In addition, the company hit on another incredibly successful innovation with the assistance of researchers at the University of Indiana. This time, it was a unique toothpaste that included stannous fluoride. This combination of fluorine and tin that could significantly reduce cavities became known as Crest toothpaste. Introduced in 1955, this product rapidly became the number one selling toothpaste in America.

The next innovation horizon for P&G was paper products, which also became popular in the 1950s. A new method of drying wood pulp led to several new products, including White Cloud, Puffs, and a reformulation for the famous Charmin brand.

But the best was yet to come. With the baby boom in full swing, the company introduced Pampers, which revolutionized the world of diapers. One of the company's researchers, Vic Mills, was changing one of his own grandchildren's leaking diapers one day when he decided that he could use his resources at P&G to do better (innovations truly come from tough times). Mills developed a three-layer paper diaper that absorbed moisture, kept it away from the baby's skin, and retained the fluid until the diaper was disposed of. This invention took the market by storm and has remained the standard of care for babies everywhere.

7.3 STRUCTURE VARIATIONS RANGING FROM CONTROL TO AUTONOMY

Enterprises are exposed to considerable dynamics created by external forces that have to do with the market, for example, or customer behavior, governmental activities, the economy, technology developments, or the geopolitical situation. In response, the enterprise creates its own dynamics, such as through reorganization, business cooperation, a merger, acquisition or new product, and service development. In the context of these dynamics and their associated uncertainty, strategic choices have to be made and operationalized; these could be in areas such as flexibility and time to market, the quality of products and services, customer satisfaction, process excellence, safety, costs, or compliance with rules and legislation. These strategic choices can only be addressed through the design (and architecture) of the enterprise itself: its organization. An enterprise organization is determined by aspects like culture (norms and values), processes and technology (e.g., IT), HR management, and employee behavior.

Thus, business domain changes or variations have an impact on the enterprise organization. For example, in e-business, offering customizable products and services to customers through a web portal requires that the internal back-office processes have been adjusted and redesigned such that integrated process execution is safeguarded. Further, collaboration with business partners and suppliers likewise requires extensive procedural and informational integration and entails significant implications for the enterprise. Collaborative, computer-supported activities and structures aid the procedural and informational integration.

The traditional organizational structure seems of lower importance; hierarchies and conventional central management become less relevant for networks of teams and individuals connected virtually and directed toward the cooperative execution of an end-to-end process. Other organizational forms are required due to increased dynamics and complexity facing enterprises. These organizational forms must aid in enhancing enterprise flexibility: the ability to change and adapt. Cooperative work structures, supported by information systems, can help considerably in avoiding rigidity and inertia associated with the traditional, formal, and hierarchical structures. Centralized data and knowledge can be used to effectuate decentralized authorities and responsibilities. Thus, centralization and decentralization are not necessarily mutually exclusive: local operational units have the freedom to act within the boundaries of centrally defined directions, norms, and values.

In this regard, the concept of enterprise architecture as embodied in enterprise systems like SAP implemented within the enterprise will turn out to be a crucial concept for ensuring, on one hand, a unified and integrated organization, on the other hand, a flexible and agile organization.

> In the following is the case history of ArcelorMittal. It illustrates ArcelorMittal's predominant focus on global growth via structure variation through acquisitions driven by proactive control and performance management of the acquired companies. As may be discerned through a careful perusal, these variations were accompanied simultaneously by variations in other dimensions like shared values (rules driven for bottom-line results), strategy (biased toward plans), stuff (products), style (biased toward administrational culture), staff (challenging people), skills (focus), systems (mandatory), and sequence (mass production).

7.3.1 CONTROLLING FOR GROWTH AT ACCELORMITTAL

ArcelorMittal is the world's largest steel business. The group employs some 330,000 people in 60 countries and makes around 130 t of steel a year—10% of world production. This is a high share of the market in a fragmented industry—the next largest players are Japan's Nippon Steel and Korea's Posco, making only about 30 t of steel a year each. However, the achievement of this scale of operations has rested on the reinvention of the mature steel industry on a global basis and can be traced largely to the strategic insight of one man—Lakshmi Mittal. Mittal spent two decades of deal making before, in 2006, combining Mittal Steel with Arcelor—the world's second largest steel business at that point, and his main rival—in 2006 at the cost of £18.1 billion. Mittal's offer for Arcelor provoked a nationalistic backlash from Arcelor management and European politicians but the hostile bid succeeded because of shareholders approval in mid-2006.

7.3.1.1 Coalescing Steel Ball Gathers Mass

Acquiring Arcelor was an audacious move because Mittal had broken continental Europe's hold on its industrial champions. The European Union has its very origins in the 1950s plan to integrate the coal and steel industries of Western Europe, which provided the springboard for political integration into the disaster that is now the European Union. However, the industry dominance of the ArcelorMittal group has little to do with simple organic growth. It results from the rapid amalgamation of a large number of small steelmakers. The Mittal side was built up from about 25 mergers, while Arcelor came into being in the early 2000s from the merger of Usinor, Arbed, and Aceralia—the national steel groups of France, Luxembourg, and Spain, respectively.

For decades, steel companies were among the worst performing in the world—steel was fragmented, financially weak, and plagued by over supply. Suppliers of coal and iron ore, and major customers like car makers, were far stronger than steelmakers and dictated terms. Each economic cycle downturn sent some steel companies into bankruptcy (see Chapter 5, Subsection 5.2.2.1, "Business Cycle"). Worse, the steel business had a nonentrepreneurial management approach, which, for many, was a legacy from state ownership. The underlying business model shared by traditional steelmakers was based on tonnages, not profitability, and regionalization—steel industry executives did not look beyond their home regions, because they never thought steel could be transported globally or supplied to global customers. Mittal's insight was that steel industry earnings could be boosted through a process of consolidation to build bigger companies that could dictate prices to customers. This is especially relevant in a market where demand was being driven up by the demands of China and India for steel. Consolidating a fragmented global business is at the center of Mittal's strategy. The thinking is that larger companies—particularly in a cyclical industry like steel—have a greater ability to moderate production to fit with demand patterns and so keep prices and profits high. Bigger companies also have the advantage of spreading costs like R&D over a larger sales base and providing a better service to global customers like the automotive industry. However, in addition to consolidation as such, Mittal's strategic vision was also to look at the steel business as a globalized sector, in which plants and customers could be tied together through shared operating procedures and market intelligence.

7.3.1.2 Becoming an Industry Leader

The implementation of Mittal's strategy saw a period through the 1980s and 1990s during which he purchased struggling and often out-of-date steel plants in countries like Trinidad and Tobago, Kazakhstan, and Mexico, transforming them into profitable businesses. He borrowed techniques from more successful industries like chemical and car making to increase quality and cut costs. The 2000s saw Mittal buying run-down state-owned plant in Eastern Europe as well as the unwanted assets of large steelmakers (in the downturn of the economic cycle, those assets were often acquired cheaply).

Until 2004, when Mittal bought the U.S.-based International Steel Group, nearly all Mittal's most important steelmaking assets were in low-cost countries, away from the world's main industrialized centers. The addition of advanced-technology steelmaking in high-cost countries illustrates the *reverse globalization* effect where businesses in the west are increasingly being acquired by rivals in Asia or other emerging nations. Key Mittal acquisitions were presented in the following:

Date Announced	Target	Value (Sterling Pounds)
1989	Iron & Steel Co., Trinidad and Tobago	N/A
1992	Sibalsa Steel, Mexico	117 m
1994	Sidbec-Dosco, Canada	250 m
1998	Karmet, Kazakhstan	522 m
2003	Nova Hut, Czech Republic	498 m
2005	KryvlyRih, Ukraine	2.6 bn
2005	International Steel, United States	2.5 bn
2006	Arcelor, Luxembourg	18 bn
2008	Bayou Steel, United States	475 m

Mittal's approach to restructuring new acquisitions as he built the global business followed a tried-and-tested plan:

- Transition *SWAT* team—remove most existing managers and replace with Mittal executives to get the company running on a commercial basis quickly
- Fix the liquidity—reestablish credit with suppliers to assure a steady flow of raw materials and end barter arrangements that encourage corruption and reduce cash flow
- Debug—bring in Mittal technicians to improve operations and rework maintenance schedules to cut down time
- Product mix—shift to production of higher-value products like cold rolled steel and try to sell to end users not middlemen
- Integrate—form regional groups to boost purchasing power and prevent plants from competing with each other for the same customers
- Prune—close or sell off noncore subsidiaries and gradually cut back on staffing

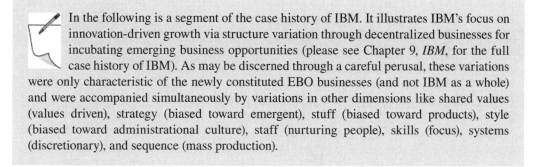

In the following is a segment of the case history of IBM. It illustrates IBM's focus on innovation-driven growth via structure variation through decentralized businesses for incubating emerging business opportunities (please see Chapter 9, *IBM*, for the full case history of IBM). As may be discerned through a careful perusal, these variations were only characteristic of the newly constituted EBO businesses (and not IBM as a whole) and were accompanied simultaneously by variations in other dimensions like shared values (values driven), strategy (biased toward emergent), stuff (biased toward products), style (biased toward administrative culture), staff (nurturing people), skills (focus), systems (discretionary), and sequence (mass production).

7.3.2 ORGANIZING FOR INNOVATION AT IBM

In September 1999, as head of corporate strategy, Harreld was given the task of looking into whether other promising new growth businesses were being abandoned. While IBM had plenty of great ideas and inventions—in fact, IBM Research was granted more patents each year than any other company in the world—Harreld found that managers had a difficult time launching and growing new businesses that would commercialize these inventions and exploit growth opportunities arising in the marketplace. Harreld's research showed that the majority of IBM employees focused on selling current products, serving current customers, and executing current operations. In fact, the focus on flawless execution and short-term results had intensified under the ruthless cost cutting necessary to survive during the 1990s. In addition, while common operating processes were enabling improvements in achieving the goal of *One IBM* in its current businesses, the innovation process continued to be focused within the silos of existing lines of business. A corporate venture fund that had been established to support internal growth opportunities had also proved problematic. The lack of experienced entrepreneurial leadership and processes caused most of these new IBM businesses to fail.

 The Alchemy of Growth advocated dividing a company's portfolio of business initiatives into three *horizons*:

- Horizon 1 (H1) businesses were mature and well established and accounted for the bulk of profits and cash flow.
- Horizon 2 (H2) businesses were on the rise and experiencing rapid, accelerating growth.
- Horizon 3 (H3) businesses were emerging and represented the *seeds of a company's future strategy*.

Each horizon required different leadership and governance, a different approach to defining and executing strategy, a different way of organizing and managing, different types of people, culture, and incentives, and a different approach to financing.

Harreld and his colleagues concluded that IBM's difficulties were largely the result of trying, unsuccessfully, to apply a single approach to organizing and leading—one that was designed for large established businesses—to its high growth and start-up businesses.

7.3.2.1 Defining a New Approach to Innovation at IBM

Over the next few months, Harreld worked with the IBM business leaders to categorize IBM's businesses as H1, H2, and H3. While it was fairly straightforward to identify current businesses and then categorize them as either mature or high growth based on historical revenue trends and industry forecasts, executives recognized that, in the turbulent high-tech industry, the assumptions behind these forecasts could be wrong and would need to be continuously monitored. This job fell to the corporate strategy group. Even more problematic, however, was the selection of H3 businesses, which would be designated as emerging business opportunities (EBOs) and the decision of where in the organization to allocate leadership and authority for these EBOs.

After much debate, the corporate executive committee (CEC) decided that a centralized model would perpetuate the organizational silos that they had been working so hard to break down. Rallying behind the *One IBM* vision and values that had helped pull together the company during crisis, the CEC decided to organize EBOs to ensure corporate guidance and oversight while maintaining business unit line manager authority and accountability. In doing so, IBM sought to build innovation capabilities where they were needed in the divisions, focus business leaders on managing different business horizons, and ensure a smooth transition for successful EBOs into their ultimate business home. More importantly, when EBOs required cross-business unit cooperation, CEC oversight would shine a spotlight on critical areas of need and would enable IBM's senior executives to work with business unit leaders to solve the organizational problems that made cooperation difficult.

Initially, seven key business opportunities were designated as EBOs. The criteria for selecting these opportunities included the need for cross-business cooperation and resources, the maturity of the business plan and strategy (e.g., key market and technology risks appeared manageable and expertise was available to build the first offering and take it to market), the forecasted size of the market, and the potential for generating over $1 billion in 3–5 years. By 2003, the number of EBOs had grown to 18 and they addressed both new technology products (e.g., grid computing, blade servers, Linux, pervasive computing) and new markets (e.g., life sciences, digital media).

7.3.2.2 Organizing for Growth

The corporate EBO process functioned effectively but relatively informally for its first 2 years. In addition to *evangelizing* the need for a commitment to innovation and growth and for developing different management processes, the core activity was a monthly review of each EBO. Fashioned on the company's traditional business review process, each EBO leader, accompanied by his or her division head, met with Thompson, Harreld, and Donofrio to report progress, discuss plans, and solve problems. But unlike traditional IBM reviews, which focused on financial performance versus plan, these sessions were intended to verify and refine business plans and to measure the progress made as the EBO moved through the innovation process. Although efforts were made to identify expenses and revenues for each EBO, most questions during the meeting—and most of an EBO leader's compensation—revolved around clarifying assumptions and risks and assessing progress against key project-based milestones. Success against these project-based milestones could include clarifying market demand and willingness to pay by interviewing key customers or reducing technology risk by completing a key phase of the product development process.

7.3.2.3 EBO Progress

Of the original 18 EBOs, Life Sciences and Business Transformation Services had become 1-billion-dollar businesses with the latter growing over 30% during 2003, Digital Media grew 60% to $1.7 billion in revenue, Linux grew to over $2 billion in revenue, and pervasive computing generated more than $2.4 billion in revenues. Three additional EBOs (blade servers, flexible hosting services, and storage software) doubled their revenues. Along the way, new EBOs were being developed, many of them around emerging markets and, during 2003, China, India, Russia, and Brazil had generated $3 billion in revenue, which represented double-digit annual growth.

> In the following is a segment of the case history of LEGO. It illustrates LEGO's focus on sustaining *creativity, quality, and fun* elements of their brands via structure variation through co-creation with customers, partnership with outsourcers, and digitization of the LEGO experience. As may be discerned through a careful perusal, these variations were accompanied simultaneously by variations in other dimensions like shared values (biased toward values driven), strategy (planned), stuff (creative products and creation experiences), style (biased toward transformational culture), staff (challenging people), and sequence (mass production).

7.3.3 Crossing Boundaries at LEGO

Ole Kirk Christiansen founded the LEGO Group in 1932 in a small carpenter's workshop in Billund, Denmark. LEGO is a simple abbreviation of two Danish words—*leg* (play) and *godt* (well). The company has since developed into a modern, global enterprise that is now the world's fifth largest manufacturer of toys in terms of sales. Its products are sold in more than 130 countries. Central to the LEGO Group's raison d'être are the concepts of *systematic creativity* and *lifelong play*. The fundamental idea of LEGO is that approximately 6000–8000 bricks apply to a broad range of LEGO models; these bricks can be combined in numerous ways to generate unimaginable variety. When thousands of different brick designs and color combinations are added to the LEGO product range, the range of creative play possibilities effectively becomes infinite. Throughout its history, the LEGO Group's strong values, at the organizational and brand level, have inspired decision making and have played a key role in the way business ideas are implemented. For example, the brand values—creativity, quality, and fun—are decisive for the group's relationship with its users via a numerous groups and websites such as LEGO Factory or LEGO Club.

The LEGO Group's products fall into the following six categories:

1. Preschool Products, such as LEGO DUPLO, consist of large brick elements that encourage children to build what comes into their minds.

2. Creative Building denotes standard LEGO sets where no instruction is needed other than the use of one's imagination.
3. With Play Theme product lines, the group added a further dimension to the joy of construction, namely, that children can spend many hours playing with finished models. For instance, with LEGO BIONICLE, the company developed a complete story that combines construction toys and action figures.
4. With MINDSTORMS NXT, LEGO users can design and program their own robot to perform various operations.
5. LEGO Education targets the educational sector and has developed materials for both teachers and pupils.
6. LEGO has a number of licensed products, which are basically play themes based on movies, that is, Star Wars and Indiana Jones, or books, for which the group has acquired the rights.

However, during the 1990s, the group extended and stretched the brand to embrace numerous product categories unrelated to the original LEGO idea of supporting fun (i.e., creativity) and learning (i.e., problem solving skills). The rise of digital games and toys, such as the Game Boy and the PlayStation, during the 1990s made the company question whether the kids of the future had the patience to engage in LEGO play and if parents had the willingness to pay for the multicolored bricks that, compared with many other kinds of plastic toys, were still very expensive. A general lack of focus on its core product, the LEGO brick, led the company to introduce new product lines and concepts that it hoped would be key growth drivers; these initiatives sought to extend and apply the LEGO brand to relatively unrelated areas, such as television programs, software games, children's clothing, and accessories.

The diversification strategy increased complexity, confused users and employees, and took the company away from its core. The number of base components was symptomatic of the various problems faced by the group. When the crisis was at its most severe, approximately 12,700 product components were used to make LEGO products. When the business transformation was nearly complete in 2007, the number of components had been reduced by almost half of the original number. By addressing the excessive proliferation of product components, the LEGO Group actually reduced the complexity of product designs. This, combined with an increased focus on customer value and the adjustment of the cost base and assets to reflect lower revenues, allowed the group to regain financial control in terms of positive bottom-line figures and rising operating margins.

7.3.3.1 Banishing Boundaries

The turnaround did not only have a financial focus. The plan also inspired a more profound transformation process related to the innovation of the LEGO Group's business model in two critical dimensions. First, it marked a shift from a traditional *bricks and mortar* company and a philosophy characterized by vertically integrated value chain activities to a more network-oriented business model that entailed a looser vertical setup. Second, the LEGO Group's new business model made use of the *open-source* concept—customers were increasingly invited to comment on products (prototypes), test them (LEGO City), codevelop them (LEGO Mindstorms), or even customize their own creations (LEGO Factory).

The company's changed business model impacted three key areas, namely, moving from vertical integration to a network configuration, co-creation of products with customers and digitization of the *LEGO experience*. The turnaround helped to establish a more sustainable, *future-proof* business platform that embraced business process optimization, while also creating room for innovativeness and creativity.

7.3.3.2 Supply Chain Optimization

As part of the turnaround plan, the LEGO Group had to optimize its cost base. Prior to 2005, the group had production and packaging facilities in Denmark, Switzerland, the Czech Republic,

Korea, and the United States. For several years, the company had been producing at its factory in Kladno, the Czech Republic, and using various subsuppliers in China. In addition, production/packaging facilities in Korea served the Asian market, including Japan. As part of the plan, production facilities were closed in Denmark, Switzerland, and Korea and transferred to Kladno and to suppliers in Eastern Europe. Moreover, the LEGO Group's European distribution centers were centralized in Eastern Europe. This, in combination with the relocation efforts, was expected to increase efficiency, improve servicing of the European market, and save costs.

The LEGO Group's decision to use relocation and outsourcing as a means of restructuring its value chain was primarily motivated by cost structure and market proximity considerations. First, the group outsourced production to reduce costs, which enhanced its competitiveness and enabled a shift to more productive, higher-value activities—namely, innovation and product development. Specifically, the labor-intensive decorating, assembly, and packaging processes within product lines characterized by a high degree of uniformity and volume (like LEGO System products) were outsourced. Second, based on a thorough analysis of the company's supply chain, Mexico and the Czech Republic were selected as key hubs from which the company could serve the European and U.S. markets. In 2006, as part of the shared vision strategy, the LEGO Group outsourced major parts of its production operations to Flextronics, a leading electronics manufacturing services (EMS) provider. The group retained ownership of the buildings and plant equipment, while Flextronics was responsible for daily operations. In addition, Flextronics took over responsibility for the company's factory in Kladno along with its 600 employees in August 2006.

While LEGO System and DUPLO products were relocated to Flextronics's facilities in Eastern Europe, the production of technically more demanding products such as LEGO Technic and BIONICLE remained at the LEGO facilities in Billund. This setup allowed the LEGO headquarters to retain a number of critical competencies in molding, processing, and packaging. By the same token, the LEGO Group established a mechanical engineering unit and a production technology R&D unit next to its remaining production facilities in Billund. This was considered crucial to enhance product development efforts.

The collaboration with Flextronics allowed the group to relocate production facilities to Kladno quickly and efficiently. While communication worked well during the outsourcing process, the LEGO Group encountered more serious challenges in globalizing its value chain in terms of process specifications and documentation, capacity utilization, effectiveness, and IT (LEGO Group used SAP while Flextronics used BAAN that was not compatible with SAP). In addition to productivity and capacity utilization issues, Flextronics wanted to relocate production to optimize scale of its own operations following its takeover of Solectron.

However, the Kladno site held strategic value for the LEGO Group, not only due to its proximity to the group's large European market but also because the plant was located next to the group's prototyping plant that created considerable synergies. Most importantly, Kladno was near the group's new pan-European distribution center in Jirny, near Prague. Consequently, in July 2008, the company announced that the existing outsourcing agreement with Flextronics would be phased out during 2009 and that headquarters would again take over LEGO production in Juárez, Mexico, and Nyíregyháza, Hungary. Reverting back to an insourced operation clearly demonstrated the challenges that face a company moving from vertical integration to a network constellation.

7.3.3.3   Co-creation of Product with Customers

A second factor in the group's transformation was related to co-creation of products with the customers. As one of the front-runners in the toy industry, the LEGO Group was experienced in involving customers in the design and product development process to varying degrees through user testing, user codevelopment, and personal customization. Today, inviting users to directly codesign new products and encouraging their involvement in online brand communities, where users discuss or seek inspiration, are integrated parts of the LEGO Group's business model. The company's main concern was whether these discussions and exchanges of ideas genuinely supported the brand and values of creativity, quality, and fun. User involvement occurred on many levels, in many programs, and with varying degrees of engagement and rules. Originally prevalent in adult user communities, LEGO Factory encouraged children to build and publish their own designs by using LEGO Digital Designer software. Another, more organized, example was the LEGO Group's Ambassador Program, which was a community based program made up of adult LEGO hobbyists who share their product and build expertise with the worldwide LEGO community and the public.

Shortly after LEGO Mindstorms was launched in 1998, it became a huge success with more than one million sets sold. This prompted plans for a second generation of robotic construction toys. Named *NXT* and launched in 2006, the second generation was partly designed by the lead users of Mindstorms. Experiments completed by core users often made the product more stimulating and exciting.

7.3.3.4 Digitization of the LEGO Experience

A third element of the group's transformation involved digitalization of the *LEGO experience*. In the mid-1990s, the group was under pressure from various computer game producers to create games for use on the Nintendo GameCube and Sony PlayStation consoles. This led to attempts to digitalize the bricks. In 1997, the LEGO Group established the subsidiary LEGO Media International In London, United Kingdom, the purpose of which was to develop and sell LEGO computer games, video films, and books. Various computer games were introduced to target different age groups— LEGO Friends for girls, LEGO Racer for boys, and LEGO Rock Racers for adults. Initially, there was an overarching belief that a LEGO user in a virtual world would be fundamentally different from original LEGO users. In reality, these users were similar and shared the same fundamental passion for the LEGO idea and brand; in fact, the LEGO Group discovered that the most hardcore LEGO users of the physical bricks were also front-runners in testing and adapting to new technologies. But the solution to make the business model sustainable still eluded them.

In the late 1990s, new digital product concepts were introduced. The strong emphasis on technology blurred the distinction between the virtual and the physical LEGO experience. The group's success with digitalization strategy was dependent on the extent to which the company could achieve seamless integration between the virtual and the physical worlds, for which it was imperative that the users pay for the integrated experience. Given the success of social communities and networks on the Internet, the LEGO Group aspired to unite its humungous number of LEGO users into a proper universe. In 2006, the company began working on what was possibly its largest digital venture in years, namely, LEGO Universe—a massive multiplayer online game (MMOG) in which thousands of LEGO fans would create, build, quest, and socialize in a game world that would constantly evolve through players' actions.

7.4 STUFF VARIATIONS RANGING FROM PRODUCTS TO EXPERIENCES

The number of new products has tripled since 1980. The shorter life cycle of products and services can also be mentioned; renewal thus occurs more frequently. For example, at the end of the 1970s, the life cycle of electronic consumer products lay between 3 and 6 years. Ten years later, this had already been reduced to 1 year; more variations of the same product also reach the market. Roughly over the same period, it was not only the product life cycle that reduced significantly but the number of electronic product variations also increased tenfold. Enormous product variations of essentially the same product resulted from more enterprises offering that type of product, but also arose from enterprises offering more product variations. Such enormous variation can be noticed in virtually all areas: from electronic equipment and cars to toothpaste.

The distinction between physical products and services is vanishing. Technology enables complementing physical products with associated services. For example, enterprise that is in the business of providing car-usage-related services could shift its focus from producing cars toward delivering movability services. Technological developments will lead increasingly to the diffusion of business boundaries. A freight carrier might, for example, grow into a producer of logistic services who controls the total end-to-end chain. Within any business domain, the use of loyalty cards for customers can lead to offering financial services associated with the loyalty card. Diffusion of business boundaries is fueled further since IT, as mentioned previously, makes it relatively easy to add complementary services to the primary product. So the sales of airline tickets can be combined (possibly through business partnerships) with services pertinent to finance, insurance, car rental, or hotel reservations.

> In the following is the case history of Harley-Davidson. It illustrates Harley-Davidson's predominant focus on stuff variations targeted at heightening of the *Harley ownership* experience. As may be discerned through a careful perusal, these variations were accompanied simultaneously by variations in other dimensions like shared values (values driven), strategy (planned), structure (biased toward control), style (biased toward transformational culture), staff (biased toward nurturing people), skills (biased toward breadth of skills), systems (mandatory), and sequence (mass production).

7.4.1 HARLEY EXPERIENCE AT HARLEY-DAVIDSON

Harley-Davidson, Inc. was founded in 1903 by William Harley and brothers William Davidson, Arthur Davidson, and Walter Davidson. In 1909, Harley introduced its first two-cylinder, V-twin engine, featuring the deep, rumbling sound for which Harley motorcycles are renowned. In the postwar, growing affluence and the rise of youth culture created a growing demand for motorcycles. However, this was satisfied primarily by imports. By the end of the 1970s, Honda had replaced Harley as market leader in heavyweight motorcycles in the United States. In 1981, following a leveraged buyout, Harley emerged as an independent, privately owned company (though heavily laden with debt). The new management team devoted themselves to rebuilding production methods and working practices in order to cut costs and improve quality. Within a year, all Harley's manufacturing operations were being converted to JIT: components and subassemblies were *pulled* through the production system in response to final demand.

Earlier, the Harley-Davidson organization had been a traditional multilayered, fragmented command-and-control system with an overly bureaucratic approach to routines and procedures. Harley revamped its organization, resulting in a flatter and better-integrated structure, systems that were less hierarchical and more inclusive, and increased flexibility in practices and procedures. Across the years, Harley's belief in the effectiveness of nonhierarchical, team-based structures in fostering motivation and accelerating innovation and learning was evident throughout the company. The 1990s saw year-on-year uninterrupted growth in the heavyweight motorcycle market and a continued increase in Harley's market share.

The new Harley-Davidson Operating System was a philosophy and a methodology for continuous improvement involving team-based efforts to identify wasted steps, pare costs, and enhance quality throughout manufacturing. Despite serious changes in its production methods and product offerings, Harley-Davidson did not deviate from its core identity: freedom, distinctiveness, passion, independence, and toughness. This identity, coupled with the country's external image as an American icon, resonated with customers and turned out to be one of the driving forces in the company's revitalization. As a result, despite a fivefold increase in production capacity since the beginning of the 1990s, demand for Harley motorcycles continued to outstrip supply.

7.4.1.1 Owning the Harley Experience

Harley-Davidson had long recognized that it was not selling motorcycles; it was selling the *Harley experience*. This appeal of the Harley brand was central, not just to the company's marketing but to its strategy as a whole. The central thrust of the strategy was reinforcing and extending the relationship between the company and its consumers. The Harley-Davidson image and the loyalty it engendered among its customers were its greatest assets. Harley-Davidson was one of the archetypes of

American style: you get a Harley and you were buying into the U.S. mystique. Together with a few other companies—Walt Disney and Levi Strauss—Harley had a unique relationship with American culture. The values that Harley represented—individuality, freedom, and adventure—could be traced back to the cowboy and frontiersman of yesteryear, and before that to the motives that brought people to America in the first place. As the sole surviving American motorcycle company from the pioneering days of the industry, Harley-Davidson represented a tradition of U.S. engineering and manufacturing.

To increase Harley's involvement in its consumers' riding experience, it formed the Harley Owners' Group (HOG) in 1983. Through HOG, the company became involved in organizing social and charity events. Employees, from the CEO down, were encouraged to take an active role in HOG activities. HOG's website described the kind of emotion and atmosphere that the company was trying to deliver to customers through its HOG organization. This quickly became, and still is, the world's largest motorcycle club, with chapters all over the world and close to one million members. Factory-sponsored rides, gatherings, parades, and charity events create a highly visible presence, serving both marketing and customer service functions. HOG also fostered community and camaraderie for which Harley-Davidson is world renowned, positioning the brand as a lifestyle, rather than just a motorcycle, enabling it to capture both market and mind share at a huge premium. HOG sponsors and runs national events and state rallies for Harley-Davidson owners every year. In 2003, more than one million people worldwide participated in hundredth anniversary events.

Through the HOG, Harley was able to extend this base and reach out to women and a younger generation of admirers—going beyond its traditional narrower focus on American men, mostly in their late 30s to late 50s. The Harley-Davidson brand is frequently cited in marketing books, top 100 lists, cult lists, and enthusiast lists for its ability to generate loyalty beyond reason and profits beyond projections.

7.4.1.2 Realizing the Harley Experience

Personalization is an essential requirement for the Harley owner. Hence, Harley offered a wide model range, and a broad set of options regarding paint, accessories, and trim. At the same time, economies in engineering, manufacturing, and purchasing required standardizing components across the model range. The result was that Harley continually broadened its range of models and for each model offered a range of options (at the same time, it based this range of product offerings upon three engine types, four basic frames, four styles of gas tank, and so on). Harley concentrated upon incremental refinements to its engines, frames, and gearboxes aimed at improving power delivery, reliability, increasing braking power, and reducing vibration. This continual upgrading of its technology and its quality was an essential requirement of Harley shifting its customer base from blue-collar enthusiasts to middle-aged professionals who lacked the time, inclination, and expertise to tune and maintain their bikes and needed *luxuries* such as electric starters and vibration control. In recent years, by implementing lean manufacturing ideas from Toyota Production System, Harley-Davidson has increased its commitment to lean production, enhanced quality, innovation, and more radical product design.

To further develop the Harley-Davidson lifestyle, the company focused on complementary products as well as motorcycles. This consisted of motorcycle parts, accessories, and general merchandise (clothing and collectibles) representing about 20% of the total revenue in 2000—much higher than for any other motorcycle company. Clothing sales included not just traditional riding apparel (like leather jackets and helmets, nonriding attire such as T-shirts and baseball hats, and household goods such as branded pet accessories and barbecue tools) but a wide range of men's, women's, and children's leisure apparel. Most of the *general merchandising* business represented licensing of the Harley name and trademarks to third-party manufacturers. Harley-Davidson Financial Services was established (by acquiring Eaglemark) to extend credit to both retail and wholesale customers and also to underwrite motorcycle insurance.

A key part of Harley-Davidson's growth strategy was expanding sales outside of the United States. A critical issue for international marketing was the extent to which the products and the Harley image needed to be adjusted to meet the needs of overseas markets. Harley's image was rooted in American culture and was central to its appeal to European and Asian customers. At the same time, the composition of demand and the customer profiles were different in overseas markets. Europe was the focal point of Harley's overseas ambitions, simply because after United States, it was the second largest heavyweight motorcycle market in the world. But, European roads and riding style were different from the United States. As a result, Harley modified some of its models to better meet the needs and tastes of its European customers. The U.S. Sportster, for example, had a straight handlebar instead of curled buckhorns and a new suspension system to improve cornering.

In the following is the case history of Southwest Airlines. It illustrates Southwest Airlines's focus on stuff variations targeted at enhancing its passenger transportation services. As may be discerned through a careful perusal, these variations were accompanied simultaneously by variations in other dimensions like shared values (values driven), strategy (planned), structure (biased toward control), style (biased toward administrational culture), staff (nurturing people), skills (breadth of skills), systems (mandatory), and sequence (mass production).

7.4.2 SOUTHWEST AIRLINES: TRANSPORTATION SERVICE RATHER THAN A TRAVEL EXPERIENCE?

In 1994, after 20 years of often-precarious existence, Southwest Airlines was in market position number eight, with only a 3.3% share. It was making money but was locked out of three of the four U.S. computer airline reservations systems. United, Continental Airlines, and Delta Airlines had blackballed Southwest in order to protect their routes. Southwest responded by using its own 800 number and later its own website to sell seats, using a ticketless and seatless (no assigned seats) model. Both were in keeping with its no-frills service model. The major carriers periodically matched Southwest's low fares, although typically for a *limited number of seats* in competing markets and with a 21-day advance purchase restriction.

However, the other major carriers saw such low fares as temporary price wars, not a paradigm shift. What, after all, had become of People Express, the prototypical discount upstart, or other insurgents such as New York Air? The incumbents had seen this act before, and those upstarts were runway kill. For the new breed of discounters, was it not therefore only a matter of time? High-cost majors like Northwest saw the industry in terms of two tiers. In one tier, from primary hubs, they served the well-heeled-business travelers and folks who wanted traditional service and didn't like scrambling for seats. In the other tier, the discounters flew budget-minded folk from one out-of-the way hub to another in low-class planes with lousy quality, safety, and service.

7.4.2.1 Making of a Black Swan

Southwest, however, saw the world in a different way. It saw itself as a short-haul, high-frequency airline. Because it saw cars, trains, and buses as its primary substitutes, it had built its cost structure to compete with them. Its business model had been built not on *this week only* or seasonal specials but on low fares forever. In keeping with such a lean cost structure, Southwest founder and boss Herb Kelleher didn't draw down a lot of long-term debt to buy new airplanes—he paid mostly cash. He paid his pilots three-fourths what the big airlines paid theirs. Those pilots flew one third more hours and occasionally pitched in to clean the cabins. In 1995, Southwest signed a 10-year pay deal with their pilots, eliminating one aspect of an issue that has been a constant headache for the majors. As a comparison, in 1996, it cost Southwest just 7.5 cents to fly one seat 1 mile, well below the industry average of about 9 cents.

Southwest also flew only Boeing 737s, which saved money on scheduling, training, and maintenance. It kept its airplanes in the air more hours per day, making better use of its capital. It turned around its planes at the gate in a fraction of industry standards, gaining extra flights each day in the process. It also avoided the entire expense and bother of providing hot airline meals—one lesson the other *premium* airlines appear to have learned.

The major carriers tried to protect their market by limiting Southwest's access to gates they controlled at important airports. But Southwest would just outflank the majors by initiating service at smaller airports like Chicago's Midway Airport and in places like Albany, New York, and Providence, Rhode Island. Southwest didn't need to run specials; it just needed to run more flights. Every year, Southwest added cities like Boise, Idaho, and Manchester, New York, to its service and new nonstop routes like Baltimore–Oakland and Kansas City–Seattle. As it sought airports away from the expensive hubs, soon smaller cities eagerly recruited Southwest to serve their communities. And just as often, the major airlines would quickly dump those routes from their schedules. In 1999, 171 U.S. cities asked Southwest Airlines to provide flights at their airports.

Southwest Airlines' market cap gives it the option to acquire any of the old-guard airlines, yet it is highly unlikely that it would ever do so. It is growing organically at an impressive pace and will likely continue to hold the leader's share of market value in the domestic airline industry. Now shifting from its regional short-haul profile to a national, long-haul model, Southwest is redefining the inner circle of the airline industry. It is in effect moving its niche position into the core of the market, transforming the mainstream in the process.

> In the following is the case history of Disney. It illustrates Disney's predominant focus on stuff variations targeted at enhancing value of the *experience assets* that in essence *celebrate life*. As may be discerned through a careful perusal, these variations were accompanied simultaneously by variations in other dimensions like shared values (biased toward rules driven), strategy (planned), structure (biased toward control), style (administrational culture), staff (nurturing people), skills (biased toward focus), systems (mandatory), and sequence (biased toward mass production).

7.4.3 Rejoicing Life at Disney

Walt Disney and his brother Roy founded the Walt Disney Company in 1923. Walt was innovative in terms of using new techniques and technologies, whereas Roy was business oriented. By mortgaging his house and taking additional loans, Walt made the first animation with sound effects. In 1928, Mickey Mouse character premiered in the famous film *Steamboat Willie* at the Colony Theater in New York. The 7½ min cartoon drew better reviews than the full-length movies released that week. *Pluto* released in 1930 and *Donald Duck* released in 1932 marked the start of the Disney formidable *experience property* juggernaut that would generate billions in future. In 1932, Walt Disney heard about a coloring technology developed by Technicolor and was convinced about its future potential to use it immediately. In 1932, *Flower and Trees* the first animation with color won the Oscar for the best cartoon for that year. From 1935 to 1941, Disney Studios won six Academy Awards for animation. Animation films provided the basis of the *Disney experience* created by Disney.

In 1986, *Who Framed Roger Rabbit* at $60 million became the most expensive film produced by Disney. Within 2 years, Disney signed 34 license agreements for 500 products including toys, dolls, brooches, leather bomber jackets, videocassettes, computer games, and joint ventures with McDonald's and Coca-Cola. Cover stories in *Newsweek* and *Time* led to $154 million in U.S. box office tickets and $174 million from overseas sales, contributing to profits more than $100 million from this single film. The timeless appeal of Disney movies like *Cinderella* and *Pinocchio* is unparalleled in the film industry. *The Little Mermaid* (1989), *Beauty and the Beast* (1991), and *Aladdin* (1992) each yielded similar or more profits. *The Lion King* broke all previous records and became the first cartoon to gross $1 billion in sales and related merchandise worldwide. This triggered a virtual cycle: the success of Disney's animated features allowed Disney to attract the best animators in the business, who in turn created breakthrough animation characters and films. As the Disney name became synonymous with success, popular film stars began to supply the voices for the characters. Disney films have included the voices of stars such as Robin Williams, Robbie Benson, and Whoopi Goldberg. In *Toy Story*, the voice for the character Buzz Lightyear was provided by Tom Hanks, a winner of two best actor Oscar awards. *The Little Mermaid*, *Beauty and the Beast*, and *Aladdin* each won the Oscar for best song. Elton John composed songs for *The Lion King*, a blockbuster, whose soundtrack sold in millions of copies.

Disney created Touchstone Pictures and Hollywood Pictures as separate entities to produce trendy films to attract teenagers and adults respectively, without affecting the company's image of a wholesome family entertainer. They also ensured optimal usage of Disney Studios by rapidly churning out movies at a fraction of the actual costs but which generated significant earnings within the first few weeks or months of their releases. However, Disney kept film classics scarce for loss of their franchise because of overexposure—they wanted to build the equity of the *Disney experience*. Disney first released its classics on cassette in 1986 when it sold one million copies of *Sleeping Beauty*. Disney releases new films on video cassette, often within 6 months after they appear in theaters. Classics such as 101 *Dalmatians* and *Snow White and the Seven Dwarfs* were rereleased on the big screen while the Disney Channel carries second-tier classics such as *The Love Bug* and *The Absent-Minded Professor*.

Few companies have been as successful as Disney in systematically creating long-lived character properties with global appeal. Popular Disney character properties in England, France, German, Japan, and Brazil, respectively, are Winnie the Pooh, Bambi and Thumper, Scrooge McDuck, Mickey Mouse, and Ze Carioca. The Disney legal team protects Disney character properties, persecuting those who attempt to infringe their copyrights. A staff of dedicated lawyers protects the overall *Disney experience*. Through 1987, Disney had filed 17 lawsuits with 700 defendants in the United States and 78 overseas defendants including toy manufacturers, T-shirt vendors, and even the day-care center that had painted Disney characters on its walls.

Through the medium of the theme parks, Disney affirmed that Disney operates as an entertainment company that plays out its story in real estate. Disneyland theme park's success was possible because of the unique rides that were linked to Disney's animated films. In mid-1950s, Disney produced a show on ABC Network called *Disneyland*, which featured the Disneyland theme park and Disney character properties every week. This was the first attempt to build an *experience platform* based on the equity of the *Disney experience*. However, the success of the park and the *Disney experience* was undermined by developers buying up miles of surrounding countryside—priced real estate in the Disney experience Platform—and converting it into a disorderly tangle of cheap hotels and low-end commerce that was incompatible with the Disney image.

To counter that, Disney purchased 287,000 acres of land near Orlando, Florida, to build its new theme park Disney World and the Epcot World Showcase. The new park had ample land to build hotels, restaurants, shops, and virtually other future extensions to the *Disney experience* platform. Disney also obtained concessions from the state of Florida, assuring sovereignty over its domain, including rights of policing, taxation, and civic administration. Disney World draws 100,000 people every day, totaling to more than 30 million visitors every year. Disney controls every aspect of the visitor's experience. Attractions—the scenery and location of a particular fantasy, like *Treasure Island*—are carefully engineered environments so that customers can immerse themselves fully into its experience without any distractions. Staying at the Disney hotels and going to character meals is a declared part of the *Disney experience*. Once registered at Disney hotels, guests are effectively captive customers; few can pass up the Disney merchandise in the gift shops. With free monorail and bus service to take them to parks, few venture to competing parks outside the company property.

In 1987, Disney opened the first company-owned retail store outside of Disney parks. Disney movies bring customers into the stores, where they are exposed to products and videos that prompt and propel customers to the parks and back to the theaters. At the stores, customers learn about upcoming animated features, buy tickets for theme parks, and watch the Disney Channel. By the mid-1990s, Disney had more than 250 stores in malls across United States and around the world that averaged three times the norm for specialized retailing.

Disney's strategy is to attract customers to Disney properties through unique and enjoyable experiences and then build other establishments to capitalize on the land values, thus expanding the *Disney experience platform*. Disney acquired the Arvida Corporation to build hotels on property owned by Disney, which they off-loaded later. It also established Disney University to train park employees to deliver a uniform *Disney experience* to its visiting customers. Disney's new hires were inducted as cast members in a show. The success of this experience platform can be judged from the fact that Disney runs a 3-day seminar, *Disney's Approach to People Management*, for which corporate executives pay $2400 to attend.

7.5 STYLE VARIATIONS RANGING FROM ADMINISTRATIONAL TO TRANSFORMATIONAL LEADERSHIP

Within an enterprise, leadership provides meaning, fulfillment, and purpose. When management is analyzed from the viewpoint of leadership, different views on the role and activities of management are obtained; the employee-centered approach to organizing entails management practices based on leadership. Two important types of relationship can be identified between the person in charge and employees:

1. Administrational (or transactional)
2. Transformational

In the case of a transactional relationship, the interaction between the person in charge—the manager—and employees is based on the exchange of valued things, as described by the economic transaction theory. No shared goal is required, while the mutual stimulation is limited, simple, and restricted by the elements of transaction, such as monetary reward in exchange for labor. In many cases, the relation between management and employees is purely transactional: a contract that stipulates mutual obligations limited to the context and duration of the contract.

In the case of transformational relationship, a more complex, deeper, and mutually stimulating relationship exists, which is directed toward the attainment of the common goals. Unlike the top-down perspective, whereby the enterprise is managed as an *object*, leader and followers are cocreating emergent outcomes. The relationship between leader and followers concerns and affects the motivation of followers, based on mutual needs, expectations, and values. This transduction rests on trust and integrity—trust is important considering that much of the enterprise context and reality is unpredictable, ambiguous, and chaotic. Leaders tolerate and can deal with the absence of structure and the presence of uncertainty and unpredictability. Empathy, seen as the capacity to identify oneself with the situation, feelings, and motives of others, is considered essential for the possibility to create trust and the ability to motivate people even under uncertain circumstances (Table 7.1).

TABLE 7.1
Comparison between Leadership and Management of Enterprises

	Leadership	Management
Assumed context	Dynamic, chaotic, uncertain	Stable, orderly
Primary focus	Vision, values, direction	Control, routinizing
Relation with employees	Transformational	Transactional
Basis of relationship	Shared values, trust, goal	Money
Communication	Mutual, two-way, bottom-up	Top-down
Style	Coach, guiding	Authoritative

One might say that management is about subordinates, but leadership is about followers. An important element of leadership therefore concerns moral aspects that shape and give meaning to the relationship with followers, since the relationship is based on more than merely transactional elements. Leadership is about the behavior of followers resulting from the mutually enhancing relationship.

Since leadership entails a fundamentally different relationship with followers than management with subordinates, the concept of leadership appears to be meaningless within the mechanistic perspective, which principally excludes the possibility of leadership. Further, although the employee-centered approach manifests itself differently in different situations, the approach itself is based on the philosophy that considers employees as the crucial core for enterprise success. It should be emphasized that this choice implies a shift from management toward leadership, since employee involvement, participation, and commitment requires more than just a transactional relationship, but a relationship based on shared goals, values, and aspirations.

In the following is a segment of the case history of Samsung. It illustrates Samsung's focus on style variations targeted at being responsive to the changing tastes of the customer and the changing trends in the market. As may be discerned through a careful perusal, these variations were accompanied simultaneously by variations in other dimensions like shared values (rules driven), strategy (planned), structure (control), stuff (products and experiences), staff (challenging), skills (focus), systems (mandatory), and sequence (mass production).

7.5.1 Being Responsive at Samsung

Samsung continued to pursue its low-cost strategy until the mid-1990s, when its chair, Lee Kun Hee, made a major decision. Sensing the emerging threat posed by China and other Asian countries whose cheap labor would rob Samsung of its low-cost advantage, Lee realized that Samsung needed to find a way to enter the big leagues and compete directly against the Japanese giants. The question was: How could Samsung do this, given that companies like Sony, Panasonic, and Hitachi were leaders in electronics research and development? Lee began his new strategy by closing down 32 unprofitable product divisions and laying off 40% of Samsung's work force. Having lowered its cost structure, Samsung could now invest much more of its capital in product research. Lee decided to concentrate Samsung's research budget on new-product opportunities in areas like microprocessors, LCD screens, and other new kinds of digital components that he sensed would be in demand in the coming digital revolution. Today, Samsung is a major supplier of chips and LCD screens to all global electronics makers, and it can produce these components at a much lower cost than electronics makers can because it is farther down the experience curve.

7.5.1.1 Fast Innovations

The focus of Lee's new strategy, however, was on developing research and engineering skills that would allow the company to quickly capitalize on the technology being innovated by Sony, Matsushita, Phillips, and Nokia. His engineers would take this technology and rapidly develop and improve it to create new and improved products that were more advanced than those offered by Japanese competitors. Samsung would produce a wider variety of products than competitors but only in relatively small quantities. Then, as its new products were sold in stores, newer electronic models that were still more advanced would replace them. One advantage of speeding products to market is that inventory does not sit in Samsung's warehouses or stores nor does Samsung need to stock large quantities of components because it needs only enough to make its budgeted output of a particular product. So by making speed the center of its differentiation strategy, Samsung was able to make more efficient use of its capital even as it introduced large numbers of new products to the market.

7.5.1.2 Faster to the Market

At the same time, Samsung's ability to innovate a large number of advanced products attracts customers and has allowed it to build its market share. Today, for example, while Nokia can claim to be a leading cell phone innovator, Samsung was the first to realize that customers wanted a color screen for their phone to allow them to play games and a built-in camera that would allow them to send photographs to their friends. Both these incremental advances have allowed Samsung to dramatically increase its share of the cell phone market. To compete with Samsung, Nokia has had to learn how to innovate new models of cell phones rapidly. Although in the 2000s Nokia has introduced new phones more quickly, Samsung has been able to do so even faster.

By making speed of new-product development the center of its business model, Samsung also was able to move ahead of its other major competitors like Sony. Because of its focus on developing new technology and because of the slow speed of decision making typical in Japanese companies, Sony was hard hit by Samsung's success, and its profitability and stock price declined sharply in the 2000s. Today, Samsung is not just imitating Sony's leading-edge technology but is also developing its own, as shown by the fact that in 2004, Sony and Samsung announced a major agreement to share the costs of basic research into improving LCDs, which run into billions of dollars.

Today, Samsung is in the first tier of electronics makers and is regarded by many as one of the most innovative companies in the world. Almost a quarter of Samsung's 80,000 employees work in one of its four research divisions—semiconductors, telecommunications, digital media, and flat-screen panels. Because many of its products require components developed by all four divisions, it brings researchers, designers, engineers, and marketers from all its divisions together in teams at its research facility outside Seoul to spur the innovation that is the major source of its success. At the same time, it can still make many electronic components at a lower cost than its competitors, which has further contributed to its high profitability.

Given the rapid technological advances in China, however, it appears that Chinese companies may soon be able to make some of their components at a lower cost than Samsung, thus doing to Samsung what Samsung did to companies like Sony. Samsung is relying on the speed of its research and engineering to fight off their challenge, but all global electronics makers are now in a race to speed their products to market.

> In the following is a segment of the case history of ABB. It illustrates ABB's focus on transformational style variations targeted at being responsive to the changing tastes of the customer. As may be discerned through a careful perusal, these variations were accompanied simultaneously by variations in other dimensions like shared values (biased toward values driven), strategy (biased toward emergent), structure (biased toward autonomy), stuff (products and services), staff (biased toward challenging), skills (focus), systems (mandatory), and sequence (biased toward mass customization).

7.5.2 Transforming Time at ABB

In 1990, ABB introduced what has become a continuing program of radical change called *Customer Focus*, which is based on the central premise that the customers' needs are central to the company. By means of the program, ABB aims to learn directly from its customers what products or performance characteristics are needed. It consists of a collection of initiatives built around three major dimensions, namely, total quality management, supply-chain management, and cycle time management. ABB states that its style or approach to business can be typified by the belief that *satisfied customers and motivated employees are the keys to competitive success.*

The Customer Focus program had lot of inherent challenges. Customers, facing their own tough markets, demand continuously higher-quality products and systems—and they want them faster, at lower prices, and with more reliable service on a continual basis. But ABB in tackling these challenges has a big advantage as well. Unlike other global companies, ABB puts a top priority on building deep local roots in the communities in which it operates. ABB hires and trains local managers who know their local markets; ABB also works in small entrepreneurial units to interact and understand the customers' requirements and decides locally on how best to meet those needs. Further, ABB supports them with a global organization and information network, equipped with advanced technological know-how, economies of scale in supplying parts and products, financial muscle to get large projects up and running, and the accumulated operational and management expertise of its large workforce spread across the whole world.

7.5.2.1 Cycle by Half

Initially, the Customer Focus program concentrated on the continual improvement of internal operational performance as a necessary step in meeting customer demands. Progressively, it graduated to *move the customer into the center of the company*, basing operational and strategic decisions on what the customer needs. An example of a Customer Focus initiative is the T50 (T − 50 = Time minus 50%) program that started in 1992 at ABB Sweden and was aimed to halve all lead times in the firm's activities by the end of 1993: the total cycle time for taking the order, through design, engineering, and manufacture to shipment for all products. This was achieved by decentralizing work responsibilities and widening individual worker skills within teams. Accordingly, ABB Sweden changed its structure from specialist departments to *horizontal product departments* of 30–100 people each, which were then further reduced into 10-person *high-performance teams.*

Time-based competition perfectly fitted Percy Barnevik's aims of speeding up ABB and installing a culture of constant change. In 1990, the Boston Consulting Group (BCG) introduced the world to the notion of *time-based competition.* To give customers what they want when they want it, enterprises were altering their measure of performance from competitive costs and quality to competitive costs, quality, and responsiveness. BCG demonstrated how focusing on responsiveness in this way could raise productivity, increase prices, reduce risks, and improve market share. Reduction of total cycle time was the new goal. The definition of *cycle time* encompassed the time from the decision to develop a new product to launching the product, from initial customer enquiry to confirm quotation, from customer order delivery to payment, as well as response times for information and service.

The restructuring and rationalization at ABB made it well suited to the new approach. T50 depended on three important themes:

1. Decentralization: This decentralization of authority was from the corporate to the company level and decentralization within the company to multifunctional target-oriented high-performance teams of 10–15 workers responsible for the entire customer order process from order reception to shipment and invoicing.
2. Competence development: The new approach demanded a big effort in competence development to heighten the skill of team members, including on-the-job training and education in such areas as scheduling, order processing, and quality control.
3. T50 relied on a communication system to spread success stories and disseminate and apply the lessons learned in one ABB company on team to another.

By the late 1990s, ABB had drastically reduced cycle times by means of the time-based strategies. In 1988, it took 3 years to build a medium-sized combined cycle plant. ABB reduced that to 2 years, and by the late 1990s, ABB was quoting 10 months for completion. ABB's top management believed that there was no end to the reductions that could be achieved; ABB was confident that after reducing by 50%, they could aim for another cycle of 50% reduction in the cycle time.

> In the following is the case history of Acer. It illustrates Acer's focus on transformational style variations targeted at instilling a sense of ownership at the business line management level. As may be discerned through a careful perusal, these variations were accompanied simultaneously by variations in other dimensions like shared values (biased toward values driven), strategy (biased toward emergent), structure (biased toward autonomy), stuff (cutting edge products), staff (biased toward challenging), skills (biased toward breadth of skills), systems (mandatory), and sequence (biased toward mass customization).

7.5.3 EMPOWERING OWNERSHIP AT ACER

In 1976, together with his wife and five other partners, Stan Shih founded Multitech International Corporation, which would later become Acer. Unlike traditional Taiwanese conglomerates that are widely diversified with businesses ranging from oil refineries to banking to high tech, Acer's founders agreed to focus only on the high-tech industry. This enabled them to design processes and shape the culture that was in sync with the fast pace of this industry and, thus, enabled them to emerge as the number one Taiwanese player in this field.

Very few Taiwanese companies are able to grow to become large enterprises because employees, after gaining some experience, tend to leave to start their own small businesses—*rather than a small fish in a big pond, they would rather be a big fish in a small pond*. To counter this, unlike the practices at traditional Taiwanese companies, Acer encouraged significant decisions to be made by people who were closest to the relevant information. Shih averred, "At Acer, everybody can be a little boss." Similarly, in traditional companies, to enhance their control and power, seniors tightly controlled knowledge and information. Acer instituted the policy of providing detailed corporate financial information and openly discussing management issues without inhibition with all employees. Secret of successes or failures were transparently shared to the benefit and learning by all employees.

In its initial years, Acer engaged primarily in technical consulting that enabled it to gradually gather knowledge and expertise in high tech. Later, the company produced microprocessor-based products like games, calculators, and watches. Acer's first IBM compatible computer was introduced in the market in early 1984. Even before IBM and just behind Compaq, Acer introduced its first 32-bit PC using the Intel 386 microprocessors in 1986. In 1988, Acer went public, successfully gaining an exorbitant market evaluation.

With an eye on becoming a global player, in 1989, Dr. Leonard Liu was hired from IBM to be Acer's President. Dr. Liu attempted to change Acer's nimble and decentralized operational architecture into an IBM-style architecture of central control. He tried to control everything; everybody had to follow his directions. His attempts met with considerable resistance from Acer's management team. The approaches that had served IBM well in the comparatively slow-moving environment of mainframe computers, when applied at Acer, had disastrous consequences in the fast-moving PC industry. Liu's quest for central control also led Acer into making a succession of costly business decisions. By 1992, after Dr. Liu had departed, Acer was experiencing major difficulties in its business. While the entire computer industry was facing a crisis, Shih felt that all decisions were tending to get made by people at the headquarters in Taiwan, who did not have the best knowledge and perspective. More importantly, Acer PCs were losing part of their value during the weeks that it took to sea-ship them to their destination. With the product lifecycle being down to 6 months, key components (such as memory chips and microprocessors) could easily lose 10% or more of their value between the time of purchase or production by Acer and the time the PCs arrived on retailer's shelves.

7.5.3.1 Networking to the Future

Shih affected an enormous turnaround by transforming the vertically integrated organization into a networked one. Shih started three initiatives that would provide a new philosophy, a new structure, and a new business model that was more flexible and better suited to the changed and dynamically fast-changing market realities:

1. *Global brand, local touch philosophy*: This philosophy is realized by Acer giving up financial control of its RBUs and letting local shareholders buy the majority of shares in each local unit. Thus, the ownership in the literal sense of the word is transferred to where the best information resides. This also automatically makes Acer into the brand of choice for all channels everywhere. By the mid-1990s, this strategy had paid great dividends, especially in the emerging markets. Acer had become the strongest player in Asia (excluding Japan and Korea) and Africa and number two or three the Latin America and Russia.
2. *Client–server structure*: Shih devised this architecture in analogy with the corresponding client–server computing architecture. SBUs, mostly located in Taiwan, are the *servers* for the regional business units (RBUs), the *clients*. Technology knowledge is concentrated at the servers (SBUs), which provide central R&D and manufacturing components, whereas the clients (RBUs) assemble Acer-brand products locally. Headquarters doesn't manage the individual SBUs and RBUs but rather sets the rules for the interactions between the units. RBUs also take care of distribution, service, and marketing in the local markets where they are closest to the relevant information and situations. This architecture also instills a strong sense of ownership into the business units mandating each unit to be competitive on its own—there is no *strategic* support for SBUs by forcing RBUs to buy from the SBUs nor will headquarters cover any losses of an individual unit. Lack of financial guarantees from headquarters forces the SBUs to leverage their resources with external customers, thereby expanding their business network beyond Acer.
3. *Fast-food business model*: The counter to the problem of PCs loosing value while they are shipped to their target market was to assemble them locally rather than in Taiwan. The difficulty was really in maintaining consistent quality of PCs wherever they were assembled. This was analogous to the problem of eating Chinese food outside of Taiwan—which prompted as a possible solution the use of the approach of global fast-food chains like McDonald's. McDonald's restaurants enjoy a strong brand name and produce hamburgers with consistent quality around the world. Central kitchens produce standardized components, and consistent procedures are used to make hamburgers locally.

Shih transferred this business model from the fast-food industry to the PC industry. Acer categorized PC components into three categories:

1. Low changeability components, like floppy disk drives or power supplies, are purchased centrally in Taiwan and sea-shipped to RBUs with a lead time of about 4 or 6 weeks.
2. Moderate changeability components like motherboards that lose value quickly are centrally produced at Acer's SBUs and air-shipped from Taiwan.
3. High changeability components or *hottest* components are purchased locally.

This allows Acer to react quickly to changes in local customer tastes and at the same time to capitalize on Acer's economies of scale for less dynamic components. As a result of these changes, the overhead costs of Acer's manufacturing operations were reduced to about one-sixth of the original level, and the inventory turnover doubled. Acer saw a significant increase in its revenues, profits, and market value.

The proof and efficacy of the changed dynamics became evident in September 1995, when Acer America introduced the Aspire, a PC with a new design that looked more like a consumer electronics device than a PC. It proved that the *new* Acer with its empowered business units was agile in bringing new products swiftly to the market. This bold move also helped improve Acer's image as an innovative company.

7.6 STAFF VARIATIONS RANGING FROM CHALLENGING PEOPLE TO NURTURING PEOPLE

Excellence in all areas requires employee involvement and participation, such that employee input is used to improve enterprise performance relative to productivity, quality, and service, as well as creating an overall order in an uncertain and unpredictable context, while enabling enterprise learning and innovation.

Principles for HR engagement geared to employee involvement, participation, and self-management are significantly different than those for the mechanist or instrumental approach. This *unitarist* view does not envisage any opposition, incompatibility, or divergence between enterprise and employee interests. The unitarist view states in essence that desired forms of human behavior based on enterprise performance, or based on human development, are not necessarily contradictory to each other. This focus would make employees able to satisfy higher-order motivational needs. Enterprise performance and people satisfaction are thus not considered as necessarily mutually exclusive but can be mutually enforcing.

The unitarist view on HR management unites enterprise issues pertinent to people management from an operational perspective, with ethical aspects regarding the responsibility toward employees. Within this approach, people-oriented aspects are thus both ends and means; this stance advocates a change from adapting the individual to the needs of the organization to adapting the organization to the needs, aspirations, and potential of the individual. Considering conditions of uncertainty, ambiguity, and unpredictability associated with the enterprise reality, these conditions not only require employee involvement and participation to give overall order, but at the same time offer opportunities to make employee involvement and participation meaningful.

In the following is the case history of Microsoft. It illustrates Microsoft's predominant focus on staff variations targeted at challenging the employees to surpass themselves to achieve enterprise goals. As may be discerned through a careful perusal, these variations were accompanied simultaneously by variations in other dimensions like shared values (biased toward rules driven), strategy (planned), structure (biased toward autonomy), stuff (leading products), style (transformational culture), skills (biased toward breadth of skills), systems (discretionary), and sequence (mass production).

7.6.1 MICROSOFT

Microsoft is the original paranoid company; it endures in its unassailable position by being paranoid about its vulnerability at every moment and step of the way. It engineered almost a monopoly on operating systems for personal computers; it garnered a dominant market share in word processors, spreadsheets, and many other markets. Microsoft sustains as a giant with a market value of several hundred billion dollars by making constant innovation an inseparable part of its life; the spirit of innovation does not come naturally to the firm but has to be sustained through a concerted effort of all the members of the enterprise.

Microsoft sustains this atmosphere of innovation through a staffing strategy consisting of three crucial components: hiring *very smart people*, maintaining a loose operating structure, and organizing workers in small, intense, task-oriented groups. One crucial component of the strategy is Microsoft's investment in intellectual talent. Since a software company is foremost a provider of solutions for people's information problems, hiring the brightest people has several benefits: smarter workers ensure faster, better, or more efficient solutions. An influx of fresh graduates, preferred by Microsoft, are likely to keep alive an atmosphere of innovation and dynamism in the company, least likely to be set in their ways and most likely to be open to exploring new ideas. Moreover, graduates who come from the best research universities learn from the leading researchers in their respective fields. Thus, in addition to an ethic of hard work, research, and innovation, they are likely to bring the latest research ideas.

The second component of Microsoft's strategy is an informal and responsive work structure; a tight structure may be detrimental for a lively, creative, and thriving enterprise; while openness and spontaneity foster creativity. Employees do not have a regimen of work hours, attire, schedules, or work habits, and they are encouraged to descent and think contrarian. The third component of Microsoft's strategy is an intense goal-oriented work ethic. The Microsoft environment demands solving tough problems, in short time frames, with limited staff, in an intense work environment. Employees often work long hours during the day, into the night, and over weekends.

As a result of these strategies, policies, and measures, Microsoft employees have brought forward a string of software applications across a wide spectrum of uses. Microsoft persists ceaselessly with innovation, even when a particular version of a product is successful or unsuccessful; it continues to introduce new versions of the program, until it becomes appealing to the users at the next level of usability, achieves competitive parity with competitive products in the market and achieves market success, and then repeats the whole process again to make them even more useful to consumers. The success of this strategy of ceaseless innovation can be judged from the fact that once Microsoft has won market leadership of a category, it has never lost that leadership, despite constant change in the market. Microsoft has not been a pioneer in any market that it currently leads: operating systems, browsers, graphical user interfaces, word processors, or spreadsheets. The first generations of Windows, Excel, and Word invariably were flops; under similar circumstances, any other company would have collapsed repetitively because of the expended colossal efforts and failed investments. But Microsoft survives, strives, and thrives because of financial cash flow support from other successful products and policy of persistent innovation. Thus, Microsoft's successful leadership of several software markets is due not to first-mover advantage in those markets but to following a policy of relentless innovation that comes from recruiting, motivating, and retaining outstanding talent.

> In the following is a segment of the case history of GE. It illustrates GE's focus on staff variations targeted at challenging the employees to achieve organizational goals. As may be discerned through a careful perusal, these variations were accompanied simultaneously by variations in other dimensions like shared values (biased toward rules driven), strategy (planned), structure (biased toward autonomy), stuff (products), style (administrational culture), skills (biased toward breadth of skills), systems (mandatory), and sequence (biased toward mass production).

7.6.2 Performance by Challenges at GE

Welch believed that a performance-driven organization would not only encourage GE's managers to perform up to the limits of their capabilities, it would also nurture those capabilities. Welch firmly believed that GE's ability to outperform its peers ultimately depended upon having out-standing employees. GE offered opportunities for career development and the acquisition of skills and expertise that no other company could match. He believed that GE's true *core competency* today was not manufacturing or services, but the global recruitment of the world's best people and the cultivation in them of an insatiable desire to learn, to stretch, and to do things better every day. By finding, challenging, and rewarding these people, by freeing them from bureaucracy, by giving them all the resources they need, and by simply getting out of their way, GE had seen them make themselves better and better every year. GE as a company was more agile than others a fraction of their size.

Maintaining a vigorous, performance-driven culture required putting managers under contin-ual pressure, including continual weeding-out of weaker performers. GE's system of evaluation was renowned for its thoroughness and its ruthlessness: In every evaluation and reward system, GE breaks its population into three categories—the top 20%, the high-performance middle 70%, and the bottom 10%. The top 20% are loved, nurtured, and rewarded in the soul and wallet because they are the ones who make magic happen. However, the top 20% and middle 70% are not permanent labels; people move between them across these categories all the time. However, the bottom 10% tend to remain there. A company that bets its future on its people must remove that lower 10%, and keep removing it every year—always raising the bar of performance and increasing the quality of its leadership. He believed that not removing that bottom 10% early in their careers is not only a management failure but also a moral failing because inevitably a new leader will come into a business and take out that bottom 10% right away, leaving them—sometimes midway through a career—stranded and having to start over somewhere else. GE leaders must not only understand the necessity to encourage, inspire, and reward that top 20% and be sure that the high-performance 70% is always energized to improve and move upward; they must develop the determination to change out, always humanely, that bottom 10%, and do it every year.

7.6.2.1 Grooming Performance

The key to GE's long-term development and performance was the development of its management talent. GE had a well-developed system of management appraisal and development, which Welch retained. He believed that giving managers greater profit-and-loss responsibility earlier in their careers would be conducive to an even greater flourishing of managerial talent. But to encourage risk taking and higher levels of performance aspiration required more powerful incentives. Welch believed in giving more recognition to individual contributors and higher rewards to those who pro-duced superior results: A flat reward system is a big anchor to incrementalism. GE wanted to give big rewards to those who do things but without going for the scalps of those who reach for the big win but fail. Punishing failure assures that no one dares.

Welch redesigned the bonus system to reach deep into middle management. The bonuses became much more discriminating. The typical 10%–15% bonuses for senior managers were replaced by 30%–40% bonuses for far fewer managers. In addition, stock options were extended from the top echelon of management to a much wider range of managerial and technical employ-ees. By 1996, Welch was able to report that the number of employees receiving stock options had increased from 400 in the early 1980s to 22,000 by the end of 1995; consequently, stock option compensation based on total GE performance is far more significant than the salary or bonus growth associated with the performance of any individual unit or business. This aligned the interests of the individual, the company, and the share owner behind always-improving company results.

One of the distinctive characteristics of Welch's system of management was his use of periodic new corporate initiatives as mechanisms to drive particular aspects of company-wide performance. Thus, while strategic planning, financial control, and HR management provided the basic systems for managing GE, about every 2 years, Welch would announce a major new initiative designed to energize the company and drive its performance in a particular direction. Over time, these initiatives would become absorbed into the ongoing management systems of GE.

7.6.2.2 Work-Out

The idea for GE's *Work-Out* process began with the no-holds-barred discussion sessions that Welch held with different groups of managers at GE's Management Development Institute at Crotonville, New York. Impressed with the energy and impetus for change that these sessions generated, Welch initiated a company-wide process called *Work-Out*. The idea was to create a forum where employees could speak their minds about the management of their business without the fear of retribution by their superiors. Typically, the sessions assembled a cross section of 50–100 of the business's employees for meetings that ran for 2 or 3 days. In an environment that Welch likened to an old New England town meeting, the group would be asked to openly and honestly review the management process and practices in their part of the operation. Initially, they focused on unproductive or bureaucratic behaviors that had limited their personal effectiveness. At the end of each work-out, the group's manager returned to hear the findings and recommendations and could either accept or reject them on the spot, or appoint a team to report back with more data by a given date. Welch believed that work-outs could achieve fundamental changes in management: the practical objective was to get rid of thousands of bad habits accumulated in GE's operating system; the intellectual objective was to expose the leaders to the vibrations of their business—opinions, feelings, emotions, and resentments, not abstract theories of organization and management. Ultimately, work-out was about redefining the relationship between boss and subordinate.

Over time, work-out sessions evolved to the evaluation and redesign of complex cross-functional processes—often involving suppliers and customers as well as GE employees.

7.6.2.3 Six Sigma

From 1998 to 2000, Welch's Six Sigma program was its dominant corporate initiative and primary driver of organizational change and performance improvement. Welch described it as his next *soul-transforming cultural initiative*. The methodology of defining, measuring, analyzing, improving, and then controlling every process that touches a company's customers until it reduces defects to 3.4 per million was borrowed from Motorola. However, at GE it was with unprecedented fervor across an unprecedentedly broad front. In 4 years, some 100,000 people were trained in its science and methodology, and by 2001, six sigma became the way we work: all employees began to speak the common language of critical to quality (CTQ), defects per million opportunities (DPMOs), failure mode effect analysis (FMEA), and Needs Assessment Maps. Across every one of GE's businesses, major gains in performance ranking from reduced waste and lower operating costs to faster customer service and improved financial management were achieved.

> In the following is the case history of Volvo. It illustrates Volvo's focus on staff variations targeted at nurturing and enriching the employees to become more productive and quality conscious. As may be discerned through a careful perusal, these variations were accompanied simultaneously by variations in other dimensions like shared values (biased toward rules driven), strategy (planned), structure (biased toward autonomy), stuff (products), style (administrational culture), skills (biased toward breadth of skills), systems (mandatory), and sequence (biased toward mass production).

7.6.3 ENRICHING WORK LIFE AT VOLVO

In the last 30 years, Volvo, the Swedish motor vehicle manufacturer, has seen repeated attempts at diversification and alliances aimed at spreading the risks and costs of operating in a highly cyclical and very capital-intensive industry. In 1993, Pehr Gyllenhammar, Volvo's long-serving chief executive, attempted to merge Volvo with Renault, the French state-controlled car company, without success. Finally, in 1999, Volvo sold its car division to the Ford Motor Corporation and became the most profitable part of Ford's Premier Automotive Group, which included Jaguar, Land Rover, and Aston Martin.

But more than an auto manufacturer, Volvo has been seen as a leader in innovations in work organization since the 1970s when it began moving away from traditional methods of car assembly. In the 1960s, Volvo was as committed as any car company to the classical approach to work organization espoused by Taylor and embodied in the assembly-line approach to car production devised by Henry Ford. Yet, in the 1970s, it chose to break away from this industry-standard approach and embark on (what has turned out to be) a long-term program of increasingly radical work reorganization.

Volvo was faced with increasing problem of absenteeism and high labor turnover. Full employment and a lack of wage flexibility precluded more traditional *stick and carrot* measures for dealing with absenteeism and labor turnover. They had to look for alternative methods of reducing absenteeism and labor turnover and, instead of trying to alleviate the symptoms, they chose to tackle the boredom and dissatisfaction that gave rise to labor problems in the first place. The decision by Volvo's management to adopt a job design approach (antithesis of Taylorism and involves designing work to fit human needs and abilities) appears to have come about owing to a combination of intense public pressure on the company to move to a more human-centered approach to assembly work and managerial preference. With the easing of this pressure in the 1980s and 1990s, however, the company could have chosen quietly to abandon this approach. The fact that they persisted with it clearly demonstrated their belief that job redesign works; so much that this commitment has even survived the Ford takeover.

The decision to adopt job design at Volvo was and remained driven by management; the move to more flexible forms of work organization at Volvo went hand in hand with its move away from corporate bureaucracy and to more decentralized, localized management of its various vehicle operations. The parallel move by Volvo to adopt a strategy of decentralizing control to plant level (which was averse to its previous centralized, bureaucratic control procedures) gave local management some freedom to experiment with new ways of working and also allowed management to experience the lessening of control that they were advocating for workers.

7.6.3.1 Kalmar

This plant opened in 1974 and was the company's first attempt to move away from assembly line work. The conventional plants across the industry, through the use of the moving assembly line with its severe division of labor and short cycle times, had taken its Taylorist work practices to their ultimate extremes. With its commitment to challenge the *inhuman* approach to work, and without any sacrifice of efficiency or the company's financial objectives, Kalmar was aiming to give employees opportunities to work in groups, to communicate freely among themselves, to switch from one job assignment to another, to vary the pace of their work, to identify with the product, to be conscious of a responsibility for quality, and to influence their own working environment. A project team composed of managers, engineers, and architects was given responsibility for designing and building the plant. Each decision of this team had to be approved by a committee that included trade union representatives, health and safety experts, doctors, and outside job design experts, including colleagues of Einar Thorsrud, the noted Norwegian work psychologist.

In a traditional car plant, the pace of work is determined by the moving assembly line, jobs are extremely fragmented and have cycle times of a few minutes or less, and workers are dedicated to one task only. At Kalmar, there was no assembly line, workers operated in teams, with each team having its own dedicated area of the factory. Within the team, workers could move between tasks, and each task had a cycle time of between 20 and 30 min. In place of the assembly line, cars were mounted on automated carriers that moved around the plant and served both as a means of transport and as a work platform—resulting in either a straight line assembly or a dock assembly. Both forms revolved around teamwork and offered variety and task completeness. But over time, changes such as new work evaluation methods, the removal of time buffers between stages, and the general speeding up of the carriers (which are controlled by a central computer) intensified the pace of work and returned the production process much closer to the assembly-line concept than was originally intended. The true measure of Kalmar's success lies not in the degree to which it achieved its *revolutionary* goal, but in the extent to which it encouraged Volvo's management to continue with and accelerate the move away from Fordist–Taylorist approaches to work. Eventually, because of the major recession in the European car industry the plant was closed in 1992.

7.6.3.2 Torslanda

This is Volvo's main car plant, which, since the late 1970s, has seen a number of increasingly radical attempts to move away from the traditional assembly-line approach to car production. In 1976, at the central assembly plant, Torslanda management experimented with the use of large, autonomous work groups to assemble an entire car using a dock-assembly approach similar to that being attempted at Kalmar. Owing to poor productivity, this was abandoned within 6 months. Management believed that the workforce lacked the necessary skills to make such an approach work, while the metal workers' trade union felt the experiment was too risky.

In 1979–1980, with the opening of the TUN facility at Torslanda to assemble the new 700 series car, management attempted to revive group-based assembly. The TUN workforce was selected from the existing production personnel at Torslanda. The original plan for TUN, initially drawn up without union involvement, envisaged car assembly being carried out by autonomous work groups who would be responsible for their own quality and pace of work. It was planned that work groups would also have responsibility for job rotation, managing material supplies and some maintenance tasks. However, because of objections from the union, workers no longer perform indirect tasks; also, the pace of work is controlled centrally.

In 1986, once again management began to consider major changes to the organization of work at Torslanda's central assembly plant; management and unions agreed on an *action plan* that emphasized the transformation of car assembly into an *attractive alternative* to the traditional methods of car manufacture. In particular, learning from the earlier failure, the plan also stressed the need for high-quality training and continuing education to allow workers to gain the skills necessary for effective group work; upward and downward communication was considered vital, and the staffs was encouraged to show initiative through formal and informal discussion groups. Again, there were union objections to blurring the demarcation between direct and indirect tasks as also between the groups and the supervisors. Nevertheless, this effort was a great success.

By the late 1990s, the workforce at Torslanda had increased to 5500 and the plant was producing 580 vehicles a day. Multiskilling was a fact of life and, in some parts of the factory, jobs were rotated every hour. Such was the perceived success of the factory that it was given responsibility for assembling Volvo's C70 car launched in 1997.

7.6.3.3 Uddevalla

This new assembly plant opened in 1990 and was the first plant built by Volvo where workers in work groups build cars from start to finish rather than on an assembly line. In accordance with

Sweden's Codetermination Law (and Volvo's practice at Torslanda), the unions were involved in the steering group responsible for designing and building the Uddevalla plant. The completed plant comprised six mini-factories, each containing eight dock-assembly areas, each with its own autonomous work group. Each work group has 10 fully trained assembly workers, each of whom can, again in theory, perform all the tasks necessary to assemble an entire car. The work groups are responsible for determining their own pace of work and internal job rotation.

In addition, the groups have responsibility for maintenance, administration, and quality control. The role of group leader rotates among the members of each group. The incorporation of so many functions within each group resulted in a very flat hierarchy; there are no layers between the groups and the factory managers. However, like at Kalmar, fluctuations in output levels led the plant management to retreat from its original ambitions and to tighten managerial control over the work process. Even though it was most efficient of the Volvo plants, because of recession and the downturn in demand, Uddevalla plant, along with the Kalmar plant, was closed in 1992. It was eventually reopened in 1995 at a much smaller scale but with its original job design.

7.6.3.4   Gent and Born

The introduction of new cars in these existing plants in the late 1980s allowed Volvo the opportunity to introduce the methods developed in its other plants, thus showing Volvo's commitment to extending its job design philosophy across all areas of its operations. When Volvo's Gent plant was chosen to build the 850 series (known internally as the VEC—Volvo European Car), it was natural for Volvo to adopt team-based assembly. The VEC teams operated very much as at the Uddevalla plant but with even greater emphasis on continuous improvement. There was also a great deal of emphasis on the teams to carry out their own maintenance as well as other support tasks. Indeed, so successful was this that Gent became the first plant outside Japan to gain the total productive maintenance award.

Volvo's Dutch plant at Born was chosen as the site of a joint venture between Volvo and Mitsubishi called Nedcar. The objective was to make cars for both companies that share the same chassis and have one-third of the parts in common. In essence, it was an attempt to blend Japanese lean production techniques with Volvo's job design approach. The aim was to achieve world class efficiency, and the plant quickly became one of Europe's most efficient car plants.

Volvo continues to look for new and different ways to organize production, in the case of Gent and Born by adopting a lean production philosophy, but ensuring that group work lies at the heart of any new developments. Volvo's adoption of job design principles began over 30 years ago. It has now reached a stage where group work has become the standard approach to work design, and assembly-line working is not considered appropriate for any new Volvo plant. Volvo's job design approach is fundamental to the way the company operates. Though most other car companies have adopted, to a lesser or greater extent, the autonomous/semiautonomous work group concept, especially the Japanese, no one else has abandoned the assembly line or given workers the degree of autonomy and control that Volvo does, especially over the pace of work.

7.7   SKILLS VARIATIONS RANGING FROM FOCUS TO BREADTH OF SKILLS

A learning enterprise is geared intentionally to the acquisition and distribution of knowledge in order to detect and remove errors and to improve enterprise processes and actions. Evidently, the process of continuous improvement identified with regard to productivity, quality, and service requires the ability to learn. Thus, a learning enterprise is an organization skilled at creating, acquiring, and transferring knowledge and at modifying its behavior to reflect new knowledge and insights. Learning is both a manifestation and a prerequisite for change; enterprises that cannot learn cannot change.

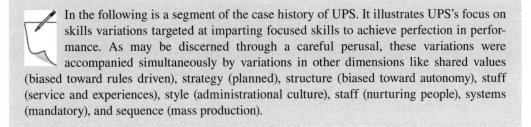

In the following is a segment of the case history of UPS. It illustrates UPS's focus on skills variations targeted at imparting focused skills to achieve perfection in performance. As may be discerned through a careful perusal, these variations were accompanied simultaneously by variations in other dimensions like shared values (biased toward rules driven), strategy (planned), structure (biased toward autonomy), stuff (service and experiences), style (administrational culture), staff (nurturing people), systems (mandatory), and sequence (mass production).

7.7.1 DRIVING FOR PERFECTION AT UPS

An urban UPS driver must make approximately 200 delivery stops in a scheduled day—and make them in a brisk, fast-paced fashion, because beginning the same time daily, 30 or so pickup stops are waiting. The pressure is on to finish, deliver, and unload everything so the package car (never called a truck by UPS) is empty to receive new pickups. From the company's very beginning, UPS has continually improved and refined its methods. Optimizing the connection between body and task is the responsibility of UPS's cadre of efficiency experts, most of whom were also drivers. They are just as tireless and never stop honing delivery into a fine art. Ergonomics professionals analyze and optimize every juncture between work and human being. Anatomy, physiology, and psychology come together to make the task fit the human and the human fit the task, harming neither the human nor the delivery. Add to those beneficial working postures, maximizing power while minimizing excessive force, nutrition, and diminishing vibration and other adverse exposures. Every motion at UPS is timed, measured, and refined to its ergonomic best, always balancing physical work rate with workload. Engineers, industrial designers, computer specialists, physicians, health and safety practitioners, and trainers strive to decrease stress, errors, and other debilitations. All movements at UPS are subject to efficiency modifications and institutionalized.

Driver training is designed to establish a cognitive match between the trainee and the tasks. Drivers are instructed to park as close to the point of delivery as possible. To minimize accidents, especially backing accidents, the simple rule *Don't Back* is part of their training. Leaving the vehicle, they are expected to grab the keys with their right hand, use the hand rail with their left hand, and then walk at a brisk pace. Upon return, they are instructed to hold their keys on their right pinky finger, grab the hand rail with the right hand, enter their package car, buckle their seat with the left hand, and insert the ignition key with their right, at each stop. It's that precise. The seconds saved become minutes over the day. Since every minute counts when a driver is trying to finish on time, and a few minutes each day mean big dollars, these methods have lasted.

Not just economy of motion and efficiency are quantified; the drivers are measured on safety too. They are gauged by numerous indices—from individual (years of safe driving without a preventable vehicle accident) to group (1,000 collective days of accident free driving) to district and company-wide (accidents per 100,000 driver hours, and so on). To help reduce accidents, safety committees exist at all levels. Today, individual safe drivers are still honored annually, and in 2006, there were more than 4000 active drivers who had driven for 25 years or more without an avoidable accident. And 87 of them had over 35 years, topped by a Kentucky district feeder driver, Ron Sowder, who had 43 years without an accident. Today's UPS drivers log more than two billion miles per year and average less than one accident for every million miles driven.

UPS drivers don't just happen. Usually, UPS novices sweat and heave their way into driver positions via other strenuous entry-level package-handling jobs, such as unloading, preloading, and sorting, most often starting out part time. Package handling in the hubs is hard and punishing job—moving hundreds of packages daily, weighing up to 150 lb each. It is not for everyone. Recruiters even show videos of package handling to prospects to prepare them. Some handlers quit early on, some even on the first day after experiencing how difficult it really is. Yet, with practice and supervision, they learn how to maneuver more and more weight, which helps prepare them to become drivers.

Finally, prospective drivers get to the head of the waiting list. There, they undergo an additional grueling training program that is so effective that government agencies and other companies use it as a model. The indoctrination includes 20 h of computer-based classroom training and on-road supervisor training, which incorporates *Space and Visibility* training from day 1. Following that, they have 30 working days to prove themselves, as a supervisor carefully scrutinizes their performance in three safety-evaluation rides. If they can't meet the demands, they must return to the other job and wait as long as 6 months before reapplying. When they don the UPS driver's uniform, it stands for reliability, strength, respect, and safety.

> In the following is a segment of the case history of McDonald. It illustrates McDonald's focus on skills variations targeted at achieving performance perfection through standardized and optimized procedures. As may be discerned through a careful perusal, these variations were accompanied simultaneously by variations in other dimensions like shared values (biased toward rules driven), strategy (planned), structure (biased toward control), stuff (product and service), style (administrational culture), staff (nurturing people), systems (mandatory), and sequence (mass production).

7.7.2 Satisfaction from Standardization at McDonald's

McDonald's designed its operating system to ensure consistency and uniformity across all outlets. Operating procedures guaranteed customers the same quality of food and service visit after visit, store after store. Every hamburger, for example, was dressed in exactly the same way: mustard first, then ketchup, onions, and two pickles. McDonald's operating system concentrated on four areas: improving the product, developing outstanding supplier relationships, training and monitoring franchisees, and improving equipment. In its quest for improvement, McDonald's revolutionized the entire supply chain, introducing innovations in the way farmers grew potatoes and ranchers raised beef, altering processing methods for both potatoes and meat, and inventing efficient cooking equipment tailored to the restaurant's needs.

Most revolutionary, perhaps, was McDonald's attention to detail. McDonald's developed the first operations manual in 1957, which, by 1991, reached 750 detailed pages. It described how operators should make milk shakes, grill hamburgers, and fry potatoes; it delineated exact cooking times, proper temperature settings, and precise portions for all food items—even prescribing the ¼ oz of onions to be placed on every hamburger and the 32 slices to be obtained from every pound of cheese. French fries were to be 9/32 of an inch, and to ensure quality and taste, no products were to be held more than 10 min in the transfer bin. McDonald's designed a potable stainless steel lazy Susan that could hold 24 hamburger buns. They developed a handheld stainless pump dispenser to automate the hamburger dressing process that required one squeeze on to a trigger to squirt the required amount of ketchup and mustard evenly on a bun. A variation of the device is still standard equipment in 20,000 McDonald's outlets worldwide.

McDonald's meticulous attention to detail and careful analysis of quality and procedures did not come from an unbending need for regimentation. Instead, McDonald's sought to study every component of its operation to learn what worked and what failed, to determine how best to offer consistently good service and food. They were continuously looking for a better way to do things and then worked on bettering the better way to do things. Nothing exemplified the success of McDonald's operating system like the development of its food. From french fries to Chicken McNuggets, McDonald's had distinguished its menu offerings by drawing both on the rigorous operating system, with its focus on uniformity and on the orchestra formed by corporate management, suppliers, and franchisees.

McDonald's had made french fries standard fare for an American meal, but more important for McDonald's, french fries became the restaurant chain's most distinctive item. McDonald's applied tender loving care in preparing its french fries. At first, the company simply monitored the way french fries were cooked in its restaurants, trying to determine the exact temperature and settings that yielded the best french fries. Each batch of fries fell to a different temperature, but, McDonald's researchers discovered, the fries were always perfectly cooked when the oil temperature rose 3° above the low temperature point. This discovery enabled the company to design a fryer that produced perfect french fried potatoes every order. The initial research team eventually learned that potatoes also need to be cured for 3 weeks to produce perfect french fries: in that period of time, the sugars within potatoes convert into starches. To prevent excessive browning and permit uniform crispness through the fry, McDonald's only accepted potatoes with a high starch content.

As the number of McDonald's outlets grew to over 400 in the early 1960s, it gave McDonald's and its suppliers sufficient purchasing power to influence growers of Idaho Russet potatoes to adhere to planting practices that yielded potatoes with high starch content. McDonald's also began looking for potato processors willing to invest in storage facilities with sophisticated temperature controls. Considering the problems of supplying fresh potatoes to their growing chain and also maintaining quality of fresh potatoes in the cold storage, McDonald's explored frozen fries to better control the quality and consistency of McDonald's potato supply. The traditional freezing process robbed structure and flavor from the french fries. McDonald's developed a process to dry french fries with air, run them through a quick frying cycle, then freeze them; this reduced the moisture in the frozen fry while preserving its crispness. McDonald's even improved the way restaurant crews filled orders for French fries. Operators had complained that employee productivity suffered because the metal tongs traditionally used to fill french-fry bags proved clumsy. In response, a McDonald's engineer, Ralph Weimer, designed a V-shaped aluminum scoop with a funnel at the end that enabled operators to fill a french-fry bag in one motion and, in addition, align the fries in the same vertical direction within the bag.

In the following is the case history of NUMMI. It illustrates NUMMI's focus on skills variations targeted at achieving performance excellence through breadth of skills resulting in ideal workmanship. As may be discerned through a careful perusal, these variations were accompanied simultaneously by variations in other dimensions like shared values (biased toward values driven), strategy (planned), structure (biased toward autonomy), stuff (product), style (biased toward transformational culture), staff (nurturing people), systems (discretionary), and sequence (biased toward mass customization).

7.7.3 FRUITS OF EMPOWERMENT AT NUMMI

NUMMI had a team-based organization with a flat, three-level management hierarchy. This contrasts with the five to three levels common in many GM plants. All employees were part of multifunctional teams composed of three to six people. Team leaders, who are selected jointly by management and the union, coordinate teamwork and training, replace team members on the line when necessary, and build a closely knit high-performance team. Each team member is responsible for the design of their own work and to rotate jobs within the team. Each team member is thus obligated to understand team concepts, accept responsibility for quality and continual improvement, perform all job functions (including housekeeping and maintenance), and work within the NUMMI philosophy.

Group leaders, the first-level managers, role includes planning for the group, training team leaders, and supporting the continuous improvement effort. The responsibilities include assisting in the resolution of engineering problems and breakdowns, implementing the suggestion system, solving problems, and supervising any corrective discipline or counseling issues that the team leaders raise. They are also expected to be available to work on the line if the need arises. Second-level managers have similar responsibilities and are expected to be more process oriented rather than result oriented. They have responsibility for budgeting, planning, and training; they are also expected to encourage openness concerning problems and to see that the problems are resolved at the lowest possible level.

The NUMMI system makes all employees responsible for quality and safety and provides a method (the *andon* cord) for any person to stop the line to get help with a quality or safety problem—even though the estimated cost of line downtime is $15,000 per minute. The cord is routinely pulled over 100 times per day because the very survival of the company depends on quality. Unlike the erstwhile GM mass production systems (or *push* system), which could tolerate conflict and adversarial relations, the new lean production (or *pull* system) minimizes the buffers of inventory and demands interdependence and cooperation throughout the assembly line. Under this approach, the emphasis is on *kaizen*, or continuous increment improvements in efficiency. The responsibility for quality does not reside in management supervision and inspection but is pushed down to the actual worker under the principle of *jidoka* or identifying problems the moment they occur and responding to them immediately. The problems are resolved at the lowest level possible. The assembly line is kept constantly alert, with the emphasis being on doing the operation correctly every time. Responsibility lies with the individual to call attention to a problem whenever a defect is observed. This places a premium on people being able to identify problems and to quickly adjust and correct errors.

In the erstwhile GM, few people beyond the superintendent had the authority to stop the production line. At NUMMI, downtime is a clear signal that workers are taking their jobs seriously. Maintaining these defect records is a team responsibility. To increase the sense of interdependence and teamwork, NUMMI makes overall plant performance highly visible. This is done in part by hanging standardized work and *kaizen* charts in public team areas. Attendance boards with individual ratings in color are displayed prominently throughout the plant. There are also daily meetings of 40–50 team leaders, group leaders, and assistant managers to discuss defects found in a random sample of cars. Managers are required to explain the reasons for these defects and the corrective measures they plan to take; the focus is on solving problems rather than holding an individual responsible. Team leaders pass on this information to all team members so that all employees understand on a daily basis how the plant is performing.

Team members are also responsible for designing and improving their jobs, including the industrial engineering. This includes generating detail definitions and sequencing of jobs, completing standardized worksheets, and adherence to such instructions. Team member often take initiative and contact suppliers to improve quality of parts.

Under the Toyota, there is continual training. The approach is characterized as a *lifetime training system*. Newly hired team members attend a 4-day orientation conducted by team members and managers. These classes are on team concept, the Toyota production system, quality principles, attendance requirements, safety policies, labor management philosophies, cultural diversity, and the competitive situation in the automobile industry. The formal training is 30 days and includes aerobics, instruction about the Toyota production system, how the suggestion system operates, the importance of standardized work processes, scrolling, welding, the team process, and lots of discussion on right attitude. It gives a realistic picture of what it is like to work on the line. NUMMI requires people who have the right attitude and are capable of performing under the demanding work conditions. After this initial training, new employees are sent out to the line for a couple of days a week, which is progressively increased across the probationary period of 90 days. Aside from the training programs in problem solving, creativity, quality improvement, industrial engineering, and leadership, there are also periodic special training sessions designed to support annual goals. Newly promoted supervisors are given 13 weeks of training on how to treat people.

7.8 SYSTEMS VARIATIONS RANGING FROM MANDATORY TO DISCRETIONARY

The IT-enabled networks of collaborating enterprises and employees, and with these networks associated collaborating customers and suppliers, create vast amounts of interconnected and interdependent tasks and functions requiring that information is shared and integrated. The productivity of knowledge thus depends on unity and integration: the enterprise must be directed toward the integration of knowledge into a common task. Creating and sharing knowledge is viewed as crucial for gaining competitive advantage; knowledge (information) must not be fragmented, but unified and integrated.

Shared knowledge will determine the enterprise *mental map* that guides behavior and determines the enterprise reaction to various internal and external circumstances. The concept of the learning enterprise emphasizes the importance of the generation, distribution, integration, and application of knowledge in enterprises in order to change behavior, as well as emphasizing the need to create conditions for adapting to new shared knowledge. Thus, enterprise learning concerns the increased capacity to address those environmental changes effectively. Enterprise learning must be a core competence and is both a manifestation as well as a prerequisite for change or variation. Rightly, enterprises that cannot learn cannot change.

The informatization of enterprises also manifests noteworthy developments concerning the relationships of enterprises with customers (or citizens). Traditionally, these relationships were merely transaction oriented: the exchange of products or services for some monetary reward. However, as indicated earlier, informatization has resulted in enormous amounts of data about customers. Effectively exploiting this data enables extending the relationship with customers beyond that of a singular transaction. Rather than a short-term transaction orientation, attention can shift toward a long-term relational orientation. It is argued that the information-intensive enterprise and society enables a shift from the *transaction economy* toward the *relationship economy*, with its focus on supporting customers, civilians, patients, etc., based on the relationships that support-giving enterprises have built across the years.

> In the following is a segment of the case history of McDonald's. It illustrates McDonald's focus on systems variations targeted at achieving performance perfection through standardized and optimized operating systems. As may be discerned through a careful perusal, these variations were accompanied simultaneously by variations in other dimensions like shared values (biased toward rules driven), strategy (planned), structure (biased toward control), stuff (product and service), style (administrative culture), staff (nurturing people), skills (focus), and sequence (mass production of standardized products or services).

7.8.1 OPERATING SYSTEMS AT McDONALD'S

McDonald's had distinguished itself in the quick-service industry through its remarkable consistency across all units. McDonald's golden arches always symbolized pleasant, fast service and tasty, inexpensive food. McDonald's had built its success on a legendary operating system that amazed competitors and the financial community by generating an average annual return on equity of 25.2% from 1965 through 1991 and an average annual earnings growth of 24.1%. The company was always faced with the dilemma of changing the company's operating system, so vital in guaranteeing uniform quality and service at every McDonald's outlet was suited to accommodate the growing need for flexibility and variety in products.

Dick and Mac McDonald opened their first drive-in restaurant in 1941, relying on carhops—waiters who went from car to car—to take orders from patrons parked in the restaurant's large lot. In 1948, the brothers abandoned their popular format and introduced self-service windows, 15-cent hamburgers, french fries, and milk shakes. They standardized their preparation methods (in what they termed the *speedee service system*) with exact product specifications and customized equipment. Every hamburger, for example, was prepared with ketchup, mustard, onions, and two pickles; the ketchup was applied through a pump dispenser that required just one squirt for the required amount. Ray Kroc, who held the national marketing rights to the multimixers used in the restaurants to make milk shakes, met the McDonald brothers in 1954. He was so impressed by their restaurant and its potential that he became a national franchise agent for the brothers and founded the McDonald's chain. Like the McDonald brothers' first restaurant in San Bernardino, California, the McDonald's chain featured a limited menu, low prices, and fast service. From the moment in 1955 when he opened his first McDonald's, in Des Plaines, Illinois, Kroc made the operating system his passion and his company's anchor.

McDonald's designed its operating system to ensure consistency and uniformity across all outlets. Operating procedures guaranteed customers the same quality of food and service visit after visit, store after store. Every hamburger, for example, was dressed in exactly the same way: mustard first, then ketchup, onions, and two pickles. Most competitors haven't been able to bring the discipline needed in fast food to get that type of consistency. McDonald's operating system concentrated on four areas: improving the product, developing outstanding supplier relationships, improving equipment, and training and monitoring franchisees. In its quest for improvement, McDonald's revolutionized the entire supply chain, introducing innovations in the way farmers grew potatoes and ranchers raised beef, altering processing methods for both potatoes and meat, and inventing efficient cooking equipment tailored to the restaurant's needs.

Most revolutionary, perhaps, was McDonald's attention to detail. Never before had a restaurant cared about its suppliers' product beyond the price, let alone the suppliers' methods of operation. McDonald's was able to spend as much time and effort as it did in perfecting its operating system because it restricted its menu to 10 items. Most restaurants in the 1960s and 1970s offered a variety of menu items, which made specialization and uniform standards rare and nearly impossible. Fred Turner, one of Kroc's original managers and later senior chairman of McDonald's, stressed the critical importance of menu size in attributing success of the company's operating system (see Subsection 7.7.2, "Satisfaction from Standardization at McDonald")

McDonald's referred to its 3500 U.S. franchisees as its partners for good reason. By 1992, McDonald's generated 39% of its revenues from franchise restaurants. When Ray Kroc first sold franchises, he made sure that his *partners* would make money before the company did, and he insisted that corporate revenue come not from initial franchise fees but from success of the restaurants themselves. That philosophy continued to be at the center of McDonald's franchise and operating practices. McDonald's patrolled suppliers and franchisees scrupulously. In 1991, McDonald's spent $26.9 million on its field service operation to evaluate and assist each of its restaurants. Each of the company's 332 field service consultants visited over 20 restaurants in the United States several times every year, reviewing the restaurants' performance on more than 500 items ranging from restroom cleanliness to food quality and customer service. Turner was the first corporate employee to visit and evaluate each restaurant, and, as early as 1957, he summarized his evaluations by assigning a letter grade to a restaurant's performance in three categories: quality, service, and cleanliness (QSC). For more than 30 years, therefore, McDonald's had prided itself on QSC and a fourth letter—V for value.

McDonald's meticulous attention to detail and careful analysis of quality and procedures did not come from an unbending need for regimentation. Instead, McDonald's sought to study every component of its operation to learn what worked and what failed, to determine how best to offer consistently good service and food. Whereas other chains ignored both franchisees and suppliers, McDonald's sought to elicit commitment from them—commitment that required not only adherence but experimentation. In 1971, he developed a sandwich and a special utensil that could, in classic McDonald's style, guarantee foolproof production of the sandwich. McDonald's rolled out a complete breakfast menu in 1976, featuring the Egg McMuffin, hotcakes, scrambled eggs, sausage, and Canadian-style bacon. McDonald's had again distinguished itself from competitors, none of whom responded until the mid-1980s, by which time McDonald's held a virtual monopoly on breakfast, which accounted for 15% of average restaurant sales.

Similarly, the collaborative effort between McDonald's and its suppliers produced a modified hamburger-patty machine that cut boneless chicken into nuggets and a special batter that gave the nuggets the taste and appearance of being freshly battered. The result was a breakthrough new and unique product, Chicken McNuggets. By March 1980, just 5 months after beginning work on McNuggets, McDonald's was testing them in a Knoxville restaurant. Within 3 years of introducing Chicken McNuggets throughout its chain, McDonald's was deriving 7.5% of domestic sales from its newest product. The giant of the hamburger business had suddenly become the second largest chicken retailer in the food-service industry, positioned behind Kentucky Fried Chicken.

> In the following is a segment of the case history of Dell. It illustrates Dell's focus on systems variations targeting direct sales on the Internet that enabled fulfillment and servicing of customer-specific orders for customized PCs. As may be discerned through a careful perusal, these variations were accompanied simultaneously by variations in other dimensions like shared values (rules driven), strategy (planned), structure (control), stuff (products and services), style (administrational culture), skills (biased toward breadth of skills), and sequence (biased toward mass customization).

7.8.2 WHY LESS IS MORE AT DELL

Operating performance or process innovations play a central role in most breakthroughs. Dell computer provides a powerful example of how innovations in operating performance carried a marginal competitor to market leadership. Dell computer was an undistinguished face in the PC crowd during the first half of the 1990s. Despite strong sales growth, Dell only held about 3% of the market for personal computer systems in 1994, and it lost $36 million that year. At the midpoint of the 1990s, Dell was busy consolidating operations, writing off assets, and booking employee severance payments. Five years later, Dell became the leading PC vendor in the United States, followed by Compaq, Hewlett-Packard, Gateway, and IBM. All of Dell's success sprang from breakthrough innovation centered in core operations. Dell tightly integrated its customer service, supply chain, production scheduling, and fulfillment functions into its direct sales front end, improving operating efficiency, cycle times, and customer service. It converted cost savings into competitive pricing that generated both growing market share and profitability.

Dell was a pioneer in PC telemarketing, but the real breakthrough occurred in 1995 when founder Michael Dell forced the company to fully focus on direct sales over the Internet via its Dell.com website. Sales over the Internet reached $50 million per day, and half of Dell's sales were booked online by the end of the decade. Dell's breakthrough was more than a sales channel innovation. It was the first to embrace mass customization of PCs. Every customized computer system was built to order on a JIT basis and shipped within days, slicing weeks off the company's inventory. Dell was the first company to perfect a now-generic breakthrough strategy that combines the following:

- Mass customization
- Customer-specific product design
- JIT supply-chain solutions
- Rapid, remote fulfillment and service

The result was typical of successful breakthroughs—rapid sales growth and rising margins.

Dell's stock was the top performer in the S&P 500 during the 1990s. It ranked number three on the Fortune list of most admired companies in 2000. Dell had joined such computer industry leaders as IBM and HP in the rarified air of high-profile brands and megamarket caps. It was extremely well positioned to maintain its market leadership as industry consolidation began to constrict the PC industry in 2001, and the rule of three began to kick in. As the PC market tightened, Dell began to pull away from its peers in the PC business. Dell's market momentum, which originated in its breakthrough business model, continues to carry it to new heights.

Dell's success shows how a small, second-tier competitor can move out of the shadow of much larger rivals and seize market leadership by embracing a breakthrough strategy. Its strategy started with a powerful performance innovation that drove dramatic gains in profits and financial value, competitive position, and profile. Dell's profile continues to expand as it moves aggressively into workstations, servers, data storage, and beyond.

In the following is a segment of the case history of eBay. It illustrates eBay's focus on systems variations targeting online auctioning of goods. As may be discerned through a careful perusal, these variations were accompanied simultaneously by variations in other dimensions like shared values (rules driven), strategy (planned), structure (control), stuff (products), style (administrational culture), and skills (focus).

7.8.3 Happy Auctioning at eBay

Until the 1990s, the auction business was largely fragmented; thousands of small city-based auction houses offered a wide range of merchandise to local buyers. And a few famous global ones, such as Sotheby's and Christie's, offered carefully chosen selections of high-priced antiques and collectibles to limited numbers of dealers and wealthy collectors. However, the auction market was not very efficient, for there was often a shortage of sellers and buyers, and so it was difficult to determine the fair price of a product. Dealers were often able to influence auction prices and so obtain bargains at the expense of sellers. Typically, dealers were able to buy at low prices and then charge buyers high prices in the bricks and mortar (B&M) antique stores that are found in every town and city around the world, so they reaped high profits.

The auction business was changed forever in 1995 when Pierre Omidyar developed innovative software that allowed buyers around the world to bid online against each other to determine the fair price for a seller's product. Omidyar founded his online auction site in San Jose on September 4, 1995, under the name AuctionWeb. A computer programmer, Omidyar had previously worked for Microsoft, but he left that company when he realized the potential opportunity to develop new software that provided an online platform to connect Internet buyers and sellers. The entrepreneurial Omidyar changed his company's name to eBay in September 1997, and the first item sold on eBay was Omidyar's broken laser pointer for $13.83. eBay's popularity grew quickly by word of mouth, and the company did not need to advertise until the early 2000s. Omidyar had tapped into a huge unmet buyer need, and people flocked to use his software.

eBay generates the revenues that allow it to operate and profit from its electronic auction platform by charging a number of fees to sellers (buyers pay no specific fees). In the original eBay model, sellers paid a fee to list a product on eBay's site and paid a percentage fee of the final price the product was sold at the end of the auction. Indeed, Meg Whitman's biggest problem was to find search engine software that could keep pace with the increasing volume of buyers' inquiries. Initially, small independent suppliers provided this software; then IBM provided this service. But as search technology has advanced in the 2000s, it partnered with Yahoo to use their search to drive buyers to eBay auctions. In fact, because eBay is one of the world's biggest buyers of web search terms, eBay manages a portfolio of 15 million keywords on different search sites, such as Google, Yahoo, and AOL.

7.8.3.1 eBay's Evolving Business Model

From the beginning, eBay's business model and strategies were based on developing and refining Omidyar's auction software to create an easy-to-use online market platform that would allow buyers and sellers to meet and transact easily and inexpensively. eBay's software was created to make it easy for sellers to list and describe their products and easy for buyers to search for, compare, and bid on the products they wanted to purchase. The essence of eBay's software is that the company simply provides the electronic conduit between buyers and sellers; it never takes physical possession of the products that are listed, and their shipping is the responsibility of sellers and payment the responsibility of buyers. Thus, eBay does not need to develop all the high-cost functional activities like inventory, shipping, and purchasing to deliver products to customers, unlike Amazon.com, for example, and so, it operates with an extremely low-cost structure given the huge volume of products it sells and the sales revenues it generates. eBay is also low cost since till recently, sellers located outside a buyer's state do not have to collect sales tax on a purchase. This allows buyers to avoid paying state taxes on expensive items such as jewelry and computers, which can save them tens or even hundreds of dollars and makes purchasing on eBay more attractive.

To make transactions between anonymous Internet buyers and sellers possible, however, Omidyar's software had to reduce the risks facing buyers and sellers. In particular, it had to convince buyers that they would receive what they paid for and that sellers would accurately describe their products online. To minimize the ever-present possibility of fraud from sellers misrepresenting their products or from buyers unethically bidding for pleasure and then not paying, eBay's software contains a method for registering feedback, converting it into a *trust score* that consolidates a buyer's reputation over time. When sellers and buyers consistently act in an honest way in more and more transactions overtime, they are able to build a stronger and stronger positive feedback score that provides them with a good reputation for honesty.

To take advantage of the capabilities of eBay's software, the company expanded the range and categories of the products it offered for sale to increase revenue. Second, it increased the number of retail or *selling* formats used to bring sellers and buyers together. For example, its original retail format was the 7-day auction format, where the last bidder within this time period *won* the auction, provided the bid met the seller's reserve or minimum price. Then, it introduced the *buy-it-now* format where a buyer could make an instant purchase at the seller's specified price, and later a real-time auction format in which online bidders, and bidders at a B&M auction site, compete against each other in real time to purchase the product up for bid. In this format, a live auctioneer, not the eBay auction clock, decides when to close an auction.

Beyond introducing new kinds of retail formats, over time eBay has continuously strived to improve the range and sophistication of the information services it provides its users—to make it easier for sellers to list, describe, present, and ship their products, and for buyers to make better purchasing decisions. For example, software was developed to make it easier for sellers to list their products for sale and upload photographs and add or change information to the listing. Buyers were able to take advantage of the services that are now offered in what is called MyeBay; buyers can now keep a list of *watched* items so that over the life of a particular auction they can see how the price of a product has changed and how many bidders are interested in it.

By creating and then continually improving its easy-to-use retail platform for sellers and buyers, eBay revolutionized the auction market, bringing together buyers and sellers internationally in a huge, never-ending yard sale. The first-mover advantage eBay gained from Pierre Omidyar's auction software created a nonassailable business model that gave eBay effectively a monopoly position in the global online auction market.

CEO Whitman looked for new ways to improve eBay's business model (i.e., continually attract more buyers and sellers to its auction site and search for ways to generate more revenue from these buyers and sellers):

- eBay began to expand the range and categories of the products it offered for sale to increase revenue enabled by the capabilities of its software.
- eBay increased the number of retail or *selling* formats used to bring sellers and buyers together. For example, its original retail format was the seven day auction format, where the last bidder within this time period *won* the auction, provided the bid met the seller's reserve or minimum price. Then, it introduced the *buy-it-now* format where a buyer could make an instant purchase at the seller's specified price and later a real-time auction format in which online bidders, and bidders at a B&M auction site, compete against each other in real time to purchase the product up for bid. In this format, a live auctioneer, not the eBay auction clock, decides when to close an auction.
- eBay has continuously strived to improve the range and sophistication of the information services it provides its users—to make it easier for sellers to list, describe, present, and ship their products and for buyers to make better purchasing decisions.
- eBay also encouraged the entry of new kinds of sellers into its electronic auction platform. It then sought to attract larger-scale sellers using its eBay Stores selling platform, which allows sellers to list not only products up for auction but also all the items they have available for sale, perhaps in a B&M antique store or warehouse. Large international manufacturers and retailers such as Sears, IBM, and Dell began to open their own stores on eBay to sell their products using competitive auctions for *clearance goods* and fixed priced buy-it-now storefronts to sell their latest products.
- eBay replicated its business model in different countries across the world customized to the needs and language of a particular country's citizens.
- eBay provided more kinds of value-chain services. One service created in the early 2000s for individual sellers is eBay Drop Off. eBay licenses reputable eBay sellers who have consistently sold hundreds of items using its platform to open B&M consignment stores where any seller can *drop off* the products they want to sell. For a commission, the owner of the Drop-Off Store describes, photographs, and lists the item on eBay and then handles all the payment and shipping activities involved in the auction process.
- Similarly, ProStores allowed any potential seller to utilize eBay's functional competencies in online retailing to create its own online storefront using eBay's software. Unlike the regular eBay Stores, ProStores sites are accessible through a URL unique to each seller and are not required to carry eBay branding.
- eBay acquired companies to augment its value chain like PayPal online payment services and Skype, a voice-over Internet provider (VOIP).
- eBay entered specialized auction business through acquisitions like Butterfield & Butterfield to facilitate its entry into the auctioning of high-priced antiques and collectibles and CARad. com, an auction management service for car dealers.

- eBay and Yahoo announced an alliance in 2006 to boost its position against Google and Microsoft; the alliance allowed eBay to use Yahoo search to drive buyers to eBay auctions.
- eBay established eBay Express, where a vast inventory of brand new, brand-name, and hard-to-find products are offered at fixed prices by top eBay sellers.

The Long Tail: Research in the late 1990s revealed power-law distributions in the structure of the Internet and the interconnectedness of the web. A power-law distribution is a curve with a very small number of very high-yield events (like the number of words that have an enormously high probability of appearing in a randomly chosen sentence, like "the" or "to") and a very large number of events that have a very low probability of appearing (like the probability that the word "probability" or "baffelgab" will appear in a randomly chosen sentence). The number of events with a very low probability creates a heavy or long tail as the probability decreases but never quite reaches zero.

In his book "The Long Tail," Wired Editor Chris Anderson argued that this distribution is an important property of the web, in particular because the content and commodities available on the web are digital. A traditional business, constrained by storage capacity and costs, focuses on the high-frequency end of the power-law distribution in order to reap the greatest profit from every transaction. Anderson uses a music shop as an example. This music shop will focus on providing popular albums because the faster they shift them, the less time the albums remain on the shelves, which in turn means the profit margin is greater. The more difficult-to-sell albums take up space and cost, especially so the longer they idle on the shelves. Such a situation enforces the power-law distribution because it ensures that customers find it harder to buy less popular albums. However, an online music shop has only virtual shelf space and can therefore virtually stock an infinite number of albums, including the least popular. It costs Amazon no more to virtually stock a highly popular album than it does to stock a niche product. As a result, the artificial barrier to users buying less popular albums is lifted and the tail of the distribution grows.

Although the number of events under the tail of the distribution is small compared to the high-frequency end, it is still a substantial number considering the total number of users of the web. Hence, there are significant advantages to businesses in supporting the tastes of those customers who make up the tail. According to Anderson, in traditional retail, new albums account for 63% of sales (in 2005), but online, that percentage is 36%.

The Long Tail is not only important for astute business people. It has significant implications for all the users of the web. By removing the traditional barriers to content production and storage, the road is open for production by anyone: the web becomes a read/write space again but this time on a massively greater scale with infinite room for endless niche markets. This mass producerism creates not only a vast amount of data but a number of possibilities that arise from the data that are exploited by savvy applications and businesses aware of its potential. In particular, they draw strength from the diversity displayed in the long tail.

7.9 SEQUENCE VARIATIONS RANGING FROM MASS PRODUCTION TO MASS CUSTOMIZATION

In the new enterprise context, the traditional distinction between customer and producer or between product and service becomes less prominent. Through interactive dialog with the supplier, a customer can determine the type of product and service. Other than mass production for anonymous customers, the product or service is delivered for a specific customer. As such, the logic of production is reversed: the customer does not come into play at the end of the production process but determines the execution of the production process right from the start. The situation typical of the first industrial revolution is reversed: mass production, based on mass demand, will shift increasingly toward individual production based on individual demand.

> In the following is the case history of Ford. It illustrates Ford's focus on sequence variations that enabled for the first time large-scale mass production. As may be discerned through a careful perusal, these variations were accompanied simultaneously by variations in other dimensions like shared values (rules driven), strategy (planned), structure (control), stuff (products), style (administrational culture), skills (focus), and systems (mandatory).

7.9.1 FORD'S MASS PRODUCTION (WHICH EVENTUALLY INSPIRED LEAN PRODUCTION)

The auto maker Henry Ford helped pioneer the concept of low-cost repetitive mass production before World War I by building the giant plant at River Rouge near Dearborn, Michigan, in 1919. The principle that Ford followed to achieve low cost was to build this facility to produce one variant of a product (black-colored Model T) and then run it without interruption at full capacity virtually around the clock year in and year out until it literally sated the public's first-time demand for a basic automobile. By 1925, the plant was producing about one vehicle per minute in a total lead time of about 3 days and 9 h from steelmaking to the finished vehicle. The flow was dictated by the plant's original design—a design that ensured efficiency by allowing work to flow continuously from beginning to end and by having it consume at every point only the required resources to advance one unit of output to the next step toward completion. Given the simplicity of the flow and the repetitive nature of tasks at each work station, there was a need to spend extra resources on activities to control and expedite the flow of material; the work more or less paced itself. Indeed, the schedule pushed material at a ceaseless pace that was sustained by having machines and workers perform repetitive tasks as fast as possible.

The system followed the ideal of a machine, where workers themselves were little more than *cogs in the gears* of the system. The relation between information regarding the work and the actual flow of the work illustrates the mechanical philosophy of the whole enterprise. The primary information regarding the flow of work originates outside the process, in the very layout of the plant and in the schedule. Neither the material nor the workers can influence the process, they can only react to the outside influence; they are literary being *pushed* by external information. Underlying that information is a design, or abstract model, that defines the laws governing the motion of the material and operations of the workers in the plant. The mass production model is characterized by the homogeneity of the inputs and outputs, high speed of throughput, uninterrupted flow of work, and large scale. The design of the work process and the quality of the incoming material insures an acceptable level of quality. The uninterrupted flow of homogenous units at *as fast as possible* rate insures the lowest possible cost per unit of output.

7.9.1.1 Evolution to Virtual Assembly Lines

Until the mid-1920s, Americans delighted in Ford's Model T, a private, enclosed, gasoline-powered alternative to bicycles and horse-drawn carriage buggies. However, as time passed, the car-buying public grew more sophisticated; they wanted cars with more features and styles. GM responded by coordinating among its several divisions so as to provide a car for *every purse and purpose*. By 1950, with faster growth in demand for varieties of products, companies like GM searched for ways to make, efficiently and profitably, two or more variants of a product in the same plant. They remained steadfastly committed to the mass production thinking that says high profits depend on producing at low cost by running operations without interruptions at full capacity for as long as possible. Thus, for catering to production of a variety of products would entail stopping the production from time to time to change over from one product to another (see Chapter 5, Subsection 5.1.3.2, "Toyota Production System").

> Ford took for granted the times it took to change over the various types of equipment used in their plants at that time. Instead of trying to focus on reducing the time it took to do individual changeovers (as was done critically at Toyota), Ford took steps to reduce the total amount of time spent changing over for different products by batching, that is, separating the various processes through which the material flowed without interruption as long as possible.

However, producing varieties in long-running batches creates new costs because mix of varieties produced in batches means becoming out of step with the flow of customer orders. Moreover, sometimes, a batch will contain more of a variety than customers want, which is a costly waste. At times, a batch will tie up capacity and prevent making something else that customers do want, which can lead to a costly loss of sales. Thus, for maintaining the low costs promised by batch-producing varieties of output, market forecasting and advertising to stimulate demand supported by discounting coupled with performance incentives for workers, etc., may become an expensive and unavoidable necessity. Most mass production manufacturers addressed these additional costs of batching varieties by speeding up the flow of output for each batch and increasing the output even further; this invariably resulted in declining quality of the outputs, leading to increase in errors or defects, rework, and rejects.

As variety proliferated after the 1950s, most large organizations separated their otherwise linked operations into separate departments and allowed each operation to perform according to its own rhythm. This *decoupled* batch production approach to mass production of variety featured uninterrupted work only in each separate operation, followed by transit to a central staging area, or warehouse, where material waited until a schedule directed it to flow in varieties to a final assembly plants. Making all the pieces in this complicated *flow* come together in the right places at the right times required additional resources (accounted as *overheads*) that were employed in activities such as scheduling, controlling, expediting, storing, inspecting, sorting, transporting, and reworking. All these resources represented an *information factory* that is parallel to the material-flow factory and is created out of the need to impose order on a batch-driven system that itself had been created to minimize the costs of producing in varieties. Order imposing information factory is usually realized by computer-based production control, scheduling, and cost accounting systems. Applying the logic of economies of scale and speed, profitability is always assured if enough output is produced to reduce unit costs below the prices customers will pay. Hence, the solution to address the added costs of building an information factory (i.e., *overheads*) was to increase the speed and amount of output (i.e., *throughput*) even more and then engage in advertising or other incentives to stimulate customer demand.

> Most companies attributed the activities associated with batch processing and the resulting costs to the complexity caused by producing varieties of product, not to the way they organized work to produce that variety. The impact of the altered way of organizing work can be judged from the fact that the overall lead time to make a vehicle went from 3 days and 9 h at Ford's River Rouge plant in the mid-1920s to several weeks in most auto organizations by the late 1970s.

Eventually, the reality of the *information factory* overtook the actual reality on the shop floor. In other words, managers increasingly considered reality to be the abstract quantitative models, the management accounting reports, and the computer scheduling algorithms that were used to make sense of decoupled batch production system. Eventually, this belief in the primacy of the information factory further reinforced the myth of the antithesis between differentiation and mass production. Most manufacturers assumed it was nearly impossible to efficiently and profitably make increasing varieties of products for large markets: you could profit by producing wide varieties or by selling in large markets but not by doing both (see Chapter 4, Subsection 4.4.2, "Enterprise Perspectives"). A company that differentiates sacrifices scale economies by multiplying the varieties of its products. Therefore, it can be profitable either by selling large varieties in small niche markets (where prices are high enough to cover the high costs of variety) or it can sell limited variety in large markets (where it can efficiently mass-produce large quantities at low prices).

> In the following is the case history of IKEA. It illustrates IKEA's focus on sequence variations that enabled for the first time self-assembly furnishings. As may be discerned through a careful perusal, these variations were accompanied simultaneously by variations in other dimensions like shared values (rules driven), strategy (planned), structure (biased toward autonomy), stuff (products), style (administrational culture), and systems (mandatory).

7.9.2 Furnishing Self-Assemblies at IKEA

Ingvar Kamprad, through his company IKEA, revolutionized home furnishing. He launched a mail-order business selling nylon stockings, marches, and cigarette lighters from a tiny shed in his hometown Almhult in northern Sweden. Lacking the resources to deliver the packages to his customers, Kamprad came up with a dependable, low-cost option for transporting goods to his customers: he arranged for his goods to be delivered by local milk trucks. This was the first of many creative approaches that he adopted to reduce costs and deliver what his customers wanted. He has moved on from its original limited product range and now offers the widest range of home furnishings to the greatest number of people around the world.

When IKEA entered the fray, the home furnishings industry was traditional and uninspiring. It was characterized by large stores usually selling cheap and low quality goods or small stores selling high-end and high-quality expensive pieces. It was all characterized by a lack of customer focus and poor value for money. IKEA changed the ground rules for competition in this traditional and dull market. IKEA combined eye-catching designs with low prices, making for a winning formula that caught the competition off-guard. Its creative cost-conscious designs, flat-pack, self-assembly products, warehouse, and mass production techniques deliver cost savings that benefit the customer through low prices. The company's convenient out-of-town locations, free parking lots, in-store playroom facilities, and long opening hours all appealed to the young and aspirational market segments.

As IKEA's business and brand grew and expanded geographically, it took on another dimension. IKEA was fast becoming more than just a store; it was being transformed into a lifestyle choice that revolves around attributes of contemporary design, low price, wacky promotions, and an unbridled enthusiasm. Just like Harley-Davidson and Starbucks, IKEA has come to reflect an individual's personality and has become a guardian of people's lifestyles. Far more than a purveyor of furniture and soft furnishings, it has become an indicator of good taste and value. By 2006, the company had close to 250 stores and 420 million shoppers across Asia, Europe, Australia, and North America.

> In the following is the case history of Scania. It illustrates Scania's focus on sequence variations that enabled for the first time modular- and component-based design. As may be discerned through a careful perusal, these variations were accompanied simultaneously by variations in other dimensions like shared values (rules driven), strategy (planned), structure (control), stuff (products), and style (administrational culture).

7.9.3 Modular Architecture and Design at Scania

Scania is a Swedish-based multinational manufacturer of heavy trucks, buses, and diesel engines. Scania created a process for designing trucks individually tailored to meet specific needs of any particular customer; Scania achieved variety at a low cost by focusing on product design. The modular strategy grew out the company's decision to after World War II to specialize its efforts on the heavy range of trucks; it wanted to export trucks to as many parts of the world as possible. To market all over the world meant designing trucks to meet an enormous range of specialized transportation purposes. To meet the unique requirements of each and every customer in widely varying conditions, and to do so at low cost, Scania devised an innovative modular design architecture. They saw modular product architecture as the key to supplying high-quality variety at the lowest possible cost.

The initial impetus for modularization came from Carl-Bertel Nathorst, a brilliant mechanical engineer and industrial economist who led Scania from 1940 to 1951. He promoted the philosophy of building trucks from a limited number of parts or components, by maximizing the number of common and standardized parts or components. This approach eventually led to a strategy and architecture that is termed today as modularization. Nathorst adopted modularized design as the primary product strategy to fulfill the company's ambitious growth plans of expansion across the world. Paradoxically, Nathorst transformed Scania's workshops from the individualistic craft-centered mode of production typical of the early industrial enterprises to the standardized mass production method that had become the norm after the World War II.

7.9.3.1 Module- and Component-Based Design and Engineering

Modularization is a principle of design that divides a mechanical system or structure into architected standardized elements called modules (and components) that can be used interchangeably by reason of the common interfaces between them. This enables one to make myriad versions of the system with relative ease and cost. Modularization reduces cost of accommodating a change because it permits one to make a change by varying the minimum number of modules and components to accomplish the required state of the system. This is akin to the structures that can be created using the blocks by the Danish toy company LEGO. Using these modular, interchangeable block, an inventive child can build a remarkable variety of wide variety of distinctive structures. Thus, from a small number of modular parts comes a wide variety of unique designs.

To modularize its trucks, Scania identifies a minimum of four distinctive but common modules: engine (used to generate motive power), transmission (the gearbox, transmission shaft, and final gears used to transmit motive power to the wheels), chassis (front and rear axels), and frame used to carry loads and cab (used to house and connect the driver with the rest of the vehicle). For instance, most heavy trucks make use of diesel engine because of its reliability, durability, overall transmission efficiency, and ease of maintenance. The challenge is to standardize these modules so that any size of one module is capable of fitting together with all sizes of the other modules. When this modular design architecture is extended to smaller and smaller parts within a system, the resultant effect is remarkable. It becomes possible by making only a very small change at the local module or component level to affect a desired difference in the character or performance of the whole system. Thus, the sales personnel can configure a different truck for each individual customer and *the company incurs no more design or production cost than if all customers were to order essentially the same vehicle.*

For example, Scania's truck modules consist of 3 cab types, 4 engine types, 4 transmission types, and 15 chassis type. Each of the three cabs will take engine of any size; cab designers put attachment mounts in all three cab designs to hold all the varieties of engine sizes. Similarly, one can construct different sizes of the engine (9, 12, and 16 L) by combining modular combustion chambers that contain identical 2 L cylinders, pistons, and cylinder heads. Resultantly, Scania will be able to rapidly meet all foreseeable government emission requirements, without having to design an entirely new engine each time the emission standards change. Further, varieties of the chassis module can be constructed with different combinations of identical axels transmitting power to the wheels. A 6×4 chassis as three axels with power transmitted to two of them and a 4 × 2 chassis has two axels with power transmitted to only one of them. In each of these cases, different combinations of identical submodules inside the engine or chassis modules produce very different performance in the truck as a whole.

Each cab design accommodates a variety of engine sizes, engine configurations, sleeping facilities, and doorway configurations; nevertheless, each of the three cab types in each series shares the same front windshield and driver compartment. Within the driver compartment, the dashboard is designed to change easily between left-hand drive and right-hand drive trucks. The dashboards on all Scania trucks can be configured for either a left-hand drive or a right-hand drive with only four different part numbers—driver-side panel, passenger-side panel, and two variants of the middle wedge. It is no accident that Scania in the early 1990s could sell as many units as its closest competitor, in many more varieties, and yet require only half as many different part numbers to make those units. This ability to produce far more varieties of end product with a fraction of the part numbers is a major reason for Scania's superior profitability among European truck makes in recent decades.

 Alternately, Scania can also design just two dashboards, one outfitted for left-hand drive vehicles and a mirror image of that one outfitted for right-hand drive vehicles. Making of two dashboards prompted by such a need is an example of an integrated design, the antithesis of modularization. The opposing needs for modularization and integration have to balance to achieve optimal capability for maximum flexibility with maximum simplicity.

7.9.3.2   Growing Modular

Having chosen modular design architecture as the best way to profitably make varieties of heavy trucks, Scania's engineers set out in the 1950s to identify and measure all the various demands that heavy trucks could face around the world. They weren't attempting to design precisely each and every truck in advance; instead they identified the main factors influencing the each function of a truck, and then they assessed the range of conditions for those factors in the various parts of the world were Scania trucks might operate. For instance, Scania focused its attention primarily on studying durability of each module, and its components, under varying operational loads in different applications across the world. Operational load took into account combination of road resistance and truck weight. Over a period of many years, durability tests were conducted in the laboratories and in the field to study the impact of operational loads on modules and components. These tests eventually led to specifying the range of component sizes that could satisfy the requirements of all operational loads with a minimum number of differing sizes. Eventually, this study was extended to encompass all functions performed by the truck, namely, generate power, transmit power for motion, carry load, and house and protect the driver. The result of this effort is a continually evolving matrix showing the specifications of each module (and submodule) and component (and subcomponent) that a truck requires to meet all possible conditions that a driver might face anywhere in the world.

 The matrix ensures avoiding duplication of effort, thus, freeing design resources to focus either on addressing new but previously unidentified solutions or on improving preexisting solutions to the present needs of the customer.

Consequently, Scania does not design trucks in advance of the customer orders. Scania's design engineers do not have to attend to the configuration of each customer's particular order. Scania's design engineers do not create bills or BOMs for finished trucks in anticipation of a sale. Sales and dealer personnel, without having to call on design engineers, work with the prospective customer to specify a truck's bill of material that meets the customer's needs with the minimum number of unique parts. Scania creates bill of materials only in response to customer orders; ultimately, a customer order *pulls* the design of a specific truck from the data in the matrix.

An obvious advantage of its unique modular architecture is that Scania requires a much smaller number of parts than any of its competitors does to make an equivalent, if not more, variety of trucks. Scania's many different varieties of trucks share a surprisingly high percentage of commonality or reusability of parts (i.e., modules and components). Indeed, reusability of parts is the major source of Scania's ability to deliver large variety of trucks at very low cost. By attaining a high reusability of parts among its great variety of trucks, Scania makes it easier to avoid costs, inflexibility, and complexity attendant on making changes in designs and, consequently, also changes in tooling, production, distribution, and servicing of their trucks. Scania undertook a comparison study for comparing the impact of its higher reusability-driven modularization and component standardization program for its European operations during the 1980s with a like competitor that produced and sold similar number of heavy tricks but required about twice as many part numbers. Scania's average spend on product development was about half of what the competitor spent on product development each year. Scania's highly reusable modules and components generated average annual savings in production and distribution amounting to about 0.4 billion SEK by reason of its focus on modularization and standardization.

7.9.3.3 Modularizing for Competitiveness

Absence of the strategy of reusability-driven modularization and standardization of components is the prime reason foremost of Scania's competitors to engage in the homogenous production of *global* products because these companies use cost targets alone to make marketing and production decisions. In an effort to profit from scale economies, many auto and truck makers mass-produce high volumes of integrated and standardized products that they refer to *world cars* or *world trucks*; for them, producing variety automatically means much higher cost structures. Consequently, for Scania's competitors, reducing part-number complexity and costs engenders the idea of sacrificing customers and revenue. As a counterexample, one can consider how Scania's designers meet a customer's need for more power. Most truck designers have traditionally believed that increasing the engine's power, because it increases the output torque of the gearbox, also makes it necessary to increase the torque capacity of the final gear that connects the gearbox to the rear drive axels. Contrary to this, years ago, Scania's engineers had discovered that under the usual range of truck operations found across the world, the torque capacity of the final gear varies with road resistance and not with the horsepower. Since road resistance is determined by surface quality of roads, and not by engine power, Scania's engineers realized that they could leave the torque capacity of the final gears untouched and concentrate on meeting customer demand for increase in horse power. In fact, since road quality across the world has continued to improve dramatically across the world, Scania actually decreased final gear torque capacities while simultaneously raising the engine power. Accordingly, Scandia's engineers met customers' demands for more horsepower with a far more commonality or reusability of parts than what their competitors have achieved.

In 1994, Scania's senior executives identified modular design architecture as the main reason for the company's sustained profitability. Scania's executives believe that this unique design architecture has enabled the company to achieve higher margins on revenue and more stable profitability for a longer period than any other truck maker in the world. In fact, despite a very cyclical market for heavy trucks, Scania has been profitable in every year since 1934. Moreover, since the 1950s, Scania has increased the multinational scope of its activities multifold. Scania trucks, buses, and engines are sold on all continents and in over hundred countries. In the 1990s, Brazil has been Scania's largest single national market for all of its products.

By designing and manufacturing all critical modules of a truck, Scania chooses to concentrate on building long-term customer loyalty with very dependable products. The company is not keen in catering to short-term purchasers, no matter how large their orders, whose demands for cost cutting outweigh the long-term beneficial consequences of systemic product design. Sensing an enormous gap between its own systemic design-oriented strategy and short-term focus on cost-minimization focus of a typical American heavy-truck buyer, Scania has chosen to generally stay away from the North American heavy-truck market. Though, its new venture into the Mexican market is based on the belief that this proxy for the American market is ready to appreciate the nuances of the Scania difference.

7.10 SUMMARY

This chapter discussed variations in one or several of these dimensions: shared values, strategy, structure, stuff, style, staff, skills, systems, and sequence. It discussed examples of businesses with shared values variations ranging from rules driven (Cisco, DuPont) to values driven (Tata); strategy variations ranging from planned (Wal-Mart) to emergent (Google, P&G); structure variations ranging from control (ArcelorMittal) to autonomy (IBM, LEGO); stuff variations ranging from products (Harley-Davidson) through services (Southwest Airlines) to experiences (Disney); style variations ranging from administrational (Samsung, ABB) to transformational (Acer); staff variations ranging from challenging (Microsoft, GE) to nurturing people (Volvo); skills variations ranging from focus (UPS, McDonald's) to breadth of skills (NUMMI); systems variations ranging from mandatory (McDonald's, Dell) to discretionary (eBay); and sequence variations from mass production (Ford) to mass customization (IKEA, Scania). Naturally, in certain cases, the variations cited are a combination of more than one variation dimension.

Section IV

Business Excellence through Variations

In this section, we look at enterprises through their entire life spans to highlight the variations they had to undergo to sustain excellence—more than case studies, these are more of life histories of these enterprises. Each of these companies has been operating for about a century or more, and they range from manufacturing to service companies. As may be discerned through a careful perusal, these case histories are replete with simultaneous variation in several dimensions of variation—ranging from one end to the other and back again a few times along each of these dimensions—like shared values (rule-driven and value-driven), strategy (planned emergent), structure (control autonomy), stuff (products to services to experiences), style (administrational to transformational culture), staff (challenging to nurturing people), skills (focus to breadth of skills), systems (mandatory to discretionary), and sequence (mass production to mass customization). While General Electric operates in the most traditional manufacturing sectors of the economy, IBM is a typical high-technology company that had to renew itself multiple times to remain at the forefront of new-era excellent companies. UPS is an example of a traditional transportation and delivery company that has reframed itself as the premier logistics and supply chain company for the burgeoning world of e-businesses.

As mentioned in the Preface, instead of newer case studies, the objective was to present the usual and long familiar case studies through the prism of the "variations" idea to experience the difference of the "case history" approach presented here. Case histories are by definition chronological but, depending on the context, have different focus: GE case history is chronological on leadership, IBM case history is chronological primarily on stuff or offerings, and, finally, UPS case history is chronological primarily on strategic or geographical expansion of business operations. Every case history has a story to tell and must be studied in larger rather than smaller numbers. It is not for nothing that case studies play such a large and critical role in the business management education. The experience represented by the cases is not generalizable: each case history has to be studied for its own sake. Culturally, this is very much in the grand tradition of elders in any society educating their children by narrating stories: no two stories are same, neither are any two stories wildly different.

8 General Electric (GE)

GE currently ranks among the top three American companies as measured by market value. Very few firms can match GE over so prolonged a period of time. Owing to its long history, GE provides an unparalleled opportunity to assess our variation-based managerial paradigm. It is one of the best illustrations of the secrets of sustained vitality—variations.

GE is a highly diversified company. Its various businesses—medical systems, major appliances, aircraft engine, plastics, financial services, NBC, etc.—have very little in common. While highly diversified, its CEOs have sought to maximize the value of the portfolio by leveraging one business to help another and by exploiting common systems and shared values. They have insisted upon an active role in

1. Allocating financial, technical, and human resources
2. Helping shape business strategy
3. Prodding businesses to remain competitive and adaptive

One of the key reasons for the company's astonishing long-term achievements has been its ability to recognize when even seemingly successful strategies need to be adapted and changed. GE's management has anticipated and responded successfully to major market shifts. Drawing on its inherent strengths and resources, the company transformed from being a leading electrical systems and products company to being a highly diversified, multi-industry global corporation, and it instituted unique management systems and human resource programs to make it work.

A good part of how GE has renewed itself over successive generations can be perceived from tracing its history and noting the compensatory actions that corrected its excesses—overtime. The overall pattern of GE's pendulum swings can be fully understood only when viewed in a historical context. The majority of GE's seven CEOs swung the pendulum to extremes. And while, as suggested earlier, there are costs along with benefits in employing this technique, GE's vitality appears to have been served by these reinvigorating shifts in emphasis. Perhaps, in a very large, highly diversified firm, one must send very strong signals to ensure the employees many levels down get the message that change is necessary. While the pendulum swings have at times done *violence* to the organization, perhaps such violence is necessary to provoke the change that is necessary, though the pain inflicted at times threatens to overshadow the gains realized. Yet if we look at the net effect of the pendulum swings across a long period of time, a more tolerant perspective emerges. GE's genius has been in its choice of successive CEOs, each of whom tended to counter the extremes of his predecessors.

 We would like to highlight that this case history is meant to highlight the variations during the life span of the company rather than to illustrate either effective or ineffective handling of an administrative situation.

GE's history begins in 1877. Thomas Edison's inventive contributions to the telephone, phonograph, and electric light bulb were secured with strong patent protection. Like a modern-day Silicon Valley entrepreneur, he sought to create a company in each of these technologies. To finance these start-ups, he assembled investors. Charles Coffin, who was part of the group that underwrote

Edison's fledgling company, recognized that the concept of the incandescent lamp provided superior illumination to the alternative technology of arch lamp. But Edison was wedded to direct current (DC) applications, whereas rival firms were demonstrating greater efficiencies with alternating current (AC). Edison in GE had a strong position in the illumination market and Thomson in the power traction market. Seizing the moment, Coffin headed a group that purchased Edison's patents, combined them with Thompson–Houston's AC patents, and formed the GE Company in 1892. This combination enabled the new GE to become the electrical systems and products leader in both of these major technologies and application segments. For the next 30 years, Coffin served as chairman and CEO.

1. There are two principal ways of generating and transmitting electricity: DC and AC. Edison selected the DC approach, while others—primarily George Westinghouse and Thomson–Houston—selected AC. AC required that the voltage be reduced, transmitted, and distributed to local users by a central electricity-generating plant, while DC technology was generated and transmitted locally. AC depended on first stepping up voltages, transmitting, and, then stepping them back down through the use of transformers. The AC approach was centralized, while DC was decentralized and comparatively inefficient.
2. Edison elected not to own and operate his own utilities but rather to just invest in them and have them as loyal customers; financing consumers became a key element in Jack Welch's successful strategies of the 1980s and 1990s.

8.1 COFFIN (1913–1922)/SWOPE (1922–1939) ERA

Coffin became president and CEO in 1892. Acquisition and mergers require leaders who are able to integrate diverse culture and technologies. Coffin's consultative and participative style of leadership was ideal for achieving this result. He was highly successful in developing long-term relationship with all key stakeholders and in dealing with financial crisis. It was during this period that GE instituted its strong and disciplined financial and accounting systems, which became hallmark of GE. This enabled the firm to improve several key metrics, such as ROI and cash flow. This was also the time when the company initiated and invested heavily in its womb-to-tomb selection, training, and development programs.

In 1893, there was a major financial collapse that threatened GE's very existence because the company was highly leveraged because Edison and Villard had taken equity positions in companies owned by their key customers. This put GE in a cash flow crunch that almost forced the company into bankruptcy. Coffin cut a critical deal with J.P. Morgan whereby Morgan agreed advanced the required money as payment for GE-held utility stocks. This traumatic event had profound effect on the financial strategies and policies of GE not only during the remaining tenure of Coffin but also for all future times.

At the turn of the century, the U.S. government began to recognize that electricity was a crucial factor in industrializing America. Coffin decided to avoid government clients; he defined instead a continuum of businesses that ranged from products that *illuminate or rotate* to those that *generate or transmit* electricity. Through the first decades of this century, federal and state governments supported the electrification of America. The electrification of America was a boon to GE's lightning business. GE instituted the practice of selling light bulbs to retailers on consignment. GE owned the bulbs until they were sold—at which time the dealer received a commission; the advantage of this arrangement was that it foreclosed discounting. GE's lightning business has been an unparalleled source of revenues and profits. To this day, more than half of all light bulbs sold in America are GE's.

> Since its inception, GE had a *make* rather than *buy* mentality. From Coffin's day, there was a distrust of being *captive* to suppliers and there was a marked preference for the *do-it-yourself* approach. This coupled with the growth during the war years generated an increasing tendency for GE to diversify into any and every area and trying to do it all in-house. World War II saw GE getting into atomic power, jet engines, radar, aerospace, and a variety of other technologies.

Gerald Swope, who was GE's CEO from 1923 to 1939, continued the strategic direction set by his predecessor. During his tenure, GE consolidated its position as a leading innovator in the electrical field as well as the dominant manufacturer in its various lines of products:

1. Swope coined the term *benign cycle* that referred to the characteristic mutually reinforcing relationship between increasing installations of electric appliances (like large and small refrigerators, heaters, toasters, lamps, irons) that increased the demand for electricity, which in turn increased the need for generated electricity requiring utilities to acquire increased power generation, transmission, and distribution equipment. It was the same strategy used by Standard Oil and other commodity industries, and variations on this are still used today by companies such as Intel and other electronics companies. GE sold its housewares to generate consumption and made its money on big-ticket generators and transformers. It was an economic engine of astonishing power. This is a very typical strategy for any network-based business (see Chapter 5, Subsection 5.2.3.2, "Bandwagon Effect"), but GE helped pioneer the model and refined it to an extraordinary degree.
2. Swope and Young joined with their key competitor, Westinghouse, to form a new venture, RCA, in an effort to break into the infant broadcasting industry. But unlike the success of a similar strategy earlier in the electrical industry, they were outmaneuvered by David Sarnoff to render it as a missed opportunity for GE. The broadcasting business was very attractive to GE because it possessed many of the same characteristics as the electrical business. Both are network and technology based, which allowed GE to build a comprehensive advantage through its technological expertise and a strong patent position. Furthermore, GE could sell to regulated customers, which provided a risk buffer and enabled the company to maintain high margins. There was a significant opportunity to develop and sell high-value radio and television sets that in turn would require new programming and more sophisticated advertising—thus creating another version of the highly successful benign cycle strategy.
3. GE licensed its technology throughout Europe, China, Japan, and Latin America in return for major positions in their electric companies. By 1935, GE owned 29% of Siemens and 10% of Philips and had joint ventures in China and Japan and throughout Latin America.

Swope's vision for GE encompassed its organizational culture that included the cornerstones of engineering and manufacturing excellence, robust accounting and financial control systems, and emphasis on the GE *family*. The integrity of GE's product lines was protected functionally by autonomous *works* managers who oversaw a geography—in effect, regional manufacturing centers making an array of GE products associated with these factory complexes that had transformed themselves into minicities with their own schools, parks, hospitals, shopping centers, etc. The fierce independence of the respective *works* was balanced against the sense of GE as a family, and in turn, the activities of the *works* managers were monitored by GE's financial system and Swope's extensive informal intelligence network. Gradually, respective works managers became more independent and insular. Culturally, GE shifted from being one *family* to a collection of sects with a common ancestry. The GE *family* was characterized by retreats for executives and progressive personnel policies that were aimed at enlisting worker's commitment and contribution to maintaining and enhancing manufacturing efficiency. The *off-sites* were held at Association Island and were attended by all managers above foreman level.

In the 1920s, Swope personally authored a number of personal policies that were decades ahead of their time:

- He established employer associations to ensure that worker interests were fairly represented.
- Introduced life insurance and disability insurance.
- Added the novel feature of cost-of-living wages increases to hourly wages.
- Pioneered the introduction of unemployment insurance and pensions.

In 1923, they established a unique pension trust that protected the worker from the problem of bankruptcy; this defined-benefit program required that both the employers and the company make contributions. The creation of the trust was highly innovative for the time, and it has helped GE avoid many of the problems faced by most of the U.S. companies. In 1929, the stock market collapsed, and the world suffered the greatest economic depression in modern times. GE's revenues dropped more than 75% during this period. In comparison to many of their peers, who instituted layoffs, Swope and Young were more pragmatic. They recognized that if they wanted to keep talented people, they would have to take steps to minimize the depression's impact on them, including unemployment benefits, guaranteed work program, and profit sharing program in 1930.

Pushed by Swope and Young, GE instituted very powerful resource systems that permitted the company to develop a *strong, loyal, and trained* bench of professionals and leaders. Both Swope and Young made major contributions to solving the social, political, and economic issues facing the United States in the Great Depression. These included being architects of Social Security and the National Recovery Administration as well as inviting the Congress of Industrial Organization (CIO) to organize and represent GE employees. This provided GE with labor peace from mid-1930s to the late 1940s, while other companies were afflicted with violent labor strikes.

The GE board named Charles Wilson as Swope's successor in 1940 and he served through 1952. The war effort flooded GE with orders; in many segments, the company sold all it could produce. After the war, the Marshall Plan underwrote the reconstruction of Europe, giving a further boost to demand for power generation and heavy industrial equipment. Even though GE lost some of the past momentum, still these were its golden years. GE's relationship was so closely associated with the government war effort that Wilson was lent to Washington as head of the War Mobilization board. During Wilson's absence, Swope returned briefly from retirement largely in the capacity of a caretaker president. This left GE somewhat in limbo during the war and resulted in a strategy and leadership vacuum.

8.2 CORDINER ERA (1950–1963)

In the postwar period, insatiable demand created an environment in which it was easy to succeed. No real *strategy* had been required; beginning with the World War II and through the postwar recovery period, GE had been drawn into wartime technologies—aircraft engines, nuclear energy, and aerospace. But the early 1950s brought reversals not only in the marketplace but also in the government. Under the Truman and Eisenhower administrations, the government began to reverse the previously adopted benign position toward GE. Antitrust infractions were investigated and people held responsible were brought to trial.

By the end of World War II, GE was no longer an electrical systems company but a highly diversified, technology-based giant. Unlike many other companies, the Cordiner/Reed team decided that GE should remain diversified and revert to focusing only on electrical systems. Since no consumer goods were manufactured during the war, almost all of the consumer goods sectors had high pent-up demand. Meeting one consumer need often created, in turn, another demand. For example, housing was in desperately short supply following the war. Developers drew on the techniques of mass production to begin building houses on a massive scale. The building of new homes, in turn, stimulated demand for household appliances as well as a new major contractor segment for GE. Entire cities were created, and massive highway and telecommunications networks were built. This caused a huge surge in the construction of manufacturing and commercial buildings, providing GE with major growth opportunities for its industrial and commercial businesses and creating a need for new electrical systems. All these trends enhanced GE's consumer businesses.

An especially attractive feature in all of this growth was that, for the most part, only American companies could take advantage of these opportunities. European competitors, for example, had been devastated by the war and were not in a position to compete. Furthermore, the Marshall Plan and other government-funded programs stipulated that only U.S. companies can participate in the supply of these programs. This meant that GE and other American companies had exclusive access to huge amounts of government funding.

Government program enabled the company to develop new products that would ultimately be used in industrial, consumer, and commercial applications. Many of the high-tech products that we are using today came almost as a result of these programs. Although government business had a few low return on sales, it had very positive cash flows, and it required little in terms of investment dollars because the government often owned the facilities and made all the investments. This gave U.S. companies such as GE a major competitive advantage.

This also resulted in a singular focus on manufacturing capacity and utilization rather than on selling, marketing, or even competing. Customer demand for almost all products was so much greater than the supply that pricing was not an issue. This was a period when companies and their leaders did not need to have long-term marketing and competitive strategies; all they needed to do was build factories, hire workers, and produce and deliver products. Effectively, strategic planning disappeared and was not revived until the 1970s.

Cordiner targeted consumer goods as a hot growth area in this postwar environment; he changed GE's slogan to *Progress is our most important product* and endeavored to build a comparatively stronger marketing capability. Later in his tenure, he embarked on an ambitious program in the capital goods sector, funding GE's foray into computers and nuclear power, which later proved to be unviable businesses. The focus was on internal development, rather on acquisitions or mergers, and GE was single minded in its pursuit of organic growth. Cordiner urged the company's decentralized management to be risk takers and to develop new products and business based on their internal strengths, or *core competencies*, rather than on acquisition or alliances. This required that the company balance the short and long range—that is, achieve the short-term numbers but look longer range for new opportunities and threats.

The consumer group's major appliance division continued to add innovative products to its cooking, dishwashing, and refrigerating product lines. This entailed developing new technologies such as the microwave oven and induction cooker and improving the quality and beauty of the appliances; innovating heating and cooling products were added to this line. Room air conditioners were developed to enable consumers to cool individual rooms. Using the product-obsolescence approaches that had been so successful in the automobile industry, the consumer was encouraged to continually upgrade these appliances by means of new features, more attractive packaging, or both. Radios, potable televisions, and stereos were also added to the product portfolio, with the company suing the appliance retailers and selected department stores to sell these new products. Since housing construction was booming, GE created a new distribution channel to sell directly to home and apartment builders. The objective was to get GE appliances installed, so that when consumers needed to upgrade, they would automatically select GE brands. In addition, GE established its own appliance service so that it would not have to rely on retailers or independent contractors. The combination of product innovation, strong retailer functions, aggressive marketing, and fair-trade pricing enabled both the major appliance and small appliance businesses to be very profitable and to continue to be leaders in their respective markets.

Postwar conditions warranted a repositioning of GE and change was overdue. But Cordiner's response was somewhat abrupt, in that, within a month of taking charge, he began to dismantle what Swope had created. A champion of the *organization as machine* mind-set of his day, Cordiner viewed decentralization as the primary remedy to GE's ills. So Cordiner broke up the works and decentralized them. Cordiner divided the company into three layers of management—group, divisions, and departments—for each of the industry sectors. The major groups included consumer, industrial, and electric utilities. Each of the departments was required to have its own engineers, sales, manufacturing, finance, and employee relations operations. No deviations were permitted; whenever a department exceeded $50 million in revenues, it triggered a split into smaller departments. As a result, by 1956, GE manufactured some 200,000 products and had 350 lines of products in nearly 100 product-manufacturing departments with average revenue between $30 and $40 million.

Over a 20-month period, he changed jobs of 2000 senior executives, introduced the concept of interchangeable *professional managers*, discontinued the tradition of retreats to Association Island, and established administrative machinery to enforce his reforms down into the ranks. The extensive decentralization was unfolded by promulgating the new concept of *management by objectives* (MBO) invented jointly with Peter Drucker. Each GE general manager was made responsible for a *profit center* and was expected to achieve a threshold of performance called *hurdle rates*: 7% return on sales and 20% return on investment. Each general manger was required to *make their numbers* even if it was unrealistic in the context and scale of their business units. This overzealous application of rigid performance benchmarks resulted in premature divesture of certain business like mobile communications and computers. This represented dramatic change from the company's traditional centralized organization. Before MBO, corporate management was responsible for setting the objectives and developing the strategies, and the operating units were expected to execute them with little or no deviation. In effect, the shift transferred power from the centralized functional units to the product department general managers.

Cordiner targeted for structural and procedural change in light of the postwar complacency that was perceived to have set within GE; it was felt that radical surgery was necessary to awaken GE to the new competitive realities. Seeking *consistency*, he imposed a dogma of decentralized profit centers, mandatory quantifiable hurdle rates, professional management, and so forth. This approach was fraught with the danger of excesses because it was implemented with unrelenting rigor and lack of compassion. He also disallowed any countervailing opinions or disagreements. However, his initiatives did not result in the entrepreneurial behavior that he envisaged. His approach was so intensely focused on breaking the entrenched loyalties within the works that it severed many effective working relationships, ruptured mutual bonding, and also undermined trust within functioning teams.

Cordiner's declaration of war upon the works disrupted the power structure of the manufacturing *warlords* and also impacted the engineering cadre. Many of these managers had started to believe that it was *their company* and they could run it as they saw fit, disregarding the concern for the investors, customers, and employees. It led to an attrition of a very large number of his key middle- and top-management managers over a 10-year period. Cordiner's chief of staff Harold Smiddy implemented the program that broke GE's traditional organization into almost hundred product departments. To connect all these business units, Smiddy engineered complex linkage systems and procedures that

- Relied on stringent financial accounting and controls to keep track of these business units
- Established a hierarchy of reporting relationships to ensure executive oversight
- Instituted a process of reviews that established checks and balances against possible excesses of delegated authority

Smiddy also issued eight blue books that were procedure manuals that tried to anticipate every possible situation. The objective was to institute layered interlocking control over processes preventing taking certain kind of decisions unilaterally. These included capital commitments, budget increases, hiring or firing, performance appraisals, and salary reviews. Everything was cross-linked with policies and procedures that were linked vertically and horizontally. This translated into uniformity in pay, organizational structure, rigid hierarchy of levels and span of control, policies and policies regardless of the size, and maturity of the business unit or its products. Thus, an outcome of Cordiner's reforms was that finance became an extremely powerful function. Charged with administering the Smiddy system, finance effectively became the final arbitrator by many a time exercising the *tiebreaking* vote in decision making. Finance rose in stature, since decentralization required, beefed up control, and, each P&L unit, needed its own manager of finance.

In place of Association Island, Cordiner established Crotonville, a management training center. The center sought to hard wire Cordiner's new approach into the collective consciousness of the management ranks. Toward this end, GE borrowed its faculty from outside sources; Peter Drucker, Chris Argyis, and a host of professors from Harvard Business School had a hand in devising the curriculum. This symbiotic relationship of GE with outside management experts created its own *benign cycle* wherein consultants laud GE's role as the pioneer of the newest management ideas put into practice that are naturally originated by the concerned consultants who have been compensated for their work with GE.

Cordiner recognized that managing a diversified, decentralized company would require a different type of manager. He believed that management was a profession just like engineering and accounting and that there were fundamental managerial principles that could be taught and should be taught. Professional managers, like engineers, were to be provided with tools and skills to attack any problems and manage any type of enterprise, regardless of its size, maturity, and technology. On the downside, this gave rise to a misplaced belief that *a great manager could manage anything.* Correspondingly, to measure effective performance, he instituted eight key result areas:

- Profitability
- Market share
- Productivity
- Product leadership
- Personnel development
- Employee attitudes
- Public responsibility
- The balance between short-term and long-term goals

Cordiner and Boulware decided that the company would need a tough-minded, talented people who could work with employees and help neutralize the power of the unions. They were instrumental in the move from the emphasis from personnel to human resources.

Overall, the period from 1950 to 1960 must be judged as highly positive for GE, since the company grew, grew profitably. However, this was marred greatly by the *great electrical conspiracy*, in 1959, when several very senior GE executives were found guilty of price fixing. It was widely believed that Cordiner's pressure to achieve the *hurdle rates* created a context in which such behavior became possible. This event hampered the company's ability to select its leaders and imposed a major drag on the company's growth.

8.3   BORCH ERA (1964–1972)

Against the backdrop of the price fixing scandal, the board selected Fred Borch, former president of GE's lightning business, as the next CEO of GE. Borch brought a refreshing change in style. Whereas Cordiner was aloof and directive, Borch tended to very involved. His approach was to solicit lot of input—then work behind the scenes through subordinates to give shape to his priorities. He softened his tone with his friendliness and accessibility. Borch's program of *calming the waters* gave line managers greater say in corporate resources allocation discussions and reemphasized the drive to recruit engineering talent. But he was not able to restore the harmonious working relationships prevalent during the prewar period nor recreate the requisite constructive tension between engineering, manufacturing, and finance.

Finance continued to overshadow other functions in most businesses. It gained still further clout when the collateral duties of strategic planning and information systems were added to its portfolio of responsibilities. GE Finance had historically maintained a strong dotted-line reporting relationship to the chief financial officer and, through him, to the CEO. This paralleled its solid-line relationship between the designated financial manager and his boss within the P&L unit. By board resolution, a manager of Finance could not be removed without approval of higher financial management. Further, the finance organization determined who filled the slot whenever vacancies occurred. To this day, a line manager at GE cannot select, hire, or fire his financial subordinate without review and concurrence of CFO.

Borch undertook an early effort at restructuring. Concluding that the P&L units were not succeeding because they were too big, he doubled their number to 300. This understandably led to excesses like GE's refrigerator unit spun off its compressor activities itself as a separate P&L unit. This precipitated so much cross-selling that this resulted in a thicket of transfer pricing. Moreover, it weakened GE's competence in sales and marketing even further in most businesses.

But Borch was more aggressive in striving to reposition GE in fields of the future. GE was back to its primary urge to diversify into new areas. Borch's major challenge was that the company had hit a $5 billion plateau; in response, he initiated a *growth council* to identify major growth opportunities. These included four product-oriented ventures (nuclear, computers, plastic, and aircraft engines) and five service opportunities (entertainment, community development, education, financial and personal services, and medical services). Borch got GE into housing, entertainment, and credit financing; he embarked on ventures in Europe and extended renewed support for aircraft engine and plastic businesses. The computer and nuclear power business were also back as strategic priorities and received an infusion of resources.

The failure of five of his nine ventures compelled Borch to rethink the company's strategies and portfolio mix. These failures had belied the commonly held belief that GE had unlimited financial, physical, and human resources and that its managers could manage anything. Borch created a task force headed by Dave Dance to determine what should be changed to make GE more successful in future. The task force recommendations resulted in the emphasis on strategic portfolio management. First, the study team recommended that the 100 product manufacturing departments be dissolved and replaced with 43 SBU based on servicing of clearly identifiable market segments and constituting customers. Second, recommendation was instituting new management and strategic planning systems that would enable the SBUs to understand the trends in their markets and anticipate external, competitive, and resource change that could impact their business. Thirdly, the Crotonville management training center needed to develop the strategic skills of its managers by instituting programs focused on strategic thinking, decision making, and planning.

Borch instituted a strategic-thinking and decision-making process that forced all of the company's businesses to critically and systematically assess their portfolios. For the first time in company's history, pruning and restructuring existing businesses became tenable. The freed resources were aggressively redeployed into more attractive and promising businesses. Accordingly, near the closure of his tenure, Borch undertook two far-reaching initiatives. First, he hired McKinsey consultants to look at organizational restructuring. GE underwent a massive recentralization by clustering its business units in 43 SBUs. Second, he implemented McKinsey-designed sophisticated system of strategic planning. While this and other state-of-the-art management techniques were well-intentioned efforts to tackle with GE's growing diversity, it was marred by the increasing tendency to apply such methodology indiscriminately resulting in suboptimal benefits.

Some of Borch's strategic thrusts paid off and reestablished avenues for future growth. The organization had begun to heal itself slowly after the turmoil of the Cordiner years. However, in course of time, Borch's multiple initiatives collectively began to represent unattainable goals—many of Borch's costly acquisitions in entertainment, modular housing, personal services, and education went nowhere. Further, GE's investments in computers were nearing a dead end; growing demands of GE's nuclear and aircraft engine businesses became sinks of major cash drains. More importantly, Borch's decentralization, as well as his endorsement of fee-based corporate services, also contributed to making GE more like a confederation of independent, often competing businesses than like a single, coherent company. Most of the GE business units had their own distinctive cultures. There has never been one *GE culture* since the company became highly diversified; each business is so different that it develops its own culture and style. Unlike GM, Ford, or IBM, there never was one GE style or culture. Employees identified more with their individual businesses than with the company as a whole. Often, there was competition among the departments, which added to the lack of company spirit. In fact, one reason the company has been able to be both diversified and successful is that more than one culture is tolerated.

8.4 JONES ERA (1973–1981)

By the end of Borch's era, the seeds for some extremely important new businesses were well planned, but debt also had increased and ROI dipped to an all-time low. In spite of the longest sustained boom of business expansion for over two decades, in constant dollar sales terms, GE was of the same size as at the end of World War II. It was only a matter of time before finance would emerge with direct control over GE's destiny. Reginald Jones spent 20 years in finance and distinguished himself on the auditing staff. He had a tour of duty in line assignments in early 1960s and returned to corporate office as chief financial officer and was elevated to the post of CEO in 1973. The era of 1970s was focused more on controls, ROI, and cash flow. Jones' foundation gave Welch the financial means to achieve growth that GE witnessed in the 1980s under Welch's leadership. He worked toward improving GE's relationship with employees and adopted a more conciliatory stance toward the union.

Jones strengthened the planning staff to more than 200 professionals and applied strategic planning methodology with great rigor. Jones implemented the SBUs that were originally instituted by Borch. While intended as a means to manage subsets of GE's portfolio, effectively he superimposed another layer of six sectors atop the layer of 43 SBUs. The sectors added finance and planning staff of their own and strove to achieve their sector numbers. The sectors became competitors, which split rather than unite the company. This led Welch to launch the *boundaryless* company initiative. However, the Sectors increased the overhead of the management layer superstructure tremendously. They imposed an overhead on GE's divisions not only in the accounting sense but also in the form of procedures for planning, reporting, and reviews. The forming of sectors complicated the strategic planning process and made planning a competitive game rather than just a development of the most appropriate strategies. This led Welch to introduce the work-out process. This layered structure also increased the *latency* or response time in making decisions compared with competitor firms who were usually CEOs of single product firms, who could decide and act unilaterally.

During this era, GE increasingly tended to view its businesses in purely financial terms and pioneered the application of portfolio management. Some decisions that were made at corporate level invariably translated into resource allocations that tended to jeopardize long-term competitiveness at the business level. Inevitably, this eventually resulted in harvesting certain core businesses like mobile communications while restricting financing in a few other high-tech businesses like factory automation. Fortuitously, aircraft engine and plastics business escaped this stranglehold as they were making their numbers.

Mobile communications was established in the late 1950s as part of Cordiner's quest for growth opportunities. The business flourished under Borch's watch to the extent that in 1972, Motorola held first position with a 40% share, GE was behind at 30% share followed further by a host of smaller players. With the market growing at 15% per year, GE was poised to exploit its strong number two position. Cellular phones were fast becoming staple of modern communications, and GE could have positioned itself as a leading player in this exploding market. However, unlike aircraft engine, GE's ability to build a significant competitive advantage in this market was thwarted by shortcomings of leadership, lack of corporate sponsorship, and underfunding. But as Jones faced the earnings pressure, the emphasis shifted to profits, and consequently, market share had to take a beating. Line management knew that its core product was increasingly vulnerable and passionately appealed for investment dollars, but in vain. Inevitably, Motorola attacked with a cheaper and technologically superior product, and by 1976, GE had fallen to a weak number two position with a market share of 17%. Japanese competitors entered the fray, and progressively mobile communications was relegated to the status of a divesture candidate and was sold to Siemens in 1989.

The GE strategic planning system was based on the reality that resources were limited and had to be allocated to those business units that had the highest potential. This was the beginning of the emphasis on human resource portfolio management. Per the new management and strategic planning system, a special session (session C) was included in the process to help ensure that the right people would be available to implement and lead the company. This entailed all of the key management and professional team members to be appraised and be put in one of three categories:

- Category I included the top 20%, that is, the *high potential people* for whom a career and succession plan had to be developed and shared with each one of them. These were the people who would be selected to attend the executive management program at Crotonville and otherwise given special assignments and mentoring.
- Category II included the next 70% of the overall population, that is, people who were considered to be meeting their job standards but were probably not going to be promoted to senior management positions.
- Category III included the bottom 10%, that is, those who were given the opportunity to improve their skills and performance or be fired.

Senior management evaluated all reviews and career plans of the top 20% and bottom 10% during the spring session C. These reviews and career plans were either accepted or modified. In October, the follow-up session C was held to review progress to ensure that the plans were being implemented. It was at this time that decisions were made about the bottom *10 percenters*; many of these individuals were pruned from the organization just as a business unit was pruned if its progress and performance were judged as inadequate.

In 1976, in an effort to push GE into the international mining sector, Jones made the most expensive acquisitions in U.S. history—Utah International (UI). But the acquisition failed to meet the company's expectation, and ultimately, it was divested by Jack Welch. During his final 5 years at the helm, Jones focused on succession planning, a process leading to the appointment of Welch as his successor.

Reginald Jones got GE's financial house in order. As he stepped down, the upside was that returns were strong and the company was widely admired. The downside was the straitjacket of strong controls that had been imposed to achieve these results and the divestures of promising businesses like mobile communications on account of aggressive harvesting. Jones placed extreme emphasis on strategic planning that created a climate in which entrepreneurial initiative was the rare exception.

8.5 WELCH ERA (1981–2001)

Jack Welch was one of the few successful in-house entrepreneurs at GE. He had almost single-handedly built a hugely successful 2-billion-dollar business in most unlikely of the fields—plastics. From there, he was promoted to group head, where he repeated his earlier success by overseeing the turnaround of GE's dying medical diagnostics business. He fought the internal battles necessary to invest in CAT-scan technology and established GE as world leader in medical imaging. Still later, as vice chairman, he began transforming GE capital from a financier of refrigerators and turbines into financial services powerhouse. Today, it is the nation's 14th largest lending institution. In short, Welch stood almost alone in his ability to grow business despite GE's controls. And Welch had done it three times.

Welch first focused on reversing the trend of declining earnings; he felt it essential to earn credibility in this domain in order to have latitude to maneuver later. GE was not under any perceived crisis; the only viable alternative was to take actions to shock GE's businesses out of their complacency. Between 1981 and 1986, Welch affected a 25% reduction of the total GE workforce amounting to elimination of 1,30,000 jobs, which exceeded even the reduction during the Great Depression; this alone generated savings of more than $6.5 billion. Reactions to these and other austerity measures were immediate and vociferous. He was nicknamed *Neutron Jack* alluding to the neutron bomb that destroys animate human beings but leaves inanimate buildings unaffected. He could not have remained insulated from the anguish and adverse reactions generated internally as well as its extensive coverage in the external media, but he endured it all hoping that the positive outcomes in future would ultimately justify these harsh measures.

Welch moved aggressively to divest weak holdings and squeeze out costs; UI was sold off for $2.9 billion. The cash generated enabled him to experiment by making a large number of small acquisitions; not all of them were successful. But earnings grew, and GE's stock reflected investor confidence in the new strategy. Welch was convinced that his best bets were in businesses in which GE was already number one or two and in which acquisitions could be made upon preexisting strengths to achieve accelerated growth. He conceptualized GE's portfolio as falling into three circles (core, services, and high technology), and those remaining outside the circles (mobile communications, housewares, TV and audio, and consumer electronics) were prime candidates for divesture. Finally, he used his reserves of cash for two major acquisitions, namely, RCA was acquired to strengthen NBC and its defense and aerospace portfolio, and employee reinsurance company was purchased to further strengthen GE capital. Overnight, GE's revenues increased by 30%. In the years since then, GE has ranked first in the world in two-thirds of its key businesses.

To sell the air-conditioning and small appliances business, Welch permitted Trane and Black & Decker to use the GE monogram for 5 years after the sale. Welch made a deal with Broken Hill properties to sell UI for $2.4 billion (after splitting out and retaining Ladd Petroleum). A few years later, Welch sold off Ladd for another half a billion dollars.

Welch's best play was reacquisition of RCA (see *The Coffin/Swope Era* earlier). As mentioned there, the broadcasting business was very attractive to GE because it possessed many of the same characteristics as the electrical business. RCA's acquisition enabled GE to move back into the TV network business and become its dominant player; it gave GE a strong position in the global satellite market and enabled GE to participate in the rapidly growing cable business. This also enabled Welch to bundle various GE and RCA businesses together to make them more attractive to divest, namely, the consumer electronic business, the semiconductor business, and the aerospace division. Welch integrated the GE and RCA consumer electronics brands, including television to make it the no. 1 brand, and then traded it (along with the GE monogram with any time limit) with Thomson of France for the medical systems business in addition to $1 billion cash. Welch packaged the GE and RCA semiconductor businesses and sold it to Harris (along with people and facilities) for $206 million. Welch combined the GE and RCA aerospace businesses and then sold them to Martin Marietta for a 25% stake.

Welch searched for avenues to breathe life and ownership into the ranks below. Hearing from his business heads that they were fettered by too many controls, he raised the signed-off limits, dramatically reduced the number of reports and indices, chopped away at headquarters staff, and embarked on a long-overdue campaign to redirect the finance and auditing staff to reposition themselves from being gatekeepers to supporters of line management. Cutting the groups and sectors eliminated communication filters enabling direct communications between the CEO and the leaders of the 14 businesses. This resulted in very short cycle times for decisions and little interference by corporate staff. A major investment decision that used to take a year or more were beginning to be taken in a matter of days.

Jack Welch operated by adopting six rules:

1. Face reality as it is, not as it was or as you wish it were.
2. Be candid with everyone.
3. Don't manage, lead.
4. Change before you have to.
5. If you don't have a competitive advantage, don't compete.
6. Control your own destiny or someone else will.

Another clear obstacle to renewal was GE's entrenched system of controls. He decided to do away with a lot of the intricate numbers and details that were causing us to miss the forest for the trees. He started this at the Corporate Executive Council (CEC) by changing the process of review for 14 of the key businesses. Each business was asked questions regarding relevant market conditions, competitor's strategies and GE's countervailing strategies, and GE's strategies for its own business. The CEC created a sense of trust, a sense of personal familiarity, and mutual obligation at the top of the company.

If the process of simplification had worked with his direct reports, there was a rationale for cascading it down through the entire organization to strip away controls, layers, and redundancy. In tandem with his head of executive development, James Baughman, Welch formalized this into a process called *work-out*. The work-out process was tailored to the specific needs of each business. It targets for obtaining clear commitments among management teams to eliminate wasteful practices. This process was facilitated by external consultants paid by corporate office. It entailed the systematic identification of productivity blocks and outdated work practices. Some businesses focus on specific problems, others of general issues, some on functional efficiencies, others on cross-functional operations. The objective was to create more fulfilling and rewarding jobs.

The second objective was on the leadership front that entailed putting the leaders of each business in front of a hundred or so of their people every month to let them hear what people think about their company, what they like and don't like about their work, about how they are evaluated, and about how they spend their time. Work-out exposed the leaders to the vibrations of their businesses—opinions, feelings, emotions, resentments, and not abstract theories of organization and management. GE would succeed if people could perceive the psychic or financial impact from the way the organization was working. He wanted GE to gain from the *differential dividend* of its employees. GE targeted to build a freer, stimulating, and creative environment, with incentives that tied directly to what people do.

Following on the work-outs, Welch launched an initiative called *boundaryless company* that was focused on promoting ideas from anywhere without any barriers between (say) domestic and foreign operations. Considering that the increase in scale and scope naturally lead to proliferation of unnecessary procedures that led to impedance or boundaries between various operations; it necessitated measures to effectively negate such divisive tendencies and increase the integration of these separated parts and motivate people to exchange ideas across the business units.

One of Welch's most famous initiatives involved GE's embrace of the *Six Sigma quality program*, which is a statistical quality control program and was imported from Motorola. Welch commissioned a cost-benefit analysis to study the approach and determine its potential payouts. They showed that if GE was running at three to four sigma, the cost-saving opportunity of raising this quality to six sigma was between $7 and $10 billion—which was a significant 10%–15% of sales. Welch clearly saw the huge bottom-line impact from pursuing the Six Sigma program, and hence, he instituted an adapted enterprise-wide program at GE.

Welch's gradual reforms at the CEC level along with processes such as work-out gradually began to address GE's most serious cultural problem: pervasive overcontrol. This was of paramount importance because corporate responsiveness increases in an organization as control decreases. A tiny change in growth has phenomenal effect on profits. But the subsequent increasingly difficult productivity gains cannot come from simple top-down edicts and movements but from bottom-up voluntary behavior, initiatives, and actions of the working teams and employees. Programs like employee involvement and chimney breaking had already gotten off the ground at GE; but GE's most far-reaching vehicle to enlist employee involvement, namely, work-out, brought it closer to achieving its objective of obtaining wholehearted worker commitment by the mid-1990s.

> A key lesson of this period was that all enterprises must be willing to challenge the status quo and make appropriate changes. GE was willing to make these kinds of far-reaching changes while it still had options and did not wait till it was too late. Most enterprises refuse to change when things are going well. They wait so long that by the time drastic change affects them, they go into a reactive mode that invariably involves unpalatable gut-wrenching maneuvers. This is a major difference between GE and other companies.

8.6 IMMELT ERA (2001–)

Jeff Immelt became GE's tenth CEO just days after the horrific events of September 2001. Immelt moved decisively to return GE to its technology-based heritage on a global scale. Up until the mid-1970s, GE obtained more patents annually than any other company. Its R&D center and product departments were encouraged to create new products that could be turned into new businesses. But when the company made the R&D center into a quasi-profit center, it shifted the focus from long-term breakthroughs to short-term applications and results. Most of the new businesses were acquired and not internally developed, and the company moved from being driven by advances in technology to being driven by its financial services and applications. Immelt restored the significance of R&D of new products as a part of the overall strategy. He believed that technology could produce high-margin products, win competitive battle, and create new markets. He invested in upgrading its Schenectady R&D labs and building research facilities in India, China, and Germany. GE began to put less focus on short-term projects and encourage more long-term research. GE Global Research consisted of more than 3000 employees working in four state-of-the-art facilities in Niskayuna (New York), Bangalore (India), Shanghai (China), and Munich (Germany).

Contrary to critics of globalization, who believed in the loss of jobs in developed economies, Immelt strongly believed that the loss of jobs would not be in the developed economies per se but more so in the low-tech industries that lack differentiation in the eyes of the customers; but in industries that are technically based and innovative, globalization will unlock decades of growth and jobs that would create wealth. GE's global revenues came majorly from Europe, followed by Pacific Basin, and the Americas; China and India are expected to provide the greatest growth globally. Other major targeted growth areas are consumer and commercial finance in Eastern Europe, the modernization of rail and power projects in Russia, and the rebuilding of Iraq's power network. However, making money in these countries would require long-term investments and commitment.

Health care has been one of the focus areas of GE's efforts since the invention of x-ray tube in 1920. As mentioned earlier, Welch traded consumer electronics business for the European Thomson medical systems business. Immelt ran this business beginning in 1997 and made many acquisitions to expand the business scope and geographic positions to build a $15 billion health-care business. This included making key acquisitions in electron beam tomography, ultrasound, 3D imaging systems, IT, diagnostic imaging agents, and life sciences.

Broadcasting and showbiz have always been high on GE's venture list. Recall that GE was one of the first companies to put together a successful transmission. The RCA windfall gave GE the opportunity to become network leader through the vehicle of NBC. NBC purchased the financial network to become the world's leading cable network known as *CNBC*. NBC established a strategic alliance with Dow Jones and combined its operations in Europe and Asia with the respective Dow Jones operations to form CNBC Europe and CNBC Asia. In the course of time, GE's showbiz business encompassed network, film, stations, entertainment, cable, TV production, sports and Olympics, and parks. Immelt believed that traditional, proven GE management and marketing processes can be used to make even the showbiz business more successful and profitable.

8.6.1   Ecomagination

GE had not been known over the years as a particularly environment-friendly company. One of the biggest environmental controversies involving GE was related to pollution of the Hudson and Housatonic rivers in the United States. Immelt felt that sustainability was a profitable business opportunity rather than a cost and hence seized on the idea of greening GE's technology and turning it into a corporate-wide strategy for growth. He felt that with creativity and imagination, it was possible to solve some of the world's most difficult environmental problems and make money while doing it. It was not a zero-sum game—things that were good for the environment were also good for business. Immelt wanted GE to support climate change and invest in creating new markets for cleaner fuels and technologies as they offered opportunities for product innovation.

In May 2005, Immelt launched the $150 billion environmental initiative of *ecomagination* signaling the transition from the traditional *infrastructure* businesses to *greening-enabled* business, which is about *greening and protecting the environment by combining ecology and imagination.* Ecomagination embodied GE's commitment to building innovative clean energy technologies and meeting customer's demands for more energy-efficient products and bringing reliable growth for the company. The main objectives of this green initiative were to reduce GHG emissions, increase energy efficiency of GE operations, improve water use, double the investment in R&D for cleaner technologies, and keep the public informed about its ecomagination efforts. GE set a target to reduce GHC emissions from its factory operations by 1% from a 2004 baseline and to improve energy efficiency by 30% by the end of 2012.

Some of the initiatives are listed in the following:

- GE rolled out several energy-efficient and renewable energy technologies at its facilities too, including products such as solar panels and advanced lightning systems that it manufactured itself.
- Within the company, GE began engaging employees to see where energy savings could be achieved.
- To reduce energy usage and GHG reductions, GE made use of the *energy treasure hunt* program developed by Toyota for similar objectives.

The ecomagination strategy covers areas like aircraft businesses, energy, oil and gas, water, wind, and energy finance. All *greening-enabled* businesses have characteristic attributes, namely, big and global, capital intensive, require financing the customer or taking an equity position, strong continuing service, and upgrade revenues.

 This put it back in the same position as the early Edison company, when the company was an equity owner of U.S. utilities. It may be that due to the continuing deregulation, the company might even move back into the ownership of major utilities—which is where it started all the way back in 1877.

Through ecomagination, GE developed products and services with lower environmental impact, such as energy-efficient engines, appliances, locomotives, and wind turbines. To ensure that ecomagination products and services improved environmental performance, GE employed a rigorous review and qualification procedure known as the ecomagination product review (EPR) process to assess which product and services should be included in the ecomagination portfolio. The evaluation process was audited by a third party. Product characteristics considered during the EPR process included environmental factors such as energy consumption, GHG emissions, and water usage, in addition to financial benefits of the product to customers, and these were analyzed relative to benchmarks such as competitor's products, regulatory standards, and also the historical performance. For each product, an extensive scorecard was created quantifying the product's environmental attributes, impact, and relative benefits relative to comparable products.

Ecomagination is one of the most successful cross-company business initiatives in GE's recent history. Since its launch in 2005, the initiative paid off in a big way as it helped GE to evolve as a sustainable enterprise and contributed to the rise in its brand value. In 2009, GE's GHG emissions were 20% below its 2004 baseline. Since its inception, the company had invested a total of U.S. $5 billion in the R&D investment and generated more than 15 times revenue through the end of 2009.

8.7 SUMMARY

This chapter explained the business variations throughout the life span of GE to unravel why it continues to reign supreme in the traditional manufacturing sectors of the economy. Very few firms can match GE over so prolonged a period of time. One of the key reasons for the company's astonishing long-term achievements has been its ability to recognize when even seemingly successful strategies need to be adapted and changed. GE's management has anticipated and responded successfully to major market shifts. The majority of GE's seven CEOs swung the pendulum to extremes. Coffin was the longest serving CEO of GE from 1892 until 1922; it was during this period that GE instituted its strong and disciplined financial and accounting systems, which became hallmark of GE. The financial collapse in 1893 put GE in a cash flow crunch that almost forced the company into bankruptcy. This traumatic event had profound effect on the financial strategies and policies of GE not only during the remaining tenure of Coffin but also for all future times. Swope's vision for GE during the period 1923–1939 encompassed its organizational culture, which included the cornerstones of engineering and manufacturing excellence, robust accounting and financial control systems, and emphasis on the GE *family*. GE licensed its technology throughout Europe, China, Japan, and Latin America in return for major positions in their electric companies.

The Cordiner/Reed team (1950–1963) decided that GE should remain diversified and revert to focusing only on electrical systems. Cordiner targeted consumer goods as a hot growth area in the postwar environment. A champion of the *organization as machine* mind-set of his day, Cordiner viewed decentralization as the primary remedy to GE's ills; an outcome of Cordiner's reforms was that finance became an extremely powerful function. Borch was more aggressive in striving to reposition GE in fields of the future—GE was back to its primary urge to diversify into new areas. Borch instituted a strategic-thinking and decision-making process that forced all of the company's businesses to critically and systematically assess their portfolios. During Jones' era (1973–1980), GE increasingly tended to view its businesses in purely financial terms and pioneered the application of portfolio management. Inevitably, this eventually resulted in harvesting certain core businesses like mobile communications. This was also the beginning of the emphasis on human resource portfolio management. Reginald Jones got GE's financial house in order. Welch's gradual reforms at the CEC level, along with processes such as work-out, gradually began to address GE's most serious cultural problem: pervasive overcontrol. This was of paramount importance because corporate responsiveness increases in an organization as control decreases. Immelt (2001–) moved decisively to return GE to its technology-based heritage on a global scale. GE began to put less focus on short-term projects and encourage more long-term research.

9 IBM

Toward the end of the nineteenth century, an engineer named Herman Hollerith invented a calculating machine that sorted cards by punched holes. Any kind of data could be recorded by punching holes according to a standard procedure, and then the data could be analyzed statistically to provide a picture of the overall results. Potential customers for this device were organizations, such as government agencies, railroads, and retail establishments, that needed a way of managing and manipulating large amounts of information. The U.S. Census Bureau, for example, saw the potential of this device for handling its national data collection efforts, and Hollerith was awarded a contract for managing the data processing of the 1890 census. Holes were punched in cards to represent different census attributes, such as age, sex, and national origin. The cards were then sorted by the punched holes, and Hollerith's calculating machine supplied the requested data, such as the statistics for the percentage of people in a certain age group in a certain state. The punch card machine required a huge number of punched cards—in the census, one for every family unit—that could be used only once, so each machine sale provided card revenue. Thus, although the machines performed quickly and accurately, they were expensive to operate. Nevertheless, the potential uses of the machine were limitless because any kind of data could be recorded on these cards.

 We would like to highlight that this case history is meant to highlight the variations during the life span of the company rather than to illustrate either effective or ineffective handling of an administrative situation.

9.1 PUNCH CARD MACHINES

James Powers, an employee of the U.S. Census Bureau, immediately saw the potential of the calculating machine. From his experience with Hollerith's machines at the Census Bureau, he developed an improved calculating machine, and, using his contacts at the Census Bureau, he managed to get the contract for the 1910 census. Having lost his principal customer, Hollerith approached Charles Flint, a financier and arms merchant, to get him to invest in the business to undertake further improvements in his machine. But Flint, seeing the opportunity to broaden his company's line of business machines, decided to acquire Hollerith's Tabulating Machine Company and merged it with ITR and Computing Scale to form the Computing Tabulating & Recording Company (CTR). This formed the seed of what was to become IBM.

Although Power's machine was technologically better, Hollerith had developed the practice of only leasing his machines to customers. Customers liked this arrangement because it lowered their operating costs. These leases provided CTR with a continuing source of revenues, but, more importantly, each of CTR's customers was required to buy their punch cards from CTR; 75% of the tabulating revenues came from the sale of the punched cards, while only 25% came from the lease of the actual machines. Also, Hollerith provided a repair service for the machines, which were prone to breakdown. Using CTR's resources, the calculating machines were continually improved over time, and the new and improved machines were leased to customers.

In 1914, Thomas Watson was hired as the general manager of CTR. Watson, who was a former employee at NCR, implemented many of NCR's sales strategies and practices at CTR that later became defining characteristics of IBM's culture for a long time in future. He began instituting many of the principles and practices for which IBM would become known: dark-suited salespeople, a strong culture of corporate pride and loyalty, implied lifetime employment, and a work ethic expressed in the slogan *THINK*. Although NCR's competitors had higher quality cash registers than NCR, NCR consistently beat the competition because of the way it organized and rewarded its sales force. NCR had a strong sales force in which salespeople were granted exclusive territories and paid on commission. This made them aggressively pursue all sales opportunities in their territories. They continually called on customers and built strong, personal relationships with them. The leadership at NCR insisted that NCR salespeople answer repair calls immediately and instilled in them that they were selling a service not just a product. NCR also established the NCR *Hundred Point Club*, which recognized and rewarded salespeople who had exceeded their quotas; members of the club received bonuses and trips to conventions in big cities, coverage in the company newspaper, and congratulations from the top guy. Watson implemented all these practices at CTR to attract and retain good employees and gain the commitment of its workforce.

Watson implemented a plan to develop new tabulators, recorders, and printers to print the output of the tabulating machine. To achieve this new plan, the company funded the development of a research laboratory to improve the tabulating machines and established a facility to train salespeople. His goal was to create a sales force like NCR's sales force and make better tabulating machines than CTR's competitors. Watson became chairman of CTR in 1924 and renamed the company International Business Machines (IBM). Its strategy was to lease its machines and then support the machines with trained service representatives who were available to handle customers' problems and make suggestions for improving customers' information processing as their individual businesses changed. Leasing gave IBM several competitive advantages over Burroughs, NCR, and Remington Rand who all sold machines. First, it allowed the company to retain control over outdated technology that could not be resold in the used market (a problem NCR had encountered). Second, leasing made it easier for the customers because they were not committed to a large capital outlay or purchasing outmoded machines. Third, leasing provided IBM with a steady cash flow. Tabulating machines were increasingly used by large companies to keep records on their employees, suppliers, and customer accounts. Companies usually leased IBM's machines; IBM developed a specific punch card system to meet the needs of each individual customer. For example, IBM developed a coding system appropriate to each client's information processing needs.

By 1939, IBM was the biggest and most powerful business machine company in the United States. IBM owned about 80% of the keypunches, sorters, and accounting machines used for tabulating purposes. By this time, Remington Rand and Burroughs were minor competitors, and the Powers company had disappeared, unable to match IBM's strengths in sales and R&D.

9.2 VACUUM-TUBE-BASED COMPUTERS

Toward the end of World War II, J. Presper Eckert and John Mauchly invented a computer called ENIAC to solve math problems for the army to compute ballistic tables for the big guns of World War II. The machine had cost $3 million to build, it was constituted of 18,000 vacuum tubes, took a long time to set up, and was very difficult to use. Realizing that computers could take the place of punch card tabulating machines and would eventually be used in business, they created a company to develop and manufacture a computer for commercial use, the UNIVAC (standing for UNIVersal Automatic Computer). In 1948, they received an order from the U.S. Census Bureau for their computer (just as Hollerith had 60 years before), and in the same year, Prudential Insurance also ordered a UNIVAC. These organizations were two of IBM's largest customers, and so IBM became interested in the new computer technology. Just as Watson had realized the potential of the punch card machine, so Remington realized the potential of the computer. In 1950, Remington Rand, which also sold typewriters, tabulators, filing cabinets, and electric shavers, forestalled IBM and bought Eckert and Mauchly's company to gain entry into the new computer market.

After looking at the ENIAC computer, which used the new electronic circuits, Watson, Jr. encouraged IBM's research laboratory managers to recruit more electronic specialists. He prodded IBM to incorporate electronic circuits in punch card machines because a primitive electronic circuit could perform 5000 additions per second compared to 4 per second for the fastest mechanism in a punch card machine. Working quickly, and with access to the company's large resource base, IBM developed a new machine in 1946 that could compute payroll in one tenth the time a punch card machine could do it. The machine's success convinced Tom Watson, Jr. and his father that electronics would perform even faster. From this time on, the company committed its resources to developing an advanced new computer system, just as 30 years before Tom Sr. had bet CTR's future on advanced punch card machines.

At the threshold of the computer era in 1952, he turned leadership over to his son, Thomas Watson, Jr. IBM's research lab had been dominated by engineers because its punch card machines operated on mechanical principles. None of its engineers understood electronics, however; so Watson, Jr. hired a new lab chief and increased the staff from 500 mechanical engineers and technicians in 1950 to more than 4000 electrical engineers by 1956. Watson, Jr. also created a smaller lab in California to specialize in storage devices. In less than 3 years, this lab invented the computer disk that stores data on magnetic tape that became the backbone of IBM's future computer systems. Watson, Jr. also led the development of the IBM 650 in 1956, which provided enough data processing power for most general commercial applications. The 650 introduced thousands of punch card customers to computers. It was designed to work with ordinary punch card equipment but made the punch card system much more powerful and versatile. For example, life insurance companies compute insurance premiums from actuarial tables based upon the age, sex, and other customer factors. Using a 650, these actuarial tables could be loaded into the computer memory, and when the punch card containing information on a customer was loaded into the machine, the computer did the calculations and furnished the total. Previously, a clerk had to figure the totals and record the information on a punch card for recording purposes; the 650 did everything.

IBM put its huge sales force behind the 650 machine, and as a result of its efforts, within a year, almost 1000 machines were sold. Most computers were used in administrative offices and in factories for controlling the manufacturing process. By the end of the 1950s, IBM had a 75% market share. The remaining market was divided among Remington Rand, Honeywell Electronics, NCR, and a few others.

9.3 TRANSISTOR-BASED COMPUTERS

In 1956, William Shockley at Bell Labs developed the transistor, weighing 100 times less than the vacuum tube, as a replacement for the vacuum tube; compared to a vacuum tube, the transistor required a lot less electrical power, could perform calculations at a much faster rate, and had the potential to miniaturize computing systems. The transistor made it feasible both to design a more complex and powerful computer and sell it at a price that most companies could afford. By 1960, IBM's computer division had a product line consisting of eight newer transistor-based computers and several older vacuum tube machines. This caused several problems for IBM's customers because the computers were not compatible. For example, if a customer expanded and wanted to upgrade to a larger or newer computer, the customer had to lease a whole new range of equipment and rewrite all the programs to make the computer work in the company. The disjointed product line was also causing problems for IBM's personnel in providing effective support and services. Its attempt to become the leader in the industry resulted in the development of a fragmented product line that was confusing its customers and employees.

IBM needed to build a line of computers that would cover the needs of the whole computer market. The project was called the System/360, representing 360° in a circle, because IBM wanted to meet the needs of a whole spectrum of users in both the scientific and business community; all of the 360 computers would be compatible with one another. Moreover, they would all use the same operating language, software, disk drives, printers, etc. The goal of this design was to lock in customers to IBM's computer systems and make it difficult for customers to change to competing products. Their incentive would be to keep buying new IBM products when they wanted to upgrade their systems. The other goal of the system was to make it easier for its sales force to be able to sell an integrated package of products to customers. The System/360 mainframe computer was launched in 1964 and captured 70% of the market. It offered the revolutionary new concept of compatibility, allowing customers to use the same printers and other peripherals with any 360 machine. The project was an immense success and put IBM way ahead of its competitors. Although before the 360, competitors such as RCA, Burroughs, Honeywell, UNIVAC, and GE sold machines that performed much better than IBM computers for the same price, the compatible design and the power of the System/360 beat all competitors. Around this time, IBM acquired the nickname *Big Blue* because of the color of its muscular blue mainframe computers (mirrored in the blue suits adopted by IBM executives). So dominant was IBM by the late 1960s that it became the target of an unsuccessful 13-year-long antitrust action by the U.S. Justice Department.

IBM created a check and balance system in IBM called *contention management*. This system forced both staff and line managers to meet and encouraged them to debate the merits of an idea; no operating plan became final without staff approval. When line and staff managers could not agree, the problem was sent to the corporate management committee—the top six executives. Over time, however, an increasing number of issues were sent to the top of the organization to resolve, and it became accepted that top management would resolve important strategic issues. Thus, despite Watson's claimed policy of decentralizing authority to divisional managers and their subordinates, much of IBM's decision making remained centralized at the top of the organization. Managers from IBM's mainframe division, its chief revenue earner, had the most power in shaping corporate decision making.

In 1970, Dick Watson resigned to become the U.S. ambassador to France, and Tom Watson, Jr. suffered a heart attack that resulted in his retirement in 1971. When Tom Watson, Jr., appointed T.V. Learson as CEO in 1971, the period of the Watson family's control over IBM came to an end. IBM was the largest, most successful computer company in the world and had achieved complete domination over the global computer industry. He initiated and oversaw the development of IBM's new, more powerful System/370 computer series. Technical advances lowered the System/370's price per calculation to 60% less than that of the System/360s, plus the 370 had a larger information storage system. Under Learson's control, and then under the control of Frank Cary who became CEO when Learson retired in 1973, IBM continued to enjoy its domination of the mainframe market. By 1980, IBM had a market value of $26 billion, four times its size in 1971.

From 1970 onward, IBM became concerned about the threat of low-cost, foreign competition in the mainframe computer market after witnessing the decline of several U.S. industries, including automobiles, due to the entry of low-cost Japanese competitors. The price of ICs, the heart of a mainframe computer, was plummeting at this time, and Japanese companies had the technical capability to build a powerful computer that could match or exceed the IBM 370. The existence of a low-cost global competitor was a major threat to IBM's domination of both the U.S. market and the global market. Its major competitors at the time like Amdahl, Honeywell, Burroughs, UNIVAC, NCR, and Control Data began offering IBM's customers mainframe systems at a lower cost than the expensive IBM systems. Initially, IBM faced competition only from companies selling IBM-compatible peripheral equipment such as disk drives, storage devices, and printers at lower prices than IBM's products. Its sales force had been able to ward off such threats. Now, however, the nature of competition was changing. IBM's competitors began selling cheaper, higher-performing,

IBM-compatible central processing units (CPUs)—the brain of the computer and the source of its processing power. For the first time, competitors were offering a low-price alternative to the IBM mainframe. Another emerging low-price threat came from leasing companies. These leasing companies would buy old 360s from IBM and lease them on better terms than IBM offered, attracting price-conscious IBM customers. While these competitive threats were small, they nevertheless gave IBM cause for concern.

In response to the threat of low-cost competition, Cary announced that IBM would spend $10 billion to build new automated plants to produce low-cost computers over a 6-year period. In this way, IBM would be able to meet the challenge of low-priced computers should the threat materialize and its customers start to switch to low-cost competitors. John Opel, who became IBM's CEO in 1981, was also concerned about competition from Japan and carried on with Cary's low-cost producer strategy. Because the computer life span was getting shorter and because of the growing low-cost competition, IBM decided to begin selling and phase out IBM's system of leasing machines to customers. IBM devoted most of its immense resources to developing technically superior mainframe products, lowering the cost of production, and supporting its very expensive but very successful sales force.

IBM's push to reduce manufacturing costs did not fit well with its strategy of offering excellent customer service and using its very expensive sales force to sell and service its machines. It was unlikely that IBM would ever be able to compete on price with its competitors because its customer service and support activities raised its costs so much. Moreover, competing on price had never been a part of its strategy; IBM always had competed on its unique ability to provide customers with an integrated, full-line computer service.

9.4 MINICOMPUTERS

Minicomputers were smaller and priced anywhere from $12,000 to $700,000, which was significantly cheaper than mainframe computers. Two researchers from the Massachusetts Institute of Technology pioneered the development of a smaller, more powerful computer. They founded the Digital Equipment Corporation (DEC), which, in 1965, launched the PDP-8, a computer that could handle the smaller information processing needs and tasks of companies such as small businesses, offices, factories, and laboratories. The venture was very successful, and by 1968, DEC's sales reached $57 million, and its earnings were $6.8 million. DEC's computer competed with the lower end of the 360 range. The computer sold well in research facilities, but it did not do as well in business, because IBM dominated this market with its powerful sales force. However, DEC had plans to develop a more powerful machine. As it grew, it was quickly expanding its own national service network, imitating IBM's.

To meet DEC's challenge, which was still seen as a minor issue, Cary formed the General Systems Division in 1969. Its goal was to produce the System/3, which was to be IBM's small, powerful minicomputer. IBM did not, however, rethink its technology or invest resources to develop new minicomputer technology to make a product to suit this new market segment. Rather, IBM tried to adapt its existing mainframe technology to the minicomputer market. The result was that when the System/3s were developed, they were too big and too expensive to compete with DEC's machine and too small to compete with IBM's own mainframes. This caused them to fail to make much inroad into what was becoming a very big market segment. As the minicomputer segment of the market continued to grow rapidly in the 1970s, Cary tried to increase the importance of the minicomputer group inside IBM's corporate hierarchy by reorganizing IBM's data processing division and splitting it into two units: general systems to make minicomputers and data systems to make the mainframes. He hoped that this change would force IBM managers to change their mindset and support the company's move into the new markets.

IBM's top managers had risen up the ranks of IBM from the mainframe division and were conditioned by the idea that the level of computing power was everything: big machines meant big revenue. IBM's mainframe managers saw the potential earning power of the minicomputer as insignificant when compared to the huge revenues generated by its mainframes. Cary's change of structure created huge divisional rivalry between mainframe and minicomputer managers. The mainframe division saw itself as being in direct competition for resources with the minicomputer division. Managers in both units failed to cooperate and share technological resources to develop the new range of machines. Nevertheless, it was successful, as many IBM customers had large sums of money invested in IBM mainframes and were reluctant to switch suppliers; they moved to adopt the IBM minicomputer system because it was compatible with their IBM mainframe systems.

Effected by the *mainframe mindset*, this situation would recur again and again during waves of technological breakthroughs in the future. IBM's responses were invariably late, suboptimal, proprietary, and entailed charging a premium—all of which was increasingly resisted and greeted unfavorably by the customers. Managers continued to be arrogant and complacent and believed completely in IBM's preeminence despite all the warning signs that it had lost its competitive edge. Its top management committee, staffed primarily by managers from its mainframe division, repeatedly misread the competitive threat posed by disruptive products that periodically burst forth in newer market segments; turf battles between autonomous divisions often absorbed more energy than marketplace battles. They seemed unable to make the type of innovative decisions that would allow IBM to respond quickly to the rapidly changing computer environment. The result was a failure to develop products fast enough and a mistaken commitment to the mainframe computer. Even its renowned salespeople had become a problem for the company: Committed to the IBM product, they had become oriented to selling and servicing the mainframe; they were not oriented toward satisfying customer needs, which was more inclined toward using a minicomputer or a workstation.

For example, IBM could not respond quickly to the price cutting moves of its rivals and introduce new kinds of PCs because of its centralized decision-making style. Whenever a competitor reduced prices, managers of the PC division had to get approval from the corporate management committee to cut prices, a process that sometimes took months. As a result, the PC division was never able to forestall its rivals. Moreover, just as in the case of minicomputers, rivalry between PC and mainframe managers hampered efforts to quickly exploit the potential of the powerful new microprocessors (and the PC). Above all, even though it was clear that new segments of the computer market were developing and that new uses for computers were being found, IBM managers still repeatedly discounted the potential threat to mainframes from either the minicomputer or the PC or the workstations and other innovations in the future.

In 1986, DEC introduced its new VAX 9000 minicomputer. This new minicomputer shocked IBM's mainframe managers because it had the same speed and capacity as IBM's largest 370 mainframe, the 3090, but cost only 25% as much. For the first time, mainframe managers were forced to accept the fact that minicomputers might be feasible substitutes for mainframes in many applications. Although DEC gained business with its new machine in market segments previously dominated solely by IBM, such as large financial service companies and corporate data processing centers, it still could not seize many of IBM's loyal customers who were locked into IBM systems.

As a result of the success of its new minicomputers, IBM increased its market share from about 16% in 1988 to 28% in 1992, while DEC's market share fell. IBM now had a $14 billion business in minicomputers, which have gross margins of 56%.

By the mid-1980s, IBM's products were universally regarded as sound solutions to a range of business problems, as was apparent from the oft-repeated dictum that "nobody ever got fired for buying IBM."

9.5 PERSONAL COMPUTERS

The microprocessor or *computer on a chip* sparked the development of the PC, which was developed in 1977 by Steven Jobs and Stephen Wozniak, the cofounders of Apple. By 1980, Apple's sales had grown to $117 million. Once again, IBM stood by and watched as a new market segment was created. This time, recognizing the mistakes it had made in the minicomputer market by not moving quickly enough to develop a machine to compete with the industry leader, it decided to move quickly to create its own machine to compete with Apple's. In an effort to enter the PC market quickly, IBM outsourced and bought the inputs it needed from other companies to make its PC. For example, Intel supplied the 8088 microchip that was the heart and Microsoft delivered MS-DOS, the programming language and software applications for the new IBM machine. Finally, computer stores, not the IBM sales force, were used to sell the new IBM PCs to get the machines to individual customers quickly.

IBM's first PC, more powerful than the first Apple computer, was introduced at a price of $1565 in 1981. Intel's 8088 chip had more main memory and was more powerful than the chip used in the Apple II computer, and Microsoft's operating system, MS-DOS, was better than the current industry standard. These features, combined with the power of the IBM brand name, made the IBM PC an immediate success; it quickly became the industry standard for all other PCs. Backed by IBM's legendary service, business users turned to the machines in the thousands. By 1984, IBM had seized 40% of the PC market.

The runaway success of the IBM PC attracted imitators; soon, clone manufacturers were selling IBM-compatible PCs as powerful or more powerful than IBM's own machines. For example, Compaq, founded in 1981, began to clone IBM PCs and produced a high-powered machine that seized a large share of the high-price business market. In 1986, Compaq beat IBM to the market with a machine using Intel's powerful new 386 chip. At the same time, other clone makers, such as Zenith and Packard Bell, attacked the low-price segment of the computer market and began producing PCs that undercut IBM's. IBM's competitors moved quickly to encourage the development of powerful new NetWare software. This software could link PCs together and to a more powerful computer, such as a minicomputer or a workstation, so that a network of PCs could work as effectively as a mainframe—but more conveniently and at only a fraction of the cost.

IBM, threatened both in the high-price and low-price end of the PC markets, fought back with the PS/2. It had a proprietary hardware channel that IBM made sure could not be imitated, as its first PC had been. However, customers resisted buying the new PS/2. They did not want to become locked into a new IBM system that was not compatible with IBM's old system and their other software or hardware investments. In the face of hostility from its customers, and losing market share, IBM was forced to back down. In 1988, IBM began producing PS/2s that were compatible with the existing industry standard—ironically, its own older standard.

It was suddenly clear to IBM that it no longer controlled the rules of the competitive game in the PC industry. Nonetheless, it was still slow to change its strategy. Despite the fact that its cheaper rivals had machines that were as powerful as its own, IBM still attempted to charge a premium price for its product. In response, its customers went elsewhere. Throughout the 1980s, IBM's PC division (which is the biggest PC operation in the world) could not respond quickly to the price cutting moves of its rivals and introduce new kinds of PCs because of its centralized decision-making style.

9.5.1 WORKSTATION COMPUTERS

While PCs are designed for individual jobs such as word processing and financial analysis, workstations essentially are very powerful PCs designed to be connected to each other and to a mainframe through software. Workstations can analyze financial results and track inventories much faster than PCs and much more cheaply than minicomputers or mainframes. A network of workstations can also be linked to an even more powerful workstation (or minicomputer) called a file server, which contains a company's files and databases or which can retrieve them from a company's mainframe computer. Workstations, usually priced from $5,000 to $100,000, were increasingly utilized by business professionals. New network software links workstations so that many people can work together simultaneously on the same project. These desktop machines have *user-friendly* graphic displays and allow people at different machines to share data and software. By 1988, the workstation market was $4.7 billion.

Underestimating the potential power of PCs and slow to develop powerful minicomputers, IBM managers once again failed to see the potential of an emerging market. Underestimating the potential power of PCs and slow to develop powerful minicomputers, IBM managers once again failed to see the potential of an emerging market. IBM had only a 3.9% market share in 1987, compared to Sun Microsystems's 29% and Apollo's 21%, the two upstart companies that were the innovators of the workstation. Once they realized the importance of this market segment, both IBM and DEC introduced workstations based on RISC processors, which make machines two to three times faster. After the failed attempt with IBM RT PC in 1986, IBM finally launched the RS/6000 workstation in 1989 and captured 18% of the $11.3 billion market by the end of 1991. But, IBM was facing severe competition from DEC, Sun, Apollo, and HP, all of which sold RISC workstations.

9.6 CORPORATE REORGANIZATION

To fight the trend toward PCs and workstations, IBM attempted to make its 370 computer the central component of a network of computers that link individual users to the mainframe. However, this move was not successful as sales growth for its biggest mainframe, the 370 dropped to half. The market for mainframe computers, IBM's principal source of revenue, was declining as machines such as PCs and workstations were able to perform mainframe tasks at lower cost. By 1990, IBM was facing stiff competition in all the developing segments of the computer market, from companies that were mainly specialized in one market niche, for example, Microsoft in the software segment or Sun Computer in the workstation niche. IBM was fighting to increase its market share in each market segment but was suffering because of tough competition from strong competitors that had developed their own loyal customer following in each of these market segments.

As a result of this shift, suppliers of computer components such as chips and software were the winners, as their share of industry profits rose from 20% in 1986 to 31% in 1991. Thus, for example, the share prices of Microsoft and Intel, which control the software and microprocessor markets, respectively, soared. Similar growth occurred in the share prices of Conner, Quantum, and Seagate, which dominated disk drives, as well as Andersen Consulting and EDS, which were the leaders in system integration (Figure 9.1).

IBM's focus was mainframes and its continuing belief that its own proprietary hardware and software would become the industry standard seems to have been the source of its reluctance to enlarge and expand its software operations. IBM has always realized the importance of developing proprietary software that can link and join its mainframes, minicomputers, workstations, and PCs to provide customers with a completely integrated computer package. It failed, however, to recognize the developing market for company-specific databases and application systems. After assessing the challenges of developing its own software applications, IBM belatedly embarked on a program to forge alliances with many small, independent software companies to develop software for IBM machines quickly. IBM embarked on a project called Systems Application Architecture

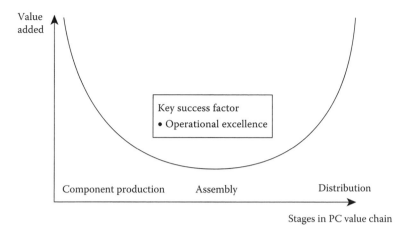

Value added

Key success factor
• Operational excellence

Component production   Assembly   Distribution

Stages in PC value chain

FIGURE 9.1   Value added in the different steps of the PC value chain (*smile curve*).

(SAA), which is a set of rules for links between programs and computers. SAA would facilitate the creation of networks with all types of machines, including mainframes and PCs. Software and services accounted for 40% of IBM's revenue in 1992. IBM wanted to achieve 50% of revenues from software and services by the year 2000.

The systems integration market and outsourcing market were now growing at 19% annually. IBM's failure to enter this market early allowed its competitors—principally EDS and Andersen Consulting, the accounting firm that early on established a computer consulting division—to gain a first-mover advantage and dominate the market. To quickly develop a presence in this lucrative market, IBM began developing alliances with various organizations. It formed a joint venture with Coopers & Lybrand to provide management consulting in selected industries. IBM also teamed with AT&T to make IBM's mainframes work better with AT&T's network management systems. IBM established the Integrated Systems Solutions Corporation subsidiary in 1991 to provide a platform for IBM to enter the data processing outsourcing market. The subsidiary did outsourcing for 30 companies, including Continental Bank. IBM would run all of a client company's systems, from mainframes and workstations to voice and data telecommunication.

In 1985, John Akers became CEO and was charged with the task of using IBM's vast resources to make it the market leader in the new lucrative market segments of the computer industry and reduce IBM's dependence on mainframes. The *mainframe mindset* coupled with the *contention system* was resulting in a failure to develop products fast enough and a mistaken commitment to the mainframe computer. Akers realized the need to restructure the company and change IBM's highly centralized style of decision making if it was to innovate the next generation of products and emerge as a market leader in the new market segments. Akers recognized that the biggest problem for IBM was its highly bureaucratic organizational structure that slowed decision making and continually frustrated attempts to be innovative and entrepreneurial.

While revenues softened, fixed costs burgeoned. Parts of the company were still operating in growth mode. New buildings were being constructed. Warranty costs reached record levels, and customers became more vocal about quality problems. At the heart of the company's problems were its evolved product complexity and the organizational silos that had developed to manage it. IBM had 20 separate business units, which collectively sold 5,000 hardware products and 20,000 software products. There were different designs for components that served exactly the same purpose in different products. Different business processes were used in different parts of the company for accomplishing the same thing. Where commonality did exist in products or processes, it was not fully exploited. Most telling was IBM's poor performance in the area in which it should have been most expert—internal IT management. The company had 125 separate data centers worldwide and 128 CIOs. There were 31 private and separate networks and literally hundreds of different configurations of PC installations. Data processing costs were a dramatic three times the industry average.

Executives were isolated from the growing problems by deep levels of hierarchy, a heavy reliance on an army of corporate staff, and a consensus driven decision-making culture. Decisions *made by committee* took an exceedingly long time and a *nonconcur* from any one member could overrule general agreement on a course of action. Executives had large staffs and little direct involvement in writing their own reports. They delivered presentations prepared by staff members during numerous *premeetings* in which the staff worked to align positions and eliminate surprises. Armies of staff members attended executive meetings, lingering in hallways or—in the case of very senior staff—seated close behind their executive in the meeting room, armed with volumes of backup material. Prepared presentations dominated even informal meetings, and most executives had projectors built into their office furniture.

As noted earlier, since the 1970s, IBM employed a *contention* system to control new product development. In this system, two or more project teams designed competing product prototypes, and a series of committees at both the divisional level and the corporate level met over a period of months to debate the merits of each project. A project would be approved after six committee members rated the two processes, which could take months or years; then the committee met to finalize the product plan. During this process, if any committee member said, "I nonconcur," meaning that he or she disagreed with the project, it would be sent back for further review or scrapped. The result of the contention system was that the projects that were approved were generally successful. However, the time frame associated with making the decision was generally so long that products were late to market, putting IBM at a competitive disadvantage. For example, the small, independent team charged with the development of the first IBM PC launched the product in 1 year. However, once the PC group was put into the information systems and communication division and decision making became constrained by IBM's contention system, the speed of the development process slowed significantly. For example, the PS/2 was not introduced until 1987, missing the 1985 target.

To speed decision making, in January 1998, Akers reorganized IBM into seven divisions based on the main product market segments in which the company was competing: PC systems, midrange systems, mainframes, information systems and communications, technology development (such as microchips), programming, and software. The idea behind the reorganization was to demolish the mainframe mindset by giving the managers of each division the autonomy and responsibility for developing new products for their respective markets.

The sales divisions would still be responsible for selling the whole range of IBM products, however, and control over sales would be centralized at corporate headquarters. The logic was that customers wanted a sales force that could handle their entire computer needs, and there were synergies from having one sales force provide a full set of products and services. IBM's traditional focus on service was still a strong competitive advantage. The disadvantage of the single sales force was that each division would not be able to devise a sales strategy specific to its own competitive environment, and salespeople would not be able to focus on a single product line. IBM felt that the economies of scale and scope provided by a unified sales force outweighed these disadvantages.

The 1988 reorganization was a failure. Although each division was supposed to become more autonomous, in reality, most decisions still required approval by IBM's corporate headquarters managers—managers who had risen through the ranks from the powerful mainframe computer division. Products that might have cannibalized the sale of mainframes were still discouraged by corporate managers, who, having achieved their success during the mainframe era, were hesitant to introduce products to compete with mainframes.

So, IBM announced another restructuring at the end of 1991, which was aimed at decentralizing decision-making authority to the divisions and reducing the role of IBM corporate headquarters in setting divisional strategy. The goal of the restructuring effort was to make the divisions independent units operating under a broad IBM umbrella, thus freeing them from corporate control, freeing up IBM's powerful resources and make it more competitive. Division heads would have control over long-term development and business level strategy. Akers' plan was that each division would be an autonomous operating unit that could freely negotiate transfer prices of inputs with other divisions and, if a division wanted to, buy from and sell to outside companies. The divisions were to treat each other as they would outside companies; no favorable prices were to be granted to IBM divisions. Moreover, the performance of each division would be reported separately, and each division would be accountable for its individual profits and losses. The heads of the divisions were responsible for developing annual business plans and were to guarantee IBM a certain return on money invested in their division. Again, the sales force was to remain a separate entity whose job would still be to sell the whole line of IBM products.

To allow the PC division to respond faster to the quickly changing PC market, Akers decided to place the PC business in a separate operating unit. In 1991, Akers formed the IBM Personal Computer Company and gave it control over the design, production, distribution, and marketing of IBM PCs. Prior to this change, distribution was performed by IBM's large sales and marketing division. To demonstrate the commitment to IBM's more autonomous and entrepreneurial approach to doing business, IBM's PC division was given total control over its own sales and named an independent unit in 1992. James Cannavino, the head of the PC unit, took total control over the PC division's strategy and organized the PC division around products instead of functions. Each product group was in charge of its own brand development, manufacturing, pricing, and marketing. This change was designed to allow the product groups to respond much more quickly to changes in the PC market, where products may have a life span of only 6 months to a year.

9.7   CORPORATE RENEWAL

Despite the 1991 organization, IBM's profits and revenues continued to decline; 1991 loss of $2.8 billion was the first loss in IBM's history. In 1992, IBM's losses increased to $5 billion on $65 billion in revenues. Pressure for change at the top was increasing. Under pressure from investors and the public, John Akers resigned in January 1993. The board of directors chose an outsider to be the CEO of IBM; Louis Gerstner, former CEO of RJR Nabisco was the first outsider to have occupied the top job; he had engineered a major turnaround in the performance of American Express and Nabisco. While many wondered how an executive with no technology background could rescue IBM, insiders knew that Gerstner was brought in not to rescue the company but to break it up for sale. In no time, however, Gerstner learned from customers, analysts, and employees that IBM's value was not in its pieces but *One IBM*. Reversing direction, he rallied support for saving IBM.

One IBM became the impetus for reorganizing the company. Gerstner and his reconstituted top management team spent all of 1993 analyzing how IBM worked, as a prelude to *reengineering the corporation*. Gerstner formed an 11-person *CEC* of IBM's top managers to spearhead the reengineering effort. Eleven task forces were formed to analyze IBM's main processes, which were modeled on the reengineering effort that Cannavino had performed in the PC division. Another group, the worldwide management council (WMC), composed of the top 35 people including geographic leaders and division presidents, met monthly to define and execute global tactical strategy and operations. Reengineering refers to a two-step process whereby an organization first identifies and analyzes each of the core business processes—manufacturing, marketing, R&D, and so on—that make a business work and then changes or reengineers them from the bottom-up to improve the way they function. Consequently, this effort led IBM to a product group structure, in which each group took control over its own manufacturing and marketing—a change that had been very successful in the PC division during Akers' stint. Gerstner hoped that a corporate-wide effort would also prove successful.

He spent his first few months as CEO on a whistle-stop tour interviewing IBM's managers; he also visited many of IBM's largest corporate customers to discover what they wanted from IBM now and in the future. Gerstner soon announced that he intended to keep IBM as a single united company. His strategic analysis led him to conclude that IBM's ability to provide clients with a complete and comprehensive computing or IT solution that could be customized to each client's particular needs was the source of its future competitive advantage. IBM's principal problem was to find a better way to integrate the activities of its hardware, software, and service (HS&S) groups to create more value for customers. In other words, Gerstner decided that IBM needed to work toward offering clients an improved, more comprehensive IT package.

Contrary to the belief of most of the analysts' about Gerstner continuing with Akers' thrust on decentralizing decision making to the divisions, and even spinning off IBM's businesses into independent companies, Gerstner moved in diametrically opposite direction, which, on the face of it, reaffirmed the traditional approach in most of the areas:

- Gerstner and his top management team believed that IBM's core strategy of being a full service company was appropriate.
- Gerstner believed that IBM should continue to follow its traditional strategy of providing customers with a full line of hardware and software products and services.
- Gerstner affirmed his support for the mainframe division.
- Gerstner announced that he would not change the current companywide sales force structure. The current sales force of 40,000 salespeople would still pursue the strategy of *one face to a customer*.
- Gerstner believed IBM needed to increase integration among divisions so that they could share skills and resources more effectively.

Gerstner resolved to reengineer the company to make better use of its resources. In a major departure from the past, Gerstner believed the company's main problem was that it was too big. To reduce size, Gerstner announced plans to shed 115,000 more jobs in 1993 and 1994, reducing the workforce to 250,000. Despite all these measures, IBM's loss in 1993 was $8.37 billion.

As cost cutting got under way, Gerstner also focused the organization on becoming *One IBM* in terms of how the company operated. In late 2003, Gerstner assigned each member of the CEC responsibility for a functional reengineering project (e.g., procurement, product development, sales). He set two priorities for these projects:

1. Get cost out as quickly as possible.
2. *Clean-sheet* the process and redesign it for global use.

The redesigned processes would form the foundation for sustained cost competitiveness and best-in-class operations as the company embarked on the growth phase of its transformation. Unwieldy executive governance structures and processes were removed, and Gerstner made it emphatically clear that senior executives were *unambiguously accountable* for making sizable and sustainable improvements in their assigned processes. Initial efforts were targeted at core processes such as procurement, engineering, manufacturing, new product development, IT, research, human resource management, and finance.

The PC division exemplified the changes made within business units. In January 1994, Gerstner hired Rick Thoman, a former colleague from Nabisco, American Express, and McKinsey, to head the troubled PC division. Thoman killed nearly all of the PC company brands, saving only the eventually very successful ThinkPad brand for the laptop computer business. Recognizing that PC manufacturing was not a core competency and that IBM's dedicated PC factories came with high fixed costs, the company outsourced PC manufacturing. Finally, by capitalizing on the successful ThinkPad brand and moving all products under that brand, the PC organization was able to move forward with one marketing team, one development team, shared synergies, and an executive team slimmed by 25%. IBM's internal IT organization contributed to the $7 billion cost reduction. Between 1994 and 1997, the cost of operating and running IT operations was cut in half, generating over $2 billion in cost savings. Key savings came from reducing the number of data centers from 155 to 3 regional *megacenters* fed by 11 *server farms* and a 60% reduction in headcount. IT leadership was centralized; 128 CIOs were reduced to 1. Networks were converted to one common protocol (TCP/IP). The systems development process was also reengineered; internal applications decreased from 16,000 to 5,200, and component reuse was increased by 34%.

The sales organization, which had been organized by geography and product, was reorganized into global sales teams. In response to numerous customer complaints, a customer relationship manager and a dedicated sales and service team were appointed for each key customer account. These teams were grouped within larger vertical industry teams, and product specialists were assigned to each. The product specialists served as boundary spanners, moving back and forth between focused product groups and key account teams, taking product knowledge to the field and customer input back to the product groups. Product specialists reported to the product organization, but incentives rewarded increased sales of their products through industry sales teams.

9.8   SYSTEMS INTEGRATOR

Gerstner focused on making IBM a customer-driven company, given that sales of mainframes were declining and PCs and servers were becoming commodity products with low-profit margins, what IBM had to do was to provide something unique so that customers would be willing to pay a premium price for its products and services. The challenge facing IBM was to learn how to customize products to the needs of customers, if it was to be able to succeed in the new highly competitive computing environment. Gerstner's business model for IBM was that the company would build such a broad and sophisticated range of computer hardware and software, backed by the best consulting and service competencies in the industry, that it would overwhelm its competitors in the future. EDS and Accenture provide consultancy and service, for example, and HP, Dell, Sun, Oracle, and Microsoft produce computer hardware and software, but none of them had the capability to match the breadth and depth of IBM's growing computer offerings. By the late 1990s, the ability to bundle products together was becoming a major advantage to clients seeking a seamless and cost-effective way of managing their IT systems; it has only become more important since.

The litany of missed opportunities continued unabated: there are concerns that Gerstner's focus on making IBM a services business, blinded him to important competitive shifts, in which IBM lost out. For example, Cisco walked away with the multibillion-dollar market for networking equipment, even though much of the technology was developed in IBM laboratories. Similarly, IBM failed to counter Sun Microsystems' spectacular late-1990s push into the Unix server market, and the company was slow to challenge Oracle in relational databases (another invention of IBM laboratories). It may also have been shortsighted to allow new upstarts, like BEA in middleware and EMC in storage, the freedom to become market leaders in these fields.

At that time, industry thinking was that the future belonged to specialist technology companies that could bring new products to market extremely quickly and change strategy in an instant. Vertically integrated giants like IBM, making everything from microprocessors through to operating systems and finished computers and software, were thought to have no place in the new fragmented world of technology. IBM's very poor performance from the late 1980s onward seemed to justify this view. Thus, his central strategy flew in the face of conventional wisdom: IBM would use its size to become an *integrator*—assembling systems from the mass of components provided by its own product divisions and by its competitors.

In fact, Gerstner's services-led strategy aimed to turn IBM into the integrator of choice for large corporations. In the 6 years up to 2001, Gerstner increased IBM's revenue by 19%, net income by 83% and earnings per share by 250%, adding 100,000 new employees to the payroll. Admittedly, a revenue growth of 4% a year is not spectacular, given this period was one of very high IT spending growth throughout the world. Nearly all the growth (and all the new jobs) came from IBM Global Services, the consulting and outsourcing unit. Sales of hardware stagnated and software did not do much better.

In implementing this business model, Gerstner recognized that in many specific computer hardware and software product areas, IBM was no longer the industry leader. So he embarked on a strategy of offering IBM's clients the *best-of-breed* or *leading-edge* products currently available, such as SAP's ERP software, PeopleSoft's HRM software, Sun's servers, or Dell's PCs when they were either clearly better or lower priced than those supplied by IBM's own divisions. Then, and crucially, IBM's consultants, as a result of its focus on developing expertise in middleware that links any computer products together, were able to guarantee clients that they could install, maintain, and integrate them so that they worked together seamlessly. In adopting this strategy, IBM was strengthening its commitment to *open standards* in the computer industry by announcing publicly that in the future, it would continue to work to make all the future software and hardware of all producers—its competitors—compatible by strengthening its expertise in middleware. In doing so, Gerstner and IBM were also assuring clients that when they used IBM's computer consulting services, they would not become locked into IBM's proprietary hardware and software—no switching costs would arise from this source. However, Gerstner hoped at the same time that clients would be impressed by IBM's ability to provide such a complete service that they would become *locked in* because of the high quality of the service that it could provide.

> One implication of this new focus was the increased importance of *middleware*, which provided the tools and technology that served as the interconnections—the glue—between disparate and distributed data sources, applications, and computers. The shift from software applications to middleware prompted the major acquisition of Lotus Development Corporation for $3.5 billion in 1995, which provided a collaborative messaging/middleware platform. The $700 million acquisition of Tivoli Systems filled the distributed systems development and management software void.
>
> IBM also recognized that SMBs were another important customer group for its computer services—especially as it had developed scalable computer hardware and software that could be sold at a price that meets a client's budget. IBM had developed less expensive software targeted at the needs of SMB clients. It now worked with the thousands of new dot.com start ups, such as Internet web design and webhosting companies, to teach these companies how to install and maintain its software in SMBs. IBM hoped that once SMBs had made the connection with IBM, they would start to buy other kinds of its software, for example, to manage their databases and functional, value-chain tasks such as bookkeeping and inventory control.

9.8.1 Renewed Computer Hardware

Gerstner instructed hardware managers to do everything possible to reduce the costs of mainframe computing while increasing the scalability of its computers. Scalability means that a computer can be customized and designed and built to suit the needs of different-sized companies or different-sized computing tasks from managing global databases to operating a small chain of restaurants. IBM began to position its smaller mainframes as *enterprise servers*. Sales reps were told to emphasize to clients that computers could be made at a size and price to suit their unique needs, but a large powerful mainframe computer was still needed at the hub of a large company's IT system. IBM deliberately set the price of its hardware low, knowing it could make more money later in providing the new software and services.

9.8.2 RENEWED COMPUTER SOFTWARE

IBM had little to offer clients in the software applications areas, where companies like Oracle, and SAP had gained a first-mover advantage that was difficult for IBM to challenge. Oracle is the market leader in database management software, and SAP is the German company whose enterprise resource planning (ERP) software was soaring in popularity. ERP software allows a company to link its value-chain activities and connects mainframes to servers and servers to PCs. It gives a company's managers at all levels extensive real-time information about a company's activities; ERP software has become the backbone of most IT systems in large companies. To catch up with competitors in these areas, Gerstner acquired software companies that possessed unique solutions to provide clients with valuable new business applications and allow them to make better use of their computer networks. One of the companies IBM acquired at a cost of more than $3 billion in 1995 was Lotus, which had developed the popular Lotus Notes collaborative software. This software created a corporate intranet, an information network inside a company that allows managers at all levels to share information quickly both inside their own department and division and between divisions.

IBM also decided to focus its efforts on developing *middleware* software that is designed to link all the different pieces of a company's hardware—mainframes, servers, PCs, and laptops—together. That is, IBM wanted to control the middleware necessary to provide customers with a *seamless* solution to their computing needs regardless of their legacy system. If IBM had the middleware necessary to link any kind of IT hardware and software, it would be able to upgrade any client that wished to improve upon its legacy system to take advantage of new and advanced IT applications offered by any company. This revolutionary approach was part of Gerstner's *open standards* strategy designed to make IBM's own services available to all kinds of customers.

9.8.3 RENEWED CONSULTING SERVICES

Gerstner was familiar with the business model that Jack Welsh, former CEO of GE, had developed for his company. GE would sell a product such as a turbine or aircraft or diesel engine at a relatively low price to increase sales because each sale would result in a profitable stream of future income from servicing and maintaining the complex equipment it sold. Gerstner recognized that this model was viable in the new IT environment; he also recognized that in the IT sector, clients need expert help to decide which kind of computer solution best meets their current and future business needs. In IT, companies such as Electronic Data Services (EDS) and Accenture were the leaders and earned huge profits by providing companies with expert help; the market was increasing by double digits each year. For example, SAP could not satisfy the demand of large global clients to install its ERP software in its client's companies. Clients were paying billions of dollars to consulting companies such as Accenture and Cap Gemini for their expert help.

In 1996, Gerstner renamed the services division to Global Services, led by Sam Palmisano; Global Services had three main lines of business:

1. Strategic outsourcing services that provide customers with competitive cost advantages by outsourcing customers' processes and operations.
2. Integrated technology services designs, implements, and maintains customers' technology infrastructures.
3. Business consulting services deliver value to customers through business process innovation, application enablement, and integration services.

Global Services was charged with the task of spearheading IBM's push into the outsourcing and value-chain management business to go head to head with competitors such as EDS and Accenture. Gerstner's business model was now that Global Services would offer clients an outsourcing and business consultancy service based on assessing a customer's current legacy system and its future computing needs. IBM consultants would then design, plan, implement, maintain, and upgrade the client's IT system over time to help reduce the client's cost structure, improve its products, and build its competitive advantage. Gerstner also hoped that providing such expert services would once again build up switching costs and keep IBM's clients loyal on a long-term basis because of its ability to show them how its comprehensive, customized computing solution could help increase their profitability over time. Global services experienced continuing success throughout the 1990s and into the 2000s.

9.8.4   e-Business

An indicator of how well Gerstner was attuned to the changing IT environment was his early recognition that the growth of the Internet and e-commerce would become a dominant force dictating which kinds of IT would be most necessary in the future. IBM coined the term e-business, and Gerstner established an Internet division in IBM in 1995 before most other IT companies. IBM's early recognition of the future possibilities of e-business allowed its engineers to adapt its software and hardware to serve Internet-related value-chain transactions before its competitors. The acquisition of Lotus helped IBM understand the potential of the Internet: Lotus Notes was a company-specific or internal software collaboration application, while the Internet provided a major channel for collaboration between different companies; IBM's acquisition of Lotus revealed how the power of the Internet could shape supply-chain transactions between companies and their suppliers.

Another significant implication of the shift to an e-business strategy was the possibility of neutralizing the advantage of any specific operating system, network, software application, or hardware platform by shifting focus from proprietary to open technology. Under this scenario, rather than providing a proprietary industry platform (as it did with the S/360), IBM would provide the integration platform. This realization implied that IBM's hardware product organizations needed to become best-in-class or risk obsolescence. More importantly, it freed the company from having to compete in every product category. Instead of funneling resources and energy into competing in categories in which its offerings were weak, IBM could partner with best-in-breed providers to meet the needs of its customers. Thus, IBM, the company most identified with the word *proprietary*, turned its back to the past and its face toward *open standards*.

9.9   e-BUSINESS ON DEMAND

When Palmisano took over in 2003, following Gerstner's dramatic strategic shifts at the company, commentators saw Palmisano as no more than a caretaker of Gerstner's strategy. In fact, Palmisano provided far more in changing IBM structure, management, and strategic direction. Early signs that Palmisano planned to manage the company differently to Gerstner came at the first IBM board meeting of 2003, when he asked the board to cut his 2003 bonus and set it aside as a pool of money to be shared by about 20 top executives, based on their performance as a team. Palmisano also put an end to the 92-year-old IBM executive management committee—the 12-person inner sanctum that had presided over IBM's strategy and initiatives. Instead, Palmisano favored working with three new teams of people, covering operations, strategy, and technology, drawn from throughout the company, to bring the best ideas to the table and to move more quickly than the old IBM bureaucracy permitted. Palmisano is building a flatter organization with fewer bureaucratic levels and allocating $100 million to teach 30,000 managers to lead, not control their staff.

His goal was to build a new strategy to put IBM back at the forefront of technology. Called *e-business on demand*, the initiative aimed to allow IBM to supply computing power as if it were water or electricity. Gerstner's reforms started the process, by shifting IBM toward software and services, but Palmisano's *e-business on demand* went much further: Palmisano was planning to extend the services strategy to software and even hardware. The customer would tap or draw on the computing services (hardware, software, programming, and support services) per requirement on pay-per-use basis (see Subsection 9.9.6, "Cloud Computing"). The strategy was to be a unifying force for IBM, bringing closer together the almost autonomous *fiefdoms* in software, chips, and computers. Palmisano planned to have IBM get back to the position where it set the industry agenda, using its R&D to leap ahead with grid computing and self-healing software. In its first year, *e-business on demand* took a third of IBM's $5 billion R&D budget. The new initiative provided Palmisano with the tool to remake IBM. He was counting on the initiative to create the best IBM sales growth since the 1990s.

The *e-business on demand* strategy had the potential to cut technology user costs by 50%, though achieving this was dependent on a decade of rolling out new technologies and new ways of doing business: Companies would have to simplify into a unified network, based on a small number of servers, using open standards so that all machines can speak to each other; to achieve efficiency in server and software usage, virtualization (a process in which many machines appear to be one) gets more work out of equipment by farming work out across them; all networks and data centers would have to be linked to create a giant computing grid, allowing access to more information and computing power; if a company ran out of capacity, it would buy computing power from a supplier, as needed, instead of building a new data center; and new web-based services will speed up tasks yet more.

Palmisano's vision also involves reinventing the services industry by injecting disciplines of product development and delivery, more usually found in product markets, and doing this on a global scale. Turning services—by definition delivered by people—into repeatable processes is a massive organizational and cultural shift for the business. The move blurs the line between the services and software business models—for example, merging services into software to allow services developed for one project to be applied to others subsequently. By 2005, in spite of early IBM successes in the outsourcing area, the success of Palmisano's services strategy was far from assured. Sales growth was slow. The era of multibillion-dollar outsourcing contracts had come to an end. Critics saw underlying weaknesses exposed in IBM's services strategy: that it did not deliver on the original promise of services; that its method of delivering services did not bring consistent benefits for customers around the world, many of whom actually face very similar problems; and that the lack of a standardized approach had led IBM to miss out on some of the hottest markets, such as security.

By 2005, IBM's performance had started to fall. The problem Palmisano soon realized was that its now dominant global services group that had grown like wildfire and provided the largest proportion of IBM's revenues and profits had run into trouble. Its global outsourcing business had come under intense competition from low-priced overseas outsourcing companies, particularly Indian companies, at a time when its cost structure was quickly rising because of the rapid growth in the number of its employees, now more than 150,000 people worldwide. With the revenues of global services group plateauing, Palmisano had to search for new strategies to grow IBM's revenues and profits and solve the problems of its global services group.

Palmisano decided to vary IBM's business model and strategies in several ways:

- First, he decided to cut the cost structure of its global services group.
- Second, to make up for slowing revenues and profits, he accelerated the strategy he had begun in 2003—changing IBM's business model so that all its operating groups

focused on investing resources to move into higher-profit-margin IT businesses in which the specialized skills of IBM's workforce could be used to develop higher value-added IT services, based on some combination of research, software, and services that would offer its customers greater value.

- Third, he decided to exit any hardware businesses in which profit margins were thin and focus resources on strengthening and growing its core mainframe business.
- Finally, he made globalization and the drive to increase IBM's presence in every country in which it operated a major priority across the company.

All IBM's business groups were instructed to focus on cooperating to grow global sales of the HS&S package they offered to customers, not just in the advanced G7 countries in North America, Europe, and Japan, but across all world regions, especially in the rapidly growing economies of India and China.

To achieve all these strategies, and especially to expand its global customer base quickly, Palmisano also changed IBM's structure. In the early 2000s, IBM's overseas divisions had operated independently on a country-by-country basis; there was little cooperation between them. IBM has worked to get rid of the command and control structure of the past, and to build a culture of connection and collaboration—within the company as well as outside. IBM is also revamping its *people supply chain*. In the twentieth century, IBM was the pioneer of the multinational business model—creating *mini-IBMs* in each country with their own administration, manufacturing, and services operations. But this approach is too top heavy at a time when lean Indian tech companies and Chinese manufacturers produced high-quality goods and services at a fraction of the costs of multinationals. IBM now pioneers what it calls *globally integrated operations*, with the goal of lowering its costs but also providing superior service. This model groups people around the world into competency centers (collections of people with specific skills), with the aim of having low costs in some places but in others having highly skilled employees close to customers. Rather than each country's business unit having its own workforce entirely, many people are drawn from competency centers. The thinking is that in areas like tech services low-cost labor is essential (to equal Indian and Chinese competitors' costs), but not sufficient (to supply high levels of specialized skills). IBM's radical makeover in its 200,000 person services workforce includes.

- Not being a multinational but a globally integrated enterprise—IBM no longer runs a mini-IBM in each country and region and has reduced administrative employee numbers and reassigned technical specialists.
- Moving beyond outsourcing—performing work for clients where it can be done most competitively; assembling A-Teams—when IBM wins a new client, it picks a team to suit that client's needs, selecting people from around the world with the right skills and costs.
- Avoiding commodity businesses—IBM cannot operate as inexpensively as Indian challengers, so focuses on taking human labor out of tech services.

Accordingly, Palmisano built a streamlined global structure in which IBM technical experts who specialized in certain business functions or industries were organized into *clusters of business expertise*. These clusters might be in any country of the world but are connected to each other and to IBM's HS&S groups through its own proprietary Lotus high-speed communications Intranet. Project managers can search worldwide for the HS&S experts with the right skills for a job located in different countries around the world and form teams of experts quickly to meet the needs of clients in any country. For example, IBM created global and regional teams of skilled experts in particular industries, from airlines to utilities, who travel as needed to consult on projects.

IBM's services business is less profitable than other IBM activities: operating margins in services in 2004 were 25%, compared to 31% for hardware and 87% for software. However, only services offer the growth on the massive scale that IBM wants. In 2007, Palmisano decided to split the global services group into two parts: the global technology services (GTS) group that was to specialize in IBM's traditional kinds of IT services such as outsourcing maintenance and database management and the global business services (GBS) group that was to specialize in developing high-margin business and industry IT solutions customized to the needs of individual clients. If the goal in its GTS group was to increase profit margins and the number of customer accounts by being able to offer global customers lower prices and high-quality customer service, the goal of its GBS group is to offer customers state-of-the-art value-creating software services that can be customized to their needs, albeit at a premium price.

9.9.1 GLOBAL TECHNOLOGY SERVICES

Palmisano assigned all of IBM's more traditional *routine* lower-margin IT services to the GTS group. The GTS group handles value-chain infrastructure services and uses IBM's global scale and its expertise in standardizing and automating transactions to manage outsourcing, integrated technology services such as logistics and data center management, and maintenance services for its global clients. This outsourcing services business was providing billions of dollars of revenues from contracts with large global companies to manage their *noncore* business functions such as distribution, logistics, and data center management. This intense competitive pressure was coming from low-cost Indian companies such as Infosys, Tata Consulting Services, and Wipro, which had grown enormously in the 2000s because of their lower labor costs.

IBM had to compete more effectively in this IT services segment, which had been a main source of the increasing revenues that had allowed it to rebuild its competitive advantage. Like most manufacturing companies, IBM was forced to eliminate 20,000 GTS jobs in Europe and the United States and move these jobs to India. Its Indian workforce grew from 30,000 in 2004 to 45,000 in 2006. Then in June 2006, IBM announced it would triple its investment in India to $6 billion over the next 3 years to take advantage of its growing importance as a market for technology products and a source of high-technology workers. By 2009, it had more than 75,000 Indian employees. IBM made the investment to establish huge, low-cost service delivery centers for its global clients, improve the software necessary to automate the management of networks and data centers, and develop IT to improve telecommunications, especially Internet services. From India, IBM runs a whole range of IT services for its global customers, including software delivery services such as upgrading and maintaining client software and managing and protecting database centers.

9.9.2 GLOBAL BUSINESS SERVICES

In creating the GBS group, Palmisano's goal was accelerate its move into higher margin service activities, especially consulting and business transformation in which IBM could use the specialized skills of its U.S. software engineers to offer customers IT services that increase their competitive advantage. Specifically, the GBS group's strategy is to offer its customers professional, innovative services that deliver value by providing them with state-of-the-art solutions that leverage IBM's industry and business process expertise. For example, one of IBM's projects involved working with a Texas utility, CenterPoint Energy, to install computerized electric meters, sensors, and software in a *smart-grid* IT project to improve service and conserve energy. Dozens of IBM's industry experts from around the country moved to work on the project to design and build advanced software tailored to the needs of a utility company. Because some of the programming work can be done in India, engineers are on the project team as well. IBM plans to use the valuable skills learned and software written for the Texas smart-grid project in new projects with utility clients around the world, thus leveraging its skills in a high-profit-margin business. Similarly, in 2009, IBM and SAP announced an agreement with British retailer Marks & Spencer (M&S) to implement a suite of SAP Retail applications. The program aims to provide M&S with accurate business intelligence data and state-of-the-art functional and industry IT solutions that will allow it to discover business improvement initiatives that will increase operating efficiency and responsiveness to customers. IBM will draw on its expertise in organization, process, and technology to provide end-to-end program management, including change management and business process consulting services. SAP will provide its *Industry Solution for Retail*, a suite of business applications designed specifically to meet the unique requirements of large and sophisticated retailers.

9.9.3 COMPUTER SOFTWARE

Since 2005, Palmisano has emphasized the central role advanced software development must play in IBM's future business model to offset the slowing revenues from global services because of low-cost global competition. By late 2006, it was apparent that software had become IBM's fastest-growing business. The $16.8 billion software division—second only to Microsoft in the world software business—was emerging as the most reliable growth engine. While the overall company grew by 1% in 2006, software grew by 5%. In part fuelled by a rapid sequence of software acquisitions—more than 30 software companies purchased in 4 years—the plan is to use the acquisitions to tap new software lines, while milking mature products for profits. Margins are significantly higher for software compared to services. Interestingly, new software products also benefit services—sales often include huge service contracts, and customers who buy new software typically spend five times as much on services to install and maintain it.

In 2008, IBM acquired Cognos, a leading maker of business intelligence software, for $4.9 billion. IBM's acquisition came after SAP's acquisition of Business Objects and Oracle's takeover of Hyperion, the other two leading makers of business intelligence software in 2007. Owning Cognos should help IBM sell more of its other middleware, including its WebSphere and DB2 database products. Business intelligence software draws data from a range of corporate systems to give managers a view across their operations. Business intelligence software sifts through huge masses of data and uses sophisticated problem-solving procedures to identify and discover crucial events such as changes in the buying habits of a customer group or the *hidden* factors reducing the efficiency of a company's value-chain functions or business processes. Recent advances in IT have increased the power of business intelligence software to identify ongoing changes and forecast likely future events, an area in which IBM had no expertise. Cognos software is used by many retailers, including Home Depot, Amazon.com, American Eagle Outfitters, and 7-Eleven.

IBM's software strategy now shows a dramatic contrast to the business models of rivals like Microsoft, Oracle, and SAP. While these companies have been rushing to create vertically integrated *stacks* of software, extending all the way up to applications used by individual workers, IBM has concentrated on creating a *horizontal* layer of middleware that lies at the center of IT systems, where most workers never encounter it. The IBM strategy rests on a single belief—that legacy corporate IT systems, measured in trillions of dollars of value, require extensive work as companies try to integrate them better, build on them, and adapt them to new business purposes.

9.9.4 SOFTWARE INTEGRATION

IBM has built five middleware brands—Lotus, Tivoli, WebSphere, Rational, and the DB2 database business—each of which as a stand-alone business would rank among the world's 25 biggest software businesses. IBM's middleware strategy aims to position the company to take advantage of the major shift taking place in the global software market—the growth of *service-oriented architecture* or broader and more flexible software platforms on which companies can build more adaptable technology, capable of changing with their business needs. This market shift vindicates

IBM's decision in the late 1990s to move away from the applications business, instead partnering with other software companies, while it builds broader platforms. However, other broad trends in the software market are more challenging for IBM. Open-source software has been championed by IBM in its support for the Linux operating system, to challenge Microsoft. However, low-margin open-source software is moving into other parts of middleware. IBM itself offers open-source versions of some of its middleware for the low end of the technology market, like application server software. If more advanced parts of middleware are commoditized, IBM's position could be threatened, unless it can continue to move up into higher value areas of software.

A second challenge for IBM comes from the emerging trend toward *software as a service*—the business of providing applications online as a service to companies, pioneered by Salesforce.com and taken up by Google. Customers buying these services will no longer need to buy IBM hardware systems and IT integration. This could pressure IBM to step up as a full service provider, which would mean reversing the decision to keep IBM out of the applications business, which has underpinned its profitable partnerships with other software producers (see Subsection 9.9.6, "Cloud Computing").

9.9.5 SYSTEMS AND TECHNOLOGY

In its hardware business, Palmisano continued his strategy of focusing on high-profit-margin products that directly complemented its service and software offerings. As noted earlier, IBM had sold off its PC business to Lenovo for $1.25 billion and its disk drive business Hitachi for $2 billion. In 2007, IBM decided to spin off its printer business, which was suffering from intense competition from HP and Xerox to Ricoh for $725 million.

Palmisano directed the systems and technology group to put its resources into developing new kinds of mainframes and servers that would appeal to a wider number of customers groups and expand global sales. IBM still receives about 25% of its $100 billion in annual revenue from sales, software, services, and financing related to its mainframes and servers. Since 2005, IBM has been pursuing the strategy of constantly upgrading the performance of its large mainframes to offer its customers a better value prospection, that is, to give them more and more power and flexibility for each IT dollar they spend. And, beginning in 2006, it began to offer customers the option of buying smaller and much-less expensive mainframes to drive sales to medium-sized global customers. In 2007, for example, it introduced its latest generation of mainframes, the powerful z10 Enterprise Class (z10EC) mainframe that retails for about $1 million and the smaller z10 Business Class (z10BC) mainframe that retails for about $100,000; it is highly attractive to smaller enterprises and midmarket companies looking to consolidate multiple server racks in many data centers with one large machine—virtualization technology results in linked server racks being able to emulate the power of mainframes.

 IBM sells its large mainframes directly to customers through its own sales force to protect the lucrative software and service revenues that accompany these sales. The smaller mainframe, however, is sold through its 20 global channel partners, who also provide the software and service package customized to each client's needs. IBM pursued this strategy to accelerate the adoption of the machines throughout the world because global customers, particularly those in India and China, are the main targets for these $100,000 machines.

9.9.6 CLOUD COMPUTING

IBM has always been interested in the idea of hosting its client's data on its own network of mainframes. By the mid-2000s, however, the cost of linked racks of servers (which might contain 10,000 powerful individual servers) was falling sharply as Intel and AMD introduced ever-more advanced microprocessors, which when combined with Oracle's database management software, made them low-cost alternatives to renting space on IBM's mainframes. Also in the mid-2000s, the idea of cloud computing had been pioneered by Internet companies such as Google, Yahoo!, and Microsoft, and the concept was gaining in popularity. In the cloud computing business model, Internet and other companies design their own customized data centers to store vast amounts of information that can be accessed and processed from afar using PCs, netbooks, cell phones, or other devices. For example, Google pioneered an online document hosting service in which both individuals and companies can upload documents that are stored in Google's data centers on server racks and then can be accessed using word processing or spreadsheet software programs and so on. Once again, these data centers are composed of tens or even hundreds of thousands of servers linked into racks, which are in turn connected together to provide immense amounts of storage and processing power.

What is unique about the cloud computing model, however, is that cloud data centers require server racks that have been configured with the right HS&S to meet the needs of each individual company. These data centers are not *off-the-shelf* standardized products, such as IBM's mainframes. Even more unique, the growing number of companies that are competing to offer these integrated server racks have developed a new business model in which these racks are housed in portable storage platforms that are housed in shipping containers similar to those used to deliver products around the world on ships and trucks. These storage platforms are then integrated into a company's physical data center using networking hardware and software. This business is growing fast; it is expected to be a multibillion-dollar business in the future.

In 2009, IBM announced a new agreement with Amazon Web Services (AWS), a subsidiary of Amazon.com, to deliver IBM's software to clients and developers via cloud computing (see below). The new *pay-as-you-go* model provides clients with access to development and production instances of IBM DB2, Informix Dynamic Server, WebSphere Portal, Lotus Web Content Management, WebSphere sMash, and Novell's SUSE Linux operating system software in the Amazon Elastic Compute Cloud (Amazon EC2) environment, providing a comprehensive portfolio of products available on AWS.

By May 2008, IBM stock was trading near its 6-year high level, and it seemed as though Palmisano's new strategies had worked. However, then came the recession in the summer of 2008. Although, as expected, revenues from its hardware group fell sharply as large companies reduced their spending on mainframes and servers, IBM was not hurt as badly as its competitors because of its major push to globalization. In 2007, for example, it had reported that it enjoyed more than 10% growth in revenues in more than 50 countries. In October 2008, analysts were surprised when IBM reported strong third-quarter profits despite the financial services industry meltdown. Although financial services is IBM's biggest customer segment contributing 28% to its revenues, and the one hit hardest by the economic downturn, 75% of that revenue came from outside the United States.

IBM exemplifies many of the strategic renewal challenges faced by companies in rapidly changing markets and the types of organizational transformation needed to implement new strategies. However, moving toward the end of the second decade of the twenty-first century, there are major concerns about the continuing transformation of IBM. While the vision of a new type of globally integrated enterprise focused on new types of service product is compelling, questions surround the ability of the company to implement that vision effectively, globally, and rapidly enough to meet competitive threats; doubts arise whether the transition to becoming a tech services company has stalled in the face of low-cost competition, aggressive competition, and market change.

Moving toward a collaborative business model, sharing R&D with customers, developers, and competitors raises the specter of another Xerox, where new ideas are exploited more effectively by others than by the originators. The commitment to open-source software development and attempts to make open source the industry standard may backfire and undermine the strength of the IBM software division, which is currently the main source of revenue growth for the company. Growth driven by acquisition, rather than organically by in-house or collaborative R&D, may undermine the coherence of the business and its knowledge generation for superior IBM service offerings.

9.10 SUMMARY

This chapter explained the business variations throughout the life span of IBM to unravel how it continues to reign supreme in the high-tech sectors of the economy. IBM began with punch card machines, but by 1939, IBM already was the biggest and most powerful business machine company in the United States. In 1964, it launched System/360 series of computers that would satisfy the needs of a whole spectrum of users in both the scientific and business community. It offered the revolutionary new concept of compatibility, allowing customers to use the same printers and other peripherals with any 360 machine. System/360 was wildly successful; so dominant was IBM by the late 1960s that it became the target of an unsuccessful 13-year-long antitrust action by the U.S. Justice Department.

But more detrimental was the *mainframe mind*set that it engendered internally: IBM's top managers, who had risen up the ranks of IBM from the mainframe division, became conditioned by the idea that the level of computing power was everything—big machines meant big revenue. IBM's mainframe managers saw the potential earning power of the minicomputer as insignificant when compared to the huge revenues generated by its mainframes. This situation would recur again and again during waves of technological breakthroughs in the future—minicomputers, PCs, workstations, systems integration, data processing or outsourcing, business process outsourcing, consulting services, and so on.

Gerstner (1980–2003) focused on making IBM a customer-driven company, given that sales of mainframes were declining and PCs and servers were becoming commodity products with low-profit margins, what IBM had to do was to provide something unique services that was chargeable at a premium. Gerstner decided to find better ways to integrate the activities of its HS&S groups to create more value for customers. In fact, Gerstner's services-led strategy aimed to turn IBM into the integrator of choice for large corporations. When Palmisano took over in 2003, his goal was to build a new strategy to put IBM back at the forefront of technology. Palmisano's *e-business on demand* went much further: Palmisano planned to extend the services strategy to software and hardware as well. The customer would tap or draw on the computing services (hardware, software, programming, and support services) per their requirements on pay-per-use basis.

 This would also be a right place to speculate on future trajectories of high-tech companies like IBM. Considering Apple's resurgence as a consumer devices company, one is tempted to wonder if this would be the likely direction for the future evolution of high-tech companies albeit with suitable variations in individual cases:

- HP has traditionally been in measurement and testing instruments and subsequently also successfully became a major player in ink-jet and laser printers business.

- Oracle (which already has a robust consulting business) acquired Sun Microsystems a few years back.
- Dell, which has traditionally been a hardware company, has made a strategic foray into services and consulting business.
- Microsoft, a software major that already has services and device businesses (like mouse, game consoles), has recently acquired the mobile device business of Nokia.
- Samsung has entered into medical device business.
- Sony has traditionally been in device businesses of cameras and TVs.
- Google entered into device business with its acquisition of Motorola's Android operating system for mobiles.

Hence, the conjecture that IBM could be on the lookout for a successful play in the electronic device business. Such a foray could also be of interest for companies like Cisco, SAP, Xerox, Lenovo, and Huawei. For the same reason, Blackberry could be of interest to these companies as also to companies like Alcatel, Ericsson, AT&T, and Nortel. In retrospect, one can only conjecture if Kodak's foray into smartphones or HDTV or a stronger thrust in medical electronics could have been a much more viable alternative to making repeated attempts to prop up the already collapsing business in photographic films and related add-on services and bridges to digital cameras.

10 UPS

Transformation is in UPS's DNA. In 1954, when almost all of UPS's revenues were coming from thousands of well-known and respected departmental stores, company President Jim Casey made the call: the company's future was in the common carrier business.

In the mid-1980s, when UPS was at the very top of its game, it designed a new business model that included global delivery.

In the late-1990s, after the emergence of Internet and UPS began to thrive as the delivery service of choice for e-commerce, it again threw out the playbook and decided to embrace a new solutions strategy.

This allows UPS to be the trusted partner for customers ranging from German high-end fabric maker JAB Anstoetz, which makes curtains and upholstery for the world's finest hotels, to Patrick Enterprises of Circleville, Ohio, the world's largest manufacturer of monster trucks. UPS's century-long success is not only to do with driving trucks, sorting packages, wiring mainframes, and flying airplanes, but it has also to do with a singular culture of never being satisfied, about the discipline to execute, about the willingness of tens of thousands of partners to pull together and transform an organization. It is finally about managing large-scale change, again and again.

 Jim Casey coined a term to describe his compulsive habit of endlessly tinkering with the status quo: *creative dissatisfaction*, which managers actively encouraged across the company. In 1937, for example, the issue was fleet maintenance efficiency. Over the years, it was progressively the efficacy of electric delivery cars in urban environments, the potential of moving packages by the New York City subway system, and the possible conversion to a monorail-based sort system. UPS engineers tested all these ideas rigorously and quantitatively, always factoring in not just the mechanical efficiencies to be gained but also ergonomics for ease of use. UPS has rarely grown by bursts of pure invention. It has built itself not by inventing so much as by engineering and then reengineering—its equipment, its systems, and itself.

We would like to highlight that this case history is meant to highlight the variations during the life span of the company rather than to illustrate either effective or ineffective handling of an administrative situation.

10.1 RETAIL SERVICES

Jim Casey and Claude Ryan launched American Messenger Company in a basement office at Seattle on August 28, 1907. The company offered *best service and lowest rates* round the clock, including evenings, Sundays, and holidays. At that time, Seattle had two independent telephone companies, but few homes had telephones or automobiles; nine messenger companies competed for the business of relaying communiqués, delivering and picking up messages, and running miscellaneous errands. Few people owned cars, so the service afforded shoppers the luxury of continuing their errands without being encumbered with earlier purchases. King Brothers Clothing was the first store to sign on with American Messenger Company, allowing the store to offer customers same-day delivery. Packages of clothing purchases arrived at the basement messenger office throughout the day and were dispatched along with messages to the same neighborhood. Effectively, this consolidation generated far greater revenue from a single trip. And retail deliveries suggested a means of getting away from the sometimes irksome and less rewarding message-and-errand business.

At that time, four major express companies (Adams Express, Wells Fargo, American Express, and United States Express) were handling interstate shipments in 1907, operating over about a dozen railroads. The express companies shipped contracted mail, goods, and other commodities, but the business of messages, parcels, and intracity retail deliveries was up for grabs. This was a period of trial and error and the entire business was learning by doing; the young team cast about for a strategy that would add substance to their business. The founders made a key move that was to establish a protocol for future expansion—partnering up.

With a plan for focusing on consolidating deliveries for departmental stores, they joined up with Evert *Mac* McCabe's Motorcycle Delivery Company that had a fleet of about a half-dozen Yale motorcycles serving the Seattle area, each rigged with baskets and saddlebags. The integrated company was renamed *Merchants Parcel Delivery*, and they decided to focus on deliveries for small retail businesses in downtown Seattle. By consolidating deliveries from several stores, the partners figured they could economize on trips. And customers could receive their purchases at one predictable time, from a single delivery person.

As department store deliveries became the core business, meticulous attention to details, concern for professional appearance of drivers, concern for impeccable standards of service, and concern for cleanliness, upkeep, and regular maintenance of vehicles and equipment became a defining aspect of UPS. By 1915, Merchants Parcel Delivery had 4 automobiles, 5 motorcycles, and 30 ft messengers; together they covered 1600 miles each day in Seattle.

For the next decade, they worked continuously on improving the deliveries and systems. They devised the policies of assigned routes, *three delivery attempts*, along with later additions like pre-work communication meeting (PCM) and Circle of Honor (reserved for those drivers with 25 years of service without an accident), which survive to present times. Jim Casey devised and implemented a new system for sorting and loading packages. It looked like a seashell with concentric circles. To load or unload packages, drivers would back their vehicles up to solid wooden wheels. On the side of the wheel opposite the vehicle, an aisle circled the loading area. There, sorters worked to deposit the packages from and to bins that surrounded the wheel. Variations on the Casey-designed wheel and bin system were used well into the 1960s.

The World War I boosted Merchants Parcel Delivery's success, because its drivers could take over deliveries that department stores could no longer staff. The flourishing department store delivery business in Seattle and ever more proficient operations convinced Jim that they had a successful delivery system that could be duplicated in other cities. Jim wrote to the chambers of commerce of every American city with a population over 100,000, asking for names of local delivery firms. He wrote to them all seeking ideas.

As a result of this groundwork, in 1919, they acquired Motor Parcel Delivery company operations in Oakland, California, to be incorporated under the name *United Parcel Service* with Jim Casey as the president. Before long, United Parcel Service was dominating deliveries in Oakland and a few other East Bay cities, with systems, operations, and drivers that were difficult for the competition to match. The subject of unionization had not confronted the partners in Seattle, but things were different in the prolabor Bay Area. Jim invited the teamsters to represent the several dozen United Parcel Service drivers and part-time hourly package-handling employees in Oakland. The relationships from this early proactive position led to future union contracts with many necessary flexible features. These included variable start times, working as directed with minimum work rules, working across job classification, combination jobs, part-time employees for half the workforce, and mandatory overtime as needed.

In the early Seattle years, the young messengers had delivered anything to anyone, but by the time the company had become Merchants Parcel Delivery, they no longer deliver business to business. Merchants Parcel Delivery specialized in store to consumer. But wholesale delivery was completely different from retail delivery and was known as *common carrier* service. Common carrier shipping was regulated by the Interstate Commerce Commission as well as various state commissions. In the decades before deregulation, shippers needed to acquire the rights to pick up and deliver packages business to business. The Russell Peck company had these rights, but only in the Southern California area; with the purchase of this company in 1922, United Parcel Service took over these rights. It was quite different from being on contract to deliver a department store's retail sales. In fact, United Parcel Service could not even mix wholesale deliveries with retail packages, and in some cities later on, including Portland, it had to use different drivers, even when they covered the same neighborhood. U.S. law stated that common carriers were required to serve any shipper, carrying any package, no matter how small, to all locations within their service territory, no matter how remote.

By 1927, United Parcel Service's common carrier service extended 125 miles from downtown L.A. in every direction. But, this also put them in direct competition with the U.S. Post Office, which had inaugurated a parcel post service in 1913. Eventually, in 1984, the United States overtook the U.S. Postal Service parcel business in the number of packages moved, 1.96–1.86 billion.

United Parcel Service augmented its new Los Angeles operation by purchasing a smaller company operated by Joe Meiklejohn, then merging the two companies. Rather than paying up front with cash, they funded these acquisitions by pledging what they had, which meant shares of United Parcel Service stock. Joe Meiklejohn stayed on with United Parcel Service in a management capacity, and with an investment to support, he worked hard to assure the merger's success. United Parcel Service was to use this strategy numerous times in the coming years.

Soon after United Parcel Service began Los Angeles operations, the company moved to a 22,500 ft^2 building at 420 West 11th Street, which remained national headquarters until 1930. The first suburban substations (operating centers) were established, beginning with Long Beach and followed by Pasadena (again buying owner delivery operation using United Parcel Service stock and asking the seller to remain as manager), and then Hollywood. Soon United Parcel Service was covering the Pomona Valley, San Fernando Valley, and Orange County. Before long, Santa Barbara, Riverside, San Bernardino, and San Diego came on line. The first long-haul service transfers, now called *feeder runs*, served those outlying facilities from 11th Street. On West 11th in the 1920s, the company got its first automatic car wash, its first conveyor belt (180 ft long), and its first brown uniforms.

Dentists, needing patient dental impression molds right away, were among United Parcel Service's biggest customers. With abundant requests for same-day service, the company launched Red Arrow Bonded Messenger Corporation in March 1925 offering *immediately dispatched, same-day service* using messengers on bicycles and motorbikes. This service took off rapidly with the establishment of Hollywood Red Arrow in 1927, followed by Portland Red Arrow in 1930 and New York Red Arrow in 1934.

In recent times, people are surprised to find that UPS handles all sorts of high-ticket items. More high-value items go through the UPS Metro New York District than any other in the world, because of its proximity to New York's Diamond District on West 45th Street; accordingly, security is rigorous and multilayered.

After Charles Lindbergh's historic transatlantic flight in 1927, talk of air express was in the air. At McCabe's suggestion, the company sent surveys out to businesses to weigh the interest in and need for an air service. The results were very encouraging. Finally, in 1929, United Parcel Service formed United Air Express. They contracted with three air companies to deliver parcels by air. At the airports, United Air Express delivered packages to carriers and picked up packages for delivery. In cities with no United Parcel Service ground delivery, local companies were hired but the partners' same high standards of service were still applicable.

The UPS founders, who had already determined a need for UPS's delivery service in New York City, desperately wanted to begin service on the East Coast as soon as possible. The offer to UPS came through the investment banking firm Bancamerica-Blair Corporation, which represented Curtiss-Wright and a few other aviation firms. The group envisioned a huge air express company, with UPS providing the ground service. Per the deal signed by all parties including UPS, the Bancamerica-Blair holding company bought United Parcel Service for $2 million and 600,000 shares of Curtiss Aeroplane stock. Using the $2 million primarily for expansion, United Parcel Service was also able to give its stockholders (employees) cash, along with Curtiss Airlines shares, for their holdings. But, due to the historic October 1929 crash and the Great Depression that followed, the grandiose plans of Bancamerica-Blair's member airline firms hoping for an air-UPS delivery system fizzled. United Air Express ceased operations after only about a year.

Yet the financial disaster created an opportunity for United Parcel Service to reinvent itself by striking a deal with Bancamerica-Blair that was looking to divest itself of some of its holdings. As a part of the deal, UPS retained the $2 million, and the investment company returned the United Parcel Service stock, but the intrepid delivery company had to assume responsibility for all outstanding obligations. One of these was the expensive lease at 331 East 38th Street in New York, which was to serve as UPS headquarters for many years. Also in 1930, UPS formed United Parcel Service of America, Inc., a Delaware corporation, and that year again made UPS stock available for senior employees in all job categories. After 4 more fretful years, all the UPS stock was returned to UPS employees in exchange for the Curtiss Airways stock they had signed back. UPS stock was again offered to the employees. When United Parcel Service made the decision to headquarter in New York City, key executives moved to Manhattan and brought their families with them; the number of UPS employees more than tripled between 1930 and 1934, from 400 to more than 1400.

In 1927, the founders made a decision that very few other companies were making in those days—to share their bounty with employees. They believed their employees deserved a stake in the significant profits that West Coast operations were then generating; the loyalty of former delivery company owners who stayed on as managers inspired this move. Specifically, the founders offered designated employees a chance to purchase *associate's shares* that gave full voting rights and dividend privileges.

While others offered limited profit sharing (P&G in 1887 and Kodak in 1912), UPS was restructuring the company to make it a much wider partnership. The P&G and Kodak programs only evolved into stock-offering plans later, whereas UPS's plan went beyond profit sharing to actual voting shares. With nearly 500 UPSers in 1927, the founders were extending equity to more than 1/10 of the employees; and from then on, these included not only executives but also frontline employees (drivers, helpers, mechanics, washers, and porters).

The offering was an immediate hit, managers began referring to each other as *partners*, and they truly were partners in the company's growing success. Most people credit that stock ownership by employees, which continued to expand over the years as new members were added, as the most important factor in the company's ascendancy. It bred enormous loyalty and became a long-standing hallmark of the company.

When UPS embarks on a major initiative—building its supply-chain business, for example— it is able to successfully undertake these large-scale changes without falling prey to the pitfalls (like covert resistance, employee insecurity, entrenched habits and methodology, low morale) that can cripple an organization during times of radical change. The stock offering assured better management—from frugality to employee motivation—which in turn contributed to increased profits. The value of the stock offered was $15 a share, and the company gave the managers 5 years to pay for it, as proof that they intended to encourage participation. Most privately held companies have illiquid stock, but UPS stock can be cashed out. Employee stockholders could always, and still can, sell shares back at the earlier board-set price or today's market price. Since UPS stock has split many times in 80 years, that one 1927 share, originally valued at $15, has become 16,000 shares today, each worth $80 (early 2013 price), for a total value of $1,280,000. Unlike some other privately held companies who made stock available too (but only among members of the family that owned those companies); UPS's employees became the family.

Participating in UPS's profit sharing program remains voluntary, with the exception of all managers and supervisors who also receive stock through the management incentive plan (MIP). The delivery business's expanding service area made it all the more important to keep great, dedicated managers on board. To ensure that the cream of the crop stayed and kept performing, by the 1940s, UPS began to issue shares of stock to managers annually. Through the MIP, each year, managers were awarded a certain amount of shares in appreciation, based on years of service, salary, and job responsibility. United Parcel Service was unique. It was the only company of its size that not only remained private but also rewarded its management team with the presentation of stock as an incentive. The MIP was never just about getting stock. It was about keeping employees.

The UPS corporate culture is unique—different from other businesses to a degree that could be characterized as archaic and even peculiar. UPSers themselves rarely question the myriad regulations they must abide by, many of which have carried over from the earliest days. Even new hires, carefully screened for their adaptability to a highly disciplined company, quickly acclimatize to the UPS way because the procedures work: they work for the employees, they work for customers, and they work for profits. Collectively, these performance expectations and methodologies constitute one of the most singular corporate cultures in the world. This conservative and apparently insular culture has supported UPS as it reinvented itself time and again in order to survive and keep growing.

Adherence to what may seem like an excessively methodical mode of doing business does not diminish UPSers' autonomy on larger matters. UPS gives individual employees responsibilities that require independent decision making and nearly superhuman performance. Yet these same employees work within controlled regulations and routines that might easily be called *obsessive-compulsive*. Somehow, UPS achieves a balance between the two extremes. To outsiders, the strict regime seems over the top. To UPSers, it is the modus operandi.

Perhaps second in importance to the partnership concept, the promotion-from-within policy—from entry-level positions to top management—has been a hallmark at UPS. From the early days of expansion and growth, managers were generally given greater and greater responsibility, the opportunity to climb the corporate ladder, make more money, and own more stock. Along with role models and on-the-job training, numerous internal training schools and materials prepare employees for higher-level positions. UPS CIO Dave Barnes started working for the company as a part-time worker in St. Louis, unloading packages on the sort; subsequently, he worked in operations, engineering, finance, and technology. Recent CEO Mike Eskew is the former head of industrial engineering, and the CEOs immediately preceding him included two operators, a marketer, an attorney, and an accountant. At UPS, a broad experience trumps a subject matter expert.

Back in Seattle in 1912, when American Messenger Company (which eventually became UPS) opened its second office, George Casey made his messenger decisions without constantly seeking permission from his elder brother Jim Casey or Claude Ryan. Early on, the founders learned that on-the-spot decisions affecting their delivery operations often had to be made, and employees had to be held accountable for these snap decisions. As the company expanded down the West Coast, local decision making became even more important. Each geographical area had its unique circumstances; decentralization of operations was critical to the success of United Parcel Service's expansion. UPS divides its operations into regions, regions into districts, and districts into divisions and operating areas. A region will generally include 5–10 districts; in turn, a district might comprise

1 state and maybe portions of another or 2 complete states. Some large states have two or more districts. The region manager and region staff provide guidance to all districts in their region. The district manager and staff are responsible for the service, cost, and the maintenance and development of their business within the district.

The district manager remains responsible for the district's making a profit and is held accountable for all sorts of production, service, and safety indices—in effect, making decisions that would get mired in the approval process in many other companies while living and breathing policies from the corporate policy bible (see the later paragraph in this section). Under the district managers, division managers have a lot of latitude running the six or seven centers in their jurisdiction. Center managers, too, make numerous autonomous decisions. They can shift drivers' routes around to accommodate a shipper wanting a later pickup. Or they can schedule their supervisors' hours to ensure overlapping coverage. Local decision making extends to the hourly ranks. Loaders, for example, know when to leave their posts for a few minutes to help a neighbor who might be getting behind. Drivers constantly make decisions—like returning to a pickup later or breaking route to deliver a misloaded package—without consulting their supervisor.

Under the decentralized operations, UPS needed a means of ensuring that autonomous managers still operated within parameters that would result in consistent, high-quality service and profitability. In 1929, United Parcel Service developed its UPS Policy Book of about 75 pages that details more than a hundred policies. While the policy book's purpose is inflexible, it is a working and living guide, updated by input from the entire management team every few years to reflect a changing world. The UPS Policy Book spells out its policies quite plainly, from dress codes to much more complicated canons such as decentralization. For instance, on decentralization, the policy book informs that to achieve greater efficiency and teamwork, UPS manages each operation on a personal, on-the-job basis and delegates appropriate decision-making authority.

UPS divides operations into smaller units to provide closer guidance and support. They have learnt that small work groups develop a spirit of teamwork, perform more effectively, and provide greater responsibility for their group's goals. Decentralization creates autonomy and strengthens responsibility at every echelon. Even today, as an example, many UPS drivers cite their ability to be on their own, making numerous job decisions daily, as a desirable element of their job. Decentralization coupled with strong common policies worked beautifully, and it has stood the test of time, even with globalization.

10.2 COMMON CARRIER SERVICES

United Parcel Service has always been efficient and economical, but the company's distribution area was at first quite restricted, limited to those delivery areas served by the large department stores of major cities. Outside those areas, people couldn't take advantage of the company's now-famous reliability as they can today because severe federal and state regulation kept that reliability from expanding beyond those retail stores and out of reach. Jim Casey's ambition, prompted by his boyhood days eyeing cargo as it arrived on Seattle's wharfs from distant ports, had long been a grand and sensible alternative: nationwide shipping, coast to coast, to every address in the 48 continental states. United Parcel Service didn't accomplish this objective in one fell swoop. Rather, the company doggedly pursued it, state by state and in some cases city by city, with applications, formidable paperwork and documentation, meetings with attorneys, and state and federal hearings, with occasional appeals, over a period of 68 years. Not until United Parcel Service focused its attention on all types of deliveries and obtained the rights to compete did it finally achieve nationwide shipping in 1975.

The war effort had changed America, changed United Parcel Service, and changed the delivery business. The postwar years found many people migrating to suburbs, with new homes near large, new shopping centers surrounded by vast parking lots. A new American lifestyle was evolving; the age of automobile was overtaking the United States and UPS. Families purchased more cars, and with second cars, the breadwinner was not the only one behind the wheel. With more and more people driving their packages home, the retail delivery business that had always defined United Parcel Service leveled off, the combination of automobile ownership, suburban stores, and parking lots that made UPS's delivery service a lot less relevant.

By the end of the 1940s, it was clear that a new direction was needed. The company had to reinvent itself once again to survive and prosper during the years following World War II. The real question was not whether to develop a new business model, but what this model would be. This was the common carrier business; UPSers already knew retail outflows; now they would have to target the retail inflows.

With the advent of car, as highways were being threaded across the continent, long-haul trucking emerged as a viable alternative to railroad freight. Casey's vision was that the economic trends were creating the possibility of carrying commerce across much bigger spans of geography via modern highways and airplanes of increasing carrying capacity.

The business of UPS, within 10 years, would be nothing less than facilitating the commerce of the continent. UPS would, in addition to continuing serving retail stores, be delivering wholesale small packages by automobile or airplane, to any city or town in the United States within 2 days.

In 1953, United Parcel Service got back into the air business it had abandoned 23 years before and was soon renamed as UPS Blue Label Air. More and more customers wanted to ship packages rapidly from one city to another, and once again, UPS looked to the skies. UPS Blue Label Air packages flew in the cargo holds of regularly scheduled domestic airlines, packed into airline hampers that were configured to fit in the bellies of the planes. The service was not labor intensive since each city in the system needed only one air manager to confirm that airline staff loaded and unloaded from the proper planes (United Airlines, American Airlines, and the rest). Add a few clerks and some drivers to move the packages to and from the UPS hubs to the airports, and you had a 2-day air service with the front end delivered by UPS package cars. Blue Label service continued to grow modestly until by 1980 it was available in the larger metropolitan areas of all 48 contiguous states.

As mentioned earlier, common carriers were in direct competition with the post office, and the rights to become a common carrier in new regions were hard to come by because they were highly regulated by both the federal and state governments. Since 1887, the ICC had tightly regulated the economics and services of carriers engaged in transportation between states. Congress created the ICC, the first regulatory commission in U.S. history, to protect against railroad malpractice, but ICC's jurisdiction extended to trucking companies, bus lines, freight forwarders, water carriers, oil pipelines, transportation brokers, and express agencies too.

Except for airlines, any business conveyance that charged money to transport goods or passengers from one state to another was under ICC regulation. The agency's roles included rights, rate making, regulation, and resolving labor disputes in interstate transport. The ICC represented a formidable challenge to UPS's expansion plans, allied as the ICC was with UPS's biggest competitor, the U.S. Post Office Department. Despite the challenges, United Parcel Service made the momentous decision to pursue wholesale package delivery, to expand United Parcel Service's *common carrier* services to deliver packages from any customer, whether private or commercial, to any other.

Casey set a goal of achieving comprehensive coverage of the United States with wholesale delivery within 10 years. What started in 1952 as an effort to add wholesale traffic became a campaign to forge the *Golden Link*, meaning contiguous states through which UPS could deliver packages from coast to the other. A road-based, truck and package car–carried network had never been built on a national scale by a commercial company before. In fact, this was akin to forging of the national rail and telegraph networks in the nineteenth century. Unlike the consolidated retail delivery business, which took shape on the ground as a series of essentially unconnected local operations, the new business would have to be tightly interconnected. In 1975, the company reached a milestone when it inaugurated overland service between the West Coast, Eastern, and Midwestern states, formally forging the *Golden Link* successfully.

UPS began its common carrier quest in 1952 by applying to the state of California for a certificate allowing common carrier service in the San Francisco Bay Area and also for transferring packages between the Bay Area and Los Angeles. Even though United Parcel Service was well established in both California cities, the company was unable to move packages between them. To do so, one had to go to the U.S. Post Office. A mere extension of UPS's operating authority in California precipitated a series of legal battles before regulatory commissions and in the courts. California's PUC granted package-transfer rights in 1953, and the company immediately began moving packages between California's two largest metropolitan areas, San Francisco and Los Angeles. However, overnight common carrier service rights between the two California cities required a separate application. Later, the PUC granted overnight common carrier service rights between the two California cities, and in 1956, that service commenced.

The common carrier vision went beyond California and was national in scope; thus, permit applications were being filed by United Parcel Service all over the country. From 1952 until 1980, the company waged legal battles before regulatory commissions and courts across the nation to secure additional permissions to expand delivery service. Every service expansion was hard earned and in many cases came about only after UPS lawyers and executives presented mountains of evidence and hours of testimony, after customers pleaded for service, and after local officials made personal appeals. Early applications requested only small expansions of territory, either just a particular city or perhaps an entire metropolitan area. Then, emboldened by growing operational success and depending upon regulatory jurisdictions, the company began to request more and larger areas, whole states, and even multistate regions in a single application.

During a span of nearly 30 years, UPS pursued over a hundred applications for common carrier operating authority. In 1953, Chicago became the first city outside California where UPS offered common carrier delivery service. Subsequent expansion was to cities where United Parcel Service had already established a flourishing retail delivery business. In 1956, first time in its history, UPS elected to start from scratch in building common carrier service in Boston. They purchased new UPS package cars, hired drivers, and initiated delivery routes. Boston was an amazing success as it moved to 10,000 packages a day within 6 months of the launch. Thereafter, Boston also became a model for hundreds of new openings all over the country. The commissioning of the Boston operations was a defining moment in the UPS's history: common carrier package delivery business transformed the company and redefined it, with retail deliveries becoming an increasingly smaller percentage of the business volume. In 1961, the company logo was also pared down to display *UPS*, announcing a new era. In 1962, Jim Casey, by then 74 years old, relinquished responsibility to George Smith.

After all those years of toil for UPS, the federal government finally deregulated interstate commerce. Just as United Parcel Service was mapping its final districts in the United States, the Motor Carrier Act of 1980 opened up the trucking industry to new carriers. UPS had won the hard-fought battle, but now it was faced with new challenges and competition. Competition was good for consumers because it offered shippers more choice. It allowed manufacturers to reduce inventories and move their products more quickly. That situation also created opportunities for UPS years later, when the company began to offer supply-chain services to help customers move their products to consumers when they needed them. The Motor Carrier Act of 1980 also meant that United Parcel Service had competition not only on the ground but also in the air; it also removed all regulatory restrictions against the ground movement of packages that were partly transported by air. But, before it even attempted to take on FedEx, it extended its brown tentacles, for the first time, into the foreign market.

FedEx was established in 1973 as an airline, not as a ground delivery, company. This is an important legal distinction, because the company was exempt from onerous common carrier regulations. Airlines fall under a different regulatory body (the FAA), not the ICC that regulated trucking companies including UPS, and even though FedEx also had trucks, its corporate structure exempted it from ICC regulation. All FedEx packages, no matter where they came from and no matter where they were bound, flew into one hub, namely, Memphis, Tennessee. It copied how UPS was using its ground hubs, a concept the passenger airlines also emulated to set up their hub-and-spoke airport layout systems. Flying and sorting at night, when air traffic was lighter, facilitated 1-day delivery. With these modifications, FedEx had revolutionized air delivery. While UPS was busy with its delivery service expansion (UPSers were still decrying the U.S. Postal Service as the number one competitor), FedEx worked out its kinks and got even further ahead in the air-transport business. It added planes, people, and, what was more important, a comprehensive ground network. FedEx was one of the factors that actually helped bring about the deregulation of the airlines—Cargo deregulation occurred in 1979 and passenger deregulation in 1980.

UPS had been in business for more than 75 years and had forged world-class ground operations. Yet it had also grown complacent, and its intense corporate culture of industrial engineering and operations was, in some sense, an obstacle for it to replicate in the air, what it had perfected on the ground. FedEx burst on the scene in 1973 with an innovative model that ultimately redefined the airfreight industry, encroached on UPS's core business, and forced UPS to rethink fundamental strategic assumptions. UPS was going to have to unlearn some of the very traits that had made it so successful.

10.3 INTERNATIONAL SERVICES

Actually, in 1975, UPS started its first operations outside the United States by commencing service within Canada's largest metropolis, Toronto, Canada. Gradually, Canadian service expansions in both ground and air service were extended throughout the country. In 1989, various Canadian regulatory agencies granted UPS additional authority to provide ground service to 90% of the population.

In Europe, UPS decided to begin in a limited way from Dusseldorf, West Germany. Germany, a country known for its punctuality and structure of order, seemed like a perfect location to establish an operation based on UPS's strong values of regimentation and strict service standards. But with the work ethic in the 1970s, Germany was not the fine-tuned Swiss watch the UPS pioneers had anticipated. The country's labor climate was institutionalized by German laws that called for extended vacations, much time off, liberal unlimited sick-day policies, assistance for loading (UPSers load their cars themselves), short work hours and weeks, and other inflexibilities. Furthermore, driving was considered a lowly job in Europe, at a lower pay scale than the U.S. standard. Unlike United States, Germans considered the familiarity of first-name basis and the lack of proper titles insulting.

After recognizing the seriousness of oversights in the German start-up, in 1980, UPS assigned a special team of 10 managers to delve into the problems. After an investigation, they implemented important culture-sensitive corrections and adjustments, such as granting the aforementioned wage increase, applying better hiring criteria (which resulted in the recruitment of more native Germans), and setting up an assimilation strategy. Benefiting from these adjustments and also enhancing benefits to the levels that Germans were used to, the big problems of turnover and absenteeism began to improve. Soon, the German operation became a productive model of a foreign extension of an American company, finally posting a profit in 1981.

From 1987 to 1992, UPS acquired 16 different trans-European transportation companies as a way of building a European UPS from the inside out, as the company had done throughout the United States. From then on, UPS did its research before making foreign expansion. Teams compared existing cultural and business practices in appealing target countries to the UPS way and then strategized how to cope with them in advance. Operations began to turn around and prosper once UPS began to move forward more cautiously, with respect for the culture into which it was expanding. UPS top leadership made a decision to hire competent management people locally and has American managers train key foreign managers in UPS systems, sometimes rotating them through assignments in the states to give them a better understanding of the UPS corporate culture. They gave them whatever help they needed to get started with acquiring good employees and customers. Then U.S. managers took a backseat, removing themselves from day-to-day operations.

It was in the Orient that UPS saw its most lucrative future. UPS formed a partnership with Yamato Transport Co., Japan's highly respected and largest package delivery company. Called UPS/Yamato Express, the new venture covered every address in Japan. China represented the biggest cultural challenge the company had ever faced. In 1988, UPS initiated an agent partnership with China's biggest freight forwarder and a state-owned delivery company popularly known as the Sinotrans Group. UPS brought the packages to China and Sinotrans delivered them. When in late 2001, after China at last joined the World Trade Organization as the 149th member, UPS became the first package delivery company to commence direct flights between the United States and China. UPS was then able to purchase its earlier service partners, such as Sinotrans in 2004. In a deal worth $100 million, UPS assumed direct control of express-delivery services in 23 locations covering 200 cities and regions throughout China—that made UPS the only express-delivery service wholly owned by non-Chinese.

UPS made what seemed like tentative steps into China in 1988, but in 1989 alone, it went from a 41-country base to more than 180 countries worldwide, covering 80% of the world's population. The approach was vintage UPS, an international version of the same method it had used to expand into the Bay Area in 1919. UPS identified existing delivery companies that had rights for one or more countries, set up partnerships with those companies, and later acquired most of these partners. This round of pioneering thus did not immediately provide the level of service to every address that UPS could offer in the United States, but it established beachheads in the major metropolitan areas in each country.

It took 15 years to develop a comprehensive, integrated air and ground network in Europe, but by 2005, UPS had established service there much like what is available in the United States and the rest of North America—it has the capability to serve any address in either of those two continents. In addition to Worldport in Kentucky, the company has other air hubs serving UPS international. Cologne, Germany, is the European Union hub. Miami serves the Latin American market. The Philippine hub at Clark Air Force Base in Pampanga takes care of the intra-Asian market. In addition, UPS built a 425,000 ft² distribution and logistics hub at the Singapore Airport, where the Asia Region headquarters is also located. The Shanghai hub, a 53,000 ft² facility with the right to expand to at least 100,000 ft², will provide UPS's direct link to Japan.

Today, in more than 200 countries, all of UPS global transportation services combined, which include UPS Supply Chain Services, can reach over four billion people or about double the portion of the world's population that can be reached by any telephone network. It's an enormous, multilingual version of UPS's earlier nationwide strategy, not *Golden Link* but *Global Link*. And the creed was *don't divide and conquer* but *consolidate and conquer*.

10.4   AIR CARRIER SERVICES

In 1981, UPS made a decision to get into the air business in a big way. The airline business is highly complex, heavily regulated, and entirely unfamiliar to UPS. Looking for a middle road, UPS decided to buy airplanes, but rely on a group of four independent carriers to handle operations. Officially, that meant that UPS wasn't an airline and wouldn't be regulated by the FAA; but the inherent limits of the strategy repeatedly left UPS hamstrung. It bought its first airplane in 1981 and began using several smaller air companies, like Evergreen and Orion, to provide the pilots and supporting airline services.

In 1982 UPS selected Louisville International Airport to be the center of its air operations and began to set up a Memphis-like hub on 550 acres between the existing airport's two parallel runways. By 1985, UPS Next Day Air service was available in all 48 states and Puerto Rico. Alaska and Hawaii were added later. That same year, UPS began its intercontinental service as it commenced flying packages and documents between the United States and six European countries. Blue Label Air service morphed into UPS 2nd Day Air, giving shippers a less expensive alternative for important packages that didn't have to be there overnight.

It wasn't until 1988, when the FAA granted UPS authorization to operate its own aircraft, that UPS Airlines was formed to take direct control over all its air operations. But, the process was fraught with risk. First, it would require a massive commitment of resources and money; second, airline labor norms were completely unfamiliar to UPS; and third, UPS knew very little about operating an airline. UPS had to hire pilots, no fewer than 800 to get the airline off the ground. UPS had to figure out how to integrate, at once, a huge number of professionals used to being the most important people in their organizations. As a small example, pilots wanted to be addressed by other UPS employees as *captain* even though the CEO and other top managers went by first names like everyone else.

It purchased aircraft from Boeing, other aircraft manufacturers, and other airlines and hired pilots and air-support loaders, sorters, and other personnel, while it accumulated all of the necessary technology and support systems. By the end of 1989, UPS owned 110 airplanes, including seven 747s, and leased an additional 247 airplanes. In its first year, UPS Airlines was the fastest-growing airline in FAA history. By its 100th anniversary in 2007, UPS owned and operated 268 jet aircraft (including 24 new planes to help cover rapidly growing Asian markets) and charters another 309 to accommodate its transport obligations, making it the world's 9th largest airline. UPS now runs the 8th largest airline in the world, serving more than 800 airports in more than 200 countries and territories around the world. A new $1 billion project will increase Worldport sorting capacity by 60%, to 487,000 packages per hour, which will swell the UPS Louisville area workforce to almost 23,000, including drivers, ground crews, and supply-chain employees. Louisville International Airport is now the fourth busiest cargo airport in the United States.

The UPS hub, on the 550 acres at the Louisville International Airport, is now called *Worldport*. It is massive with 122 miles of upward, downward, north-, east-, south-, and westbound conveyor belts, chutes, and ramps. The 4 million square foot facility is 75 ft high, too big to air-condition. Most of the action—over a million packages a day's worth—takes place between 11 p.m. and 4 a.m. Each night over a hundred planes from all over the world swoop down to Louisville. UPS has invested $35 million in FAA-endorsed new satellite-based navigation system called ADS-B that gives precise information about where a plane is and where it is headed. The ADS-B devices interface with UPS's advanced information systems like Computerized Operations Monitoring, Planning and Scheduling System (COMPASS) that not only provides planning, scheduling, and load-handling information but can also plot optimum flight schedules as well as the most efficient routes to land in Louisville.

Approximately 5000 employees come nightly to *the sort*. Some unload packages from the planes, making sure to put each package label-side up, onto one of three conveyors: One conveyor is for small parcels like envelopes that are mostly Next Day Air and 2nd Day Air packages, another conveyor is for irregularly shaped packages, and the third is for normal six-sided boxes. The boxes' labels must be pointed upward so that the system's infrared image sensor can read the recipient's address as well as register the parcel's dimensions and weight. Small rubber mallets, called *hockey pucks*, line one side of a belt. Based on the scanned directions, the pucks push packages onto a belt going to the appropriate direction. Scanning occurring as many as six times as the parcel courses through Worldport determines its trajectory till the exit. A package that enters Worldport with *smart label* technology can take as little as 8 min to make its proper journey from inbound to outbound plane. When labels aren't electronically scannable, Telecode Office employees rectify the label from their desks, else they reroute the packages into the *exceptions* circuit where other employees correct the label manually. If package lines jam, there are 30 mechanics on call to undertake on-demand repairs. A belt that can't be fixed quickly gets its packages rerouted to others on the matrix. Propelled by all such technology, packages exit Worldport automatically sorted by destinations and placed in appropriate *cans*. Loaders place the cans in the refueled UPS jets that take off in the early morning darkness for airports all over the world.

10.5 e-COMMERCE SERVICES

On November 9, 1999, Atlanta-based United Parcel Service of America made financial history when it made what was then the largest U.S. IPO in history—$5.47 billion worth at $50 a share. Immediately prior to the opening, the stock had split two for one, creating a total 1.1 billion shares. The stock was $3 higher than its previous valuation due to the strong demand from institutional investors. Shares sold to the public were class B stock, with one vote per share. The existing employee-owned shares would become class A stock, with 10 votes per share. Two years after the IPO, class A shares gradually became eligible to be sold, and if sold, they would become class B shares and carry a single vote. This was in the spirit of the ownership company in that it reinforced the central message that the most important owners at UPS were still those who had invested their lives in the company—the employees.

The approaching end of the millennium had marked the beginning of point-and-click online ordering. Brandishing its new *Moving at the Speed of Business* slogan, UPS was already the industry leader in shipping e-commerce. It had the infrastructure and methodologies to deliver electronic commerce solutions to businesses. Its accounts included 6 of the top 10 Internet retailers, including Amazon.com. During the 1998–1999 holiday season, UPS delivered over half of all online purchases.

It had the resources to become a full-service vendor, offering a wide range of services to manage the flow of information, goods, and funds business to business, retailer to customer, and household to household. Not only has customer service dramatically improved, but the cost per tracking request has dropped from the $2 it was in 1994 to less than 10 cents. UPS uses its technological advantages and its integrated network of air and ground transport (helped out by machinery that sorts more than 350,000 packages per hour) to keep pace with the home delivery boom created by the Internet and with business-to-business commerce.

UPS had invested more than $10 billion in IT over the 5 years prior to the IPO and wasn't finished yet. At the time of the IPO, UPS already dominated the large business-to-business e-commerce market. It had only to refine the software to capture a large percentage of business-to-household e-commerce. UPS used a chunk of its cash to develop an information network supported by formidable electronics technology, which includes real-time Internet tools—UPS online—to help customers track their goods.

Today, information—primarily input from the 96,000 Delivery Information Acquisition Device (DIAD IVs) in use every day for recording pickups and deliveries and receiving UPS dispatcher messages—is available to all. Almost 19 million people check out the www.ups.com (online since the mid-1990s) website each day, making an average of 10 million tracking requests. With a budget of $1 billion a year, he manages 4700 employees who develop much of the company's software, watches over a website that draws close to 19 million visitors a day, maintains 8700 servers, and monitors 15 mainframes capable of processing millions of instructions per second. Barnes's job—just like all the others at UPS—is to exact more efficiency from an already efficient operation that moves an average of 15 million packages a day across the world.

> Mahwah's nine IBM mainframes, and six more located in a data center near Atlanta called Windward, process 27 million instructions per second, track 15 million packages each day, coordinate the operations of an entire airline, collect and distribute package delivery data from 96,000 DIADs, and connect 149,000 workstations through 8,700 servers. UPS owns the largest IBM relational database in the world. It is the biggest user of cellular minutes in the world. It is the biggest purchaser of PCs in the world. And, it employs 4000 of its own software engineers!

On Barnes's watch, UPS is pushing automation to the summit with *package flow technology*. Computerization determines the order in which packages are loaded on a truck and the most efficient route for delivering them, and it makes tracking packages directly available to customers and UPSers. The flow begins when the customer generates a digital *smart label* on the UPS website or with help from clerks at a UPS shipping outlet, such as The UPS Store. That request transmits customer and package information to a central processing unit, where it is linked with several other systems—including GPS to pinpoint its exact position. The moment that label is generated, the center that delivers that address is notified when it will arrive. The label, of course, is printed and affixed to the parcel. The parcel is loaded into a feeder (a big rig that transports packages) at the nearest UPS package center, taken to a nearby hub for sorting, and sent on its way. Information on shipments for every UPS package is stored in databases at a facility in Mahwah, New Jersey, and then backed up by a second data center outside Atlanta. Besides allowing UPS to track packages, the databases allow for rerouting as necessary.

With enterprise-wide access to the data, each of the 1100 U.S. delivery centers knows what's coming in, from several days out to the Next Day Air deliveries. At the package center, a scanner validates the smart label and then issues another label, dubbed a preload assist label (PAL), so loaders know how to route the package. The preload assist system (PAS) tells the loader where that package should be placed in the package car, in stop-by-stop order. This makes the preloader's job very easy (preloaders are generally part-timers, and the positions have relatively high turnover). The PAS reduces preloader training from a 30-day marathon of chart memorizing to a few hours of learning to place the packages in the vehicles; the reduced training alone should help the PAS pay for itself immediately.

Now, instead of a driver arriving at the center and scanning all the packages in the delivery vehicle and planning the day's route, all that information has already been transmitted to a wireless handheld computer, the DIAD. This device is now in its smaller, lighter fourth-generation avatar known as the *DIAD IV*. The new DIAD IV system designs delivery routes built from this *inbound package knowledge*. The enhanced DIAD download (EDD) system knows exactly what is loaded in each vehicle and will remind drivers if they're forgetting a package or are about to misdeliver one. EDD also gives UPS dispatchers specific driver location information so they can select the most convenient driver to send for an on-call pickup. Today's DIAD IV instantly records deliveries and captures signatures, confirming receipt of packages immediately. It can also display critical information about deliveries nationwide, in a specific geographic area or even to an individual recipient.

10.6 LOGISTIC SERVICES

UPS had always been operations oriented, but globalization and competition forced the company to become market driven. Kent *Oz* Nelson, CEO 1989–1997, came from the company's business development and engineering sectors. Keeping in mind the forward-thinking UPS founder Jim Casey, Nelson and his team had begun steering the mammoth shipping firm into as yet uncharted territory—logistics. With that act, the company's focus shifted. Thanks to electronics, commerce and tracking could be virtual, but delivery must remain actual. Electronics also had capabilities that could greatly enhance transportation, as UPS was being reminded by competitors FedEx and Roadway Packaging System (later purchased by FedEx) during the 1990s. In 1995, UPS turned its ROADNET division into the UPS Logistics Group to help fulfill the needs of individual customers. In 1999, the logistics group became UPS Logistics Technologies. UPS essentially packaged itself, wrapped up what it already did so well—thanks to its armies of efficiency experts—and started selling logistics services to businesses.

By 1999, UPS had revised its charter to change the company's mission for the first time in history, from serving customers' small package needs to enabling global commerce. The logistics business could piggyback off the hard-won national infrastructure that UPS had already built.

UPS decided to stretch its *core capabilities* tied to its delivery infrastructure, network planning, operational excellence, industrial engineering firepower, and growing IT integration.

UPS has built a comprehensive electronic network and has applied this to its massive international transportation network, facilitated by what may be the largest technological infrastructure in commercial history. This incredible infrastructure, plus the global staff that supports it, constitutes UPS's innovative supply-chain and logistics services. Electronics gave UPS industrial engineers the tools to reassess and redefine their role and function. So, in addition to auditing, doing time measurements, motion studies, and reports designed for an internal audience, the department's efforts could also be reengineered for the customer: looking at customer logistics, customer volume development, and customer satisfaction. UPS Logistics Technologies takes the kinks out of transportation for businesses like Frito-Lay, Costco, and SYSCO. Its transportation and logistics software—called ROADNET—supports route optimization, territory planning, mobile delivery execution, real-time wireless dispatch and scheduling, and GPS tracking. Other products include daily and territorial route planners, delivery trackers, and loading tools. UPS Logistics Technologies offers significant reduction in transportation, distribution, and inventory costs, as well as predictable and expeditious delivery times.

Soon after the IPO, the Ford Motor Company came to UPS asking for help in getting its cars from assembly plants to the showrooms of America. UPS Logistics signed a deal with Ford to optimize the transportation of Ford vehicles from factory to dealer. UPS redesigned everything, the entire delivery network, and even pasted bar codes on windshields. The end result was not only better tracking of each vehicle, but shaving a whopping 40% off the time in transit. That added up to big dollars. Even the Harley-Davidson Motor Company, an American motorcycle manufacturer since 1903, sought the aid of UPS. The company had logistical challenges, primarily inbound transportation and getting parts and accessories to dealerships. Consultation revealed that hundreds of suppliers were shipping components to one of the company's three factories in different states. Then components were stockpiled and consolidated for delivery. UPS helped Harley-Davidson optimize its entire transportation operation by having everything sent to one UPS cross-docking facility and shipped out immediately.

10.7 SCM SERVICES

By the mid-1990s, many businesses were already outsourcing or offshoring much if not all of their manufacturing to operations in other cities and other countries. If someone in England could get a book delivered to San Clemente, California, faster than another bookstore in Los Angeles, the order went out to the British store. If sweatshops in Manila could make a T-shirt faster than a manufacturer in Philadelphia, the order went out to the Philippines. Physical proximity was no longer an important factor in the supplier–customer equation. This trend created global supply chains. Outsourcing was cost-effective but presented a set of complex challenges for businesses, coupled with the unpredictability inevitable with anything that is out of sight and foreign. Trying to keep track of multisource manufacturing and shipping, foreign currencies, customs duties, and wide distribution can be like trying to juggle a bunch of spinning plates—things that UPS had perfected for decades. Better supply-chain management and solutions are the answer. Before 1999, UPS already had the insights and the will to create a supply-chain revolution. It only needed the means.

UPS strategy is focused on complementing and growing the core package delivery business with new, innovative SCS. They will accomplish that by inserting their unmatched capabilities in managing the flow of goods, information, and funds across their customers' supply chains. Their strategy has been manifested by the launch or acquisition of new logistics, freight forwarding, customs brokerage, financial services, mail, and consulting businesses that expand the scope and power of the distribution and SCS. The company decided to position itself at the head of the rapidly growing world commerce by establishing UPS SCS.

In 1996, UPS SCS went into the business of synchronizing commerce. To support SCS, UPS was strategically buying companies in the late 1990s and even creating them if they did not exist. Under CEO Oz Nelson and then Jim Kelly, the enterprise was determined to grow in uncharted territory by managing the movement of goods, the accompanying flow of information, and even providing the financing if necessary. UPS SCS assists customers with logistics, global freight, mail services, consulting, and financial services. The new mantra at UPS would be the heady and ambitious catch phrase *enable world commerce*. SCS was all about reducing inventories, optimizing JIT manufacturing processes, and getting those cardboard boxes to hustle along. Say you have customers in Massachusetts whose products are manufactured in China. After these products are manufactured, they need to be distributed, but maybe sending them back to Massachusetts is an unnecessary middle step. That is where *integrated delivery* comes in. SCM helps businesses by eliminating unnecessary shipping steps. Domestic and international deliveries are still the largest segments of UPS's current business, but its SCS segment is the fastest growing and, together with UPS Freight, reflects 14% of the company's revenue, or approximately $6 billion a year.

As an *integrated carrier*, the new UPS offers shipping products and services to streamline the distribution process. Timex began in Waterbury, Connecticut, in the nineteenth century, and that's where its headquarters still are. Yet 7500 Timex employees—in Connecticut and Arkansas, as well as Brazil, France, Germany, the People's Republic of China, Israel, India, and the Philippines—contribute to the end product. This means shipping goods between one continent and another. The various components converge in Cebu, Philippines, where 80% of the watches are assembled. There, Timex's Global Distribution Center daily distributes 170,000 watches, shelf-ready with pricing and security measures already in place, not to Waterbury, but to their retail customers.

Neil Pryde Sails, another Connecticut-based business, designs and sells approximately 4000 boat sails a year. Neil Pryde designs in Connecticut; manufactures in Shenzhen, China; and ships finished sails to customers around the globe and customers who want their sails immediately. Neil Pryde Sails uses UPS OnLine WorldShip software. The time-saving database provides automated shipping forms for tracking and tracing. UPS Worldwide Express guarantees the pickup, drop-off, and in-transit times for all Neil Pryde Sails shipments from Hong Kong and ensures door-to-door deliveries internationally. UPS Customhouse Brokerage makes sure that products clear customs quickly and reduces duties by billing all customers in their local currency. UPS imports allows the company easy-to-follow billing in U.S. dollars. So much shipping can be handled online that Neil Pryde Sails no longer needs to warehouse products, because UPS is providing what it refers to as a *warehouse in motion*.

In another case, Nikon, the world leader in precision optics, wanted to help retailers meet customer demand for the new, high-tech digital cameras. It called on UPS SCS to help streamline the distribution process. UPS coordinated Nikon's manufacturing centers in Japan, Indonesia, and Korea with air and ocean freight and customs brokerage. It designed everything to go to Louisville, Kentucky, where Nikon-related tasks joined those of hundreds of other companies at UPS SCS Logistics Center. There, UPS employees prepare Nikon kits, adding accessories like batteries and chargers, and then repackage them and send them on their way to thousands of retailers throughout the United States, Latin America, and the Caribbean. UPS SCS participation significantly shortened Nikon's supply chain, increased the speed of product to market, and created a higher level of service to the retailers.

UPS not only sorts and delivers business clients' products; it may, through UPS SCSs, help assemble, repair, and store them. UPS employees can be found servicing broken computers, mixing pet food, quality checking sports footwear, troubleshooting and repairing cameras, gathering and consolidating motorcycle components, and even custom-dressing teddy bears for shipment, all as services to other businesses. UPS has become a multitasker par excellence. Businesses then achieve a better turnaround time and better customer service. UPS can even interact with businesses' customers in place of the businesses' own staffs. Sometimes SCS eliminate extra transportation steps. UPS has minimized the transport in the repair industry. Say your Toshiba laptop goes on the fritz.

You call Toshiba's 1-800 number. Either you take it to The UPS Store or your UPS driver shows up at your door to whisk away the laptop, padded box in hand. The box flies to the Louisville hub and from there, not to Japan, but 2 miles down the road to another UPS building where UPS employees specially trained and certified by Toshiba—not Toshiba employees—fix it. Within 3 days, your Toshiba is back at your house in tip-top shape. When it turned to UPS SCSs, Toshiba saw its customer complaints instantly drop.

To keep the household-to-household business, UPS toyed with a network of UPS pack and ship stores across the country, but instead, it finally joined forces with Mail Boxes Etc. in 2001, buying the parent company out from the brink of bankruptcy, for $191 million cash. In 2003, Mail Boxes Etc. franchises began rebranding as The UPS Store, and presently, there are more than 5600 franchises in 40 countries around the world. Customers can access UPS from home too. When you order merchandise online, it triggers a supply-chain algorithm that may click several times across the globe. In a likely scenario, the item you ordered from a U.S. company is sourced from a Chinese warehouse, routed to the Hong Kong hub, and voilà!—3 business days later, the UPS driver stands at your door, merchandise in hand. And when The UPS Store processes that box you just left there, the hubs and destination center *feel* its presence electronically, triggering seamless physical actions that further it along its journey.

10.8 SUMMARY

UPS century-long excellence and success is mainly about managing large-scale change again and again. When UPS embarks on a major initiative—building its supply-chain business, for example—it is able to successfully undertake these large-scale changes without falling prey to the pitfalls (like covert resistance, employee insecurity, entrenched habits and methodology, low morale) that can cripple an organization during times of radical change. UPS has evolved a Built-for-Variation enterprise on the bedrock of such ingredients like the concept of partners entailing stock ownership by employees, conservative corporate culture, promotions-from-within policy, and decentralized and autonomous style of operations. When it decided to commence air carrier services, the challenges were formidable. First, it would require a massive commitment of resources and money; second, airline labor norms were completely unfamiliar to UPS; and third, UPS knew very little about operating an airline. But UPS went ahead to launch UPS Airlines; and by its 100th anniversary in 2007, with 268 jets, UPS now runs the 8th largest airline in the world. By 1999, UPS had revised its charter to change the company's mission for the first time in history, from *serving customers' small package needs* to *enabling global commerce*. UPS then went one step further into the business of synchronizing commerce, that is, providing SCM solutions and services.

Section V

Industry Excellence through Variations

This section presents an overview of the variations witnessed by the automobile industry in automobiles, manufacturing technologies, new product development, manufacturing operations, production operations, and also the market operations. It provides a snapshot of the emergence of Ford's T Model as the *dominant design* leading to GM's differentiated range of models, the transition from Ford's *mass production* to Toyota's *lean production* system, and decades of convergence of design and technologies occurring across market segments, categories of vehicles, manufacturers, and even countries. As noted in the introduction to Section IV, with regard to any company, there is no generalizability. Similarly, every industry is different at every stage and from each other. For the focus at industry level, we have selected the automobile industry only because it has been widely witnessed and participated by everyone across the world in the last century.

11 Automobile Industry

The first internal combustion-powered vehicles were produced in Europe—notably by Gottlieb Daimler and Carl Benz in Germany during the 1880s. But the emergence of the modern industry dates back to 1913 and Henry Ford's first implementation of the production technology—the continuously moving assembly line—that would revolutionize so much of industrial capitalism over the next few decades. Ford quickly became the master of mass production, churning out thousands of black Model T Ford from his Highland Park plant in Michigan. Mass production dramatically lowered the costs of building cars and paved the way for the emergence of a mass consumer market. It was not Ford, however, but Alfred Sloan, the CEO of GM, who in the mid-1920s realized that the key to success in this industry was serving customers by offering them *a car for every purse and purpose*. Under Sloan, GM segmented the market, producing a differentiated range of models to consumers. In doing so, the company seized market leadership from Ford and has not relinquished it since.

By the 1960s, GM, Ford, and Chrysler dominated the U.S. market, then by far the world's largest. GM at one point made more than 60% of all automobile sales in the United States, and collectively, the three companies accounted for more than 90% of sales. Moreover, the companies were now multinationals, with significant operations outside of North America, particularly in Europe, the world's second largest car market. This, however, was all about to change. Riding the wave of economic disruption caused by the OPEC oil price hikes of the 1970s, foreign manufacturers of fuel-efficient cars began to invade the U.S. market. First there was Volkswagen, with its revolutionary VW Beetle, followed by a slew of Japanese manufacturers, including, most notably, Honda, Nissan, and Toyota.

It was the invading Toyota that was to usher in the next revolution in car making. Faced with a small and intensely competitive home market and constrained by a lack of capital, Toyota started to tweak the mass production system first developed by Ford. Engineers tried to find ways to build cars efficiently in smaller volumes and with less capital. After years of experimentation, by the 1970s, a new production system emerged at Toyota. Later dubbed *lean production*, it was based on innovations that reduced setup times for machinery and made shorter production runs economical. When coupled with the introduction of JIT inventory systems, flexible work practices, an organization-wide focus on quality, and the practice of stopping the assembly line to fix defects (which was the antithesis of Ford's continually moving assembly line), the lean production system yielded significant gains in productivity and product quality. In turn, it lowered costs, improved brand equity, and gave Toyota a competitive advantage. Toyota capitalized on its lean production system to grow faster than its rivals; by 2008, the company had replaced GM as the world's largest automobile manufacturer.

As was the case with mass production earlier, Toyota's innovation of lean production was imitated, with varying degrees of success, by other volume carmakers. Japanese competitors were the first to try to adopt Toyota's innovation. During the 1990s, the American volume carmakers jumped on the bandwagon, but the sluggish American response to Japanese and European invasions of their home market allowed the foreigners to capture even more market share. Consequently, Toyota still enjoys an advantage in the automobile industry, based on production excellence, although the gap has closed significantly.

By the end of the first decade of the twenty-first century, America's big three were rapidly losing their grip on the domestic market. Even in light trucks (which include pickup trucks and sports utility vehicles [SUVs], both segments in which the big three have traditionally been very strong), the big three share declined from 74% in 1997 to 61.8% in 2003 to further reduction to 47.9% in 2008. In contrast, the foreign carmakers were up from 26% in 1997 to 52.1% in 2008, with one major difference—unlike in the 1980s when most foreign cars were imported into the United States, by 2008, most foreign nameplates were built in *transplant* factories located in North America.

11.1   EVOLUTION OF THE AUTOMOBILE

The early years of the industry were characterized by considerable uncertainty over the design and technology of the motorcar. Early *horseless carriages* were precisely that—they followed design features of existing horse-drawn carriages and buggies. Early motorcars demonstrated a bewildering variety of technologies. During the early years, the internal combustion engine vied with the steam engine. Among internal combustion engines, there was a wide variety of cylinder configurations. Transmission systems, steering systems, and brakes all displayed a remarkable variety of technologies and designs, as well as considerable ingenuity.

However, interestingly, the carriage manufacturers did not innovate to automobiles; the first automobile manufacturers were from the bicycle industry. Carriage manufacturers traditionally worked with wood, whereas the new bicycle manufacturers worked with steel. Bicycles themselves were an innovation in the 1880s, made possible by three things, namely, the cheapness of steel from the earlier innovations in steel production, the paving of city streets, and the discovery of vulcanized rubber for tires. To invent the automobile, the idea was to put some kind of engine onto a carriage made of bicycle components, for the bicycle provided steering, gearing, and wheels. Three kinds of engines were tried: (1) steam engine and wood fuel, (2) electric motors and battery power, and (3) internal combustion engine and gasoline fuel.

Prior to the introduction of the internal combustion engine, steam engines and electric motors were used to power the so-called horseless carriage. In fact, by the close of the nineteenth century, some 30 manufacturers in the United States were offering an array of vehicles powered by gasoline, steam, or electricity with electric vehicles outselling all other types of cars. Steam engines, however, proved too heavy to be practical for road vehicles, plus they had long start-up times and their need for plenty of water limited their range, so they soon faded from the scene. Electric vehicles of that era also had limited range and were very expensive and slow, which ultimately led to the declining popularity of electrically powered cars. Races were held between the three principle configurations of automobiles as steam, electric, or gasoline powered. In 1902, a gasoline-powered car defeated electric and steam cars at a racetrack in Chicago, establishing the dominance of the gasoline engine. Thereafter, this engine was to become the core technology for the automobile.

Forerunners of the modern automobile actually first appeared in the eighteenth century—notably a steam-powered three-wheeled vehicle invented in France in 1769 by Nicolas Joseph Cugnot—but self-propelled vehicles didn't become commercially viable until the introduction of the internal combustion engine in the nineteenth century. Etienne Lenoir, a Belgian inventor, developed the first internal combustion engine, which he demonstrated in Paris in 1862. Then, in 1878, Nikolaus Otto, a German inventor, developed a four-stroke coal-gas engine that was quieter and smoother running (see Chapter 6, Subsections 6.2.1, "Lenoir Internal Combustion Engine;" 6.3.1, "Otto Four-Stroke-Cycle Internal Combustion Engine;" and 6.4.1, "Wankel Rotary Engine"). In 1885, Germans Karl Benz and Gottlieb Daimler built the first gasoline-powered vehicles, and in 1889, Frenchman Armand Peugeot built the first automobile for commercial sale. American brothers Charles and Frank Duryea began production in 1896 of the first commercially available gasoline-powered car in the United States.

Early gasoline-powered vehicles also had their drawbacks, including noise, the smell of the fuel, complicated shifting requirements, and difficult hand cranking needed to start the engine. Several developments in the early years of the twentieth century propelled the gasoline internal combustion engine to prominence and made possible the personal transportation revolution, most notably the invention of the electric starter by Charles Kettering in 1912, which eliminated the hand crank and initiated the mass production of the gasoline engine by Henry Ford. It was the introduction in

1908 of the very affordable Model T by Henry Ford with its $950 price tag that really marked the beginning of the personal transportation revolution. That price dropped as low as $280 when Ford revolutionized automotive production in 1913 with the constantly moving assembly line and $5 per day wages in 1914. These developments made cars affordable for the average person, gave factory workers increased buying power, and triggered the explosive growth of the global automotive industry, which by 2006 was selling nearly 64 million vehicles annually.

Over the years, technologies and designs tended to converge as competition relegated many once-promising designs to the scrapheap of history. The Ford Model T represented the first *dominant design* in automobiles—the technologies and design features of the Model T set a standard for other manufacturers to imitate. Convergence of technologies and designs was the dominant trend of the next 90 years. During the 1920s, all manufacturers adopted enclosed, all-steel bodies. During the last few decades of the twentieth century, most models with distinctively different designs disappeared: the VW Beetle with its rear, air-cooled engine, the Citroen 2-CV and its idiosyncratic braking and suspension system, Daf with its *variomatic* transmission, and the distinctive models made by Eastern European manufacturers, such as the three-cylinder Wartburg and the two-cycle Trabant. Engines became more similar: typically four or six cylinders arranged in line, with V-6 and V-8 configurations for larger cars. Front-wheel drive and antilock disk brakes became standard on smaller cars; suspension and steering systems became more similar; body shapes became increasingly alike. Although the automobile continued to evolve, technological progress was incremental: innovations primarily involved new applications of electronics and new safety features.

In terms of automotive engineering, the main advances were multivalve cylinders, traction control systems, all-wheel drive, variable suspensions, and intercooled turbos. The quest for fuel economy resulted in the substitution of lighter materials (aluminum, plastics, ceramics, and composites) for iron and steel. Despite continuing advances in the application of electronics—including satellite navigation systems, communications technology (telematics), emergency signaling, collision-avoidance radar, and intelligent monitoring systems—little in today's family cars was radically new.

Designs and technologies also converged among manufacturers. While different categories of vehicle (family cars, sports cars, passenger minivans, SUVs) retained distinctive design features, within each category, the manufacturers' product offerings became increasingly similar. Convergence also occurred across countries. U.S. cars downsized; Japanese and Italian cars became larger. The same market segments tended to emerge in different countries. The major differences between countries were in the sizes of the various segments. Thus, in the United States, the *midsize* family sedan was the largest segment, with the Ford Taurus, Honda Accord, and Toyota Camry the leading models. In Europe and Asia, small family cars (*subcompacts*) formed the largest market segment. Other national differences were also apparent. In North America, pickup trucks, used as commercial vehicles in most of the world, increasingly displaced passenger cars.

The top 15 global manufacturers, including their affiliates and subsidiaries, account for 85% of the world vehicle production. These companies and their global affiliate and subsidiary operations are the following:

- GM, which includes Daewoo (Korea) and Holden (Australia)
- Toyota Motor Corp., which includes Daihatsu (Japan) and Hino (Japan)
- Ford Motor Company, which includes Aston Martin (United Kingdom), Jaguar (United Kingdom), Land Rover (United Kingdom), and Volvo Car Corp. (Sweden)
- Volkswagen AG, which includes Audi (Germany), Bentley (United Kingdom), Bugatti (Italy), Lamborghini (Italy), Skoda (Czech Republic), and Seat (Spain)
- DaimlerChrysler AG, which includes Chrysler division, Dodge, Jeep, Mercedes-Benz (Germany), Smart (Germany) and Commercial Vehicle Division, EvoBus GmbH (Germany), Freightliner (United States), and Mitsubishi Fuso Truck and Bus Corp. (Japan)
- Hyundai-Kia Automotive, which includes Hyundai Motor (Korea) and Kia Motors (Korea)
- Nissan Motor Co. (Japan)

- Honda Motor Co. (Japan)
- PSA/Peugeot-Citroen SA (France)
- Renault SA (France), which includes Dacia (Romania) and Renault-Samsung Motors (Korea)
- Suzuki Motor Corp (Japan), which includes Maruti Udyog Ltd. (India)
- Fiat S.p.A. (Italy), which includes Fiat Auto (Italy), Ferrari (Italy), Maserati (Italy), and Iveco (Italy)
- Mitsubishi Motor Corp. (Japan)
- BMW Group (Germany) which includes Rolls-Royce (United Kingdom)
- Mazda Motor Corp. (Japan)

11.1.1 EVOLUTION OF AUTO SPECIES

In today's world, personal transportation includes pickup trucks, some capable of carrying up to five passengers, as well as SUVs and vans, both mini and full sized. Pickups and SUVs also come in compact and full-sized models. Since the story of both cars and light trucks is so interwoven and complex, for the purposes of this section, we will explore the automobile in the broader context of being any light vehicle used for passenger transportation.

As the name implies, a pickup is a small truck with an open cargo-carrying bed. Traditional SUVs function like station wagons with passenger and cargo-carrying capabilities but are built on pickup truck platforms. A new breed of downsized compact SUVs appeared early in the twenty-first century based on car rather truck platforms. These more car-like SUVs are an example of the blurring of lines between cars and trucks and will be covered later in this essay. Full-sized vans include commercial-style passenger vans and van conversions that provide living room comfort for its passengers, while minivans are primarily factory-built smaller versions of van conversion designed.

The history of pickup trucks generally follows a timeline similar to cars. Gottlieb Daimler, the German automobile pioneer, built the first pickup truck in 1896, a four-horsepower belt-driven vehicle with somewhat limited capability. The first truck company to go into business in the United States, the Rapid Motor Vehicle Company, was opened in Detroit in 1902 by two brothers, Max and Morris Grabowski. The previous year, they had designed and built a single-cylinder chain-driven dray machine that was basically a motorized version of a horse-drawn wagon. Rapid and the Reliance Motor Company, also of Detroit, which also began building trucks in 1902, were purchased in 1908 and 1909, respectively, by William C. Durant, founder of GM Corporation (GMC). Both Rapid and Reliant trucks were big gas-powered machines designed to replace horse-drawn wagons, so in the early years, GMC used electric vehicles for light-duty delivery. However, in 1916, GMC converted everything to gasoline engines. Light-duty Chevrolet trucks appeared on the scene in 1918 and GMC-badged trucks were introduced in 1927, a product that originated with Pontiac but was badged a GMC to avoid the prospect of three GM branded trucks. The other top selling American pickup truck pioneers, Dodge and Ford, introduced their pickup truck models in 1918 and 1925, respectively.

Compact pickup trucks, which today are among the best-selling vehicles in the world, first appeared in the United States in 1959 when the Nissan Motor Company, a small Japanese manufacturer, exported the Datsun 1000, which had a load capacity of only a quarter-ton and a 1000 cc, 37 hp engine. While initial models only sold a few hundred vehicles per year, sales jumped to more than 15,000 in 1965 with the importation of the Datsun 520 pickup. Nissan eventually phased out the Datsun model name and badged all subsequent models as Nissan. Toyota jumped into the compact pickup fray in the U.S. market in 1964 by exporting its Stout, followed in 1969 by the Hilux.

The popularity of the compact pickups caught the attention of the domestic big three (GM, Ford, and Chrysler) in the United States, and they countered in the early years with imports of their own: Chevrolet with the LUV from Isuzu Motors Ltd. in 1972, Ford with the Courier from Mazda at about the same time, and Dodge from Mitsubishi in 1979. These models evolved into the domestically built Chevrolet S-10, Ford Ranger, and the Dodge Dakota, introduced in the mid-1980s as the first midsize pickup trucks.

Both SUVs and station wagons trace their heritage to the 1920s when cars called depot hacks or suburbans were used to carry passengers and their luggage from train stations. Chevrolet and GMC applied the name to a utility vehicle introduced in 1936 as a passenger-carrying vehicle based on a commercial panel truck. Another early SUV forerunner was the Willy's Jeep Wagon introduced in 1940 as a utility vehicle for the family and eventually redesigned as the Jeep Wagoneer in 1963. The British Land Rover, another icon of the SUV industry, was inspired by the World War II Willy's Jeep and introduced by Rover Company Ltd. at the 1948 Amsterdam Motor Show.

While SUVs evolved as truck-based vehicles, the classic station wagon is a rear-wheel-drive car with a stretched wheelbase to accommodate a cargo-carrying compartment accessible via a rear tailgate. The first production station wagon was the 1923 wood-bodied Star built by the Star Motor Company, which had been purchased by the Durant Motor Company. Ford made the station wagon affordable to the general public with the introduction of a mass-produced Model A version in 1929.

Passenger vans have been part of the light vehicle automotive scene since the 1920s, but minivans did not emerge until they were introduced in 1983 by Chrysler Corporation, the market leader in full-size vans. The company recognized the desirability of a downsized van that fits in a typical garage and offers all the comforts and handling ease of a station wagon with a lot more room for passengers and cargo. Ford and GM followed suit in 1985 with the Aerostar and Astro/Safari, respectively.

11.1.2 Evolution of New Product Development

The declining importance of scale economies in assembly did not make life easier for smaller automobile producers. The critical scale economy was the ability to amortize the huge costs of new product development over a large enough number of vehicles. The cost of developing new models had risen steeply as a result of increasing complexity of automobiles, the application of electronics and new materials, higher safety requirements, quality improvements, new environmental standards and the need for increased fuel efficiency. By the late 1980s, the cost of creating an entirely new, mass production passenger car from drawing board to production line was about $1.25 billion. By the early 1990s, costs had escalated substantially above this level. Smaller manufacturers could survive only by avoiding these massive product development costs.

One way was to avoid new model changes: at the time of its acquisition by Ford, Jaguar's two models, the XJ6 and XJS, were almost two decades old, and almost no investment had been made in developing a new model. The tiny Morgan car company has made the same model since the late 1930s. The alternative was to license designs from larger manufacturers. Thus, Tofas of Turkey built Fiat-designed cars, Proton of Malaysia built Mitsubishi-designed cars, and Maruti of India produced Suzuki-designed cars.

During the 1990s, new product development emerged as the critical organizational capability differentiating car manufacturers. Designing, developing, and putting into production a completely new automobile was a hugely complex process involving every function of the firm, up to 3000 engineers, close collaboration with several hundred suppliers, and up to 5 years from drawing board to market launch. By 2004, the leading Japanese manufacturers, Toyota and Honda, were still viewed as industry leaders in new product development. Attempts to lower product development costs focused around modular designs and *virtual prototyping*—the use of 3D computer graphics to design and test prototypes.

The cost of new product development has been the major reason for the wave of mergers and acquisitions in the industry. Over the past two decades, the industry has consolidated through mergers and acquisitions. The financial problems of Japanese and Korean auto companies during the late 1990s accelerated this process. As a result, U.S. and European carmakers had acquired significant proportions of the Japanese and Korean auto industries by 2004. Economies from sharing development costs also encouraged increased collaboration and joint ventures: Renault and Peugeot established joint engine manufacturing; GM established collaborations with Suzuki, Daewoo, Toyota, and Fiat to build cars and share components. In China and India, most new auto plants were joint ventures between local and overseas companies.

11.1.3 Evolution of Manufacturing Operations

11.1.3.1 Manufacturing Systems

At the beginning of the twentieth century, car manufacture, like carriage making, was a craft industry. Cars were built to order according to individual customers' preferences and specifications. In Europe and North America, there were hundreds of companies producing cars, few with annual production exceeding 1000 vehicles. When Henry Ford began production in 1903, he used a similar approach. Even with fairly long runs of a single model (e.g., the first version of the Model T), each car was individually built. The development of more precise machine tools permitted interchangeable parts, which ushered in mass production: batch or continuous production of components that were then assembled on moving assembly lines by semiskilled workers. The productivity gains were enormous. In 1912, it took 23 man-hours to assemble a Model T; just 14 months later, it took only 4. The resulting fall in the price of cars opened up a new era of popular motoring.

If *Fordism* was the first major revolution in process technology, then Toyota's *lean production* was the second. The system was developed by Toyota in postwar Japan at a time when shortages of key materials encouraged extreme parsimony and a need to avoid inventories and waste through defects. Key elements of the system were statistical process control, JIT scheduling, quality circles, teamwork, and flexible production (more than one model manufactured on a single production line). Central to the new manufacturing was the transition from static concepts of efficiency optimization toward continuous improvement to which every employee contributed. During the 1980s and 1990s, all the world's car manufacturers redesigned their manufacturing processes to incorporate variants of Toyota's lean production.

During the 1960s and 1970s, it was believed that efficiency required giant assembly plants with outputs of at least 400,000 units a year. During the past decade, most of the new plants established had output capacities of between 150,000 and 300,000 units. New manufacturing methods required heavy investments by the companies in both capital equipment and training. The 1980s were a period of unprecedented high investment expenditures. However, as GM was to learn after spending more than $10 billion in upgrading its plants, the essence of the Toyota system was not new manufacturing *hardware* in the form of robotics and computer-integrated manufacturing systems; the critical elements were the *software*—new employee skills, new methods of shop floor organization, redefined roles for managers, and new relationships with suppliers. The new flexible manufacturing technology together with modular designs reduced the extent of scale economies in assembly. The quest for flexibility was a central feature of Bill Ford's revitalization strategy. Starting in Ford's North American plants, reorganizing for flexibility would enable the manufacturing of multiple models in individual plants, which would allow capacity totaling one million units to be closed.

11.1.3.2 Relationships with Suppliers

Henry Ford's system of mass production was supported by heavy backward integration. In Ford's giant River Rouge plant, iron ore entered at one end and Model Ts emerged at the other. Ford even owned rubber plantations in the Amazon basin. The trend of the past 20 years has been toward increasing outsourcing of materials, components, and subassemblies. This has been led primarily by the desire for lower costs and increased flexibility. Again, leadership came from the Japanese: Toyota and Nissan have traditionally been much more reliant upon their supplier networks than their U.S. or European counterparts. At the end of the 1990s, GM and Ford both spun off their component manufacturing businesses as separate companies: Delphi and Visteon, respectively.

Relationships with suppliers also changed. In contrast to the U.S. model of arm's length relationships and written contracts, the Japanese manufacturers developed close, collaborative long-run relationships with their *first-tier* suppliers. During the 1990s, the Japanese model of close collaboration and extensive technical interchange with a smaller number of leading suppliers became the model for the entire global auto industry—all the world's manufacturers outsourced more manufacturing and technology development while greatly reducing the number of their suppliers. As the leading component suppliers have gained increasing responsibility for technological development—especially in sophisticated subassemblies such as transmissions, braking systems, and electrical and electronic equipment—they have also grown in size and global reach. By 2004, Bosch, Johnson Controls, Denso, and Delphi were as big as some of the larger automobile companies.

11.1.3.3 Cost-Reduction Efforts

Different companies have faced different cost issues. While European manufacturers were constrained by rigid working conditions, restrictions on layoffs, and generous benefits, U.S. companies were hit by increased provisions for pensions and health care. In Japan, the critical cost issue of the past decade was the strength of the yen. The quest for economies of scale and scope in relation to product development meant that companies sought to spread rising development costs over larger production and sales volumes. Increasingly, during the 1990s, the auto manufacturers attempted to introduce single global products. After more than a decade of coordinating its European and U.S. models, Ford's Mondeo/Contour was the company's first truly global model.

Increasing competition in the industry has intensified the quest for cost reduction among automobile manufacturers. Cost-reduction measures have included the following:

- Worldwide outsourcing. The tendency for increased outsourcing of components has been noted earlier. In addition, auto firms have developed OEM supply arrangements among themselves: Daewoo supplies several of GM's models; GM supplies components to Fiat; Mitsubishi and Chrysler supply engines for the BMW Mini.
- JIT scheduling, which has radically reduced levels of inventory and work in progress.
- Shifting manufacturing to lower-cost locations. VW's North American production is based in Mexico, and it moved production from Germany to the Czech Republic, Spain, and Hungary; Japanese companies have moved more and more production to lower-cost locations in Southeast Asia; Mercedes and BMW developed greenfield plants in the deep south of the United States.
- Automation. In high-cost locations (North America, Western Europe, and Japan), increased automation has reduced labor input.

This desire for scale economies in development, manufacture, and purchasing also resulted in the standardization of designs and components across the different models of each manufacturer. Ford's platform strategy is evolving out of the company's desire to cut costs by spreading its technology across as many brands as possible: the idea is to share systems in areas that customers can't see and feel and differentiate the brands in areas they can (see Chapter 5, Subsection 5.2.4.2, "Platform Effect"). Ford realized valuable efficiencies in manufacturing, engineering, and product costs for new vehicles by sharing vehicle platforms and components among various models and the reuse of those platforms and components from one generation of a vehicle model to the next. During the late 1990s, Ford synchronized platforms with Mazda and by 2000 was building its luxury models on the same platforms used for its volume models. Thus, the Jaguar X-type used the Mondeo platform, while the Jaguar S-type and the Lincoln LS also shared the same platform. Similar standardization occurred in engines. Ford moved to just five basic engine designs whose modular structure allowed many common components and multiple variations. Thus, Ford's Global inline 4-cylinder engine family, launched in 2003 in the Mazda 6, had 100 possible variations and consolidated 8 engine families into 1 (see Subsection 11.1.3.4, "Patterns of Variations").

The rise of foreign competitors in the U.S. market has been attributed to a number of factors, including better designs and more fuel-efficient offerings (particularly in the passenger car segment), superior product quality, higher employee and capital productivity, and lower costs due to smaller pension and health-care commitments. Despite the closing of the productivity gap, American vehicle makers still lost money on every car they made in 2007, while their Japanese competitors made money. The main reason was higher labor costs at the big three. This was due not just to higher wage rates but also to the pension and health-care obligations that American manufacturers have long borne not just for their current employees but also for their retirees. GM, for example, has 2.4 pensioners for every current employee. As a consequence of such factors, in 2007, the average labor cost at the American big three was $75 an hour, compared to $45 an hour at Toyota's American assembly plants. However, all three American companies have been renegotiating their contracts with the UAW and trying to shift the obligations for retirees onto the union. Indeed, bankruptcy protection has enabled Chrysler and GM to accelerate this process.

11.1.3.4 Patterns of Variations

In an effort to cope with the tough competitive conditions in the North American market and elsewhere, automobile companies are looking hard at additional ways to take costs out of their system or capture more of the available demand. Among the most notable initiatives underway have been industry-wide attempts to streamline product development, offer a wider range of niche cars, work more closely with suppliers, develop systems for building cars to order, and introduce a new breed of hybrid cars. Historically, it took 4 years and cost as much as $1 billion to develop a new car model and prepare a factory for its production. To recoup those fixed costs, automobile companies needed high-volume sales, which required selling cars without a major update for 4 years and sometimes as long as 7 years. To attain maximum economies of scale, automobile manufacturers tried to run their plants at full capacity, producing 240,000 units a year. The ideal was to have each plant produce just one model.

In recent years, the automobile market has become increasingly fragmented. Models are now updated more frequently to keep pace with changing consumer tastes and competitive pressures, shortening product life cycles. Customers have demanded more variety, and automobile companies have been willing to give it to them, bringing a wider variety of niche cars to the market. For example, the Ford Taurus was once the best-selling passenger car in America with annual sales of approximately 500,000 (equivalent to two plants running at full capacity). As sales slipped, Ford decided to kill the Taurus and replace it with two models, one smaller than the Taurus and one bigger.

However, to recoup the costs of such variety of offerings, development and manufacturing costs have to be reduced. Automobile companies are trying to do this by using a common platform and parts in a wider range of cars.

11.1.3.4.1 Product Platforms

An example depicting the industry's evolving philosophy is GM's 2005 roadster, the Pontiac Solstice. Under the old economics, for a car costing $20,000 and forecasted to sell only 25,000 units a year would never have made it off the drawing board. To make the car economically viable, GM revolutionized its product design philosophy:

- By digitalizing much of the design of the car and tools, GM was able to cut $50 million out of the design costs. It used to take 12 design engineers 3 months to produce a clay model, an essential step in the design process. Now, a single designer can take an idea on a computer screen to an animated video of a vehicle in 3 weeks. GM saved another $80 million by designing the car so that it could use existing tools at its factory.
- More money was saved by a decision to base the car on a common platform architecture called Kappa, which would be used for other small rear drive cars. According to GM, the company could make an almost unlimited number of bodies on the Kappa architecture, and each vehicle would be profitable with a volume of 20,000–25,000 a year.

Using the same platform across a wide model range is fast becoming industry standard practice. As with so many other industry trends, the Japanese pioneered the practice. Honda, for example, builds its Odyssey minivan, the Pilot SUV, and the Acura MDX SUV on the same platform.

11.1.3.4.2   Extensively Reusable Parts

Another design goal is to try and use the same parts in a wider variety of car models and, where appropriate, use parts from old models in new cars. Detroit auto designers formerly boasted that new models were completely redesigned from the floor up with all new parts. Now, that is seen as costly and time-consuming. At GM, the current goal is to reuse 40%–60% of parts from one car generation to the next, thereby reducing design time and tooling costs.

Hand in hand with changes in design philosophy, automobile companies are retooling their factories to reduce costs and make them capable of producing several car models from the same line. By doing so, they hope to be able to reduce the break-even point for a new car model. With the Solstice, for example, GM cut design costs by using a common platform and parts. It has cut tooling and production costs by investing in flexible manufacturing technologies that can be used to produce multiple designs based on the Kappa platform from the same basic line.

11.1.3.4.3   Enhanced Production Flexibility

Automobile companies are retooling their factories to reduce costs and make them capable of producing several car models from the same line. By doing so, they hope to be able to reduce the break-even point for a new car model. With the Solstice, for example, GM cut design costs by using a common platform and parts. It has cut tooling and production costs by investing in flexible manufacturing technologies that can be used to produce multiple designs based on the Kappa platform from the same basic line. GM has also worked hard to get unions to agree to changes in inflexible work rules. Assembly line workers now perform several different jobs, which reduces waste and boosts productivity.

As a result of all these changes, the costs and time for bringing new cars to market are shrinking. Most of GM's new development projects are now on 24-month schedules—a far cry from the late 1980s when GM engineers rejoiced when they were able to bring out the Chevrolet Corsica in just 45 months.

11.1.3.4.4   Redefined Supplier Relationships

At one time, the American automobile companies were highly vertically integrated, producing as much as 70% of their component parts in-house. Those parts that were not made in-house were often purchased using an annual competitive bidding process. Both Ford and GM have sold off major chunks of their in-house suppliers: GM spun off its in-house suppliers in 1999 as Delphi Automotive; Ford spun off its in-house suppliers the following year as Visteon Corporation. Delphi and Visteon are now the number one and two auto parts suppliers in the United States.

The big three have also been reconfiguring their relationships with independent suppliers. The automobile companies are now expecting their tier 1 or major suppliers to produce modules—larger vehicle parts that comprise several components such as fully assembled chassis, finished interiors, and *ready-for-the-road* exterior trim. These modules are then bolted and welded together to make finished vehicles, rather like toy models being snapped together. For such an approach to work, the suppliers have to get involved earlier in the process of designing and developing new models and engineering assembly tools. To create an incentive for them to do so, the automobile manufacturers have been entering into longer-term contracts with their tier 1 suppliers.

Another trend has been to encourage major suppliers to locate new facilities next to assembly plants. Ford's refurbished plant in Chicago has a supplier park located next door. The idea is to get suppliers to deliver inventory to the assembly line on a JIT basis. At the Chicago plant, the average component now needs to travel only ½ mile, as compared to 450 mile in the past. The proximity has saved suppliers transportation costs, which are passed onto Ford in the form of lower prices. In addition, Ford has reduced inventory on hand at its Chicago plant from 2 to 3 days' worth to just 8 h worth.

11.1.3.4.5 Rapid Production and Deliveries

Once a car is built, it spends between 40 and 80 days sitting in factory lots, distribution centers, and dealers' forecourts before it is actually sold. This represents a huge amount of working capital that is tied up in inventory. Most of the automobile companies have been trying to reduce the time between ordering and delivery. The ultimate goal is to have cars built to order, with cars being assembled and shipped to a dealer within days of a customer placing an order. This is similar in conception to the way that Dell sells computers, with customers ordering a computer and paying for it, online, while the machine is shipped out within days. Toyota, too, is trying to build more cars to order. By the mid-2000s, Toyota was building about 12% of the cars it sold in the United States to order, with a build time of just 14 days.

11.1.3.4.6 Sharper Forecasting

One of the biggest problems in the automobile industry is predicting what demand will be. If automobile companies could predict demand more accurately, they might be able to reduce the mismatch between inventories and demand—and hence the need to resort to incentives.

11.1.4 EVOLUTION OF PRODUCTION OPERATIONS

11.1.4.1 Globalization

Although the logic of maximizing volume in order to spread the costs of developing new models and new technologies pushed companies into expanding into all three of the world's major markets—North America, Europe, and Asia (Japan in particular)—many sizable companies remained regional players. Renault had effectively merged with Nissan and Samsung Motors, but lacked any presence in North America, while Fiat and Peugeot were essentially European manufacturers.

The driving force behind capacity expansion was internationalization. Although multinational growth extends back to the 1920s (when Ford and GM established their European subsidiaries), until the 1970s, the world auto industry was made up of fairly separate national markets. Each of the larger national markets was supplied primarily by domestic production, and indigenous manufacturers tended to be market leaders. For example, in 1970, the big three (GM, Ford, and Chrysler) held close to 85% of the U.S. market, VW and Daimler-Benz dominated the market in Germany, as did Fiat in Italy, British Leyland (later Rover) in the United Kingdom, Seat in Spain, and Renault, Peugeot, and Citroen in France. By 2004, the industry was global in scope—the world's leading manufacturers were competing in most of the countries of the world.

Internationalization required establishing distributors and dealership networks in overseas countries and often building manufacturing plants. Foreign direct investment in manufacturing plants had been encouraged by trade restrictions. Restrictions on Japanese automobile imports into North America and Europe encouraged the Japanese auto makers to build plants in these regions. Similarly, the high tariffs protecting the motor vehicle markets of most Asian and Latin American countries obliged the major auto makers to set up local assembly.

Different companies pursued different internationalization strategies:

- Toyota and Honda had expanded throughout the world by establishing wholly owned greenfield plants.
- Ford, which had initially internationalized by creating wholly owned subsidiaries throughout the world, extended its global reach during 1987–1999 by acquiring Mazda, Jaguar, Aston Martin, Land Rover, and Volvo.
- GM extended its global reach through a series of alliances and minority equity stakes: notably with Fiat, Suzuki, Saab, and Daewoo.

- DaimlerChrysler was created through a transatlantic merger in 1998 and established a position in Asia by acquiring equity in Mitsubishi Motors and Hyundai.
- Volkswagen made a series of acquisitions in Europe (Seat, Skoda, and Rolls Royce) and had focused heavily on investing in manufacturing capacity outside the advanced industrial countries, notably in Eastern Europe, Latin America, and China.

Despite the tremendous internationalization of the auto industry, it was the home market that remained the most important market for every car maker: that was where they typically exercised market leadership. For example, Fiat was the market leader in Italy, VW in Germany, Renault and PSA in France, and Hyundai and Daewoo in Korea. This was partly a legacy of earlier import protection, partly due to national preferences of domestic consumers, and partly a result of well-developed local dealership networks and intimate local knowledge.

11.1.4.2 Production Locations

Given the shift in demand to the emerging market countries and the auto makers' quest for lower production costs, it might be expected that the geographical distribution of the industry would have changed substantially over recent decades (in the same way that other manufacturing industries—consumer electronics, small appliances, textiles, and semiconductors—have relocated in newly industrializing countries). Yet, in automobiles, such shifts have been surprisingly small. The main feature of 1950–1980 was the rise of production in Japan, but since 1980, variations have been small, with the three major manufacturing regions—Western Europe, North America, and Japan—each accounting for close to 30% of world production. The continuing dominance of this triad is despite the attempts of newly industrializing countries to develop their domestic industries, either by protecting domestic manufacturers or by encouraging inward investment.

The advantages of these countries lie primarily in labor costs, which were often a fraction of those in the older industrialized countries. Nevertheless, with the exception of Korea, none of the new auto-manufacturing countries has emerged as a major world center for motor vehicle production. The ability of the established auto-manufacturing countries to sustain their leadership points to the importance of factors other than wage rates in driving international competitiveness in the auto industry. For example, although wage costs were much lower in Mexico than in the United States, this cost advantage was outweighed by other factors.

11.1.4.3 Excess Capacity

A major problem for the industry was the tendency for the growth of production capacity to outstrip the growth in the demand for cars. During the 1980s and early 1990s, Japanese companies were major investors in new capacity with a number of greenfield *transplants* in North America and Europe. During the 1990s, all the world's major car companies responded to the quest for globalization with new plants (many of them joint ventures) in the growth markets of Southeast Asia, China, India, South America, and Eastern Europe. During 1990s, the Korean car companies were especially aggressive investors in new capacity. It was particularly worrying that, even in the markets where demand was growing fastest (such as China, where sales grew by over 50% in early 2000s), growth of production capacity outstripped growth in demand. The resulting overhang of excess capacity was a key factor exacerbating intense competition in the industry.

11.1.5 EVOLUTION OF MARKET OPERATIONS

As already noted, despite the globalization of the leading auto makers, the world market by 2004 was still composed of many national markets due to differences in national regulations and customer preferences, differences in affluence and infrastructure, trade restrictions, and the need for each manufacturer to build a dealership network in each market it served. The world market was also segmented by types of product. The market for passenger vehicles was traditionally segmented by size of automobile. At the top end of the market were *luxury cars* distinguished primarily by their price. There were also specific types of vehicle: sports cars, SUVs, small passenger vans (*minivans*), and pickup trucks. Although industry statistics distinguish between automobiles and trucks—the latter being for commercial use—in practice, the distinction was less clear. In the United States, small pickup trucks were a popular alternative to automobiles; SUVs were also classed as trucks.

Margins varied considerably between product segments. Chrysler's position as one of the world's most profitable auto manufacturers for much of the 1990s was primarily a result of its strong position in SUVs (through Jeep) and minivans (through its Dodge Caravan and Plymouth Voyager models). The luxury car segment, too, was traditionally associated with high margins. By contrast, small- and medium-sized family cars have typically lost money. However, mobility barriers between segments tend to be low. Modular product designs and common platforms and components have facilitated the entry of the major manufacturers into specialty segments. As the pressure of competition has increased across all market segments, manufacturers have sought differentiation advantage through introducing models that combine design features from different segments. In early 2000s, an increasing number of *crossover* vehicles were introduced into the U.S. market, notably: SUVs that adopted the integrated body and frame of the typical automobile, such as the BMW X5, Honda Pilot, and Saturn Vue; minivan, SUV hybrids such as the Chrysler Pacifica and Pontiac Aztec; sports utility station wagons such as the Cadillac SRX; four-wheel drive minivans; luxury SUVs; and smaller SUVs based on small-car platforms such as the Honda CR-X and Toyota RAV4.

Vertical segmentation was also an issue for the industry. Profitability varied across the different stages of the auto industry's value chain. The prevailing wisdom was that downstream activities offered better profit potential than manufacturing activities—certainly financial services (mainly customer and dealer credit) were far more profitable than vehicle manufacturing. It was this logic that had encouraged the auto companies to outsource and spin off most of their production of components. It also motivated Ford's previous CEO, Jacques Nasser, to acquire downstream companies such as the repair and parts supplier Kwik Fit and Hertz car rental.

11.2 RECESSION 2008

The recession started in the U.S. housing market. Over the prior decade, mortgage lenders had been making increasingly risky loans to American homebuyers, some of whom clearly could not afford the loans that they were taking on. However, low *teaser rates* that expired after 1–5 years, to be replaced by much higher interest rates, persuaded many borrowers to take on mortgage debt obligations. Moreover, many believed, incorrectly as it turned out, that if they could not meet their mortgage payments, they could always sell their home and pay off the loan. For their part, mortgage lenders were encouraged to make risky loans by the development of a market for mortgage-backed securities. This enabled them to bundle mortgages into bonds and sell them off to other finan cial institutions, thereby shifting the risk. The institutions that purchased these mortgage-backed securities were themselves able to buy insurance that protected them against the risk of default by mortgage payees, which would have significantly reduced the value of the bonds they held. This insurance took the form of complex derivatives, known as collateralized debt obligations, or CDOs, that were then traded between institutions. CDOs were viewed as relatively safe investments because default rates on mortgages were low.

The entire system seemed to work as long as housing prices continued to rise and defaults on mortgages stayed low. But in 2007, a two-decade rise in U.S. housing prices came to an abrupt end. Furthermore, the interest rates were starting to rise on many adjustable rate mortgages that had been sold with low teaser rates. As rates started to rise, defaults surged, homes were foreclosed at record rates, and an increase in the supply of homes for sale drove prices down even further. At this point, the U.S. financial system went into a tailspin. The value of mortgage-backed securities and derivatives such as CDOs plunged, damaging the balance sheets of many financial institutions.

Because financial institutions from all over the world had been purchasing American mortgage-backed securities and derivatives, the crisis immediately became global. With assets on their balance sheets, financial institutions had no choice but to dramatically reduce the new loans that they made, and after decades of easy credit, suddenly, it became very difficult to borrow money.

The credit squeeze hit the automobile industry particularly hard because cars are, for many people, their second-biggest purchases after homes and are often financed with loans. Moreover, even for those people who used cash to buy cars, the financial crisis suddenly made them very nervous; they responded by putting off any purchases of big-ticket items such as automobiles as they waited for the crisis to resolve. As a consequence, demand for automobiles plunged. For 2008, U.S. automobile sales were down 18% from 16.1 million units in 2007 to 13.2 million units in 2008, the monthly sales figures recording some of the lowest levels since the 1960s.

What complicated the situation was that at the same time the financial crisis was unfolding, oil prices surged to record highs, hitting $150 a barrel in mid-2008. As prices at the gas pump rose, people who were buying cars switched to more fuel-efficient vehicles, many of which were made not by American producers, but by smaller foreign firms such as Hyundai and Kia of Korea and Subaru of Japan. Even though oil prices subsequently fell as the recession took hold, the perception had taken hold that once the economy recovered, oil prices would again increase and demand for pickup trucks and SUVs remained weak.

The global financial crisis caused credit contraction and increased uncertainty about the future, which hit automobile sales particularly hard. Two factors made the sharp sales declines particularly painful for automobile manufacturers:

- High level of fixed costs: As sales fall below break-even run rates, high fixed costs imply rapidly rising losses.
- Overcapacity: Between 2004 and 2008, some 19 million units of new productive capacity had been added to the global industry.

The combination of expanding global capacity, followed by a sharp drop in demand, when coupled with a demand shift to smaller cars, proved toxic for several companies. Hardest hit were GM and Chrysler. Both companies were forced to seek government aid in an attempt to stave off bankruptcy. In total, the U.S. government had committed $17.4 billion in aid to GM and Chrysler by early 2009. Despite the aid, both Chrysler and GM were forced into bankruptcy. Under an agreement negotiated after Chrysler's bankruptcy, the Italian company Fiat will take over management of the company's assets. Fiat itself had undergone a dramatic turnaround between 2004 and 2008 under the leadership of Sergio Marchionne, primarily through a combination of production efficiencies and new product launches, including small cars that have sold well in an environment of high fuel prices. As of May 2009, Fiat was also reported to be bidding for Opel, the European arm of GM.

In contrast, Ford, who had raised significant capital from private investors in 2007, declined government aid and signaled that, despite operating losses, it would be able to survive the recession.

While the slump in demand was most dramatic in America, other markets also saw sharp declines, and for many of the same reasons. However, while decline in demand was the norm in developed nations, the story in developing nations was different. In China, India, and Brazil, for example, the sales declines were much smaller, and growth had already resumed by early 2009. In all of these countries, relatively low levels of automobile ownership, coupled with fast underlying economic growth rates, indicated that sales will continue to grow at a robust rate in coming years.

11.3   CURRENT PATTERNS OF VARIATIONS

The automobile, which first appeared commercially in the nineteenth century and went on to revolutionize personal transportation during the twentieth century, is evolving through a series of fundamental changes early in the twenty-first century in order to achieve two somewhat incompatible goals. On the one hand, there is a growing mandate among many governments to minimize the automobile's impact on the environment and nonrenewable natural resources. On the other hand, it must maintain its utility and affordability if it is to remain attainable by the general public.

Three dominant trends that are determining its growth and direction in the twenty-first century are the following:

1. The blurring of the line between cars and trucks as truck-like vehicles become increasingly popular.
2. The drive to make vehicles more environmentally friendly by cleaning their emissions, making them more recyclable and lighter, and eliminating their consumption of nonrenewable resources; a serious effort has been expended to eventually replace the internal combustion engine with an alternative power train and energy source, possibly the space age version of the fuel cell, in order to minimize or eliminate undesirable exhaust emissions.
3. The desire to make vehicles as safe as possible by improving their crash avoidance capabilities, crash worthiness, and occupant protection.

Within each of these trends, the driving force is the continuing application of advanced technologies, notably the continuing increase of mobile and in-vehicle electronics, automotive-grade semiconductors, and automotive telematics and navigation.

The demand for vehicles that incorporate the comfort and performance of the automobile with the utilitarian benefits of a truck has created a new type of vehicle built from the ground up as a cross between car and truck with unibody construction; relatively high seating positions; two-, four-, or all-wheel drive; and capability of carrying up to eight passengers plus reasonable cargo space—the only missing ingredient is an ability to go off-road. This new breed of personal transportation vehicles is known generically as crossovers—built on car chassis with car-like suspension systems and power trains, yet with the ruggedness, storage, and utilitarian features of SUVs, vans, and pickup trucks. The suburban vehicles of the 1920s and 1930s were the forerunners of this movement, especially as embodied in the early Chevrolet and GMC Suburban models. The modern crossover emerged late in the twentieth century, experiencing quick acceptance among the motoring public in the United States, growing 62% from 1999 to 2003 and predicted to continue at a 10% rate into the future, according to some forecasters.

The R&D efforts of the automotive industry are primarily focused on technologies that will make the automobile as environmentally compatible, as economical to operate, and as safe as possible, goals that in many ways are mutually exclusive. Safety and emission reductions all add cost, while efforts to improve fuel economy by reducing weight can make the vehicle less safe and crashworthy. To make vehicles more environmentally compatible, the major emphasis has been on emission reduction, although there is increasing interest in making the vehicle as recyclable as possible. The latter is being improved by using recyclable materials as much as possible and making it easier to disassemble and extract recyclable materials at the end of its useful life.

The primary efforts, however, have been on power train technology, with the emphasis on cleaning up emissions and reducing fuel costs and consumption. This has included constantly improving the venerable gasoline internal combustion engine so that it runs as cleanly as possible without an undue sacrifice of power and performance. But by the end of the twentieth century, it had become apparent that further improvements were providing only marginal emission improvement. Alternative power and fuel sources have been the primary goal ever since.

Ironically, one of those alternative sources is a reintroduction of the electric motor, either as the primary motive force or as part of a hybrid system mated with an internal combustion engine. In hybrid versions, the internal combustion engine may be used in any of three ways: strictly as part of a generating system to charge the batteries; as an auxiliary to the electric motor providing extra power when needed, as well as for recharging the batteries; or as the main motive force while the batteries are used to power all other systems in the vehicle, reducing demands on the internal combustion engine. Hybrids have been a major research effort by virtually all of the major manufacturers for use in both cars and trucks.

In hybrid cars, at low speed, the power comes from an electric motor that gets electricity from an onboard battery. At higher speed, the internal combustion engine kicks in and provides power, while simultaneously recharging the battery through a generator. When braking, energy from the slowing wheels is sent back through the electric motor to charge the batteries. The result can be substantial savings in fuel consumption, with little in the way of a performance penalty. Toyota's Prius hybrid can go from a standstill to 60 mph in 10 s and averages 60 mpg in the city and 51 mpg highway driving. This makes the Prius an ideal commuting car. The big drawback is that the hybrid propulsion system adds about $3,000–$5,000 to a vehicle's sticker price and the battery has to be replaced about every 100,000 miles at a cost of about $2,000. At a gas price of $2 a gallon, it takes some 5 years for a hybrid to repay the additional investment. In addition to the Prius, Toyota also sells hybrid versions of some of its other models, including the Lexus SUV, the Highlander SUV, and the Camry sedan. The company aims to increase its overall hybrid sales to $1 million by 2010–2012 and offer hybrid versions of all of its vehicles by 2020.

Electric vehicles reappeared in the 1990s with conversion vehicles from Ford, GM, DaimlerChrysler, and Toyota, plus two cars built from the ground up as electric cars, GM's EV1 and Honda's EV Plus. Cost and short range imposed by the limitations of battery technology have kept pure electric vehicles out of the mainstream, although promising developments with advanced lithium ion battery packs and GM's development of the Chevrolet Volt, an electric car concept vehicle introduced at the North American International Auto Show in 2007, could bring electric vehicles back into a more prominent position. The Volt uses GM's patented E-Flex Propulsion System that consists of an electric drive system, lithium ion battery, and an onboard generator powered by a 1 L turbocharged internal combustion engine to keep the batteries charged.

Introduced in 2010, the Chevy Volt is a compact four-door electric car with a reserve gasoline-powered engine. The primary power source is a large lithium ion battery. The battery can be charged by plugging it into a wall socket for 6 h, and fully charged, it will fuel the car for 40 miles, which is less than most people's daily commute. After that, a gasoline engine kicks in, both providing drive power and recharging the lithium ion battery. GM estimates fuel economy will be about 100 miles a gallon, and charging the car overnight from a power outlet would cost about 80% less.

Yet another power train technology that dates to the early days of the automobile and has been around ever since may in the end be the technology to trump all the others. That is the lowly diesel, an internal combustion engine used extensively in Europe and Asia in small cars, yet largely looked down upon in the United States because of the perception that it is inherently noisy, dirty, hard to start, and expensive to buy, although more fuel-efficient and longer-lasting than gasoline engines. The diesel engine was invented in the late 1880s by Rudolf Diesel, a German looking for an alternative to steam power. He developed an internal combustion engine based on compression ignition principles capable of running on biomass fuel—peanut oil in initial demonstrations. Early diesels were too large and heavy for use in vehicles, and it was not until the 1920s when smaller, lighter versions were introduced for lorries in Europe. Mercedes began using diesels in cars in 1936, and such use in cars has grown ever since. By the early twenty-first century, for example, Europeans were buying diesel-powered cars 35% of the time—45% if you include light trucks.

A further plus of the diesel is its ability to operate on nonpetroleum-based fuels. Diesel owners have the option of using biodiesel, a domestically produced renewable fuel that reduces U.S. oil dependence and contributes to the national economy. American consumers are turning to diesel-powered vehicles to help them save money on fuel costs without having to sacrifice the power and performance that they have come to expect. A great deal of R&D effort among diesel engine builders has been focused on addressing the negatives associated with classic diesel engines, including improved engine management systems, common rail fuel systems, direct injection, high-pressure injectors, multiple spray patterns, turbocharging, particulate filters, and new biomass fuels.

Long-term, fuel cells are considered to be the next revolution in automotive power trains. Fuel cell is an electrochemical device that combines hydrogen and oxygen to produce electricity (with water and heat as its by-product). Fuel cell vehicles (FCVs) are propelled by electric motors, but unlike battery-electric vehicles that use stored electric energy, FVCs create their own. They can be fuelled by pure hydrogen gas stored on board in high-pressure tanks or by hydrogen-rich fuels such as methanol, a natural gas.

11.4   SUMMARY

This chapter explained the business variations throughout the life span of the automobile industry. The automobile industry is a defining industry in the global economy. The automobile has shaped our landscape, changed our atmosphere, and exerted a profound influence on the global economy: modern cities, with their attendant suburban sprawl, have been designed around the automobile, and the industry consumes nearly half the world's output of rubber, 25% of its glass, and 15% of its steel; its products are also responsible for almost half of the world's oil consumption and are a major source of rising carbon dioxide levels in the atmosphere, the GHG implicated in global warming; the industry makes over 50 million cars and trucks a year, employs millions of people in factories located across the globe, and accounts for about 10% of the gross domestic product in many developed countries. The rise of foreign competitors in the U.S. market has been attributed to a number of factors, including better designs and more fuel-efficient offerings (particularly in the passenger car segment), superior product quality, higher employee and capital productivity, and lower costs due to smaller pension and health-care commitments. The gap has narrowed substantially in recent years as American-owned producers have worked to improve their productivity by implementing improved manufacturing techniques based on Toyota's model, but in the meanwhile, the competition has moved on from determinants like quality, productivity, and manufacturing excellence to other determinants of excellence like smaller fuel-efficient cars, hybrids, services, and marketing where the American car manufacturers are again playing catch-up with the foreign competitors.

Section VI

Business Excellence and SAP

This section starts with a chapter explaining the business variations throughout the life span of SAP, the world's premier vendor of enterprise resource planning software that is implemented by most corporations today. We witness the seismic shift that SAP had to undergo because of the corresponding shifts in dynamics of the market with the advent of the Internet. The competitiveness of enterprises today is predicated on the competitiveness of their enterprise systems in terms of their ability to simultaneously attain efficiency, flexibility, and innovativeness. The book then introduces SAP's vision of an enterprise-wide, integrated, and near real-time performance platform called SAP Business Suite that is empowered for realizing these variations for reframing and reconfiguring enterprises. SAP provides a solution to help meet the three central requirements of an enabling business platform, namely, a software platform that fulfills the demand for flexibility and innovation at manageable costs. In the last chapter, we describe how business variations in all dimensions of variations—strategy, structure, shared values, stuff, style, staff, skills, systems, and sequence—can be achieved by using SAP. In this context, Chapter 14, Subsection 14.7, "Enterprise Variations using SAP" (see page number 398), is the most significant subsection of this part.

Chapter 14 discusses the change-enablement (i.e., *Built-for-Variation*) aspects of a SAP implementation. SAP enables the essential changing of processes that are so critical to the success of the enterprise. Business processes that *reside* or are internalized within an organization's employees are difficult to change simply because human beings naturally find it more difficult to change. However, processes that reside within any computerized systems are easy to change because they are not impeded by problems of inertia, fatigue, or lack of motivation.

There is a severe lack of appreciation of the power and potential of enterprise systems like SAPs to enable changeability of enterprises, which is evidently critical for their continued growth and commercial success.

I don't feel my integrity is lessened to any degree if I include discussions on SAP in the discourse. On the contrary, discussions on relevant architecture and capabilities of SAP give it a concrete edge.

Moreover, many of the corporations—who are major players of the world economy, and, sponsor and support research in the academies across the world—have huge installations of SAP.

12 Business Excellence at SAP

In 1972, five former IBM employees, Hasso Plattner, Dietmar Hopp, Claus Wellenreuther, Klaus Tschira, and Hans-Werner Hector, launch a company called SAP. Their vision was to develop standard application software for real-time business processing. These have been involved in the provisional design of a software program that would allow information about cross-functional and cross-divisional financial transactions in a company's value chain to be coordinated and processed centrally—resulting in enormous savings in time and expense. They observed that other software companies were also developing software designed to integrate across value chain activities and subunits. Using borrowed money and equipment, the five analysts worked day and night to create an accounting software platform that could integrate across all the parts of an entire corporation.

 We would like to highlight that this case history is meant to highlight the variations during the life span of the company rather than to illustrate either effective or ineffective handling of an administrative situation.

12.1 SAP R/1

In 1973, SAP unveiled an instantaneous accounting transaction processing program called R/1, one of the earliest examples of what is now called an ERP system.

Today, ERP is an industry term for the multimodule applications software that allows a company to manage the set of activities and transactions necessary to manage the business processes for moving a product from the input stage, along the value chain, to the final customer. As such, ERP system scan recognize, monitor, measure, and evaluate all the transactions involved in business processes such as product planning, the purchasing of inputs from suppliers, the manufacturing process, inventory and order processing, and customer service itself. Essentially, a fully developed ERP system provides a company with a standardized IT platform that gives complete information about all aspects of its business processes and cost structure across functions and divisions. Right from the beginning, SAP's goal has been to create the global industry standard for ERP by providing the best business applications software infrastructure.

In its first years, SAP not only developed ERP software, but it also used its own internal consultants to install it physically on-site at its customers' corporate IT centers, manufacturing operations, and so on. Determined to increase its customer base quickly, however, SAP switched strategies in the 1980s. It decided to focus primarily on the development of its ERP software and to outsource, to external consultants, more and more of the implementation services needed to install and service its software on-site in a particular company. It formed a series of strategic alliances with major global consulting companies such as IBM, Accenture, and Cap Gemini to install its R/1 system in its growing base of global customers.

To some degree, its decision to focus on software development and outsource at least 80% of installation was a consequence of its German founders' *engineering* mind-set. Founded by computer program engineers, SAP's culture was built on values and norms that emphasized technical innovation, and the development of leading-edge ERP software was the key success factor in the industry. SAP poured most of its money into R&D to fund projects that would add to its platform's capabilities; consequently, it had much less desire and money to spend on consulting and building consulting expertise. Essentially, SAP was a product-focused company and believed R&D would produce the technical advances that would be the source of its competitive advantage and allow it to charge its customers a premium price for its ERP platform. By 1988, SAP was spending more than 27% of gross sales on R&D.

As SAP's top managers focused on developing its technical competency, however, its marketing and sales competency was ignored because managers believed the ERP platform would sell itself. Many of its internal consultants and training experts began to feel they were second-class citizens, despite the fact that they brought in the business and were responsible for the vital role of maintaining good relationships with SAP's growing customer base. It seemed that the classic problem of transitioning a growing business from the entrepreneurial to the professional management phase was emerging. SAP's top managers did not understand the criticality of executing a rapidly growing company's strategy on a global basis; the need to develop a sound corporate infrastructure as a foundation for sustained growth and profitability was being neglected.

12.2   SAP R/2

In 1981, SAP introduced its second-generation ERP software, R/2. Not only did it contain many more value chain/business process software modules, but it also linked its ERP software to the databases and communication systems used on mainframe computers, thus permitting greater connectivity and ease of use of ERP throughout a company. The R/1 platform had been largely a cross-organizational accounting/financial software module; the new software modules could handle procurement, product development, and inventory and order tracking. Of course, these additional components had to be compatible with each other so that they could be seamlessly integrated together at a customer's operations on-site. SAP's system was made compatible with Oracle's DBMS; this was to have repercussions later, when Oracle began to develop its own ERP software.

As part of its push to make its R/2 software the industry standard, SAP had also been in the process of customizing its basic ERP platform to accommodate the needs of companies in different kinds of industries. The way value chain activities and business processes are performed differs from industry to industry because of differences in the manufacturing processes and other factors. ERP software solutions must be customized by industry to perform most effectively.

Its push to become the ERP leader across industries, across all large global companies, and across all value chain business processes required a huge R&D investment. In 1988, the company went public on the Frankfurt stock exchange to raise the necessary cash.

By 1990, with its well-received multilingual software, SAP had emerged as one of the leading providers of business applications software, and its market capitalization was soaring. SAP began to dominate ERP software sales in the high-tech and electronics, engineering and construction, consumer products, chemical, and retail industries. Its product was increasingly being recognized as superior to the other ERP software being developed by companies such as PeopleSoft, S. D. Edwards, and Oracle. One reason for SAP's increasing competitive advantage was that it could offer a broad, standardized, state-of-the-art solution to many companies' business process problems, one that spanned a wide variety of value chain activities spread around the globe. By contrast, its competitors, like PeopleSoft, offered more focused solutions aimed at one business process, such as HRM.

ERP installation is a long and complicated process. A company cannot simply adapt its information systems to fit SAP's software; it must use consultants to rework the way it performs its value chain activities so that its business processes, and the information systems that measure these business processes, became compatible with SAP's software. SAP's ERP system provides a company with the information needed to achieve best industry practices across its operations. The more a particular company wishes to customize the SAP platform to its particular business processes, the more difficult and expensive the implementation process and the harder it becomes to realize the potential gains from cost savings and value added to the product.

SAP's outsourcing consulting strategy allowed it to penetrate global markets quickly and eliminated the huge capital investment needed to provide this service on a global basis. For consulting companies, however, the installation of SAP's software became a major money-spinner, and SAP did not enjoy as much of the huge revenue streams associated with providing computer services, such as the design, installation, and maintenance of an ERP platform on an ongoing basis. It did earn some revenue by training consultants in the intricacies of installing and maintaining SAP's ERP system.

> By focusing on ERP software development, SAP did not receive any profits from this highly profitable revenue stream and made itself dependent on consulting companies that now became the experts in the installation/customization arena. This decision had unfortunate long-term consequences because SAP began to lose first-hand knowledge of its customers' problems and an understanding of the changing needs of its customers, especially when the Internet and cross-company integration became a major competitive factor in the ERP industry. For a company whose goal was to provide a standardized platform across functions and divisions, this outsourcing strategy seemed like a strange choice to many analysts. Perhaps SAP should have expanded its own consulting operations to run parallel with those of external consultants, rather than providing a training service to these consultants to keep them informed about its constantly changing ERP software.

12.3 SAP R/3

In 1991, SAP had presented its R/3, or third-generation solution, for the first time at the CeBIT in Hannover and was released to the general market in 1992. The product met with an overwhelming approval due to its client/server concept, uniform appearance of graphical interfaces, consistent use of relational databases, and the ability to run on computers from different providers. Essentially, expanding on its previous solutions, R/3 offered seamless, real-time integration for over 80% of a company's business processes. It had also embedded in the platform hundreds and then thousands of industry best practice solutions, or templates, that customers could use to improve their operations and processes. The R/3 system was initially composed of seven different modules corresponding to the most common business processes. Those modules are PP, materials management (MM), financial accounting, AM, HRM, project systems (PS), and sales and distribution (SD).

R/3 was designed to meet the diverse demands of its previous global clients. It could operate in multiple languages and convert exchange rates on a real-time basis. SAP, recognizing the huge potential revenues to be earned from smaller business customers, ensured that R/3 could now also be configured for smaller customers and be customized to suit the needs of a broader range of industries. Furthermore, R/3 was designed to be *open architectured*, meaning that it could operate with whatever kind of computer hardware or software (the legacy system) that a particular company was presently using. Finally, in response to customer concerns that SAP's standardized system meant huge implementation problems in changing their business processes to match SAP's standardized solution, SAP introduced customization opportunity into its software. However, the costs of doing this were extremely high and became a huge generator of fees for consulting companies.

SAP used a variable-fee licensing system for its R/3 system depending upon

- The cost to the customer was based on the number of users within a company
- The number of different R/3 modules that were installed
- The degree to which users utilized these modules in the business planning process

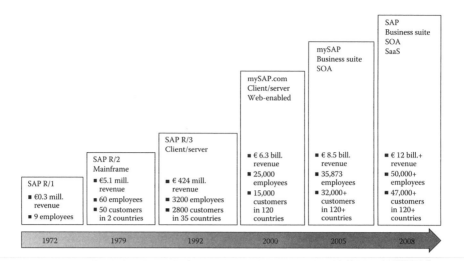

FIGURE 12.1 SAP product history.

SAP's R/3 far outperformed its competitors' products in a technical sense and once again allowed it to charge a premium price for its new software. It was seeking to establish R/3 as the new ERP market standard and lock in customers before competitors could offer viable alternatives. This strategy was vital to its future success because, given the way an ERP system changes the nature of a customer's business processes once it is installed and running, there are high switching costs involved in moving to another ERP product—costs that customers want to avoid (Figure 12.1).

12.4   DECENTRALIZED OPERATIONS

R/3's growing popularity led SAP to decentralize more and more control of the marketing, sale, and installation of its software on a global basis to its foreign subsidiaries. While its R&D and software development remained centralized in Germany, it began to open wholly owned subsidiaries in most major country's markets. By 1995, it had 18 national subsidiaries; today, it has over 50. In 1995, SAP established a U.S. subsidiary to drive sales in the huge U.S. market. Its German top managers set the subsidiary a goal of achieving $1 billion in revenues within 5 years; the American company Burger King, Inc., became the 1000th HR customer. Microsoft also began to use SAP. To implement this aggressive growth strategy, and given that R/3 software needs to be installed and customized to suit the needs of particular companies and industries, several different regional SAP divisions were created to manage the needs of companies and industries in different U.S. regions. Also, the regional divisions were responsible for training an army of both internal and external consultants, from companies such as Accenture, on how to install and customize the R/3 software. For every internal lead SAP consultant, there were soon about 9–10 external consultants working with SAP's customers to install and modify the software.

 In 1995, Deutsche Telekom AG implemented R/3, which required 30,000 R/3 workstations and represented the largest contract in the company's history. The next year, Coca-Cola, the largest soft drinks manufacturer in the world, decided to implement SAP R/3.

This policy of decentralization was somewhat paradoxical because the company's mission was to supply software that linked functions and divisions rather than separated them, and the characteristic problems of too much decentralization of authority soon became evident throughout SAP. In its

U.S. subsidiary, each regional SAP division started developing its own procedures for pricing SAP software, offering discounts, dealing with customer complaints, and even rewarding its employees and consultants. There was a total lack of standardization and integration inside SAP America and indeed between SAP's many foreign subsidiaries and their headquarters in Germany. This meant that little learning was taking place between divisions or consultants, there was no monitoring or coordination mechanism in place to share SAP's own best practices between its consultants and divisions, and organizing by region in the United States was doing little to build core competences. These problems slowed down the process of implementing SAP software and prevented quick and effective responses to the needs of potential customers and dissatisfaction of the existing customers.

> To a large degree, SAP's decision to decentralize control of its marketing, sales, and installation to its subsidiaries was due to the way the company had operated from its beginning. Its German founders had emphasized the importance of excellence in innovation as the root value of its culture, and SAP's culture was often described as *organized chaos*. Its top managers had operated from the beginning by creating as flat a hierarchy as possible to create an internal environment where people could take risks and try new ideas of their own choosing. If mistakes occurred or projects didn't work out, employees were given the freedom to try a different approach. Hard work, teamwork, openness, and speed were the norms of their culture. The pressure was on software developers to create superior products. Primarily, it wanted to be the world's leading innovator of software, not a service company that implemented it.

On the other hand, SAP's R/3 was criticized as being too standardized because it forced all companies to adapt to what SAP had decided were best industry practices. When consultants reconfigured the software to suit a particular company's needs, this process often took a long time, and sometimes, the system did not perform as well as had been expected. Many companies felt that the software should be configured to suit their business processes and not the other way around, but again SAP argued that such a setup would not lead to an optimal outcome. For example, SAP's retail R/3 system could not handle Home Depot's policy of allowing each of its stores to order directly from suppliers, based upon centrally negotiated contracts between Home Depot and those suppliers. SAP's customers also found that supporting their new ERP platform was expensive and that ongoing support cost three to five times as much as the actual purchase of the software— although the benefits they received from its integrated R/3 system usually exceeded these costs substantially.

However, the problems with a policy of decentralized business operations soon caught up with SAP:

a. Because SAP was growing so fast and there was so much demand for its product, it was hard to provide the thorough training consultants needed to perform the installation of its software. Once SAP had trained an internal consultant, that consultant would sometimes leave to join the company for which he or she was performing the work or even to start an industry-specific SAP consulting practice, with the result that SAP's customers' needs were being poorly served. Since the large external consulting companies made their money based on the time it took their consultants to install a particular SAP system, some customers were complaining that consultants were deliberately taking too long to implement the new software to maximize their earnings and were even pushing inappropriate or unnecessary R/3 modules.

b. The word started to circulate that SAP's software was both difficult and expensive to implement, which hurt its reputation and sales. Some companies had problems implementing the

R/3 software; SAP usual response was that the problem was not with the software but the way the company had tried to implement it, but SAP's reputation was harmed nevertheless.

c. Although the United States had become SAP's biggest market, the explosive growth in demand for SAP's software had begun to slacken by 1995. Competitors such as Oracle, Baan, PeopleSoft, and Marcum were catching up technically, often because they were focusing their resources on the needs of one or a few industries or on a particular kind of ERP module (e.g., PeopleSoft's focus on the HRM module). Indeed, SAP had to play catch-up in the HRM area and develop its own to offer a full suite of integrated business solutions. Oracle, the second largest software maker after Microsoft, was becoming a particular threat as it expanded its ERP offerings outward from its leading database systems and began to offer more and more of an Internet-based ERP platform.

12.4.1 Centralization

As new aggressive competitors emerged and changed the environment, SAP found it needed to change as well. Competitors were increasing their market share by exploiting weaknesses in SAP's software. They began to offer SAP's existing and potential customers' ERP systems that could be customized more easily to their situation; systems that were less expensive than SAP's, which still were charged at a premium price; or systems that offered less expensive module options. SAP's managers were forced to reevaluate their business model and their strategies and the ways in which they implemented them.

In 1997, it established an HRM department and gave it the responsibility to build a more formal organizational structure. Previously, it had outsourced its own HRM. Increasing competition led SAP's managers to realize that they were not capitalizing on its main strength—its HR. HRM managers started to develop job descriptions and job titles and put in place a career structure that would motivate employees and keep them loyal to the company. They also put in place a reward system, which included stock options, to increase the loyalty of their technicians, who were being attracted away by competitors or were starting their own businesses because SAP did not seem to offer a career path. For example, SAP sued Siebel Systems, a niche rival in the customer relationship software business, in 2000 for enticing 12 of its senior employees, who it said took trade secrets with them.

SAP's top managers realized that they had to plan long term and that innovation by itself was not enough to make SAP a dominant global company with a sustainable competitive advantage. It started to operate more formally:

a. It became more centralized to encourage organizational learning and to promote the sharing of its own best implementation practices across divisions and subsidiaries. Its goal was to standardize the way each subsidiary or division operated across the company, thus making it easier to transfer people and knowledge where they were needed most. Not only would this facilitate cooperation, but it would also reduce overhead costs, which were spiraling because of the need to recruit trained personnel as the company grew quickly and the need to alter and adapt its software to suit changing industry conditions. For example, increasing customer demands for additional customization of its software made it imperative that different teams of engineers pool their knowledge to reduce development costs and that consultants should not only share their best practices but also cooperate with engineers so that the latter could understand the problems faced by the customers.

b. It adopted a more standardized and hierarchical approach recognizing the stream of income it could get from both the training and installation sector of the software business. It began to increase its team of consultants. By having them work with its software developers, they became the acknowledged experts and leaders when it came to specific software installations and could command a high price. SAP also developed a large global training function to provide the extensive ERP training that consultants needed and charged both individuals and consulting companies high fees for attending these courses so that they would be able to work with the SAP platform.

c. SAP's U.S. subsidiary also moved from a regional to a more market-based focus by realigning its divisions, not by geography, but by their focus on a particular sector or industry, for example, chemicals, electronics, pharmaceuticals, consumer products, and engineering.

Once again, however, the lines of authority between the new industry divisions and the software development, sales, installation, and training functions were not worked out well enough, and the hoped-for gains from increased coordination and cooperation were slow to be realized.

Globally, too, SAP was still highly decentralized and remained a product-focused company, thus allowing its subsidiaries to form their own sales, training, and installation policies. Its subsidiaries continued to form strategic alliances with global consulting companies, thus losing the majority of revenues from servicing SAP's growing base of R/3 installations. SAP's top managers, with their engineering mind-set, did not appreciate the difficulties involved in changing a company's structure and culture, either at the subsidiary or the global level. They were disappointed in the slow pace of change because their cost structure remained high, although their revenues were increasing.

 In 1997, customers like Daimler-Benz and GM decided to implement SAP R/3 and more than two million users worldwide were working with SAP products.

12.5 INTERNET'S IT INDUSTRY RECONFIGURATION

By the mid-1990s, despite its problems in implementing its strategy, SAP was the clear market leader in the ERP software industry and the fourth largest global software company because of its recognized competencies in the production of state-of-the-art ERP software. However, there were several emerging problems posing major threats to its business model.

In essence, the Internet was changing both industry- and company-level business processes and providing companies and whole industries with many more avenues for altering their business processes at a company or industry level so that they could lower their cost structure or increasingly differentiate their products. Clearly, the hundreds of industry best practices that SAP had embedded in its R/3 software would become outdated and redundant as e-commerce increased in scope and depth and offered improved industry solutions. SAP's R/3 system would become a dinosaur or a *legacy system* within a decade unless it could move quickly to develop or obtain competencies to develop web-based software. One source of SAP's competitive advantage was based on the high switching costs of moving from one ERP platform to another. However, if new web-based platforms allowed both internal and external integration of a company's business processes, and new platforms could be customized more easily to answer a particular company's needs, these switching costs might disappear. SAP was at an inflection point in its history.

Rivalry among major software makers in the new web-based software market became intense. Rivalry between the major players and new entrants, like Netscape, Siebel Systems, Marcum, i2 Technology, and SSA, was intensifying. The major software makers, each of which was a market leader in one or more segments of the software industry, such as SAP in ERP, Microsoft in PC software, and Oracle in DBMS, sought to showcase their strengths to make their software compatible with web-based technology. Thus, Microsoft strove to develop its Windows NT network–based platform and its IE web browser to compete with Netscape's Internet browser and Sun Microsystems' open-standard Java web software programming language, which was compatible with any company's proprietary software (unlike Microsoft's NT).

New companies like Siebel Systems, Commerce One, Ariba, and Marcum, which began as niche players in some software applications such as SCM, CRM, intranet, or website development and hosting, also began to build and expand their product offerings so that they now possessed ERP modules that competed with some of SAP's most lucrative R/3 modules. Commerce One and Ariba, for example, emerged as the main players in the rapidly expanding B2B industry SCM market. B2B is an industry-level ERP solution that creates an organized market and thus brings together industry buyers and suppliers together electronically and provides the software to write and enforce contracts between them. Although these niche players could not provide the full range of services that SAP could provide, they became increasingly able to offer attractive alternatives to customers seeking specific aspects of an ERP system. Also, companies like Siebel, Marcum, and i2 claimed that they had the ability to customize their low-price systems, and, consequently, prices for ERP systems began to fall rapidly.

In the new software environment, SAP's large customers started to purchase software on a *best-of-breed* basis, meaning that customers purchased the best software applications for their specific needs from different, leading-edge companies rather than purchasing all of their software products from one company with a monolithic package—such as SAP offered. Sun began to promote a free Java computer language as the industry *open architecture* standard, which meant that as long as each company used Java to craft their specific web-based software programs, they would all work seamlessly together and there would no longer be a need or an advantage, to using a single dominant platform like Microsoft's Windows or SAP's R/3. Sun was and is trying to break Microsoft's hold over the OS industry standard, Windows.

12.5.1   mySAP.com

In 1997, SAP sought a quick fix to its problems by releasing new R/3 solutions for ERP Internet-enabled SCM and CRM solutions, which converted its internal ERP system into an externally based network platform. SCM, identified as the *back end* of the business, integrates the business processes necessary to manage the flow of goods, from the raw material stage to the finished product. SCM programs forecast future needs and plan and manage a company's operations, especially its manufacturing operations. CRM, identified as the *front end* of the business, provides companies with solutions and support for business processes directed at improving sales, marketing, customer service, and field service operations. CRM programs are rapidly growing in popularity because they lead to better customer retention and satisfaction, and higher revenues. In 1998, SAP followed with industry solution maps, business technology maps, and service maps, all of which were aimed at making its R/3 system dynamic and responsive to changes in industry conditions. In 1998, recognizing that its future rested on its ability to protect its share of the U.S. market, it listed itself on the New York Stock Exchange that fueled its expansion in the U.S. market.

In May 1999, Co-Chairman and CEO Hasso Plattner announced the mySAP.com strategy, heralding the beginning of a new direction for the company and its product range. mySAP.com connects e-commerce solutions with existing ERP applications using up-to-date web technology. In the same year, numerous mySAP.com customers are won, among them HP and the pharmaceutical company Hoechst Marion Roussel. The mySAP initiative was a comprehensive e-business platform designed to help companies collaborate and succeed, regardless of their industry or network environments.

First, to meet its customers' needs in the new electronic environment, SAP used the mySAP platform to change itself from a vendor of ERP components to a provider of e-business solutions. The platform was to be the online portal (SAP enterprise portal [EP]) through which customers could view and understand the way its Internet-enabled R/3 modules could address their evolving needs. SAP recognized that its customers were increasingly demanding access to networked environments with global connectivity, where decisions could be executed in real time through the Internet. Customers wanted to be able to leverage new e-business technologies to improve basic business goals like increasing profitability, improving customer satisfaction, and lowering overhead costs. In addition, customers wanted total solutions that could help them manage their relationships and supply chains.

Second, mySAP provided the platform that would allow SAP's product offerings to expand and strengthen over time—an especially important feature because web-based software was evolving into ever more varied applications. SAP was essentially copying other software makers, who were branching out into high-growth segments and to prevent obsolescence should demand for their core software erode because of technological developments. Henceforth, SAP was not offering product-based solutions but customer-based solutions. Its mySAP e-business platform solutions are designed to be a scalable and flexible architecture that supported databases, applications, OS, and hardware platforms from almost every major vendor.

Third, SAP realized that cost was becoming a more important issue because competition from low-cost rivals demonstrated that customers could be persuaded to shift vendors if they were offered good commercial deals. Indeed, major companies like Oracle often offered their software at discount prices or even gave it away free to well-known companies to generate interest and demand for their product (and wean them away from SAP). SAP focused on making mySAP more affordable by *unbundling* its modules and business solutions into smaller, separate products. Customers could now choose which particular solutions best met their specific needs; they no longer had to buy the whole package. All mySAP offerings were fully compatible with the base R/3 system so that customers could easily expand their use of SAP's products. SAP was working across its whole product range to make its system easier and cheaper to use. SAP realized that repeat business is much more important than a one-time transaction, so they began to focus on seeking out and developing new, add-on solutions for their customers to keep them coming back and purchasing more products and upgrades.

Fourth, mySAP was aimed at a wider range of potential customers. By providing a simpler and cheaper version of its application software coupled with the introduction of the many mySAP e-business solution packages, SAP broadened its offerings targeted to not only large corporations but also small- and medium-sized companies. mySAP enabled SAP to provide a low-cost ERP system that could be scaled down for smaller firms. For example, for small- to midsized companies that lack the internal resources to maintain their own business applications on-site, mySAP offered hosting for data centers, networks, and applications. Small businesses could benefit greatly from the increased speed of installation and reduced cost possible through outsourcing and by paying a fee to use mySAP in lieu of having to purchase SAP's expensive software modules. SAP also focused on making its R/3 mySAP offerings easier to install and use and reduced implementation times and consulting costs that in turn reduced the costs of supporting the SAP platform for both small and large organizations.

To support its mySAP initiative, SAP had continued to build in-house training and consulting capabilities to increase its share of revenues from the services side of its business. SAP's increasing web software services efforts paid off because the company was now better able to recognize the problems experienced by the customers. This result led SAP to recognize both the needs for greater responsiveness to customers and customization of its products to make their installation easier. Its growing customer awareness had also led it to redefine its mission as a developer of business solutions, the approach embedded in mySAP, rather than as a provider of software products.

To improve the cost-effectiveness of mySAP installations, SAP sought a better way to manage its relationships with consulting companies. It moved to a parallel sourcing policy, in which several consulting firms competed for a customer's business, and it made sure a SAP consultant was always involved in the installation and service effort to monitor external consultants' performance. This helped keep service costs under control for its customers. Because customer needs changed so quickly in this fast-paced market and SAP continually improved its products with incremental innovations and additional capabilities, it also insisted that consultants undertake continual training to update their skills, training for which it charged high fees. In 2000, SAP adopted a stock option program to retain valuable employees after losing many key employees—programmers and consultants—to competitors.

Fifth, SAP increasingly embraced the concept of open architecture, and its mySAP offerings are compatible with the products of most other software makers. It had already ensured that its mySAP platform worked with OS such as Microsoft NT, Sun's Java, and UNIX, Linux. Now, it focused on ensuring that its products were compatible with emerging web applications software from any major software maker—by 2001, SAP claimed to have over 1000 partners.

Indeed, strategic alliances and acquisitions became increasingly important parts of its strategy to reduce its cost structure, enhance the functionality of its products, and build its customer base. Because of the sheer size and expense of many web-based software endeavors, intense competition, and the fast-paced dynamics of this industry, SAP's top managers began to realize they could not go it alone and produce everything in-house. SAP had never seemed to be able to enjoy sustained high profitability because changing technology and competition had not allowed it to capitalize on its acknowledged position as the ERP industry leader.

Given existing resource constraints and time pressures and the need to create a more profitable business model, in the 2000s, SAP's managers realized that they needed to partner with companies that now dominated in various niches of the software market. By utilizing already developed best-of-breed software, SAP would not have to deploy the capital necessary if it were to go it alone. In addition, synergies across partner companies might allow future development to be accomplished more efficiently and enable it to bring new mySAP products to the market more quickly.

Sixth, SAP used acquisitions to drive its entry into new segments of the web software market. For example, SAP acquired Top Tier Software Inc. in 2001 to gain access to its iView technology. This technology allows seamless integration between the web software of different companies and is critical for SAP because it lets customers drag-and-drop and mix information and applications from both SAP and non-SAP platform-based systems and thus enables the open systems architecture SAP has increasingly supported. Top Tier was also an EP software maker, and in 2001, SAP teamed up with Yahoo to use these competencies to create a new U.S. subsidiary called SAP Portals, which would deliver state-of-the-art EP products that would enable people and companies to collaborate effectively and at any time. It also launched SAP hosting to provide hosting and web maintenance services.

By 2002, SAP believed that its partnerships and alliances had maneuvered it into a position of continued market dominance for the twenty-first century. Many of the major vendors of the databases, applications, and OS became SAP partners. In essence, SAP was treating these other products as complementary products, which added to the value of its own, promoted mySAP as the industry standard, and increased its dominance of the ERP web software market (see Chapter 5, Subsection 5.2.3.2, "Bandwagon Effect").

SAP's number of software installations and customers increased steadily between 1998 and 2002. The number of software installations grew at a faster pace than the number of customers, a characteristic of the lock-in feature of investment in one ERP platform. In 2002, SAP was still the number 1 vendor of standard business applications software, with a worldwide market share of over 30%. Oracle was next with a 16% share of the market. SAP claimed that it had 10 million users and 50,000 SAP installations in 18,000 companies in 120 countries in 2002 and that half of the world's top 500 companies used its software.

12.5.2 Reorganization: Verticalization

SAP's problems were not just in the strategy area, however. Its mySAP initiative had increased its overhead costs, and it still could not find the appropriate organizational structure to make the best use of its resources and competencies. It continued to search for the right structure for servicing the growing range of its products and the increasing breadth of the companies (in terms of size, industry, and global location) it was now serving. Recall that in the mid-1990s, SAP had begun to centralize authority and control to standardize its own business processes and manage knowledge effectively across organizational subunits. While this reorganization resulted in some benefits, it had the unfortunate result of lengthening the time it took SAP to respond to the fast-changing web software ERP environment.

To respond to changing customer needs and the needs for product customization, SAP now moved to decentralize control to programmers and its sales force to manage problems where and when they arose. SAP's managers felt that in an environment where markets are saturated with ERP vendors and where customers want service and systems that are easier to use, it was important to get close to the customer. SAP had now put in place its own applications software for integrating across its operating divisions and subsidiaries, allowing them to share best practices and new developments and thus avoid problems that come with too much decentralization of authority.

12.5.3 TRIFURCATION OF DEVELOPMENT GROUP

In 2000, to speed the software development process, SAP divided its central German software development group into three teams. One team works on the development of new products and features, the second refines and updates functions in its existing products, and the third works on making SAP products easier to install. Also, to educate its customers and enhance customer acceptance and demand for mySAP, SAP changed its global marketing operations in late 2000. Following its decentralized style in the mid-1990s, each product group once had its own marketing department that operated separately to market and sell its products. This decentralization had caused major problems because customers didn't understand how the various parts of mySAP fit together. It also wasted resources and slowed the sales effort. Signaling its intent to have a focus on marketing in contrast to its previous focus on its engineering competency, SAP's top managers centralized control of marketing at its U.S. subsidiary and put control of all global marketing into the hands of one executive, who was now responsible for coordinating market efforts across all mySAP product groups and all world regions.

12.5.4 RECONSOLIDATION

Soon after, in 2001, once again to speed up the implementation of the mySAP initiative, SAP folded the SAP Markets and SAP Portals subsidiaries into SAP's other operations and split the SAP product line into distinct but related mySAP product groups, each of which was to be treated as an independent profit center, with the head of each product group reporting directly to SAP's chairperson: the type of web software application or ERP industry solution being offered to the customer differentiates each product group.

SAP also changed the way its three German engineering groups worked with the different mySAP products groups. Henceforth, a significant part of the engineering development effort would take place inside each mySAP product group so that program engineers, who write and improve the specific new mySAP software applications, were joined with the sales force for that group. Now, they could integrate their activities and provide better customized solutions. The software engineers at its German headquarters, besides conducting basic R&D, would be responsible for coordinating the efforts of the different mySAP engineering groups, sharing new software developments among groups, providing expert solutions, and ensuring all the different mySAP applications worked together seamlessly.

Each mySAP product group is now composed of a collection of cross-functional product development teams focused on their target markets. Teams are given incentives to meet their specific sales growth targets and to increase operating effectiveness, including reducing the length of installation time. The purposes of the new product group/team approach were to decentralize control, make SAP more responsive to the needs of customers and to changing technical developments, and still give SAP centralized control of development efforts. To ensure that its broadening range of software was customizable to the needs of different kinds of companies and industries, SAP enlisted some of its key customers as *development partners* and as members of these teams. Customers from large, midsized, and small companies were used to test new concepts and ideas. Within every mySAP product group, cross-functional teams focused on customizing its products for specific customers or industries. SAP opened the development process to its competitors and allowed them to work with SAP teams to make their products compatible with SAP's products and with the computer platforms or legacy systems already installed in their customers' operations. Through this implementation approach, SAP was striving to pull its actual and potential customers and competitors toward the single, open standard of SAP. The company also instituted stricter training and certification methods for consultants to improve the level of quality control and protect its reputation.

12.5.5 Global Operations

At the global level, SAP grouped is national subsidiaries into three main world regions. Europe, the Americas, and Asia/Pacific. This grouping made it easier to transfer knowledge and information between countries and serve the specific demands of national markets inside each region. Also, this global structure made it easier to manage relationships with consulting companies and to coordinate regional marketing and training efforts, both under the jurisdiction of the centralized marketing and training operations.

Thus, in the 2000s, SAP began to operate with a loose form of matrix structure. To increase internal flexibility and responsiveness to customers while at the same time boosting efficiency and market penetration, the world regions, the national subsidiaries, and the salespeople and consultants within them constituted one side of the matrix. The centralized engineering, marketing, and training functions and the 20 or so different mySAP product groups constituted the other side. The problem facing SAP is to coordinate all these distinct subunits so that they will lead to rapid acceptance of SAP's new mySAP platform across all the national markets in which it operates.

In practice, a salesperson in any particular country works directly with a client to determine what type of ERP system he or she needs. Once this system is determined, a project manager from the regional subsidiary or from one of the mySAP groups is appointed to assemble an installation team from members of the different product groups whose expertise is required to implement the new client's system. Given SAP's broad range of evolving products, the matrix structure allows SAP to provide those products that fit the customer's needs in a fast, coordinated way. SAP's policy of decentralizing authority and placing it in the hands of its employees enables the matrix system to work. SAP prides itself on its talented and professional staff that can learn and adapt to many different situations and networks across the globe.

12.5.6 R/3 Enterprise

In April 2002, SAP announced that its revenues had climbed 9.2%, but its first-quarter profit fell steeply because of a larger-than-expected drop in license revenue from the sale of new software. Many customers had been reluctant to invest in the huge cost of moving to the mySAP system, given the recession and continuing market uncertainty. Accordingly, SAP announced it would introduce a product called R/3 Enterprise; it was an interim product, which would be targeted at customers not yet ready to make the leap to mySAP. R/3 Enterprise is a collection of web software that can be added easily to the R/3 platform to provide a company with the ability to network with other companies and perform many e-commerce operations. SAP hopes this new software will show its R/3 customers what mySAP can accomplish for them once it is running in their companies.

12.6   SAP NETWEAVER

SAP's managers believed these initiatives would allow the company to jump from being the third largest global software company to being the second, ahead of main competitor Oracle. They also wondered if they could use its mySAP open system architecture to overcome Microsoft's stranglehold on the software market and bypass the powerful Windows standard. Pursuing this idea, SAP put considerable resources into developing a new business platform called SAP NetWeaver that is a web-based, open integration and application platform that serves as the foundation for enterprise SOA and allows the integration and alignment of people, information, and business processes across business and technology boundaries. Enterprise SOA utilizes open standards to enable integration with information and applications from almost any source or technology and is the technology of the future. SAP NetWeaver is now the foundation for all enterprise SOA SAP applications and mySAP Business Suite solutions; it also powers SAP's partner solutions and a customer's custom-built applications. Also, NetWeaver integrates business processes across various systems, databases, and sources—from any business software supplier—and is marketed to large companies as a service-oriented application and integration platform. NetWeaver's development was a major strategic move by SAP for driving enterprises to run their business software on a single SAP platform.

12.6.1   OUTSOURCING

As a part of its major push to reduce costs, SAP began to outsource its routine future programming development work overseas to low-cost countries such as India. By 2003, SAP employed 750 software programmers in India and had doubled that number by 2004. To help boost global revenues, SAP also began to use its expanding Indian research center to develop new ERP modules to serve new customers in more and more industries or vertical markets, and by 2003, it had mySAP systems designed for about 20 industry markets. At the same time, SAP used its growing army of low-cost Indian programmers to work the bugs out of its SAP modules and to increase their reliability when they were installed in a new company. This prevented embarrassing blowups that sometimes arose when a company implemented SAP's ERP for the first time. Fewer bugs also made it easier to install its modules in a new company, which reduced the need for consulting and lowered costs, leading to more satisfied customers. By 2006, SAP had doubled its Indian workforce again, and its Indian group was now bigger than its research group in Walldorf, Germany. Outsourcing has saved the company billions of Euros a year and has been a continuing contributor to its rising profitability in the 2000s.

12.6.2   mySAP BUSINESS SUITE

In 2003, SAP changed the name of its software from mySAP.com to mySAP Business Suite because more and more customers were now using a suite licensing arrangement to obtain its software rather than buying it outright. Part of the change in purchasing was because of the constant upgrades SAP was rolling out; in a licensing arrangement, its clients could expect to be continually upgraded as it improved its ERP modules. This also had the effect of locking its customers into its software platform for its raised switching costs. However, while SAP continued to attract new large business customers, the market was becoming increasingly saturated as its market share continued to grow—it already had around 50% of the global large business market by 2003. So, to promote growth and increase sales revenues, SAP began a major push to increase its share of the small and medium business enterprise (SME) market segment of the ERP industry.

12.7   SMALL AND MEDIUM BUSINESS ENTERPRISE

The small size of these companies, and so the limited amount of money they had to spend on business software, was a major challenge for SAP, which was used to dealing with multinational companies that had huge IT budgets. Also, there were major competitors in this market segment that had specialized in meeting the needs of SMEs to avoid direct competition with SAP, and they had locked up a significant share of business in this ERP segment. By focusing primarily on large companies, SAP had left a gap in the market that large software companies like Oracle, Microsoft, and IBM took advantage to develop their own SME ERP products and services to compete for customers and revenues in this market segment—one also worth billions of dollars in the years ahead and the main growth segment in the future ERP market. So, to reach this growing market segment as quickly as possible, SAP decided to develop two main product offerings for SMEs: SAP All-in-One and SAP Business One.

SAP is facing competition in the SME market, especially from CRM companies such as salesforce.com that specializes in on-demand software downloaded directly from the Internet. Complementing SAP's existing portfolio for midsized companies, a new solution, Business ByDesign (BBD), was introduced to leverage on-demand and hosted delivery at a significantly lower cost and that will allow them to *try–run–adapt* the software to meet their needs.

12.7.1 SAP All-in-One

SAP All-in-One is a streamlined version of its R/3 mySAP Business Suite, it is much easier to install and maintain and much more affordable for SMEs. To develop All-in-One, SAP's software engineers took its mySAP Business Suite modules designed for large companies and scaled them down for users of small companies. All-in-One is a cutdown version of SAP's total range of products like SAP customer relationship management (CRM), SAP ERP modules, SAP product life-cycle management (PLM), SAP SCM, and SAP supplier relationship management (SRM). Despite its reduced size, it is still a complex business solution and one that requires a major commitment of IT resources for an SME.

12.7.2 Business One

So, recognizing the need to provide a much simpler and more limited and affordable ERP solution for smaller companies, SAP decided to also pursue a second SME ERP solution. To speed the development of a new suite of programs, SAP decided not to develop a new software package from scratch based on its leading R/3 product, as it did with its All-in-One solution. Rather, it took a new path and bought an Israeli software company called Top Manage Financial Solutions in 2002 and rebranded its system as SAP Business One. SAP Business One is a much more limited ERP software package that integrates CRM with financial and logistic modules to meet a specific customer's basic needs. However, it still provides a powerful, flexible solution and is designed to be easy to work and affordable for SMEs. Business One software works in real time; no longer does an SME need to wait until the end of the month to do the accounts. The system manages and records the ongoing transactions involved in a business such as cost of goods received, through inventory, processing and sale, and delivery to customers, and automatically records transactions in a debit and credit account. Despite its streamlined nature, Business One contains 14 important core modules:

1. Administration module that configures and links the activities involved in a business' value creation system
2. Financials module that controls accounting and financial activities
3. Sales opportunities module that maintains contact with existing customers and tracks potential customers
4. Sales module that tracks when orders are entered, shipped, and invoiced
5. Purchasing module that issues purchase orders (POs) and records goods received into inventory
6. Business partners module that maintains record and contact with customers and sellers
7. Banking module that tracks and records where cash is received and paid out

8. Inventory module that records and values inventory
9. Production module that tracks cost of materials and manufacturing
10. MRP module that increases the efficiency of input purchase and PP
11. Service module that manages after-sales service activities and records
12. Human resources module that records all employee information
13. Reports module that generates user-defined reports (as printouts or Excel files)
14. E-commerce module that allows customers to buy and sell online to consumers or other businesses

To speed the development of its new Business One solution, SAP chose its management team from engineers outside the company. Many of these managers came from Top Manage, and one of these, Shai Agassi, has since risen in SAP to become its chief technology officer for all of its products and technologies. One reason is because of the growing importance of the SME segment, which became clear in 2005 when SAP began reporting revenues from the SME market segment separately from revenues for its larger customers, one way of showing its commitment to SME customers.

12.8 ERP MARKET SATURATION

As mentioned earlier, one of the major reasons for SAP to enter and compete in the SME segment was that the large company segment was becoming increasingly mature and saturated. By 2004, achieving rapid growth by increasing the number of new large business customers was becoming more and more difficult, simply because SAP's share of the global ERP market had already grown to 58%. As a result, SAP reported that it expected single-digit growth in the future—growth worth billions in revenues but still growth that would not fuel a rapid rise in its stock price. However, competition in the SME market was also increasing as its business software rivals watched SAP develop and introduce its All-in-One and Business One solutions to dominate this segment. Now SAP's rapid growth in this segment led to increasing competition and to a wave of consolidation in the ERP industry.

In 2003, PeopleSoft, the leader in the HRM software module segment, bought J. D. Edwards, a leader in SCM, to enlarge its product offerings and strengthen its market share against growing competition from SAP and Oracle. However, Oracle, the dominant business software database management company, and its chairman, Larry Ellison, also realized the stakes ahead in the consolidating business software market. While SAP had never made large acquisitions to acquire new products and customers, preferring *organic growth* from the inside or small acquisitions, this was not true of Oracle. Ellison saw major acquisitions as the best way to expand Oracle's range of business modules to complement the suite of ERP modules it had been developing internally and so gain market share in the SME market segment. Through acquisitions, it could quickly develop an ERP suite with the breadth of SAP's to meet the needs of SMEs. Also, it could use its new competencies and customers to attack SAP in the large company segment, which Oracle now regarded as a major growth opportunity.

So, Oracle began a hostile takeover of PeopleSoft. PeopleSoft's managers battled to prevent the takeover, but Oracle offered PeopleSoft's customers special low-cost licensing deals on Oracle software and guaranteed them the changeover to its software would be smooth. It finally acquired PeopleSoft—and the resources and customers necessary to gain a large market share in the SME segment at the expense of SAP and Microsoft—in 2005. Oracle has kept up the pressure. Since January 2005, it acquired 25 more business software companies in a huge acquisition drive to build its distinctive competencies and market share in ERP software. PeopleSoft brought Oracle expertise in HRM, and J. D. Edwards, expertise in SCM; and in a major acquisition of Siebel Systems, Oracle bought a leading CRM software developer. These acquisitions have allowed Oracle to dramatically increase its market share, particularly with SMBs. Before purchasing Seibel, for example, Oracle had a 6.8% share of this market; now, it could add Seibel's 11% market share to become one of the top three CRM suppliers.

Oracle developed a new e-business suite called Oracle Fusion middleware that allows them to seamlessly connect different ERP packages from different companies; this enables companies to leverage their existing investments in the software applications of other companies, including SAP, so that they can work seamlessly with Oracle's newly acquired ERP modules. Fusion is Oracle's answer to SAP NetWeaver and is seen as a major threat to SAP, for it obviates the need for customers to move to SAP's All-in-One or Business One suite. Oracle hopes that because some of its modules, like PeopleSoft's HRM software module, have been regarded as stronger offerings than SAP's, many companies will be inclined to keep their existing PeopleSoft installations and then choose more offerings from Oracle's growing business applications suite. Also, Oracle hopes that SAP customers will now be able to keep any existing SAP application but still add on Oracle modules.

The third leading SME ERP supplier, Microsoft, is also keeping up the pressure. Using the competencies from its acquisition of Great Plains and Navision, it subsequently released a new business package called Microsoft Dynamics NAV, which is ERP software that can be fully customized to the needs of SME users, to their industries and scaled to their size. Microsoft's advantage lies in the compatibility of its ERP offerings with the Windows platform, which is still used by more than 85% of SMEs, especially as it can offer a discount when customers choose both types of software and upgrade to its Windows Vista software in 2007 and beyond.

12.8.1 Restrategizing

In 2005, SAP established five new broad corporate goals: agility, high performance, simplicity, talent development, and co-innovation. Agility was becoming vital as new technological developments, particularly due to the Internet, were rapidly changing the value of its software to customers. For example, a new approach to delivering business software to customers by direct download from the Internet, along with constant upgrading from the Internet, was being pioneered by Internet start-ups such as salesforce.com, which offered its customers CRM software online at prices that undercut SAP and its competitors. High performance meant ensuring that SAP's software worked seamlessly with its customers and was bug-free and that all the complex parts of its business suite worked totally in tandem. Simplicity meant that its software engineers should continuously work to make its modules easier to install and use by its clients.

Co-innovation means cooperating with partners and customers to improve products and solutions, a strategy SAP had always pursued. For example, SAP and Microsoft formed an alliance to ensure interoperability between Microsoft's.Net platform and SAP's NetWeaver platform and create a new suite of software that will leverage each others' business applications. To help companies manage complex regulations, SAP also made small acquisitions like Virsa Systems that have expertise in U.S. accounting laws and standards. Its software was then incorporated into SAP products to provide a complete approach to allowing compliance with the Sarbanes–Oxley Act, which mandates openness and conformity to strict accounting reporting requirements through their governance, risk, and compliance (GRC) solutions. Also, SAP's modules now contain customized software that allows companies to manage trade compliance according to the regulations of different countries, for example, environmental, pharmaceutical, and banking requirements. Finally, the new RFID that uses wireless ID tags to improve SCM and the tracking of shipments and inventory has required SAP incorporate software to manage this into its business applications. As all aspects of the environment change, so must SAP's software.

12.9 SAP HANA

SAP is also working to be able to offer all of its customers the advantage of cloud computing as it matures and becomes a more reliable and secure option. SAP business objects solutions are continually being upgraded and developed to help companies optimize business processes on premise, on demand, and on device.

More recently, SAP was the first company to introduce in-memory technology to enable both online transaction processing (OLTP) and online analytical processing (OLAP) with full enterprise data loaded in memory through its product SAP high-performance analytic appliance (HANA). HANA is designed to speed up analysis of business data. Post the 2008 recession, SAP expects HANA to be a game changer solution in light of the increasing focus of enterprises *to do more with less* entailing focus on enterprise performance management and analytics.

12.10 SUMMARY

This chapter explained the business variations throughout the life span of SAP to unravel how it became the world's premier enterprise resources planning software company. It described the initial generations of SAP applications, namely, R1, R/2, and R/3. It then explains the variations SAP underwent in the wake of emergence of the Internet. We visit the next milestone in SAP's history when it introduced SAP NetWeaver, its new operating environment. It describes its solutions for the SME market: SAP All-in-One and Business One.

13 Understanding SAP ERP

13.1 INTRODUCTION TO SAP ERP

SAP has become the preeminent vendor of standard business applications software. Throughout the last decade, it has reported sales and profit growth rates in excess of 40% every year. The sales for 2009 were reported to be $10 billion. As reported by SAP, there are more than 36,000 customers with more than 100,000 installations of SAP across the world. And, worldwide, more than seven million users work on SAP systems. By any standards, these are impressive numbers coming from a company that has a great vision and is destined to play a significant role even in the Internet-driven markets of this century as well. SAP's main product is SAP Business Suite. Throughout this book, we will refer to SAP as a company as well as its enterprise products by the same term *SAP*. This should not lead to any confusion because, at any point, the context would make it clear which meaning is intended.

The phenomenal success of SAP comes from the fact that SAP systems are comprehensive but at the same time configurable to the specific needs of any company. Companies prefer off-the-shelf packages like SAP because it is flexible and can be configured to satisfy most requirements of any company in any industry. SAP can be deployed on various hardware platforms providing the same comprehensive and integrated functionality and flexibility for addressing individual company-specific requirements, as well as ensuring independence from specific technologies deployed in the company. Above all, SAP implements a process-oriented view of the enterprise.

It is remarkable that right from the beginning, SAP focused on developing enterprise-wide software to integrate all business processes within the enterprise. This integration was also to result from real-time processing of data rather than the batch-mode processing that was dominant at that time. And they also adopted very early on the layered model for the application architecture as a fundamental design principle that promised inherent flexibility and openness. At every stage in its history, SAP made critical decisions in adopting barely emerging ideas and technologies as the core strategies for its products even though these concepts had not proven themselves in the market. For instance, in the beginning, they decided on the concept of an enterprise-wide centralized database as well as real-time updates into this centralized database. They embraced the truth about GUIs being the focus of all interactions between the system and the users long before hardware and technologies made this viable without sacrificing the critical virtue of scalability. Also, SAP always kept internationalization and related issues like multicurrency on its active agenda while developing and enhancing its products. The SAP systems were fundamentally architectured to be multilingual right from their initial offerings and versions. More recently, SAP was the first company to introduce in-memory technology to enable both OLTP and OLAP with full data loaded in memory through its product SAP HANA.

SAP is one of the best ERP packages there is on the market, but it also shares this market space with a handful of other packages. In the last few years, the characteristics of such packages called ERP have become well established. In this chapter, we will look in detail at the nature of ERP packages and the reason for their predominant position in the IT landscape since the 1990s.

13.1.1 History of ERP

In the early days, the most important systems in manufacturing companies were known as MRP-based systems. After two decades, MRP systems evolved into MRP II, but it was many years before ERP systems were first implemented, and these systems continue to evolve.

In the 1960s, MRP emerged with the rapid evolution of computers. The main emphasis of these systems was to manage inventory, and the use of MRP helped companies control their inventory based on actual demand rather than reorder points. To do this, MRP used a set of techniques that took into account bills of material data, inventory data, and the master production schedule to predict future requirements for materials. A finished product was subdivided into its components, and for every component, a time schedule was developed. Based on this list, using computers, all necessary information required for the production of this specific product could be obtained in a very short time. The critical subcomponents could be tracked easily and, if necessary, could be obtained quickly to support on-time production. The critical path (time, resources, etc.) could be defined, and orders could be organized in order to prevent time delays in receipt of materials. However, even this simple procedure became tedious once the number of parts increased. Thus, a computer was essential to carry out these features of MRP. To sum up the benefits of MRP, it reduced the level of inventory a company needed to maintain, reduced production times by improving coordination and avoiding delays, and increased the company's overall efficiency.

In the 1980s, companies transitioned to MRP II. This system allowed manufacturers to optimize materials, procurement, manufacturing processes, and so forth, while at the same time providing financial and planning reports. The underlying idea behind the MRP II concept was to integrate MRP with further manufacturing functions and other business functions. MRP II was designed to assist in the effective planning of all the resources available to a manufacturing company. Ideally, it addressed operational planning in units and financial planning in dollars and included a simulation capability with which to answer *what-if* questions. It included business planning, sales and operations planning, production scheduling, MRP (as in the original MRP), and capacity requirements planning, along with executive support systems that could be used to balance capacities and materials.

Toward the end of the 1980s, many business processes such as logistics, procurement, and financial accounting needed to be integrated to allow companies to operate at their maximum efficiency. Actually, software systems to automate each of these internal business processes already existed, and these were very efficient in their own areas. However, their relative autonomy and limited real-time interaction was a major problem that had to be solved. The divisions did not exchange data with each other, or even if they did exchange data, it was poorly coordinated, which caused substantial problems that decreased the efficiency of the systems. For example, it was impossible for accounting systems to exchange data with manufacturing systems, and the time lag for exchanging data was so large that it brought no benefits for either division.

The main focus of ERP has been to integrate and synchronize the isolated functions into streamlined business processes. ERP has evolved considerably over the next 30 years as a result of continuous improvements in business management and the development of new information technologies. The ERP concept was first implemented at the end of the 1980s with the development of better client/server technology that enabled the implementation of an ERP system. Figure 12.1 shows how the systems have expanded to encompass more areas of operations in a company. ERP is a cross-functional enterprise backbone that integrates and automates many internal business processes and information systems within the sales and distribution, production, logistics, accounting, and HR functions of a company.

ERP not only coordinates several divisions but also enables companies to enter data only once for the information to be distributed to all the integrated business processes. ERP systems consist of several integrated suites of software modules, which share common data and provide connectivity.

Once the data have been recorded, they are available for all the company's divisions. The information about the processes in the company is represented consistently and is up to date in all business divisions at all times.

13.2   WHAT IS ERP?

There is no generally accepted definition of ERP in the offerings in the market. Not only is there little agreement on what it really stands for, there is even less agreement on what constitutes an ERP package, how it should be used, the potential of productivity gain, the impact on the organization, the costs involved, the personnel needed, or the training needed for the ERP personnel. Its characteristics are not limited to the ERP products and tools that are currently available in the market, and it is certainly not a technique or methodology. It is preferable not to contain ERP within a single set of current ideas but to look at ERP as a developing area of enterprise computerization with expanding boundaries. There is every reason to believe that the boundaries described for ERPs in this book will be constantly enlarging in the coming years. Notwithstanding all this caveats, ERP could be defined reasonably as follows:

> Enterprise Resources Planning (ERP) software applications package is a suit of pre-engineered ready-to-implement integrated application modules catering to all of the business functions of an enterprise and which possesses the flexibility for configuring and customizing dynamically the delivered functionality of the package to suit the specific requirements of the enterprise. ERP enables an enterprise to operate as an integrated enterprise-wide process-oriented information-driven real-time enterprise.

ERPs can provide this comprehensiveness and flexibility because at the heart of the system resides a computer-aided software engineering (CASE)-like repository that stores all details of these predeveloped applications. These details include every single data item, data table, and software program that is used by the complete system. For instance, SAP has more than 800 application process definitions stored in about 8000 tables within its repository. It also has additional support subsystems that help it to manage, secure, and maintain the operations of this package on a day-to-day basis. ERPs are a major development based on the initial ideas about information engineering put forward by Clive Finkelstein in Australia around 1980. He crystallized the basic idea that systems analysis could be engineered. Information engineering approaches essentially treat application development environment as an application in itself. The development can be designed and managed with an expectation that the users will request many changes; the systems are designed to accommodate such changes. The integrated application repository holds a full set of correlated information regarding the application, which also greatly facilitates documentation, testing, and maintenance. The major development of the ERPs over the information engineering approaches was in terms of providing predefined already-built-in comprehensive functionality of the application systems.

The success of ERP packages is based on the principle of reusability. It is not a very new concept in the computer industry. The origin of reusability goes back almost to the beginning of the computer era in the middle of the last century when it was recognized early that far too much program code was being written and rewritten repeatedly and uneconomically. Very soon, most of the programming languages provided for routines or packets of logic that could be reused multiple times within individual programs or even by a group of programs. Databases enabled the reuse of data, resulting in a tremendous surge in programmer productivity. Similarly, networks permitted reuse of the same programs on different terminals or workstations at different locations. ERP basically extended the concept of reusability to the functionality provided by the package. For instance, SAP R/3 was based on the essential commonality that was observed in functioning of companies within an industry. SAP built a reusable library of normally required process in a particular industry; and all that implementing SAP customers had to do was to select from this library all those processes that were required by their company. From a project effort and cost that was essential for the development and implementation using the traditional software development life cycle (SDLC), ERP reduced the project effort and cost only to that associated with the implementation phase of the SDLC. A comparison of the traditional SDLC and postmodern ERP implementations is shown in Figure A.1. Even though the cost of implementing ERP may seem higher than that for the traditional systems, ERP get implemented sooner and, therefore, start delivering all the benefits much earlier than the traditional systems. The fabled library of 800 best-of-class processes made available by SAP R/3 is like building blocks or components that can be reused by any customer to build their system quickly and at a considerably reduced cost.

In the early 1990s, all software crisis situations underwent a dramatic change with the arrival of ERP systems. ERPs changed the basic developmental model of implementing computerized systems within organizations to that of implementing off-the-shelf ready-made packages that covered every aspect of the function and operations of an enterprise. It provided an integrated set of functional modules corresponding to all major functions within the organization. It engendered the concept of implementing all these modules as an integrated whole rather than in a piecemeal fashion. Although there have not been any published results as yet, it became an accepted fact that enterprises that implemented ERPs only for a part of their organizations or only for a few select functions within their organizations did not benefit greatly. And, for the first time in the history of IT, ERPs gave indication of the recognition of the fact that business processes of an organization were much more fundamental than time-invariant data characterizing various aspects of the organization. And, most importantly, ERPs elevated information systems (IS) from a mere enabler of business strategy of an organization to a significant part of the business strategy itself. Thus, ERPs brought to an end the subsidiary and support role that IT had played throughout the last few decades. But in turn, the very nature of IS has also undergone a complete transformation (see Subsection 13.2.6, "ERP Elevates IT Strategy as a Part of the Business Strategy"). Implementation of an ERP within an enterprise was no longer a problem of technology; it was a business problem. ERPs have been the harbingers of a paradigm shift in the role of the IS/IT function within an enterprise. The writing of this book was also motivated by the need to address these fundamental changes in the very nature of IS/IT activity within an enterprise.

The distinguishing characteristics of ERP are as follows:

1. ERP transforms an enterprise into an information-driven enterprise.
2. ERP fundamentally perceives an enterprise as a global enterprise.
3. ERP reflects and mimics the integrated nature of an enterprise.
4. ERP fundamentally models a process-oriented enterprise.
5. ERP enables the real time enterprise.
6. ERP elevates IT strategy as a part of the business strategy.
7. ERP represents a major advance on the earlier manufacturing performance improvement approaches.
8. ERP represents the new departmental store model of implementing computerized systems.
9. ERP is a mass-user-oriented application environment.

In the remaining part of this section, we introduce the concept of ERP and deal with each of these characteristics of ERP systems. There is also a need of a unifying framework that would bring together the various aspects of an ERP implementation. These include aspects of business competitiveness, information-based organizations, integrative and collaborative strategies, process-oriented real-time operations, employee empowerment, information capital and knowledge assets, organizational learning, business engineering, change management, and virtual value chains and strategic alliances.

13.2.1 ERP Transforms the Enterprise into an Information-Driven Enterprise

All computerized systems and solutions in the past were using past-facing information merely for the purpose of referring and reporting only. ERP, for the first time in the history of computerized systems, began treating information as a resource for the operational requirements of the enterprise. But, unlike the traditional resources, information resource as made available by ERPs can be reused and shared multiply without dissipation or degradation. The impressive productivity gains resulting from the ERPs truthfully arise out of this unique characteristic of ERPs to use information as an inexhaustible resource.

13.2.2 ERP Fundamentally Perceives an Enterprise as a Global Enterprise

In these times of divestitures, mergers, and acquisitions, this is an important requirement. Unlike some of the earlier enterprise-wide solutions available on mainframes, ERPs cater to corporate-wide requirements even if an organization is involved in disparate businesses like discrete industries (manufacturing, engineering, etc.), process industries (chemicals, paints, etc.), and services industries (banking, media, etc.). ERP enables the management to plan, operate, and manage such conglomerates without any impediments of mismatch of systems for different divisions.

Although it may seem a minor point, ERP also permits the important functionality of enabling seamless integration of distributed or multilocation operations; we consider this aspect in the next section.

13.2.3 ERP Reflects and Mimics the Integrated Nature of an Enterprise

Notwithstanding the different ways in which the enterprises are structured and organized, enterprises function essentially in an integrated fashion. Across the years, the turf-preservation mentality has been rigidified even in the computerized systems deployed for the various functions. Under the garb of fundamentally different nature of the activities and functions, motley of information systems had mushroomed within organization reenforcing rather than lessening the heterogeneity of systems. This had led to problems of incompatibility, differing standards, interfacing issues, limited functional and technological upgrade paths, costly maintenance, high operating costs, costly training and support activities, inconsistent documentation, and so on. Instead of providing the strategic leverage necessary for the business operations of the enterprise, IS/IT systems were constant drain on the enterprise and, truthfully, reduced their reaction times to the changes observed in the market space.

ERP with its holistic approach and its demand for integration dissolve all such efficiency dissipating spurious processes not only in their IS/IT aspects but also in their actual functions. With a single centralized transparent, current, consistent, and complete database of all enterprise-related data, ERP in a masterstroke eliminated all wait times associated with all intracompany interactions. Integration as embodied in ERP eliminates many a non-value-added (NVA) processes. With its laser-like focus on best-of-business practices, SAP demonstrates glaringly the essential futility of routine bureaucratic mechanization within organizations; it brings in consistency, discipline, and fast reaction times in the operations of a company. Thus, whereas finance may aim for minimizing stock, the purchasing function may want to maintain a buffer stock to avoid out-of-stock situations. Similarly, marketing may want production of more varied product models to cater to the requirements in the market, whereas production function will want to lessen the number of different kinds of products for reducing setup times and related costs. By promoting cross-functional processes and work teams, ERP like SAP provides a powerful medium for supporting, reconciling, and optimizing the conflicting goals of different functions of the organizations.

13.2.4   ERP Fundamentally Models a Process-Oriented Enterprise

As organizational and environmental conditions become more complex, globalized, and, therefore, competitive, processes provide a framework for dealing effectively with the issues of performance improvement, capability development, and adaptation to the changing environment. Process modeling permits the true comprehension of the characteristic structure and dynamics of the business. Business processes are the most important portions of the reality that had been ignored by the traditional information systems. The traditional IT process modeling techniques, methodologies, and environments are a misnomer, for they truly model only the procedures for operating on the data associated at various points of the business subprocesses, which themselves are never mirrored within the system.

Conventional systems primarily store only snapshots of discrete group of data at predefined or configured instants of time along a business process within an organization. This predominating data-oriented view of the enterprise as implemented by the traditional IT systems is the most unnatural and alien way of looking at any area of human activity. The stability of the data models, as canonized in the conventional IT paradigm, may have been advantageous for the systems personnel, but for the same reason, they would have been unusable (and unacceptable) to the business stakeholders within the organizations. Traditional systems could never really resolve this simple dichotomy of the fact that systems based on leveraging on the unchanging data models, although easy to maintain, can never describe the essentially dynamic nature of businesses. The lack of facilities for modeling business processes and business rules was the root cause of the resulting productivity paradox mentioned in the beginning of this section.

ERPs for the first time recognized the fundamental error that was being perpetuated all these past decades. Although many of the ERP packages still carry the legacy of the data-oriented view, the parallel view of business process and business rules is gaining prominence rapidly. This can also be seen to be the reason for the rapidly maturing groupware and workflow subsystems within the core architecture of current ERP systems.

13.2.5   ERP Enables the Real-Time Enterprise

ERP has engendered the earlier imagined-only possibility of a real-time enterprise. Even before the arrival of ERPs, companies had witnessed the power and perils of operating an online system, which provided on-the-system direct registration of business transactions as well as immediate updates or posting to the relevant master and transaction data files. ERP has made this possible on enterprise-wide scale and has realized tremendous gains in efficiencies and productivity by extending, as it were, the concept of JIT to the whole of the organization. Every system is a collection of many subsystems and processes with life-cycle times of varying durations. A system that can respond effectively within the life-cycle time of some of the smaller life cycles can be considered to be functioning essentially in a real-time mode. As per this definition, for example, as far as the solar system is concerned, with reference to a life cycle of earth's rotation period of 365 days, forecasting the climatic conditions anytime within a period of 365 days could be termed as functioning in a real-time mode! In analogy with this, for better appreciation of real-time responsiveness, enterprises could define enterprise standard time (EST). This could be defined based on the following:

- A central reference location within the organization
- An optimal cycle time in days or weeks suitable for all functions within the organization

All responses within the enterprise could be measured with reference to this EST. Enterprises that can cut down their EST relentlessly would be able to sustain their competitiveness in the market. And this would become achievable to a large extent because of the instant availability of relevant information to all concerned members of the company provided by the ERP. Information is only relevant when it is available within a cycle of EST; information furnished after this period ceases to act as a resource and rapidly ends up being of value only for recording and reporting purposes (see last paragraph in Subsection 13.5.1, "Information as the New Resource"). A continuous effort for reducing EST would result in kind of customer responsiveness that would be unimaginable in earlier times.

Furthermore, the real-time responsiveness of the enterprise coupled with the earlier mentioned enterprise-wide integration also enables enterprises the powerful capability of concurrent processing that would be impossible without ERPs like SAP. Enterprises can obtain tremendous efficiencies and throughputs because of this ability to administer in parallel many a related processes that are not interdependent fully or partially. In non-ERP enterprises, such closely related processes are typically done sequentially because they are usually handled by the same set of personnel, who may be obviously constrained to address them only in a sequence. An illustration of this could be ad hoc analysis that may have to be done simultaneously on a set of POs and corresponding vendors/suppliers, deliveries, invoices, and so on. ERPs like SAP can perform all these concurrently because of ready availability of all relevant, complete, and consistent information at the same time.

13.2.6 ERP Elevates IT Strategy as a Part of the Business Strategy

The coming of SAP heralded enhanced role for the IT systems. They are no longer the support functions of the earlier years. If someone is under that illusion, they will pay a very high price, maybe even in terms of the corporeal death of the enterprise itself. Now the real focus of IS/IT systems is no longer its alignment with the business strategy of the enterprise but on how to give it a competitive edge; it is part of the business necessities and priorities. Because of the complexity of increasing business change and uncertainty, IS/IT is business strategy incarnate!

And this arises primarily from the fact that information itself has become a vital resource for an enterprise in the same league as the traditional resources like manpower, materials, money, and time.

13.2.7 ERP Represents a Major Advance on the Earlier Manufacturing Performance Improvement Approaches

ERP is the latest in the succession of approaches that have been adopted throughout the history of enterprises for the improvement of enterprise-level performances. ERPs have realized the failed dream of improvements that were expected from the MRP II-based manufacturing resources planning systems of the 1970s. ERPs have enabled combining the *hard* approach of MRP II with the much broad-scoped *soft* approaches of World Class Manufacturing (WCM) that were widely adopted during the 1980s in the last century. The WCM included such powerful approaches like JIT, TQM, benchmarking, lean manufacturing, HR development movement, and, later in the 1990s, BPR. Table 13.1 gives a list of major enterprise performance improvement movements during the last century. ERPs provide the basic platform for devising techniques and tools for better implementations of the earlier approaches.

13.2.8 ERP Represents the Departmental Store Model of Implementing Computerized Systems

The coming of ERP has been the death knell of the development model of IS systems and, along with it, has gone the concept of requirements capture, modeling languages, development of software programs, testing, and so on that have usually been associated with the conventional

TABLE 13.1

Timeline of Performance Improvement Movements in the Twentieth Century

1690	Division of Labour	Adam Smith
1890	Scientific Measurement	Fredderick Taylor
1900	Mass Production	Henry Ford
1920	Industrial Engineering	F. Gilbreth and Fredrick Taylor
1930	Human Relations Movement	Elton Mayo
1950	Japanese Quality Revolution	J. M. Juran and W. E. Demming
1960	Materials Requirement Planning	William Orlicky
1970	Manufacturing Resources Planning	Oliver Wright
1970	Focused Factory	Wickham Skinner
1980	Total Quality Management	Philip Crosby
1980	Just In Time	Taiicho Ohno
1980	Computer Integrated Manufacturing	
1980	Optimised Production Technology	Eliyahu Goldratt
1980	ISO 9000	NASI
1980	World Class Manufacturing	Richard Schonberger
1990	Mass Customisation	Stan Davis and B. Joseph Pine II
1990	Lean Manufacturing	Jones & Roos
1990	Business Process Re-engineering	Michael Hammer
1990	Enterprise Resources Planning	
1990	Customer Relationship Management	Frederick Reichheld

developmental model. In its place, for the first time, is the end-user-friendly model of what one could call as the departmental store model of computerized systems. The reference here is to the fact that rather than going through the complexities of specifying and getting a job done for you, you walk into a departmental store and from the array of functional goodies on display, *pick and choose* the functionality required by you. An ERP is the analog of the great departmental store of functionalities or processes required within an organization. ERP makes the transition from the world of carefully engineered and running systems to, as if were, the world of consumers where the value of the delivered functionality is based not on its pedigree but only on what, how, where, and when it can be used gainfully.

This then is the final commoditization of the IS/IT products and services!

13.2.9 ERP Is a Mass-User-Oriented Application Environment

Compared to the degree of involvement of functional managers and end users into traditional software project implementations, their participation in SAP implementations may definitely seem unusual. SAP brings computerization to desktops and in this sense is an end-user-oriented environment in the true sense of the word. Unlike the traditional systems, where users accessed the system directly only in well-defined pockets within the enterprise, in SAP, end users are truly the personnel actually involved with the operations of the business. Because of the intense involvement of a sizable portion of the workforce of the company with the SAP implementation right from the beginning, the probability of them embracing the system and not struggling against the system is much higher. They also act as the advocates and facilitators during and after the implementation phase.

13.3 WHY USE ERP?

The implementation of ERP engenders the following business and technical advantages:

- Reconciling and optimizing the conflicting goals of different divisions or departments; the transparent sharing of information with all concerned departments also enables cross-functional collaboration that is essential for the success of the millennium enterprise standardization of business processes across all the constituent companies and sites, thus increasing their efficiencies.
- Ability to know and implement global best practices.
- Altering the function-oriented organization toward more team-based cross-functional process-oriented organization, thus leading to more flexible, flatter, and tightly integrated organization.
- ERP provides a responsive medium for undertaking all variants on process improvement programs and methodologies including PI, process improvement, and business process.
- ERP also provides a responsive medium for quality improvement and standardization efforts including QC, QA, and TQM.
- ERP being process-oriented is a fertile ground for implementing activity-based management (ABM) efforts, be it for budgeting, costing, efficiency, or quality.
- ERP provides the best conduit for measuring the benefits accruing to the organizations by their implementation by monitoring the ROI of not only money but also manpower, materials, time, and information. This could be in terms of various parameters like cost, quality, responsiveness, and cycle time. Thus, ERP could assist in the implementation of, for instance, the balanced scorecard within the enterprise.
- ERPs, because they customarily implement best-of-class practices, provide the best means for benchmarking the organization's competitiveness.
- An ERP enables an enterprise to scale up its level of operations drastically or even enter into different businesses altogether without any disruption or performance degradation.
- Real-time creation of data directly during the actual physical transaction or processes by the persons who are actually responsible for it.
- Pushing latest data and status to the actual operational-level persons for better and faster decisions at least on routine issues; empowering and ownership to the operational personnel at the level of actual work (this automatically does away with problems associated with collection of voluminous data, preparation, entry, corrections of inaccuracies, backup, etc.)
- Integration of data of the organization into a single comprehensive database.
- Online availability of correct and up-to-date data.
- ERP provides the most current, correct, consistent, complete operational data that could be populated into the enterprise data warehouse for analysis and reporting.
- ERP greatly reduces the cost of maintaining systems. The vendor shoulders the responsibility of enhancing functionalities, providing technical upgrades as well as incorporating the latest country-specific regulations and statutory requirements.

As mentioned in Subsection 13.1, "Introduction to SAP ERP," all these characteristics of SAP-implemented organizations arise primarily from the fact that what they handle is not merely organizational data but a resource that is of strategic significance to the enterprise.

In the next section, we turn to this aspect of the postmodern integrated organizations.

13.4 MANAGEMENT BY COLLABORATION

The business environment has been witnessing tremendous and rapid changes in the 1990s. There is an increasing emphasis on being customer focused and on leveraging and strengthening the company's core competencies. This has forced companies to learn and develop abilities to change and respond rapidly to the competitive dynamics of the global market.

Companies have learned to effectively reengineer themselves into flatter organizations, with closer integration across the traditional functional boundaries of the organization. There is increasing focus on employee empowerment and cross-functional teams. In this book, we are proposing that what we are witnessing is a fundamental transformation from the manner in which businesses have been operating for the last century.

This change, which is primarily driven by the information revolution of the past few decades, is characterized by the dominant tendency to integrate across transaction boundaries, both internally and externally. The dominant theme of this new system of management with significant implications on organizational development is collaboration. We will refer to this emerging and maturing constellation of concepts and practices as management by collaboration (MBC). ERP packages such as SAP are major instruments for realizing MBC-driven organizations.

MBC is an approach to management primarily focused on relationships; relationships by their very nature are not static and are constantly in evolution. As organizational and environmental conditions become more complex, globalized, and, therefore, competitive, MBC provides a framework for dealing effectively with the issues of performance improvement, capability development, and adaptation to the changing environment. MBC, as embodied by ERP packages such as SAP, has had a major impact on the strategy, structure, and culture of the organization.

The beauty and essence of MBC are that it incorporates in its very fabric the basic urge of humans for a purpose in life, for mutually beneficial relationships, for mutual commitment, and for being helpful to other beings, that is, for collaborating. These relationships could be at the level of individual, division, and company or even between companies. Every relationship has a purpose and manifests itself through various processes as embodied mainly in the form of teams; thus, the relationships are geared toward attainment of these purposes through the concerned processes optimally.

Because of the enhanced role played by the individual members of a company in any relationship or process, MBC not only promotes their motivation and competence but also develops the competitiveness and capability of the organizations as a whole. MBC emphasizes the roles of both the top management and the individual member. Thus, the MBC approach covers the whole organization through the means of basic binding concepts such as relationships, processes, and teams. MBC addresses readily all issues of management, including organization development. The issues range from organizational design and structure, role definition and job design, output quality and productivity, communication channels, and company culture to employee issues such as attitudes, perception, values, and motivation.

The basic idea of collaboration has been gaining tremendous ground with the increasing importance of business processes and dynamically constituted teams in the operations of companies. The traditional bureaucratic structures, which are highly formalized, centralized, and functionally specialized, have proven too slow, too expensive, and too unresponsive to be competitive. These structures are based on the basic assumption that all the individual activities and task elements in a job are independent and separable. Organizations were structured hierarchically in a *command and control* structure, and it was taken as an accepted fact that the output of the organization as a whole could be maximized by maximizing the output of each constituent organizational unit.

On the other hand, by their very nature, teams are flexible, adaptable, dynamic, and collaborative. They encourage flexibility, innovation, entrepreneurship, and responsiveness. For the last few decades, even in traditionally bureaucratic-oriented manufacturing companies, teams have manifested themselves and flourished successfully in various forms as superteams, SDWTs, quality circles, and so on. The dynamic changes in the market and global competition being confronted by companies necessarily lead to flatter and more flexible organizations with a dominance of more dynamic structures like teams.

People in teams, representing different functional units, are motivated to work within constraints of time and resources to achieve a defined goal. The goals might range from incremental improvements in efficiency, quality, and productivity to quantum leaps in new-product development. Even in traditional businesses, the number and variety of teams instituted for various functions, projects, tasks, and activities has been on the increase.

Increasingly, companies are populated with worker teams that have special skills, operate semi-autonomously, and are answerable directly to peers and to the end customers. Members must not only have higher level of skills than before but also be more flexible and capable of doing more jobs. The empowered workforce with considerably enhanced managerial responsibilities (pertaining to information, resources, authority, and accountability) has resulted in an increase in worker commitment and flexibility. Whereas workers have witnessed gains in the quality of their work life, corporations have obtained returns in terms of increased quality, productivity, and cost improvements.

Consequently, in the past few years, a new type of nonhierarchical network organization with distributed intelligence and decentralized decision-making powers has been evolving. This entails a demand for constant and frequent communication and feedback among the various teams or functional groups. An ERP package such as SAP essentially provides such an enabling environment through its modules like SAP Office, SAP Workflow, and SAP Business Warehouse.

13.4.1 Information-Driven Enterprise

The combined impact on companies of increasing product complexity together with increased variety has been to create a massive problem of information management and coordination. Information-based activities now constitute a major fraction of all activities within an enterprise. Information-based organizations alone can enable companies to survive in the dynamically changing global competitive market. Only integrated, computer-based, postmodern information systems such as SAP are (and can be) enablers for this kind of enterprise-level collaboration.

The information-based organization as proposed by management theorist Peter Drucker is a reality today; correspondingly, companies are compelled to install both end-user and work-group-oriented enterprise-level integrated computing environments. Only information-based organizations can possibly store, retrieve, analyze, and present colossal amount of information at the enterprise level, which is also up to date, timely, accurate, collated, processed, and packaged dynamically for both external and internal customers. It should be noted that this section title uses the phrase *information driven* rather than *information based*. The primary reason for that is technology in the 1990s permits us to use information as a resource that is a legitimate substitute for conventional resources. We visit this aspect in Subsection 13.5.1, "Information as the New Resource".

13.4.2 Process-Oriented Enterprise

ERP packages enable an organization to truly function as an integrated organization: integration across all functions or segments of the traditional value chain, sales order, production, inventory, purchasing, finance and accounting, personnel and administration, and so on. They do this by modeling primarily the business processes as the basic business entities of the enterprise, rather than by modeling data handled by the enterprise (as done by the traditional IT systems). Every ERP might not be completely successful in this; however, in a break with the legacy enterprise-wide solutions, every ERP treats business processes as more fundamental than data items.

Collaborations or relationships manifest themselves through the various organizational processes. A process may be generally defined as the set of resources and activities necessary and sufficient to convert some form of input into some form of output. Processes are internal, external, or a combination of both; they have cross-functional boundaries; they have starting and ending points; and they exist at all levels within the organization.

The significance of a process to the success of the company's business is dependent on the value, with reference to the customer, of the collaboration that it addresses and represents. In other words, the nature and extent of the value addition by a process to a product or services delivered to a customer is the best index of the contribution of that process to the company's overall customer satisfaction or *customer collaboration*.

Thus, MBC not only recognizes inherently the significance of various process-related techniques and methodologies such as PI, business process improvement (BPI), business process redesign (BPRD), and BPR but also treats them as fundamental, continuous, and integral functions of the management of a company itself. A collaborative enterprise enabled by the implementation of an ERP is inherently amenable to business process improvement, which is also the essence of any TQM-oriented effort undertaken within an enterprise. We will deal with such process improvement–related issues in Chapter 14, Subsection 14.4, "BPR and SAP Implementation".

13.4.3 VALUE-ADD-DRIVEN ENTERPRISE

Business processes can be seen as the very basis of the value addition within an organization that was traditionally attributed to various functions or divisions in an organization. As organizational and environmental conditions become more complex, globalized, and competitive, processes provide a framework for dealing effectively with the issues of performance improvement, capability development, and adaptation to the changing environment.

Along a value stream (i.e., a business process), analysis of the absence or creation of added value or (worse) destruction of value critically determines the necessity and effectiveness of a process step. The understanding of value-adding and NVA processes (or process steps) is a significant factor in the analysis, design, benchmarking, and optimization of business processes in the companies leading to the BPR.

Values are characterized by both value determinants such as time (cycle time, lead time and so on), flexibility (options, customization, composition, and so on), responsiveness (lead time, number of hand-offs, and so on), quality (rework, rejects, yield, and so on), and price (discounts, rebates, coupons, incentives, and so on). We must hasten to add that we are not disregarding cost (materials, labor, overhead, and so forth) as a value determinant. However, the effect of cost is truly a result of a host of value determinants such as time, flexibility, responsiveness, and so on.

Consequently, in this formulation, one can understand completely the company's competitive gap in the market in terms of such process-based, customer-expected value and the value delivered by the company's processes for the concerned product or service. We will refer to such customer-defined characteristics of value as critical value determinants (CVDs). Therefore, we can perform market segmentation for a particular (group of) product or service in terms of the most significant of the customer values and the corresponding CVDs.

13.4.4 VIRTUAL ENTERPRISE

Along with the general economic growth and globalization of markets, personal disposable incomes have increased, so the demand for product variety and customization has increased appreciably. Additionally, technological progress driven by the search for superior performance is already increasing the complexity of both products and processes. Because volume, complexity, and variety are mutually exclusive, this has invariably led to collaborative endeavors for achieving this with greater flexibility in terms of enhancing of capabilities, minimization of risks, lower costs of investments, shortened product life cycles, and so on.

These collaborative endeavors, which have been known variously as partnering, value-added partnering, partnership sourcing, outsourcing, alliances, virtual corporations, and so on, recognize the fact that optimization of the system as a whole is not achievable by maximization of the output at the constituting subsystem levels alone. Only mature ERP packages such as SAP can provide a backbone for holding together the virtual value chain across all these collaborative relationships.

Outsourcing will become a dominant trend in the millennium enterprise, whereby the enterprise concentrates only on being competitive in its core business activities and outsources the responsibility of competitiveness in noncore products and functions to third parties for mutual benefit. The development and maintenance of its core competencies are critical to the success of its main business; an enterprise cannot outsource these because it is these core functions that give it an identity. On the other hand, competitiveness in noncore functions, which is also essential for overall efficiencies, is outsourced to enterprises that are themselves in business of providing these very products or services; the outsourced products and services are their core competencies.

Most of the major manufacturers over the world have become to a large extent *systems integrators*, providing only some of the specialized parts and final assembly of subsystems from a network of suppliers. Their economic role has transformed mainly into the basic design, marketing, and service, but not complete production per se. For the existence and growth of such virtual organizations, it is important that the company be able to manage the complexities of managing such relationship on day-to-day basis. An ERP system provides all the functionality and processes for managing and accounting for such outsourced jobs. But, more significantly, only an ERP can make it possible for such a collaborative enterprise to exist and grow to scales unimaginable with traditional organizational architectures.

13.5 ENTERPRISE KNOWLEDGE AS THE NEW CAPITAL

Adam Smith started the industrial revolution by identifying labor and capital as the economic determinants of the wealth of a nation. In this century, however, the size of the land, mass of labor, and materials that you may possess might be worthless if you do not control the related know-how. In the twenty-first century, know-how will reside and flourish in people's minds; what might matter more are how many enterprising and innovative people you have and the freedom that they have in realizing their dreams. It will be the century of information economics.

ERP like SAP also acts as transformers of the knowledge, which resides in the heads of the operational and subject experts into a more explicit and accessible form. This corresponds exactly to the tacit knowledge talked about by I. Nonaka and H. Takeuchi in their book titled *The Knowledge Creating Company*. These could be learning experiences, ideas, insights, innovations, thumb rules, business cases, concepts or conceptual models, analogies, and so on. They exhort companies to convert the illusive, unsystematized, uncodified, and *can-be-lost* knowledge of the corporation into explicit knowledge that can be codified, collated, and managed like any other capital investment. This could be in the form of documents, case studies, analysis reports, evaluations, concept papers, internal proposals, and so on. Most importantly, it is available for scrutiny and can be improved on an ongoing basis. SAP performs the invaluable service of transforming the implicit knowledge into the explicit form.

13.5.1 INFORMATION AS THE NEW RESOURCE

Having covered the context of ERP in this chapter, it is time now to state that the importance of ERP packages like SAP is not because of the total integration of various modules, single-point data entry, data integrity, ad hoc reporting, instant access to information, end-user computing, etc., provided by them. But it arises primarily from the fact that information is by now the fifth resource (the first four being manpower, materials, money, and time). And, unlike other resources, this resource is inexhaustible—it can be shared infinitely without any reduction. Thus, if we can use information as substitute for other resources (which we can see below), we can use it many times over without any appreciable further cost. Among all resources, this is one resource that in practical terms almost defies the universal law of increase of entropy as understood in the physical sciences.

Traditionally, competitive advantage came from strategies based on following value determinants:

Cost   (ownership, use, training support, maintenance, etc.)
Time   (cycle time, lead time, etc.)
Response time   (lead time, number of hand-offs, number of queues, etc.)
Flexibility   (customization, options, composition, etc.)
Quality   (rework, rejects, yield, etc.)
Innovation   (new needs, interfaces, add-ons, etc.)

But because everyone has squeezed (and continue to do so) as much as one can from the preceding value determinants in the last few decades, now, the only source for competitive strategy of substantial value, which remains to be exploited in a major way, is from the latest new-found resource:

Information (correctness, currency, consistency, completeness, clarity, compliance, availability, security, etc.)

Traditionally, the basic resources have been manpower (before the agricultural revolution), materials (before industrial revolution), capital (before information revolution till the mid-twentieth century), and time (since the mid-1950s). In certain sense of the term, these basic resources are considered interchangeable. Likewise, since the mid-twentieth century, information has become the fifth resource, and it is almost a substitute for manpower, materials, capital, and even time.

For instance, JIT permits us to order for just the right kind of material at the right time at the right place, therefore reducing inputs of manpower in ordering, handling, storing, etc. It also results in reduced materials inventory and, hence, cost of storage mechanisms, cost of locked capital, etc.

The availability of detailed and up-to-the-minute information on production runs can result in up-to-the-minute information on

- Production plan for the next run
- Hence, material requirements for the next run
- Hence, issue of materials from the main stores for the next run
- Hence, stock at hand in the stores for the next run
- Hence, material to be ordered for the next run

It is not difficult to see that this ultimately results in drastically increased throughputs and reduced business cycle times, which is equivalent to improved production or technological processes through use of improved resources. Traditionally, appreciably higher throughputs and lower production/business cycles could only be possible through innovation in technology and/or production methods or process. How information as provided by ERPs is a resource of an organization can be seen from the analogy with fuel that drives automobiles: information as made available by SAP greatly increases the speed of business processes within the organization. Evidently, this is a class apart from what is achievable with the manual or even fragmented legacy computerized systems. Enterprise-wide JIT, and not just the one confined primarily to the production department only, is impossible without integrated postmodern computerized systems like ERPs for correct, current, consistent, and complete information.

Thus, information is a practical and tangible substitute for manpower, materials, and money in real commercial terms. And though manual JIT systems are possible, only computerized ERP systems can give you JIT even in industries like airlines, credit cards, electronic banking, and courier services, which do not work in batch mode of production but are essentially functioning in a real-time mode.

We can take this analogy even further. In any industry, like that for any other traditional raw materials, companies need the *information* resource preprocessed in massive amounts that has to be correct, current, consistent, and so on. And only complete and integrated ERP packages like SAP can provide this operational raw material required by in massive amounts. It should be specially noted that only an ERP implemented within an enterprise enables the optimal utilization and efficient conversion of such a seemingly intangible resource like information into tangible commercial product(s), which is also a highly perishable resource!

13.6 ERP AS THE NEW ENTERPRISE ARCHITECTURE

ERP provides the architecture for the realization of the dimensions of variations discussed in Chapter 7.

Shared values: ERP truly makes it possible to operate as a collaborative value-add-driven organization. It is difficult to imagine such a company operating on manual or even non-integrated systems, which, because of the inherent delays of information transfer between them, would not function in the real-time mode. SAP permits learning happening in any part of the enterprise to be incorporated into the system even on a daily basis.

Strategy: ERP enables the realization of an organization that has a vision to be competitive by raising the level of skills and competencies of its personnel so that they can respond better, faster, and at the optimal cost to the changing business situations every day.

Structure: For the millennium enterprise, the ERP system provides visibility to the responsibility-oriented organization structure rather than the designation-oriented structure of the earlier times. It provides instant communication and interaction with all members who are involved in a particular activity or process irrespective of their reporting department or designation.

Stuff: ERP enables the definition, management, planning, production, and delivery of products or services. They empower the enterprise to compose or develop new products or services and add them seamless to the traditional processes established for defining, manufacture, and delivery of products to the end customers.

Style: ERP enables access to data to all concerned personnel to keep track of the organization's overall performance with reference to the company's goals as well as their own contribution to the same on a daily basis. This engenders a sense of involvement and transparency that had not been achievable earlier.

Staff: ERP enables access to data to all concerned personnel to keep track of the organization's overall performance with reference to the company's goals as well as their own contribution to the same on a daily basis. This engenders a sense of involvement and transparency that had not been achievable earlier.

Skills: ERP is equipped to fully maintain a repository of skills (and skill sets) across the whole base of employees. It can query for a specific skill or shortlist for upgrade of skills or register acquisition of new skills at an individual or group level. ERP can also help plan and schedule skills that need periodic refresh on systematic basis.

Systems: ERP implements all essential systems and procedures to their bare-minimum necessity level. It provides for adequate control without encumbering the work that directly contributes in the value add delivered to the external or internal customers. ERP enables the process-oriented enterprise that may not always be feasible to realize physically, for instance, by locating all concerned members of a team in one place. It also makes it possible for members to participate efficiently and effectively in more than one business-critical process.

Sequence: ERP can enable the handling of discrete or continuous process requirements of any enterprise. ERP also enables the handling of any or a mix and match of both modes of production depending on the enterprises' requirement. Any changes planned in the production flow by reason of changes of products, materials, production process, quality, and so on can be accommodated readily.

13.7   ENTERPRISE BUSINESS PROCESSES

Businesses take inputs (resources) in the form of material, people, and equipment and transform these inputs into goods and services for customers. Managing these inputs and the business processes effectively requires accurate and up-to-date information. For example, the sales function takes a customer's order, and the production function schedules the manufacturing of the product. Logistics employees schedule and carry out the delivery of the product. If raw materials are needed to make the product, production prompts purchasing to arrange for their purchase and delivery. In that case, logistics will receive the material, verify its condition to accounting so that the vendor can be paid, and deliver the goods to production. Throughout, accounting keeps appropriate transaction records.

Most companies had unintegrated information systems that supported only the activities of individual business functional areas. Thus, a company would have a marketing information system, a production information system, and so on, each with its own hardware, software, and methods of processing data and information. This configuration of information systems is known as silos because each department has its own stack, or silo, of information that is unconnected to the next silo. Silos are also known as stovepipes. Such unintegrated systems might work well within individual functional areas, but to achieve its goals, a company must share data among all the functional areas. When a company's information systems are not integrated, costly inefficiencies can result. For example, suppose two functional areas have separate, unintegrated information systems. To share data, a clerk in one functional area needs to print out data from another functional area and then type the information into her area's information system. Not only does this data input take twice the time, it also significantly increases the chance for data-entry errors. Alternatively, the process might be automated by having one information system write data to a file to be read by another information system. This would reduce the probability of errors, but it could only be done periodically (usually overnight or on a weekend), to minimize the disruption to normal business transactions. Because of the time lag in updating the system, the transferred data would rarely be up to date. In addition, data can be defined differently in different data systems, such as calling products by different part numbers in different systems. This variance can create further problems in timely and accurate information sharing between functional areas.

The functional business model illustrates the concept of silos of information, which limit the exchange of information between the lower operating levels. Instead, the exchange of information between operating groups is handled by top management, which might not be knowledgeable about the functional area (see Figure 13.1a). In the quickly changing markets of the 1990s, the functional model led to top-heavy and overstaffed organizations incapable of reacting quickly to change. This led to view a business as a set of cross-functional processes, as illustrated in Figure 13.1b. In the process-oriented model, the flow of information and management activity is *horizontal* across functions, in line with the flow of materials and products. This horizontal flow promotes flexibility and rapid decision making and stimulated managers to see the importance of managing business processes. Now information flows between the operating levels without top management's involvement.

13.8   SAP BUSINESS SUITE

mySAP Business Suite is a comprehensive family of business applications that allow companies to manage their entire value chain. mySAP applications describe processes and functions from a process point of view. The business applications provide users with consistent results throughout the entire company network and give your company the flexibility needed in today's dynamic market situations. It consists of a number of different products that enable cross-company processes.

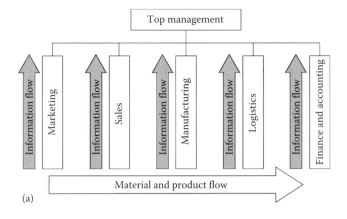

(a)

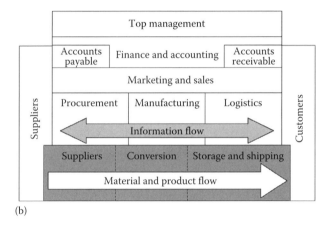

(b)

FIGURE 13.1 Information and material flows in (a) a functional business model and (b) a business process model.

mySAP Business Suite consists of individual applications. Each application has its own focus area and provides functions to map this area in a flexible and comprehensive way. These applications can be purchased as an entire suite or individually. All the applications are based on the SAP NetWeaver technology platform, an integration and application platform that reduces total cost of ownership across the entire IT landscape and supports the evolution of mySAP Business Suite to a service-based architecture.

Business experience, strategies, and know-how are incorporated in SAP software. The flexibility and comprehensive integration and adaptation options offered by SAP software result in high-performance, industry-specific, and cross-industry e-business applications, namely,

1. mySAP applications describe processes and functions from a process point of view. Applications are SAP's products seen from the point of view of the customer, with an outside-in focus on company processes.
2. Components are not the actual company solutions, simply the technical building blocks; components represent SAP's technical view of software with an inside-out focus (Figure 13.2).

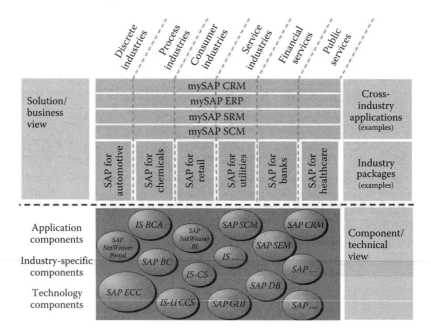

FIGURE 13.2   SAP applications and SAP components.

13.8.1   mySAP Applications

SAP ERP provides several solutions that assist firms in achieving operational excellence through process efficiencies, business agility, and streamlined business operations. There is quite a bit of overlap between particular solutions and modules. Although it can be confusing, this flexibility is one of SAP's greatest strengths—the ability to customize a business solution in this way makes it possible to create innovative business processes capable of meeting the needs of most of any organization's finance and executive leadership teams.

1. SAP provides a breadth of products, each targeted a bit differently at addressing the requirements of customer enterprises. The *best* solution depends on many factors, including cost, required functionality, features, preference for onsite versus hosted solutions, size, and complexity of the business processes to be configured.
2. With the changing market dynamics and concomitant changes in SAP's go-to-market strategy, the SAP suite of products undergoes changes in structures, compositions or reconfigurations, etc. The reader should keep in mind the broad subdivision between Internet-based applications (described in this section) and the underlying core functional components (see Subsection 13.8.2, "SAP Components"). The background behind the emergence of two levels of applications is explained in earlier chapter (see Chapter 12, Subsection 12.5.1, "mySAP.com").

13.8.1.1   mySAP ERP

13.8.1.1.1   mySAP ERP Financials

SAP ERP Financials package enables financial transformation. New general ledger capabilities streamline the financial reconciliation process, reduce the cost of administration and control, and minimize user error. This in turn frees up an organization to focus strategically—another area SAP

ERP Financials enables. By offering more effective collaboration with its customers, vendors, and suppliers, SAP ERP Financials enables governance, helps manage risk and compliance, increases inventory turns, frees up cash and working capital, provides greater financial transparency, and simplifies other complex invoicing and payment processes. The ability to drill down into areas such as profitability analysis and take advantage of built-in analytic solutions empowers end users as they make better decisions faster across many different financial domains and, therefore, address financial matters as described in the following.

13.8.1.1.1.1   Governance, Risk, and Compliance   SAP provides a solution for GRC called SAP GRC. With its integrated SAP ERP back end, SAP provides the visibility and transparency organizations demand in response to various regulatory body and internal control requirements. SAP GRC enables a firm to effectively manage risk and increase corporate accountability, thereby improving the firm's ability to make faster, smarter decisions and protect its assets and people. By giving end users a tool to simply recognize critical risks and analyze risk–reward trade-offs, the time and expense required to implement SAP GRC is quickly recouped in cost savings. SAP GRC's business benefits include the following:

- Well-balanced portfolios boasting well-vetted risk/reward analyses. Through GRC's transparency, visibility, and company-wide hooks, the solution can enable a firm's decision makers to make smart decisions—decisions based on risk and the probability of return.
- Improved stakeholder value, yielding preserved brand reputation, increased market value, reduced cost of capital, easier personnel recruiting, and higher employee retention.
- Reduced cost of providing GRC. GRC is no longer an optional service a firm should provide on behalf of its stakeholders but rather a mandatory part of doing business in a global world tainted by less than ethical business practices. Effective GRC is a differentiator today.
- Enhanced business performance and financial predictability. SAP GRC provides executive leadership teams the confidence they need in their numbers and methods to quickly rectify issues.
- Organizational sustainability despite the risks associated with poorly managed GRC, particularly legal and market ramifications.

All of this amounts to increased business agility, competitive differentiation, and other brand-preserving and company-sustaining benefits.

13.8.1.1.1.2   Financial and Managerial Accounting   The Financial and Managerial Accounting module enables end users to enhance company-wide strategic decision-making processes. It allows companies to centrally manage financial accounting data within an international framework of multiple companies, languages, currencies, and charts of accounts. The Financial and Managerial Accounting module complies with international accounting standards (IAS), such as generally accepted accounting principles (GAAP) and IAS, and helps fulfill the local legal requirements of many countries, reflecting fully the legal and accounting changes resulting from Sarbanes–Oxley legislation, European market and currency unification, and more.

The Financial and Managerial Accounting module contains the following components:

- General ledger accounting—Provides a record of the company's business transactions. It provides a place to record business transactions throughout all facets of the company's business to ensure that the accounting data being processed by SAP is both factual and complete.
- Accounts payable—Records and administers vendor accounting data.
- Accounts receivable—Manages the company's sales activities and records and administers customer accounting data through a number of tools specializing in managing open items.

- Asset accounting—Manages and helps a company supervise its fixed assets and serves as a subsidiary ledger to the general ledger by providing detailed information on transactions specifically involving fixed assets.
- Funds management—Supports creating budgets by way of a toolset that replicates a company's budget structure for the purpose of planning, monitoring, and managing company funds. Three essential tasks include revenues and expenditures budgeting, funds movement monitoring, and insight into potential budget overruns.
- Special-purpose ledger—Provides summary information from multiple applications at a level of detail specified according to business needs. This function enables companies to collect, combine, summarize, modify, and allocate actual and planned data originating from SAP or other systems.

Accounts payable and accounts receivable subledgers are integrated both with the general ledger and with different components in the SD module. Accounts payable and accounts receivable transactions are performed automatically when related processes are performed in other modules.

13.8.1.1.1.3 Cost Controlling Cost accounting is facilitated by the Controlling (CO) module, which provides functions necessary for effective and accurate internal cost accounting management. Its complete integration allows for value and quantity real-time data flows between SAP Financials and SAP Logistics modules. The CO module contains the following:

- Overhead cost controlling—Focuses on the monitoring and allocation of your company's overhead costs and provides all the functions your company requires for planning and allocation. The functionality contained within the CO module supports multiple cost-controlling methods, giving you the freedom to decide which functions and methods are best applied to your individual areas.
- Activity-based costing—Enables you to charge organizational overhead to products, customers, sales channels, and other segments and permits a more realistic profitability analysis of different products and customers because you are able to factor in the resources of overhead.
- Product cost controlling—Determines the costs arising from manufacturing a product or providing a service by evoking real-time cost-control mechanisms (capable of managing product, object, and actual costing schemes).
- Profitability analysis—Analyzes the profitability of a particular organization or market segment (which may be organized by products, customers, orders, or a combination thereof).

13.8.1.1.1.4 Enterprise Controlling SAP's Enterprise Controlling module is divided into a number of components:

- Business planning and budgeting—Comprises high-level enterprise plans that allow for the adaptable representation of customer-specific plans and their interrelationships. This also takes into consideration the connections between profit and loss statements, balance sheet, and cash flow strategies.
- Consolidation—Enables a company to enter reported financial data online using data-entry formats and to create consolidated reports that meet your company's legal and management reporting mandates.
- Profit center accounting—Analyzes the profitability of internal responsibility or profit centers (where a profit center is a management-oriented organizational unit used for internal controlling purposes).

13.8.1.1.1.5   Treasury Management   The Treasury Management module provides functionality needed to control liquidity management, risk management and assessment, and position management. It includes the following components:

- Treasury management—Supports a company's financial transaction management and positions through back-office processing to the Financial Accounting module. It also provides a versatile reporting platform that your company can use to examine its financial positions and transactions.
- Cash management—Identifies the optimum liquidity needed to satisfy payments as they come due and to supervise cash inflows and outflows.
- Market risk management—Quantifies the impact of potential financial market fluctuations against a firm's financial assets. The cash management package, in combination with the treasury management package, helps a firm control for market risks, account for interest and currency exposure, conduct portfolio simulations, and perform market-to-market valuations.
- Funds management—Helps create different budget versions, making it possible to work with rolling budget planning. It is tightly integrated with the Employee Self-Services (ESSs) online travel booking function to track estimated and real costs.

13.8.1.1.1.6   Global Trade Services   In reality, the component of SAP GRC known as SAP Global Trade Services (GTS) is also a SAP ERP Financials solution that further qualifies as a SAP Corporate Services solution and global supply-chain enabler. GTS makes it possible for international companies to connect and communicate with various government systems using a company-wide trade process. In this way, SAP GRC GTS enables the following:

- Meet international regulatory requirements
- Manage global trade by integrating company-wide trade compliance across financial, supply-chain, and human capital management (HCM) business processes
- Facilitate and expedite the import/export process for goods traveling through different country customs organizations
- Facilitate increased supply-chain transparency by sharing cross-border trade-related information with partners (insurers, freight handlers, and so on)

SAP GRC GTS thus enables a firm to mitigate the financial and other risks associated with doing business around the globe. By ensuring compliance with international trade agreements, SAP GRC GTS customers can optimize their supply chain, reduce production downtime, and eliminate errors that otherwise yield expensive penalties. In a nutshell, SAP GRC GTS makes it possible for firms to do business across country borders and to do so more consistently and profitably.

13.8.1.1.1.7   Financial Supply Chain Management   With all the attention today on driving inefficiencies out of an organization's supply chain, there's little wonder why SAP continues to optimize functionality geared toward financially streamlining supply chains. The Financial Supply Chain Management (FSCM) module facilitates

- Credit limit management and control
- Credit rules automation and credit decision support
- Collections, cash, and dispute management
- Electronic bill presentment and payment
- Treasury and risk management

13.8.1.1.2   mySAP ERP Human Capital Management

SAP HCM also facilitates an HR shared-services center augmented by reporting and analytics capabilities. In this way, HCM marries what the organization needs to measure internally (e.g., related to how well its own HR teams are performing against targets and other metrics such as hiring goals) with the organization's services to its customers—the firm's employees, long-term contractors, and others. This self-service functionality includes or supports a number of roles and company needs, including the following:

- A centralized employee interaction mechanism, which is nothing more than a central point of contact for employees that acts as a single source of company, HR, and other related information. As the primary venue for interacting with the employer, this tool becomes a ubiquitous source of *the answers* company-wide. Meanwhile, the company's HR team uses the tool to access and help manage the information needed behind the scenes.
- ESS, which is perhaps best known as a tool used to maintain personal data and book travel and conduct other administrative activities that lend themselves to an *online* support environment.
- SAP developed ESS, an effective means of providing real-time access and data upkeep capabilities to employees.
- Workforce Process Management (WPM) or the bundling of common country-specific employee master data. This might include time entry, payroll, employee benefits, legal reporting, and organizational reporting—all of which are brought together and standardized to meet local regulations or country codes. The majority of WPM is not done via self-services but rather by an administrator or through a shared-services function.
- Manager Self-Service (MSS), a cockpit of data used by leadership to identify, retain, and reward the firm's top performers; manage budgets, compensation planning, and profit/loss statements; sort and conduct keyword searches of employees' records; conduct the annual employee review process; and address other administrative matters quickly and from a centralized location.
- Workforce deployment, geared for project teams rather than individuals. Teams are created based on projects, and individual team member competencies and availabilities may then be tracked along with time, tasks, and so on.

Several of these HCM services actually fall into two broad focus areas that SAP still tends to use as labels: personnel administration (PA) and personnel planning and development (PD). Each addresses different aspects of a company's HR functions; the integration of the two creates a well-oiled HR machine that, when integrated with a firm's other business processes, creates a competitive advantage for the business.

13.8.1.1.2.1 Personal Administration The PA module of HCM manages functions such as payroll, employee benefits enrollment and administration, and compensation. Beyond PA, SAP's Talent Management enables recruiters and managers visibility into the various phases of employment, from employment advertising and recruitment through onboarding, employee development/training, and retention activities. It also provides a company-wide profile of the firm's human capital (people), making it possible to seek out and manage the careers of people holding particular skills, jobs, or roles. Underlying solutions include the following:

- Enterprise compensation management is used to implement a company's pay, promotion, salary adjustments, and bonus plan policies. Functions managed by this solution include salary administration, job evaluations, salary reviews, salary survey results, compensation budget planning and administration, and compensation policy administration. Use it to create pay grades and salary structures and make compensation adjustments—an important piece of functionality to help companies retain their top talent. SAP accomplishes this by marrying performance ratings with compensation standards, industry trends, performance-based pay standards, bonus payouts, and more, which not only helps create bulletproof justifications but reduces the time, the effort, and therefore the risk otherwise germane to such time-sensitive matters.

- E-recruiting helps companies manage their employee recruiting process. Recruitment initiates from the creation of a position vacancy through the advertisement and applicant tracking of potentials, concluding with the notification of successful and unsuccessful applicants and the hiring of the best candidate. E-Recruiting also ties all the data associated with attracting, acquiring, educating, and developing talent and future leaders into a single system of record.
- Time management provides a flexible way of recording and evaluating employee work time and absence management. Companies can represent their time structures to reflect changing conditions, using the calendar as a basis. Flextime, shift work, and normal work schedules can be used to plan work and break schedules and manage exceptions, absences, and holidays.
- Payroll efficiently and accurately calculates remuneration for work performed by your employees, regardless of their working schedule, working calendar, language, or currency. Payroll also handles fluctuating reporting needs and the regularly changing compliance requirements of federal, state, and local agencies.

13.8.1.1.2.2 Personal Planning and Development In contrast to these solutions, SAP provides tools to better manage people and traditional HR functions, including organizational management and workforce planning. Some of these include the following:

- Organizational management—Assists in the strategizing and planning of a comprehensive HR structure. Through the development of proposed scenarios using the flexible tools provided, you can manipulate your company's structure in the present, past, and future. Using the basic organization objects in SAP, units, jobs, positions, tasks, and work centers are all structured as the basic building blocks of your organization.
- SAP enterprise learning—Helps a company coordinate and administer company-wide training and similar events and also contains functionality to plan for, execute, confirm, and manage cost allocations and billing for your company's events. By creating an efficient and personalized learning process and environment, SAP enterprise learning takes into account an employee's job, tasks, qualifications, and objectives to create a custom training regimen that aligns with preestablished career development goals.
- SAP learning solution—A component of SAP enterprise learning that also falls under the talent management umbrella (discussed previously), the SAP learning solution links employee learning to a firm's business strategy and objectives. To pull this off, the SAP learning solution brings together SAP ERP HCM with knowledge management and collaboration solutions and provides this in an innovative Learning Portal. Intuitive in form and function, the Learning Portal encompasses not only specialized learning management software but also tools to author test and to manage content through a customizable taxonomy and collaborate across an enterprise.

13.8.1.1.3 mySAP Operations
Essentially logistics, these solutions encompass all processes related to a firm's purchasing, plant maintenance, sales and distribution, manufacturing, materials management, warehousing, engineering, and construction. SAP Manufacturing and SAP ERP Operations (an aging but still useful term) include the following solutions:

- Procurement and logistics execution, enabling end users to manage their end-to-end procurement and logistics business processes as well as optimizing the physical flow of materials

- Product development and manufacturing, from production planning to manufacturing, shop floor integration, product development, and so on
- Sales and service, which range from actual sales to managing the delivery of services and all the processes necessary to pay out commissions and other sales incentives

13.8.1.1.3.1 Manufacturing   SAP manufacturing connects a firm's manufacturing processes with the rest of its business functions: logistics, financials, environmental health and safety (EHS) requirements, and more. It also allows a firm to manage its manufacturing operations with embedded Lean Sigma and Six Sigma, both of which help create and improve competitive advantage. SAP manufacturing allows discrete and process manufacturing firms to better plan, schedule, resequence, and monitor manufacturing processes so as to achieve higher yields and greater profitability. This is accomplished through partner and supplier coordination, exception management, embracing Lean and Six Sigma, complying with EHS requirements, and so on—all facilitated by SAP manufacturing. Through continuous improvement, SAP seeks to provide management and shop floor teams alike the ability to view and optimize real-time operations. SAP manufacturing's powerful analytics support the firm's ability to make changes on the fly. Thus, SAP manufacturing allows a company to transform itself through enhanced manufacturing capabilities such as the following:

- SAP lean planning and operations—Accelerate and maintain lean operations (through high throughput, high quality, and low overhead)
- SAP manufacturing integration and intelligence—Obtain the data that a manufacturing team needs to take the proper action at the proper time
- SAP supply chain management—Optimize the supply chain hosted by SAP ERP
- SAP solutions for RFID—Further optimize the supply chain through more efficient asset tracking and management
- SAP ERP Operations—Enable the manufacturing team to gain greater visibility into its operations and in turn increase control and business insight

13.8.1.1.3.2 Production Planning and Control   Within SAP ERP Operations, the focus of SAP's Production Planning and Control module is to facilitate complete solutions related to production planning, execution, and control. The PP module includes a component called Sales and Operations Planning, which is used for creating realistic and consistent planning figures to forecast future sales. Depending on your method of production, you can use SAP's production order processing, repetitive manufacturing, or *kanban* production control processing. *Kanban* is a procedure for controlling production and material flow based on a chain of operations in production and procurement. In the end, PP and Control helps manage the following:

- Basic data
- Sales and operations planning, master planning, and capacity and material requirements planning
- *Kanban*, repetitive manufacturing, assembly orders, and production planning for process industries
- Production orders and product cost planning
- Plant data collection, production planning, and control information system

The implementation of the PP and Control module makes it possible to eliminate routine tasks for the end users responsible for production scheduling. The related reduction in time allows for additional time to be dedicated to more critical activities within the company.

13.8.1.1.3.3 Materials Management   A firm's inventory and materials management business processes are essential to the success of the company. Streamlined day-to-day management of the company's consumption of materials, including company purchasing, managing warehouses and their inventory, and tracking and confirming invoices, is all part of the MM module. Its components include inventory management, warehouse management, purchasing, invoice verification, materials planning, and purchasing information system. In this way, MM saves time and money, conserves resources, and helps optimize the company's supply chain.

13.8.1.1.3.4 Plant Maintenance The main benefit to SAP's Plant Maintenance (PM) module is its flexibility to work with different types of companies to meet differing designs, requirements, and workforces. Different management strategies are supported within the application, including risk-based maintenance and total productive maintenance. Some benefits that your company will derive from the implementation of the PM module involve reduced downtime and outages, the optimization of labor and resources, and a reduction in the costs of inspections and repairs. The PM module includes

- Preventative maintenance
- Service management
- Maintenance order management
- Maintenance projects
- Equipment and technical objects
- Plant maintenance information system

On the whole, the integration of the PM module supports a company in designing and executing its maintenance activities with regard to system resource availability, costs, materials, and personnel deployment.

13.8.1.1.3.5 Sales and Distribution The SD module arms a firm with the necessary instruments to sell and to manage the sales process. SD provides a wealth of information related to a company's sales and marketing trends, capabilities, and so on. An SD end user can access data on products, marketing strategies, sales calls, pricing, and sales leads at any time to facilitate sales and marketing activity. The information is online, up-to-the-minute support to be used to service existing customers and to mine for potential customers and new leads. Also included within the SD module is a diverse set of contracts to meet diverse business needs. Agreements concerning pricing, delivery dates, and delivery quantity are all supported within this module.

13.8.1.1.4 mySAP ERP Corporate Services

The final SAP ERP business solution, Corporate Services, assists companies with streamlining internal life-cycle processes. Modules of Corporate Services include the following:

- Global Trade Services (GTS)—Manages international trade activity complexities, from regulatory compliance to customs and risk management
- Environment, Health, and Safety (EHS)—Assists firms with managing how they comply with matters of product safety, hazardous substance management, waste and emissions management, and so on
- Quality Management (QM)—Reflects the controls and gates necessary to proactively manage the product life cycle
- Real Estate Management—Manages the real estate portfolio life cycle, from property acquisition through building operations, reporting, maintenance, and disposal
- Enterprise Asset Management—Addresses design, build, operations, and disposal phases
- Project and Portfolio Management—Manages a firm's project portfolio (including tracking and managing budget, scheduling, and other resource-based key performance indicators)
- Travel Management—Processes travel requests to managing planning, reservation changes, expense management, and specialized reporting/analytics

13.8.1.1.4.1   Real Estate Management   SAP's Real Estate module integrates real estate processes into your company's overall organizational structure. The Corporate Real Estate Management model is divided into two components: Rental Administration and Settlement and Controlling, Position Valuation, and Information Management. For a company to successfully use the Real Estate component, special configurations are required in the MM, PM, PS, and Asset Accounting modules.

13.8.1.1.4.2   Quality Management   The QM module improves product and to some extent process quality. To produce high-quality products, the QM system ensures product integrity, which in turn helps foster good client relations and company reputation. QM services include the following:

- Quality planning, inspections, and quality control
- Quality notifications and quality certificates
- Test equipment management
- Quality management information system

The QM module enables a company to analyze, document, and improve its processes across several dimensions.

13.8.1.1.4.3   Project and Portfolio Management   Once simply called the PS module, the Project and Portfolio Management module is an important component of SAP ERP corporate services and assists a company in managing its portfolio of projects. Such high-level cross-project insight allows for outstanding planning, execution, and financial oversight, facilitating true project management in the process. As such, it is centered on managing the network of relationships within the system and establishing project management links.

Project and portfolio management is used to manage investments and marketing, software and consulting services, R&D, maintenance tasks, shutdown management, plant engineering and construction, and complex made-to-order production. The components of the PS module include basic data, operational structures, project planning, approvals, project execution and integration, and project system information system. Like most project management approaches, the system is based on work breakdown structures (WBSs). A WBS is a structured model of work organized in a hierarchical format; work or tasks are managed in a stepwise manner during the course of conducting a project, where large tasks are broken down into key elements that represent the individual tasks and activities in the project.

13.8.1.2   mySAP CRM

mySAP CRM is a comprehensive solution to the management of your customer relationships. It supports all customer-oriented business divisions, from marketing to sales to service, and even customer interaction channels, such as the interaction center, the Internet, and mobile clients. SAP CRM brings together a company's sales, services, and marketing functions. In this way, CRM helps a company focus on three related customer-related areas: driving topline revenue growth, achieving operational excellence, and increasing customer-facing business agility. Key business scenarios include the following:

13.8.1.2.1   Marketing Support

Marketing support enhances marketing effectiveness, maximizes resource use, and empowers the sales team to develop and maintain long-term profitable customer relationships. From a user's perspective, this includes marketing resource management, campaign management, trade promotion management, market segment management, lead/prospect management, and marketing analytics.

13.8.1.2.2   Sales Support

Sales support helps remove barriers to productivity by enabling teams to work with their customers in a consistent manner. CRM sales empowers and provides the team with the tools they need to close deals. For example, territory management, account and contact management, lead and opportunity management, and sales planning and forecasting help sales forces identify and manage prospects. Then, by leveraging quotation and order management, product configuration, contract management, incentive and commission management, time and travel management, and sales analytics, the team has the information it needs to keep customers happy while hopefully increasing sales volume and margins and decreasing the costs of doing all this.

13.8.1.2.3   Service Support

Service support assists service management teams in maximizing the value obtained from postsales services. This enables teams to profitably manage a broad range of functions geared toward driving successful customer service and support, including field service, Internet-enabled service offerings, service marketing and sales, and service/contract management. These happier customers benefit from improved warranty and claims management and effective channel service and depot repair services. And the company's service team benefits from insight gleaned from service analytics, which enable the team to maximize profit per customer.

13.8.1.2.4   Web Channel

Web channel increases sales and reduces transaction costs by turning the Internet into a service channel (or sales and marketing channel) geared toward effectively connecting businesses and consumers. This makes it possible to increase profitability of existing accounts while also reaching new markets.

Interaction center (IC) management support complements and arms a company's field sales force. This functionality supports marketing, sales, and service activities such as telemarketing, telesales, customer service, e-service, and interaction center analytics.

13.8.1.2.5   Partner Channel Management

Partner channel management improves processes for partner recruitment, partner management, communications, channel marketing, channel forecasting collaborative selling, partner order management, channel service, and analytics. In this way, a company can attract and retain a more profitable and loyal indirect channel by managing partner relationships and empowering channel partners.

13.8.1.2.6   Business Communications Management

Business communications management enables inbound and outbound contact management across multiple locations and communications channels. Business communications management integrates multichannel communications with a firm's customer-facing business processes to create a seamless communications experience across several different communications mediums (including voice, text messaging, and e-mail).

13.8.1.2.7   Real-Time Offer Management

Real-time offer management helps manage the complexities of marketing offers in real time, using SAP's advanced analytical real-time decision engine. This functionality also optimizes the decision-making process across different customer interaction channels, enabling a company to quickly and intelligently enhance its customer relationships.

13.8.1.3   mySAP SRM

mySAP SRM is a solution that enables the strategic planning and central control of relationships between a company and its suppliers. It allows very close connections between suppliers and the purchasing process of a firm, with the goal of making the procurement processes simpler and more effective. SAP SRM supports processes such as ordering, source determination, the generation of invoices and credit memos, supplier qualification, and Supplier Self-Services.

SAP SRM helps to optimize and manage the relationship between a company and its suppliers. As another one of SAP's more mature offerings, SRM integrates seamlessly with PLM, enabling a high degree of collaboration between product buyers and parts suppliers.

13.8.1.4 mySAP SCM

By transforming a supply chain into a dynamic customer-centric supply-chain network, mySAP SCM enables companies to plan for and streamline the firm's network of logistics and resources that merge to form a supply chain enabling better service, increased productivity, and improved profitability. A supply chain comprises three areas: procurement, production, and distribution. The supply portion of a supply chain focuses on the raw materials needed by manufacturing, which in turn converts raw materials into finished products; the distribution aspect of a supply chain focuses on moving the finished products through a network of distributors, warehouses, and outlets. mySAP SCM enables increased velocity and improved profitability resulting from cross-company collaboration; enhanced visibility into a company's suppliers, vendors, and customers makes it easier to create a more predictable supply chain capable of capitalizing on circumstances, minimizing costs, and maximizing margins through the following:

- Improving responsiveness via real-time insight into the entire supply chain
- Improving inventory turns by synchronizing balancing supply with demand
- Encouraging collaboration by providing visibility into trends as seen through supply-chain monitoring, analysis, and business analytics

13.8.2 SAP COMPONENTS

13.8.2.1 SAP ECC

Enterprise Central Component 6.0 (SAP ECC 6.0) consists of the following modules:

1. SD module records sales orders and scheduled deliveries. Information about the customer (pricing, how and where to ship products, how the customer is to be billed, and so on) is maintained and accessed from this module.
2. MM module manages the acquisition of raw materials from suppliers (purchasing) and the subsequent handling of raw materials inventory, from storage to work-in-progress goods to shipping of finished goods to the customer.
3. PP module maintains production information. Here, production is planned and scheduled, and actual production activities are recorded.
4. QM module plans and records quality control activities, such as product inspections and material certifications.
5. PM module manages maintenance resources and planning for preventive maintenance of plant machinery, to minimize equipment breakdowns.
6. AM module helps the company to manage fixed asset purchases (plant and machinery) and related depreciation.
7. Human Resources (HR) module facilitates employee recruiting, hiring, and training. This module also includes payroll and benefits.
8. PS module allows the planning for and control over new R&D, construction, and marketing projects. This module allows for costs to be collected against a project, and it is frequently used to manage the implementation of the SAP ERP system. PS manages build-to-order items, which are low-volume, highly complex products such as ships and aircrafts.
9. Financial Accounting (FI) module records transactions in the general ledger accounts. This module generates financial statements for external reporting purposes.

10. CO module serves internal management purposes, assigning manufacturing costs to products and to cost centers, so that the profitability of the company's activities can be analyzed. The CO module supports managerial decision making.
11. Workflow (WF) module is not a module that automates a specific business function. Rather, it is a set of tools that can be used to automate any of the activities in SAP ERP. It can perform task-flow analysis and prompt employees (by e-mail) if they need to take action. WF is ideal for business processes that are not daily activities but that occur frequently enough to be worth the effort to implement workflow, such as preparing customer invoices.

13.8.2.2 SAP SCM

SAP SCM complements SAP ERP with important components offering planning-based as well as execution-based functions for logistics processes. The components mentioned only briefly here will be examined in more detail in a subsequent chapter:

- SAP Extended Warehouse Management (SAP EWM) is the functionally very extensive successor to the SAP ERP component Warehouse Management (WM). It can be employed as a stand-alone system for complete warehouse management, including all contiguous processes.
- SAP Transportation Management (SAP TM) offers complete transportation processing, from order acceptance, transportation planning, and subcontracting to invoicing customers and service providers. It can be operated as a stand-alone system and was also conceived for use by logistics service providers.
- SAP Event Management is a tool with which processes can be tracked in several ways (such as transport tracking) and critical conditions in a process can be actively determined and reported to users. SAP Event Management can be configured and used for all status management and tracking tasks.
- SAP Auto-ID Infrastructure (SAP AII) integrates RFID technology into business processes. It allows users to establish a bridge between RFID readers and business processes in the application.

Another important component is SAP Advanced Planning and Optimization (SAP APO) consisting of the following:

- Supply Chain Monitoring serves to monitor the logistics chain.
- Supply Chain Collaboration enables collaboration with suppliers and customers.
- Demand Planning (DP) allows medium-term planning of requirements based on a prognosis for demand of your company's products on the market.
- Supply Network Planning (SNP) integrates the areas of procurement, production, distribution, and transport. It thus enables tactical planning decisions and those pertaining to procurement sources based on a global model.
- Global Availability Check (ATP) (global ATP [gATP]) allows product-availability checks on a global basis. It also supports product substitutions and place-of-delivery substitutions.
- Transportation Planning (Transportation Planning and Vehicle Scheduling) enables optimal intermodal planning for incoming and outgoing deliveries. The actual transportation processing, however, takes place in ERP.

13.8.2.3 SAP PLM

SAP PLM supports your company in product development, the maintenance of assets, and service processing for your products. PLM enables a company to offer the right products at the right time and at the right prices for the customer. Delays increase costs and decrease your competitive ability; costs can often be reduced for service processing through preventative maintenance.

And throughout all these activities, the early involvement of customers and subcontractors reduces costs and increases profitability. A company can achieve higher productivity by quickly introducing new products to the market.

SAP PLM has the advantage of being an integrated solution: product development, quality management, asset management, maintenance, and service management are all integrated, and the life cycle is mapped in its entirety. SAP Product Lifecycle Management offers all the functionality needed by any company for integrated product and asset management:

1. Program and Project Management: Provides advanced capabilities to plan, manage, and control the complete product development process.
2. Life-Cycle Data Management: Provides an environment for managing specifications, bills of materials, routing and resource data, project structures, and related technical documentation throughout the product life cycle.
3. Life-Cycle Collaboration: Supports collaborative engineering and project management, employing XML-based web standards to communicate information such as project plans, documents, and product structures across virtual development teams.
4. Quality Management: Provides integrated quality management for all industries throughout the entire product life cycle.
5. Enterprise Asset Management: Manages physical assets and equipment, covering all components of an enterprise asset management system.
6. Environment, Health, and Safety: Provides a solution for environment, health, and safety issues by enhancing business processes to comply with government regulations.

13.8.3   SAP NetWeaver

SAP NetWeaver is the technological platform for all SAP applications, including SAP xApps and the mySAP Business Suite, and forms the basis of solutions of selected partners. Reliability, security, and scalability are the characteristics that ensure that business-critical enterprise processes are processed smoothly using SAP NetWeaver (Figure 13.3).

Most organizations have clearly identified the benefits of an integrated enterprise and want to profit from this integration. However, integrating heterogeneous systems is always a significant challenge for the IT department. Combining separate systems for individual projects using a point-to-point integration is expensive and means that IT environments of this type become ever more inflexible. To reduce complexity and costs requires a single platform that includes all people, information, and business processes. SAP NetWeaver provides this platform.

SAP NetWeaver is a comprehensive integration and application platform that helps to reduce your total cost of ownership. It combines all users, information, and business processes on a cross-company and cross-technology basis. SAP NetWeaver is also an integrated platform based on web services. Preconfigured business content reduces the amount of customer-specific integration that needs to be carried out. Unlike other platforms, SAP NetWeaver is compatible and extendible with Microsoft.NET and IBM WebSphere and supports Java 2 Platform Enterprise Edition (J2EE). In this way, the SAP platform contributes to protecting existing investments in IT systems and employee qualifications. These advantages mean that the total cost of ownership can be considerably reduced not only for SAP solutions but for the entire IT landscape. SAP NetWeaver helps you to use existing IT investments in a way that adds value while also representing the foundation for future cross-enterprise processes.

13.8.3.1   People Integration

People Integration ensures that your employees have the information and functions that they require to perform their work as quickly and efficiently as possible. The functions of the SAP NetWeaver Portal play a central role here.

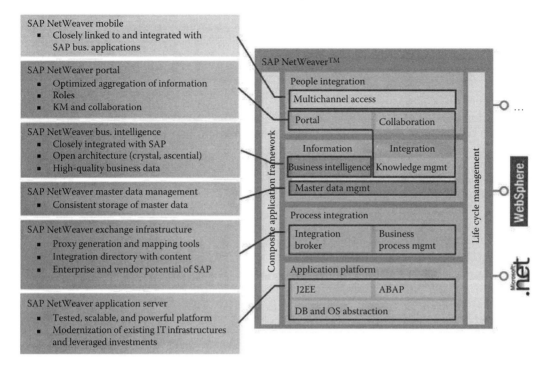

FIGURE 13.3   SAP NetWeaver components.

The subareas of People Integration are as follows:

1. Portal: Delivers unified, personalized, and role-based user access to heterogeneous IT environments. Business processes in which customers, vendors, partner companies, and employees are involved become significantly more efficient.
2. Collaboration: Promotes dynamic and cost-effective communication within teams or communities. This includes virtual collaboration rooms and tools for collaborating in real time, such as message forums, chat, team calendars, application sharing, and document storage.
3. Multichannel access: Allows access to enterprise systems through PCs, the Internet, mobile devices, and speech-controlled systems. In this way, you can relocate your business processes to where the business is transacted.

13.8.3.1.1   SAP Enterprise Portal

The SAP NetWeaver Portal gives you access to all relevant data over a service-friendly interface. It also allows you to convert unstructured knowledge into concrete knowledge. SAP NetWeaver Portal brings together information from SAP and non-SAP systems, data warehouses, and desktop documents, as well as web content and services on a central, unified platform.

The SAP NetWeaver Portal offers a central point of entry to all applications, BI functions, documents, and web services in a company. Users are central players. Users can use information from different sources and collaborate with one another inside and outside the company. Each portal is organized so that an optimal working environment for quickly realizing business opportunities and solving problems is created. This guarantees an extensive provision of predefined content, business packages, a fast implementation, and a higher ROI than for comparable products. This makes the portal into a user-oriented platform for companies and their business partners.

One of the main aims of an enterprise portal is facilitating and accelerating access to information, applications, and services. This happens by allowing users access using a *single sign-on*. The target group does not have to be limited to employees of one particular company. You can use external portals to reach partners, customers, or other interested parties.

SAP NetWeaver Portal solution enables

- The integration of all kinds of company data and applications, as well as the opportunity to control heterogeneous IT landscapes
- The optimal use of open standards for securing existing investments
- The conversion of unstructured information into concrete knowledge and cross-company collaboration
- The provision of enterprise portal content for users, according to their particular role within the company

13.8.3.2 Information Integration

The Information Integration subarea provides access to all structured and unstructured information in your company. The core component in this subarea is SAP NetWeaver BI, which provides data from a large number of different systems for evaluation.

The subareas of Information Integration are as follows:

1. Business Intelligence: Enables companies to include, analyze, and distribute business-critical information. This includes an extensive package of tools to develop and publish customized and interactive reports and applications. In this way, decision making is supported at every level.
2. Knowledge Management: Manages unstructured information such as text files, presentations, or audio files and allows access to this content. This includes an integrated search, content management, distribution of information, classification and workflow functions, and an open architecture for integrating external content.
3. Master Data Management: Ensures company-wide unification of data and information in heterogeneous IT environments. Master Data Management provides services for consolidation, harmonization, and central management of your master data, including business partner information, product master data and structures, and information about technical systems.

13.8.3.2.1 SAP Business Intelligence

SAP NetWeaver BI allows the evaluation of data from operative SAP applications, from any other business applications, and from external data sources (databases, online services, and the Internet). The Administrator Workbench provides functions for controlling, monitoring, and maintaining all data retrieval processes.

Data from various sources (SAP systems, non-SAP systems, flat files, XML data, databases, and so on) are loaded into the SAP NetWeaver BI using extraction processes and, where necessary, are then transformed. For example, this may take the form of technical modifications or business modifications (such as currency translation). After being processed, the data are saved in InfoProviders. InfoProviders are created with specific business considerations in mind. This simplifies the process of evaluating and analyzing data later for reporting purposes. InfoProviders are objects that make data available for reporting. You can access an InfoProvider and generate reports based on it using the reporting tools provided by the Business Explorer (BEx). This allows you to get a focused readout of your data.

The SAP NetWeaver BI allows OLAP for preparing large quantities of operative and historical data. OLAP technology makes multidimensional analysis possible from various business perspectives. The Data Warehouse, preconfigured with business content for core areas and processes, guarantees that you can view information in an enterprise-wide context. With business content, the information that employees need to fulfill their particular tasks is made available based on roles selected for an enterprise.

With the BEx, SAP NetWeaver BI makes flexible reporting and analysis tools available. This enables strategic analysis and supports decision making within a company. Authorized employees can access and evaluate historic and current data in different levels of detail.

13.8.3.3 Process Integration

Process Integration ensures that business processes run across system boundaries in a heterogeneous system landscape. This is achieved using XML data packages and workflow scenarios, for instance. The SAP NetWeaver Exchange Infrastructure (SAP NetWeaver XI) plays a central role here.

The subareas of Process Integration are as follows:

1. Integration Broker: Realizes XML/SOAP-based communication between application components from various sources. The Integration Broker enables the definition of software components, interfaces, mappings, and content-based routing rules based on open standards.
2. Business Process Management: Allows the modeling and acceleration of processes in a dynamic IT environment. It allows you to combine existing applications with adaptive integrated processes across the entire value creation chain.

13.8.3.3.1 SAP Exchange Infrastructure

SAP NetWeaver is the integration and application platform for mySAP applications; SAP NetWeaver XI represents the Process Integration layer of the NetWeaver stack and is a crucial element of the Enterprise Services Architecture (ESA).

Many components in customer system landscapes are directly connected using point-to-point connections, with all integration capabilities hardwired directly into the application components and individual mapping programs. These systems have been integrated over time using whatever integration technology or middleware was available. The integration knowledge is hidden within the different applications or within the used middleware tools and the interface descriptions. This results in a wildly grown integration landscape with different application systems and multiple individual connections between different interfaces increasing its complexity and renders it very difficult and costly to maintain. The overall key concept of the SAP NetWeaver XI is to drive integrated business processes across heterogeneous and highly dynamic IT landscapes in a more manageable and cost-effective way.

The Integration Repository provides integration scenarios, routing objects, mappings, interfaces, and components at design time. It is built in Java and follows Java 2 Enterprise Edition (J2EE) standards. The Integration Directory starts with the same knowledge captured in the Integration Repository, but it adds configuration-specific information that is needed for execution. The collaboration run time environment enlists all runtime components relevant for exchanging messages among the connected software components and business partners. At the center of execution is the Integration Server, which includes the Integration Engine. The Integration Engine exchanges all messages between the different connected components.

13.8.3.4 Application Platform

The Application Platform supports J2EE and Advanced Business Application Programming (ABAP) in a single environment. It guarantees the independence of databases and operating systems, the complete support of platform-independent web services and company applications, and an open environment that is based on recognized standards. The central component of the Application Platform is the SAP NetWeaver Application Server (SAP NetWeaver AS).

In addition to the traditional runtime environment for ABAP programs, SAP NetWeaver AS also has a runtime environment for J2EE-based Java programs: the SAP J2EE Engine. Together with functions to control the operating system and database, SAP NetWeaver AS forms the application platform of SAP NetWeaver.

SAP NetWeaver AS offers

- A reliable and thoroughly tested runtime environment, which has evolved for the past decade
- A framework for executing complex business processes that meets the highest security standards
- A reliable and user-friendly development environment
- Support for open technical standards such as HTTP(S), SMTP, Unicode, HTML, and XML
- High scalability, inherited from SAP Basis
- Support for various operating systems and databases

Benefits of SAP NetWeaver AS are as follows:

1. Openness and extendibility: SAP NetWeaver features complete compatibility and extendibility with IBM WebSphere and Microsoft.NET technologies in which companies have made significant investments. SAP will ensure interoperability with IBM and Microsoft solutions and assist in development strategies, sales activities, and competence and support centers. The integration of SAP NetWeaver with IBM and Microsoft solutions spans all levels and therefore applies to the integration of people, information, and processes. This means that optimal benefit can be gained from existing IT investments in systems and employee qualifications.
2. Immediate integration: SAP NetWeaver enables complete enterprise integration at all critical levels. SAP NetWeaver also provides valuable preconfigured business content. This ready-to-use content is available at all levels of SAP NetWeaver, drastically reducing implementation time and therefore speeding up ROI. Among other things, the following business content is provided with SAP NetWeaver:
   a. Preconfigured portal content and predefined roles for better integration of people
   b. Reports and analyses for fast integration of information
   c. Interfaces for linking the business processes in your various back-end systems
3. Lower total cost of ownership: The technology platform leverages your existing IT investments, since it integrates these and profitably includes systems that are already used in your company. SAP NetWeaver supports the entire software life cycle of business-critical applications with the lowest total cost of ownership. The technology platform is the result of SAP's 30 years of experience with reliable enterprise solutions. This means that you profit from high scalability, continuous uptime, and high security standards.

13.8.4 SAP Enterprise Performance Management (EPM)

SAP EPM is SAP's solution for defining, executing, and monitoring the corporate strategy of an enterprise. EPM, which was known as strategic enterprise management (SEM) before 2005, addresses corporate strategy areas like setting of corporate goals, enabling alignment, communicating priorities, empowering collaboration of stakeholders, and defining, managing, and monitoring of the corporate scorecard.

It consists of the following:

1. Business Planning: This entails areas like budgeting; sales, revenue, and capital expenditure planning; staffing and headcount; expense and cash flow planning; and forecasting and consensus building.
2. Business Profitability Management: This entails activity-based costing for informed management decisions that optimize customer and product profitability, reduce the cost to serve, and optimize cost of key processes; shared-services costing and cross charging to

align resources and capacities with demand, reduce delivery costs, and gain process transparency; on-demand, what-if scenario analysis; driver-based and activity-based budgeting; and ongoing dynamic monitoring of the drivers of cost and profitability.

3. Business Consolidation: This entails consolidation including intercompany matching reconciliation, intercompany eliminations, management roll-ups, and legal consolidation and financial reporting and analysis including ad hoc analysis, automated variance analysis, and driver analysis (industry, growth, capacity, etc.).

13.8.5 SAP INDUSTRY-SPECIFIC APPLICATIONS

1. Automotive: SAP for Automotive is designed to streamline and improve disjointed business practices, enabling you to closely manage multitiered networks of customers, suppliers, and partners. This solution set facilitates seamless integration and collaboration across multiple internal and external organizations. It also includes best practices that support critical business processes, providing full visibility into enterprise data and increasing speed and flexibility worldwide.

2. Banking based on a flexible, scalable infrastructure, SAP for Banking provides a robust environment for incorporating new technologies, controlling core banking processes, and extending operations to the Internet. Innovative core banking capabilities seamlessly connect front-office activities with back-office systems; enable low-cost, real-time processing of key financial transactions; and speed the development of multichannel products and services that meet the needs of your demand-oriented market.

3. Chemicals: SAP for Chemicals delivers capabilities for sales and operations planning, quality management, recipe and batch management, and supply chain operations. Also included is detailed profit reporting by customer, product, or segment, along with integrated hubs that let you unify process control systems and monitor production execution.

4. Healthcare: Healthcare is a high-pressure industry facing demands for higher-quality patient care, cost controls, government regulations, and increasing competition. SAP for Healthcare integrates your health-care processes—from staffing and inventory to financials and patient-centric processes—on an open platform designed for growth. And when combined with leading, complementary components, SAP for Healthcare provides an end-to-end application for all administrative and clinical processes.

5. Logistics Service Providers: Designed in collaboration with many of the industry's leading companies, our comprehensive set of proven solutions, applications, technology, and services helps you manage your logistics business efficiently and profitably. SAP for Logistics Service Providers handles all order volumes and supports complex business processes in procurement, fulfillment, returns management, warehousing, and value-added logistics.

6. Mining: Mining consists of multiple processes, each with its own set of challenges, and mining operations must optimize these processes to reduce costs. What's more is that mining operations need to ensure regulatory compliance and commit to sustainability, even as commodity prices shift based on global demand and supply. SAP for Mining enables you to meet the specific challenges of the mining industry by helping you manage your assets and operations and leverage global supply chain networks. As a result, you can increase efficiency and reduce costs.

7. Oil and Gas: In today's oil and gas industry, companies are caught between rising hydrocarbon prices and ever-growing pressure from customers and regulators. You make every effort to reduce production and distribution costs, but the need for profitability and accountability to your shareholders continues to increase. With SAP for Oil and Gas solutions, you can face the challenges of cost and profitability head on. This set of solutions gives you comprehensive tools that enable you to leverage key data, manage assets effectively, and maximize cash flow.

8. Public Sector: SAP for Public Sector creates fast, flexible, and responsive e-government by electronically connecting public administrations with citizens, businesses, suppliers, and other organizations via the Internet, enhancing communications, streamlining services, and cutting costs. With rich functionality tailored to the unique demands of the public sector, this set of solutions helps you meet the challenge of serving the public today.

9. Retail consumers have never been more in control. They have come to expect superb quality, selection, and service, and they're perfectly willing to abandon any retailer that can't deliver. In today's market, there's no margin for error. SAP for Retail provides a comprehensive solution designed specifically for the new retail environment, where every piece of your retail value chain from forecasting and planning to allocation and replenishment must be focused on meeting and surpassing customer expectations.

13.8.6 SAP COMPOSITE APPLICATIONS

SAP xApps are a new breed of applications that enable you to drive improvements and innovations in your company more easily. With their ability to combine existing, heterogeneous systems to form cross-functional processes, SAP xApps bring people, information, and business processes together to make your company more dynamic and competitive. This flexibility allows you to implement business-wide strategies more easily and efficiently. SAP xApps increase the value of existing investments in the core business area and maximize the return on strategic assets, including employees, knowledge, products, business relationships, and IT.

SAP xApps realize strategies by using previously unparalleled functions that bring employees, data, and processes in a company together on one interface. SAP xApps provide both continuity and discontinuity. Continuity is ensured by increasing effectiveness and improving productive business transactions; discontinuity is provided in the sense that a company can perform an innovative change in an unusually flexible manner.

By using xApps, a company can optimize a sales process across multiple systems. Functions such as a credit check from the accountancy system or delivery time and availability (ATP) from the logistics systems are used to design an integrated sales process. The employee works on just one interface, whereas before they had to perform separate checks in three different systems. The defining characteristics of SAP xApps are as follows:

1. Cross-functional: SAP xApps can be implemented with a multitude of applications and information sources. This allows you to run critical integrated processes across heterogeneous systems in compliance with your company's business strategy.
2. Composite: SAP xApps execute flexible workflow and business processes independently of the underlying infrastructure. Furthermore, SAP xApps synchronize and improve existing business processes. This makes your company more flexible and, by improving the use of existing investments, it also increases your ROI.
3. Cross-system: SAP xApps support a complex transfer of information (context, relevance), as well as the communication within the business itself, thereby simplifying the collaboration of working groups and sound decision making.
4. Information-driven: SAP xApps enable intelligent processes that are driven by decision-relevant business information. This enables a company to make informed, strategic decisions, which you can continually evaluate and, if applicable, amend.

Some examples of available xApps are as follows:

- SAP xApp Cost and Quotation Management (SAP xCQM): This solution enables the creation of a quotation through the upload of a BOM, automatic pricing of existing components, streamlined eRFQ processing for new components, and execution of consolidated costs reports.

- SAP xApp Resource and Portfolio Management (SAP xRPM): SAP xRPM integrates information from existing project management, HR, and financial systems to provide an overview of the project portfolio with easy drilldown to details for portfolio managers, project managers, resource managers, and project members.
- SAP xApp Product Definition (SAP xPD): SAP xPD is a simple, easy-to-use solution that addresses the hurdles and inefficiencies at the critical front end of product development processes, such as idea management and concept development.
- SAP xApp Emissions Management (SAP xEM): To comply with environmental regulations such as the Kyoto Protocol or the U.S. Clean Air Act, emissions management is a must for all energy-consuming and carbon dioxide–producing businesses. SAP xEM helps corporations improve their compliance with emerging emissions regulations worldwide and increase revenue through trading of emissions credits.

13.8.7 SAP SMALL- AND MIDSIZE BUSINESS APPLICATIONS

13.8.7.1 mySAP All-in-One

Each qualified mySAP All-in-One partner solution is a prepackaged, industry-specific version of mySAP Business Suite with built-in content, tools, and methodologies for a cost-effective, turnkey implementation. mySAP All-in-One partner solutions offer out-of-the-box flexibility combined with the power of SAP's world-class business applications.

Qualified mySAP All-in-One partner solutions provide the following advantages:

1. Rapid implementation and transparent costs: mySAP All-in-One is provided by selected, qualified partners who are familiar with the challenges of the respective market segment and industry. The software is implemented using a special implementation method that is based on experience gained from more than 15,000 customer installations in more than 20 industries worldwide. In comparison to traditional implementation projects, customers are able to save costs by 40% and reduce implementation time by 30%. Due to its scalability, the enterprise solution can be readily extended when the company grows and can thus keep pace with any company changes.
2. Increased productivity and cost control: The comprehensive, preconfigured mySAP All-in-One industry solutions integrate financials, HR, logistics, and customer relationships. As a result, the customer profits from increased transparency and simplified administrative processes. This also means more efficiency not only for the company but also for partners and vendors.
3. Reliable partners: For several years, SAP's technological know-how has been complemented by the industry knowledge of selected and qualified partners. The mySAP All-in-One partner solutions reflect this valuable experience. SAP partners offer comprehensive solutions consisting of hardware, software, and consulting, all of which are tailored to small- and midsize business needs.
4. Scalability: The flexible and powerful system technology, which is also used in big enterprises, supports the growth of small- and midsize companies. The reason for this is simple: mySAP All-in-One can be easily adapted to changing business requirements.

13.8.7.2 SAP Business ByDesign

The newest of SAP's SME offerings, SAP BBD, includes preconfigured best practices for managing financials, customer relationships, HR, projects, procurement, and the supply chain. BBD allows customers to focus on their business, leaving SAP to worry about maintaining hardware and software, running database backups, addressing performance and capacity planning, implementing updates and fixes, and so on. SAP takes care of system installation, maintenance, and upgrades so that you can focus on your business rather than IT. BBD targets to address the market of customers seeking to avoid investing in business software and all the necessary infrastructure and support personnel associated with such an investment.

SAP BBD solution provides the following advantages:

1. Hosted solution: SAP hosts your BBD system in an enterprise class data center designed to provide high availability and reliability.
2. Lower efforts and costs: A company deploying BBD does not necessarily require SAP partners or consultants for implementation.
3. Increased productivity and ease of maintenance: A major advantage of BBD is its ease of configuration for changes and maintenance. Nontechnical users can build business processes using visual modeling tools and web services.

13.8.7.3 SAP Business One

SAP Business One is an easy-to-use business and operational management application for emerging and dynamic businesses ranging in size from ten to several hundred employees. The application is simple yet powerful, allowing an immediate and complete view of both business operations and customer activities.

SAP Business One provides the following advantages:

1. Rapid implementation: SAP Business One can be implemented within a few days and can be easily maintained. In addition, its familiar Microsoft Office environment allows occasional users to rapidly learn to use the software. The application is based on open technologies and can be readily extended with special functions, if required.
2. Lower costs: Because it is cost-effective, SAP Business One offers a wide range of functions for an integrated data processing. Thus, decision makers in small- and midsize companies benefit from new value potential without exceeding their budgets.
3. Increased productivity and cost control: As the user interface of SAP Business One is simple and easy to understand, users will quickly learn how to work with the system. This will increase their productivity and help reduce the costs. The Drag and Relate technology enables flexible access to business information. For example, on clicking the content of the Customer or Item Number field in the Quotation window and dragging it to another screen, the relevant data will be evaluated. This technology relates different data to each other.
4. Sound business decisions: SAP Business One allows managers to quickly and effectively access strategic information from all enterprise areas and gives them full control of the relevant information and activities.
5. Scalability: When a company grows, processes usually become more complex and software requirements change. SAP Business One's flexible and efficient system technology can easily keep pace with the company's growth. SAP Business One can be extended by the functions your company requires. It also facilitates the transition to a more comprehensive IT system, such as the mySAP Business Suite.

13.9 SUMMARY

This chapter introduced the concept of ERP and the reason for their popularity. It unravels the mystery of ERPs like SAP and their power and potential to transform business enterprises. Customary discussions on ERP systems do not address the key differentiator of ERPs from the earlier mission-critical systems: ERPs, for the first time, are able to treat enterprise-level information not merely as records of information but as a tangible resource. We then looked at the difference between functional business model and business process model. Following this, we described SAP Business Suite along with its main constituents like cross-industry applications, components, financial performance management, industry-specific solutions, composite applications, and SAP small- and midsize business applications.

14 Business Excellence through Variations Using SAP

14.1 ENTERPRISE CHANGE MANAGEMENT WITH SAP

Strategic planning exercises can be understood readily in terms of devising strategies for improving on these process-oriented CVDs based on the competitive benchmarking of these values. The strategies resulting from analysis, design, and optimization of processes would in turn result in a focus on the redesign of all relevant business process at all levels. This could result in the modification or deletion of the concerned processes or even the creation of new process.

Initiating change and confronting change are the two most important issues facing the enterprises of today. The ability to change business processes contributes directly to the *innovation* bottom line. The traditional concept of change management is usually understood as a one-time event. But if an organization is looking for the capability not only to handle change management but also management of changes on a continual basis then ERP like SAP is a must!

SAP enables the essential changing of processes that are so critical to the success of the enterprise. Business processes that *reside* or are internalized within an organization's employees are difficult to change simply because human beings naturally find it more difficult to change. However, processes that reside within any computerized systems are easy to change.

14.1.1 THE LEARNING ORGANIZATION

MBC also underlies the contemporary notion of the learning organization. To compete in an ever-changing environment, an organization must learn and adapt. Because organizations cannot think and learn themselves, it is truly the individuals constituting the organization who have to do this learning. The amount of information in an organization is colossal. A single individual, however intelligent and motivated, cannot learn and apply all the knowledge required for operating a company. Moreover, even this colossal amount of information does not remain constant but keeps changing and growing.

The only effective solution is collaborative learning; that is, sharing this learning experience among a team of people. This not only caters to differences in the aptitudes and backgrounds of people, but they all can also do this learning simultaneously, thus drastically shortening the turn-around time on the learning process itself. If organizational learning is seen in terms of the creation and management of knowledge, it is very easy for us to see the essential need to share the learning experience among the various member teams at the company level and, within each team, among the members of the teams.

SAP provides facilities and tools for quickly incorporating such learned variations on the primary business processes. Moreover, while incorporating these variations of the basic process in terms of various parameters, SAP would automatically suggest the selection of parameters for configuration that would permit the variation to become as generic as possible. Thus, ERP would not only assist in solving the immediate problem—solving problems in the present—but would also define the problem (and, hence, the solution) in a more generic way. The essential difference between the two types of learning is between being adaptive and having adaptability. ERP provides and increases the adaptability of an enterprise. This also automatically transforms the tacit knowledge within an enterprise to its explicit form for everyone to know it, feel it, analyze it, and, if possible, improve it further.

Thus, we see another reason for collaboration among and within teams for contributing effectively in the learning process of the organization as a whole. Furthermore, what distinguishes learning from mere training is the transformation that results from the former. This, again, can be implemented successfully only by collaborations between various teams as becomes apparent when such collaborations are embodied in the form of an ERP package, such as SAP R/3, and are implemented within enterprises.

14.2   BACKGROUND OF BPR

Although BPR has its roots in IT management, it is basically a business initiative that has major impact on the satisfaction of needs of both the internal and external customer. Michael Hammer who triggered the BPR revolution in 1990 considers BPR as *radical change* for which IT is the key enabler. BPR can be broadly termed as "the rethinking and change of business processes to achieve dramatic improvements in the measures of performances such as cost, quality, service and speed."

Some of the principles advocated by Hammer are as follows:

- Organize around outputs, not tasks.
- Put the decisions and control and, hence, all relevant information into the hands of the performer.
- Have those who use the outputs of a process to perform the process, including the creation and processing of the relevant information.
- Location of user, data, processes, and information should be immaterial—it should function as if all of it were in a centralized place.

As will become evident on perusing the aforementioned points, the big-bang implementation of SAP does have most of the characteristics mentioned previously.

The most important outcome of BPR has been viewing business activities as more than a collection of individual or even functional tasks; it engendered the process-oriented view of business. However, BPR is different from quality management efforts like TQM and ISO 9000, which refer to programs and initiatives that emphasize bottom-up incremental improvements in existing work processes and outputs on a continuous basis. In contrast, BPR usually refers to top-down dramatic improvements through redesigned or completely new processes on a discrete basis. In the continuum of methodologies ranging from ISO 9000, TQM, ABM, etc., on one end to BPR on the other, SAP implementation definitely lies on the BPR side of the spectrum of the corporate change management efforts.

14.2.1   VALUE-ADDED VIEW OF BUSINESS PROCESSES

Business processes can be very easily seen as the basis of the value addition within an organization that was traditionally attributed to various functions or division in an organization. As organizational and environmental conditions become more complex, globalized, and therefore competitive, processes provide a framework for dealing effectively with the issues of performance improvement, capability development, and adaptation to the changing environment. Along a value stream (i.e., a business process), the analysis of the absence, creation, addition of value, or (worse) destruction of value critically determines the necessity and effectiveness of a process step. The understanding of value-adding and non-value-adding processes (or process steps) is a significant factor in the analysis, design, benchmarking, and optimization of business processes in the companies, leading to the BPRD or BPR.

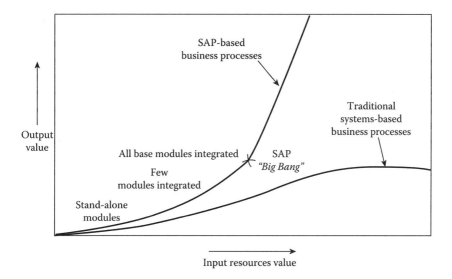

Output value

Input resources value

SAP-based business processes

Traditional systems-based business processes

All base modules integrated

SAP "Big Bang"

Few modules integrated

Stand-alone modules

FIGURE 14.1 Relationship between output value versus input resources value for SAP-based business processes.

As organizational and environmental conditions become more complex, globalized, and therefore competitive, processes provide a framework for dealing effectively with the issues of performance improvement, capability development, and adaption to the changing environment.

Value added can be defined typically as

$$\text{Value added} = \frac{\text{Output value}}{\text{Input resource value}}$$

Figure 14.1 shows the relationship between *output value* and *input resource value* for SAP-driven business processes as compared with business processes based on traditional IT systems.

> Big-bang implementation of SAP module: The organization should consider a *big-bang* implementation of SAP, wherein all the base modules of SAP are implemented and put in production together. As pointed out elsewhere in this book, by implementing only certain modules of the system, the company should not hope to reap more significant benefits than those accruing from the traditional systems. If SAP is not to be used as a past-facing system merely for recording and reporting purposes but more as a future-facing handler of an important enterprise resource, implementation of all the basic modules corresponding to the businesses of the company is essential. SAP system is modular and allows module-wise implementations. However, this is one feature that we recommend that should be ignored unless it is unavoidable because of extreme circumstances. A piecemeal approach of progressive implementation should be abandoned because delaying the implementations of all basic modules together only delays the benefits of a fully functional SAP and, therefore, incurs opportunity costs.

As discussed in Chapter 13, Subsection 13.5.1, "Information as the New Resource," information made available by ERP like SAP is not only a substitute for tangible resources like money, manpower, materials, and time but is also employable many times over. This clearly explains why the value added in Figure 14.1 shoots almost vertically for SAP-driven organizations. This also indicates that only when the basic modules of SAP are operational and fully integrated does the system truly begin to utilize information as a resource resulting in massive gains in productivity. Until then, the system is only functioning as a recording system albeit an efficient one.

Values are characterized by VDs like

- Time (cycle time, etc.)
- Flexibility (options, customization, composition, etc.)
- Responsiveness (lead time, number of handoffs, etc.)
- Quality (rework, rejects, yield, etc.)
- Price (discounts, rebates, coupons, incentives, etc.)

I must hasten to add that we are not disregarding cost (materials, labor, overheads, etc.) as a VD; however, the effect of cost is truly a resultant of a host of VDs like time, flexibility, and responsiveness.

The nature and extent of the value addition done by a process to a product and/or services delivered to an external or internal customer is the best index of the contribution of that process to the company's overall goal for competitiveness. Such value expectations are dependent upon, firstly, the customer's *use experience* of similar product(s) and/or service(s); secondly, the value delivered by the competitors; and thirdly, the capabilities and limitations of the base technological platform.

However, value as originally defined by Michael Porter in the context of introducing the concept of the value chain is meant more in the nature of the cost at various stages; rather than the value chain, it was more of a cost chain! Porter's value chain is also a structure oriented and hence a static concept. Here, we mean value as the satisfaction of not only external but also internal customers' requirements as defined and continuously redefined (dynamically by the customer) as the least total cost of acquisition, ownership, and use.

Consequently, in this formulation, one can understand completely the company's competitive gap(s) in the market in terms of such process-based customer-expected level of value and the value delivered by the company's process(es) for the concerned product(s) and/or service(s). Therefore, we can perform market segmentation for a particular (group of) product(s) and/or services(s) in terms of the most significant of the customer values and the corresponding VDs or what we term as CVDs. We look at CVDs in detail in the next section.

Strategic planning exercises can then be understood readily in terms of devising strategies for improving on these process-based CVDs based on the competitive benchmarking of these *collaborative* values and processes between the company and customers. These strategies, and the tactics resulting from analysis, design, and optimization of processes, would in turn focus on the restrategizing of all relevant business process at all levels. This may result in the modification or deletion of the processes or creation of a new process.

14.3   ENTERPRISE BPR METHODOLOGY

In this section, we look at the full life cycle of an enterprise BPR methodology. This will indicate opportunities where SAP could be of assistance in an ongoing BPR effort within the company. We present an overview of the seven-step enterprise BPR methodology. It starts with the context for undertaking the BPR and, in particular, reengineering of business process within the company. In the next step, it identifies the motivation of the redesign of processes to be the value as perceived by the customer. Following this, it suggests a method for selecting the business processes for the reengineering effort and describes a method for mapping of the selected processes. The process maps are then analyzed for discovering opportunities for reengineering. The penultimate step involves suggestions on redesigning of the selected processes for increased performance. And finally, it talks about implementing and measuring the implementation of the reengineered processes.

BPR effort within a company is not a one-time exercise but an ongoing one. One could also have multiple BPR projects in operation simultaneously in different areas within the company. The BPR effort involves business visioning, identifying the value gaps, and hence selecting the corresponding business processes for the BPR effort. The reengineering of the business processes might open newer opportunities and challenges, which in turn trigger another cycle of business visioning followed by BPR of the concerned business processes. Figure 14.2 shows the iteration across the alternating activities without end.

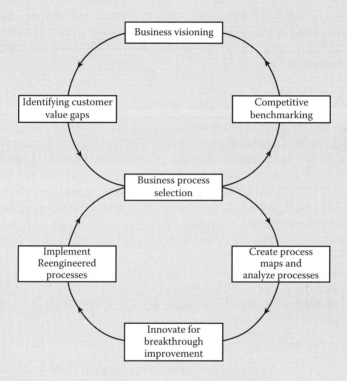

FIGURE 14.2 The alternating activities of business visioning and BPR.

14.3.1 STRATEGIC PLANNING FOR ENTERPRISE BPR

All markets are fluid to some degree, and these dynamic forces and shifting customer values necessitate changes in the company's strategic plans. The significance of a process to the success of the company's business is dependent on the nature and extent of the value addition done by this to a product and/or services delivered to a customer. Consequently, one can understand the competitive value gap in terms of the customer-expected level of value and the value delivered by the company for the concerned product(s) and/or service(s).

The competitive gap can be defined as the gap between the customer's minimum acceptance value (MAV) and the customer value delivered by the company. Companies that consistently surpass MAVs are destined to thrive; those that only meet the MAVs will survive; and those that fall short of the MAVs may fail.

CVDs are those business imperatives for business process, similar to the critical success factors (CSF) at the company level, that have to happen if the company wants to close the competitive gap. CVDs are in terms of factors like

- Time (lead time, cycle time, etc.)
- Flexibility (customization, options, composition, etc.)
- Responsiveness (lead time, number of handoffs, number of queues, etc.)
- Quality of work (rework, rejects, yield, etc.)

Market segmentation is performed based on the customer value and the corresponding CVDs. Such a market segmentation helps in suggesting corrective strategic and tactical actions that may be required, that is, to devise a process-oriented strategic business plan. The strategic plan will in turn help in identifying major processes that support these CVDs and which must be innovatively improved and reengineered.

14.3.2 IDENTIFYING THE BUSINESS PROCESSES WITHIN THE COMPANY

All business processes in the organization are identified and recorded.

A process can be defined as a set of resources and activities necessary and sufficient to convert some forms of inputs into some forms of outputs. Processes can be internal or external or a combination of both; they have cross functional boundaries; they have starting and ending points; and they exist at all levels within the organization, namely, section, department, division, and even at the company level. In fact, processes exist across company boundaries as well. Processes evolve and degrade in terms of efficiency and effectiveness.

A process itself may be constituted of various substeps. The substeps in a process could be

- Value-added steps
- Non-value-added steps
- Legal and regulatory steps (which are treated as value-added steps)

14.3.3 SELECTING BUSINESS PROCESSES FOR BPR

Selecting the right processes for innovative process reengineering effort is critical. The processes should be selected by reason of their high visibility, relative ease of accomplishing goals, and at the same time potential for great impact on the VDs.

Customers will evidently take their custom to the company that can deliver the most value for their money. Hence, the MAVs have to be charted in detail. MAV is dependent upon several factors like

1. The customer's prior general and particular experience base with an industry, product, and/or service
2. What competition is doing in the concerned industry, product, or service
3. What effect technological limitations have on setting the upper limit

As mentioned earlier, MAVs can be characterized in terms of the CVDs—only four to six VDs may be necessary to profile a market segment. CVDs can be defined by obtaining data through

- The customer value survey
- Leaders in noncompeting areas
- Best in class
- Internal customers

A detailed customer value analysis would analyze the value gaps and help in further refining the goals of the process reengineering exercise:

- Gaps that result from different value perceptions in different customer groups
- Gaps between what the company provides and what the customer has established as the minimum performance level
- Gaps between what the company provides and what the competition provides
- Gaps between what the organization perceives as the MAV and what the customer says are MAVs

It must be noted that analyzing the value gaps is not a one-time exercise; neither is it confined to one iteration of a cycle of the breakthrough improvement exercise. Like the BPR exercise itself, it is an activity that would have to be done on an ongoing basis.

As a goal for the improvement effort, a clear competitive advantage can be gained if best-in-class performance levels can be achieved in some key customer value areas and at least MAVs can be achieved in all others.

14.3.4 CREATING PROCESS MAPS

A process map documents the flow of one unit of work (the unit may be one item, one batch, particular service that is the smallest unit possible to follow separately)—what actually happens to the work going through the process. The process map is developed at several process levels starting at the highest level of the company. It documents both value-added and non-value-added steps. Process map could either be sequential or concurrent in nature.

Process could be mapped in two forms:

1. WF chart form
2. WBS form

Process workflows could be any of following kinds: continuous workflows, balanced workflows, and synchronized workflows.

Workflow becomes nonsynchronized because of

- Steps or tasks produced at different rates, that is, are imbalanced workflow
- Physical separation of operations causing work to move in batches, that is, noncontinuous workflow
- Working in batches, causing intermittent flow
- Long setup or changeover times resulting in batched work along with its problems
- Variations in process inputs in terms of quality availability on time

All these add time and costs to the process and reduce flexibility and responsiveness.

Using the value-added workflow analysis of the process map, we can

- Identify and measure significant reengineering opportunities
- Establish a baseline of performance against which to measure improvement
- Determine which tools may be most useful in the reengineering effort

Evidently, the major goal in reengineering the process is to eliminate non-value-added steps and wait times within processes. A good rule of thumb would be to remove 60%–80% of the non-value-added steps resulting in the total number of remaining steps to be not more than 1½ to 3 times the number of value-added steps. Even this would be a credible goal for the first iteration of the BPR effort.

SAP's strategy is to integrate all business operations in an overall system for planning, controlling, optimizing, and monitoring a given business. SAP has included over 800 best-of-business practices or scenarios that could help company to restructure its processes. These scenarios provide logical models for the optimization of the specific business processes and can be modeled around primary and support business activities. SAP guides a company to automatically integrate all primary and support functions of logistics like customer order, production, procurement, packaging, warehousing, delivery, service, and accounting. Companies can simply print out the relevant process models and analyze the most critical processes quickly and efficiently. The customizing features of SAP can then help in implementing the required changes.

The SAP Reference Model can help companies define their process needs and develop solutions; business solutions are already built into the reference model, eliminating the need for enterprises to start from scratch. The components of the Reference Model not only cover the process view but also the function view, information view, data view, and organization view.

For the purpose of modeling business process, SAP permits use of any of the following: ARIS toolset from IDS Scheer, Microsoft Visio, Live Model from IntelliCorp, and Enterprise Charter. They are based on Reference Model and provide a direct interface with the system functionality. The Reference Model and the tools mentioned previously use the modeling technique recommended by SAP called event-driven process chain (EPC) diagrams. An EPC, as the name suggests, is a sequence of predefined processes that is triggered by the occurrence of a predefined event. These events could be a user-centered event, a database update event, or another EPC itself.

A typical EPC diagram consists of the following symbols:

Events	Indicated by a hexagonal block
Functions	Indicated by rectangle with rounded corners
Information or material objects	Indicated by a rectangle
Organizational units	Indicated by an ellipse
Control flows	Indicated by a continuous line with arrowhead
Logical operators	Indicated by circle enclosing a symbol
Assignment	Indicated by a continuous line

14.3.5 ANALYZING PROCESSES FOR BREAKTHROUGH IMPROVEMENT

A company's competitive strength lies in eliminating as many costly non-value-added steps and wait times as possible. The key to eliminating any non-value-added step is to understand what cause it to exist and then eliminate the cause.

For breakthrough improvement, the process maps are analyzed for the following:

1. Organization complexity: Commonly, organizational issues are a major deterrent to efficiency of the processes.
2. Number of handoffs.
3. Work movement: Workflow charts are utilized to highlight move distances, that is, work movements.
4. Process problems: There are several factors that may have a severe effect on the continuity, balance, or synchronicity of the workflow. Examples are loops of non-value-added steps designed to address rework, errors, scraps, etc.

These may be on account of

- Long changeover times
- Process input/output imbalances

- Process variabilities
- Process yields

These problems need to be identified, measured, analyzed, and resolved through innovative problem-solving methodology.

14.3.6 INNOVATIVE BREAKTHROUGH IMPROVEMENT IN PROCESSES

The steps involved in innovative problem-solving methodology are as follows:

1. Define a problem.
2. Find alternate solutions.
3. Evaluate the solutions.
4. Implement the best solution.
5. Measure and monitor the success.

Business problems that need to be solved fall into three basic categories:

1. System problems (methods, procedures, etc.).
2. Technical problems (engineering, operational, etc.).
3. People problems (skills, training, hiring, etc.): These problems arise because if you change what a person does, you change what he or she is.

14.3.7 IMPLEMENTING REENGINEERED PROCESSES

This involves the following:

1. Reengineered vision and policies
2. Reengineered strategies and tactics
3. Reengineered systems and procedures
4. Reengineered communication environment
5. Reengineered organization architecture
6. Reengineered training environment

14.3.8 MEASURING PERFORMANCE OF REENGINEERED PROCESSES

Measurement of the performance of any processes is very important because lack of measurement would make it impossible to distinguish such a breakthrough effort from an incremental improvement effort of a TQM program.

Measurements are essential because they are

1. Useful as baselines or benchmarks
2. Motivation for further breakthrough improvement, which is very important future continual competitiveness

Measures for innovative process reengineering should be

- Visible
- Meaningful
- Small in number
- Applied consistently and regularly
- Quantitative
- Involve personnel closest to the process

14.4 BPR AND SAP IMPLEMENTATION

While perusing the various steps of a BPR methodology presented previously, it becomes evident that SAP can play a critical role in enabling and assisting any BPR effort in an organization in a major way.

14.4.1 SAP Reference Model

SAP's business blueprints (BBPs) that are available in the SAP reference model successfully integrate business reengineering with information technology. The reference model can help companies define their needs and develop solutions; business solutions are already built into the reference model, eliminating the need for organizations to start from scratch. The components of the reference model not only cover the functional model but also the process model, data model, organization model, information flow model, communication model, and distribution model. SAP's strategy is to integrate all business operations in an overall system for planning, controlling, optimizing, and monitoring a given business. SAP has included over 800 best-of-business practices or scenarios that could help company to restructure its processes. These scenarios provide logical models for the optimization of the specific business processes and can be modeled around primary and support business activities. SAP guides a company to automatically integrate all primary and support functions of logistics like customer order, production, procurement, packaging, warehousing, delivery, service, and accounting. Companies can simply print out the relevant process models and analyze the most critical processes quickly and efficiently. The customizing features of SAP can then help in implementing the required changes.

14.4.2 Relevant Significant Concepts of SAP

Three significant components that concern the basic functions and applications of SAP NetWeaver as well as the SAP Business Suite are

1. The client concept
2. The ability to establish organizations
3. The adaptation of the systems to customer-specific business processes (called customizing and the Implementation Guide [IMG] in the SAP system)

The client in a SAP system is a concept for the comprehensive logical separation of various work areas within the system. Technically speaking, a client is the first key field of every application database table. When a user logs into a SAP system, he or she always enters a client number (000–999). For this, the user has to be defined in that particular client. After a successful login, the user only has access to the data and processes present in that client. Data of other clients are not accessible (it can neither be displayed nor edited). This enables separately operating organizations to work parallel to one another in their own client areas within a single SAP system without influencing one another (but a maximum of 150 clients per system is recommended for performance reasons). Via integration processes, data transfer can also take place between clients. Thus, the client is a strict, organizational separating criterion for users working independently on a SAP system. Figure 14.3 displays the organizational layers of a SAP system.

For users working in separate organizations within the same company, further organizational layers are available that are developed in the applications:

- Separate systems for corporate subsidiaries and/or regions: Such a case is characterized by complete logical and technical system separation, uniform usage, data integration via SAP NetWeaver PI, and common or separate technical financial processing.
- Separate system internal clients for corporate subsidiaries and/or regions: This case is characterized by complete logical separation with common usage of technical system resources, uniform usage, data integration via SAP NetWeaver PI, and common or separate financial processing.

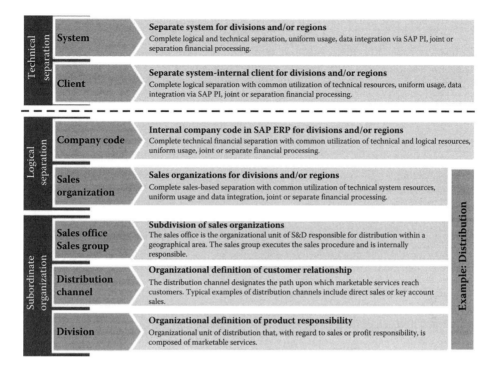

FIGURE 14.3 Organizational layers of a SAP system.

- Internal company code for corporate subsidiaries and/or regions: This case is characterized by complete technical financial separation with a common use of technical system and logistics resources, uniform usage, and common or separate financial processing.
- Sales organization for divisions and/or regions: This case is characterized by complete technical sales separation with common usage of technical system resources, uniform usage, data integration, and common or separate financial processing.
- Subdivision of sales organizations: The sales office is the organizational unit of the sales and distribution department, responsible for distribution within a geographical area. The sales group executes the sales procedure and is internally responsible.
- Organizational definition of customer relationship: The distribution channel designates the path upon which marketable services reach customers. Typical examples of distribution channels include direct sales or key account sales.
- Organizational definition of product responsibility: This case is characterized by the distribution department forming an organizational unit, which, with regard to sales or profit responsibility, is composed of marketable services.

There are further specific organizational hierarchies within the individual applications. For instance, in purchasing, there are purchasing organizations and purchasing groups. In distribution, there are sales organizations, distribution channels, etc. These organizational layers enable users to work together within a single client of the SAP system while, on the other hand, being limited to their respective organizational areas.

14.4.3 IMPLEMENTATION GUIDE

SAP IMG plays a critical role in the customization of SAP delivered to a customer to the specific requirements of the customer. This is achieved through configuration of the SAP software without modifying the base SAP software. SAP provides the implementation environment called Business Engineer, which manages and assists this effort for the configuration of SAP. This contains tools like the Business Navigator, IMG, Business Workflow, and IDES.

IMG tool is similar to the initialization modules of the traditional systems except that, in comparison, the number of parameters that are definable here is very large. In fact, it is the most vital tool for successful configuration of SAP for specific requirements of different companies. Over a course of time, the IMG exists in the following versions:

1. Reference IMG
2. Enterprise IMG
3. Project(s) IMG

The Reference IMG is the initial IMG that has the base set of configuration options from which all SAP functionality can be derived as per specific requirements. It is the most generic version of the system available. All other IMGs are derived from this basic version.

In contrast, the Enterprise IMG is a subset of the Reference IMG, which represents only the functionality that is needed by a particular enterprise implementing the system. Configuration options related to these excluded modules get filtered out at the time of generation of the Enterprise IMG.

Further down, since SAP implementations could be undertaken in waves or phases, the Enterprise IMG is specified for each of these projects separately resulting in the corresponding Project IMG for each of these projects. All configurations for a particular project are executed on the corresponding Project IMG. The access to Reference IMG and Enterprise IMG is restricted so as to avoid inadvertent changes being effected on them. Whenever required, the scope of the Project IMG can be increased at any time, and hence, such architecture rather than being a hindrance is very helpful in the management of the customization effort. We will refer only to the Project IMG for the rest of this section.

14.4.4 Features of Project IMG

A Project IMG contains multiple configuration transactions. Configuration transactions are the means for configuring the various processes or functionality delivered by the SAP system. A particular business process could be configured in terms of more than one configuration transaction. In conventional terms, each configuration transaction is 1 of 8000 parameter tables existing within SAP. They could be parameters like company code, type of G/L accounts, ranges of account numbers, A/P and A/R control account codes, posting codes, location codes, vendor or customer categories, tax codes, fiscal calendar, currencies and conversion factors to the base currency, and accounting transaction number ranges.

For each configuration transaction, the *configuration help text* provides explanation on a particular configuration transaction, why it is needed, and how it affects the functionality for a particular process.

The *configuration status* can be maintained at every level of the Project IMG hierarchy. It helps in the visual tracking of the customizing effort. The status flag can be configured to represent user-defined statuses. SAP provides standard status values like complete and in process. Statuses have to be maintained manually.

The *configuration Documentation* provides facility for recording annotations, notes, issues, problems, etc., on the various configuration settings for each configuration transaction. It is usually in the freeform text but could be standardized based on the requirements of different projects.

14.4.5 Using Project IMG for Customizing SAP

The basic structure of Project IMG is hierarchical. The various configuration transactions are grouped in a hierarchy of folders that are broadly arranged in the order that the customizations are undertaken within a SAP module. Among the various SAP modules, the IMG folders are arranged in the order that the modules get implemented in real life. However, there are some parameters or configuration transaction that are independent of any specific modules and are relevant to all modules and functionality of the system. All such configuration transactions are arranged within the top most IMG folder termed as Global Settings. Obviously, further down the hierarchy, it becomes fairly difficult to maintain strictly the order in which the transactions may be required to be configured. And therefore, this ordering is only a general guidance; otherwise, it could degenerate into a huge list of configuration transactions at a single level, which would certainly become unmanageable.

For any SAP implementation, a small selection of the initial parameters or configuration transaction that needs to be defined is as follows:

- Client: The highest organizational level in SAP R/3, not to be confused with a customer or client as defined in SAP Basis environment.
- Company code: The lowest legal entity for external reporting purposes of balance sheet, P/L statement, etc. There can be multiple company codes for a client but not the other way around.
- Chart of accounts: This is useful for legal reporting. Every client has only one chart of account; all company code within one client must use only this chart of account.
- Credit control area: This is useful for credit control management and reporting.
- Business areas: It is useful for flexible financial reporting.
- Controlling area: The highest entity for internal reporting and accounting purposes. A controlling area can have multiple company codes.
- Operating concern: There is only one operating concern for each controlling area. It is used if the profitability analysis module is implemented (this module may not be implemented by all customers). Controlling area is assigned to an operating concern.
- Valuation area.
- Plant: A unit where inventories are stored, accounted, processed, or manufactured. There can be multiple plants for a company code as well as a purchasing organization.
- Sales organization: The highest level for managing and reporting sales.
- Sales distribution channel: This characterizes different modes of supplying to end customers (retail sales, distribution agents, factory outlets, Internet sales, and so on). There can be multiple distribution channels for a sales organization.
- Sales division: This is useful for management and reporting of a group of products. There can be multiple product divisions for multiple sales organization as well as a distribution channels.
- Sales area: It is useful for flexible management and reporting. It is a combination of a sales organization, distribution channel, and division.
- Purchasing organization: This is an organizational unit for purchasing activities and generation of purchase orders.
- Storage locations: The physical location where a company's inventory is stored. There can be multiple storage locations for multiple plants.
- General ledger (G/L) account: G/L accounts are used for legal, external reporting through the chart of accounts.
- Housing bank and bank account: These organization structures reflect a company's banking institutions and their individual bank accounts.
- Vendor master: This contains important information on the company's vendors. For example, a vendor's name, address, telephone number, fax number, contact person, purchasing information, bank information, and accounting information are stored in the vendor master data. This information saves on transaction entries; when a transaction is made with the vendor, the vendor master data can automatically be used by default in the transaction.

- Customer master: Similar to the vendor master data, the customer data contain important information on the company's customers. Information such as customer's name address, buying habits, marketing information, and accounting information is stored here. When a transaction is made with a customer, the customer master data can automatically be used by default in the transaction.

As may have been noted, some of the IMG transactions actually correspond to the programs for the creation of master data like G/L account, vendor master data, and customer master data. Programs or the functionality for the creation and maintenance of master data and transaction data is also available through the respective modules.

14.4.6 IMPLEMENTATION OF SAP STANDARD FUNCTIONALITY

As far as possible, avoid the bugbear of customization by altering and additional programming in ABAP. Additional programming should be evaluated and adopted only as a last resort. SAP keeps upgrading its suite of products and if custom software is built for a particular version, it will have to be upgraded every time SAP releases new upgrades. Like any other product, SAP goes through oscillating cycles between major functional upgrades followed by technical upgrades and vice versa. The best solution is to

- Use SAP standard functionality
- Accommodate the variation of the business process by using SAP's flexibility for configuring variant processes
- Adopt a workaround that indirectly takes care of the required functionality; for example, in the absence of the HR module, some accounts interfacing HR functions can be managed by treating employees as customers
- Use third-party products that are properly certified and qualified by SAP

14.4.7 SELECTING THE MOST CRITICAL PROCESSES

A company should evaluate and select the processes that are critical to its business and focus on implementing them effectively to add maximum value for optimal effort.

14.4.7.1 Implementing Best-of-Business Processes

SAP has a library of 800 best-of-business processes derived from companies throughout the world. The success of SAP in providing comprehensive functionality within a shorter time frame compared with traditional implementations is based on the strategy of leveraging the commonality that is found in similar processes prevalent in companies within an industry.

Reusability has been a powerful concept in enhancing productivity and the quality of delivered software in the areas of traditional software development. SAP, in particular, extends this concept of reusability to the design of mission-critical systems. It packages such universal commonalities of functionality for rapid and successful implementations.

Before adding reusability to the library of the best-of-business processes, however, the company should document, rationalize, and standardize the company's select group of processes that are to be implemented using SAP.

14.4.7.1.1 Documentation of Processes

Documenting the various business processes permits the true comprehension of the characteristic structure and dynamics of the business environment within a company. This involves recording various details on the business processes like name, purpose, responsible function, process description, including inputs and outputs, and subprocesses. This also includes interfaces with other functions and systems, exceptional conditions, areas for improvement, and impact analysis of suggested scenarios.

14.4.7.1.2   Rationalization of Processes

Many of the systems and procedures adopted by traditional systems were influenced by the architecture of the systems themselves. For instance, these earlier systems were designed to be used by IT-literate personnel managed and supported by a centralized IT function. In contrast, because of the end-user orientation of ERP packages like SAP as well as the online availability of data on all aspects of company operations, SAP permits the rationalizing of many processes. This could be in terms of eliminating sequential wait periods for approvals, acknowledgments prior to further processing, collating status updates from various departments before compiling the latest positions on inventory, and so on.

In enterprise-wide integrated packages like SAP, many of these facilities and features become available automatically as a part of the architecture of the system. Thus, such process steps could be eliminated entirely from the business processes.

14.4.7.1.3   Standardization of Processes

Every plant or office site of a company develops its own character and culture, which is a result of the company's recommended corporate environment blending with the local situations. Such local practices have strong adherents and generate loyalty and pride. These factors often harm the progress of implementing a fairly uniform system, even if it is a computerized system like SAP, across the organization at all of its sites and offices.

The CPO must take ample measures to ensure the broad acceptance within the organization of standardized implementation. This can be ensured by

- The rapid implementation at the pilot site
- The rapid rollout of SAP at other company sites and offices
- The deputation of key personnel from all sites for the teams at the pilot sites, even at the risk of overstaffing these teams
- The judicious selection and documentation of functionalities for implementation at the pilot sites
- The democratic and transparent process of standardization based on the predefined criteria of value addition in terms of customer friendliness, quality, timeliness, costs, and so on
- Configuring and customizing the maximum possible functionality at the pilot site, keeping in view the businesses and practices prevalent at all other sites and offices

14.4.7.2   Centralized Base Reference Configuration

A company can experience the real payoff of implementing an ERP like SAP only when it has implemented SAP at all of its plants, facilities, and offices. Traditional computerized systems have a much more difficult time implementing standardized processes across all locations of their organizations. Since a SAP project entails implementing both best-of business and standardized processes, it leads to fairly standard implementation solutions across all of its sites.

A company should plan to implement a fairly comprehensive functionality at its pilot site. This is termed as the centralized base reference configuration (CBRC). This can simply be transplanted at each of the rollout sites in the subsequent stages of the project. Such an approach engenders faster customization, training, integration testing, and, finally, go-live stages.

14.5   CHANGEABILITY OF SAP-DRIVEN ENTERPRISES

SAP-driven enterprises are fundamentally enabled for managing changes in the operations of the business. Their changes could be driven by external market conditions, or they could also be planned and generated internally. You have already seen many aspects of this in the beginning of this chapter. In this section, we highlight two characteristics of SAP-driven enterprises that achieve a measure of BPR simply by implementing SAP in the first place.

14.5.1 REAL-TIME SAP OPERATIONS MAKE PROCESSES TRANSPARENT

SAP transactions are immediately updated into the concerned functional areas, be they inventory, party ledgers, accounting, and so on. SAP reengineers the business immediately to eliminate all wait times and minimize time period required for communication between various functions. And all of these postings are done simultaneously so that a consistent view is always available for any transactions—there is no lag between material, management, and financial accounting of any transactions. All these add up to tremendous transparency and visibility in the functioning of the SAP system and hence the organization.

With traditional systems, which were not integrated and had batch-oriented processing cycles, a consistent picture was available only for a short period of time near the close of a month or a year. It also permitted different functions of certain latitude in exercising a manner of ownership and degree of authority even to the detriment of the overall functioning of the company's operations

By effecting all transaction in real time, SAP also enables the organization to minimize reaction time to changing situations in the market and take immediate corrective action. This automatically also makes the organization more efficient, which is discussed in the following subsection.

14.5.2 INTEGRATED SAP OPERATIONS ELIMINATE HANDOFFS

The integration of all organization functions and processes engendered by SAP eliminates various kinds of handoffs between departments, wherein tasks and copies of related documents are handed over to the next department for further processing. At every stage, this generates the need for inwarding, reconciliation, negotiations, and follow-up with upstream and downstream activities along the process path, and so forth. All these merely add more overheads, elapsed time, manpower effort, information overload, and therefore costs. The inherent integration provided by SAP eliminates all such overheads and non-value-added activities. Reduced time cycles encourage various operational decision makers not to pad heavily plans, projections, estimates, requisitions, material and purchase orders, production orders, etc., to accommodate contingencies. Overall, implementing SAP makes companies to become more lean and efficient. However, one cannot discount the possibility of an organization under some misguided zeal, for accountability may enforce highly restrictive authorization and access profiles that may essentially negate the advantages arising out of basic transparency, real-time interfaces, and integration provided by SAP.

14.5.3 CONVERTING CHANGED BUSINESS PROCESSES INTO SAP FUNCTIONALITY

Implementing SAP solutions to meet business requirements is always a daunting task. It gets even more challenging when the business processes within an organization are complex and the standard functionality provided within the SAP solution is not enough to meet even 80% of the business requirements.

Changed functional development with regard to SAP solutions can be broadly categorized as follows:

- Configuration—This involves setting up the SAP solution by adding, selecting, and configuring a certain set of available parameters for the business processes to be executed in SAP without making any programming updates.
- Customization—This involves making programming changes to the standard software solution provided by SAP so that the standard business processes will not behave in a manner different from what is expected, primarily to meet the customer requirements.

During the BBP phase of the SAP implementation methodology, business processes are converted into a SAP-specific functional plan—a blueprint. One of the first steps in this process is to understand the current business processes existing within an enterprise. The functional specialist spends the next few days diving deeply into each functional area, understanding all the current business processes and describing any additional processes identified as part of the visioning exercise described in the previous section. Existing business process documentation is analyzed and discussed with the project team members. Business process flow charts are developed as a means to capture the information shared by the business process owners and SMEs. Each process flow diagram contains its subprocesses and decision trees depicted together in a visual format where each row of activity is described as a swim lane. The flow chart depicts not only the business process in detail but also links to other functional areas, such as inventory management, MRP, and finance. Additionally, it shows the processes that will be executed in SAP ERP, those that are carried out manually, and those being executed in a non-SAP system. Effectively, the flow chart depicts the business process mapping to the SAP ERP solution and clearly identifies any gaps that might exist within the business process.

The corresponding BBP consists of the following:

- Policies and procedures, instructions
- Exclusions, if any
- Decisions
- Change management items
- Business process description including business process flow diagrams
- Business process mapping to the SAP ERP solution
- Local business process requirements (if different from earlier requirements for legal reasons)
- Gap analysis
- RICEFS (reports, interfaces, conversions, enhancements, forms, and SAP scripts)
- Authorization
- Data volume per site
- Archiving details
- BBP acceptance of results—sign-off by leads

Gaps are processes or functionality that does not exist within the standard SAP solution. These gaps are categorized as either critical or *nice to have*. A gap can be mitigated with a workaround within the SAP solution or through the process of customization in which the actual SAP programs are changed to accommodate these gaps in business processes or functionality. A cost–benefit analysis is carried out to conclude whether this gap can be mitigated with a workaround or through customization. In some cases, even if a workaround exists, it might not be beneficial because it might be time consuming and/or might result in human errors that an organization cannot afford to make. If the decision is made to add new functionality into the standard SAP solution, then the solution is designed and a detailed design document for this new functionality is developed. This detail design will also include functional specifications of the new functionality to be developed.

14.5.3.1 SAP Configuration

SAP configuration is a two-step process. The first step is to develop the baseline configuration, which involves configuring SAP ECC based on the information provided during the BBP phase. The second step is to fine-tune the configuration further based on the outcome of each unit and integration test scenario. As noted earlier, this is achieved through SAP IMG.

14.5.3.2 SAP Customization

The term customization refers to developing programs not available within the SAP standard functionality to cater to an organization's business requirements.

Such customized programs could be used to create the following:

- Enhancements to the standard SAP programs for additional business requirements
- Reports required to run the business and not available within the SAP solution
- Interfaces between SAP and non-SAP systems
- Conversion programs to transfer data from the legacy to the SAP solution

14.5.4 ADVANCED BUSINESS APPLICATION PROGRAMMING

SAP solutions have primarily been developed using ABAP, which dates back to the 1980s. ABAP programs communicate with the database management system of the central relational database and with the presentation layer, which could be a SAP-specific GUI (such as the fat client SAP GUI) or, in the case of web-based SAP applications, a web browser.

The ABAP tools can be accessed via the ABAP Development Workbench.

The ABAP Development Workbench provides the following primary functions:

- Package Builder
- Object Navigator
- Web Application Builder for ITS (Internet Transaction Server) services
- Web Application Builder for BSPs (Business Server Pages)
- Web Dynpro
- Web Services
- ABAP Dictionary
- ABAP Editor
- Class Builder and Function Builder
- Screen Painter and Menu Painter
- Testing tools such as ABAP Debugger for runtime analysis and performance trace
- Transport Organizer

14.5.5 LEGACY SYSTEM MIGRATION WORKBENCH

Legacy System Migration Workbench (LSMW) is a tool that supports data migration from legacy systems, such as non-SAP systems, to SAP systems. Instead of using individual tables or field contents, this tool migrates user-defined data sets or objects, combined according to business criteria. The following primary features and functions are available:

- Read data from an input file
- Display the data (for review purposes)
- Convert this data to make it compatible to the target system (SAP) requirements
- Display the converted data (again, for review)
- Create a batch input session for data transfer
- Execute the data transfer into SAP

Log files are created for every step executed during the data migration process, and each step can be controlled by authorization so that only the appropriate person having access to a step can execute that step.

To transfer data (master data as well as transactions) between clients in a SAP system or from a non-SAP system into an SAP system, or to set up this data automatically, other tools may be used, such as Application Link Enabling (ALE), Computer-Aided Test Tool (CATT), or the application interfaces provided in the Business Object Repository (BOR).

14.5.6 Java and the SAP NetWeaver Development Studio

SAP offers the SAP NetWeaver Developer Studio to create, build, and deploy applications that are compliant with the Java Platform, Enterprise Edition 5 (Java EE 5). Through this toolset, developers have the flexibility to design user interfaces, use web services, and handle XML-based messages across heterogeneous environments based on the new Java EE 5 standard. The following features and functions are available:

- Use of the latest Java standards makes development of business applications easier.
- Service Data Objects (SDO) 2.1 standards make data programming easier.
- Architecture provides scalability and robustness.
- Connectivity capabilities make it possible to interface with all SAP systems adherent to the latest open standards.

14.5.7 SAP NetWeaver Composition Environment

The SAP NetWeaver Composition Environment (SAP NetWeaver CE) provides a service-oriented and standards-based development environment in which developers can easily model and develop composite applications. These applications, commonly known as *composites* (because they combine previously available functions and data sets in a new way), accelerate business process innovation. Composite applications provide data and functions as services. The developer accesses and combines these from the underlying repository to combine them into a new solution for a business process, to add functionality to an already existing application, and so on.

As an example of a composite application, consider a typical end-to-end process within a manufacturing organization that starts with demand creation, wherein a sales order is created for a product ordered by a customer. Based on this demand signal, material requirement planning is executed. Here, the BOM for this product is exploded; the stock at each level of the BOM is checked for its material availability, and if there are shortages, a purchase and a production plan is created. This plan consists of purchase requisitions created for raw materials and planned orders created for manufacturing parts, namely, the semifinished and finished parts. Purchase orders are created from these requisitions and sent to the supplier. The suppliers will fulfill the purchase order requirements, and the raw materials will be received into inventory at the manufacturing plant. The manufacturing process will start with the receipt for the raw materials from stock. The raw materials will be processed to subassemblies or semifinished parts and then will be manufactured further to get the final finished product ordered by the customer. The finished product is then picked, packed, and shipped to the customer. The suppliers are paid for their raw materials, and the customer is billed for the product they ordered. The customer then pays the manufacturer of the product.

This end-to-end process consists of sales, planning, procurement, manufacturing, and financial processes. All of these processes are executed in one or more online transaction systems. The product executive wants to monitor the progress of this product through all these processes and needs one view. A developer can develop a composite application using tools and technologies such as the SAP NetWeaver Visual Composer or SAP Composite Application Framework Guided Procedures (CAF GP). A good example is a dashboard-type application residing on the portal. The data extracted from the OLTP systems will be formatted to provide the view, as per the product executive's requirements, where he or she can monitor this end-to-end process from the desktop.

The SAP NetWeaver CE is a must-have in our eyes because it is a key innovation enabler; SAP NetWeaver CE allows an organization to take its SAP business application to the next level and adopt real-world SOA principles. Its model-driven development tools enable developers to create custom services as well as custom user interfaces. And by combining these, a custom workflow or complex business process can be assembled not only quickly but in a manner that enables it to be decomposed and changed again later as business changes dictate. It is this innate flexibility of SAP

NetWeaver CE—combined with access to a robust set of existing services and the capability to create new services—that makes this tool an indispensable asset for any contemporary SAP developer tasked with quickly standing up new business solutions.

14.6   SAP AND CHANGE MANAGEMENT PROGRAM

In the last chapter, which gave an overview of a SAP implementation project, we identified the fact that a SAP implementation project is like any other business performance improvement program. Because of the enterprise-wide character of these projects, the issues arising out of SAP project necessitate that a formal change management program be undertaken within the enterprise.

14.6.1   CHANGE CHAMPIONS: CORE TEAM

The key members from the various functional departments of the SAP team are the ideal *change champions* for the SAP project. They can best communicate to the end users of their department with whom the key members already have a good standing. After mapping and configuring the processes in SAP suitable for their requirements, the key members are also in the best position to talk to the other members of their respective departments and quickly address their particular common requirements and apprehensions. The change process is furthered by the core team members being directly involved in training the super users from their respective departments.

14.6.2   CHANGE FACILITATORS: SUPER USERS

Super users are the key to a full-scale implementation and subsequently the productive operation of SAP. Super users are trained by the key members of their respective departments. Their training consists of an overview of their module (and related modules) and all the critical processes of interest within their departments.

   Under the guidance of the key users, the super users participate in the full-scale validation and integration testing with other departments. This helps them to see the power and potential of SAP through actual experience with the system. It also helps them to understand the practical implications of the tight integration, immediate updates, and transparency available in the SAP system. The super users can then convey the real power of the system as experienced by them, especially during the integration testing phase, to the end users in their respective departments. The super users would be the messengers who would not only advocate changes in the processes but also demonstrate its actual functioning and benefits.

14.6.3   CHANGE AGENTS: END USERS

The super users train the end users in their respective departments, covering an overview of the processes in their area of operation, the details of the process, and programs of direct relevance to their daily operations.

   The transparent and instant access to relevant information that SAP provides from other departments is always a great motivator, but the implications of instantaneous updates and integration also make all members conscious of the enhanced responsibility and discipline that the system demands from all the concerned participants. Although new systems are always viewed with suspicion, the sense of involvement and ownership inherited from contacts and interaction far outweighs all misgivings about using a SAP system in production.

14.6.4   WHY ARE SAP IMPLEMENTATION PROGRAMS SO COMPLEX?

The prime reason for the longer duration of SAP implementation projects was the peculiar complexity of the product and, hence, its implementation. Let me explain. The contradictory demands of comprehensibility and flexibility were satisfactorily addressable in SAP because of its repository-oriented architecture (in this chapter, we will mainly focus on the functionality aspects of this repository rather than the technical ones, which also are substantial). Fundamentally, this was not much different from the trend of parameterized packages that had been gaining ground among application software packages since the 1980s. The main difference was the extent or degree of parameterization: SAP was parameterized to an extreme. It was this property that enabled it to be flexible enough to be configurable to requirements suitable to several industries.

The difficulty in implementing SAP arose from the fact that the success of the implementation project depended on correctly mapping all of the company's business process onto the SAP system. This entailed correct configuration of all the required process right in the beginning or the initial stages of the project. As we have seen earlier, SAP addressed the problem of providing usable application software systems by effectively short-circuiting the problematic requirements analysis phase, which was the bane of the traditional SDLC. But because of the demand for correct configuration right at the beginning, we were back confronting essentially the same problem. The majority of the risk for the ultimate success of the project was also dependent again on this initial mapping being completed correctly, consistently, and completely. Unlike in the SDLC, where the end users were expected to know only their requirements thoroughly, in the new dispensation, they had the additional burden of being required to become quite familiar with the functionality provided by SAP. Thus, SAP was very flexible, but also for configuring it correctly to use its power, not only was one required to know the business process requirements of the company, but one also required to be well acquainted with the SAP functionality even before starting on the configuration. And in typical SAP projects, this was right in the initial stages of the project! This was the root cause for the large amount of effort and time required for completing the mapping and configuration of the base SAP system in all SAP projects. Although all the required functionality may have been available in SAP all along, it takes everyone a long time to discover and use it correctly.

14.6.5 CONFIGURATION THROUGH IMPLEMENTATION GUIDE

Like in SAP's older implementation methodology called Procedure Model, all configuration in SAP is also done through an environment called IMG. IMG is not unlike the initialization modules of the traditional computerized systems, except that it is very large by comparison. SAP has more than 8000 configuration tables. All business processes of the company could be mapped onto the SAP system functionality by configuring the parameters in IMG. For implementing any process, one had to identify the parameters that may have to be defined before this process could become operational into the system. For example, for creation of an invoice document, it was important to identify tax parameters and define them first through the IMG. The whole process of specifying the parameters suitable of the specific requirements of a company is also known as customization, which is accomplished using IMG. However, the essential problem was that for an integrated system like SAP, there was no systematic way in the earlier methodology to identify all the relevant parameters quickly and completely for implementing these processes.

As noted in Subsection 14.4.3, "Implementation Guide," IMG is structured in a manner that does reflect to a certain extent the sequence in which these parameters have to be defined, but for most part, this was not adequate for customizing SAP quickly. For typical SAP implementation teams, locating hundreds of these parameters correctly, completely, in a proper sequence and also in a timely manner was an intractable problem. Rather than a systematic process, it was more of an experience in discovery, and the number of parameters to be identified and defined was simply overwhelming. To be on the safe side, typical project teams were always on the defensive, invariably confirming and reconfirming every small aspect (although this did not guarantee avoiding missing something) before proceeding further in the effort, and all this simply added to a large time frame for completing the project. And, along the way, the benefit of using the departmental store model of computerization was being lost completely (see Chapter 13, Subsection 13.2.8, "ERP Represents the Departmental Store Model of Implementing Computerized Systems").

The obvious remedy was to address the following two issues for achieving faster SAP implementations:

1. Enable bridging the gap between the know-how of the to-be-mapped company processes and/or requirements, on one hand, and the functionality provided by SAP or that was configurable in SAP through IMG, on the other.
2. Quick transfer of know-how, expertise, and experience to newer implementation teams on experience gained from numerous earlier implementations.

As was seen earlier in the book, repository-oriented systems like SAP are in continuation with the tradition of computer-aided software engineering (CASE) environments. By the same token, the later point truly corresponds to a computer-aided software implementation (CASI) environment, which we consider next.

14.6.6 Computer-Aided Software Implementation

AcceleratedSAP is a classic illustration of CASI environment that assists in speeding up the implementation effort based on expertise and experience gained from thousands of past SAP implementation projects and will continue the same in future to improve its performance further. There are two aspects to a CASI: one is CASE and the other is intelligent assistance.

Traditionally, implementing software application systems was constituted of familiar phases like feasibility analysis, requirements analysis, effort estimation, project plan, design, development, testing, integration, documentation, training, data uploads, interfaces, and, finally, cut over to production. Right from the inception of the computerization activity, there have been efforts toward employing computerized systems to aid in this effort at different stages. There has been the usual profusion of software applications addressing the requirements of the various phases of the SDLC. Among these program generators, screen painters, report painters, prototyping, and automated/assisted testing tools to assist in the software development have been the most common ones. But there have been solutions for every phase in SDLC. Many of these environments also embodied the corresponding methodologies for speeding up the effort at respective phases of SDLC. Some of these environments or accelerators also became generic that made them adaptable to any methodology deployed for a particular project rather than being confined to specific methodologies including for analysis, system design, data modeling, and database design. The history of computerization in the last century has been littered with numerous examples of such environments that, many a time, have followed differing standards and have been incompatible with each other.

14.6.7 SAP as Populated CASE Environment

In their most developed form in the later part of the last century, CASE technology was constituted of the following components:

1. Methods
2. Tool environment

The CASE environment was a set of integrated tools that were designed to work together and to assist or possibly automate all phases of the SDLC.

SAP environments like Basis system, Repository (constituted of advanced tools like the ABAP Dictionary, ABAP Development Workbench, CATT, and Workbench Organizer), and Business

Engineer (constituted of Reference Model, Business Navigator, Procedure Model superseded now by ASAP, IMG, IDES, etc.) form a state-of-the-art CASE environment.

However, as noted earlier, SAP is not only one of the best of the CASE environments, but it is also a populated CASE in that its repository is populated with the details of the most comprehensive application system, namely, SAP consisting of financials, logistics, and HR systems.

14.6.8 SAP IMPLEMENTATIONS AND EXPERT SYSTEMS

Expert systems (ESs) were environments that extended the realm of reusability into the areas of operations and usage of the computerized systems. These knowledge-base-driven systems applied inferences processing to a knowledge-base-containing data and business or decision rules that matured depending on the veracity of the produced results.

In their most advanced form around the late 1980s, ES technology was constituted of the following components:

- Knowledge base.
- Inference engine that *learned* and fine-tuned its performance based on some predefined criteria with reference to the usefulness of the inferred results. This learning could be in terms of generating new rules or modifying the strengths of the current rules or even updating the knowledge base itself.

AcceleratedSAP is not an ES in the traditional sense; however, it does have the basic ingredients of a knowledge base and production of inferences or suggested actions. In fact, in certain cases, it affects these actions automatically onto the SAP system. The knowledge base of AcceleratedSAP keeps on getting upgraded based on the latest reported experiences and expertise gleaned from SAP implementations. Presently, this is not an online, dynamic, and automatic update like some of the other services provided by SAP like GoingLive Check or EarlyWatch Alert service; SAP releases periodic upgrade of this knowledge base through CD-ROMs. But it is easy to imagine that AcceleratedSAP may become an online service like GoingLive Check and other services accessible through the Internet in near future. And it may also become a full-featured ES with its characteristic features and user interface.

14.6.9 WHY SAP PROGRAMS MAY SOMETIMES BE LESS THAN SUCCESSFUL

There are various reasons why SAP implementation programs may be less than successful. These may be because of the following reasons:

- Top management involvement and interest falters or is perceived as such.
- Lack of clear project scope and strategies; project is too narrowly focused.
- Implementation of nonoptimized processes in SAP.
- Decisions on changes in processes and procedures may not get effected; they may be ignored or subverted.
- Lack of proper visibility and communication on the SAP project at all stages.
- Lack of adequate budget and resources like for training of large group of envisaged end users.
- Not deputing the key managers on the implementation team.
- Support infrastructure and systems are delayed inordinately.
- Disputes and conflicts in the team are not resolved quickly.
- Company members of the team may not get along with the external consultants.
- External consultants may have differences with end users or user managers.

- Core team members may have differences with user departments.
- A company-wide change management plan is not implemented.
- Too much gap between the implementation at the pilot site and rollout sites.
- Members of the company do not participate actively because
  - Members may feel the system has been implemented in haste and that it does not address their requirements; they feel they have not been taken in confidence
  - Members may feel they have not been given adequate training
  - Members of the company are apprehensive of their future roles
  - Members of the company are afraid that they may not be able to learn the new system and perform satisfactorily
  - Members of the company feel unsettled by the lack of hierarchy in the system
  - Members may feel they have been reduced to data entry operators
  - Members of the core implementation team may resign and leave the company
  - Members of the core team may be averse to move on projects at rollout sites

14.7 ENTERPRISE VARIATIONS USING SAP

Having built all the requisite bases, we are now ready to tackle the primary issue of enabling various enterprise variations using SAP.

1. Shared values variations enabled by SAP: Any variations in shared values can be realized in terms of corresponding variations in policies and procedures, which in turn can be affected in the relevant constituents or components of the SAP Business Suite including the mySAP ERP HCM (see Chapter 13, Subsection 13.8, "SAP Business Suite").
2. Strategy variations enabled by SAP EPM: As explained in Chapter 13, Subsection 13.8.4, "SAP Enterprise Performance Management (EPM)", company's business strategy can be varied using SAP EPM, and the corresponding profitability can be managed and monitored and consolidated to produce to assess the enterprise performance on an ongoing basis.
3. Structure variations enabled by SAP IMG: As explained in Subsection 14.4.3, "Implementation Guide", any variations in strategy can be affected using the IMG—though in certain cases, this may be a fairly elaborate exercise. The majority of variations could be merger and acquisitions of another company: depending on the circumstances and requirements, this could be accomplished by defining the company code in a new *client* or a new company code in the existing *client*. In the case of a split or formation of a new division, a new division code can be defined.
4. Stuff variations enabled by SAP PLM: Any variations in existing *stuff* or introductions of new products or services can be affected using SAP PLM (see Chapter 13, Subsections 13.8.2.1, "SAP ECC" through 13.8.2.3 "SAP PLM").
5. Style variations enabled by SAP: Any variations in shared values can be realized in terms of corresponding variations in policies and procedures, which in turn can be affected in the relevant constituents or components of the SAP Business Suite including the mySAP ERP Financials (see Chapter 13, Subsection 13.8, "SAP Business Suite").
6. Staff variations enabled by SAP HR: Any variations in existing *staff* or introductions of new policies and procedures, which in turn can be affected in the mySAP ERP HCM (see Chapter 13, Subsection 13.8.1.1.2, "mySAP ERP Human Capital Management").
7. Skill variations enabled by SAP: Any variations in existing *staff* or introductions of new policies and procedures, which in turn can be affected in the relevant constituents or components of the SAP Business Suite including the mySAP ERP HCM (see Chapter 13, Subsection 13.8, "SAP Business Suite").

8. System variations enabled by SAP IMG and ABAP: Any variations in existing functionality or creation of new functionality for addressing the company-specific requirements can be affected by configuring in IMG or customizing by programming in ABAP (see Subsections 14.4.3, "Implementation Guide" and 14.5.4 "Advanced Business Application Programming").

9. Sequence variations with SAP SCM, APO, PP: Any variations in production plans and systems can be affected in SAP SCM, APO, and PP (see Chapter 13, Subsections 13.8.1.4, "mySAP SCM," 13.8.2.1 "SAP ECC," and 13.8.2.2 "SAP SCM").

14.8 SUMMARY

The competitiveness of enterprises today is predicated on the competitiveness of their enterprise systems in terms of their ability to simultaneously enable efficiency, flexibility, and innovativeness. In this final chapter of the book, we described how enterprises can achieve business excellence through variations enabled by SAP. We introduce the concept of BPR and describe the full cycle of an enterprise BPR methodology. SAP enables the essential changing of processes that are so critical to the success of the enterprise. We explain the changeability of SAP-driven enterprises. We describe how business variations can be achieved by using SAP in all dimensions of variations, namely, strategy, structure, shared values, stuff, style, staff, skills, systems, and sequence.

Appendix: Traditional Software Development versus Complete Off-the-Shelf Applications

In the past few decades, all of us have witnessed a procession of different methodologies, tools, and techniques emanating from the software industry that have had a tremendous impact on the very nature and operations of business enterprises. But in the midst of all this turmoil, one fact has remained constant and that has been the lack of productivity improvements, irrespective of the extent and nature of computerization.

But right from the start, there was an even more basic problem in terms of the number of software applications that were actually completed and implemented successfully. Much has been written on the software crisis that engulfed information service groups in the 1980s. The reasons were multifold:

- With the advent of PC-like functionalities, users were becoming more aware and demanding.
- Consequently, applications were becoming bigger and more complex.
- Correspondingly, productivity was reducing rather than increasing.
- Software development times were increasing and cost and time overruns were fairly routine.
- Quality trained professionals were always in short supply, resulting in increased costs for programmers; hence, systems development costs were ever-increasing.
- Mortality of systems was very high.

On average, out of the total number of IT systems under development, more than half used to be canceled; of the remaining half, only about two-thirds were delivered. Half the delivered systems never got implemented, while another quarter were abandoned midway through the implementation. Of the residual quarter of the delivered systems, half failed to deliver the functionality required by the management and were therefore scrapped. Only the remaining half of the systems was used after great modifications, which entailed further delays and costs in an almost never-ending process.

One of the root causes identified for these problems was the inherent weakness of the phase in which requirements were captured and analyzed. This phase never seemed to get the correct and complete requirements. As a result, completed projects never seemed to deliver on the promised functionality and had to be recycled for more analysis and development. Maintenance and enhancements were called for indefinitely and became harder to undertake as time went by. Because individuals often changed midway, both on the development and user sides, system requirements changed frequently and the whole process continued indefinitely. This is primarily because there is a fundamental disconnect between the business and the IT/IS people. Notwithstanding how much both the parties try to bridge the gap, there is a fundamental chasm between the perception of a business user and what is understood by the systems staff; both classes of people speak different languages. Even if the systems personnel tried to increase precision by using methodologies and specification tools, they were never able to ratify the documented requirements completely because users were unfamiliar with these tools.

Typically, surveys found that 50%–80% of the IT/IS resources were dedicated to application maintenance. The ROI in IT was abysmally low by any standard of measurement and expectation. With IT/IS budgets stretching beyond the capabilities of most organizations, there was a compelling need for a radically new approach that could result in actual usable functionality that was professionally developed, under control, and on time.

The traditional software implementation involving the development of applications was characterized by the following:

- Requirement-driven functional decomposition
- Late risk resolution
- Late error detection
- Use of different language or artifacts at different phases of the project
- Large proportion of scrap and rework
- Adversarial stakeholder relationship with non-IT users
- Priority of techniques over tools
- Priority of quality of developed software rather than functionality, per se
- Greater emphasis on current, correct, complete, and consistent documentation
- Greater emphasis on testing and reviews
- Major effort on change control and management
- Large and diverse resource requirements
- Schedules always under pressure
- Greater effort on projected or estimated target performance
- Inherent limitations on scalability
- Protracted integration between systems

Many alternate strategies were devised like CASE and prototyping; however, none were able to cross this basic hurdle. CASE provided a more rigorous environment for requirement analysis and design, and automated to a large extent the subsequent development of code, testing, and documentation efforts. The increased time spent on requirement definition with the users was envisaged to lead to systems that were closer to the user's actual requirements. On the other hand, prototyping was designed to address the requirement capture issue by making the users directly participate in the process of defining the requirements. This was mainly focused on the screen and reports design because these were the elements that could be visualized directly by the user. However, none of these strategies really resolved the problem. Packages like ERP and CRM adopted a totally different approach by providing the most comprehensive functionality within the package. Company personnel were only expected to pick and choose whatever was required by the company actually using the package. Thus, ERP/CRM packages effectively short-circuited the whole issue of capturing requirements. The traditional project life cycle consisting of analysis, design, development, testing, and implementation was transformed to the ERP/CRM implementation life cycle consisting merely of requirement mapping, gap analysis, configuring and customizing, testing, and implementation.

Figure A.1 shows a comparison of effort expended during ERP/CRM and the traditional software development life cycle.

This ultimately led to the ERP revolution that we are witnessing today.

Unlike the traditional systems, the ERP software implementations involving the implementations of pre-engineered ready-to-implement application modules are characterized by the following:

- Primacy of the architecture, process-oriented configurability
- Primacy and direct participation of the business user
- Early risk resolution
- Early error and gap detection
- Iterative life-cycle process, negligible proportion of scrap and rework

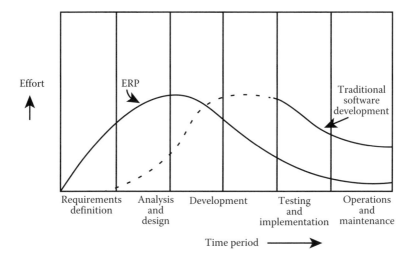

FIGURE A.1 Comparison of effort expended during ERP and the traditional software development life cycle.

- Changeable and configurable functionality
- Participatory and cohesive stakeholder relationship with non-IT users
- Priority of functionality over tools followed by techniques
- Quality of the functional variability and flexibility of the available functionality
- Greater emphasis on current, correct, complete, and consistent documentation of customizations
- Greater emphasis on integration testing
- Actual demonstration of functionality at all phases of the project
- Twin categories of resource requirements—functional and technical
- Schedules devoid of long-term cascading impact
- Demonstrated performance
- Larger span of scalability
- Efficient integration between systems

Off-the-shelf packages, and especially enterprise-wide solutions such as ERP, were considered as the best approach for confronting the software crisis of the 1980s. This was because of the following:

- ERP ensures better validation of user requirements directly by the user.
- ERP ensures consistent quality of delivered functionality.
- ERP provides a cohesive and integrated information system architecture.
- ERP ensures a fair degree of standardization.
- ERP provides a consistent and accurate documentation of the system.
- ERP provides outstanding quality and productivity in the development and maintenance of the system.

As companies are reporting their couple of decades of experience in implementing and operating on ERP, a base of experience seems to support the fact that companies that plan and manage the use of ERP are usually successful. It is no longer a matter of learning only new technology; it is now about applying the new technology effectively and addressing the problems of inertia and resistance to change across the enterprise. Today, the recognized management decision is not *whether* to use ERP but rather *when* to use ERP and which ERP package to use. After going through the later part of this book, it will become evident that SAP is the preeminent product in this genre.

References

Afuah, A., *Business Models: A Strategic Management Approach* (New York: McGraw-Hill, 2003).

Anderson, C., *The Long Tail: Why The Future of Business is Selling Less of More* (Hyperion, 2008).

Anupindi, R., Chopra, S. et al., *Managing Business Process Flows* (London, U.K.: Prentice-Hall, 2011).

Barham, K. and Heimer, C., *ABB: The Dancing Giant* (London, U.K.: FT Pitman Publishing, 1998).

Beinhocker, E.D., *Origin of Wealth: Evolution, Complexity and the Radical Re-Making of Economics* (New York: HBS Press, 2006).

Bejan, A. and Peder Zane, J., *Design in Nature: How the Constructal Law Govern Evolution in Biology, Physics, Technology and Social Organization* (New York: Doubleday, 2012).

Bell, S., *Lean Enterprise System: Using IT for Continuous Improvement* (Hoboken, NJ: John Wiley & Sons, 2006).

Besanko, D. et al., *Economics of Strategy* (New York: Wiley, 2009).

Bowler, P.J., *Evolution: The History of an Idea* (Berkeley, CA: University of California Press, 1989).

Buckminster Fuller, R., *Critical Path*, 2nd ed. (New York: St. Martin's Griffin, 1982).

Collins, J. and Porras, J.I., *Built to Last: Successful Habits of Visionary Companies* (New York: Harper Business, 2002).

Coyne, R., *Logic Models of Design* (London, U.K.: University College of London, 1988).

Dasgupta, S., *Design Theory and Computer Science* (Cambridge University Press, 2009).

David, A. and Anderson, L., *Beyond Change Management: How to Achieve Breakthrough Results through Conscious Change Leadership* (San Francisco, CA: Pfeiffer, 2010).

David, H., *Entrepreneurship and the Market Process* (London, U.K.: Routledge, 1996).

Davis, F.W. and Mandrodt, K.B., *Customer-Responsive Management: The Flexible Advantage* (Cambridge, MA: Blackwell, 1996).

Day, L. and Mcneil, I. (eds.), *Biographical Dictionary of the History of Technology* (New York: Routledge, 1998).

Dennett, D.C., *Darwin's Dangerous Idea: Evolution and Meanings of Life* (New York: Simon & Schuster, 1996).

Di Sciullo, A.M. and Boeckx, C., *The Biolinguistic Enterprise: New Perspectives on the Evolution and Nature of the Human Language Faculty* (Oxford University Press, 2011).

Dove, R., *Response Ability: The Language, Structure, and Culture of the Agile Enterprise* (New York: Wiley, 2001).

Easley, D. and Kleinbarg, J., *Networks, Crowds and Markets: Reasoning about a Highly Connected World* (Cambridge University Press, 2010).

Foster, R. and Kaplan, S., *Creative Destruction: Why Companies That Are Built to Last Underperform the Market–And How to Successfully Transform Them* (Crown Business, 2001).

Fritz, T., *The Competitive Advantage Period and the Industry Advantage Period* (Wiesbaden, Germany: Gabler, 2009).

Goldratt, E.M., *Theory of Constraints* (New York: North River Press, 1990).

Goranson, T., *The Agile Virtual Enterprise: Cases, Metrics*, (Praeger, 1999).

Grant, R., *Cases to Accompany Contemporary Strategic Analysis*, 6th ed. (Chichester, U.K.: Wiley-Blackwell, 2007).

Handy, C., *The Empty Raincoat* (London, U.K.: Hutchinson, 1994).

Harbold, R., *Seduced by Success* (New York: McGraw-Hill, 1997).

Harford, T., *Adapt: Why Success Always Starts with Failure* (London, U.K.: Little, Brown Book, 2011).

Hill, C.W.L. and Jones, G.R., *Strategic Management Theory: An Integrated Approach* (Boston, MA: Houghton-Mifflin Co., 2008).

Hunt, S.D., *Foundations of Marketing Theory: Toward a General Theory of Marketing* (New York: M.E. Sharpe, 2002).

Ingrassia, P., *Crash Course: The American Automobile Industry's to Bankruptcy, and Bailout and Beyond* (Random House, 2011).

Kale, V., *Implementing SAP R/3: The Guide for Business and Technology Managers* (Indianapolis, IN, Sams, 2000).

Kirchmer, M., *High Performance through Process Excellence: From Strategy to Execution with Business Process Management*, 2nd ed. (Berlin, Germany: Springer, 2011).

Kitcher, P., *The Advancement of Science: Science without Legend, Objectivity without Illusions* (New York: Oxford University Press, 1995).

Klein, T.D., *Built for Change: Essential Traits of Transformative Companies* (Santa Barbara, CA: Praeger, 2010).

Koren, Y., *The Global Manufacturing Revolution: Product-Process-Business Integration and Reconfigurable Systems* (Hoboken, NJ: Wiley, 2010).

Kuhn, T., *The Structure of Scientific Revolutions*, 3rd ed. (London, U.K.: University of Chicago Press, 1996).

Lewis, T., *Network Science* (Hoboken, NJ: Wiley, 2009).

Manzi, J., Uncontrolled: *The Surprising Payoff of Trail-and-Error for Business, Politics, and Society*, Basic Books 2012.

McGahan, A.M., *How Industries Evolve: Principles for Achieving and Sustaining Superior Performance* (Boston, MA: HBS Press, 2004).

McKelvey, M.D., *Evolutionary Innovations: The Business of Biotechnology* (New York: Oxford University Press, 1996).

Mckenzie, R., *Digital Economics: How Information Technology has Transformed Business Thinking* (Westport, CT: Praeger, 2003).

Niemann, G., *Big Brown: The Untold Story of UPS* (San Francisco, CA: Jossey-Bass, 2007).

Normann, R.A., *Reframing Business: When the Map Changes the Landscape* (Chichester, U.K.: John Wiley & Sons, 2001).

Page, S.E., *The Difference: How the Power of Diversity Creates Better Groups, Firms, Schools and Societies* (Oxfordshire, U.K.: Princeton University, 2008).

Peters, T.J. and Waterman, R.H., *In Search of Excellence: Lessons from Americas Best-Run Companies* (New York: Oxford University Press, 1980).

Picken, J. and Dess, G., *Mission Critical: The 7 Strategic Traps that Derail Even the Smartest Companies* (Chicago, IL: Irwin, 1997).

Popper, K., *The Logic of Scientific Discovery* (London, U.K.: Routledge, 1992).

Postrel, V., *The Future and Its Enemies: The Growing Conflict Over Creativity, Enterprise and Progress* (New York: Free Press, 1998).

Rasche, A., *The Paradoxical Foundation of Strategic Management* (Heidelberg, Germany: Physica-Verlag, 2008).

Raynor, M.E., *The Strategy Paradox: Why Committing to Success Leads to Failure (And What to do About It)* (Crown Business, 2007).

Resoenzweig, P., *The Halo Effect: ...and Eight other Business Delusions that Deceive Managers* (New York: Free Press, 2007).

Rothschild, M., *Bionomics: The Inevitability of Capitalism* (New York: Henry Holt, 1990).

Rothschild, W., *The Secret to GE's Success: A Former Insider Reveals the Leadership Lessons of the World's Most Competitive Company* (New York: McGraw-Hill, 2007).

Rugase, O., *Identity Strategy: How Individual Visions Enable the Design of a Market Strategy that Works* (Northampton, MA: Edward Elgar, 2006).

Oosterwal, D., *The Lean Machine* (New York: AMACOM, 2010).

Samson, D. and Challis, D., *Patterns of Excellence: Discover New Principles of Corporate Success* (Upper Saddle River, NJ: Pearson, 1999).

Schnaars, S.P., *Managing Imitation Strategies: How Later Entrants Seize Markets from Pioneers* (New York: Free Press, 2002).

Schwaninger, M., *Intelligent Organizations: Powerful Models for Systemic Management*, Springer, 2nd Edition 2009.

Screpanti, E. and Zamagni, S., *An Outline of the History of Economic Thought*, Revised 2nd ed. (New York: Oxford University Press, 2005).

Sheth, J., *The Self Destructive Habits of Good Companies... and How to break Them* (New York: Wharton School Publishing, 2007).

Smith, R., *Business Process Management and the Balance Scorecard* (Hoboken, NJ: Wiley, 2007).

Stacey, R.D., *Strategic Management and Organizational Dynamics* (London, U.K.: Pitman, 1996).

Stickland, F., *The Dynamics of Change: Insights from Natural World into Organizational Transition* (London, U.K.: Routledge, 1998).

Stratfield, P.J., *The Paradox of Control in Organizations. Complexity and Emergence in Organizations* (London, U.K.: Routledge, 2001).

Terry Win, *Manufacturing Strategy* (Macmillan, 1985)

Thomke, S.H., *Experimentation Matters: Unlocking the Potential of New Technologies for Innovation* (Boston, MA: Harvard Business School Press, 2003).

Thompson, K., *The Networked Enterprise: Competing for the Future Through Virtual Enterprise Networks* (Meghan Kiffer, 2008).

Witzel, M. (ed.), *Tata: Evolution of a Corporate Brand* (New Delhi, India: Penguin Portfolio, 2010).

Witzel, M., *A History of Management Thought* (London, U.K.: Routledge, 2012).

Zanders, E., *The Science and Business of Drug Discovery* (New York: Springer, 2011).

Index

A

ABAP, *see* Advanced Business Application Programming (ABAP)
ABB, style variations, 210–212
Acer, style variations, 212–214
ADS-B devices, 291
Advanced Business Application Programming (ABAP), 367, 388, 392
Advanced Research Projects Agency (ARPA), 136
Altair 8800, 146
Amazon Web Services (AWS), 278
Antipatterns of excellence
  self-destructive habits
    arrogance, 37–38
    competency dependence, 38
    competitive myopia, 39
    complacency, 38
    denial, 37
    territorial impulse, 39–40
    volume obsession, 39
  strategic traps
    arbitrary and inflexible goals, 35–36
    assumptions and premises, 31–32
    competitive advantage, 33–34
    environmental changes, 31
    leadership failure, 36–37
    organizational barriers, 34–35
  success-induced traps
    bloat, 41
    boredom, 41
    complexity, 41
    confusion, 42
    lethargy, 42
    mediocrity, 41
    pride, 40–41
    timidity, 42
    unique business model, 40
Apple II, innovation variations, 172
Apple iPod, 168–169
Apple MessagePad, 158
ArcelorMittal, structure variations, 195–197
ARPA, *see* Advanced Research Projects Agency (ARPA)
Asynchronous transfer mode (ATM) technology, 176–177
Automobile industry
  bicycles, 300
  electronic applications, 301
  engine system, 300–301
  Ford Model T, 301
  gasoline-powered vehicles, 300
  global manufacturers, 301–302
  horseless carriages, 300
  manufacturing operations
    cost-reduction efforts, 305–306
    Ford, 304
    supplier relationship, 304–305

    Toyota's lean production, 304
  variation patterns (*see* Variation patterns, automobile industry)
  market operations, 309–310
  new product development, 303–304
  pickup trucks, 302–303
  production operations
    excess capacity, 309
    globalization, 308–309
    location based, 309
  recession 2008, 310–311
  SUVs, 302–303
AWS, *see* Amazon Web Services (AWS)

B

Bandwagon effect, 106–108
BBD, *see* Business ByDesign (BBD)
BBPs, *see* Business blueprints (BBPs)
Bell Labs germanium transistor, 139
Bell System, 101
Bill of material (BOM), 92
BPR enterprise
  breakthrough improvement, 382–383
  business process, 380–381
  process maps, 381–382
  reengineered process, 383
  strategic planning, 379–380
Built-for-Variation enterprise
  corporate culture, 121
  directed dynamics, 120
  generating value
    best planning approach, 91
    BOM, 92
    definition, 70
    EOQ model, 92
    MRP, 92–93
    product flow planning, 90–91
    supply-chain management, 90–91
    Toyota Production System, 93–94
  identity, 72
  organizing
    activity-based costing, 88
    Charles Schwab's market capitalization, 89–90
    definition, 70
    performance-based information systems, 88
    skills, 87–88
    staff, 86–87
    style, 84–86
  reconfigurable principles, 120
  refreezing, 69
  reusable principles, 119–120
  scalable principles, 120
  self-organizing dynamics, 120
  strategic adjustments, 70
  strategic reorientations, 70